Contents

Introduction

Whether you're here for a long weekend or a lifetime, there's so much to love about Rome: its colours, raking mid-season light and sunsets; its agelessness, artistic wealth and cocksure sense that it is the world's most beautiful city.

There's quite a lot to rile you too: traffic chaos, stroppy shopkeepers and less-than-reliable public transport.

The Eternal City and its eternal contradictions can be challenging for first-time visitors. But Rome more than repays the effort of getting to know it: once you've got a handle on this city, you'll find there's so, so much to revel in.

There are few places in the world that offer such artistic riches on a plate, many of them free to enjoy. Six magnificent Caravaggios, for example, hang in three of Rome's churches, gratis. Music rings out around Rome – from churches and obscure institutions, to the magnificent Auditorium-Parco della Musica. Any stroll around the city centre (and central Rome, being small, is great for walking) is likely to take you past millennia of architecture, from the Pantheon (AD 126) to Richard Meier's shell for the Ara Pacis (2006), from the Roman Forum's Temple of Vesta (seventh century BC) to the MAXXI contemporary art and architecture gallery (2010).

Add to all this some very fine food and wine, some extremely chic shopping and much scope for pavement-table lounging and people-watching, and the impulse to moan about life-threatening driving styles will fade away.

Take it as it is – rough, ready and infinitely fascinating – and you too will enjoy this infuriating, fabulous city.

The Roman Forum

ABOUT THE GUIDE

This is one of a series of Time Out guidebooks to cities across the globe. Written by local experts, our guides are thoroughly researched and meticulously updated. They aim to be inspiring, irreverent, well-informed and trustworthy.

Time Out Rome is divided into five sections: Discover, Explore, Experience, Understand and Plan.

Discover introduces the city and provides inspiration for your visit.

Explore is the main sightseeing section of the guide and includes detailed listings and reviews for sights and museums; restaurants ⑩; cafés, bars and pubs ⑩; bakeries, pasticcerie and gelaterie ⑩ and shops ⑩, all organised by area with a corresponding street map. To help navigation, each area of Rome has been assigned its own colour.

Experience covers the cultural life of the city in depth, including festivals, film, LGBT, music, nightlife, theatre and more.

Understand provides in-depth background information that places Rome in its historical and cultural context.

Plan offers practical visitor information, including accommodation options and details of public transport.

Hearts

We use hearts ❤ to pick out venues, sights and experiences in the city that we particularly recommend. The very best of these are featured in the Top 20 (*see p10*) and receive extended coverage in the guide.

Maps

A detachable fold-out map can be found on the inside back cover. There's also an overview map (*see p8*) and individual streets maps for each area of the city. All the venues featured in the guide have been given a grid reference so that you can find them easily on the maps and on the ground.

Prices

All our **restaurant listings** are marked with a euro symbol category from budget to blow-out (**€-€€€€**), indicating the price you should expect to pay for two courses (from *antipasto, primo, secondo* and *dolce*) plus wine: **€** = under €20; **€€** = €20-€40; **€€€** = €40-€60; **€€€€** = over €60.

A similar system is used in our **Accommodation** chapter based on the hotel's standard prices for one night in a double room, mid-week and mid-season: **Budget** = up to €100; **Mid-range** = €100-€250; **Expensive** = €250-€400; **Luxury** = over €400.

Discover

Trajan's Column and Basilica Ulpia

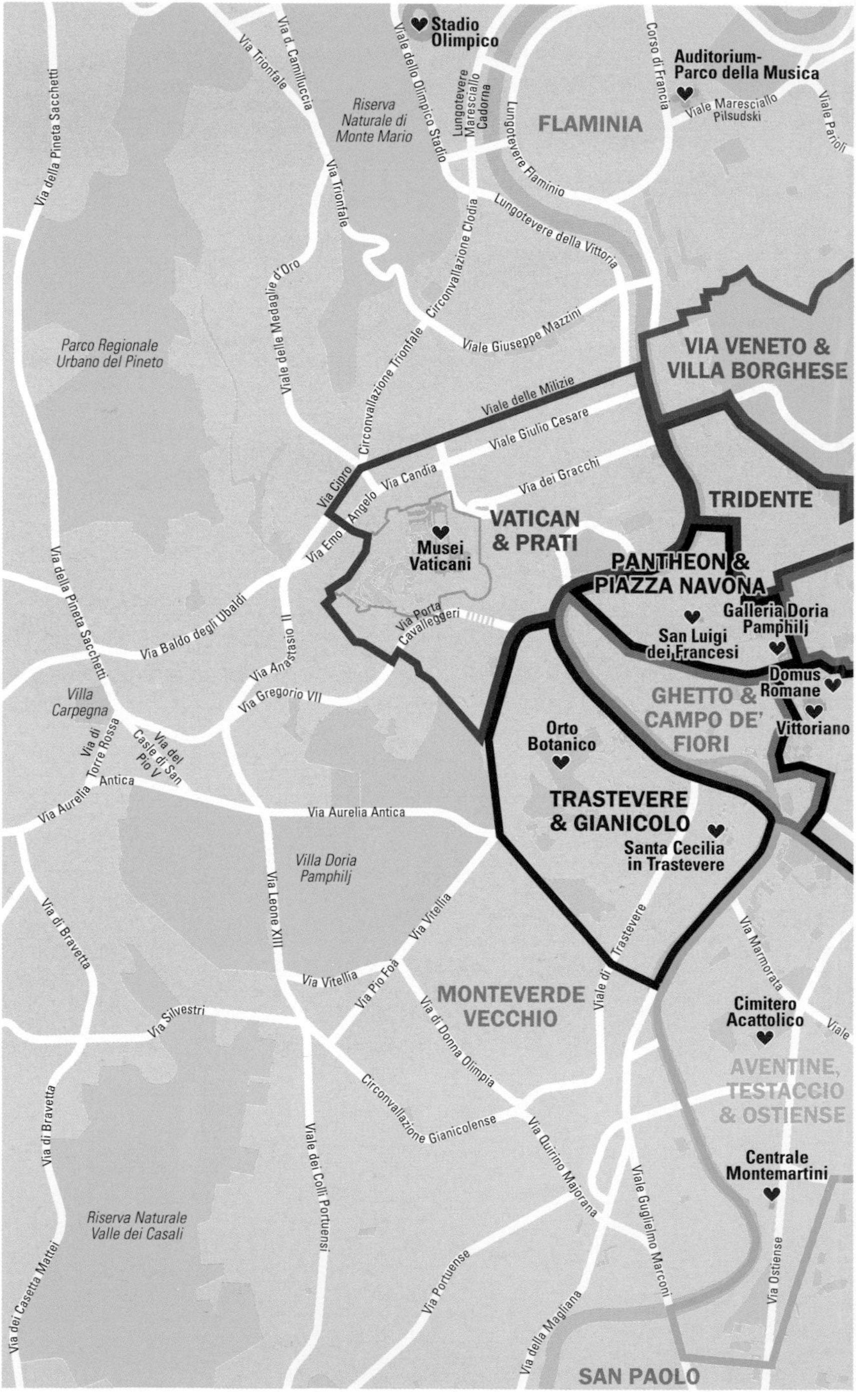
Stadio Olimpico
Auditorium-Parco della Musica
FLAMINIA
Riserva Naturale di Monte Mario
Parco Regionale Urbano del Pineto
VIA VENETO & VILLA BORGHESE
TRIDENTE
VATICAN & PRATI
Musei Vaticani
PANTHEON & PIAZZA NAVONA
Galleria Doria Pamphilj
San Luigi dei Francesi
Domus Romane
Vittoriano
GHETTO & CAMPO DE' FIORI
Orto Botanico
TRASTEVERE & GIANICOLO
Santa Cecilia in Trastevere
Villa Carpegna
Villa Doria Pamphilj
MONTEVERDE VECCHIO
Cimitero Acattolico
AVENTINE, TESTACCIO & OSTIENSE
Centrale Montemartini
Riserva Naturale Valle dei Casali
SAN PAOLO
Via della Pineta Sacchetti
Via Trionfale
Via d. Camilluccia
Viale dello Olimpico Stadio
Lungotevere Maresciallo Cadorna
Lungotevere Flaminio
Corso di Francia
Viale Maresciallo Pilsudski
Viale Parioli
Lungotevere della Vittoria
Circonvallazione Clodia
Viale delle Medaglie d'Oro
Viale Giuseppe Mazzini
Circonvallazione Trionfale
Viale delle Milizie
Viale Giulio Cesare
Via dei Gracchi
Via Candia
Via Cipro
Angelo
Via Emo
Via Baldo degli Ubaldi
Via Porta Cavalleggeri
Via Anastasio II
Via Gregorio VII
Via di Torre Rossa
Via del Casale di San Pio V
Via Aurelia Antica
Via Leone XIII
Via di Bravetta
Via Vitellia
Via Pio Foa
Via di Donna Olimpia
Viale di Trastevere
Via Marmorata
Viale
Via Silvestri
Circonvallazione Gianicolense
Via Quirino Majorana
Viale dei Colli Portuensi
Viale Guglielmo Marconi
Via Ostiense
Via Portuense
Via della Magliana
Via dei Casetta Mattei

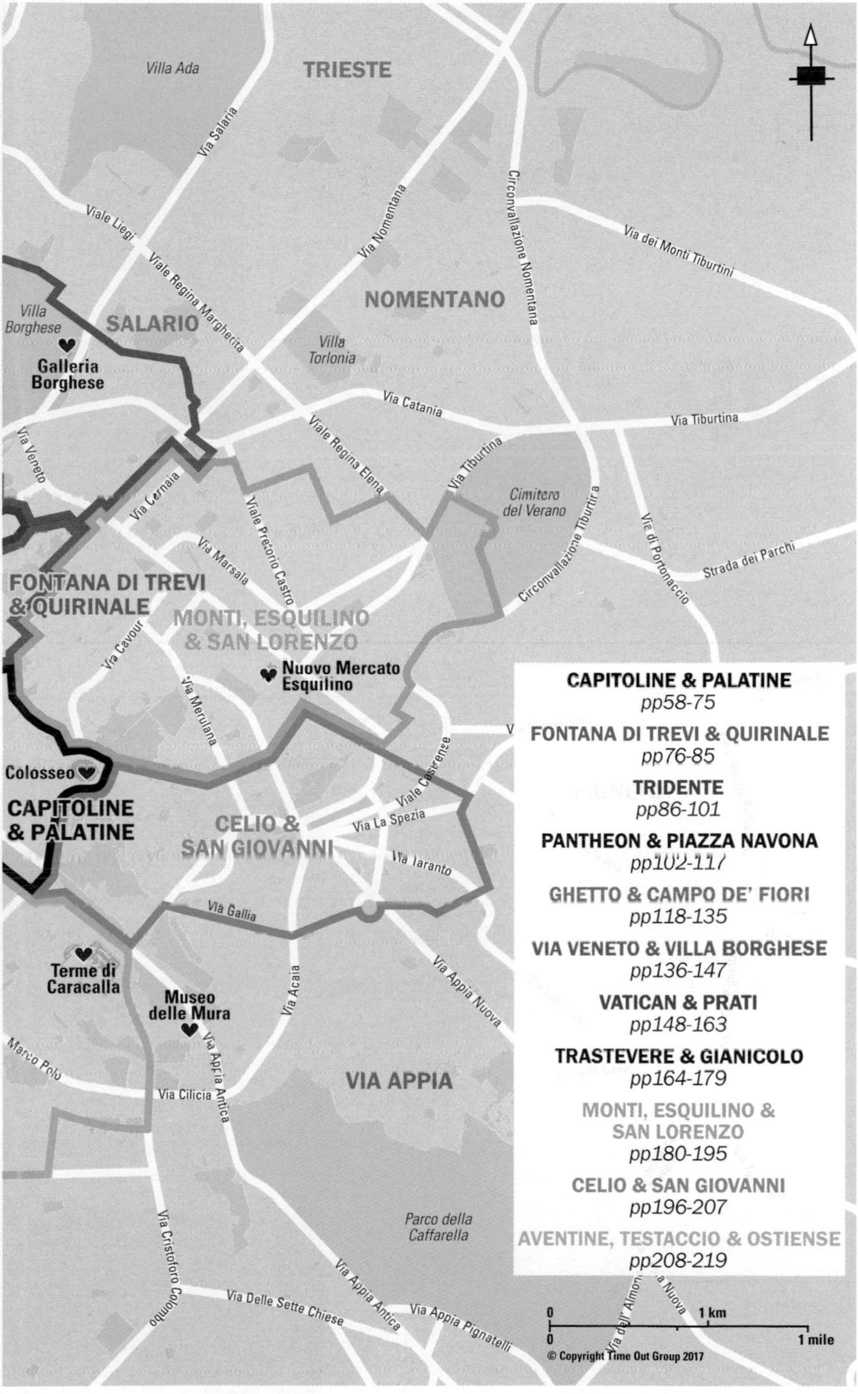
Villa Ada
TRIESTE
Via Salaria
Viale Liegi
Via Nomentana
Circonvallazione Nomentana
Via dei Monti Tiburtini
Viale Regina Margherita
NOMENTANO
Villa Borghese
SALARIO
Galleria Borghese
Villa Torlonia
Via Catania
Via Tiburtina
Viale Regina Elena
Via Veneto
Via Tiburtina
Via Cernaia
Cimitero del Verano
Viale Pretorio Castro
Circonvallazione Tiburtina
Via di Portonaccio
Via Marsala
Strada dei Parchi
FONTANA DI TREVI & QUIRINALE
MONTI, ESQUILINO & SAN LORENZO
Via Cavour
Nuovo Mercato Esquilino
Via Merulana
Viale Castrense
Colosseo
CAPITOLINE & PALATINE
CELIO & SAN GIOVANNI
Via La Spezia
Via Taranto
Via Gallia
Terme di Caracalla
Via Acaia
Via Appia Nuova
Museo delle Mura
Marco Polo
Via Appia Antica
Via Cilicia
VIA APPIA
Via Cristoforo Colombo
Parco della Caffarella
Via Delle Sette Chiese
Via Appia Antica
Via Appia Pignatelli
Via dell' Almone
CAPITOLINE & PALATINE
pp58-75
FONTANA DI TREVI & QUIRINALE
pp76-85
TRIDENTE
pp86-101
PANTHEON & PIAZZA NAVONA
pp102-117
GHETTO & CAMPO DE' FIORI
pp118-135
VIA VENETO & VILLA BORGHESE
pp136-147
VATICAN & PRATI
pp148-163
TRASTEVERE & GIANICOLO
pp164-179
MONTI, ESQUILINO & SAN LORENZO
pp180-195
CELIO & SAN GIOVANNI
pp196-207
AVENTINE, TESTACCIO & OSTIENSE
pp208-219
0
1 km
0
1 mile
© Copyright Time Out Group 2017

Top 20

From the Colosseo to Caravaggio, we count down the city's finest

01

Colosseo *p74*

No other landmark says 'Rome' quite like the Flavian Amphitheatre – aka the Colosseo (Colosseum) – a symbol of influence, clout and skillful manipulation of the people, in an architectural marvel which has withstood the passage of time. Inaugurated in AD 80 with 100 days of wild-animal carnage, the 50,000-seater Colosseum kept social unrest at bay with free gory entertainment.

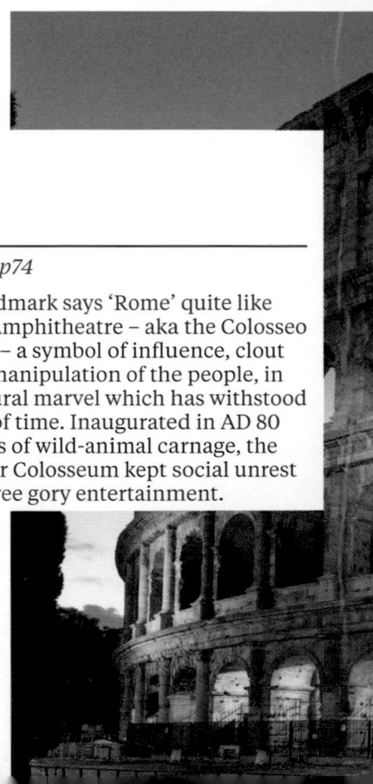

02

Centrale Montemartini *p213*

A decommissioned power station hosting a beautifully displayed collection of ancient statuary, the Centrale Montemartini is arguably Rome's most under-visited, under-appreciated gem. Admittedly, it's less than central. But the striking setting and the glorious selection of pieces – including the engaging muse Polimnia and a remarkable ivory doll with jointed limbs – make it unique.

03

Cimitero Acattolico *p216*

Rome's utterly lovely non-catholic cemetery celebrated its 300th anniversary in 2016. Nestling beneath the Pyramid and sheltered by umbrella pines, this is the flower-filled final resting place of poets (Keats, Shelley, Gregory Corso), philosophers (Antonio Gramsci) and Grand Tourists galore. For sheer atmosphere, the cemetery is hard to beat, especially at sunset, bathed with golden light through the pines.

04

A match at the Stadio Olimpico *p223*

For sheer decibels, matches at the Stadio Olimpico are cup winners. Whether you're here to see SS Lazio (diehard fans in the Curva Nord) or AS Roma (Curva Sud), for a Serie A match or the Coppa Italia, you'll enjoy great crowd choreography and – in general – much audience camaraderie, at surprisingly low ticket prices.

05

Galleria Borghese *p142*

A superb container for a superlative collection, Galleria Borghese is the 17th-century pleasure house where Cardinal Scipione Borghese stashed his Bernini statues and Caravaggio paintings. Two Bernini works alone – Daphne turning into a bay tree as she flees lustful Apollo, and Pluto seizing the grain goddess Proserpine – make the (obligatory) process of pre-booking a visit worthwhile.

06

Musei Vaticani *p154*

Sprawling, overwhelming and with something for everyone, the Musei Vaticani (Vatican Museums) offer far more than the Sistine Chapel and a handful of Raphael frescoes. There are sections covering – among other things – Egypt (complete with mummies), the Etruscans, ethnographical artefacts collected by adventuring missionaries, and modern art.

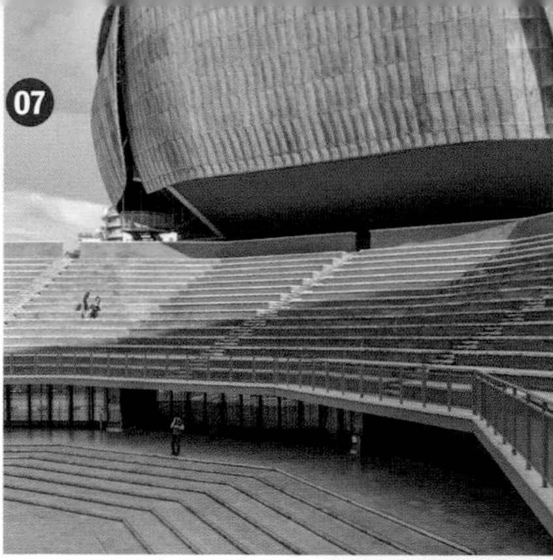

07

Auditorium-Parco della Musica *p273*

The three beetle-shaped blocks of this pulsating performing arts centre in the northern suburbs are the venue for music concerts from classical to contemporary, for meetings with authors, science festivals, Rome's annual film fest and endless other events. The outdoor *cavea* (enclosure) is a skating rink in winter and the perfect concert spot in summer.

08

Roma Incontra il Mondo *p259*

This long-running festival embodies the mood of summer in Rome: on July and August evenings, strains of folk, reggae, world music and more resound through the greenery of the Villa Ada gardens. It's a laid-back kind of happening, with play spaces for kids, an emphasis on organic in its food stalls and some good craft beer.

09

Museo delle Mura *p227*

With 12.5km (7.5 miles) of the third-century BC Aurelian Walls still standing, you'll come face to face with them all over the city. Only in this overlooked little museum can you walk on them. From the San Sebastiano gatehouse – where exhibits explaining ancient wall and road construction will fascinate detail-orientated visitors – there's access to a 350m (1150ft) stretch with magnificent views.

10

Nuovo Mercato Esquilino *p193*

Strolling the streets of central Rome, you may wonder at the city's lack of ethnic mix. But not in the Esquilino district. At the heart of this vibrant multicultural zone lies the Nuovo Mercato Esquilino – still known as piazza Vittorio market after its venue until 2002 – where stalls purvey ingredients from all over the globe to clients of every nationality.

11

Domus Romane *p61*

Archaeological wonders never cease coming to light in Rome. Recently added to the roster, the Domus Romane – remains of several richly decorated ancient Roman houses – stands out for its superb use of avant-garde technology to enhance our appreciation of the ancient. Computer-generated images 'grow' up the monumental brick walls, adding Roman Empire decor and filling the spaces with the sounds of inhabitants.

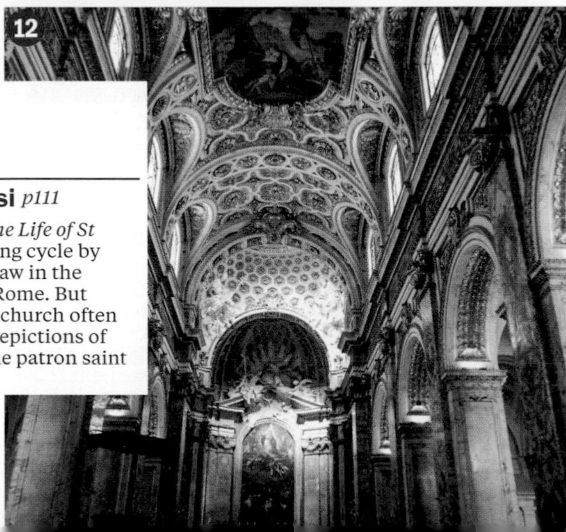

12

San Luigi dei Francesi *p111*

The dramatic *Scenes from the Life of St Matthew* (1600-1602) painting cycle by Caravaggio is the biggest draw in the French national church in Rome. But visitors to the 16th-century church often overlook a series of lovely depictions of *Histories of Cecilia* (1615), the patron saint of music, by Domenichino.

13

Ostia Antica *p232*

A trip to Pompeii out of the question this visit? Never fear: Ostia Antica is a worthy substitute. Ancient Rome's port is less daunting than many better-known sites but equally satisfying. There's a frescoed bar/grocer's shop, rows of municipal loos, a glorious theatre where performances are still staged and shipping company offices with mosaics depicting their wares.

14

Opera at Terme di Caracalla

p269

The beetling ruins of Emperor Caracalla's great bath complex never fail to impress, but seen on a summer's night, startlingly illuminated, to the notes of an opera, concert or dance performance, they are sheer magic. Gone are the heydays of *Turandot* complete with elephants, but productions remain impressive.

15

Santa Cecilia in Trastevere *p177*

Reputedly built over the home of St Cecilia, this church – of fifth-century origins with later additions – is a treasure trove. From the Cosmatesque decoration in the crypt, to Stefano Maderno's moving sculpture of St Cecilia beneath the altar, to the magnificent *Last Judgement* (c1300) mural by proto-Renaissance dark horse Pietro Cavallini upstairs in the choir, it's an essential stopover.

16

Gelato *p41*

Ice-cream is Rome's great leveller. From scurrying nuns to pompous politicians and chic boutique staff... everyone can be caught slurping a cone on a hot day. Recent years have seen a revolution in gelato culture. Sure, you can still get the highly coloured processed variety; but now there's also organic, gluten- and lactose-free and gourmet to choose from.

17

Rome Marathon *p243*

One April Sunday each year, Rome grinds to a halt as runners professional and amateur pound through the city streets towards a finishing line in the shadow of the Colosseum. Those cobblestones can be hard on the ankles but that doesn't seem to cool the ardour of the almost 14,000 who stayed the course in 2017.

18

Orto Botanico *p170*

Plants have been cultivated since the 13th century in the area where Rome's botanical garden now flourishes, and the Orto has a lush timelessness to it that restores the spirits after an overdose of sightseeing. Officially it's a university research department, but the vibe is more genteel disarray than scientific rigour. There's a scent garden for visually impaired garden-lovers.

19

Galleria Doria Pamphilj *p115*

The Doria Pamphilj family is part of Rome's papal aristocracy, with a *centro storico palazzo* covering a whole city block and a superlative art collection still in private hands. Besides the Velazquez portrait of the Pamphilj pope Innocent X, there are works by Caravaggio and Titian, Filippino Lippi and Lorenzo Lotto... plus sumptuous interiors fit for a *principe*.

20

Vittoriano *p64*

This monument to Italian unification is a jingoistic bit of kitsch, glaringly out of whack with its surroundings. Exhibition spaces in its cavernous interior host so-so events. But slog up its daunting white steps or – even better – whizz in the glass lift up to the roof of the pile for a magical experience: Rome laid out in glory below.

Itineraries

Get the most out of the city, whatever your timescale or budget

ESSENTIAL WEEKEND

Rome in two days
Budget €400 for two
Getting around Walking

► *Budgets include transport, meals and admission prices, but not accommodation and shopping.*

DAY 1

Morning

Ancient Rome permeates the modern city in many ways, and getting to grips with the very old will help you appreciate the many layers added through ensuing centuries to make the glorious jumble that greets you today.

An overview shows the extent to which the hub of the ancient city is still with us. Climb the steep steps up to the forecourt of **Santa Maria in Aracoeli** (*see p63*), from where you can take a lift to the very top of the white **Vittoriano** monument in piazza Venezia (*see p64*). If it's a clear day, you'll feel you can see forever.

Cross to the south-east side of the Michelangelo-designed piazza del Campidoglio and enjoy the view over the **Foro Romano** (*see p67*) as you make your way to its entrance: queues here are generally less daunting than at the Colosseum (one ticket covers both). You'll have your work cut out for you to see the whole site before lunch. But it's worth slogging up the **Palatine hill** (also included on the ticket) for another wild view over Rome – not to mention a little welcome shade – at the verdant **Horti Farnesiani** gardens.

Vittoriano

Afternoon

At the piazza Venezia end of the Imperial Fora, **Terre e Domus** (*see p65*) serves produce and wine from Rome's surrounding Lazio region; try to get a table overlooking Trajan's marvellous column.

If you've been very efficient – and if you've pre-booked – you may make the 2pm or 2.30pm visit in English of the fascinating **Domus Romane** (*see p61*). If not, press on.

Stroll up past **Mercati di Traiano** (*see p73*), then down salita del Grillo and pretty via degli Ibernesi for an unexpectedly quiet glimpse of Rome's medieval heart in the Monti district. You might want to tack along via della Madonna dei Monti to grab a gelato at **Fatamorgana** (*see p186*) to keep energy levels up before tackling the **Colosseum** (*see p74*).

Evening

Ready for *aperitivi*? Head back into the warren of streets in Monti to join tipplers at one of the innumerable wine bars, such as **Ai Tre Scalini** (*see p186*). If you've got the energy, head to the outskirts of town to the stunning **Auditorium-Parco della Musica** (*see p273*) for a cultural feast, whatever your music taste.

Mercati di Traiano

Horti Farnesiani

DAY 2

Morning

The complicated geography of Rome's *centro storico* reflects the city's history. Roman foundations were used for medieval re-building; urban planning sprees by Renaissance popes remain intact; baroque *piazze* follow the lines of ancient constructions. The *centro* is conveniently compact and walkable.

The **Spanish Steps** (*see p92*) are a grandiose monument, especially after a recent restoration. At the foot of the steps, the **Keats-Shelley Memorial House** (*see p91*) will be of interest to lovers of Romantic poetry.

Via del Babuino is lined with chic antique and furnishing shops; running parallel to the east and far less trafficked, via Margutta was full of artists' studios, one of which featured as Gregory Peck's bachelor pad in the movie classic *Roman Holiday*, and is now occupied by chi-chi galleries and high-rent pieds-à-terre. Via del Babuino emerges in piazza del Popolo with its obelisk, magnificent gate in the Roman wall and the Caravaggio-filled church of **Santa Maria del Popolo** (*see p98*).

With some art under your belt, you deserve a coffee. Elegant café **Rosati** (*see p99*) is a Roman classic.

Via Ripetta leads out of the square and along to the **Museo dell'Ara Pacis** (*see p101*). Besides the beautiful Altar of Peace, this museum has exhibits explaining the layout of the ancient city.

Obelisk, piazza del Popolo

Afternoon

Head down via della Croce for a cheap and cheerful – and very tasty – pasta lunch at **Pastificio Guerra** (*see p93*). Continue back along via Ripetta, which becomes via della Scrofa. In piazza **Sant'Agostino**, the church (*see p110*) of the same name contains another superb Caravaggio. And if you still have an appetite for this bad boy of the baroque, his St Matthew series in the nearby church of **San Luigi dei Francesi** (*see p111*) is a must.

Piazza Navona, which follows the lines of Emperor Domitian's great stadium, merits a saunter; Gianlorenzo Bernini's **Fontana dei Quattro Fiumi** dominates the space. At the south end of the square, the **Museo di Roma** (*see p107*) is a minor museum but its depictions of Rome through the ages put the city into vivid historical context.

Fontana dei Quattro Fiumi (Gian Lorenzo Bernini, 1651)

Evening

Join the crowd at the **Antica Vineria** (*see p128*) in campo de' Fiori – a fantastic place for an *aperitivo*. **Ditirambo** (*see p126*) is a lively place for dinner. Skip over to the nearby **Shari Vari Playhouse** (*see p258*) to dance the night away.

FAMILY DAY OUT

Keeping the kids amused

Budget €130 for two adults, two children
Getting around Walking, bus

Morning

Rome doesn't go out of its way to entertain your children. There's a zoo (*see p141*) but it's nothing to write home about. What it does offer is endless curiosities and hidden surprises, each of which has a fascinating tale behind it. Then, when even those fail... there are parks and ice-creams (*see p41* Gelato).

Begin in **piazza Navona** (*see p108*) – a magnificent space with splashing fountains, street 'artists' and tales of artistic rivalry. Remind kids that summer entertainment until the mid 19th century included flooding this square so overheated Romans could cool their feet off. If you're here over the Christmas period, it will be full of stalls and merry-go-rounds.

A short walk eastwards, the **Pantheon** (*see p113*) is that rare thing: an ancient Roman building in its gob-smacking entirety. Yes, that hole in the roof is open: come during a storm if you have any doubts. In neighbouring piazza della Maddalena is a handy branch of **Il Gelato di San Crispino** (*see p81*), Rome's original gourmet ice-cream maker.

It's worth tacking south here for a look at a most unexpected bit of the ancient world. Where via del Gesù meets via Pie di Marmo there's a massive sandal-clad marble foot. Occasionally pranksters paint its toenails bright colours.

Not far away, the church of **Sant'Ignazio di Loyola** (*see p114*) was built without a dome when neighbours complained that a cupola would ruin their view. So a fake one was painted on the ceiling. The optical illusion only works from one (marked) spot though: stand on it and the pretend-dome goes from distressingly wonky to perfect.

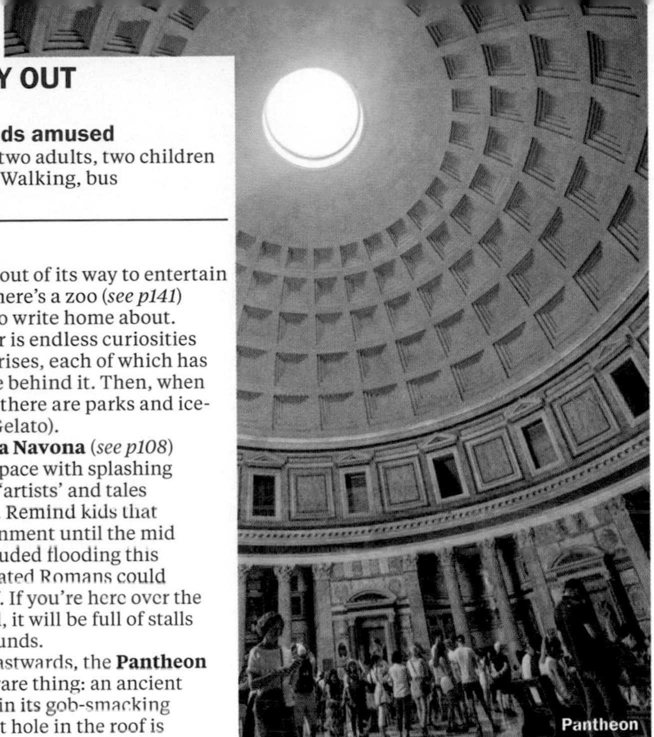
Pantheon

Gelato

Afternoon

Cross busy via del Corso to via di San Marcello. The **Antica Birreria Peroni** (*see p81*) is a big, noisy, inexpensive place to refuel for an afternoon's exploring. And it's a short stroll from the **Fontana di Trevi** (Trevi Fountain, *see p78*) where throwing three coins into the water guarantees a return to the city... if you can make it to the fountain's edge through the crowds.

You might want to hop on one of the buses plying via del Tritone to the next stop on this itinerary: the **Cripta dei Cappuccini** (*see p146*) – not the frothy coffee but the Capuchine friars' church and museum. Note that this is not for the over-sensitive. After an exhibition glorifying the deeds of this minor Franciscan order, visitors reach the crypt – a burial-ground with limited space where older bones have been dug up over the centuries and arranged in curlicues around the walls.

After which you'll be ready for the leafy spaces of the **Villa Borghese** gardens (*see p140*). Walk (or take a bus) to the park's entrance at the top of via Veneto. Once there, you'll find bikes for hire, swings, a lake with rowing boats and acres of room for letting off steam.

BUDGET BREAK

For the euro-conscious visitor
Budget €70 for two
Getting around Walking

Morning

So many of Rome's wonders are out there in the open for all to see that it's easy to feel you've 'done' the city without spending a *centesimo*. There's no charge to enter even the most masterpiece-packed churches. And the *centro* is sufficiently compact to navigate without much recourse to (its admittedly really very inexpensive) public transport.

Begin in piazza Santa Maria in Trastevere, admiring the 13th-century mosaics in the **church** (*see p169*). A couple of blocks to the south of here, the morning **market** in piazza di San Cosimato (*see p169*) is the perfect place for grabbing some picnic lunch ingredients and lots of Roman atmosphere.

Santa Maria in Trastevere

Tiber Island

Across thundering viale di Trastevere, the church of **San Francesco a Ripa** (*see p176*) has one of Bernini's most sensuous statues (*see p174* Bernini's Babes) and the cell where St Francis stayed on a visit in 1229. **Santa Cecilia in Trastevere** (*see p177*) conceals a spectacular fresco by Pietro Cavallini (open until 12.30pm): well worth paying €2.50 to see.

Villa Magistrale dei Cavalieri di Malta

Afternoon

A wander through the maze of streets will lead you to the **Tiber island** (*see p133*): down on the water-level promenade, the din of rushing water replaces traffic sounds, making it a fine place for your picnic.

North of the island, descend from the end of via del Portico d'Ottavia for a close-up look at the **Teatro di Marcello** (*see p135*) from the rather neglected, rather pretty archaeological area that skirts it.

Via Petroselli descends to **Santa Maria in Cosmedin** (*see p134*), with its hand-munching 'mouth of truth' and gorgeous Romanesque interior.

From here, continue south, taking time to stop and admire the vast proportions of the **Circo Massimo** (*see p67*). Climb the well-heeled residential **Aventine hill** by which time a sit-down in orange tree-filled **Parco Savello**, with its glorious view over the city, will be most welcome. Right next door, starkly beautiful **Santa Sabina** (*see p212*) is well worth a visit. And don't forget to peer through the keyhole (*see p212*) in piazza dei Cavalieri di Malta.

Back down the hill, still further south, lies the Testaccio district where the *aperitivo* spread at **L'Oasi della Birra** (*see p215*) on central piazza Testaccio is remarkably generous. If that doesn't satisfy your hunger, the pizzas at nearby **Da Remo** (*see p217*) are as good as they are cheap. On a Sunday evening, Testaccio's salsa club **Caruso Café de Oriente** (*see p260*), offers free entry and a friendly atmosphere.

Da Remo

When to Visit

Rome by season

Rome's artistic, archaeological and architectural treasures are a year-round draw, but how you appreciate them will be dictated by your choice of season. During the colder months you may have to contend with some bitter weather but crowds will be decidedly thinner. Some may find hordes in the summer heat unbearable, but the fine weather brings a plethora of splendid outdoor events (*see pp240-247* Events).

Rome Marathon

Spring

Spring in Rome can be dreamily warm. Or it can be weirdly wintery. Usually it's a bit of both. With glorious wisteria flowers cascading over walls and pergolas, and the Judas trees in bloom, the city is at its lushest. You might find the *centro* completely car-free for the **Rome Marathon** (*see p243*), or with a host of normally shuttered *palazzi* and churches open for the **Giornate FAI** (*see p242*). Easter brings throngs for religious festivities, including the pope's Stations of the Cross in the Colosseum during **Settimana Santa** (*see p244*) on Good Friday.

Summer

July and August in Rome will test the tolerance of the greatest heat-lover, but there's respite to be found in the city's leafy parks and in a fantastic series of outdoor evening concerts: from **Postepay Rock in Roma** (*see p245*), to world music at **Roma Incontra il Mondo** in Villa Ada (*see p259*), or the usual eclectic mix at the **Auditorium-Parco della Musica** (*see p273*). A vast

Roma Incontro il Mondo

Jovanotti at 11th Rome International Film Festival

choice of goodies in lovely venues around Rome comes under the **Estate Romana** (*see p245*) summer entertainment umbrella. If none of that appeals, the air-conditioning in spectacular museums and galleries, and the dark freshness of innumerable churches offer a chance to cool off.

Autumn

November is tops for average monthly rainfall in the Eternal City, but occasional stolen days of summery warmth and sunshine make up for the damp. Visiting crowds begin to thin at this time of year. But there are still outstanding offerings, from the **RomaEuropa Festival** (*see p246*) with its programme of world-class avant-garde theatre and dance, to the **Rome Film Festival** (*see p246*) which, though no rival for its big brother in Venice, offers the public a chance to see not-yet-released titles, usually in the original language.

Winter

When the northerly *tramontana* wind whips down from snow-covered mountains, Rome can be icy. It can also be brilliantly blue: if you can take the cold, the view from the top of the **Vittoriano** (*see p64*) on a crystal winter's day is unbeatable. So wrap up warm if you're coming to enjoy the Christmas celebrations, or, later in the season, the **Carnevale** fun (*see p247*, though it should be said, this is a minor event here compared to Viareggio and Venice). Until the Easter rush brings new-season crowds, a relatively quiet Rome may seem very intimate.

Christmas in piazza San Pietro

Rome Today

Beset with problems, yet eternally fascinating

Imposing and fascinating, scruffy and infuriating – Rome at the end of the second decade of the 21st century means very different things to different people.

Visitors – perhaps with modest expectations – enjoy averagely well-run museums with the occasional stand-out one-off show, excellent dining opportunities, a varied hotel scene and all the beauty of a *centro storico* dotted with the accretions of several bustling millennia. Residents, on the other hand, bemoan a disastrous transport situation, iffy refuse collection services, low-grade corruption and general tetchiness. The Eternal City today, it could be argued, offers more for the visitor than for the locals.

Spanish Steps and Fontana della Barcaccia

A steady stream of visitors

As the list of potential destinations around the Med and in the rest of Europe is whittled away by conflict, terrorist threats and niggling security misgivings, Rome grows in popularity year by year. Some 14 million tourists stayed in Rome's hotels in 2016 – a 6.7 per cent increase on the previous year – and anything up to five million more opted for Airbnb-type accommodation.

The early years of this millennium brought an impressive parade of new attractions (the Auditorium-Parco della Musica, the Zaha Hadid-designed MAXXI museum) and a roster of ancient sites re- or newly opened (Domus Romane, the hypogea of the Colosseum and the Baths of Caracalla), since when there's been much resting on laurels, and not a little slacking. But... *pazienza*. If there's a city with a gift for comebacks, it's Rome.

If there's a city with a gift for comebacks, it's Rome

Ups and (way) downs

Underlying the general feeling of grinding stasis is a political situation that has gone from almost-comic to dire, leaving Rome's credibility slightly tarnished (to be generous). First, a

The arrival of Virginia Raggi as Mayor in 2016 ushered in yet more city hall-paralysing chaos.

centre-left regional council president was forced to resign in a squalid tale of transvestite prostitution; then a centre-right mayor was beset by allegations that hundreds (literally) of friends, relations, political supporters and their offspring had been eased into plum council jobs; next up, a centre-right regional council became embroiled in a funds-fiddling scandal and a left-leaning mayor was forced out of office on tenuous suspicions of receipts-fiddling and more than a hint of *et tu Brute?* about his own party's involvement in his downfall.

If this is all sounding very *Decline and Fall*-ish, it hasn't stopped there. Aged just 37 when elected in 2016, Virginia Raggi was Rome's first female mayor, and its first from the populist new-broom Five Star Movement; far from being a breath of fresh air, her arrival ushered in still more city hall-paralysing chaos. All in all, not the brightest of pictures.

It should be said, of course, that even in those heady days around the turn of the millennium, Rome was never wholly a paragon of streamlined efficiency. Far from it. Then as now, you could ask any taxi driver what state he thought his city was in, and chances were that your trip wouldn't be long enough for his litany of woes: the relentless year-on-year increase in vehicles bumping over the city cobbles (2.3 million – that's more than 0.7 cars per inhabitant against a European average not far above 0.5 – in 2015, according to the Automobile Club d'Italia); skyrocketing pollution levels; the disruption caused when the pope or the president or some foreign VIP is whisked through the streets in high-speed, high-security dashes, or when demonstrators process through the city centre; the chaos – occasionally violence – when key football matches are played at the Stadio Olimpico; the transport strikes that bring the city to gridlock; the treacherous potholes; the never-ending works on never-ready new metro

Chaotic parking and cobblestone streets make driving in the centre a chore.

Romans can't abide the disruption caused by the pope or some foreign VIP being whisked through the streets in high-speed, high-security dashes

lines; the nose-to-tail tour buses disgorging ever more people into the narrow medieval streets.

All, to some extent, true. But also to be taken with a pinch of salt, for Romans are inveterate moaners, with very short memories. Many won't admit that when large sums of money were funnelled towards the capital for the 2000 Holy Year, the city took on a new lease of life and began once again to look like a world capital. Rome is still – just – coasting on that positive turnaround. Historic buildings are still looking well maintained. Museums are competently run with user-friendly visiting hours. There's an efficient service (muovi.roma.it) for tracking bus arrivals and city planning journeys. And free wi-fi is the norm throughout the city centre.

The Renzo Piano-designed Auditorium-Parco della Musica (*see p273*), which was inaugurated in 2002, continues to offer an intelligent, all-embracing programming philosophy. And the Teatro Palladium (*see p272*) – like the Auditorium, located in a suburb with little or no arts 'tradition' – is equally lively. The trickle-down effect on the whole cultural and entertainment scene can still be felt.

True, Rome slipped to 17th place in the 2016 Mastercard list of the world's most visited cities, but in fairness this may reflect the varied choices of ever-increasing numbers of global travellers

There's an efficient service for tracking bus arrivals and planning journeys.

City- and state-owned galleries are, on the whole, beautifully organised and lit. A good example is the Museo dei Fori Imperiali.

as much as the Eternal City's failure to attract. The number of people paying to enter city-run museums in 2016 was up 6.5 per cent. In 2015 the Colosseum was second only to the Great Wall of China in world rankings of most-visited archaeological sites.

But this fairly healthy tourism prospect wallpapers over a worrying state of affairs, boding far from well for the future. Milan has taken over as Italy's most successful city, producing 20 per cent of the country's GDP; in 2015 Rome slipped to seventh place for per capita GDP, according to a report from the UIL (Italian Labour Union). The mood among *romani* is grim.

Whatever is happening in the higher echelons, the important bits of Rome are still there to share: from the ever-popular Fontana di Trevi to the splendidly re-housed bronze statue of Marcus Aurelius in the Musei Capitolini.

What's in it for us?

So much for the Rome of the Romans. And the Rome of the visitor? As you hesitate on the kerb, cowed before life-threatening traffic, you might be forgiven for thinking that nothing much has changed in Rome since *Roman Holiday*. But it has.

The bad old days of museums and galleries opening for a few hours in the morning only are a distant memory – though occasionally staff shortages in less-visited sites can upset the smooth running. City- and state-owned galleries are on the whole beautifully organised and lit, and book/gift shops are well stocked, though many venues are still without cafés. Sloppy maintenance creates inexcusable problems in some larger attractions (the Roman Forum and Palatine are a case in point). But online booking has become increasingly easy. And an on-going replacement of bureaucrats in museum directorships with a more dynamic crew of curatorial experts – including, controversially, non-Italians – is expected to produce still more innovative benefits.

There's also a greater range of things to see. Already at the beginning of the millennium the Eternal City was given a host of new attractions: the Ara Pacis (*see p101*) with its Richard Meier-

designed case that – love it or hate it – restores its sense of monumentality; the bronze statue of Marcus Aurelius in its airy pavilion in the Musei Capitolini (*see p60*); the revamped Museo dei Fori Imperiali (*see p71*) which has given Trajan's remarkable markets a new lease of life; the new-look MACRO (*see p222*) and the stunning, buzzing MAXXI (*see p224*) for contemporary art. State-of-the-art technology is used to great effect at the Domus Romane (*see p61*); a similar approach has been introduced to Nero's golden house – the Domus Aurea (*see p187*).

The Estate Romana (*see p245*) umbrella organisation for summer events is holding up fairly well given budget cuts; the Rome International Film Festival (*see p246*) in autumn tries hard to rival more illustrious fests elsewhere. The RomaEuropa Festival (*see p246*) continues to offer a world-class programme of avant-garde performing arts goodies. And the programming at the Auditorium-Parco della Musica maintains a high standard of something-for-everyone.

Yet there's a feeling that the city needs to be shaken up, dusted down, smartened up and started over. With political in-fighting and administrative stasis the order of the day,

The beginning of the millennium saw a host of new attractions including the Ara Pacis (top) and Auditorium-Parco della Musica (above).

Shiftingly Hip

What do Rome's neighbourhoods signify to Romans?

The *centro storico* is an intriguing hybrid, with artisans' workshops nestling against treasure-filled patrician palaces, and spit-and-sawdust trattorias with *mamma* in the kitchen surviving against all the *alta cucina* odds. But however genteely crumbling or throbbing with *folkloristico* life a street or *piazza* may seem, don't be fooled: even a fairly humble pad here sells for upwards – in some prestigious areas such as around the Pantheon and piazza Navona very much upwards – of €7,500 per square metre; and though prices Rome-wide have plummeted by over 25 per cent since 2008, property on sale in the hub of the *centro* today is snatched up by the very rich indeed.

The city bucks international trends as far as the creeping gentrification of its suburbs goes. With the exception of the 'historic' modern suburbs whose identity changed decades ago and has remained fairly stable, the picture is one of ebb and flow rather than inexorable advance. Rome's *cognoscenti* move base, flocking en masse to San Lorenzo (*see p194*), Ostiense (*see p215*), Pigneto (*see p226*) or Flaminio (*see p222*). But in time the trend-setting pack tends to move on: the cool bars and chi-chi restaurants lose their lustre, leaving a depressed property market and a district feeling not much different to how it was when the boom began. There's little in the way of lasting legacy.

Meanwhile those more established non-*centro* haunts are stuck in their respective ruts – which is not *always* a bad thing. Monteverde Vecchio (*see p229*) is graciously residential; Parioli is the haunt of electric car-driving, designer label-wearing rich kids, their overwhelmingly right-leaning families and their Filipino house staff; retail-heaven Prati (*see p160*) is packed with well-heeled professionals and media types; and Testaccio's (*see p215*) hip side is kept refreshingly grounded by the continued presence of the denizens of low-rent council houses handed down from generation to generation.

Romans are tiring of the slow erosion of what's best about their superb city.

There's a feeling that the city needs to be shaken up, dusted down, smartened up and started over

Even so, there are great some oh-so-Roman things that – thankfully – just keep plodding on, propelled by something between affection and inertia. The morning chaos in the local café as half the neighbourhood piles in demanding *cappuccino*; the appreciation of substance and the healthy scepticism about style where food is concerned; the immense pride (often masked by a bluff grumpiness) over their very special city. Whatever is happening in the higher echelons, the important bits of Rome are still there to share.

Back streets of Trastevere

Eating & Drinking

The Roman trattoria still drives the city's fresh, local, seasonal cuisine

Rome has always taken its food seriously, valuing substance over style where eating is concerned. So, although plenty of high-end and design-driven restaurants exist, most Romans, even the well-heeled ones, will opt for tradition and hearty portions over fusion and fashion. Simple, good-value restaurants (which generally go by the name of trattoria or osteria) remain the stalwarts of Rome's eating scene – more and more as times get harder. Some are unreconstructed family-run operations that have been serving up the same dishes for generations – but still do them so well that they pack in the punters day after day. Others are revamped old-school trattorias or bistros – places that take a tried-and-tested formula (informal service, unfussy cooking based on market-fresh ingredients) but give it a twist by upping the creativity quotient in the kitchen and offering a range of fine wines.

Eat like a Roman

With only 150 years of unification under its belt, the food in Italy has remained primarily regional. The Italians' inherent respect for tradition is usually manifested on the menu, and the history and landscape of each region uniquely shapes the ingredients and preparation of its signature dishes. *Cucina romana* takes its lead from the produce historically available in the Lazio countryside; namely *pecorino romano* (sheep's cheese) and *guanciale* (cured pork jowl) which form the basis for the classic Roman pasta quartet of *carbonara, amatriciana, gricia* and *cacio e pepe* (*see p43* Decoding the Menu).

The slaughterhouse of Rome, which was situated in Testaccio throughout the 20th century, also greatly influenced eating habits among the lower-classes as offal became popular as a cheap and nutritious meal: *trippa* (tripe), *coda* (oxtail), *pajata* (calf intestine) and *cervello* (brain) can still often be found in Roman trattorias, usually accompanied by locally grown seasonal greens such as *cicoria* (chicory) or *broccoletti* (turnip tops). Rome's Jewish population, which can be traced back more than 2000 years, also contributed its own recipes to the city's cuisine. Roman favourites such as *carciofi alla giudia* (deep-fried artichokes), *fiori di zucca* (stuffed, battered courgette flowers), *filetti di baccalà* (battered salt cod) and *torta di ricotta e visciole* (cherry and ricotta pie) all have their roots in the Jewish Ghetto.

The standard Roman running order is: *antipasto* (hors d'oeuvre), *primo* (usually pasta, sometimes soup or risotto), *secondo* (the meat or fish course) with optional *contorno* (vegetables or salad, served separately), and *dolce* (dessert). You're under no obligation to order four courses – few locals do. It's perfectly normal, for example, to order a pasta course followed by a simple *contorno*. Top-flight places sometimes offer a *menu degustazione* (tasting menu) in

❤ Best traditional Italian

Armando al Pantheon *p114*
Authentic food and an unbeatable location.

Da Enzo al 29 *p176*
The quintessential Trastevere trattoria.

Flavio al Velavevodetto *p217*
Roman classics in a mountain of ancient amphorae.

Sora Margherita *p132*
No-frills traditional fare in the heart of the Ghetto.

Da Enzo al 29

In the know
Reading the listings

Average restaurant prices are what you are likely to spend per person for two courses (from *antipasto, primo, secondo* and *dolce*) plus wine; while for pizzerias they cover a starter (such as bruschetta), a pizza and a medium beer.

€ = under €20

€€ = €20-€40

€€€ = €40-€60

€€€€ = over €60

the evening, but most venues offering a *menu turistico* should be avoided.

Central restaurants tend to be packed on Friday and Saturday nights and Sunday lunchtime, so do book ahead. Romans eat late (usually around 8.30-9pm) so proper restaurants open at 7-7.30pm. Places which open earlier are usually aimed at tourists, offering poor food at high prices.

The street food revolution

As Romans increasingly search for dining options which are not only delicious but easy on the wallet, the city has seen an invasion of street food establishments. Both **Mordi e Vai** (*see p219*) and **Da Simo Pane e Vino** (*see p107*) have repackaged traditionally home-cooked dishes in sandwich form, while Stefano Callegari's **Trapizzino** (*see p217*) brand has expanded from humble beginnings to become a worldwide export with branches in Japan and the US. The humble *pizza al taglio* (pizza-by-the-slice) has been revamped by superstar pizzamaker Gabriele Bonci of **Pizzarium** (*see p162*) whose focus on prime ingredients and creative combinations have prompted a loyal following.

Cafés, bars and pubs

Almost every Italian starts their day with a coffee and *cornetto* (breakfast pastry) in their local café or bar (in Italy these amount to the same thing since alcohol and coffee are served all day long in both) and will often make several trips throughout the day for a galvanising *caffè* (espresso), to grab a snack or sandwich or merely to catch up on the local gossip after work over an *aperitivo* or *digestivo*.

The action takes place at the counter with most locals preferring to stand. This is partly to participate in the lively banter but also because it is considerably cheaper than sitting down. There are usually two price lists at the bar: *al*

In the know
Vegetarians in Rome

Rome has few bona fide vegetarian restaurants; but even in traditional trattorias (*trattorie*), waiters will no longer look blankly when you say *non mangio la carne* ('I don't eat meat'). Try *penne all'arrabbiata* (pasta in a tomato and chilli sauce), *tonnarelli cacio e pepe* (thick spaghetti with sheep's cheese and black pepper) and *melanzane parmigiana* (aubergine layered with mozzarella and tomato sauce).

❤ Best blow-out restaurants

Antico Arco *p179*
Creative fine dining without an exorbitant price tag.

Glass Hostaria *p172*
Contemporary cuisine with an Italian flourish.

La Pergola *p224*
Pure decadence with three Michelin stars.

Il Sanlorenzo *p127*
Fresh fish and seafood in pristine surroundings.

Antico Arco

banco (at the counter) and *al tavolo* (at the table) with the latter often costing twice or three times the former. Protocol is vague but common practice when consuming standing up is to pay first at the cash desk and then take your receipt to the counter; be prepared to stand your ground and catch the eye of the *barista* as there is no discernible queue system. Table service should involve somebody coming to take your order but again, in busy spots, you may have to work hard to gain their attention.

With the exception of the ever-present Irish pub, until recently the *enoteca* (see below) was the backbone of drinking culture in wine-centred Italy. However, the global trend for artisanal beers has not passed Rome by and locals are now searching out more than the usual Peroni or Moretti. Italian-style pubs such as **Open Baladin** (*see p126*) and **Ma Che Siete Venuti a Fà** are a good place to start.

Enoteche

The term *enoteca* encompasses everything *vino*-related: from dusty old bottle shops, to modern wine bars. Confusingly, restaurants in Italy may also be referred to as *enoteche*, generally denoting that they have a particular focus on the wine list or double as a wine bar. The small, charming *enoteche* of the *centro storico* offer a glimpse of local life as well as serving good-value wines *alla mescita* (by the glass). Where the food is particularly good *enoteche* have been listed here as restaurants; if it is better to stick to drinking they can be found listed under bars. Wine lists in *enoteche* and restaurants are organised by region and can be somewhat overwhelming to the uninitiated so don't be afraid to ask for recommendations.

Bakeries, pasticcerie and gelaterie

Every *zona* of Rome has its *forni* (bakeries) and *pasticcerie* (cake shops) selling freshly baked

❤ Best wine bars/ enoteche

Ai Tre Scalini *p186*
Monti's top hang-out for arty wine-lovers.

Enoteca Ferrara *p173*
Chic and sleek with an encyclopaedic selection.

Il Goccetto *p128*
Rustic, wood-lined bar in the backstreets of Campo de' Fiori.

Terre e Domus Enoteca della Provincia di Roma *p65*
Locally produced wine in the shadow of Trajan's Column.

Il Goccetto

In the know
Eating with kids

Taking children into restaurants – even the smartest – is never a problem in Rome. Waiters will usually produce a high chair (*un seggiolone*) on request and are generally happy to bring *una mezza porzione* – a half-portion. Also, just about any kitchen in the city will do those off-menu standbys, *pasta al pomodoro* (with tomato sauce) or *pasta in bianco* (plain, dressed with oil or butter and parmesan).

❤ Gelato

No trip to Rome would be complete without gelato. Although thought to have been invented in 17th-century Florence, the Romans are serious fans of the icy stuff and there are now over 2000 gelaterie throughout the city, albeit of varying degrees of quality. Real gelato, made the proper way with fresh ingredients, is a true joy and locals always have their favourite neighbourhood spot which will be visited on an almost daily basis in the warmer months. As a general rule Italian gelato is made with more milk and less cream than conventional ice-cream, it is lower in fat but a higher sugar content makes it sweeter. Most fruit flavours contain no dairy, placing them closer to sorbet in both flavour and texture.

Sadly, as tourism in Rome boomed, as did the number of quick-fix gelato shops strategically placed by the main attractions and aimed at weary tourists. These eschewed traditional methods and fresh ingredients for time-saving, money-making industrial chemical mixes and machinery. Thankfully, the last two decades have seen a gradual shift towards higher quality options. The opening of **Il Gelato di San Crispino** (*see p81*) in 1992 saw owners the Alongi brothers take things back to basics, revolutionising the Romans' expectation of gelato and setting the bar for the new wave of gourmet gelaterie which continue to expand through the Eternal City. Small chains such as **Fatamorgana** (*see p186*), **Claudio Torcé** (*see p214*) and **Gelateria del Teatro** (*see p108*) have all opened multiple branches, and their experimental, often weird and wonderful, flavours are now held in just as high regard as the old-style stalwarts such as **Alberto Pica** (*see p128*).

Luckily there are some tell-tale signs that help punters to spot the bad stuff: unnaturally bright colours, a puffy texture and extravagant decoration can all be signs of fake gelato. To avoid disappointment, take a moment to scope out the selection before handing over your cash; colours should look natural and muted (a good benchmark is pistachio which should be a sludgy, almost brownish green), the texture should be thick, dense and creamy, and the flavours, particularly the fruits, should mirror the seasons.

► *When you have exhausted the gelato, try some traditional Roman* grattachecca. *Sold only in the summer months it consists of grated ice with flavoured syrup poured over the top and served in a plastic cup. Try* **Sora Mirella** *(see p178) and* **Chiosco Testaccio** *(see p218).*

Fatamorgana

goodies including bread, pizza, pastries, cakes and biscuits. Many *pasticcerie* are also bars where a sweet pick-me-up can be consumed in situ accompanied by coffee or drinks. There can be huge variations, however, in quality and freshness; the places listed are always reliable.

Gelato is sold on almost every corner of the city, particularly in summer. Sadly, the majority of city centre gelaterie cut-corners by preparing industrial gelato mixes packed with colourings and chemicals. Real gelato is a truly memorable experience and it is worth hunting down the good stuff (*see p41* Gelato). Ice-cream is served in a *cono* (cone) or *coppetta* (tub) of varying sizes, usually costing from €2 to €4.

Coffee customs

Italians take their coffee very seriously and are very particular about what they like and how they like it. It is not uncommon to hear dozens of diverse orders shouted across the bar as locals specify everything from the temperature to the amount of froth to even what kind of cup it should be served in.

The staple order is a *caffè* (espresso) which may be *normale, lungo* (with a touch more water), *ristretto* (with less water), *macchiato* (with a little milk) or *decaffeinato* (decaf). After dinner you may hear the request for a *caffè corretto,* an espresso with the addition of a dash of alcohol (usually grappa or sambuca). *Caffè americano* is an espresso diluted with hot water and served in a larger cup either *con o senza latte* (with or without milk).

Milky beverages such as cappuccino and caffè latte are strictly for breakfast time. The digestion-obsessed Italians would never dream of consuming warm milk after lunch so expect some stares if ordering after 11am.

In the warmer months the Romans stick to *caffè freddo* (cold espresso) or *caffè shakerato* (espresso shaken with ice cubes in a cocktail shaker or whizzed in a blender).

❤ Best street food

Da Simo Pane e Vino *p107*
Traditional Roman stews in *panino* form.

Pizzarium *p162*
Outstanding pizza, sold by the slice.

I Supplì *p173*
Delectable fried snacks to devour on-the-go.

Trapizzino *p217*
The locals' favourite street-food craze.

In the know
Pizza pizza

The city's *pizzaioli* have always been proud of their thin, crisp *pizza romana*, but nowadays there are plenty of Neapolitan-style pizzerias serving the puffier *pizza napolitana*. Note that the classic, round pizza is an evening thing – during the day, the Romans prefer to stop by the *forno* (bakery) for a slice of *pizza al taglio* (slices of pizza sold by weight).

Decoding the Menu

A crash course in restaurant Italian

aceto balsamico balsamic vinegar; **acqua** water – either still (*liscia*, *naturale*) or sparkling (*gassata*, *frizzante*); **olio d'oliva** olive oil; **pane** bread; **pepe** pepper; **sale** salt; **zucchero** sugar; **vino** wine.

Sughi, condimenti e ripieni – Sauces, toppings & fillings

alle vongole with clams; **al pesto** with a sauce of pine nuts, parmesan and basil; **al ragù** with minced meat and tomatoes (ie 'bolognese', a term not used in Italy); **al sugo** with puréed cooked tomatoes; **all'amatriciana** with tomato, chilli and bacon; **all'arrabbiata** with tomato and chilli; **alla carbonara** with bacon, egg and pecorino; **alla puttanesca** with tomatoes, anchovies, olives, capers, chilli and garlic; **cacio e pepe** with pecorino and black pepper; (ravioli) **ricotta e spinaci** stuffed with ricotta and spinach; **agnolotti**, **tortellini** pasta like ravioli but usually meat-filled.

Carne – Meat

abbacchio, **agnello** lamb; **capra**, **capretto** goat, kid; **coniglio** rabbit; **guanciale** cured pork jowl; **maiale** pork; **manzo** beef; **pancetta** similar to bacon; **pollo** chicken; **prosciutto cotto** ham; **prosciutto crudo** Parma ham; **tacchino** turkey; **vitello** veal.

Piatti di carne – Meat dishes

carpaccio, **bresaola** thinly sliced cured beef; **coda alla vaccinara** oxtail stew; **ossobuco** veal shins with marrow jelly inside; **polpette** meatballs; **porchetta** slow-roasted pork; **salsiccia** sausage; **saltimbocca** veal strips with ham and sage.

Formaggi – Cheeses

cacio, **caciotta** cow or sheep's milk cheese; **parmigiano** parmesan; **pecorino romano** hard, tangy sheep's cheese; **ricotta** crumbly white soft cheese; **stracchino** creamy, soft white cheese.

Pesce – Fish

sarago, **dentice**, **marmora**, **orata**, **fragolino** bream of various kinds; **alici**, **acciughe** anchovies; **baccalà** salt cod; **branzino**, **spigola** sea bass; **cernia** grouper; **merluzzo** cod; **pesce San Pietro** John Dory; **pesce spada** sword-fish; **rombo** turbot; **salmone** salmon; **sarde**, **sardine** sardines; **sogliola** sole; **tonno** tuna; **trota** trout.

Frutti di mare – Seafood

astice, **aragosta** lobster; **calamari** squid; **cozze** mussels; **crostacei** shellfish; **gamberi**, **gamberetti** shrimps, prawns; **granchio** crab; **mazzancolle** king prawns; **moscardini** baby octopus; **ostriche** oysters; **polipo**, **polpo** octopus; **sepple**, **seppioline** cuttlefish; **telline** small clams; **totani** baby flying squid; **vongole** clams.

Verduri/contorni – Vegetables/sides

asparagi asparagus; **basilico** basil; **broccoli siciliani** broccoli; **broccolo romanesco** green cauliflower; **broccoletti** tiny broccoli sprigs; **carciofi** artichokes (*alla romana* steamed; *alla giudia* deep-fried); **carote** carrots; **cavolfiore** cauliflower; **cicoria** chicory; **cipolle** onions; **fagioli** haricot or borlotti beans; **fagiolini** green beans; **fave** broad beans; **funghi** mushrooms; **funghi porcini** porcini mushrooms; **insalata** salad; **lattuga** lettuce; **melanzane** aubergine; **patate** potatoes; **patatine fritte** french fries; **peperoncino** chilli; **peperoni** peppers (capsicum); **piselli** peas; **pomodori** tomatoes; **puntarelle** bitter Roman salad usually dressed with an anchovy vinaigrette; **rughetta**, **rucola** rocket; **spinaci** spinach; **verza** cabbage; **zucchine** courgettes.

Frutta – Fruit

albicocche apricots; **ananas** pineapple; **arance** oranges; **cachi** persimmons; **ciliege** cherries; **coccomero**, **anguria** watermelon; **fichi** figs; **fragole**, **fragoline** strawberries; **frutti di bosco** woodland berries; **mele** apples; **nespole** loquats; **pere** pears; **pesche** peaches; **prugne**, **susine** plums; **uva** grapes.

Dolci – Desserts

gelato ice-cream; **pannacotta** 'cooked cream', a very thick, blancmange-like cream; **sorbetto** sorbet; **tiramisù** mascarpone and coffee sponge; **torta della nonna** flan of pâtisserie cream and pine nuts; **torta di mele** apple flan; **millefoglie** flaky pastry cake.

Pizza & toppings

calzone a sealed pizza pie, usually filled with cheese, tomato and ham; **capricciosa** ham, hard-boiled eggs, artichokes and olives; **funghi** mushrooms; **marinara** plain tomato with garlic and herbs; **margherita** tomato and mozzarella; **napoli**, **napoletana** tomato, anchovies and mozzarella; **quattro formaggi** four cheeses.

Pizzeria extras

bruschetta toast with garlic rubbed into it and oil on top, often with diced raw tomatoes; **crochette** potato croquettes; **crostini** slices of toast, usually with a grilled cheese and anchovy or ham topping; **filetto di baccalà** deep-fried salt cod in batter; **fiori di zucca** deep-fried battered courgette flowers stuffed with mozzarella and anchovy; **olive ascolane** deep-fried olives stuffed with meat; **supplì** deep-fried rice balls with mozzarella inside (may contain minced meat).

Shopping

The Eternal City may be losing its vintage feel, but there are still gems to be found

---

Until not that long ago, shopping in Rome was a rather refreshing, old-fashioned experience with mainly independent, family-run establishments offering personal service and quality products. Huge department stores were rare and high street chains were largely absent. But these days the city's historic shops struggle to cling on in the harsh economic climate as rents rise and consumers become more willing to sacrifice service and quality for bargain prices.

However, the old-fashioned world hasn't disappeared completely – there are still plenty of unique gems buried among the now-ubiquitous international brands.

Centro storico

Look carefully and Rome's shopping scene can satisfy almost every need. While the Tridente's via del Corso is the closest thing that Rome has to a high street, just a short wander off the main drag into the narrow surrounding streets, or a trip to the smaller, up-and-coming neighbourhoods of Monti, Trastevere and Testaccio will reward you with one-off boutiques by emerging designers, quaint family-run delis and artisanal artists and craftsmen. Rome's markets, from the daily neighbourhood produce markets to the weekly flea markets, remain one of the most authentic ways to both shop and experience a slice of local life, while a stroll down the exclusive via dei Condotti will take you to the heart of the capital's high-fashion aristocracy.

Clothes and shoes

To splash the cash head to **via dei Condotti** (Tridente) where the major Italian labels such as Gucci, Prada and Dolce e Gabbana are interspersed with international names including Louis Vuitton, Jimmy Choo and Burberry. The surrounding streets in the Spanish Steps part of the Tridente are home to some smaller, but no-less exclusive, high-end boutiques. For more wallet-friendly options, **via del Corso** (Tridente) is: lined with well-known chains including Zara, H&M and Mango as well as large sports brands; similar mid-range shops can also be found on **via Nazionale** in the Quirinale. Over in the Prati district, **via Cola di Rienzo** is a less-crowded, slightly higher-end version of via del Corso, with the addition of the glamorous **COIN Excelsior** (*see p163*) department store.

Jewellery and watches

The big names in glitter production, like Bulgari, Cartier and **Damiani** (*see p94*) cluster around piazza di Spagna in the Tridente area. Even if you don't plan to purchase, it's

❤ Best Italian accessories

Borsalino *p116*
Historic hatmaker to the stars.

Ibiz *p129*
Leather bags handmade onsite.

Laboratorio Marco Aurelio *p129*
Unique handcrafted jewellery.

Sermoneta *p95*
Exquisite artisanal gloves.

High fashion and world-class brands can be found on via dei Condotti.

In the know
Seeking out boutiques

For unique purchases explore the small streets of the Ghetto, Monti and Trastevere districts to find up-and-coming designers and independent boutiques, or check out the vintage shops on **via Governo Vecchio** near piazza Navona.

worth straying along diamond lane for a look at enviable and original baubles.

Lingerie and underwear

Lingerie chains like Intimissimi, Tezenis and Yamamay have multiple branches throughout town and cater for men and women looking for cheap-and-cheerful undies. Upmarket lingerie shops including **La Perla** (*see p100*) cluster around the Tridente.

Food and drink

Supermarket chains can be found throughout the city but for higher-quality cured meats, cheese and bread visit the *alimentari* (delicatessen) or *forno* (bakery) where food is sold by the *etto* (100 grams). **Beppe e I suoi Formaggi** in the Ghetto, **Antica Caciara** in Trastevere and **Volpetti** (*see p219*) in Testaccio are some of the best in town. Most neighbourhoods have a fresh produce market which takes place in the mornings from Monday to Saturday. While the **campo de' Fiori market** (*see p123*) is the most central, it has become rather touristy in recent years; for a more authentic experience head to the newly renovated **Mercato Testaccio** or the **Mercato San Cosimato** in Trastevere (*see p175*). Wine and liquor are sold at the *enoteca* (off-licences) which sometimes also have a bar for downing a

❤ Best for foodies

Antica Caciara *p175*
Delectable delicatessen dating back to 1900.

Beppe e I Suoi Formaggi *p132*
Cheese, cheese and more cheese.

C.U.C.I.N.A *p94*
Kitchenware, crockery and gadgets.

Eataly *p219*
The best of Italian cuisine at your fingertips.

The Mercato Testaccio provides a much more authentic experience than the touristy campo de' Fiori market.

glass or two, try **Les Vignerons** (*see p176*) in Trastevere or **Trimani** (*see p194*) in Esquilino.

Cosmetics and perfumes

Beauty superstores Sephora, Limoni and Beauty Point stock big-name ranges plus basic toiletries at non-rip-off prices at many central locations. Popular Italian cosmetics chain Kiko has stores in every corner of the city selling bright, fun products at great prices. For a more refined experience, follow your nose to one of the city's elegant *profumerie* such as **L'Olfattorio** (*see p101*) in the Tridente.

Antiques and homewares

Among the best areas for antiques are **via del Babuino** (Tridente), **via Giulia** (campo de' Fiori) and **via dei Coronari** (piazza Navona). Dealers/restorers thronging **via del Pellegrino** near campo de' Fiori may be cheaper, but quality dips too. Bargains can occasionally be picked up at the **Porta Portese** flea market in Trastevere. For homeware **via delle Botteghe Oscure** and **via Arenula** located between campo de' Fiori and the Ghetto are full of shops that sell linen, fabric, laces and curtain ribbons.

Life's essentials

Most traveller essentials – including bus tickets, stamps and maps – can be found at the *tabacchi* (tobacconists). Identifiable by a large white T on a blue or black background, they not only sell tobacco products but often carry stationery, games and souvenirs. Many also have a postbox outside.

Rome's *edicole* (newsstands) are cute green kiosks which, aside from selling newspapers and magazines, also dispense transport tickets. They are also handy for directions and exchanging large notes for small change. The larger *edicole* will usually sell a selection of international newspapers and magazines.

❤ Best markets

Borghetto Flaminio *p225*
The best bet for vintage designer finds.

Mercato Monti *p187*
Original fashion, creative accessories and unique homeware.

Mercato Testaccio *p219*
Top quality produce and delicious street food.

Nuovo Mercato Esquilino *p193*
Shoppers and foodstuffs from around the globe.

Porta Portese *p178*
Rome's sprawling Sunday flea market.

Most neighbourhoods have a fresh produce market which takes place in the mornings from Monday to Saturday.

Opening times

Opening hours aren't as traditional as they once were and now most central-Rome shops operate *'no-stop'* opening hours, from 9.30-10am to 7.30-8pm every day. The occasional independent still clings to the traditional 1-4pm shutdown but will then reopen until 8-8.30pm, and in smaller neighbourhoods family-run businesses will generally close on Sundays.

The majority of clothing shops are closed, or open later, on Monday mornings. Some smaller shops shut down for at least two weeks each summer (generally in August) and almost all are shut for two or three days around the 15 August public holiday. If you're shopping with something particular in mind and you want to avoid finding a particular shop *chiuso per ferie* (closed for holidays), be sure to ring ahead.

The Piaggio Ape, with its small engine, is ideal for carrying all sorts of goods around Rome's narrow back streets.

Shopping practicalities

Non-EU residents are entitled to a sales tax (IVA) rebate on purchases of goods over €155, providing they are exported unused and bought from a shop with the 'Europe Tax Free' sticker. The shop will give you a receipt and a 'Tax Free Shopping Cheque', which should be stamped by customs before leaving Italy.

When you purchase anything, you should be given a *scontrino* (receipt). If you aren't, ask for it: by law, shops are required to provide one, and they and you are liable for a fine in the (wildly unlikely) event of your being caught without it. Major credit cards are accepted just about everywhere, although it's worth checking before queuing.

The rules on returning items are infuriatingly vague. Faulty goods, obviously, must be refunded or replaced. Most shops will also accept unwanted goods that are returned unused with a receipt within seven days of purchase, though this is not obligatory.

In the know
Shop talk

In general shop assistants will greet customers with a *buongiorno* ('good morning') or *buonasera* ('good evening') as they enter and *arrivederci* ('goodbye') as they leave. It is good custom to reciprocate in the same way. The essential lines *mi può aiutare, per favore?* ('Can you help me please?') and *volevo solo dare un' occhiata* ('I'm just looking') will stand you in good stead when dealing with reticent or over-insistent staff.

Explore

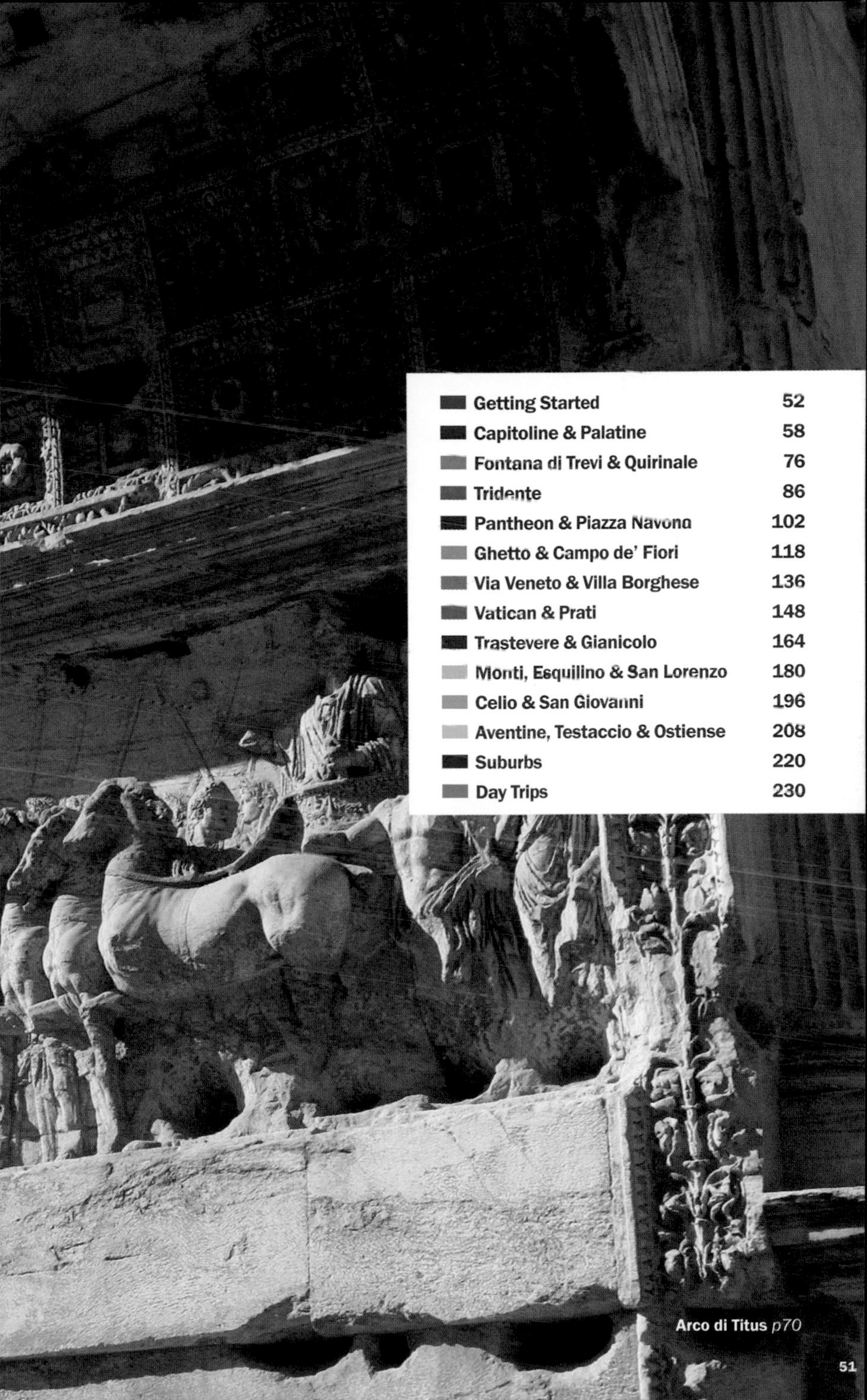

Arco di Titus *p70*

Getting Started

Central Rome is compact, and the areas covered by this guide are mostly very close to one another. The *centro storico* (historic centre) stretches from the Forum to the Vatican and was the hub of the city after the fall of the Empire. It is a densely built-up network of cobbled streets, medieval and Renaissance churches and palaces, and opulent Baroque piazzas, with traces of the Imperial city permeating the entire area: a column here, the Pantheon there. It is probably where you'll be spending most of your time, and where you may choose to stay. To make it easier to navigate, we've subdivided it into distinct areas, each of which has its own chapter. We've also strayed a little further afield to explore some especially interesting neighbourhoods both within and outside the ancient city walls.

Overview of the city

We begin with the two most important of the seven hills upon which Ancient Rome was built: the **Capitoline & Palatine** (*see pp58-73*), separated by a valley containing the Roman Forum, where you'll find some of the world's best archaeological remains.

Just north-east of piazza Venezia, the Quirinale was the tallest of Ancient Rome's

❤ Best churches

Gesù *p124*
Mother church of the Jesuits, home to a spectacular ceiling.

San Carlo alle Quattro Fontane *p84*
The tiny masterpiece of tortured Baroque genius, Francesco Borromini.

Santa Cecilia in Trastevere *p177*
A fabulous fresco, a decorated crypt and a moving sculpture of the saint herself.

San Clemente *p200*
A church upon a church upon a mithraic temple: a veritable time machine.

San Luigi dei Francesi *p111*
Come for the Caravaggios, but don't miss the Domenichinos.

Colosseo *p74*

seven hills. Today, the **Fontana di Trevi & Quirinale** area (*see pp76-85*) has a mass of Baroque treasures and art galleries to be discovered, not to mention the spectacular Trevi fountain.

Enclosed by the 'trident' of roads which radiate south from piazza del Popolo, just within the ancient city walls, the **Tridente** (*see pp86-101*) is the heartland of high-end shopping and has a significant portion of ancient heritage. Following one of the main roads, via del Corso, south, the area housing the **Pantheon & Piazza Navona** (*see pp102-117*) was first incorporated into the city limits by Augustus and is littered with imperial monuments.

Bounded by the fume-filled corso Vittorio Emanuele II to the north and the River Tiber to the south, the picturesque tangle of cobbled streets that makes up the **Ghetto & Campo de' Fiori** (*see*

❤ Best museums

Musei Capitolini *p60*
The world's oldest public museum, with a fantastic view over the Forum.

Museo dell'Alto Medioevo *p228*
Trek out to EUR to admire a recreated room decorated with marble inlay from Ostia. Trust us, it's worth it.

Museo delle Mura *p227*
Scale the city's Aurelian walls.

Musei Vaticani *p154*
Vast repository for treasures collected over many centuries.

Palazzo Doria Pamphilj *p115*
A charming papal stately home, whose art collection includes Raphael, Titian, Bernini, Velazquez and Caravaggio.

Piazza del Popolo *p97*

pp118-135) is crammed with late medieval apartment buildings, punctuated by elegant Renaissance *palazzi*: here, papal grandeur lies cheek by jowl with the area in which Rome's Jews were effectively imprisoned for over three centuries.

A stone's throw from the cobbled streets of the *centro storico* is the elegant sweep of the **Via Veneto** (*see pp136-147*). At the top of this road the is the vast **Villa Borghese** park, providing acres of green and splendid views.

On the west side of the river sits the independent state of the **Vatican** (*see pp148-163*). The *prati* (meadows) surrounding the Vatican were built upon to provide housing for the new nation's civil servants. Its stolidly elegant avenues have a certain fin de siècle bourgeois pomposity.

Overlooking the Vatican is the **Gianicolo** hill – climb up for great views. On the other side of the hill, **Trastevere** (*see pp164-179*) retains a villagey vibe; its cobbled streets and ancient churches are full of charm.

❤ Best museums *(cont)*

Villa Farnesina *p172*
A jewel decorated by Raphael and chums nestling in charming Trastevere.

Villa Giulia *p144*
The national Etruscan museum is in a villa designed in part by Michelangelo.

In the know
Free Sundays

On the first Sunday of the month, entrance to all Italian state museums is free; save the packed Colosseum for another day and take advantage at less-busy sites.

On the east side of the *centro storico* sits **Monti & Esquilino** (*see pp180-195*), and Termini railway station. In ancient times the Esquiline hill was a grand residential district, but today it's a little rough around the edges. Monti was the ancient city's slum; today its cobbled streets are full of hip boutiques, spots to eat and drink and the child-friendly Colle Oppio park, right across from the Colosseum. Outside the city walls, **San Lorenzo** is the city's university district.

South-east of the Colosseum are the altogether less-touristed areas of **Celio & San Giovanni** (*see pp196-207*). In Celio, 19th-century apartment buildings lead up to the delightful Villa Celimontana park and to some of Rome's finest early Christian churches. Further east sits Rome's cathedral, San Giovanni in Laterano.

South of the *centro storico* are **Aventine, Testaccio & Ostiense** (*see pp208-219*). Elegantly residential Aventine contrasts with the noisy atmosphere at the foot of the hill in Testaccio, which was the ancient city's river port. It remains a solidly salt-of-the-earth neighbourhood with an excellent market. Further south is student-heavy Ostiense, with its buzzing nightlife.

Beyond the Aurelian walls, in Rome's extensive **Suburbs** (*see pp220-229*), there is much of interest, both ancient and vehemently not: Zaha Hadid's MAXXI; edgy Pigneto; the bucolic sites of the Appian Way; the Fascist-era EUR. Further afield are some extraordinary sites that are worth a special trip; these are covered in **Day Trips** (*see pp230-237*).

Stele of gladiator

Flavio al Velavevodetto *p217*

Cimitero Acattolico *p216*

Getting around

Although Rome suffers from chronic traffic congestion, much of the compact central area is either pedestrianised or has restricted access to traffic, which means that walking is by far the best and most pleasant way to get around.

When you do use public transport, the bus is your best bet; the atac.roma.it journey planner is useful, and the Roma Bus app (www.muovi.roma.it) gives arrival times at bus stops in real time. The metro has two main lines (line C at present doesn't reach the centre) and is far from exhaustive. There are, however, some strategic central stops (Spagna, Barberini, Colosseo).

Children travel free on Rome's city transport until their tenth birthday; older children pay the full price for single-journey and one- or three-day bus passes. A bus tour (*see p318*) with English commentary is a good way to whisk your family past the major sights. Taxis can be found at taxi stands, and are tricky to hail on the street. Uber is, for the moment, legal in Rome.

► *For further information on all forms of transport, see p315 Getting Around.*

Tourist information

Rome's city council operates a number of green-painted tourist information kiosks (PIT) that are open 9.30am-7.30pm daily. *See p329* for their exact locations. The excellent, exhaustive 060608.it website is the city council's one-stop shop for information on museums, galleries, events, hotels and much more besides. For Rome tourist information on your mobile, see www.turismoroma.it. For other useful websites, *see p334* Further Reference.

Tickets

Expect to pay *diritti di prevendita* (booking fees) on tickets bought anywhere except at the venue on the day or night. Tickets for concerts of all descriptions, sporting events, cultural happenings and queue-free or guided visits to artistic or archaeological sites can be booked online through a number of agencies, the largest of which are: **Ticket One** (www.ticketone.it, 892 101) for concerts, sports and culture; **Hello Ticket** (www.helloticket.it, 800 907 080) for theatre and dance; **Coop Culture** (www.coopculture.it) for galleries, archeological sites and guided tours.

Tourist passes

The **Roma Pass** (€38.50, www.romapass.it) is a three-day pass including buses and metro, free entrance to two sites (choose the pricier ones to make it worthwhile) and reduced entrance to many more. There is also a seven-day **Archeologia Card** (€23, €13 reductions), which is great value if you're visiting several sites and want to avoid queues; it covers Appian Way sites, the Roman Forum, Colosseum and the Palatine. For details, see 060608.it.

Tours

The most popular sites for guided tours are the Vatican Museums and the Colosseum/Forum archeological areas. Both sites are vast and can be confusing; a good guided tour will help you to navigate the crowds, find the quiet spots and maximise your time.

Context Travel (06 9672 7371, www.contexttravel.com) runs small group (maximum six people) and private tours led by highly qualified guides, largely archaeologists and art historians. **Understanding Rome** (www.understandingrome.com) tailor-makes private tours of Rome, including 'off the beaten track' itineraries. For something different, **A Friend in Rome** (www.afriendinrome.it) gives you an opportunity to explore Rome à la Audrey Hepburn, with a private Vespa tour.

If you would like to take an open top bus, **City Sightseeing Roma** and **Roma Cristiana** (*see p318* Getting Around) are the best of the bunch, the latter especially for visiting slightly further-flung churches if you'd rather not take the metro.

Food writer Katie Parla (www.katieparla.com) runs private gastronomical tours and erstwhile London restaurateur Carla Tomasi arranges cooking classes in Trastevere (cookingwithcarlablog.wordpress.com).

In the know
Cycling in the city

Occasionally, parts of the *centro storico* are closed to traffic on a Sunday, providing an opportunity for visitors to explore the city on two wheels in relative safety. It's a weekly occurrence further out: the Appian Way offers especially serene (if somewhat bumpy) pedalling on traffic-free Sundays. For bike hire outlets, *see p320*. For information on other cycle-able bits of Rome, see www.piste-ciclabili.com/comune-roma.

Capitoline & Palatine

In the eighth century BC, a collection of grass huts was built on a hill overlooking the marshy flood plain of a tributary of the River Tiber. In the following century the land was drained and the settlement expanded down the slopes into what would become the Roman Forum. A thousand years of expansion later, this had become the heart of the ancient world's most powerful city, the capital of an empire that stretched from Scotland to the Sahara. These huts were replaced with splendid Imperial palaces (the Palatine), great temples were constructed on the neighbouring hill (the Capitoline) and emperors kept public discontent to a minimum with gory entertainment in the Colosseum.

❤ Don't miss

1 Colosseo *p74*
The mother of all stadia.

2 Domus Romane *p61*
A fascinating multimedia tour bringing grand Roman townhouses back to life.

3 Vittoriano *p64*
The national monument is an exercise in bombastic rhetoric, and there's a great view from the top.

4 Foro Romano & Palatino *p67*
The heart of Ancient Rome.

In the know
Getting around

This area is very walkable, and densely packed with some of Rome's most celebrated sites. The following buses pass through piazza Venezia: 30Exp, 40Exp, 44, 46, 53, 60, 62, 63, 64, 70, 81, 83, 85, 87, 117, 160, 170, 492, 628, 715, 716, 780, 781, 810, 916, H. Get off at piazza Venezia and make your way south-west to visit the Forum and continue to the Palatine and Colosseum. Alternatively, take metro line B to Colosseo and start at the Colosseum before walking the short distance to the entrance to the Palatine/Forum site on via di San Gregorio.

Emperor Constantine in the Musei Capitolini *p60*

PIAZZA VENEZIA & CAPITOLINE

Heavily trafficked **piazza Venezia** is dominated by a brash monument to a dynasty that produced five kings. The **Vittoriano** (*see p64*) – aka *l'altare della patria* – is a piece of nationalistic bombast made of unsuitably dazzling marble brought at vast expense from Brescia. Totally out of proportion with everything around, it was constructed between 1885 and 1911 to honour the first king of united Italy, Vittorio Emanuele II of Savoy. Centred on a colossal equestrian statue of the king (before the statue was welded together, metalworkers held a dinner for 20 in the horse's belly), it's also Italy's memorial to the 'unknown soldier'.

On the western side of piazza Venezia stands **Palazzo Venezia** (*see p63*). Constructed by the Venetian Pope Paul II in the 15th century, it was to become Mussolini's HQ: *il Duce* addressed the crowds from the central balcony. To the south of the *palazzo* is **San Marco** (*see p63*), a church founded in the fourth century and remodelled in the 15th century for Pope Paul II.

Across the piazza, the **Domus Romane** (*see p61*) beneath the Metropolitan City HQ at Palazzo Valentini gives a fascinating multimedia insight into life here in the late Imperial era.

To the right as you face the Vittoriano are the remains of a Roman *insula* (apartment building) that survived the bulldozers that devastated the area to make way for the Vittoriano. Further to the right, steep steps lead up to **Santa Maria in Aracoeli** (*see p63*), built on the spot where, legend says, a sybil prophesied the birth of Christ. Next to that, the ramped *cordonata* (sloping road) ascends to **piazza del Campidoglio.**

The **Campidoglio** (Capitoline) was, politically and religiously speaking, the most important of ancient Rome's hills and was the site of the two major temples. Chunks of the base of one to Jupiter Optimus Maximus, symbolic father of the city – whose cult chambers also included shrines to Minerva, goddess of wisdom, and Juno, wife of Jupiter – can now be seen inside the **Musei Capitolini** (**Capitoline Museums**; *see p60*). The other, to Juno Moneta ('giver of advice'), stood on the site of Santa Maria in Aracoeli. It housed the sacred Capitoline geese, whose honking raised the alarm when Gauls attacked Rome in 390 BC; so failsafe was this alarm system that Rome's first mint was built beside it – from *moneta* comes the word 'money'.

The *piazza* on the Campidoglio was designed in the 1530s by Michelangelo for Pope Paul III, a symbolic rebuilding of the heart of the city after centuries of degradation. It took about a hundred years to complete; some of Michelangelo's ideas were modified along the way, but it is still very much as he envisaged it. At the top of Michelangelo's *cordonata* are two giant Roman statues of the mythical twins Castor and Pollux, found near piazza Cenci and placed here in 1583. Looking straight ahead from the top of the steps, you'll see **Palazzo Senatorio**, Rome's city hall, completed by Giacomo della Porta and Girolamo Rainaldi to Michelangelo's design. To the left is **Palazzo Nuovo** and to the right **Palazzo dei Conservatori**, both of which house the **Musei Capitolini**.

For four centuries the piazza's central pedestal supported a magnificent second-century gilded bronze equestrian statue of Emperor Marcus Aurelius. The statue there now is a copy, with the original inside the Palazzo dei Conservatori.

From the top of the *cordonata*, take a right on the road that skirts this *palazzo*: it leads to a little park with a fantastic view. Beyond a gate, a series of pathways hugs the side of the hill (as dusk falls this is Rome's most central gay cruising area). The upper road continues to that part of the hill known as the **Rupe Tarpea** (Tarpeian Rock), where traitors and murderers were flung to their death. There's a great view of the Roman Forum (with the Colosseum in the distance) and, to your left, the back of the Palazzo Senatorio, which incorporates the great stone blocks of the Tabularium, where the archives of the ancient city were once held.

Sights & museums

Musei Capitolini

Piazza del Campidoglio 1 (06 0608, www.museicapitolini.org). See p58 Getting around. ***Open*** *9am-7.30pm Tue-Sun.* ***Admission*** *€15; €13 reductions.* ***Map*** *p68 K10.*

Housed in the twin palaces of Palazzo Nuovo and Palazzo dei Conservatori, standing on opposite sides of Michelangelo's piazza del Campidoglio, the Capitoline Museums constitute the oldest public gallery in the world. Their collection was begun in 1471, when Pope Sixtus IV presented the Roman people with a group of classical sculptures. Sixtus's successors continued to enrich the collection with examples of ancient art (mostly sculptures) and, at a later date, some important Renaissance and post-Renaissance paintings. The entire collection was finally opened to the public in 1734, by Pope Clement

❤ Domus Romane

Piazza Foro Traiano 85 (06 32 810, www.palazzovalentini.it). See p58 Getting around. ***Open*** *9am-6.30pm Mon, Wed-Sun.* ***Admission*** *€12; €8 reductions (plus €1.50 booking fee). Pre-booking obligatory.* ***Map*** *p68 K9.*

Discovered beneath the offices of the government of the Metropolitan City of Rome (formerly the Province of Rome until recent modifications to local government), the excavations of the Domus Romane offer a glimpse into the richly decorated houses of well-heeled citizens of the Roman Empire.

Since the inauguration in 2010, modern technology has been used with great success to bring back to life the domestic surroundings and lifestyles of the movers and shakers of ancient Rome, a stone's throw from their public lives in the Forum. Beneath the street level, surviving traces of mosaics, multi-coloured marble floors, and wall paintings provide the point of departure for projected reconstructions, detailing the various periods of the buildings' histories.

The visit also includes a great view and virtual reconstruction of Trajan's Forum, including his column, libraries, and the Basilica Ulpia (law court). The column is a spectacular monument of triumph carved with a relief which records Trajan's conquest of Dacia (modern-day Romania), culminating in the death of King Decebalus.

The site is definitely the best that central Rome offers for putting the ancient world in context – a veritable time machine.

Visits in English begin at 9.30am, 1.30pm, 2pm, and 2.30pm and advance booking is essential. Any disabled visitors or those with mobility difficulties should make this known when booking as there is provision for assistance.

Domus Romane di Palazzo

XII. Many statues remain frustratingly labelless but there is a decent audioguide.

Entrance to the Musei Capitolini is by the **Palazzo dei Conservatori**, on the right as you come up Michelangelo's stairs. The courtyard contains what's left of the colossal statue of Constantine (the rest was made of wood) that originally stood in the Basilica of Maxentius in the Roman Forum.

Upstairs, the huge Sala degli Orazi e Curiazi is home to a statue (1635-40) by Bernini of his patron Urban VIII in which everything about the pope seems to be in motion; at the opposite end of the hall is Urban's successor Innocent X. The Sala dei Capitani has late 16th-century frescoes of great moments in ancient Roman history and Renaissance military folk in ancient garb. In the Sala dei Trionfi, the first-century BC bronze of a boy removing a thorn from his foot, known as the *Spinario*, is probably an original Greek work. There's also a rare bronze portrait bust from the fourth or third century BC, popularly believed to be of Rome's first consul, Brutus.

The Sala della Lupa is home to the much-reproduced *She-Wolf* (*lupa*), the symbol of the city. This statue had long been supposed to be a fifth-century BC Etruscan bronze, with the suckling twins added in the Renaissance (attributed to Antonio del Pollaiolo). But further studies, released in 2012, revealed that it actually dates from the Middle Ages.

In the Sala delle Oche is Bernini's pained-looking Medusa and an 18th-century bronze portrait of Michelangelo, believed to have been based on the great master's death mask. The Sala delle Aquile is frescoed with 16th-century Roman scenes amid faux-ancient 'grotesque' decorations. In the Sala degli Arazzi a marvellous marble group shows the Emperor Commodus dressing up as Hercules and being adored by two tritons. The Sala di Annibale still has original early 16th-century frescoes that show Hannibal riding on an elephant of which Walt Disney would have been proud.

The second-century AD gilded bronze equestrian statue of Marcus Aurelius that for centuries stood in the centre of piazza del Campidoglio has now found a worthy home in an airy new wing of the museum, which also contains large sections of a temple to Jupiter (Giove). Though the statue now on the plinth in the piazza outside is a 'perfect' computer-generated copy, it can't compare with the sheer delicacy and majesty of this original.

Marforio (Oceanus), Musei Capitolini

On the second floor, the **Pinacoteca Capitolina** (Capitoline art gallery) contains a number of significant works. The most striking is Caravaggio's *St John the Baptist* (1596; in the Sala di Santa Petronilla), who has nothing even remotely saintly about him. There's a weepy *Penitent Magdalene* (c1598) by Tintoretto, a *Rape of Europa* by Veronese, and an early *Baptism of Christ* (c1512) by Titian in Room 3. There are also some strangely impressionistic works by Guido Reni in Room 6, various busy scenes by Pietro da Cortona in the room named after him, and some luscious portraits by Van Dyck in the Galleria Cini. While you're up here, check out the café; the coffee is so-so but the view from the terrace is spectacular.

To get to the other side of the Musei Capitolini, housed in the Palazzo Nuovo, visitors pass through the **Tabularium**, the ancient Roman archive building upon which the Palazzo Senatorio was built. This houses an epigraphic collection, with inscriptions translated into English. The tufa vaults of the Tabularium date back to 78 BC, and the view from here over the Forum is simply breathtaking (take the stairs on the right two thirds of the way along the corridor).

Palazzo Nuovo houses one of Europe's most significant collections of ancient sculpture. The three ground-floor rooms have portrait busts of Roman citizens, the endearing *Vecchio ubriacone* ('old drunk', part of Bacchus's entourage) and a huge sarcophagus with scenes from the life of Achilles, topped by two reclining second-century AD figures. Dominating the courtyard is the first-century AD river god known as Marforio, reclining above his little fountain.

Upstairs in the long gallery (Room 1), the wounded warrior falling to the ground with his shield is probably a third-century BC discus thrower's top half, turned on its side and given a new pair of legs in the 17th century. Room 2 (Sala delle Colombe, on your right) contains a statue of a little girl protecting a dove from a snake, a much-reworked drunken old woman clutching an urn of wine, and a dove mosaic from **Hadrian's Villa** (**Villa Adriana**; *see p235*) at Tivoli. Room 3 (Gabinetto della Venere) is home to the coy first-century BC *Capitoline Venus*. This was probably based on Praxiteles' *Venus of Cnodis*, considered so erotic by the fourth-century BC inhabitants of Kos that one desperate citizen was caught *in flagrante* with it. In Room 4 (Sala degli Imperatori), portrait busts of emperors, their consorts and children are arranged chronologically, providing a good insight into changing fashions and hairstyles. Next door in Room 5 (Sala dei Filosofi) are ancient portraits of philosophers and poets. Larger statues of mythical figures grace the huge Salone (Room 6). Room 7 (Sala del Fauno) is named after an inebriated faun carved from *rosso antico* marble in the late second century BC; the smirking, pointy eared statue inspired Nathaniel Hawthorne's *The Marble Faun*. In Room 8 (Sala del Gladiatore) is the moving *Dying Gaul*, probably based on a third-century BC Greek original.

► *Part of the ancient sculpture collection from the Musei Capitolini can be seen at the* Centrale Montemartini; *see p213. A combined ticket for both is €16 (€14 reductions), valid for seven days.*

Museo di Palazzo Venezia

Via del Plebiscito 118 (06 678 0131, www.museopalazzovenezia.beniculturali.it). See p58 Getting around. ***Open*** *8.30am-7.30pm Tue-Sun.* ***Admission*** *Museum €10; €5 reductions. Exhibitions extra. No cards.* ***Map*** *p68 J9.*

This collection contains a hotchpotch of everything from terracotta models by Bernini to medieval decorative art. In Room 1 are Venetian odds and ends, including a double portrait by Giorgione, while in Room 4 you'll find a glorious zodiac motif on the ceiling. Amid the early Renaissance canvases and triptychs in Room 6 is a breastfeeding *Madonna dell'Umiltà* – a racy show of anatomy for the 14th century, and quite a contrast to the pastel portraits of 18th-century aristocrats adorning Room 8. Collections of porcelain line the long corridor leading to Rooms 18-26, where you'll find Bernini's terracotta musings for the **Fontana del Tritone** (*see p83*) and the angels on Ponte Sant'Angelo. A lapidarium occupies the upper level of the cloister of the 'secret garden of Paul II'. As the name suggests, it houses a collection of stone: ancient, medieval and Renaissance sarcophagi, coats of arms, funerary monuments and assorted fragments. The eastern half of the *palazzo* occasionally hosts exhibitions that are sometimes worth checking out but that don't always live up to expectations. But if you stump up the extra fee you at least get to see Mussolini's old office, the huge Sala del Mappamondo, so-called because of an early map of the world that was kept there in the 16th century.

San Marco

Piazza San Marco 48 (06 679 5205). See p58 Getting around. ***Open*** *8.30am-12.30pm, 4-7pm Tue-Sun.* ***Map*** *p68 J9.*

There's a strong Venetian flavour to this church, which, according to local lore, was founded in 336 on the site of the house where St Mark the Evangelist – the patron saint of Venice – stayed. There are medieval lions, the symbol of St Mark, by the main entrance door; inside are graves of Venetians and paintings of Venetian saints. Rebuilt during the fifth century, the church was further reorganised by Pope Paul II in the 15th century when the neighbouring Palazzo Venezia was built. San Marco was given its Baroque look in the mid 18th century. Remaining from its earlier manifestations are the 11th-century bell tower, a portico attributed to Leon Battista Alberti, the 15th-century ceiling with Paul II's coat of arms, and the ninth-century mosaic of Christ in the apse. Among the figures below Christ is Gregory IV, who was pope when the mosaic was made: his square halo marks him out as bound for sainthood though still alive. In the portico (on the right as you enter) is the gravestone of Vannozza Catanei, mistress of Rodrigo Borgia – Pope Alexander VI – and mother of the notorious Cesare and Lucrezia which, after the Borgias were disgraced, was for centuries repurposed inscription-side-down in the floor of San Marco where it was found in the 1940s.

Santa Maria in Aracoeli

Piazza del Campidoglio 4 (06 6976 3839). See p58 Getting around. ***Open*** *May-Sept 9am-7pm daily. Oct-Apr 9.30am-5.30pm daily.* ***Map*** *p68 K10.*

At the head of a daunting flight of 120 marble steps, the Romanesque Aracoeli ('altar of heaven') stands on the site of an ancient temple to Juno Moneta. There is also a side exit accessible from the piazza del Campidoglio, tucked behind the Palazzo Nuovo. It was here, legend has it, that the Tiburtine Sybil whispered to the Emperor Augustus *haec est ara primogeniti Dei* ('this is the altar of God's first-born'). Though there is an altar purporting to be the one erected by Augustus in the chapel of St Helena (to the left of the high altar), there's no record of a Christian church here until the sixth century. The current basilica-form church was designed (and reoriented to face St Peter's) for the Franciscan order in the late 13th century, perhaps by Arnolfo di Cambio.

Dividing the church into a nave and two aisles are 22 columns purloined from Roman buildings. There's a cosmatesque floor punctuated by marble gravestones and a richly gilded ceiling commemorating the

Top 20

❤ Vittoriano

Piazza Venezia/via di San Pietro in Carcere/piazza Aracoeli (06 678 3587, www.ilvittoriano.com). See p58 Getting around. ***Monument, lift & Museo del Risorgimento*** *9.30am-6.45pm daily.* ***Sacrario delle Bandiere*** *9.30am-3pm Tue-Sun.* ***Ala Brasini*** *(06 678 0664, open during exhibitions only) 9.30am-7.30pm Mon-Thur; 9.30am-10pm Fri, Sat; 9.30am-8.30pm Sun.* ***Admission*** *Monument, Sacrario free; Museo del Risorgimento €5; €2.50 reductions. Lift €7; €3.50 reductions. Ala Brasini varies.* ***Map*** *p68 K10.*

It's worth climbing to the top of this monument, not only to appreciate the enormity of the thing, but also to see the Art Nouveau mosaics in the colonnade and – most importantly – to enjoy the view from the only place where you can see the whole city centre without the panorama being disturbed by the bulk of the Vittoriano itself.

Even more impressive than the view after a hike up the steps is the panorama from the very top level of the monument, reached by a glass elevator accessed from behind the monument, by the side of the Aracoeli church (*see p63*). Choose a clear day: extending over the whole city and out to countryside and hills beyond, the panorama is simply breathtaking.

The building also contains various exhibition spaces: on the south-east side of the monument the **Museo Centrale del Risorgimento** (www.risorgimento.it, entrance on via San Pietro in Carcere) has all kinds of exhibits on the 19th-century struggle to unify Italy, including the rather fancy boot worn by Giuseppe Garibaldi when he was shot in the foot in 1862, and panels (in English) explaining the key figures and events of the period. The museum also often hosts modern art exhibitions in the **Ala Brasini**. (Any exhibition advertised as held at the Complesso del Vittoriano will be here.)

The **Sacrario delle Bandiere** (entrance in via dei Fori Imperiali) contains standards from many Italian navy vessels. It also has a couple of torpedo boats, including a manned *Maiale* (Pig) torpedo.

Vittoriano

Christian victory over the Turks at the Battle of Lepanto in 1571. The two stone pulpits in front of the altar have intricate cosmatesque mosaic work – a rare case of work signed by Lorenzo Cosma and his son Jacopo, originators of this much-copied style. Just inside the main door, on a pilaster to the right, is the worn tombstone of a certain Giovanni Crivelli, carved and signed (c1432) by Donatello.

On the main altar is a tenth-century image of Mary. To the left of the altar, eight *giallo antico* columns mark the round chapel of St Helen, where relics of this redoubtable lady – mother of the Emperor Constantine – are kept in a porphyry urn. An ancient stone altar, said to be that erected by Augustus, can be seen behind and beneath the altar. Beyond the chapel, at the back of the transept, is the Chapel of the Holy Child. It contains a much-venerated, disease-healing *bambinello*, which would traditionally be whisked to the bedsides of moribund Romans. The original – carved, it is said, in the 15th century from the wood of an olive tree from the Garden of Gethsemane – was stolen in 1994 and replaced by a copy, just as holy as the other according to the custodian. The Gothic tomb opposite the Chapel of the Holy Child entrance is that of Matteo d'Acquasparta, who was mentioned by Dante in his *Paradiso*. Over the altar in the third chapel from the main door (along the left aisle) is a fresco of St Anthony of Padua (c1449) by Benozzo Gozzoli.

Restaurants

Terre e Domus Enoteca della Provincia di Romana €€

Largo del Foro Traiano 84 (06 6994 0273, www.palazzovalentini.it/terre-domus). See p58 Getting around. ***Open*** *12.30-3pm, 7.30-11pm daily.* ***Map*** *p68 K9* ① *Enoteca*

Buried round the back of the Rome provincial government offices, overlooking Trajan's Column, this local-government-sponsored wine bar and restaurant is located inside Palazzo Valentini, which also houses the Domus Romane (*see p61*). This *enoteca* serves wines and produce exclusively from the area immediately surrounding the capital. The atmosphere is warmly cordial; the small blackboard menu changes regularly to focus on traditional, seasonal food with fresh vegetables coming from the garden of the city's Rebibbia prison, while the wine menu (with large by-the-glass choice) is full of pleasant surprises. The hordes who pack the place at lunch (local office workers) and dinner (everyone) seem happy to have such a valid option right here in the *centro*. Book ahead for a table.

ZONA ARCHEOLOGICA

South from the Capitoline hill lies what is arguably the world's most extraordinary concentration of archaeological riches.

The oldest of Rome's fora, the **Foro Romano** (**Roman Forum**), started life as a swampy valley that was used for burials. Tradition says it was drained in the early seventh century BC by the Cloaca Maxima (great drain) masterminded by Tarquinius Priscus, in legend the fifth king of Rome. Subsequently the Forum would become the centre of state ceremony, commerce, law and bureaucracy.

As the Republic fell and the Empire grew, and this area became too small to cope with the legal, social and economic life of the city, emperors combined philanthropy with propaganda and created new ones of their own: the **Fori Imperiali** (**Imperial Fora**). Clearly visible on either side of **via dei Fori Imperiali**, there are five separate fora, each built by a different ruler. Mussolini saw fit to slice the road straight through them (propaganda for empire-building of his own) to connect his balcony at **Palazzo Venezia** (*see p63*) with the Colosseum, demolishing the medieval and early Renaissance buildings that had grown up out of the Roman ruins. Since the 1990s work has been underway to recover tens of thousands of square metres of the ancient remains. Part of Vespasian's forum is incorporated into the church of **Santi Cosma e Damiano** (*see p73*). The slightly wonky **Torre delle Milizie**, behind the **Mercati di Traiano** (**Trajan's Markets**; *see p71*), is a picturesque memento of what the area once looked like.

Arch of Titus in the Roman Forum with Colosseum behind

To reach the Roman and Imperial Fora from piazza del Campidoglio, skirt Palazzo Senatorio to the left. At the bottom of the stairs, on the left, is the entrance to the **Carcere Mamertino** (**Mamertine Prison**; *see p67*); beyond, to the right, stretches the **Foro Romano**; further to the left the road sweeps down to via dei Fori Imperiali.

At the end of this wide avenue towers the **Colosseo** (Colosseum, *see p74*) with the **Arco di Costantino** beside it. These monuments were hemmed in by the Palatine, Celian and Oppian hills (a spur of the Esquiline), as well as the Velia, the saddle of land which joined the Oppio to the Palatine. (What was left of the Velia, behind the Basilica of Maxentius, was bulldozed by Mussolini when he made his via dell'Impero – now via dei Fori Imperiali.)

Above the Colosseum to the west (and able to be visited on a cumulative ticket with the Foro Romano and the Colosseum) is Rome's birthplace, the **Palatine** (*see p67*).

The basket holding infant twins Romulus and Remus was found, legend says, on the other side of the Palatine hill in the once swampy area near the Tiber where **San Giorgio in Velabro** (*see p133*) now stands. Later, on 21 April 753 BC, the uncannily specific story continues, the luckier/fratricidal brother Romulus climbed the Palatine hill and founded Rome.

In fact, proto-Romans had already settled on the Palatine hill well over a century before that (and on the Capitoline as early as the fifteenth century BC). The presence of Rome's earliest temples on the Palatine hill made the area into illustrious real estate; commerce and bureaucracy were pushed down into the Foro Romano as the Palatine became increasingly residential. When Augustus had his house built here he was seeking credibility as the direct descendent of the founder of the city. His relatively modest residence would be extended by later emperors until the palace complex occupied the entire hill.

To the south of the Palatine, the **Circo Massimo** (**Circus Maximus**, *see p67*) is believed to have opened for races in the early seventh century BC.

Sights & museums

Carcere Mamertino

Clivio Argentario 1 (06 698 961, www.tullianum.org). See p58 Getting around. ***Open*** *Oct-Mar 8.30am-3.30pm daily. Apr-Sept 9am-6pm daily.* ***Admission*** *€10; free under-10s.* ***Map*** *p68 K10.*

Just off the steps leading from the Capitoline hill down to the Roman Forum is the Mamertine Prison (aka Carcer Tullianum). Into this prison went anyone thought to pose a threat to the security of the ancient Roman state. A dank, dark, tiny underground dungeon, its lower level (built in the fourth century BC) was once only accessible through a hole in the floor. Innumerable prisoners starved to death here, or drowned when the water table rose and flooded the cell. The most famous of the prison's residents, according to legend, were Saints Peter and Paul. Peter caused a miraculous well to bubble up downstairs in order to baptise his prison guards, whom he converted. Once an atmospheric minor stopover, the prison has now become a rather tawdry 'audio-visual experience' which takes about an hour.

Circo Massimo

Via del Circo Massimo. Metro Circo Massimo/bus 75, 80, 81, 118, 160, 628, 673,715/tram 3. ***Map*** *p68 K13.*

The oldest and largest of Rome's ancient arenas, the Circus Maximus hosted chariot races from at least the fourth century BC. It was rebuilt by Julius Caesar to hold as many as 300,000 people. Races involved up to 12 rigs of four horses each; the first charioteer to complete the seven treacherous, sabotage-ridden laps around the *spina* (ridge in the centre) won a hefty prize and the adoration of the populace. The circus was also used for the ever-popular fights with wild animals, and the occasional large-scale execution.

► *For restaurants and cafés close to the Colosseum, see p204* Celio.

❤ Foro Romano & Palatino

Via di San Gregorio 30/Largo della Salaria Vecchia 5/6 (06 3996 7700, archeoroma.beniculturali.it). Metro Colosseo/bus 53, 75, 80, 81, 85, 87, 117, 673, 810/tram 3. ***Open*** *daily, see p74 Colosseo.* ***Admission*** *(incl Forum & Palatine) €12; €7.50 reductions; free under-18s.* ***Map*** *p68 K11.*

Numbers (❶) refer to the map on p68.

► *Entrances at the Arch of Titus and by the Mamertine Prison are for ticket holders only; there is no ticket office.*

While you may not believe the story that Romulus killed his twin brother Remus for crossing the property line he had staked out on the Palatine, archaeological evidence shows that this spot was probably the site of the settlement that would become Rome. Remains have been found of a wall near the Forum area and of primitive huts on the top of the hill dating from the eighth century BC; tradition says one of these latter was Romulus' home.

Later, the Palatine became the home of the movers and shakers of both the Republic and the Empire as sumptuous palaces were built. The choice of location was understandable: the Palatine overlooks the Foro Romano, yet is a comfortable distance from the disturbances and riff-raff down in the valley. But the area really came into its own after Augustus built his new home next to the house of Rome's founder. Throughout the first century, successive emperors extended the palace complex until the Palatine became one enormous Imperial dwelling and seat of government. With Rome's decline it became a rural backwater, home to monasteries and their vegetable gardens, its precious marble and statuary toted off by looters.

In the 1540s much of the area was bought by Cardinal Alessandro Farnese, who turned it into a pleasure villa and garden, the Horti Farnesiani.

Wending your way uphill from the Palatine from the via di San Gregorio entrance, you pass the remains of the **baths of Septimius Severus** (❶) to the left. They are some of the best-preserved buildings in the area.

Next come the remains of the Imperial palaces built by Domitian in the late first century AD, which became the main residence of the emperors for the next three centuries. The nearest, oval section (❷), sometimes referred to as the 'stadium', was a garden courtyard. It was surrounded by a portico, visible at the southern end. Next to it stands the emperor's private residence, the **Domus Augustana** (❸). This name is a modern one, and derives from *augustus* (meaning 'favoured by the gods' it was the title given to the first of the emperors and used by his successors; Augustus himself never saw these rooms, they were built nearly a century after his death). Next door is the **Domus Flavia** (❹), which contained more public rooms. According to Suetonius, Domitian was so terrified of assassination that he had the walls faced with shiny black selenite so he could see anybody creeping up behind him. It didn't work. The strange-looking room with what appears to be a maze in the middle was a colonnaded fountain courtyard; next to this was the (roofed) dining room, where part of the marble floor has survived, its undulations

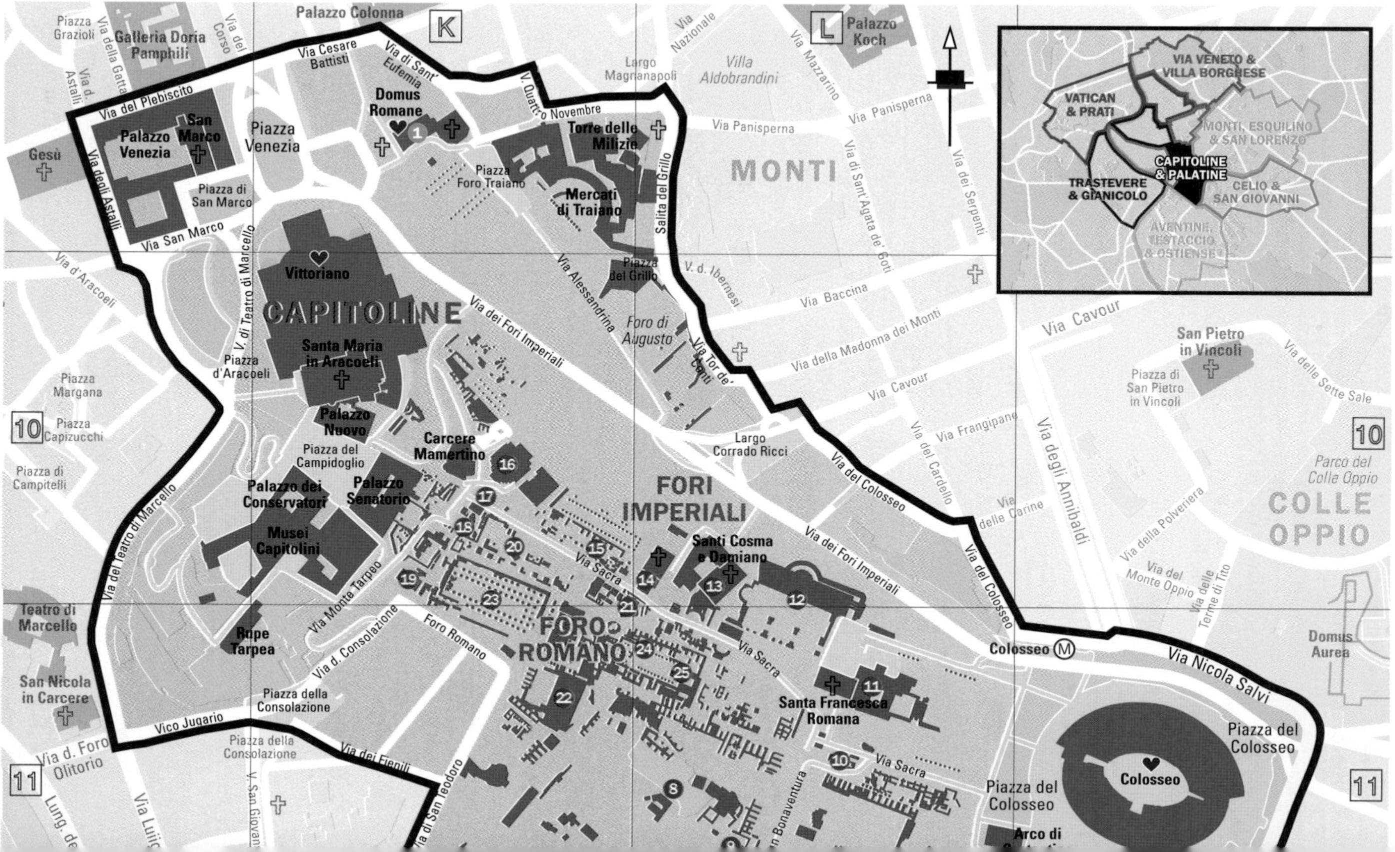
K
L
10
11
Palazzo Colonna
Palazzo Koch
Piazza Grazioli
Galleria Doria Pamphili
Via del Corso
Via della Gatta
Via d. Astalli
Via Cesare Battisti
Via di Sant' Eufemia
Domus Romane
Via del Plebiscito
Palazzo Venezia
San Marco
Piazza Venezia
Piazza di San Marco
Via San Marco
Via degli Astalli
Gesù
Largo Magnanapoli
Via Nazionale
Villa Aldobrandini
Via Mazzarino
Via Panisperna
MONTI
Via di Sant'Agata de' Goti
Via dei Serpenti
V. Quattro Novembre
Torre delle Milizie
Piazza Foro Traiano
Mercati di Traiano
Salita del Grillo
Piazza del Grillo
Via Alessandrina
Foro di Augusto
V. d. Ibernesi
Via Tor de' Conti
Via Baccina
Via della Madonna dei Monti
Via Cavour
Via Frangipane
Via del Cardello
Via degli Annibaldi
Vittoriano
CAPITOLINE
V. di Teatro di Marcello
Via d'Aracoeli
Piazza d'Aracoeli
Santa Maria in Aracoeli
Piazza Margana
Piazza Capizucchi
Piazza di Campitelli
Palazzo Nuovo
Piazza del Campidoglio
Carcere Mamertino
Palazzo dei Conservatori
Palazzo Senatorio
Musei Capitolini
Via del Teatro di Marcello
Teatro di Marcello
Rupe Tarpea
Via Monte Tarpeo
Via d. Consolazione
Foro Romano
Piazza della Consolazione
Vico Jugario
San Nicola in Carcere
Via d. Foro Olitorio
Lung. de
Via Luig
V. San Giovan
Via dei Fienili
Via di San Teodoro
Via dei Fori Imperiali
Largo Corrado Ricci
FORI IMPERIALI
Via del Colosseo
Via delle Carine
Santi Cosma e Damiano
Via Sacra
FORO ROMANO
Santa Francesca Romana
Via di San Bonaventura
Colosseo
Via Nicola Salvi
Piazza del Colosseo
Arco di
San Pietro in Vincoli
Piazza di San Pietro in Vincoli
Via delle Sette Sale
Parco del Colle Oppio
COLLE OPPIO
Via della Polveriera
Via del Monte Oppio
Via delle Terme di Tito
Domus Aurea
1
8
10
11
12
13
14
15
16
17
18
19
20
21
22
23
24
25
VIA VENETO & VILLA BORGHESE
VATICAN & PRATI
MONTI, ESQUILINO & SAN LORENZO
CAPITOLINE & PALATINE
TRASTEVERE & GIANICOLO
CELIO & SAN GIOVANNI
AVENTINE, TESTACCIO & OSTIENSE

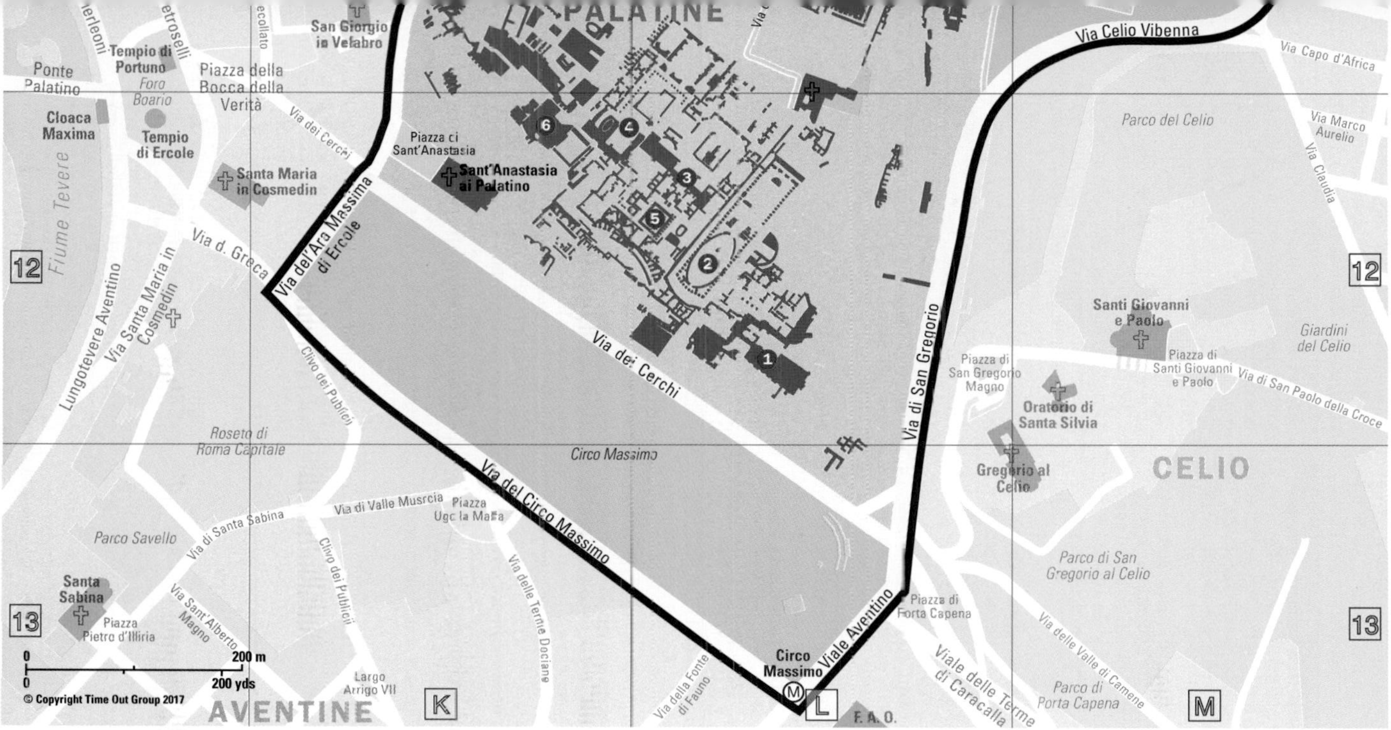

CAPITOLINE & PALATINE

Restaurants

1 Terre e Domus Enoteca della Provincia di Romana

1 refer to the Foro Romano & Palatino walking tour on p67

belying the hypocaust (underfloor heating) that once allowed hot air to circulate below.

Sandwiched between the Domus Flavia and Domus Augustana is a modern building that houses the **Museo Palatino**, (closed for restoration at time of writing, ❺). Downstairs are human remains and artefacts from the earliest communities of Rome, founded in the Forum and Palatine areas from the ninth century BC. Emerging from the floor are the foundations of Domitian's dwelling. Upstairs are decorations from the Imperial period: busts, gods and some fascinating inlaid marble decoration which gives a sense of the opulence of the palace's decoration.

North-west of here are the 'huts of Romulus', the **Domus Augusti** (❻) and the **Domus Livia** (❼). (At the time of writing they are both closed until further notice.)

North of here are the **Horti Farnesiani** (❽) – once the Domus Tiberiana – on the right. These gardens – a shady haven of orange trees and roses – were originally laid out in the 16th century, making them one of the oldest botanical gardens in Europe; what you see now is an 'interpretative re-creation' from the early 20th century. Passing beneath the gardens is the **Cryptoporticus** (❾), a partially accessible semi-subterranean tunnel built by Nero either for hot-weather promenades or as a secret route between the Palatine buildings and his palace, the **Domus Aurea** (*see p187*). Lit only by slits in the walls, the Cryptoporticus is welcomingly cool in summer. Continue to descend and you'll end up at the Forum.

After its period of glory, the **Foro Romano** was relentlessly attacked for centuries by barbarians, after which it was gradually dismantled by anyone – from popes to paupers – who needed building materials. There is, clearly, a lot missing; but if you bear in mind that for a thousand-plus years this was treated as little more than a quarry, what's really incredible is how much has survived. With a bit of patience (and a lot of imagination), it's possible to reconstruct what was once the heart of the Western world.

During the early years of the Republic an open space with shops and a few temples sufficed, but from the second century BC, ever-spreading, ever-conquering Rome needed to give an impression of authority and wealth and so expressed its political ambitions through its architecture. Out went the food stalls; in came law courts, offices and immense public buildings with grandiose decorations to proclaim the power of Rome. Space soon ran out, and emperors began to build the new **Imperial Fora** (*see p67*). But the Foro Romano remained the symbolic heart of the Empire, and emperors continued to renovate and embellish it until the fourth century AD. After taking the brunt of barbarian violence, the low-lying land of the Forum was gradually buried by centuries of flood sediment that rose unchecked in a city dramatically depopulated by plague, pestilence and war. The ancient heart of *caput mundi* came to be known as the *Campo Vaccino* (cow field). Major excavation didn't begin until the 18th century, when digging for antiquities became the hobby of choice for aristocrats from across Europe.

Framing the Forum is the **Arco di Tito** (Arch of Titus, (❿), built in AD 81 to celebrate the sack of Jerusalem by the Emperor Vespasian and his son Titus ten years earlier. One of the reliefs inside the arch shows Roman soldiers with their plundered prize from the Temple of Jerusalem: the menorah and the sacred silver trumpets. The triumphal procession is shown on the east interior wall, with Titus himself accompanied by a winged Victory driving a four-horse chariot. In the centre of the vault there's a square panel that shows Titus riding to the heavens on the back of an eagle, an allusion to his apotheosis.

Between the Arch and the Colosseum (remaining within the archeological site) is the great platform of the **Temple of Venus and Roma** (⓫), two protecting goddesses of the city. This area gives splendid views of the Colosseum.

Continue on to the towering brick ruins of the **Basilica of Maxentius** (⓬), begun in 306 by Maxentius but completed in 312 by Constantine. The last really magnificent building to be constructed in the Forum before Rome began her decline, its once marble-clad walls supported vaults which spanned three times the roofed space we see today. The great vaults are considered to have inspired Michelangelo when he was designing St Peter's.

From here, retrace your steps to via Sacra. Passing the brick remains of a medieval portico you come to a building with a set of bronze doors: this is the so-called **Temple of Romulus** (⓭), built in the fourth century and named after the Emperor Maxentius' son, to whom it may or may not have been dedicated. The interior of the temple is visible from the church of Santi Cosma e Damiano (*see p73*).

Slightly further along, and also on the right, are the great columns of the **Temple of Antoninus and Faustina** (⓮) honouring Hadrian's successor, Antoninus Pius, and his wife Faustina, both of whom were deified. In the seventh or eighth century it became part of the church of San Lorenzo in Miranda, which was heavily remodelled in the 17th century. The distance between the level you're standing on and the bottom of the church's (now-redundant) door is an example of the difference between the ancient ground level and that of the 16th century when the new façade was added; the low lying valley was subject to flooding and the accumulation of rubble for over a millenium after the fall of the Empire.

Continuing towards the Capitoline, what's left of the giant **Basilica Aemilia** (⓯) takes up nearly a whole block. Finished in 34 BC by Lucius Aemilius Lepidus Paullus with cash he got from Julius Caesar in exchange for his support, it was once a bustling place for administration, courts and business. A large chunk of a dedicatory inscription can be seen on the via Sacra corner. Beyond is the **Curia** (⓰). The home of the Senate, it was begun in 45 BC by Julius Caesar and finished in 29 BC by Augustus. (Still under construction on the Ides of March – 15 March 44 BC – it wasn't here that Julius Caesar was assassinated but at the Curia of Pompey.) It was rebuilt after the fire that heavily damaged the Forum in AD 283; in the seventh century AD it became the church of St Hadrian, almost all trace of which was removed during Mussolini's restoration of 1935-1938, although some fresco fragments still cling on inside. The Curia is rarely open, but if it is take a look inside – the floor is a fabulous example of late Imperial *opus sectile* (marble inlay). The doors aren't the originals, though – those found their way to **San Giovanni in Laterano** (*see p206*) in 1660. Opposite, directly in front of the Arch of Septimius Severus, is a fenced-off covered area where excavations have been underway for years within which lies the *lapis niger* (black stone) that was believed to mark the tomb of Romulus (not visible at time of writing).

The **Arch of Septimius Severus** (⓱) was built in AD 203 to celebrate a victory in Parthia (modern-day Iran). The reliefs of military exploits are now blurred, but some of those at the base of the columns are better preserved, having been buried until the 19th century. These show Roman soldiers (no head-gear and in shoes) leading away their Parthian prisoners (with downcast faces and floppy Smurf hats).

To the left of the arch (at time of writing one cannot pass this way, so either double back and take the left hand path, or admire from a distance) a low brown stone wall is what survives of the ***rostra*** (⓲), a platform for the declamation of speeches. To the left, closer to the Capitoline hill, the eight massive columns of the **Temple of Saturn** (⓳) bear an inscription that says it was rebuilt after a fire (probably around AD 360). The cult of Saturn was an ancient one: the first temple to him was built here around 497 BC. The feast dedicated to Saturn, the *Saturnalia*, was celebrated for three days beginning on 17 December and turned the social order on its head, with slaves and servants being served by their masters. In front of the temple of Saturn, the solitary **column of Phocas** (⓴) is clearly visible. The last monument erected in the Forum before the area became a quarry for Christian structures, it was dedicated to the murderous emperor of Byzantium, Phocas. The inscription on the pedestal records a gold statue erected on top in 608 by Smaragdus, Exarch of Ravenna (although the column itself is recycled, probably dating from the second century).

Back towards the centre of the Forum is the **Temple of Divus Julius** (㉑). A nondescript mass of concrete masonry beneath a low-pitched green roof is all that remains of the temple dedicated to the memory of the deified Julius by Augustus in 29 BC. It's popularly held to be the place of Caesar's cremation, and flowers are still left here on 15 March (the Ides) each year.

Rising beside the Temple of Divus Julius are three elegant columns. These formed part of the **Temple of Castor and Pollux** (㉒), twin sons of Jupiter who, according to legend, appeared to Roman troops in 499 BC, helping the Republic to victory over the Latins. To the right of this temple a path leads to lavatories.

On the other side of this path, opposite the site of the Basilica Aemilia, stand the foundations of the **Basilica Julia** (㉓) built by Julius Caesar in 55 BC and once a major – and by all accounts very noisy – law court.

Between the temples of Castor and Divus Julius are the scant remains of the arch of Augustus, believed to be the arch built in 29 BC to commemorate his victories, including that at Actium over Antony and Cleopatra in 31 BC. Just beyond, three small columns arranged in a curve mark the round **Temple of Vesta** (㉔) where the vestal virgins tended the sacred fire. Next door the rectangular house of the **Vestal Virgins** (㉕) was where they lived chastely around a picturesque courtyard: if not they could expect to be buried alive in the 'field of wickedness' (*campus sceleratus*) by the Quirinal.

Mercati di Traiano & Museo dei Fori Imperiali

Via IV Novembre 94 (06 6992 3521, www.mercatiditraiano.it). Bus 40, 60, 64, 70, 117, 170, H. ***Open*** *9.30am-7.30pm Tue-Sun.* ***Admission*** *€13; €11 reductions.* ***Map*** *p68 K9.*

The Imperial Fora is the grouping of extensions to the Roman Forum built first by the dictator Julius Caesar, and then by emperors Augustus, Vespasian, Nerva and Trajan. The area is split in two by the 1930s via dei Fori Imperiali. Excavations carried out in the 1990s opened up massive amounts of archaeological space to the public: the via dei Fori Imperiali offers a good view over all of the fora. An excellent permanent display inside the magnificent Trajan's Markets explains the development and structure of the whole Imperial complex, different areas are dedicated to finds from the various fora, and well-presented exhibitions are often staged here.

Foro di Cesare (Caesar's Forum)
The earliest of the Fori Imperiali, the Forum of Caesar lies on the south-west side of via dei Fori Imperiali, closest to the Foro Romano. Begun by Julius Caesar in 51 BC after the Gallic wars, the Forum contained the Temple of Venus Genetrix (three columns of which have been reconstructed) and the *basilica argentaria*, hall of the money-changers.

Foro & Mercati di Traiano (Trajan's Forum & Markets)
On the north-east side of via dei Fori Imperiali are the extensive remains of Trajan's forum, the last of the fora, laid out in the early second century AD. At the northern extremity of this forum rises the white marble **colonna traiana** (Trajan's column), an amazingly well-preserved work of Roman sculpture, dedicated in AD 113 to celebrate the triumph over the Dacians. The spiral reliefs, containing over 2,500 figures, depict the campaigns against Dacia (more or less modern-day Romania) in marvellous detail, from the building of forts to the launching of catapults. The higher sections of the column are difficult to discern today, but would have been easily viewed by the ancients from galleries that used to stand nearby. At the top of the column is a bronze statue of St Peter, added in 1587 by Pope Sixtus V to replace the original one of Trajan (now lost). So beloved by the Roman people was Trajan that, when he died in AD 117, his funerary urn was placed in a chamber at the column base; this made him and his wife, Plotina, the only Romans whose remains were allowed to be placed inside the city's boundary. The height of the column, 38 metres (125 feet), is believed to mark the elevation of that part of the Quirinal hill that extended into this area before it was cleared away to make room for Trajan's forum.

The Temple of Trajan, mentioned by ancient sources, was also around here, although the exact location is unknown. The rectangular foundation to the south of

Foro di Cesare

Trajan's column, where several imposing granite columns still stand, was the basilica Ulpia, an administrative building. Part of the floor of the basilica is occasionally visible at the gallery space acquired and restored by Alda Fendi, of fashion fame (Foro Traiano 1, 06 679 2597, www.fondazionealdafendi.it, open for exhibitions only); another sector is visible from the **Domus Romane** (*see p61*). To the west, under the walls that support via dei Fori Imperiali, are the remains of one of the libraries that also formed part of Trajan's forum.

The most distinctive feature of the forum complex is the multi-storey brick crescent to the south-east of the basilica Ulpia. This great hemicycle, forming part of the **Mercati di Traiano** (Trajan's Markets), was built in AD 107, in part to shore up the slope of the Quirinal hill. Some scholars now argue that it was more of an administrative than a commercial space.

Entering from via IV Novembre, the first room is the Great Hall, a large space possibly used for the corn dole in antiquity. To the south of the Great Hall are the open-air terraces at the top of the great hemicycle, offering spectacular views across to the Capitoline and Foro Romano. To the east of the Great Hall, stairs lead down to the so-called via Biberatica, an ancient street flanked by well-preserved shops. The shops here were probably *tabernae* (bars), hence the name 'Biberatica' (*bibere* is Latin for 'to drink'). More stairs lead down through the various layers of the great hemicycle, where most of the 150 shops or offices are still in perfect condition, many with doorjambs still showing the grooves where shutters slid into place when the working day was over. South of the hemicycle, the structure with a loggia with five large arches is the 15th-century **Casa dei Cavalieri di Rodi** (**House of the Knights of Rhodes**); its somewhat Venetian look is due to having been built by Venetian Pope Paul II. The tower beyond the hemicycle is the 13th-century **Torre delle Milizie**.

Foro di Augusto (Augustus' Forum)
To the south of the House of the Knights of Rhodes is the Forum of Augustus, the second of the Imperial Fora chronologically (inaugurated in 2 BC). The dominant feature here was the Temple of Mars Ultor ('the avenger'), built to commemorate the Battle of Philippi in 42 BC, in which Augustus (then called Octavian) avenged Caesar's death. Three marble columns of the temple are visible on the right side, as is the towering tufa firewall behind it, built to protect the Imperial space from the Suburra slum district just beyond.

Foro di Nerva (Nerva's Forum)
The next forum to the south, which is bisected by via dei Fori Imperiali, is the Forum of Nerva (or *Forum transitorium* because of its connective function from the sprawling Suburra slum to the Foro Romano). It was dedicated by Nerva in AD 97. Vestiges of a podium are all that remain of the Temple of Minerva that once stood at the east end of the elongated space, although the frieze around two marble columns of the portico (visible just before via Cavour) depicts Minerva, goddess of household skills, weaving and spinning.

Foro di Vespasiano (Vespasian's Forum)
The *Templum pacis*, third of the Fori Imperiali to be built but the last to be unearthed (on the west side of via dei Fori Imperiali), was dedicated by Vespasian in AD 75 but devastated by a fire in 192. On display inside this 'Temple of Peace' were the spoils of various wars, including treasures looted from the Temple of Herod during the Sack of Jerusalem in AD 70. The temple's library is now part of the church of Santi Cosma e Damiano. The immense *Forma urbis*, a marble map of the city made in 193 by Septimius Severus, once adorned the brick wall to the left of the church's façade. Taking his cue (as always) from the ancient emperors, Mussolini made some maps of his own: four white-and-black marble maps are still visible against the brick wall on the west side of the road. They show an area that includes Europe, North Africa and the Near East, charting the growth of the Roman Empire through antiquity. There used to be a fifth map too, which showed Mussolini's Fascist 'empire', but it was removed after the war. These maps are not presently visible while the work on the new Metro line C continues its glacial progress.

Santi Cosma e Damiano

Via dei Fori Imperiali 1 (06 692 0441). Metro Colosseo/bus 53, 75, 80, 85, 87, 117, 810. ***Open*** *9am-1pm, 3-7pm daily.* ***Map*** *p68 L10.*

This small church on the fringe of the Forum incorporates the library of Vespasian's Temple of Peace and the Temple of Romulus (visible through the glass panel that forms the front wall; the drop in level is a reminder of the centuries of sediment and muck that swallowed up the Forum). It has a wonderful sixth-century mosaic in the apse: Saints Peter and Paul stand one on each side of the vast figure of Christ descending from the clouds, presenting Saints Cosma and Damian (the patron saints of doctors) to Jesus. On the far left, Pope Felix IV holds a model of the church; on the far right stands St Theodore in memory of Theodoric the Great, who donated the temple of Romulus to the Pope.

Colosseo

Piazza del Colosseo (06 0608/06 3996 7700, www.coopculture.it). Metro Colosseo/bus 53, 75, 80, 81, 85, 87, 117, 673, 810/tram 3. ***Open*** *late Oct-mid Feb 8.30am-4.30pm. Mid Feb-mid Mar 8.30am-5pm. Mid Mar-end Mar 8.30am-5.30pm. End Mar-Aug 8.30am-7.15pm. Sept 8.30am-7pm. Oct 8.30am-6.30pm daily. Last entry 1hr before close.* ***Admission*** *(incl Forum & Palatine) €12; €7.50 reductions; free under-18s.* ***Map*** *p68 M11.*

Vespasian began building the Colosseum in AD 72 on the site of a newly drained lake in the grounds of Nero's Domus Aurea (*see p187*).

Properly called the Amphitheatrum Flavium (Flavian amphitheatre), the building was later known as the Colosseum not because it was big, but because of a gold-plated colossal statue, now lost, that stood alongside. The arena was about 500 metres (a third of a mile) in circumference, could seat over 50,000 people – some scholars estimate capacity crowds numbered as many as 87,000 – and could be filled or emptied in ten minutes through a network of *vomitoria* (exits) that remains the basic model for stadium design today.

Nowhere in the world was there a larger or more glorious setting for mass slaughter. If costly, highly trained professional gladiators were often spared at the end of their bloody bouts, not so the slaves, criminals and assorted unfortunates roped in to do battle against them. And just to make sure there was no cheating, when the combat was over, corpses were prodded with red-hot pokers to ensure no one tried to elude fate by playing dead.

It was not only human life that was sacrificed to Roman blood-lust: wildlife, too, was legitimate fodder. Animals fought animals; people fought animals. In the 100 days of carnage held to inaugurate the amphitheatre in AD 80, Martial tells that 5,000 beasts perished. By the time wild animal shows were finally banned in AD 523, the animal population of North Africa and Arabia was severely depleted. On occasion, however, the tables turned and the animals got to kill the people: a common sentence in the Roman criminal justice system was *damnatio ad bestias*, when thieves and other miscreants were turned loose, unarmed, into the arena, where hungry beasts would be waiting for them.

Entrance to the Colosseum was free for all, although a membership card was necessary, and a rigid seating plan kept the sexes and social classes in their rightful places. The emperor and senators occupied marble seats in the front rows; on benches higher up were the priests and magistrates, then above them the foreign diplomats. Women were confined to the upper reaches – all of them, that is, except the pampered Vestal Virgins, who had privileged seats right near the emperor.

By the sixth century, with the fall of the Roman Empire, bloodsports in the Colosseum were less impressive: chickens pecked each other to death here. The Roman authorities discontinued the games and the Colosseum became little more than a quarry for the stone and marble used to build and decorate Roman *palazzi*. The pockmarks all over the Colosseum's masonry date back to the ninth century, when Lombards pillaged the iron and lead clamps that until then had held the blocks together. This irreverence toward the Colosseum was not halted until the mid 18th century, when Pope Benedict XIV consecrated it as a church. For another century it was left to its own devices, becoming home to hundreds of species of flowers and plants, as well as to a fair number of Roman homeless. After Unification in 1870 the flora was yanked up and the squatters kicked out, in what 19th-century English writer Augustus Hare described as 'aimless excavations'. 'In dragging out the roots of its shrubs,' he moaned in his *Walks in Rome* (1883), 'more of the building was destroyed than would have fallen naturally in five centuries.'

The hypogeum (underground cells), where animals were held and combatants warmed up, and the upper tier of the stalls in the Colosseum can now be visited on guided tours, including night-time tours affording fantastic views over the lights of the city from the top of the arena. Guided tours cost €9 (under-12s free) and must be booked in advance (through the website above).

Standing beside the Colosseum, Constantine's triumphal arch was one of the last great Roman monuments, erected in AD 315, and is the best preserved of Rome's triumphal arches.

In front of the arch, the round foundation sunk in the grass is all that remains of an ancient fountain called the *Meta sudans* ('sweating cone'). More of this implausibly phallic object – almost all of it, in fact – would have been visible today if it hadn't been for Mussolini's bulldozing in the 1930s.

In the know
Ticket advice

The Forum, Palatine and Colosseum are visited on the same ticket: one entrance to the Palatine and Forum (counted as a single site), and one to the Colosseum over a two-day period. Save yourself a wait and buy tickets at the quieter via di San Gregorio Forum & Palatine entrance. Alternatively, pre-purchase your ticket (€14 including booking fee) from www.coopculture.it.

If you already have a ticket, enter on via di San Gregorio or by the Mamertine Prison on the Capitoline hill. On entering, queues for security are divided between ticket holders and non, but can be equally long, especially at weekends and in high summer. The best advice is to pre-buy tickets and arrive between 8.45 and 9.30am, or in the last hour or two before closing.

Fontana di Trevi & Quirinale

The roaring waters of the *acqua vergine* were fundamental to the development of this area: they supplied the popes' Palazzo del Quirinale, and still feed the towering Fontana di Trevi in the valley below. On Monday mornings when workmen turn the water off to clean the fountain, the quarter turns eerily silent. Water continues to be a key feature of the area: in addition to the fountain, you can hear the rush beneath the ruins of a Roman street at the Città dell'acqua, while a miraculous well inside the ancient church of Santa Maria in Via still provides healing cupfuls for sick parishioners.

But this area is also home to art aplenty, notably in the *gallerie* Barberini and Colonna, and at the Accademia di San Luca. And there are two small but superb churches – San Carlo and Sant'Andrea – by the geniuses of Baroque Rome, Bernini and Borromini.

❤ Don't miss

1 Fontana di Trevi *p78*
This example of 18th-century hydraulic bling lives up to the hype.

2 Palazzo Barberini *p84*
A Baroque palace with an extraordinary ceiling, and a world class art collection far from the throng.

3 Sant'Andrea al Quirinale *p82*
Small but perfectly formed, this Jesuit church is the project of which Bernini was proudest.

4 San Carlo alle Quattro Fontane *p84*
Classical architecture seen through a hall of mirrors by Bernini's great rival, Borromini.

5 Galleria Colonna *p80*
A bite-sized and elegant glimpse into the Roman aristocracy.

In the know
Getting around

Not far from the Termini central station, and served by the Barberini stop on metro line A, this is a very walkable area close to other major central sites such as the Pantheon.

Fontana di Trevi

AROUND THE FONTANA DI TREVI

The high walls of the presidential **Palazzo del Quirinale** loom over a tangle of medieval streets, all of which seem in the end to lead to the **Fontana di Trevi** (Trevi Fountain). The *acqua vergine* that feeds it is said to be the best water in Rome: Grand Tourists (*see p90*) used it to brew their tea. Nowadays you'd be hard pressed to get your kettle anywhere near for the coin-tossing hordes elbowing their way through serried ranks of tacky souvenir vendors.

Names such as via della Dataria (Ecclesiastical Benefits Office Street) and via della Stamperia (Printing Works Street) recall the era when the whole of the Trevi district acted as a service area for the palace: here were the bureaucratic departments, presses and service industries that oiled the machinery of the Papal States. To keep close to the hub of power, aristocratic families such as the Odescalchis, Grimaldis and Barberinis built their palaces close by, as did the Colonna, whose art collection can be seen at the **Galleria Colonna** (*see p80*).

Under the stern eye of the papal authorities, the **Galleria dell'Accademia di San Luca** (*see p81*) kept the flame of artistic orthodoxy.

Sights & museums

❤ Fontana di Trevi

Piazza di Trevi. Bus 52, 53, 62, 63, 71, 80Exp, 81, 83, 85, 116, 160, 492, 628. ***Map*** *p79 K8.*

For recent generations, it was Anita Ekberg who made this fountain famous when she plunged in wearing a strapless black evening dress in Federico Fellini's classic film *La Dolce Vita*. Don't even think about trying it yourself – wading, washing and splashing in fountains are strictly against local by-laws. And unlike the Grand Tourists, you don't want to drink from it either: channelled from the ancient *acqua vergine* spring – legend says the source was revealed to the troops of Agrippa by a virgin – the sparkling water of the fountain is full of chlorine (though there's a chlorine-free spout hidden in a bird-bath-shaped affair at the back of the fountain to the right).

It was an altogether different affair in 19 BC, when spring water – 100,000 cubic metres (3.5 cubic feet) of the stuff daily – was transported here by an aqueduct from the 12th kilometre of the via Collatina, to the east of Rome. The only aqueduct to pass underground along its whole route into the city, it was the sole survivor of barbarian destruction and other horrors of the early Middle Ages. In 1570 Pius V restored the conduit but it wasn't until 1732

Fontana di Trevi

❤ Time well spent

Santa Maria in Via

Largo Chigi (06 6994 0380). ***Open*** *7.15am-12.45pm, 4-8pm Mon-Fri; 8.30am-1pm, 4-9pm Sat, Sun.* ***Map*** *p79 J7.*

Perk yourself up with a cupful of miraculous water in the church of Santa Maria in Via. In 1286 a stone bearing an image of the Virgin's face floated to the surface of a well, over which this church was later built.

Santa Maria in Via

FONTANA DI TREVI & QUIRINALE

Restaurants

1. Baccano
2. Colline Emiliane

Cafés, bars & pubs

1. Antica Birreria Peroni

Bakeries, pasticcerie & gelaterie

1. Il Gelato di San Crispino

Shops & services

1. Kami Spa

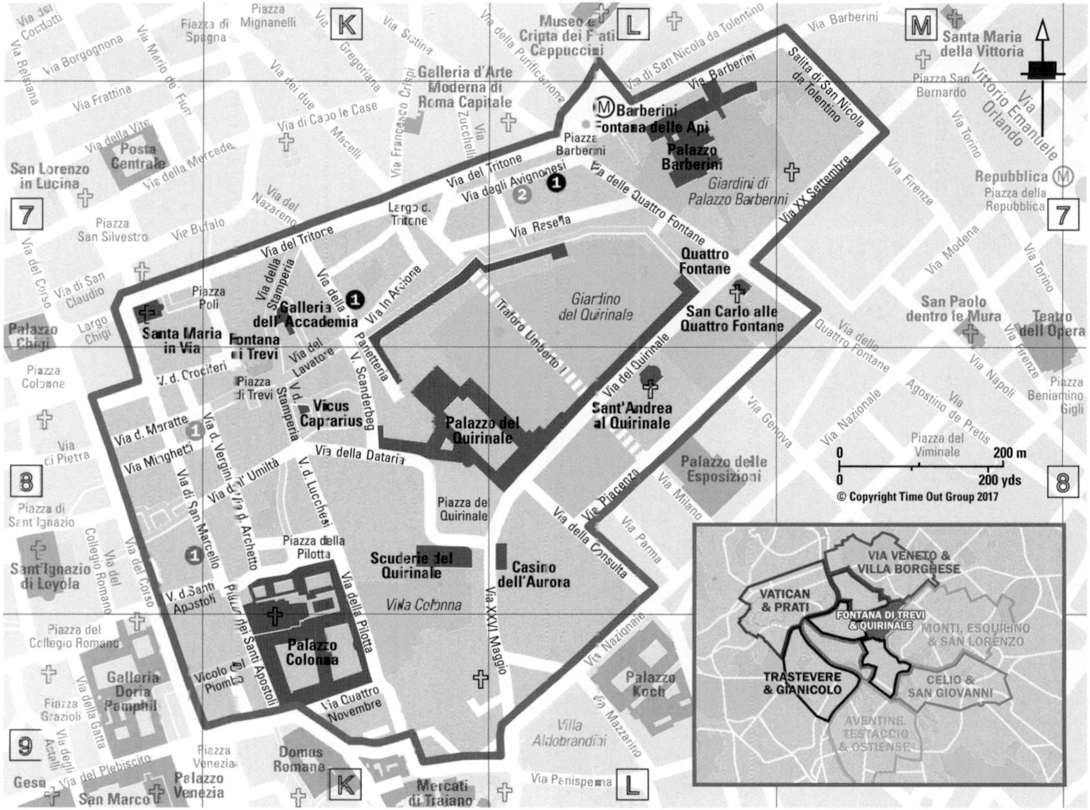

Sala Grande, Galleria Colonna

that Pope Clement XII called for designs for a new *mostra* – a magnificent fountain to mark the end of the aqueduct. Completed decades later to a design by Nicolò Salvi, the *mostra* – the Trevi Fountain – immediately became a draw for tourists who drank the prized waters to ensure a return to Rome, as folklore has it.

Tucked away in a tiny piazza and almost always surrounded by jostling crowds, the fountain's stark travertine (cleaned in 2016 in a project sponsored by Fendi) gleams beneath powerful torrents of water and constant camera flashes. It's a magnificent rococo extravaganza of rearing sea horses, conch-blowing tritons, craggy rocks and flimsy trees, erupting in front of the wall of Palazzo Poli. Nobody can quite remember when the custom started of tossing coins in to the waters. The fountain is drained every Monday morning and the money goes to the Red Cross. Visit as early or as late as you can to have a chance of avoiding the crowds.

In the know
The city of water

A stone's throw from the Trevi Fountain are the excavations that came to light during the remodelling of the Cinema Trevi. The **Vicus Caprarius**, the City of Water (vicolo del Puttarello 25, www.vicuscaprarius.com, open 11am-5.30pm Tue-Fri, 11am-7pm Sat, Sun, admission €3, €1 reductions) incorporates the remains of an Imperial-age apartment building, part of a Roman street and a holding tank for the waters of the *acqua vergine*, which can be heard rushing by underneath.

❤ Galleria Colonna

Via della Pilotta 17 (06 678 4350, www.galleriacolonna.it). Bus 40Exp, 60Exp, 64, 70, 117, 170, H. ***Open*** *9am-1.15pm Sat, or by appt. Closed Aug.* ***Admission*** *€12; €10 reductions. No cards.* ***Map*** *p79 K9.*

Saturday mornings are your only chance to see this splendid gallery, completed in 1703 by Prince Filippo II Colonna whose descendants still live in the palace. (Among others, the Colonnas produced a pope, a saint and an excommunicated cardinal.) The entrance leads to the Room of the Column, originally the throne room of Prince Filippo and his successors, who would have sat in state by the ancient column, back-lit by light shining through the window behind, and with a view across to a triumphal arch dedicated to Marcantonio Colonna, the family hero. (Audrey Hepburn behaved regally here, too, in *Roman Holiday*.) The cannonball embedded in the stairs down to the Great Hall lies where it landed during the French siege of Rome on 24 June 1849. The mirrored hall may be the work of Gian Lorenzo Bernini, inspired by his visit to Versailles in 1665, while the immense frescoed ceiling pays tribute to Marcantonio, who led the papal fleet to victory against the Turks in the great naval battle of Lepanto in 1571. The gallery's most famous and much-reproduced picture is Annibale Caracci's earthy peasant *Bean Eater*. Private tours can be arranged of the gallery as well as the private apartments at other times during the week. When the weather permits the café on the pleasant terrace is worth a visit.

Galleria dell'Accademia di San Luca

Piazza dell'Accademia 77 (06 679 8850, www.accademiasanluca.eu). Bus 52, 53, 62, 63, 71, 80Exp, 81, 83, 85, 160, 492, 628. ***Open*** *10am-7pm (last entry 6pm) Mon-Sat. Closed 3wks Aug.* ***Admission*** *free.* ***Map*** *p79 K7.*

The illustrious Accademia di San Luca (patron saint of artists; St Luke was said to have painted the Virgin and Child from life), housed in Palazzo Carpegna, was founded in 1577 to train artists in the grand Renaissance style. From the courtyard, Borromini's beautiful staircase is clever and very practical (at least for sedan chairs and mules): the elliptical brickwork ramp to the upper floors of the palace was inspired by the winding ramp inside Hadrian's mausoleum within **Castel Sant'Angelo** (*see p161*). Access to the ramp is behind a virtuoso piece of stucco work: cornucopiae of overblown buttercups and daisies denote the riches of the earth, while crowns, mitres and chains symbolise what can be achieved by hard work in the course of a long and fortunate career. But without progeny, the allegory continues (the offspring is symbolised by a small child peering out of the herbiage), it is all worthless endeavour; it's not on record whether the few women members of the Academy, such as artistic prodigies Lavinia Fontana (1551-1614) and Angelica Kauffman (1741-1807), agreed with these sentiments. The gallery displays a charming collection of paintings and sculptures by former students and visitors to the Accademia, including Canova and Thorwaldson. But the real charm lies in the exquisite scenes of 17th- and 18th-century Roman life.

Restaurants

Baccano €€€

Via delle Muratte 23 (06 6994 1166, www.baccanoroma.com). Metro Barberini/bus 52, 53, 62, 63, 71, 80, 83, 85, 492, 590. ***Open*** *11am-12.30am daily.* ***Map*** *p79 J8* ❶ Bistro

An all-day bar and bistro just a few steps from the Trevi Fountain, Baccano clearly aims to copy the kind of multi-faceted dining and drinking experience more frequently found in London or New York, with its contemporary surroundings and a plethora of menus which are shuffled throughout the day. The food is loosely billed as 'Mediterranean' and swings between somewhat pricey pasta classics, to gourmet burgers and a rather fancy oyster and champagne bar.

Cafés, bars & pubs

Antica Birreria Peroni

Via di San Marcello 19 (06 679 5310, www.anticabirreriaperoni.net). Bus 53, 62, 63, 80, 81, 83, 85, 117, 492, 628, C3. ***Open*** *noon-midnight Mon-Sat. Closed 2wks Aug.* ***Map*** *p79 J8* ❶ Birreria

This long-standing *centro storico birreria* is the perfect place to grab a quick beer or an informal lunch or dinner. Service is rough-and-Roman but generally friendly, and the food – a few hot pasta dishes, fried snacks and some cold cuts – is good and relatively cheap. Sausage, though, is the main act: three different types of German-style *wurstel* are on offer. The *birreria* still retains its original art nouveau decor, with a chiaroscuro frieze featuring such slogans as 'drink beer and you'll live to be 100'.

Bakeries, pasticcerie & gelaterie

Il Gelato di San Crispino

Via della Panetteria 42 (06 679 3924, www.ilgelatodisancrispino.it). Bus 52, 53, 62, 63, 71, 80, 83, 85, 117, 492, 590, C3. ***Open*** *noon-12.30am Mon-Thur, Sun; noon-1.30am Fri, Sat.* ***No cards. Map*** *p79 K7* ❶ *Gelateria*

A few years ago, when Rome's ice-cream sector languished in a mire of self-satisfaction, Il Gelato di San Crispino came along to shake things up. Obsessive control over the whole production process, from the choice of superlative raw materials to every stage of mixing and freezing, resulted in an ice-cream that reached new heights and prompted a wave of imitations. Although, in recent years, it has lost a little of its loyal following to some of the new kids on the block, for many punters San Crispino remains one of the best ice-creams anywhere.
Other locations piazza della Maddalena 5, Pantheon (06 9760 1190); via Acaia 56, Suburbs: south (06 7045 0412); Fiumicino airport, Terminal A.

AROUND THE QUIRINALE

The origins of the name 'Quirinale' are lost in the mists of time; it may refer to a temple of Quirinus that stood here, or perhaps it comes from Cures, a Sabine town north-east of Rome from where, legend relates, the Sabines under King Tatius came to settle on the hill. Throughout the Republican era, the hill was covered in gardens and villas where the great and the good could escape from the malarial heat of the marshy valleys. In the 16th century the pope thought it would be a good idea to do the same thing and the summer **Palazzo del Quirinale** *(see p82)* was begun in 1574 for Gregory XIII (of Gregorian calendar and chant fame). After the collapse of the Papal States in 1870, Pope Pius IX, who was holed up inside the palace, refused to hand over his keys to the troops of King Victorio Emanuele; they had to force their way in. Just 76 years later, the reigning Savoia family were forced to quit the palace following a referendum in which the monarchy, disgraced by association with the inter-war Fascist regime, was despatched into exile. Today a constant stream of motorcades swishing across the cobbles serves as a reminder that the Quirinale – now the official residence of the Italian president – is still very much at the decision-making hub of 21st-century Italy.

The space in front of the palace is officially the **piazza del Quirinale**, though it's generally referred to by locals as piazza di Monte Cavallo – Horse Hill Square – on account of the two towering Imperial-era equestrian statues. The giant horses rear up beside the five-metre-high (16 feet) heavenly twins Castor and Pollux. The statues, which had been lying in the nearby ruins of the Baths of Constantine, were artistically arranged by Domenico Fontana, the favourite architect of the city-planner Pope Sixtus V, in the 1580s. It was Pius VI who dragged the obelisk *(see p85)* now standing here from outside Augustus' mausoleum in 1786; Pius VII added the big granite basin that had been a cattle trough in the Forum. On the far side of the square are the papal stables, now an elegant exhibition space, the **Scuderie del Quirinale** *(see right)*.

Across the road from the palace's long wing stands the splendid church of **Sant' Andrea al Quirinale** *(see right)*, by Bernini.

Sights & museums

Palazzo del Quirinale

Piazza del Quirinale (06 3996 7557, www.quirinale.it). Bus 40Exp, 52, 53, 60, 61, 62, 63, 64, 70, 80Exp, 85, 170, 492, 590, C3, H. ***Open*** *8.30am-noon Sun. Closed July, Aug.* ***Admission*** *€10.* ***Map*** *p79 K8.*

The new St Peter's still wasn't finished when Pope Gregory XIII started building this pontifical summer palace on the highest of Rome's seven hills; begun in 1573, the Quirinale was not completed until over 200 years later. The risk that a pontiff (they were not, on the whole, renowned for their youthful vigour) might keel over during the holidays was such that it was decided to build somewhere that was also suitable to hold a conclave to elect a successor. The Quirinale's Cappella Paolina (named after Paul V) was designed by Carlo Maderno and finished in 1617; it is a faithful replica of the Vatican's Sistine Chapel, minus the Michelangelos. Accommodation for the cardinals was provided in the *Manica lunga*, the immensely long wing that runs the length of via del Quirinale to the rear of the palace. Bernini added the main entrance door in 1638.

Concerts are held in the Pauline chapel of the Palace at noon on Sundays throughout much of the year. Concerts are free but advance booking is required (palazzo.quirinale.it).

The presidential guard changes with a flourish on the piazza del Quirinale at 4pm on Sundays from October to May, and at 6pm from June to September. The palazzo is closed during the summer months of July and August, and occasionally in April and December, so do check before visiting.

❤ Sant'Andrea al Quirinale

Via del Quirinale 29 (06 487 4565, santandrea.gesuiti.it). Bus 40Exp, 52, 53, 60, 61, 62, 63, 64, 70, 80Exp, 85, 170, 492, 590, H. ***Open*** *8.30am-noon, 2.30-6pm Tues-Sat; 9am-noon, 3-6pm Sun.* ***Map*** *p79 L8.*

With funding from Prince Camillo Pamphilj, the Jesuits commissioned Gian Lorenzo Bernini to build a church for novices living on the Quirinale. The site was small and awkward, but Bernini solved the problem by designing an oval church (1658) with the entrance and the high altar very unusually on the short axis. Above the door, a section of the wall seems to have swung down on to the columns, creating an entrance porch. Inside, the church is richly decorated with the figure of St Andrew (by Antonio Raggi, Bernini's star pupil) floating heavenwards through a broken pediment above the high altar.

Scuderie del Quirinale

Via XXIV Maggio 16 (06 692 042, www.scuderiequirinale.it). Bus 40Exp, 52, 53, 60, 61, 62, 63, 64, 70, 80Exp, 85, 170, 492, 590, H. ***Open*** *during exhibitions only 10am-8pm Mon-Thur, Sun; 10am-10.30pm Fri, Sat.* ***Admission*** *varies.* ***Map*** *p79 K8.*

In the know

A monthly opportunity

First day of the month? Rush over to the **Casino dell'Aurora conference centre** (via XXIV Maggio 43, 06 481 4344, www.casinoaurorapallavicini.it) to gawp as the Grand Tourists did at *Aurora Scattering Flowers Before the Chariot of the Sun*. Guido Reni painted it in 1614 on the ceiling of the summer house of the 17th-century Palazzo Pallavicini Rospigliosi. The rest of the Pallavicini picture collection is off-limits.

The former stables of the Palazzo del Quirinale, this large space for major exhibitions retains original features such as the brickwork ramp to the upper floors, as well as acres of chic marble flooring and space-age lighting. There is a good art bookshop and a café and – best of all – a breathtaking view of Rome's skyline from the rear staircase as you leave. It's worth finding out what's on here as exhibitions are generally very high standard. At peak periods or when a show has just opened, it's advisable to book in advance, through 06 3996 7500 or www.coopculture.it.

Restaurants

Colline Emiliane €€

Via degli Avignonesi 22 (06 481 7538, www.collineemiliane.com). Metro Barberini/bus 52, 53, 62, 63, 71, 80, 83, 85, 492, 590. ***Open*** *12.45-2.45pm, 7.30-10.45pm Tue-Sat; 12.45-2.45pm Sun.* ***Map*** *p79 L7* ❷ *Trattoria*

This friendly, family-run trattoria celebrates the hearty cuisine of the region of Emilia-Romagna which means tortellini in broth, tagliatelle with Bolognese ragù and all forms of beef (boiled, roasted and made into meatballs). Priding themselves on their home-made pasta and carefully crafted desserts it is a pleasant escape from the somewhat repetitive Roman menus in the area. Be sure to try the regional sparkling Lambrusco wine: a far cry from the sickly sweet fizz found outside of Italy.

PIAZZA BARBERINI & QUATTRO FONTANE

Art-packed **Palazzo Barberini** towers above piazza Barberini – once a semi-rural idyll and now a woeful example of the sledge hammer school of urban planning. Traffic hurtles north into via Veneto or south-east towards the Quattro Fontane, while marooned in the midst of the belching fumes is the last commission Gian Lorenzo Bernini received from the Barberini Pope Urban VIII: the **Fontana del Tritone**. The fountain is covered with the bees of the Barberini family emblem, and shows four dolphins supporting a huge open shell on their tails. On the shell sits a Triton blowing into a conch shell to tame the flooding seas, as in a tale recounted by Ovid in his *Metamorphoses*.

Ringing with the noise of life-threatening *motorini*, narrow **via Barberini** climbs past the **Palazzo Barberini gallery** to the crossroads, which – for very obvious reasons – is known as the **Quattro Fontane** (four fountains). Four delightful Baroque fountains have stood here since 1593. It's a life-threatening task trying to see them through the traffic, but they clearly represent four river gods: the one accompanied by the she-wolf is the Tiber; the females are probably Juno (the one with the duck) and Diana. But it's anybody's guess who the fourth figure is: some claim it's an allegory of the Nile while others make

The Vestal Virgin Tuccia (Antonio Corradini, 1743), Palazzo Barberini

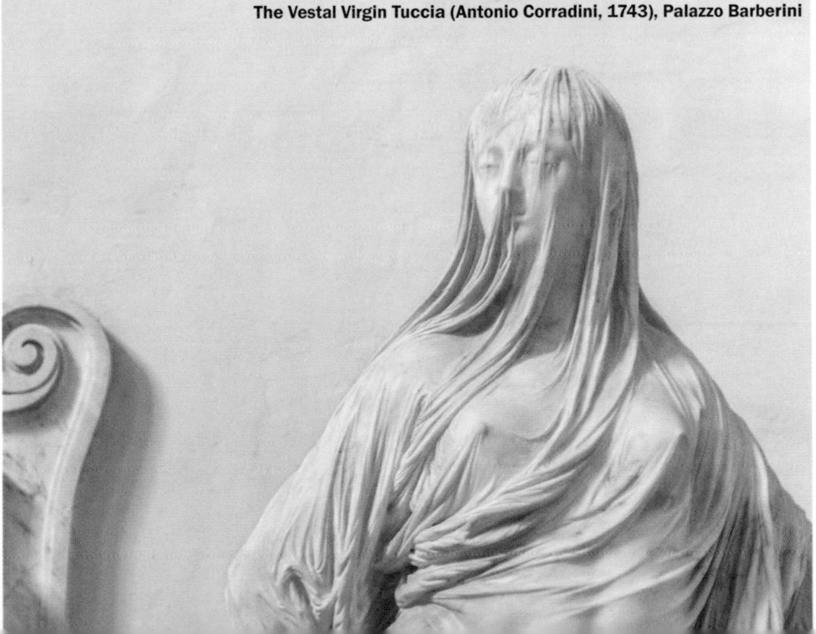

a case for the Florentine Arno. From here, the staggering view down both sides of the hill takes in three Egyptian obelisks (*see right*) – part of the city's remodelling under obelisk-mad Sixtus V. On one corner stands the little church of **San Carlo alle Quattro Fontane**, one of the great masterpieces of tortured genius Carlo Borromini.

Sights & museums

❤ Palazzo Barberini – Galleria Nazionale d'Arte Antica

Via delle Quattro Fontane 13 (06 481 4591, bookings 06 32 810, barberinicorsini.org). Metro Barberini/bus 52, 53, 61, 62, 63, 80Exp, 85, 492, 590. ***Open*** *8.30am-7pm (last entry 6pm) Tue-Sun.* ***Admission*** *€10 incl Palazzo Corsini (ticket valid 10 days, see p169); €5 reductions.* ***Map*** *p79 L7.*

Top architects like Maderno, Bernini and Borromini queued up to work on this vast pile, which, despite its size and attention to detail, was completed in just five years, shortly after Maffeo Barberini became Pope Urban VIII in 1623. Bernini did the main staircase, a grand rectangular affair now marred by an ill-placed lift. Borromini, whose uncle Carlo Maderno drew up the original palace plans, added the graceful oval staircase. After lengthy restoration and extension of the gallery into newly acquired parts of the palace, three floors of paintings are now visible. The main show is the splendid first floor *salone* with the extraordinary ceiling painting by Pietro da Cortona. The *Allegory of Divine Providence* (1629) is the most Baroque of all Baroque extravanganzas and worth the ticket price all by itself. Highlights of the main first-floor 16th- and 17th-century collection are Raphael's *Fornarina* (said, probably wrongly, to be a portrait of the baker's daughter he may have been engaged to at the time of his death in 1520), Holbein's pompous *Henry VIII*, Caravaggio's *Judith and Holofernes* and Titian's *Venus and Adonis*.

❤ San Carlo alle Quattro Fontane

Via del Quirinale 23 (06 488 3261, www.sancarlino.eu). Metro Barberini/bus 40Exp, 52, 53, 60, 61, 62, 63, 64, 70, 80Exp, 85, 170, 492, 590, C, H. ***Open*** *10am-1pm Mon-Sat; 11am-1pm Sun.* ***Map*** *p79 L7.*

Carlo Borromini's first solo composition (1631-41), and the one of which he was most proud, San Carlo (often called Carlino, due to its diminutive scale) is one of the star pieces of the Roman Baroque. The most remarkable feature is the dizzying oval dome: its geometrical coffers decrease in size towards the lantern to give the illusion of additional height – Borromini is all about illusion – and the subtle illumination, through hidden windows, makes the dome appear to float in mid-air. There is also an austere adjoining courtyard and a sobering crypt.

Shops & services

Kami Spa

Via degli Avignonesi 11-12 (06 4201 0039, www.kamispa.com). Bus 61, 62, 80, 83, 85 492, 590. ***Open*** *10am-10pm daily.* ***Map*** *p79 L7* ❶ *Spa*

Massages, scrubs and a wide selection of beauty treatments are available in this gloriously spice-scented haven of minimalist oriental decor. There's a small swimming pool and a shop. Booking ahead is recommended.

San Carlo alle Quattro Fontane

Obelisks

Finding your way around Rome's 13 obelisks

For the Egyptians, obelisks were needles channelling the energy of the sun. For the Romans, they became a symbol both of their conquest of a far more ancient civilisation, and of the elements of Egyptian culture embraced in the *caput mundi*. Late Renaissance popes began unearthing these impressive monuments, dusting them off, and topping them with crosses to serve as sign posts for pilgrims. The message was clear: Christian Rome had triumphed over its pagan past.

Palazzo Massimo alle Terme (*see map p182 N7*): an obelisk that came from Heliopolis and which dates to the reign of Rameses II. Discovered in 1883, it probably once stood in Domitian's temple to Isis, east of the Pantheon.

Piazza della Minerva (*see map p104 H9*): also from the temple to Isis, this obelisk was originally erected at Sais by the Pharaoh Apries. In 1667 Bernini mounted it on an elephant.

Piazza di Montecitorio (*see map p89 J8*): made for King Psammetichus II, this sixth-century BC obelisk was brought from Heliopolis by Augustus in 10 BC and set up in the *Campus martius* as the gnomon for a giant sundial. It was placed in front of Palazzo di Montecitorio in 1792.

Piazza Navona (*see map p104 G8*): a Roman knock-off, this obelisk was custom-made in Egypt for Domitian; its hieroglyphs were cut in Rome (and are largely invented). It stood at the temple to Isis, then later at the Circus of Maxentius, where it remained until being brought to piazza Navona in 1651.

Piazza del Popolo (*see map p89 H4*): brought from Heliopolis to Rome in 10 BC by Augustus, and placed at the centre of the Circus Maximus, this obelisk was later found in three pieces, and reassembled here in 1589.

Piazza del Quirinale (*see map p79 K8*) and **Piazza dell'Esquilino** (*see map p182 N8*): brought to stand at the entrance to Augustus' mausoleum, one was placed in piazza dell'Esquilino (behind Santa Maria Maggiore) and the other was erected in piazza del Quirinale by Pius VI in 1786.

Piazza della Rotonda (*see map p89 H8*): the obelisk in front of the Pantheon, from Heliopolis, is dedicated to Rameses the Great and dates from the 14th century BC. Domitian moved it to the temple of Isis in around AD 80. It was placed here in 1711.

Piazza San Pietro (*see map p150 D7*): erected in Alexandria by the Romans in the first century BC and dedicated to Augustus, it was brought on a vast ship to Rome; the ship was then sunk to form a new jetty at Ostia (*see p232*). Caligula placed it in his Vatican circus, where it remained standing (the only one not to fall) until Sixtus V had it moved (with the help of 8,000 men) to its current spot in 1587.

Piazza Trinità dei Monti (*see map p89 K6*): erected at its current site in 1789 by Pius VI, it originally stood in the splendid Horti Sallustiani.

San Giovanni in Laterano (*see map p198 P12*): the largest obelisk in the world was erected by Thutmose III in the 15th century BC in front of the Temple of Ammon at Thebes. Constantine brought it down the Nile to Alexandria; later (in AD 357), Constantius transported it to Rome. The last of the obelisks to be brought to the city, it was set up on the *spina* of Circus Maximus. In 1587 it was shifted here by Sixtus V.

Viale dell'Obelisco (*see map p138 J4*): inside the Villa Borghese is a monolith brought to Rome by Hadrian. Dedicated to the emperor's dead lover Antinous, it may have been erected on the site of Antinous' burial. Discovered near Santa Croce in Gerusalemme in the 16th century, it was erected here in 1822.

Villa Celimontana (*see map p198 N13*): this obelisk was presented in 1582 by the Senate to the villa's owner Ciriaco Mattei, who placed it here. Previously it had been at the foot of the steps leading to Santa Maria in Aracoeli, but had probably been moved there from the temple to Isis.

▸San Giovanni in Laterano

Tridente

The Tridente has a long history of welcoming visitors: it was a home-from-home for the Grand Tourists of the 18th and 19th centuries, when English '*Milords*' took up lodgings around piazza di Spagna. And today it's as popular as ever – there are still people who visit Rome without ever straying out of the Tridente.

But resist the allure of the area's Fendis and Armanis and there is plenty to admire, from modern-day Roman romance on the Spanish Steps, to Romanticism at the Keats-Shelley Memorial House. More ancient attractions can be found, too, in the shape of Augustus' mausoleum, the Ara Pacis and Marcus Aurelius' column in piazza Colonna.

❤ Don't miss

1 Museo dell'Ara Pacis *p101*
Augustan propaganda at its best.

2 Keats-Shelley Memorial House *p91*
Channel the Romantics in the apartment where poor doomed Keats breathed his last.

3 Santa Maria del Popolo *p98*
A gallop through the history of art, from Pinturricchio to Bernini, by way of Raphael, Carracci and Caravaggio.

4 Colonna di Marco Aurelio *p96*
As stoic as the man whose victories it commemorates.

5 Spanish Steps *p92*
A clever piece of 18th-century town planning.

In the know
Getting around

Enclosed by the *vie* Ripetta and Babuino which radiate from piazza del Popolo, the 'Trident' is a very walkable area. It is served by two stops on Metro line A, Spagna and Flaminio, and at its southernmost end it is a hop, skip and a jump from the Pantheon and the Trevi Fountain.

Colonna di Marco Aurelio

AROUND TRIDENTE

Presumably hoping to keep his favoured haunts to himself, Federico Fellini set his film *La Dolce Vita* on via Veneto (*see p250*), where gawpers from the provinces then flocked in droves for a glimpse of the jet-set. The A-class, however, favoured the Tridente, the triangle enclosed by the three prongs – *vie* **Ripetta**, **del Corso** and **del Babuino** – emanating from piazza del Popolo.

The super-smart grid of streets at the foot of the Spanish Steps was no stranger to the attentions of the rich and famous: as long ago as the 18th century it had a *dolce vita* all of its own when this was the little St James' of the Grand Tourists, who met for coffee at the (long gone) Caffè degli Inglesi on the corner where via delle Carrozze meets the piazza.

VIA DEL BABUINO & PIAZZA DI SPAGNA

Piazza di Spagna is where everybody meets, congregating in the summer on whichever side of the grand staircase is in the shade. In spring the loafers, couples, exhausted tourists and those whose dates are seriously late are temporarily turfed off the steps while an army of gardeners arranges a display of azaleas.

❤ Time to eat & drink

Morning coffee
Antico Caffè Greco *p93*, Caffè Canova-Tadolini *p93*

Lunch
Pastificio Guerra *p93*

Afternoon tea
Babington's Tea Room *p93*

Cocktails
Hotel Locarno Bar *p101*, Stravinskij Bar *p93*

❤ Time to shop

Kitchenware
C.U.C.I.N.A *p94*

Leather accessories
Furla *p95*, Sermoneta *p95*

Marble souvenirs
Bottega del Marmoraro *p94*

Perfume
L'Olfattorio – Bar à Parfums *p101*

Via del Babuino

TRIDENTE

Restaurants

1. Enoteca Buccone
2. Ginger
3. Il Margutta
4. Matricianella
5. Pastificio Guerra
6. Trattoria dal Cavalier Gino

Cafés, bars & pubs

1. Antica Enoteca
2. Antico Caffè Greco
3. Babington's Tea Room
4. Caffè Canova-Tadolini
5. Hotel Locarno Bar
6. Rosati
7. Stravinskij Bar

Bakeries, pasticcerie & gelaterie

1. Venchi

Shops & services

1. Anglo-American Book Co
2. AS Roma Store
3. Bottega del Marmoraro
4. C.U.C.I.N.A
5. Damiani
6. Enoteca al Parlamento
7. Furla
8. La Nuova Pesa
9. L'Olfattorio – Bar à Parfums
10. La Perla
11. Pro Fumum
12. Sermoneta

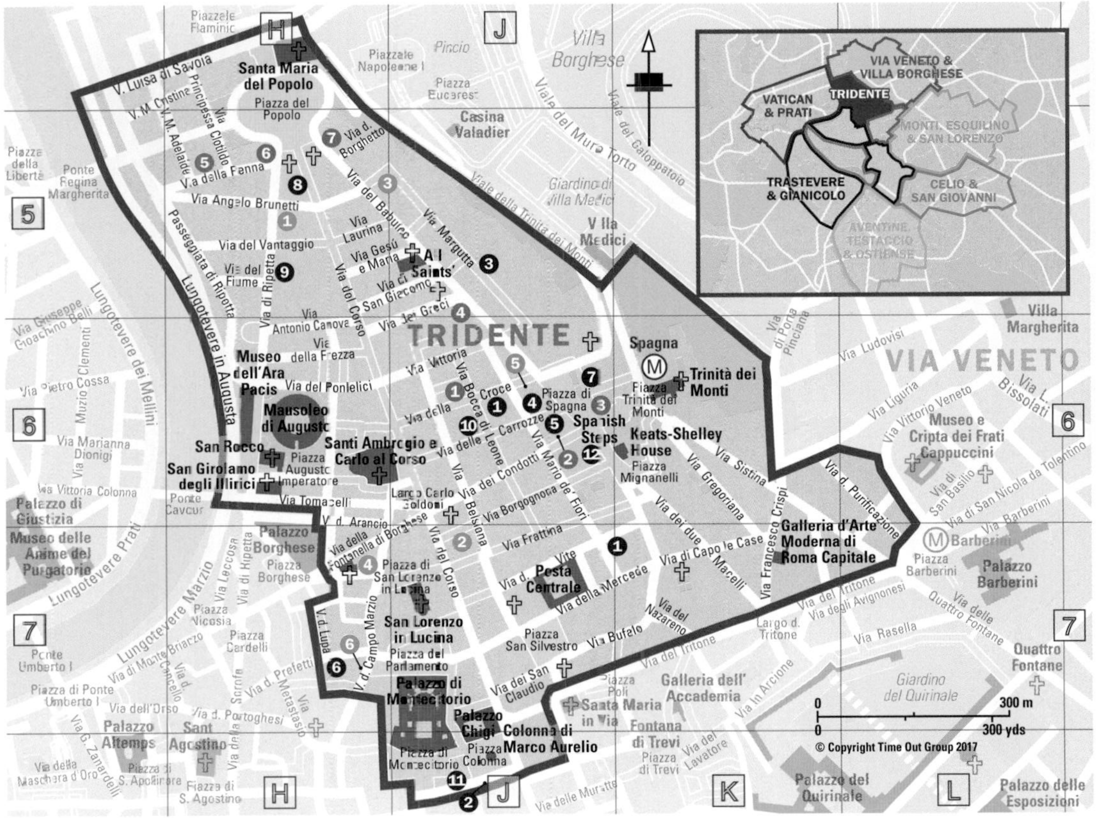

Grand Tourists

Well-to-do gentlemen flock to Rome

A burgeoning fascination with the classical world brought a procession of international travellers to Rome. The 17th century saw the arrival of artists such as Nicholas Poussin and Claude Lorrain who parlayed Roman decay into dreamy landscapes punctuated by the ruins of vanished greatness.

But it was in the 18th and early 19th centuries that the trickle turned into a flood.

A stopover in Rome was an essential part of any young gentleman's education, with English *milords* leading the pack. They put up in the smartest part of the city, between via del Corso and piazza di Spagna, where they could find hotels, cafés, carriage repair workshops (in via delle Carrozze) and an ever-growing band of *ciceroni* (tour guides) who would accompany them around the city.

Inspired by the great art around them, many would take up a brush themselves. To cater to them, a whole art industry sprung up, with artists' models hanging out on the Spanish Steps or in vicolo dei Modelli waiting to pose in return for payment, and impoverished artists both Italian and northern European keen to show them the rudiments.

Writers – particularly of the Romantic variety – flocked too. Byron claimed that Rome was the city of his soul, but he spent less than a month here. Keats came in the hope that the climate would cure his consumption. It didn't. He coughed his last at the bottom of the Spanish Steps, in what is now the **Keats-Shelley Memorial House** (*see p91*); he is buried in the wonderfully romantic **Cimitero Acattolico** (*see p216*). Shelley's ashes are interred there too, though he drowned in a sailing mishap off the Tuscan coast.

Goethe, whose Roman abode on via del Corso is one of the city's most charming house-museums, was less than impressed by the city which he described as intolerably noisy and prone to messy murders.

Shelley composing 'Prometheus Unbound' in the Baths of Caracalla (Joseph Severn, 1845)

Despite the crowds it's a lovely spot, but while here, spare a thought for the coughing, consumptive 25-year-old Keats, who spent a few wretched months in the winter of 1820-21 in the Casina Rossa, now the **Keats-Shelley Memorial House**.

Though the Spanish have a magnificent embassy in the square, it is the French who should be thanked for creating this sophisticated urban landscape with its grand **Spanish Steps** (*see p92*), which lead down from the French preserve of **Villa Medici** (*see p141*) – the glorious Renaissance villa that hosts *Prix de Rome* winners – and the **Trinità dei Monti** church and convent at the top. Don't be daunted by the steep climb, though one of the best-kept secrets of the area is the passenger lift, concealed on the left just inside the main entrance to the Spagna metro station. (This is also the easiest way up to the **Villa Borghese**; *see p140*.)

From the top of the steps you can get the lie of the land: just beyond the *barcaccia*, a charming fountain in the shape of a half-sunken boat designed by Gian Lorenzo Bernini's father Pietro (possibly with the help of his more famous son), is **via dei Condotti** with its high-fashion boutiques, the Gucci and Prada emporia immediately recognisable even at this distance by the neat lines of Japanese tourists clutching lengthy shopping lists for cult-status leather goods. Here, too, is the **Antico Caffè Greco** (*see p93*), where clientele included Casanova and mad King Ludwig of Bavaria. If it's tea you crave, try **Babington's Tea Room** (*see p93*) – located on piazza di Spagna – which has been serving reviving beverages and English-style snacks for more than 120 years.

To the south-east, the **Galleria d'Arte Moderna** (*see p91*), has an intriguing collection of 20th-century Roman artists.

To the north-west the incongruously neo-Gothic spire of **All Saints' English church** pokes up above the rooftops along **via del Babuino**. The origin of this oddly named street lies in the ugly statue draped over an old drinking trough, which reminded inhabitants of a member of the monkey family – another incongruity in the street to which all Rome's most beautiful people flock for their shopping.

Parallel to via del Babuino is **via Margutta**, focus of the 1960s art scene. Fellini lived here until his death in 1993. This was always an artists' quarter: models would ply for trade on the Spanish Steps.

Keats-Shelley Memorial House

Sights & museums

Galleria d'Arte Moderna di Roma Capitale

Via Francesco Crispi 24 (06 0608, www.galleriaartemodernaroma.it). Metro Spagna/bus 52, 53, 62, 63, 71, 80Exp, 83, 85, 117, 160, 492, 590. ***Open*** *10am-6.30pm Tue-Sat.* ***Admission*** *€7.50; €6.50 reductions. Exhibition price varies. No cards.* ***Map*** *p89 K7.*

All spruced up and with proper lighting, Rome's collection of 20th-century art has opened its doors once again in this former monastery. There are works by Giorgio de Chirico, Gino Severini, Giorgio Morandi and Giacomo Manzu, among many others.

♥ Keats-Shelley Memorial House

Piazza di Spagna 26 (06 678 4235, www.keats-shelley-house.org). Metro Spagna/bus 52, 53, 62, 63, 71, 80Exp, 83, 85, 117, 160, 492, 590, C3. ***Open*** *10am-1pm, 2-6pm Mon-Sat.* ***Admission*** *€5; €4 reductions.* ***Map*** *p89 K6.*

The house at the bottom of the Spanish Steps where 25-year-old John Keats died in 1821 is crammed with mementos. A lock of Keats' hair and his death mask, a minuscule urn holding tiny pieces of Percy Bysshe Shelley's charred skeleton, along with copies of documents and letters, and a massive library make this a Romantics enthusiast's paradise.

Bring a box of tissues: even the hardest-hearted can be moved to tears by the sight of manuscripts written by consumptive poets with shaky hands.

On the floor directly above the museum, an apartment, replete with period decor and now managed by the Landmark Trust (www.landmarktrust.org.uk), can be rented for holiday stays.

► *Devotees should also make the pilgrimage to the Cimitero Acattolico (Protestant Cemetery; see p216) where both Keats and Shelley are buried.*

❤ Spanish Steps

Metro Spagna/bus 52, 53, 62, 63, 71, 80Exp, 83, 85, 117, 160, 492, 590. ***Map*** *p89 K6.*

Piazza di Spagna takes its name from the Spanish Embassy to the Vatican, but is chiefly celebrated for the elegant cascade of stairs down from the church of Trinità dei Monti. Known in Italian as the Scalinata di Trinità dei Monti, the English Grand Tourists referred to them as the Spanish Steps. Completed in 1725, they might more accurately be called French: they were funded by French diplomat Etienne Gueffier, who felt the muddy slope leading up to the church – itself built with money from a French king – needed a revamp. At the foot of the stairs is a delightful boat-shaped fountain, the *barcaccia*, designed in 1627 by Gian Lorenzo Bernini and/or his less famous father Pietro; it's ingeniously sunk below ground level to compensate for the low pressure of the delicious *acqua vergine* that feeds it. The steps are best seen first thing in the morning before the crowds arrive.

Restaurants

Il Margutta €€

Via Margutta 118 (06 3265 0577, www.ilmargutta.bio). Metro Spagna or Flaminio/bus 117. ***Open*** *12.30-3.30pm, 7.30-11.30pm daily. Closed lunchtime 3wks Aug.* ***Map*** *p89 H5* ❸ Vegetarian

Il Margutta – one of Rome's very few vegetarian restaurants – occupies a prime piece of real estate on the corner of Rome's

Spanish Steps

gallery alley, and the decor pays homage to the area, with plenty of modern art. Variations on the buffet brunch – 'Green' during the week, and a more abundant weekend spread accompanied by live music on Sundays and holidays – are pile-your-plate affairs including soup and fruit juice. The more formal evening restaurant is less crowded and offers a range of tasting menus as well as à la carte dishes. Between lunch and dinner the WiFi Drink Bar allows you to get online over a *caffè* or something a little stronger.

❤ Pastificio Guerra €

Via della Croce 8 (06 679 3102). Metro Spagna/bus 52, 53, 62, 63, 71, 80, 81, 83, 85, 117, 160, 492, 590, 628. ***Open*** *1-9pm daily.* ***No cards. Map*** *p89 J6* ❺ *Streetfood*

This tiny purveyor of fresh pasta has gained fame as a cheap and cheerful lunch destination in one of the priciest parts of the city. There are no frills here, just a choice of two pasta dishes (which change daily) served on plastic plates to eat at the counter or take away. But at €4 a portion, which includes water and a cup of house wine, you would be hard pushed to find a better deal round here.

Cafés, bars & pubs

❤ Antico Caffè Greco

Via Condotti 86 (06 679 1700, www.anticocaffegreco.eu). Metro Spagna/bus 52, 53, 62, 63, 71, 80, 81, 83, 85, 117, 492, 590, 628. ***Open*** *9am-9pm daily.* ***Map*** *p89 J6* ❷ *Café*

Founded in 1760, this venerable café – the oldest in Rome – was once the hangout of Casanova, Goethe, Wagner, Stendhal, Baudelaire, Shelley and Byron. Opposition to the French Occupation of 1849-70 was planned here. Today its elegant interior is the very expensive hangout of bus-loads of tourists; locals, when they come, cram the foyer and down coffee on the hoof.

❤ Babington's Tea Room

Piazza di Spagna 23 (06 678 6027, www.babingtons.com). Metro Spagna/bus 52, 53, 62, 85, 117, 160, 301, 492, 628. ***Open*** *10am-9.15pm daily.* ***Map*** *p89 J6* ❸ *Tea room*

Homesick British expats have been heading to this quaint establishment at the foot of the Spanish Steps for a little taste of home ever since it opened its doors in 1893. The first place to serve tea in the Eternal City, it became a favourite meeting spot of visiting film stars and celebrities: Elizabeth Taylor and Richard Burton came here for romantic trysts during the filming of *Cleopatra* and even famed film director Federico Fellini was partial to the English muffins. Everything from breakfast, lunch and dinner is served here but it is the classic afternoon tea that draws the crowds with cucumber sandwiches and proper scones served on delicate patterned china.

❤ Caffè Canova-Tadolini

Via del Babuino 150A (06 3211 0702, www.canovatadolini.com). Metro Spagna/bus 117. ***Open*** *8pm-midnight daily.* ***Map*** *p89 J5* ❹ *Café/Bar*

Sculptor Antonio Canova signed a contract in 1818 to ensure that this property, in the heart of the old artists' quarter, would remain an atelier for sculpture. The master's wishes were respected until 1967: the workshop passed through many generations of the Tadolini family, descendants of Canova's favourite pupil and heir, Adamo Tadolini. Now refurbished as a museum-atelier, Canova's workshop has café tables among its stunning marble sculptures and a refined old-world feel: dark hardwood floors, wood-beamed ceilings, chandeliers and mustard-yellow leather banquettes and chairs. The small bar offers cocktails and assorted drinks, as well as tasty titbits, from canapés to cookies and pastries. The restaurant serves from noon to 11pm daily, but we recommend sticking to the café.

❤ Stravinskij Bar

Via del Babuino 9 (06 328 881, www.hotelderussie.it). Metro Spagna or Flaminio/bus 81, 117, 590, 628, 926. ***Open*** *9am-1am daily.* ***Map*** *p89 H5* ❼ *Bar*

Inside the swanky Hotel De Russie, this bar is divided into three sections: the small bar, a larger lounge area with sofas, and the outdoor patio. The first two are filled in cooler months with international business people, the hotel's celebrity guests and a gaggle of deep-pocketed regulars. But the real draw here is the fabulous patio, a sunken oasis of shady tables surrounded by orange trees and a gorgeous terraced garden. The drinks menu is pricey but interesting and the cocktails are well executed by some of Rome's top mixologists; try the signature Stravinskij Spritz: prosecco mixed with a secret recipe of berries, citrus and spices.

Bakeries, pasticcerie & gelaterie

Venchi

Via della Croce 25/26 (06 6979 7790, www.venchi.com). Metro Spagna/bus 117, 301, 628, 913. ***Open*** *10.30am-11.30pm Mon-Thur, Sun; 10.30am-12.30am Fri, Sat.* ***Map*** *p89 J6* ❶ *Chocolatier*

Stravinskij Bar, Hotel de Russie *p93*

Otherwise known as chocolate heaven, Venchi originated in Turin in 1878 and now has branches throughout Italy including several in Rome. The glistening shelves display an enticing array of cocoa-based products, from decadent individual truffles and jars of *gianduia* (chocolate hazelnut spread) to some of the thickest, richest chocolate gelato in town.

Shops & services

Anglo-American Book Co

Via della Vite 102 (06 679 5222, www.aab.it). Bus 52, 53, 62, 63, 80, 81, 83, 85, 117, 160, 492, 590, 628. ***Open*** *Sept-June 3.30-7.30pm Mon; 10.30am-7.30pm Tue-Sat. July, Aug 10am-7.30pm Mon-Fri; 10.30am-2.30pm Sat. Closed 2wks Aug.* ***Map*** *p89 J7* ❶ *Books*

A good selection of books in English from novels to non-fiction. There's a vast selection of scientific and technical texts for students at the other branch further down the road. The shop also organises frequent events and book signings.

❤ Bottega del Marmoraro

Via Margutta 53B (06 320 7660). Metro Spagna/bus 117. ***Open*** *8am-1pm, 3.30-7.30pm Mon-Sat.* ***No cards. Map*** *p89 J5* ❸ *Gifts & souvenirs*

Stepping into this hole-in-the-wall shop, you'd be forgiven for thinking you'd been teleported back to the workroom of an ancient Roman craftsman: the tiny space is crammed with pseudo-classical inscriptions, headless statues and busts. The jolly *marmoraro* Enrico Fiorentini can make to order.

❤ C.U.C.I.N.A

Via Mario de' Fiori 65 (06 679 1275, www.cucinastore.com). Metro Spagna/Bus 52, 53, 61, 62, 63, 80, 83, 85, 116, 116T, 150, 160, 175, 492, 590, C3. ***Open*** *11.30am-7.30pm Mon, Sun; 10.30am-7.30pm Tue-Sat.* ***Map*** *p89 J6* ❹ *House & home*

Even the most adventurous cooks will find a utensil their kitchen lacks at this culinary gadgetry shop. It sells a vast range of kitchenware, from bamboo rice steamers to a fine selection of jelly moulds.

Damiani

Via Condotti 84 (06 6920 0477, www.damiani.it). Metro Spagna/bus 52, 53, 62, 63, 80, 81, 83, 85, 117, 492, 590, 628. ***Open*** *10.30am-7.30pm Mon-Sat.* ***Map*** *p89 J6* ❺ *Jewellery*

Exquisite gems and luxury watches with that celebrity seal of approval: high-profile clients and collaborators include international royalty and Hollywood superstars such as Gwyneth Paltrow, Sharon Stone and Sophia Loren.

❤ Furla

Piazza di Spagna 22 (06 6920 0363, www.furla.com). Metro Spagna/bus 52, 53, 62, 63, 80, 81, 83, 85, 116, 116T, 117, 119, 160, 175, 492, 590, 628, C3. ***Open*** *10am-8pm Mon-Sat; 10.30am-8pm Sun.* ***Map*** *p89 J6* ❼ *Accessories*

In eye-popping colours or as elegantly subdued classics, Furla's bags have spread like wildfire all over the city, not to mention the world. Prices won't reduce you to tears, and the line extends to shoes, sunglasses and wallets as well as watches.

❤ Sermoneta

Piazza di Spagna 61 (06 6791 960, www.sermonetagloves.com). Metro Spagna/ bus 117, 301, 492, 628, 913. ***Open*** *9.30am-8pm Mon-Sat, 10.30am-7pm Sun. Closed Sun in July & Aug.* ***Map*** *p89 J6* ⓬ *Accessories*

Sermoneta's exquisite gloves are still made in the traditional method involving 10 skilled artisans and no fewer than 28 steps to produce each pair. The service is frosty but the choice is dizzying, with a selection of leathers from classic kidskin to more unique styles in suede, ostrich and boar, which come in every colour of the rainbow.

VIA DEL CORSO & PIAZZA DEL POPOLO

Via del Corso is the last urban stretch of the ancient via Flaminia, which linked Rome with the north Adriatic coast. Over the past 2,000 years it has been a processional route for Roman legions, a country lane, a track for *carnevale* races and, from the late 1800s, a principal showcase street for the capital.

The street's liveliest period began in the mid 15th century, when Pope Paul II began to fret over the debauched goings-on at the pre-Lenten *carnevale* celebrations in Testaccio (*see p247*). He decided to move the races and processions somewhere more central, where he and his troops could keep an eye on things. The obvious spot was via Flaminia – then known simply as via Lata ('wide street') – at the end of which he built his **Palazzo Venezia** (*see p63*). The pope had the stretch of the street within the city walls paved (using funds from a tax on prostitutes) and renamed il Corso. For over four centuries Romans flocked there at *carnevale* time to be entertained by such edifying spectacles as races between press-ganged Jews, hunchbacks, prostitutes and horses with hot pitch squirted up their recta to make them run faster.

Via del Corso

These grotesqueries only stopped after Italian unification in the 1870s, when the new national government set up shop halfway along via del Corso, setting the tone for what remains the country's political heart. The Lower House (Camera dei deputati) is in **Palazzo di Montecitorio** (*see p96*), in the piazza of the same name, and **Palazzo Chigi**, the prime minister's office, is next door in **piazza Colonna**, so named for the magnificent second-century AD **colonna di Marco Aurelio** (Column of Marcus Aurelius, *see p96*) that graces it.

North from Palazzo Chigi, imposing aristocratic *palazzi* give way to lower-end clothing outlets, which attract a seething mass of teenagers at the weekend. The pedestrianised **piazza di San Lorenzo in Lucina**, with its church (*see p97*) is a welcome retreat.

At the top of via del Corso, the symmetrically elegant, and now largely pedestrianised, **piazza del Popolo** (*see p97*) – once the papacy's favourite place for executions – is graced by the Caravaggio-packed church of **Santa Maria del Popolo** (*see p98*).

Sights & museums

❤ Colonna di Marco Aurelio

Piazza Colonna. Bus 52, 53, 62, 63, 71, 80Exp, 81, 83, 85, 117, 492, 590, 628, C3. ***Map*** *p89 J8.*

The 30-metre (100-foot) column of Marcus Aurelius was built between AD 180 and 196 to commemorate the victories on the battlefield of that most intellectual of Roman emperors. Author of the *Meditations*, he died while campaigning in 180. The reliefs on the column, modelled on the earlier ones on Trajan's Column (*see p72*) in the Imperial Fora, are vivid illustrations of Roman army life. In 1589 a statue of St Paul replaced that of Marcus Aurelius on top of the column.

Palazzo di Montecitorio

Piazza di Montecitorio (06 67 601, www.camera.it). Bus 52, 53, 62, 63, 71, 80Exp, 81, 83, 85, 117, 160, 492, 590, 628. ***Open*** *10.30am-3.30pm 1st Sun of mth. Closed Aug.* ***Admission*** *free.* ***Map*** *p89 J8.*

Since 1871 this has been the Lower House of Italy's parliament, which is why police and barricades sometimes prevent you from

Piazza del Popolo

getting near its elegantly curving façade. (It's best to check the website: open days can be cancelled for important parliamentary events.) Designed by Bernini in 1650 for Pope Innocent X, much of the building has been greatly altered, but the clock tower, columns and window sills of rough-hewn stone are his originals. In piazza di Montecitorio stands the tenth-century BC obelisk of Psammeticus. It was brought from Heliopolis by Augustus to act as the gnomon (projecting piece) for the emperor's great sundial (*see p85* Obelisks).

Piazza del Popolo

Metro Flaminio/bus 61, 89, 117, 490, 495, 628, 926/tram 2. ***Map*** *p89 H4.*

For centuries, piazza del Popolo was the first glimpse most travellers got of Rome. If Grand Tourists arrived during *carnevale* time, they were likely to witness condemned criminals being tortured here for the edification and/or entertainment of the populace. The obelisk in the centre was brought from Egypt by Augustus and stood in the Circo Massimo until 1589, when it was moved to its present site by Pope Sixtus V. It appears to stand at the apex of a perfect triangle formed by via Ripetta, via del Corso and via del Babuino, although this is an illusion. The churches on either side of via del Corso – Santa Maria dei Miracoli and Santa Maria di Monte Santo – look like twins, but are actually different sizes. Carlo Rainaldi, who designed them in the 1660s, made them and the angles of the adjacent streets appear symmetrical by giving one an oval dome and the other a round one. The immense Porta del Popolo gate was given a facelift by Bernini in 1655 to welcome Sweden's Queen Christina, who had shocked her subjects by abdicating her throne to convert to Catholicism. The plaque wishing *felice fausto ingressui* ('a happy and blessed arrival') was addressed to the Church's illustrious new signing. By the gate stands the church of Santa Maria del Popolo (*see right*).

San Lorenzo in Lucina

Piazza San Lorenzo in Lucina 16A (06 687 1494). Bus 52, 53, 62, 63, 71, 80Exp, 81, 83, 85, 117, 160, 492, 590, 628, C3. ***Open*** *Church 8am-8pm daily. Roman remains guided tour 5.15pm 1st Sat of mth.* ***Admission*** *Church free. Roman remains €2. No cards.* ***Map*** *p89 J7.*

Fountain of Neptune in piazza del Popolo

Santa Maria del Popolo

This 12th-century church was built on the site of a *titulus*, which in turn is believed to stand on the site of an ancient well sacred to Juno. The church's exterior incorporates Roman columns, while the 17th-century interior contains a Bernini portrait bust of a papal physician in the Fonseca Chapel, a kitsch 17th-century *Crucifixion* by Guido Reni and a monument to French artist Nicolas Poussin, who died in Rome in 1665. In the first chapel on the right is a grill, reputed to be the one on which the martyr St Lawrence was roasted to death.

❤ Santa Maria del Popolo

Piazza del Popolo 12 (06 361 0836, www.santamariadelpopolo.it). Metro Flaminio/ bus 61, 89, 117, 160, 490, 495, 628, 926/tram 2. ***Open*** *7am-noon, 4-7pm Mon-Thur; 7am-7pm Fri, Sat; 7.30am-1.30pm, 4.30-7.30pm Sun.* ***Map*** *p89 H4.*

According to legend, Santa Maria del Popolo occupies the site of a garden where the ashes of the hated Emperor Nero were scattered. The site was still believed to be haunted by demons 1,000 years later; in 1099 Pope Paschal II built a chapel there to dispel them. Nearly four centuries later, beginning in 1472, Pope Sixtus IV rebuilt the chapel as a church.

In the choir (behind the high altar, ask the custodian for permission to pass beyond the curtain) are, unusually for Rome, stained-glass windows, a northern touch created by French artist Guillaume de Marcillat in 1509. The apse itself was designed by Bramante, while the choir ceiling and first and third chapels in the right aisle were frescoed by Pinturicchio, the favourite artist of the Borgias. In Pinturicchio's exquisite works (1508-10), the Virgin and a host of saints keep company with some very pre-Christian sibyls. Most intriguing is the Chigi Chapel, designed by Raphael for wealthy banker Agostino Chigi. The mosaics in the dome depict God creating the sun and the seven planets, and Agostino's personal horoscope: with binoculars you can just about make out a crab, a bull, a lion and a pair of scales. The chapel was finished by Bernini, who, on the orders of Agostino's descendant Pope Alexander VII, added the statues of Daniel and Habakkuk. The church's most-gawped-at possessions, however, are the two masterpieces by Caravaggio to the left of the main altar, in the Cerasi Chapel. On a vast scale, and suffused with lashings of the maestro's particular light, they show the martyrdom of St Peter and the conversion of St Paul. To the left of the main door is a memorial to 17th-century notable GB Gisleni: grisly skeletons, chrysalids and butterflies remind us of our brief passage through this life before we exit the other end.

Restaurants

Ginger €€

Via Borgognona 43-44 (06 9603 6390). Metro Spagna/bus 52, 53, 62, 63, 71, 80, 81, 83, 85, 117, 160, 492, 590, 628. ***Open*** *10am-11pm daily.* ***Map*** *p89 J7* ② International

The apotheosis of the juice bar, this eco-chic all-day diner lies in the heart of the fashion shopping district. If you're craving a salad in carb-oriented Rome, this is the place to come. It also serves gourmet baguettes, deli platters (salami, prosciutto, daily-delivered mozzarella), exotic fruit and muesli mixes and a few standard *primi* and *secondi* with plenty of vegan and vegetarian options on offer. Alternatively, you can just swing by for a smoothie or a glass of organic wine. Huge skylights keep things bright even on the darkest winter day.

Matricianella €€

Via del Leone 3-4 (06 683 2100, www.matricianella.it). Bus 52, 53, 62, 63, 71, 80, 81, 83, 85, 116, 116T, 117, 119, 160, 175, 492, 590, 628, C3. ***Open*** *12.30-3pm, 7.30-11pm Mon-Sat. Closed 3wks Aug.* ***Map*** *p89 H7* ④ Trattoria

This is a friendly, bustling upscale *trattoria* with fair prices – for the *centro storico*. The menu is cover-to-cover Roman with pasta classics such as *bucatini all'amatriciana* (thick spaghetti with bacon, tomatoes and pecorino) and *rigatoni con coda alla vaccinara* (rigatoni with braised oxtail) while, for the more adventurous, there are also the local *quinto quarto* (offal) dishes featuring tripe, intestine and sweetbreads. The well-chosen wine list is a model of honest pricing; service is friendly but no-nonsense. It's almost always packed so be sure to book ahead. There are a few, highly sought-after tables outside.

Trattoria dal Cavalier Gino €€

Vicolo Rosini 4 (06 687 3434). Bus 52, 53, 62, 63, 71, 80, 81, 83, 85, 117, 160, 492, 590, 628. ***Open*** *1-2.45pm, 8-10.45pm Mon-Sat. Closed Aug.* ***No cards. Map*** *p89 H7* ⑥ Trattoria

You might seek out this hard-to-find *trattoria* in a lane off piazza del Parlamento for the food: hearty, traditional dishes such as pasta with porcini mushrooms, and rabbit cooked in white wine are prepared in good, honest time-honoured style. But it's the atmosphere that really attracts thanks to the amusing contrast between the rustic *trattoria* decor, complete with flamboyant Arcadian murals, and the clientele, made up largely of politicos and bag carriers from the nearby parliament building. Desserts include home-made *crostate* (jam tarts) and an excellent tiramisù. Come early, or be prepared to wait for a table.

Cafés, bars & pubs

Antica Enoteca

Via della Croce 76B (06 679 0896). Metro Spagna/bus 52, 53, 62, 63, 71, 80, 81, 83, 85, 117, 160, 492, 590, 628, 926. ***Open*** *11am-midnight daily. Closed Tue in Aug.* ***Map*** *p89 J6* ① Bar

When this place opened in 1842 it was the favourite haunt of the Scandinavian painters who lived on nearby via Margutta. A revamp has retained most of the original fittings, including the marble wine vats and a venerable wooden cash desk, which makes it a great place to sip one of the many wines that are offered by the glass here. There's a cold *antipasto* buffet at the bar, and a restaurant with tables in the long back room offering a full range of hot dishes at mealtimes – though the food is generally uninspiring and far from cheap.

Rosati

Piazza del Popolo 5 (06 322 5859, www.barrosati.com). Metro Flaminio/bus 81, 117, 590, 628, 926. ***Open*** *7am-11.30pm daily.* ***Map*** *p89 H5* ⑥ Café/Bar

Rosati is the traditional haunt of Rome's intellectual left: Calvino, Moravia and Pasolini were regulars. The art nouveau interior has remained unchanged since its opening in 1922. The coffee and *pasticceria* are excellent as are the cocktails; splash out on a pavement table with ringside view of stately piazza del Popolo to enjoy some serious people-watching.

Shops & services

AS Roma Store

Piazza Colonna 360 (06 6992 4643, www.asromastore.it). Bus 53, 62, 63, 80, 81, 83, 117, 119, 160, 175, 492, 628. ***Open*** *10am-7pm Mon-Sat; 11am-7.30pm Sun.* ***Map*** *p89 J8* ❷ Sports

AS Roma stores have a seemingly endless array of club merchandise, from strips to scarves and baby booties and more – all of it emblazoned with the highly recognisable red-and-yellow AS Roma logo. **Other locations** via del Corso 25; piazza B Cairoli 119, Campo (06 6880 9775).

Enoteca al Parlamento

Via dei Prefetti 15 (06 687 3446, www.enotecaalparlamento.it). Bus 52, 53, 62, 63, 80, 81, 83, 85, 117, 160, 492, 590, 628. ***Open*** *10am-midnight Mon-Sat. Closed 2wks Aug.* ***Map*** *p89 H7* ❻ *Food & drink*

Hundreds of bottles of spirits and the best Italian wines fill the wooden shelves of this warm shop. There's also delectable honey, balsamic vinegar and regional specialities. At lunchtime there is a limited menu of snacks and wine at stools and tables set up in the shop, while the back room hosts a Michelin-starred restaurant with a creative gourmet menu.

La Nuova Pesa

Via del Corso 530 (06 361 0892, www.nuovapesa.it). Metro Flaminio/bus 117, 119. ***Open*** *10.30am-1pm, 4-8pm Mon-Fri. Closed Aug.* ***No cards. Map*** *p89 H5* ❽ *Gallery*

In the 1950s, La Nuova Pesa organised the first post-war Italian shows of Picasso, Gris and Léger. The gallery now works with upcoming Roman artists and big international names alike.

La Perla

Via Bocca di Leone 28 (06 6994 1934, www.laperla.com). Metro Spagna/bus 52, 53, 62, 63, 80, 81, 83, 85, 117, 160, 492, 590, 628, C3. ***Open*** *10am-7.30pm Mon-Sat.* ***Map*** *p89 J6* ❿ *Lingerie*

From the lace and silk that have made La Perla a favourite for 50 years, to some slightly more affordable lines, this is knicker heaven.

Pro Fumum

Via della Colonna Antonina 27 (06 679 5982, www.profumum.com). Bus 52, 53, 62, 63, 80, 81, 83, 85, 117, 492, 590, 628. ***Open*** *mid Sept-June 3.30-7.30pm Mon; 10am-7.30pm Tue-Fri; 10am-1.30pm, 2.30-7.30pm Sat. July-mid Sept 10am-7.30pm Mon-Fri; 10am-1.30pm Sat. Closed 2wks Aug.* ***Map*** *p89 J8* ⓫ *Health & beauty*

The rare-brand creams, lotions and perfumes you will find in this sophisticated shop are highly tempting... but such high-class pampering certainly doesn't come cheap. **Other locations** via di Ripetta 248 (06 320 0306); viale Angelico 87-89, Prati (06 372 5791).

VIA RIPETTA

Halfway down the third arm of the Tridente, via Ripetta, is stark **piazza Augusto Imperatore**, built by Mussolini around the **Mausoleo di Augusto** (Mausoleum of Augustus) – the funerary monument of the Emperor Augustus (at the time of writing under restoration after decades of neglect). Next to it is the Ara Pacis Augustae, erected by Augustus to celebrate peace after his conquest of Gaul and Spain, housed in the gleaming structure purpose built by Richard Meier, the **Museo dell'Ara Pacis** (*see right*). South of the square stand two fine churches: **San Girolamo degli Illirici**, serving Rome's Croatian community, and **San Rocco**, built for local innkeepers and Tiber boatmen by Alexander VI (1492-1503). Heading back

Museo dell'Ara Pacis

towards via del Corso, the giant, curving walls of the **Palazzo Borghese** come into view; acquired in 1506 by Camillo Borghese, the future Pope Paul V, it was later the home of Napoleon's sister Pauline.

Sights & museums

Mausoleo di Augusto

Piazza Augusto Imperatore/via Ripetta. Bus 30Exp, 70, 81, 87, 117, 280, 492, 628, 913. Not open to the public. ***Map*** *p89 H6.*

It's hard to believe that this forlorn-looking brick cylinder was one of the most important monuments of ancient Rome. The mausoleum was built in honour of Augustus, who had brought peace to the city and its Empire, and was begun in 28 BC. The first person whose ashes were interred here was Augustus' nephew, favourite son-in-law and heir apparent, Marcellus. Augustus himself was laid to rest in the central chamber in AD 14, and many more emperors went on to join him there. In the Middle Ages, the mausoleum was used as a fortress; during the Renaissance, it housed gardens; until the 19th century it served as a theatre. Mussolini had it restored, reportedly because he thought it a fitting place for his own illustrious corpse. At the time of writing a new restoration project sponsored by the TIM phone company had just begun.

❤ Museo dell'Ara Pacis

Via Ripetta/lungotevere in Augusta (06 0608, www.arapacis.it). Bus 30Exp, 70, 81, 87, 117, 280, 492, 628, 913. ***Open*** *9.30am-7.30pm daily.* ***Admission*** *€10.50, €8.50 reductions. Exhibition price varies.* ***Map*** *p89 H6.*

Now in a striking and luminous container – designed by Richard Meier and opened amid great controversy – Augustus' great monument, the Ara Pacis Augustae, was inaugurated in 9 BC; this altar of Augustan peace celebrated the end of the civil war and strife that had characterised the last years of the Republic, and the wealth and security brought by Augustus' victories. Originally located a few hundred metres away (off via in Lucina, behind the church of **San Lorenzo in Lucina**; *see p97*), the *ara* was designed to overlook the urban stretch of via Flaminia (now via del Corso) by which Augustus had re-entered the city after three years' absence in Spain and Gaul. The altar as we see it now was reconstructed in the 1930s (by Mussolini who called himself 'the New Augustus') – after major excavations under the *palazzo* that had been built over the altar – its position known from fragments discovered during building work in the 16th century, and an equally major trawl through the world's museums looking for missing bits.

Outside, the flank of the building towards piazza Augusto Imperatore bears the Fascist Era inscription of the *Res Gestae*, Augustus' testament to his 'things done'.

Restaurants

Enoteca Buccone €€

Via Ripetta 19-20 (06 361 2154, www.enotecabuccone.com). Bus 81, 224, 590, 628, 926. ***Open*** *12.30-3pm Mon-Fri; 12.30-3pm, 7.30-10.30pm Sat; 11am-6pm Sun. Closed 1wk Aug.* ***Map*** *p89 H5* ❶ *Enoteca*

For years Il Buccone operated as a takeaway *enoteca* (wine shop) with a few wines available by the glass at the marble counter; but now tables are arranged among the high wooden shelves, and in a little room at the back, for full meals. There are always three or four pasta dishes or soups, followed by a range of meaty seconds and creative salads. The cooking is more than competent, the prices reasonable by Roman standards, and the service friendly.

Cafés, bars & pubs

❤ Hotel Locarno Bar

Via della Penna 22 (06 361 0841, www.hotellocarno.com). Metro Flaminio/bus 81, 117, 590, 628, 926. ***Open*** *7am-1am daily.* ***Map*** *p89 H5* ❺ *Bar*

The glorious art nouveau bar of the Hotel Locarno is a treat at any time of day for coffee or tea in surroundings of slightly faded elegance, much favoured by visiting actors and film directors, and local intellectuals. But around 7pm the panorama changes as the bar itself and the delightful leafy terrace outside (patio heaters keep it open through the year) become the venue for one of the city's hottest *aperitivo* scenes. Trendy young Romans rub shoulders with in-the-know out-of-towners, vying for a terrace perch.

Shops & services

❤ L'Olfattorio – Bar à Parfums

Via Ripetta 34 (bookings 06 361 2325, information 800 631 123, www.olfattorio.it). Metro Flaminio/bus 81, 117, 119, 224, 590, 628, 926. ***Open*** *10.30am-7.30pm daily. Closed Sun July, Aug & 2wks Aug.* ***Map*** *p89 H5* ❾ *Health & beauty*

It's strictly personal shopping at this innovative perfumery. A 'bartender' will awaken your olfactory organs and guide you expertly towards your perfect scent. Once determined, exclusive lines of hand-made English and French fragrances are available on site. Paradise for perfume-lovers.

Pantheon & Piazza Navona

After the fall of the Roman Empire, this area of the *Campus martius* in the loop of the river north of corso Vittorio Emanuele became prime construction territory, with great marble *palazzi* scattered among the modest homes of ordinary folk. Today, this picturesque section of the *centro storico* retains its historical mix of the very grand and the very humble: mink-coated *contesse* mingle with wrinkled pensioners and tradesmen, often living, or making a living, in parts of the same *palazzo*. It's a chic area after dark, with smart restaurants and hip bars. Next morning, however, it's back to business, with wheeling and dealing taking place against a stunning backdrop: two squares, both living links to ancient Rome, dominate the district: piazza della Rotonda – home to the Pantheon – and the magnificent piazza Navona.

❤ Don't miss

1 Galleria Doria Pamphilj *p115*
A papal stately home, complete with a couple of Caravaggios, a Bernini and a Velazquez.

2 San Luigi dei Francesi *p111*
More splendid Caravaggios in his first major church commission, the Contarelli Chapel.

3 Piazza Navona *p108*
An ancient athletics track converted into an elegant Baroque piazza with a fabulous fountain.

4 Pantheon *p113*
Quite simply the most influential building ever constructed, and the best preserved ancient building in the city.

In the know
Getting around

Perhaps the centre of the *centro storico*, this area is densely packed with cobbled streets and ancient ruins. The best way to explore the narrow and winding streets is most definitely on foot. The closest metro station is Spagna (line A), a walk away through the Tridente.

Pantheon

PANTHEON & PIAZZA NAVONA

Restaurants

1 Armando al Pantheon
2 Casa Bleve
3 Il Convivio Troiani
4 Coromandel
5 Da Francesco
6 Da Simo Pane e Vino
7 Enoteca Corsi
8 Grano

Cafés, bars & pubs

1 Bar del Fico
2 Caffè Sant'Eustachio
3 Cul de Sac
4 Etabli
5 Salotto 42
6 Scholar's Lounge
7 Tazza d'Oro

Bakeries, pasticcerie & gelaterie

1 La Caffettiera
2 Gelateria del Teatro

Shops & services

1 Antica Erboristeria Romana
2 Borsalino
3 Cartoleria Pantheon
4 Ditta G Poggi
5 Eclectica
6 Fox Gallery
7 Moriondo & Gariglio
8 Officina Profumo-Farmaceutica di Santa Maria Novella
9 Il Papiro
10 Le Tartarughe
11 Tempi Moderni

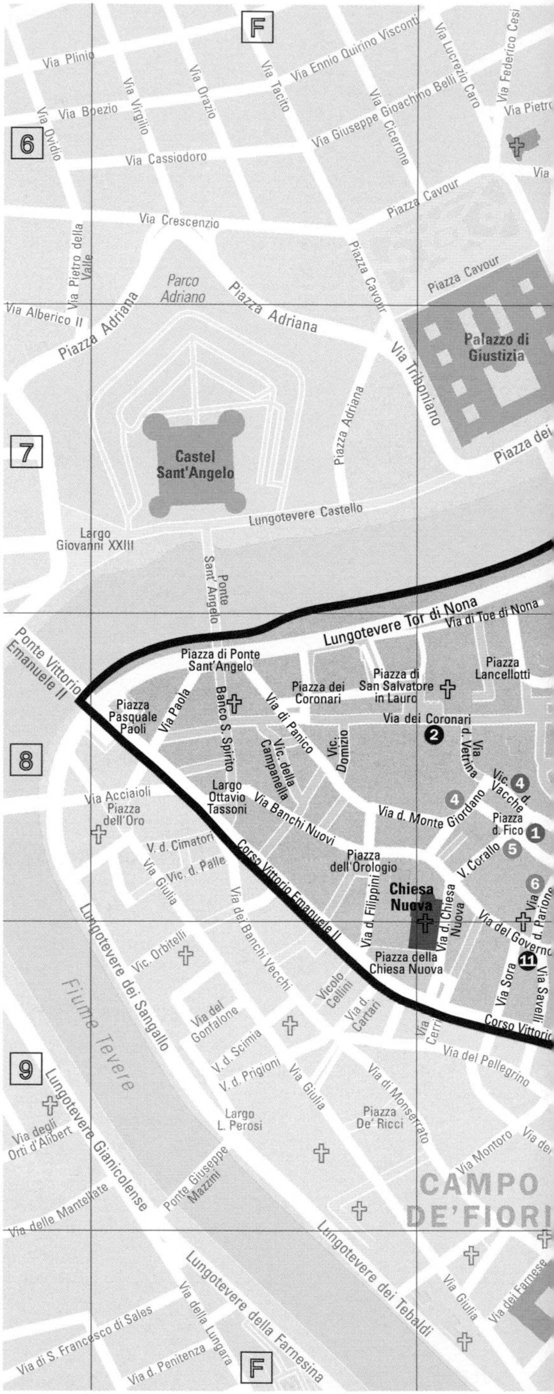

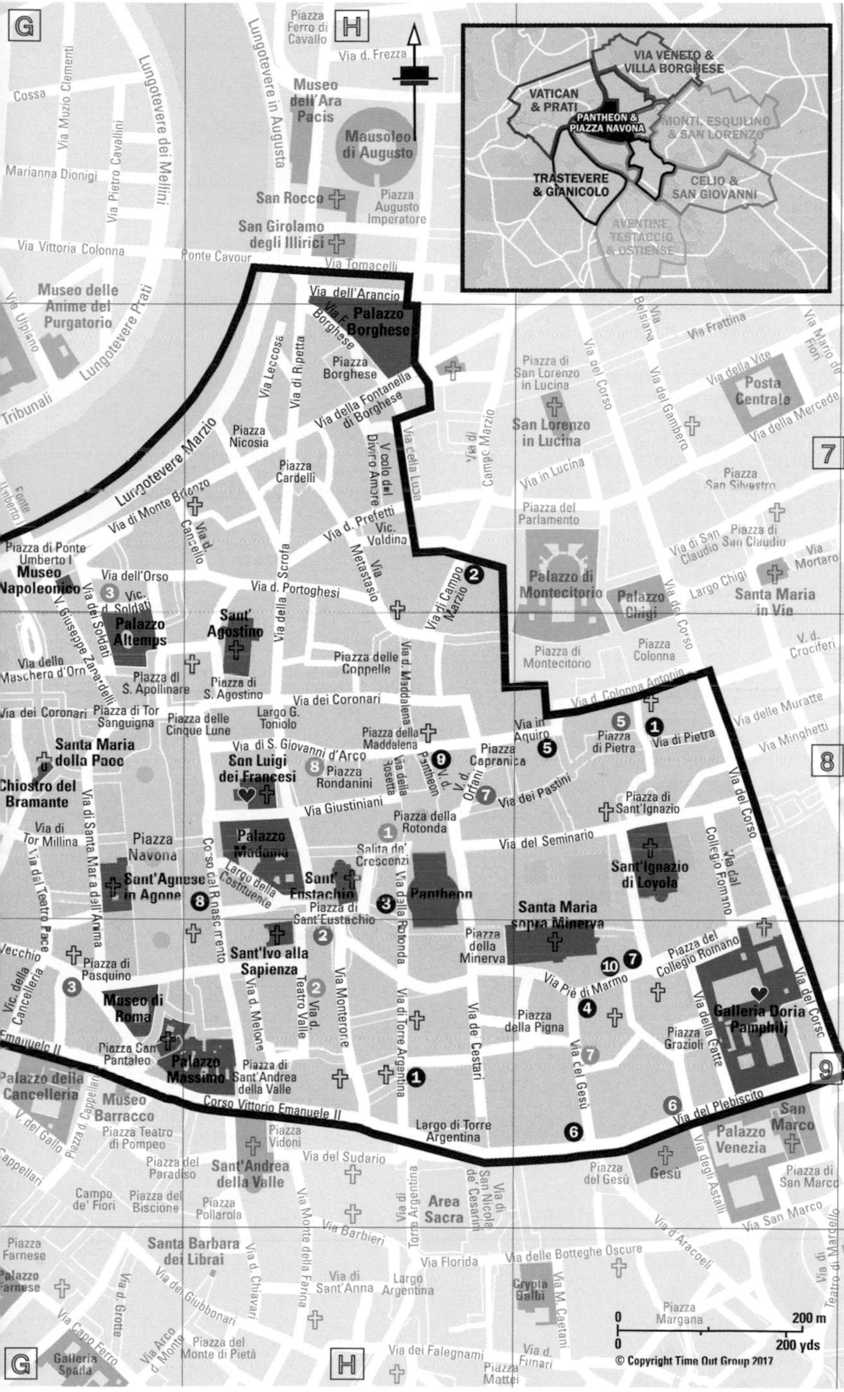

G
H
7
8
9
VIA VENETO & VILLA BORGHESE
VATICAN & PRATI
PANTHEON & PIAZZA NAVONA
MONTI, ESQUILINO & SAN LORENZO
TRASTEVERE & GIANICOLO
CELIO & SAN GIOVANNI
AVENTINE, TESTACCIO & OSTIENSE
Piazza Ferro di Cavallo
Via d. Frezza
Museo dell'Ara Pacis
Mausoleo di Augusto
San Rocco
Piazza Augusto Imperatore
San Girolamo degli Illirici
Lungotevere in Augusta
Lungotevere dei Mellini
Via Muzio Clementi
Cossa
Marianna Dionigi
Via Pietro Cavallini
Via Vittoria Colonna
Ponte Cavour
Via Tomacelli
Museo delle Anime del Purgatorio
Lungotevere Prati
Via Ulpiano
Tribunali
Via dell'Arancio
Palazzo Borghese
Via F. Borghese
Piazza Borghese
Via Leccosa
Via di Ripetta
Via della Fontanella di Borghese
Lungotevere Marzio
Piazza Nicosia
Piazza Cardelli
Via della Lupa
V. colo del Divino Amore
Via di Campo Marzio
Via d. Prefetti
Vic. Valdina
Via Metastasio
Via di Monte Brianzo
Via d. Cancello
Via della Scrofa
Piazza di Ponte Umberto I
Museo Napoleonico
Via dell'Orso
Vic. d. Soldati
Via dei Soldati
V. Giuseppe Zanardelli
Via d. Portoghesi
Palazzo Altemps
Sant' Agostino
Via della Maschera d'Oro
Piazza di S. Apollinare
Piazza di S. Agostino
Piazza delle Coppelle
Via d. Maddalena
Via dei Coronari
Piazza di Tor Sanguigna
Piazza delle Cinque Lune
Largo G. Toniolo
Piazza della Maddalena
Santa Maria della Pace
Chiostro del Bramante
Via di S. Giovanni d'Arco
San Luigi dei Francesi
Piazza Rondanini
Via della Rosetta
V. d. Pantheon
V. d. Orfani
Piazza Capranica
Via in Aquiro
Via dei Pastini
Via Giustiniani
Piazza della Rotonda
Via di Tor Millina
Via di Santa Maria dell'Anima
Piazza Navona
Palazzo Madama
Salita de' Crescenzi
Corso del Rinascimento
Largo della Costituente
Sant'Agnese in Agone
Sant' Eustachio
Pantheon
Piazza di Sant'Eustachio
Via della Rotonda
Via del Teatro Pace
Sant'Ivo alla Sapienza
Piazza della Minerva
Santa Maria sopra Minerva
Vic. della Cancelleria
Piazza di Pasquino
Museo di Roma
Via d. Melone
Via d. Teatro Valle
Via Monterone
Via di Torre Argentina
Via de Cestari
Via Piè di Marmo
Piazza della Pigna
Via del Gesù
Piazza San Pantaleo
Palazzo Massimo
Piazza di Sant'Andrea della Valle
Corso Vittorio Emanuele II
Palazzo della Cancelleria
Museo Barracco
V. del Gallo
Piazza d. Cappellari
Piazza Teatro di Pompeo
Piazza Vidoni
Largo di Torre Argentina
Via del Sudario
Piazza del Paradiso
Sant'Andrea della Valle
Campo de' Fiori
Piazza del Biscione
Piazza Pollarola
Via Monte della Farina
Via di Torre Argentina
Area Sacra
Via di San Nicola de' Cesarini
Via Barbieri
Piazza Farnese
Palazzo Farnese
Santa Barbara dei Librai
Via d. Chiavari
Via dei Giubbonari
Via Capo Ferro
Via d. Grotte
Via Arco d. Monte
Piazza del Monte di Pietà
Galleria Spada
Via di Sant'Anna
Largo Argentina
Via Florida
Via delle Botteghe Oscure
Crypta Balbi
Via M. Caetani
Piazza Margana
Via dei Falegnami
Via d. Funari
Piazza Mattei
Via Belsiana
Via Frattina
Via Mario de' Fiori
Piazza di San Lorenzo in Lucina
Via del Corso
Via di Campo Marzio
San Lorenzo in Lucina
Via del Gambero
Via della Vite
Posta Centrale
Via della Mercede
Via in Lucina
Piazza San Silvestro
Piazza del Parlamento
Via di San Claudio
Piazza di San Claudio
Via Mortaro
Palazzo di Montecitorio
Palazzo Chigi
Largo Chigi
Santa Maria in Via
Piazza di Montecitorio
Piazza Colonna
V. d. Crociferi
Via d. Colonna Antonina
Via delle Muratte
Via Minghetti
Piazza di Pietra
Via di Pietra
Piazza di Sant'Ignazio
Via del Seminario
Via del Collegio Romano
Sant'Ignazio di Loyola
Piazza del Collegio Romano
Via della Gatta
Piazza Grazioli
Galleria Doria Pamphilj
Via del Plebiscito
San Marco
Palazzo Venezia
Gesù
Piazza del Gesù
Via degli Astalli
Piazza di San Marco
Via San Marco
Via d'Aracoeli
Via del Teatro di Marcello
0 200 m
0 200 yds
© Copyright Time Out Group 2017

WEST OF PIAZZA NAVONA

After arriving at the northern entrance to the city at **piazza del Popolo** (*see p97*), pilgrims were funnelled past a succession of rosary-makers (*coronari*) – the hard-selling souvenir touts along **via dei Coronari** – who vied to empty the travellers' pockets before they reached St Peter's. The faithful also paid a swingeing toll to cross the **Sant'Angelo bridge** to reach their final destination.

Nowadays, in the golden triangle that extends between via dei Coronari and via del Governo Vecchio, humanity flows along in a continuously moving wave. Here, VIPs and wannabe movie stars parade their assets (but never before midnight) in *dolce vita*-style bars before a backdrop of dazzling Renaissance beauty, including the stunning façade of **Santa Maria della Pace** (*see p107*).

At the south-western tip of piazza Navona, in **piazza di Pasquino**, a severely truncated classical statue nestling against the back wall of Palazzo Braschi – now home to the **Museo di Roma** (*see p107*) – is the most famous of Rome's 'talking' statues; in days gone by when Vatican walls had ears and you could lose your head for an offhand irreverent remark, Romans let off steam by pinning scurrilous verse to sculptures rather than risk their lives by being vocally critical. Facts are thin on the ground but rumour had it that Pasquino (after whom the piece was named in 1501) was a tailor to the Vatican and that much of papal Rome's gossip emanated from his nearby shop. The cutting witticisms came to be known as pasquinate (pasquinades).

Nearby, **corso Vittorio Emanuele II** (simply 'corso Vittorio' to locals) shoots north-west towards the river. When it was hacked through the medieval area after Unification in the 1870s, only the most grandiose of homes – such as **Palazzo Massimo alle Colonne** (no.141) and **Palazzo Braschi** (piazza di San Pantaleo 10) – were spared.

Sights & museums

Chiesa Nuova

Piazza della Chiesa Nuova/via del Governo Vecchio 134 (06 687 5289, www.vallicella.org). Bus 30Exp, 40Exp, 46, 62, 64, 916. ***Open*** *8am-noon, 4.30-7pm daily.* ***Map*** *p104 G8.*

Filippo Neri (1515-95) was a wealthy Florentine who abandoned the cut and thrust of the business world to live and work among the poor in Rome. He experienced an 'ecstasy' of divine love at the Catacombs of San Sebastiano in 1544, after which he founded the Oratorian order. In 1575 work began on the order's headquarters, the Chiesa Nuova, on the site of Santa Maria in Vallicella (donated by Gregory XIII). Neri wanted a large, simple building; the plain walls were covered with exuberant frescoes and multicoloured marbles only after his death. Pietro da Cortona painted *Neri's Vision of the Virgin* (1665) in the vault, the *Trinity in Glory* (1647) in the cupola and the *Assumption of the Virgin* (1650) in the apse. *The Virgin and Child*, over the altar, and saints Gregory and Domitilla, to the left and right, are by Rubens (1607-08). Neri was canonised in 1622, and his body lies in an ornately decorated chapel to the left of the main altar. His rooms are open to all on 26 May (his feast day) – though you can also occasionally book on a guided tour (email oratoriopiccolo@gmail.it). Singing was an important part of Oratorian worship, and oratory as a musical form developed out of the order's services: check the programme of *concerti spirituali* on the church's website.

► *Borromini designed the brick Oratorio dei Filippini (1637-52) located next to the Chiesa Nuova.*

❤ Time to eat

Breakfast
Coromandel *p107*

Morning coffee
Caffè Sant'Eustachio *p112*, Tazza d'Oro *p116*

Lunch
Cul de Sac *p112*, Da Simo Pane & Vino *p107*

Aperitivo
Bar del Fico *p107*

Dinner
Armando al Pantheon *p114*

❤ Time to shop

Chocolate
Moriondo & Gariglio *p117*

Italian fashion
Borsalino *p116*, Le Tartarughe *p117*

Stationery
Cartoleria Pantheon *p117*, Il Papiro *p117*

❤ Time well spent

Visit the **Chiostro del Bramante** (Arco della Pace 5, 06 6880 9036, www.chiostrodelbramante.it, *map p104 G8*), which was built by Urbibo-born architect Donato Bramante in 1500-1504. His work is credited with kick-starting the High Renaissance in Rome.

Museo di Roma

Palazzo Braschi, piazza San Pantaleo 10 (06 6710 8346, www.museodiroma.it). Bus 30Exp, 40Exp, 46, 62, 64, 70, 81, 116, 168, 492, 628, 916. ***Open*** *10am-7pm Tue-Sun.* ***Admission*** *€9; €7 reductions. Exhibition price varies.* ***Map*** *p104 G9.*

A rotating collection displayed over two floors recounts the evolution of the Eternal City from the Middle Ages to the early 20th century. Paintings and drawings include portraits of Roman movers and shakers, and views of what the city looked like before 17th- and 19th-century building projects, such as the *banchine* flood walls along the Tiber, dramatically changed it. Sculpture, clothing, furniture and a great collection of 19th-century photographs help to put the city's monuments in a human context, and oddities like the Braschi family sedan chair (used by Pius VI) and the papal railway carriage (used by more recent pontiffs) round out the collection. The *palazzo* was built by Luigi Braschi (nephew of 18th-century Pope Pius VI) in one of the last great flurries of papal nepotism. Sold to the Italian state in 1871 and intended to house the Interior Ministry, the *palazzo* later became the Fascist party HQ. The bookshop is well stocked, there's a café and the reading room has a selection of Rome-oriented reference books.

Santa Maria della Pace

Vicolo del Arco della Pace 5. Bus 30Exp, 70, 81, 87, 116, 130, 186, 492, 628, C3. ***Open*** *9am-noon Mon-Wed, Sat. Mass 11am Sun.* ***Map*** *p104 G8.*

Built in 1482 for Pope Sixtus IV, Santa Maria della Pace was given its theatrical Baroque façade by Pietro da Cortona in 1656. The church's most famous artwork is just inside the door: Raphael's *Sibyls*, painted in 1514 for Agostino Chigi, the playboy banker and first owner of the **Villa Farnesina** (*see p172*). Even if the church is closed, you can visit the beautifully harmonious cloister by Bramante, his first work after arriving in Rome in the early 16th century. **Note** that opening hours depend on the presence of the custodian, but the church is always open for Mass on Sundays from 11am to 12.30pm.

Restaurants

❤ Coromandel €€

Via di Monte Giordano 60-61 (06 68802461, www.coromandel.it). Bus 40, 46, 62, 64, 628, 916. ***Open*** *8.15am-3pm, 8-11pm Tue-Sat. Closed 2wks Aug.* ***Map*** *p104 G8* ❹ *International*

The brunch menu at Coromandel has earned it a loyal following among foreign expats needing an occasional change from the ubiquitous Italian breakfast pastries, thanks to its pancakes, waffles, bagels and eggs Benedict as well as a good choice of teas and fresh juices. There is also a daily lunch blackboard and a full à la carte selection for dinner, all served in the cosy dining room on pretty mismatched china.

Da Francesco €€

Piazza del Fico 29 (06 686 4009, www.dafrancesco.it). Bus 40, 46, 62, 64, 916. ***Open*** *11.50am-3pm, 7pm-12.30am daily.* ***Map*** *p104 G8* ❺ *Trattoria/Pizzeria*

Accept no imitations: Da Francesco is the genuine *centro storico* pizzeria article. If you're looking for quiet and calm, go elsewhere; this is Rome eating at its most chaotic. The pizzas are old-school simple, the atmosphere is crushed and rushed, service is brisk and there's a range of fairly competent classic *primi* and decent steaks if pizza isn't your thing: no gourmet treat, but incredibly central in its pretty square and definitely a slice of Roman life. You can try booking but your reservation is likely to be forgotten; get there well before 8pm if you don't want to queue.

❤ Da Simo Pane e Vino €

Via di Parione 34 (06 8670 9955, www.facebook.com/dasimopaneevino). Bus 40, 46, 62, 64, 916. ***Open*** *noon-11pm daily.* ***Map*** *p104 G8* ❻ *Sandwich bar*

This tiny place cooks up hearty Roman casseroles and salads which are generously stuffed into panini and served on the ramshackle outside tables. The selection changes daily but there are always at least 8-10 choices from traditional *trippa alla romana* (tripe in tomato sauce) and *coda alla vaccinara* (oxtail stew) to aubergine parmigiana and owner Simona's grandmother's recipe of sausage stew with grapes. The exuberant staff and extremely affordable prices (panini start at €4.50 and bottles of beer are just €1) make Da Simo a hidden gem in one of the most touristy parts of town.

Cafés, bars & pubs

❤ Bar del Fico

Piazza del Fico 26-28 (06 6889 1373, www.bardelfico.com). Bus 40, 46, 62, 64, 916. ***Open*** *8.30am-2.30am daily.* ***No cards.*** ***Map*** *p104 G8* ❶ *Bistro*

This long-established *centro storico* fixture – named after the ancient fig tree (*fico*) outside – underwent a refurbishment a few years back and transformed from an old-school local bar to a vintagey French-style bistro with a laid-back boho ambience. Not that this has deterred the regulars however, and the old blokes can still be found playing chess outside. Open from breakfast until the small hours, it is the perfect central meeting place.

Etabli

Vicolo delle Vacche 9 (06 9761 6694, www.etabli.it). Bus 40, 46, 62, 64, 190, 571, 916. ***Open*** *7.30am-1am Mon-Wed, Sun; 7.30am-2am Thur-Sat.* ***Map*** *p104 G8* ❹ *Bar*

Pared-back decor, twiddly chandeliers and deep leather armchairs around a fireplace draw some seriously hip locals to this bar and restaurant in the super-chic *triangolo della pace*. The welcome is suave-warm, the vibe intimate and, with regular live music and DJs, the music is funky.

Bakeries, pasticcerie & gelaterie

Gelateria del Teatro

Via dei Coronari 65/66 (06 4547 4880, www.gelateriadelteatro.it). Bus 70, 81, 87, 115, 492. ***Open*** *10.30am-11.30pm daily.* ***Map*** *p104 G8* ❷ *Gelateria*

One of Rome's most esteemed gelato shops prides itself on the quality of the ingredients as well as the transparency of the production (take a peek through the window to see employees prepping the fresh produce). The flavours verge on the experimental with unique choices such as chocolate and red wine, raspberry with sage and white peach and lavender sitting alongside the stalwarts of lemon, pistachio and vanilla. **Other location** Lungotevere dei Vallati 25, Campo.

Shops & services

Tempi Moderni

Via del GovernoVecchio 108. Bus 30, 40, 46, 62, 64, 70, 81, 87, 116, 116T, 130, 186, 190, 492, 571, 628, 916, C3. ***Open*** *10am-7.30pm Mon-Sat. Closed 2wks Aug.* ***Map*** *p104 G9* ⓫ *Jewellery*

There's an eclectic assortment of 20th-century pieces in this boudoir-like shop: elegant art deco necklaces are displayed alongside 1950s Bakelite brooches and chunky retro bangles. A selection of jewel-bright kimonos adds to the effect.

PIAZZA NAVONA & EAST

Piazza Navona was the great theatre of Baroque Rome: at times it would be flooded in order to amuse the aristocracy with mock naval battles. Its graceful sweep – with Bernini's fountains, Borromini's church of **Sant'Agnese in Agone** (*see p110*) and picturesque pavement cafés – is now frequented by more prosaic denizens, from tarot-readers, caricaturists, buskers and suburban smoothies to tourists, nuns and businessmen.

Just north of piazza Navona are **Palazzo Altemps**, with its spectacular collection of antique statuary; **Sant'Agostino** (*see p110*), with its Caravaggio masterpiece; and the **Museo Napoleonico** (*see p108*). Due east from the piazza are the Italian Senate, **Palazzo Madama**; the church of **San Luigi dei Francesi** (*see p111*), with yet more Caravaggios; and Borromini's breathtaking **Sant'Ivo alla Sapienza** (*see p110*).

Sights & museums

Museo Napoleonico

Piazza di Ponte Umberto I (06 6880 6286, www.museonapoleonico.it). Bus 30 Exp, 70, 81, 87, 492, 628. ***Open*** *10am-6pm Tue-Sun.* ***Admission*** *free.* ***Map*** *p104 G7.*

Blink and you could miss any mention of Napoleon's reign in Rome – from 1798 to 1814 – in standard accounts of the city. But dreams of empire were the Corsican's fatal fantasy; he even shipped in Pope Pius VII for his imperial coronation in Paris in 1804. Rome was mostly an opportunity for grabbing as much loot as his army could carry, hauling back cartloads of marbles and old masters. But the emperor's mother Letizia lived happily in the Palazzo Bonaparte on piazza Venezia for many years, and his sister Pauline posed in the nude for sculptor Canova (*see p142* Galleria Borghese) and ran up huge bills for her millionaire Roman husband, Prince Camillo Borghese. The small Museo Napoleonico contains pieces relating to the Frenchman's family and is an intriguing glimpse into an often overlooked period in the city's history.

Palazzo Altemps

Piazza Sant'Apollinare 46 (06 3996 7700). Bus 30Exp, 70, 81, 87, 492, 628. ***Open*** *9am-7.45pm Tue-Sun.* ***Admission*** *€7; €3.50 reductions. Exhibition price varies.* ***Map*** *p104 G8.*

The 15th- to 16th-century Palazzo Altemps has been beautifully restored to house part of the state-owned Museo Nazionale Romano stock of Roman treasures. Here, in perfectly lit salons, loggias and courtyards, you can admire gems of classical statuary from the formerly private Boncompagni-Ludovisi, Altemps and Mattei collections.

The Ludovisis were big on 'fixing' statues broken over the ages or which simply didn't appeal to the tastes of the day. In Room 9, for example, a stately *Athena with Serpent* was revamped in the 17th century by Alessandro Algardi, who also 'improved' the *Hermes Loghios* in Room 19 upstairs. In Room 20, the former dining room with pretty 15th-century frescoes on foody themes, is an *Ares* touched up by Bernini. Room 21 has the *Ludovisi Throne*, the museum's greatest treasure... or its greatest hoax, if you subscribe to the theory of the late, great art historian and polemicist Federico Zeri. (On what may – or, then again, may not – be a fifth-century BC work from Magna Grecia, Aphrodite is being delicately and modestly lifted out of the sea spray from which she was born; on one side of her is a serious lady burning incense, and on the other is a naked one playing the flute.) In Room 26, a Roman copy of a Greek *Gaul's Suicide* was commissioned, recent research suggests, by Julius Caesar. Also here is the Ludovisi sarcophagus, which bears some action-packed high reliefs that depict Roman soldiers trouncing barbarians.

Four newly opened rooms contain more of the Mattei collection plus some remarkable Egyptian artefacts from ancient sites in and around Rome, including the recently discovered Artemis of Ephesus statue, displayed for the first time. These rooms can be seen on guided tours at 11am, noon, 4pm and 5pm from Tuesday to Saturday, and all day Sunday.

► *See also p187 The Museo Nazionale Romano collection for more on your combined ticket.*

Palazzo Madama

Corso Rinascimento (06 67 06 2177, www.senato.it). Bus 30Exp, 70, 81, 87, 492, 628. ***Open*** *(guided tours only) 10am-6pm 1st Sat of mth. Closed Aug.* ***Admission*** *free.* ***Map*** *p104 H8.*

Home to the Italian Senate since 1871, this *palazzo* was built by the Medici family in the 16th century as their Rome residence. Its rather twee façade, with a frieze of cherubs and bunches of fruit, was added a hundred years later. The 'Madama' of its name refers to Margaret of Parma (1522-86), the illegitimate daughter of Emperor Charles V, who lived here in the 1560s before moving to the Netherlands, where she instigated some of the bloodiest excesses of the religious wars. Tickets can be reserved at piazza Madama 11 from 8.30am on open days.

❤ Piazza Navona

Bus 30Exp, 40Exp, 46, 62, 64, 70, 81, 168, 492, 628, 916. ***Map*** *p104 G8.*

This tremendous theatrical space, centred on the gleaming marble composition of Bernini's Fontana dei Quattro Fiumi (Fountain of the Four Rivers), is the hub of the *centro storico*. The piazza owes its shape to an ancient athletics stadium, built in AD 86 by Emperor Domitian, which was the scene of sporting events, and at least one martyrdom.

The piazza acquired its current form in the mid 17th century under Pope Innocent

Fontana dei Quattro Fiumi (Gian Lorenzo Bernini, 1651)

X of the Pamphilj family. Its western side is dominated by Borromini's façade for the church of **Sant'Agnese in Agone** (*see p110*) and the adjacent **Palazzo Pamphilj** (now the Brazilian embassy), built in 1644-50. The central fountain, finished in 1651, is one of the most extravagant masterpieces designed – though only partly sculpted – by Bernini. Its main figures represent the longest rivers of the four continents known at the time: the Ganges of Asia, Nile of Africa, Danube of Europe and Plata of the Americas, surrounded by geographically appropriate flora and fauna. The figure of the Nile is veiled, because its source was unknown. For centuries, the story went that Bernini designed it that way to show the river god recoiling in horror from the façade of Sant'Agnese, designed by his arch-rival Borromini; in fact, the church was built after the fountain was finished. The obelisk at the fountain's centre, moved here from the Circus of Maxentius on the Appian Way, was carved in Egypt under the orders of Domitian (the hieroglyphics are a Roman addition describing him as 'eternal pharaoh'). The less-spectacular Fontana del Moro is at the southern end of the piazza. The central figure of the Moor was designed by Bernini in 1653, and executed by Antonio Mari.

Sant'Agnese in Agone

Piazza Navona/via Santa Maria dell'Anima 30A (06 6819 2134, www.santagneseinagone.org). Bus 30Exp, 40Exp, 46, 62, 64, 70, 81, 168, 492, 571, 628, 916, C3. ***Open*** *9am-1pm, 3.30-7pm Tue-Fri; 10am-1pm, 3-8pm Sat, Sun.* ***Map*** *p104 G8.*

Legend has it that teenage Agnes was cast naked into the stadium of Domitian around AD 304 when she refused to renounce Christ and marry some powerful local buck (possibly Romulus, the son of Emperor Maxentius), but her hair grew miraculously to save her from embarrassment. She was condemned to burn but when the fire refused to catch light, her pagan persecutors chopped her head off, supposedly on the exact spot where this church now stands. Carlo and Girolamo Rainaldi began the church for Pope Innocent X in 1652; after they quarrelled with the pope, Borromini was appointed in their place. He revised the design considerably, adding the splendidly fluid concave façade. The trompe l'oeil side chapels contain statues of St Agnes and another victim of a botched martyrdom, St Sebastian. The doorway in the chapel to the left of the high altar contains a reliquary with Agnes's implausibly small skull. Around the church are reliefs with cherubs holding symbols associated with the martyrdom, including the lamb most commonly used to represent her. Admire Borromini's sacristy during a Friday evening concert.

> **In the know**
> **Piazza di Tor Sanguigna**
>
> Just north of piazza Navona, at piazza di Tor Sanguigna 16, you can still see remains of the original ancient arena, sunk below street level. You can also visit the excavations; entrance includes an audioguide (piazza di Tor Sanguigna 3, www.stadiodomiziano.com, 10am-7pm Sun-Fri, 10am-8pm Sat, admission €8).

Sant'Agostino

Piazza Sant'Agostino (06 6880 1962). Bus 30Exp, 70, 81, 87, 492, 628. ***Open*** *7.30am-noon, 4-7pm daily.* ***Map*** *p104 H8.*

Built over a ninth-century church that marked the burial place of St Monica, St Augustine's mother, the 15th-century church of Sant'Agostino has one of the earliest Renaissance façades in Rome, fashioned out of travertine filched from the Colosseum. Inside, the third column on the left bears a fresco of Isaiah by Raphael from 1512 (when its commissioner complained that the artist had charged him too much for the work, Michelangelo is said to have snapped: 'the knee alone is worth that'). Immediately below is a beautiful sculpture of Mary, her mother Anne and the Christ-child by Andrea Sansovino (also 1512). In the first chapel on the left is Caravaggio's depiction of the grubbiest, most threadbare pilgrims ever to present themselves at the feet of the startlingly beautiful *Madonna of the Pilgrims* (1604). So dirty were they, in fact, that the church that originally commissioned the picture refused to have it. The two highest angels of the main altar are the work of Bernini (1628); below is a Byzantine Madonna.

Sant'Ivo alla Sapienza

Corso Rinascimento 40 (06 361 2562). Bus 30Exp, 70, 81, 87, 492, 628. ***Open*** *9am-noon Sun.* ***Map*** *p104 H9.*

You can peer, and wander, into the magnificent Renaissance courtyard of the state archives, but visit on a Sunday morning to do real justice to this crowning glory of Borromini's tortured imagination, wehn you can go inside. The concave façade of Sant'Ivo is countered by the convex bulk of the dome, which terminates in a bizarre corkscrew spire. The floor plan is based on a six-pointed star, but the forms of classical architecture (solid pediments, columns and logical arches, squares and circles) melt into an altogether more fluid play of convex and concave surfaces on the walls and up into

❤ San Luigi dei Francesi

Piazza San Luigi dei Francesi (06 688 271, www.saintlouis-rome.net). Bus 30Exp, 70, 81, 87, 492, 628. ***Open*** *9.30am-12.45pm Mon-Fri; 9.30am-12.15pm Sat; 11.30am-12.45pm Sun.* ***Map*** *p104 H8.*

Completed in 1589, San Luigi (St Louis) is the church of Rome's French community. Most visitors ignore the gaudily lavish interior, and make a beeline for Caravaggio's spectacular scenes from the life of St Matthew in the last chapel on the left, the funerary chapel of Matheiu Cointrel. Italianised as the Contarelli Chapel, it was the first of Caravaggio's major church commissions. He was awarded the contract thanks to the intervention of his patron, the Cardinal del Monte, a retainer of the Medici whose Rome palace, the Palazzo Madama (now the Italian Senate), was next to the French church.

Painted in 1600-02, the scenes depict Christ singling out a very reluctant Matthew in a contemporary tavern setting (left), Matthew attacked by his assassins, clearly reluctant to succumb to martyrdom (right) and an angel briefing the evangelist about what he should write in his gospel (over the altar).

Don't let Caravaggio's brooding brilliance and dramatic effects of light and shade blind you to the lovely frescoes of scenes from the life of St Cecilia by Domenichino (1615-17), which are in the second chapel on the right. Take a few coins for instant meter-operated illumination.

Contarelli Chapel, San Luigi dei Francesi

the dome, in a dizzying whirl that soars up to the unknowable, intangible realm of the heavens... leaving you feeling as if someone spiked your cappuccino.

► *Round off your meal with a superlative ice-cream from the branch of Il Gelato di San Crispino (see p81) in nearby piazza della Maddalena.*

Restaurants

Casa Bleve €€€

Via del Teatro Valle 48-49 (06 686 5970, www.casableve.it). Bus 30, 40, 46, 62, 63, 64, 70, 81, 87, 492, 628, 916, H/tram 8. ***Open*** *12.15-3pm, 7-10.30pm Mon-Sat. Closed 2wks Aug.* ***Map*** *p104 H9* ❷ *Wine bar*

Wine merchants Anacleto and Tina Bleve's wine bar-restaurant is in a huge colonnaded courtyard roofed over with coloured glass: impressive, though the tables feel a little lost in all this space. The buffet the place was known for has been done away with in favour of an à la carte menu. Excellent ingredients are carefully sourced, as reflected in the bill: this is never a cheap option for a quick bite. But wine remains the star turn here, with a tremendous selection, both by the bottle and by the glass.

Il Convivio Troiani €€€€

Vicolo dei Soldati 31 (06 686 9432, www.ilconviviotroiani.com). Bus 30Exp, 70, 81, 87, 492, 628. ***Open*** *8-11pm Mon-Sat. Closed 1wk Aug.* ***Map*** *p104 G7* ❸ *International*

The Troiani brothers run a high-class act in this temple of foodie excellence just north of piazza Navona. The Michelin-starred creations of chef Angelo are ultra-gourmet, some tempered by his origins in the Marche region but others – such as crab with coconut milk and asparagus – reflecting an international approach. *Secondi*, where meat, game and seafood take equal billing, are also fine, and the desserts are spectacular. The wine list is extensive and has a few affordable bottles. For Convivio beginners the six-course tasting menu (€125) is a good place to start.

Grano €€

Piazza Rondanini 53 (06 6819 2096, www.ristorantegrano.it). Bus 30, 70, 81, 87, 492, 628. ***Open*** *12.30-3pm, 7.30-11.30pm daily.* ***Map*** *p104 H8* ❽ *Italian*

The name (meaning 'wheat') suggests a concept restaurant, and indeed pasta and delicious home-made bread make their presence felt in this country-chic eaterie with southern Italian influences. The menu juggles fresh fish and hearty meat dishes with a few unusual touches such as red shrimp with passion fruit and sliced lamb with blue cheese and porcini. The desserts are excellent and the position, in a square right by the Pantheon, perfect.

Cafés, bars & pubs

❤ Caffè Sant'Eustachio

Piazza Sant'Eustachio 82 (06 6880 2048, www.santeustachioilcaffe.it). Bus 30, 40, 46, 62, 63, 64, 70, 81, 87, 190, 492, 628, 810, 916, H. ***Open*** *7.30am-1am Mon-Thur, Sun; 7.30am-1.30am Fri; 7.30am-2am Sat.* ***No cards. Map*** *p104 H9* ❷ *Coffee shop*

This is one of the city's most famous coffee bars, and its walls are plastered with celebrity testimonials. The coffee is quite extraordinary, if pricier than elsewhere; the barmen turn their backs while whipping up a cup so as not to let their secret out (though a pinch of bicarbonate of soda is rumoured to give it its froth). Try the *gran caffè*: the *schiuma* (froth) can be slurped out with a spoon or finger afterwards. Unless you specify (*amaro* means 'no sugar'; *poco zucchero* means 'a little sugar'), it comes very sweet.

❤ Cul de Sac

Piazza Pasquino 73 (06 6880 1094, www.enotecaculdesacroma.it). Bus 40, 46, 62, 64,492, 628, 916. ***Open*** *noon-midnight daily.* ***Map*** *p104 G9* ❸ *Wine bar*

Rome's first ever wine bar, the Cul de Sac was founded in 1977. Looking very traditional nowadays, it's cramped inside and out, with long pine benches and tables, and is decidedly no-frills. But the location – just off piazza Navona, with a ringside view of the 'talking' statue of Pasquino – coupled with fairly reasonable prices and an encyclopaedic wine list, ensures full occupancy all the time. The food is standard wine-bar fare including a selection of home-made pâtés as well as generous sharing plates of cured meats and cheeses.

Shops & services

Officina Profumo-Farmaceutica di Santa Maria Novella

Corso Rinascimento 47 (06 687 2446, www.smnovella.it). Bus 30, 70, 81, 87, 492, 628. ***Open*** *10am-7.30pm Mon-Sat. Closed 1wk Aug.* ***Map*** *p104 H8* ❽ *Health & beauty*

From quiet beginnings – it was founded in Florence in 1612 by a group of enterprising Dominican monks – the chic Officina's all-natural products have gained themselves a global following. The handcrafted potions are exquisite; prices, needless to say, don't reflect the products' humble origins.

PANTHEON TO VIA DEL CORSO

With the Pantheon as backdrop, all human life plays out in ever-bustling **piazza della Rotonda**. A 16th-century fountain is topped by an Egyptian obelisk dedicated to Rameses II. On the steps of the fountain, pierced punks with dogs on limp string hang out with hippies who forgot to go home. All seem oblivious to the bemused tour groups taking photographs and the well-heeled tourists paying through the nose for a cappuccino-with-a-view at the piazza's cafés.

South of the Pantheon, central Rome's only Gothic church, **Santa Maria sopra Minerva** (*see p114*), stands in piazza della Minerva. In front is *il Pulcino della Minerva*, aka '**Bernini's elephant**'. This cuddly marble animal, with wrinkled rear end and benign expression, has stood here since 1667. It was designed by Bernini as a tribute to Pope Alexander VII: elephants were both a symbol of wisdom and a model of abstinence. They were believed to be monogamous and to mate only once every five years, which, the Church felt, was the way things should be. Bernini perched a 12th-century BC Egyptian obelisk on its back; like its neighbour in piazza della Rotonda, this obelisk came from a temple to the Egyptian goddess Isis that had stood nearby (*see p85* Obelisks).

Further east, **piazza del Collegio Romano** contains one of Rome's finest art collections in the **Galleria Doria Pamphilj** (*see p115*). The charmingly rococo **piazza Sant'Ignazio** looks just like a stage set despite its severe Jesuit church, **Sant'Ignazio di Loyola**. In neighbouring piazza di Pietra, the columns of the Temple of Hadrian can be seen embedded in the walls of Rome's ex-stock exchange, where the occasional exhibition is now held. The quieter lanes close to **via del Corso** contain outposts of the parliament; journalists, MPs and assorted hangers-on haunt the area's bars. On the lower reaches of via del Corso is the privately owned **Museo del Corso**.

Sights & museums

❤ Pantheon

Piazza della Rotonda (06 6830 0230). Bus 30Exp, 40Exp, 46, 53, 62, 63, 64, 70, 81, 85, 87, 117, 160, 492, 571, 628, 810, 916/ tram 8. ***Open*** *8.30am-7.15pm Mon-Sat; 8.30am-5.45pm Sun; 8.30am-12.45pm public hols.* ***Admission*** *free.* ***Map*** *p104 H8.*

The Pantheon is the best-preserved ancient building in Rome. It was built (and possibly designed) by Hadrian in AD 119-128 as a temple to the 12 most important classical deities; the inscription on the pediment records an earlier Pantheon built a hundred years earlier by Augustus' general Marcus Agrippa (which confused historians for centuries). Its fine state of preservation is due to the building's conversion to a Christian church in 608, when it was presented to the pope by the Byzantine Emperor Phocas. The

Pantheon

Pantheon has nevertheless suffered over the years – notably when bronze cladding was stripped from the roof in 667, and when Pope Urban VIII allowed Bernini to remove the remaining bronze from the beams in the portico to melt down for his *baldacchino* in St Peter's in 1628. The simplicity of the building's exterior remains largely unchanged, and it retains its original Roman bronze doors. Inside, the Pantheon's real glory lies in the dimensions, which follow the rules set down by top Roman architect Vitruvius. The diameter of the hemispherical dome is exactly equal to the height of the whole building; it could potentially accommodate a perfect sphere. At the exact centre of the dome is the oculus, a circular hole 9 metres (30 feet) in diameter, the only source of light and a symbolic link between the temple and the heavens. The building is still officially a church, and contains the tombs of eminent Italians, including the artist Raphael and united Italy's first king, Vittorio Emanuele II. Until the 18th century the portico was used as a market: supports for the stalls were inserted into the notches still visible in the columns.

Santa Maria sopra Minerva

Piazza della Minerva 42 (06 679 3926, www.basilicaminerva.it). Bus 30Exp, 40Exp, 46, 62, 63, 64, 70, 81, 87, 492, 628, 810, 916/tram 8. ***Open*** *Sept-June 8am-7pm Mon-Fri; 8am-12.30pm, 3.30pm-7pm Sun. July, Aug 10.30am-12.30pm, 3-7pm daily.* ***Map*** *p104 J9.*

Central Rome's only Gothic church was built on the site of an ancient temple to the goddess Minerva in 1280 and modelled on Santa Maria Novella in Florence. It was (over-) restored in the 'Gothick' style in the mid 19th century. The best of its works of art are Renaissance: on the right of the transept is the superb Carafa chapel, with late 15th-century frescoes by Filippino Lippi (1457-1504), commissioned by Cardinal Oliviero Carafa in honour of St Thomas Aquinas. Carafa took Renaissance self-assurance to extremes: the altar painting shows him being presented to a patient Virgin, right at the moment when Gabriel informs her she has conceived. The tomb of the Carafa Pope Paul IV (reigned 1555-59) is also in the chapel. He was one of the prime movers of the Counter-Reformation, chiefly remembered for the institution of the Jewish Ghetto and ordering Daniele da Volterra to paint loincloths on the nudes of Michelangelo's *Last Judgement* (1565). A bronze loincloth was also ordered to cover Christ's genitals on a work by Michelangelo here: the statue was finished by Pietro Urbano (1514-21) and depicts a heroic Christ holding up a cross. An early Renaissance work is the *Madonna and Child* (c1449), attributed to Benozzo Gozzoli. Close by is the tomb of a contemporary artist, Fra Angelico. On either side of the altar are the tombs of Medici popes: corpulent Leo X and the nemesis of Henry VIII, Clement VII.

In the know
St Eustace

Legend has it St Eustace was a Roman soldier converted to Christianity while hunting at Tivoli, where he had a vision of a stag with a cross between its antlers. He is said to have been martyred where the church now stands. Antlers decorate the church's 18th-century façade.

Most people come here for the legendary *gran caffè* across the piazza at the **Caffè Sant'Eustachio** (*see p112*) – its walls are covered in snaps of visiting celebrities.

Sant'Ignazio di Loyola

Piazza Sant'Ignazio (06 679 4406). Bus 53, 62, 63, 80, 81, 83, 85, 117, 160, 492, 628, C3. ***Open*** *7.30am-7pm Mon-Sat; 9am-7pm Sun.* ***Map*** *p104 J8.*

Sant'Ignazio was begun in 1626 to commemorate the canonisation of St Ignatius, founder of the Jesuit order. Trompe l'oeil columns soar above the nave, and architraves by Andrea Pozzo open to a cloudy heaven. Trickery was also involved in creating the dome: the monks next door claimed that a real dome would rob them of light, so Pozzo simply painted a dome on the inside of the roof. The illusion is fairly convincing if you stand on the disc set in the floor of the nave. Walk away, however, and it dissolves.

Restaurants

❤ Armando al Pantheon €€

Salita de' Crescenzi 31 (06 6880 3034, www.armandoalpantheon.it). Bus 30, 40, 46, 62, 63, 64, 70, 81, 87, 492, 628, 810, 916, H/tram 8. ***Open*** *12.30-3pm, 7.15-11pm Mon-Fri; 12.30-3pm Sat. Closed Sat, Sun in July, Aug.* ***Map*** *p104 H8* ➊ *Trattoria*

Armando is a no-frills trattoria of the kind that once was common in Rome but now is like gold dust, especially when its location is taken into account – just a few yards from an A-league attraction. A recent renovation has spruced up the interior but all the hallmarks of authenticity remain, including indifferent artworks and wonderfully friendly service from the family that has run it since 1961. The menu sticks with tried-and-tested Roman

❤ Galleria Doria Pamphilj

Via del Corso 305 (06 679 7323, www.dopart.it). Bus 53, 62, 63, 80, 81, 83, 85, 117, 492, 628. ***Open*** *10am-7pm daily.* ***Admission*** *€12; €8 reductions.* ***Map*** *p104 J9.*

The collection of one of the great families of Rome's aristocracy (spelled either Pamphili or Pamphilj), now headed by two half-British siblings, is a very personal one: hung according to an inventory of 1760, some extraordinarily good paintings are packed in with the occasional bad copy to give a unique view of the tastes of late 18th-century Rome.

The entrance is through the state apartments planned by Camillo Pamphilj in the mid 16th century. The nephew of Pope Innocent X, Camillo escaped the College of Cardinals to marry fabulously wealthy Olimpia Aldobrandini, to whom the oldest part of the palace belonged, and who had already been left a widow by a member of the Borghese family. The family chapel was designed in 1689 by Carlo Fontana but heavily altered in the 18th and 19th centuries when the trompe l'oeil ceiling was added. The star turns are the corpses of two martyrs: St Justin, under the altar, and St Theodora, visible to the right of the door. The main galleries are on all four sides of the central courtyard. Hard-nosed Olimpia is shown in Algardi's stylised portrait bust by the windows in the first gallery.

Velázquez's portrait of a no-nonsense Pope Innocent X is the highlight of the collection. With Bernini's splendid bust next to it, it's difficult to see how the vital presence of Innocent X could be bettered. Other highlights include two paintings attributed to Caravaggio: *Rest on the Flight into Egypt* (1597) and *Penitent Magdalene* (c1595), shown alongside the *Portrait of Two Men* by Raphael (c1516) in the Aldobrandini room (at the end of the third gallery, down a few steps and home also to ancient sculpture). This leads onto a dark room which contains a beautifully tragic *Deposition* by Hans Memling (c1485-90). On the way, keep an eye out for Guercino's *St Agnes* (1652).

pasta and meat classics executed with love by smiley chef Claudio Gargioli. Unusually attentive to special dietary requirements, they will gladly substitute in gluten-free pasta.

Enoteca Corsi €€

Via del Gesù 87-88 (06 679 0821, www. enotecacorsi.com). Bus 30, 40, 46, 62, 63, 64, 70, 81, 87, 492, 571, 628, 916, H. ***Open*** *noon-3.30pm Mon-Sat, 7-10.30pm Fri, Sat. Closed 3wks Aug.* ***Map*** *p104 J9* 7 *Enoteca*

This wine shop, lined with shelves heaving with bottles, was the first in Rome to begin serving lunch. Prices aren't as low as they used to be, but it's still a good bet for a filling stopover. The daily changing menu offers a few pastas (€9) and a good selection of meat and fish *secondi* (€13). Dishes follow the traditional Roman order – gnocchi on Thursdays and stewed *baccalà* (salt cod) on Fridays. A slice of ricotta tart followed by a jolt of espresso makes a fitting end to a hearty meal. This *enoteca* is a popular venue for local workers looking for a filling lunch so get there early on weekdays or be prepared to queue.

Cafés, bars & pubs

Salotto 42

Piazza di Pietra 42 (06 678 5804, www. facebook.com/salotto42.it). Bus 52, 53, 62, 63, 71, 80, 83, 85, 117, 492, 59. ***Open*** *10.30am-2am daily. Closed Aug.* ***Map*** *p104 J8* 5 *Bar*

This spot on lovely piazza di Pietra, opposite the ancient temple of Hadrian, is open morning till late. The bar's Roman/Swedish/ New York pedigree is seen in little touches throughout. Incredibly comfortable chairs and sofas provide a cosy feel during the day, when a smörgåsbord of nibbles is available. By night, the sleek room becomes a gorgeous cocktail bar with a great soundtrack, excellent drinks and local sophisticates. All this plus a selection of books on fashion, art and design.

Scholar's Lounge

Via del Plebiscito 101B (06 6920 2208, www. scholarsloungerome.com). Bus 40, 46, 60, 64, 70, 87, 117, 170, H. ***Open*** *11am-3.30am daily.* ***Map*** *p104 J9* 6 *Pub*

Rome's largest Irish pub also happens to sit bang in the middle of the *centro storico* making it a convenient spot for a pit-stop and pint while sightseeing thanks to the 15 beers and ciders on tap and an award-winning selection of whiskies. Big-screen TVs stream sports events from across the globe throughout the day while after midnight the music gets louder as the international students arrive for cocktails and dancing.

❤ Tazza d'Oro

Via degli Orfani 84 (06 678 9792, www. tazzadorocoffeeshop.com). Bus 52, 53, 62, 63, 71, 80, 83, 85, 117, 160, 492, 590. ***Open*** *7am-8pm Mon-Sat, 10.30am-7.30pm.* ***Map*** *p104 H8* 7 *Coffee shop*

The powerful aroma wafting from this ancient *torrefazione* (coffee-roasters) overlooking the Pantheon is a siren call to coffee-lovers. The place is packed with coffee sacks, tourists and regulars, who flock for *granita di caffè* (coffee sorbet) in summer, and *cioccolata calda con panna* (hot chocolate with whipped cream) in winter. It sells speciality teas too.

Bakeries, pasticcerie & gelaterie

La Caffettiera

Piazza di Pietra 65 (06 679 8147, www. grancaffelacaffettiera.com). Bus 52, 53, 62, 63, 71, 80, 83, 85, 117, 160, 492, 590. ***Open*** *7.30am-10pm daily. Closed 1wk Aug.* ***Map*** *p104 J8* 1 *Tea room*

Politicians and mandarins from the parliament buildings nearby lounge in the sumptuous tea room of this temple to Neapolitan goodies, while lesser mortals bolt coffees at the counter. The rum babà reigns supreme, but ricotta-lovers rave over the crunchy *sfogliatella*, which is flavoured with cinnamon and orange peel.

Shops & services

Antica Erboristeria Romana

Via di Torre Argentina 15 (06 687 9493, www. anticaerboristeriaromana.com). Bus 30, 40, 46, 62, 63, 64, 70, 81, 87, 492, 628, 780, 916, H/tram 8. ***Open*** *9am-7.30pm Mon-Sat. Closed Sat pm in Aug.* ***Map*** *p104 H9* 1 *Health & beauty*

Visit this charming 18th-century apothecary-style shop if only to admire the carved wood ceilings and banks of tiny wooden drawers – some etched with skull and crossbones – in which herbal remedies are hidden safely away.

❤ Borsalino

Via Campo Marzio 72/A (06 679 6120, www. borsalino.com). Bus 70, 81, 117, 301, 913, 628. ***Open*** *10am-7.30pm daily.* ***Map*** *p104 H7* 2 *Hats*

Hat maker extraordinaire Giuseppe Borsalino created his brand in 1857 and since then the label's signature designs have donned the heads of such diverse names as Winston Churchill, Giuseppe Verdi, Audrey Hepburn and Leonardo di Caprio. Still created using the original techniques, craftsmanship and quality at this level certainly doesn't come cheap.

❤ Cartoleria Pantheon

Via della Rotonda 15 (06 687 5313, www. pantheon-roma.com). Bus 30, 40, 46, 62, 63, 64, 70, 81, 87, 492, 628, 780, 916, H/tram 8. ***Open*** *10.30am-8pm Mon-Sat; 1-8pm Sun.* ***Map*** *p104 H8* ❸ *Gifts & souvenirs*

Bring out your literary soul with leather-bound notebooks, hand-painted Florentine stationery and rare paper from Amalfi. Nearly everything for sale has been handcrafted. **Other locations** via della Maddalena 41 (06 679 5633); piazza Navona 42.

Ditta G Poggi

Via del Gesù 74-75 (06 678 4477, www. poggi1825.it). Bus 30, 40, 46, 62, 63, 64, 70, 81, 87, 190, 492, 628, 780, 810, 916, C3, H/tram 8. ***Open*** *9am-7.30pm Mon-Sat. Closed Sat, Sun in Aug.* ***Map*** *p104 J9* ❹ *Art supplies*

This wonderfully old-fashioned shop has been selling paints, brushes, canvases and artists' supplies of every description since 1825. **Other locations** via Cardinale Merry del Val 18-19, Trastevere (06 581 2531).

Eclectica

Via in Aquiro 70 (06 678 4228, www. eclecticaroma.com). Bus 30, 53, 62, 63, 70, 80, 81, 83, 85, 87, 117, 160, 492, 628. ***Open*** *4.30-7.30pm Mon; 10.30am-7.30pm Tue-Sat. Closed Aug.* ***Map*** *p104 J8* ❺ *Gifts & souvenirs*

An assortment of talking-point collectibles and antique toys jostles for space with a vast selection of militaria. Magic fans take note: the shop also stocks an array of tricks and hats for the professional magician. But take note: it's not half pricey.

Fox Gallery

Corso Vittorio Emanuele II 5 (06 6992 1298, www.facebook.com/pg/foxgalleryroma). Bus 30, 40, 46, 62, 63, 64, 70, 81, 87, 492, 628, 780, 916, H/tram 8. ***Open*** *10.30am-8pm Mon-Sat; 11am-2pm, 4-8pm Sun.* ***Map*** *p104 J9* ❻ *Gifts & souvenirs*

Two floors of postcards, posters and prints showcasing art from all ages from the Renaissance and Impressionism to modern and contemporary works and spanning museums and collections across the globe. There are also books, stationery, souvenirs and gifts all with an arty theme.

❤ Moriondo & Gariglio

Via del Piè di Marmo 21 (06 699 0856). Bus 30, 40, 46, 53, 62, 63, 64, 70, 80, 81, 83, 85, 87, 117, 160, 190, 492, 628, 916. ***Open*** *9am-7.30pm Mon-Sat. Closed Aug.* ***Map*** *p104 J9* ❼ *Chocolatier*

This fairytale chocolate shop with beautiful gift-boxes is especially lovely at Christmas, when you'll have to fight to get your hands on the excellent *marrons glacés*. The prices are as extravagant as the packaging.

❤ Il Papiro

Via del Pantheon 50 (06 679 5597, www. ilpapirofirenze.it). Bus 30, 40, 46, 62, 63, 64, 70, 81, 87, 492, 628, 780, 916, H/tram 8. ***Open*** *10am-7.30pm daily.* ***Map*** *p104 H8* ❾ *Gifts & souvenirs*

A great place to buy something for the writer in your life, at Il Papiro Florentine paper is incorporated into albums, notebooks and more. Don't ruin the effect with a biro: the shop also stocks quill pens and ink in a range of jazzy colours. **Other locations** Salita de' Crescenzi 28 (06 686 8463).

❤ Le Tartarughe

Via Pie' di Marmo 17 (06 679 2240, www. letartarughe.eu). Bus 30, 40, 46, 53, 62, 63, 64, 70, 80, 81, 83, 85, 87, 117, 160, 190, 492, 628, 916. ***Open*** *noon-7.30pm Mon; 10am-7.30pm Tue-Sat. Closed 2wks Aug.* ***Map*** *p104 J9* ❿ *Fashion*

Susanna Liso's sumptuous designs fill this chic boutique near the church of Santa Maria sopra Minerva. The lines of these eminently wearable garments – ranging from cocktail dresses to elegant workwear – are classic with a twist; the colours are eye-catching but never garish.

Le Tartarughe

Ghetto & Campo de' Fiori

Campo de' Fiori lies at the heart of labyrinthine medieval Rome. Within this web of cobbled alleys, life is characterised by markets and washing-lines draped across courtyards, just as it always has been (bar the odd satellite dish). Yet despite the fact that daily rituals have changed little over the years, this is an area of striking contrasts. Campo de' Fiori – with its lively morning market and partying crowds at night – stands alongside the solemn, dignified piazza Farnese.

Meanwhile, in the north-east, largo Argentina is a hub of useful bus stops, with an excavation of ancient temples in the centre. South-east of campo de' Fiori lies the Ghetto – pretty now, but historically a place of prejudice, isolation and deportation.

❤ Don't miss

1 Crypta Balbi *p123*
This small museum offers an exciting glimpse into the layers that make up Rome.

2 Gesù *p124*
The mother church of the Jesuit order, and with a fabulously opulent ceiling, as well as the tomb of Saint Ignatius himself.

3 Museo Ebraico *p131*
Discover the ancient history of Rome's Jewish community.

4 Museo Barracco di Scultura Antica *p124*
A small and eclectic collection of pre-Roman art.

In the know
Getting around

Like most areas of Rome, distances are small, and it is best to explore the higgledy piggledy cobbled streets and *piazze* on foot. The main bus routes such as corso Vittorio Emanuele are best left to the buses.

Giordano Bruno (Ferrari, 1889)

GHETTO & CAMPO DE' FIORI

Restaurants

1. Ditirambo
2. Emma
3. Open Baladin
4. Il Pagliaccio
5. Pianostrada Laboratorio di Cucina
6. Roscioli
7. Il Sanlorenzo
8. Sora Margherita

Cafés, bars & pubs

1. L'Angolo Divino
2. Barnum Café
3. Il Goccetto
4. Il Vinaietto – Antica Vineria

Bakeries, pasticcerie & gelaterie

1. Alberto Pica
2. Il Boccione
3. Il Forno Campo de' Fiori
4. Pasticceria de Bellis
5. Zum

Shops & services

1. Acquamadre
2. Arsenale-Atelier Patrizia Pieroni
3. Beppe e i suoi formaggi
4. Borini
5. Farnese Fitness
6. Ibiz
7. Laboratorio Marco Aurelio
8. Leone Limentani
9. Marta Ray
10. Momento
11. Il Ponte Contemporanea
12. Valentina Bonomo Arte Contemporanea

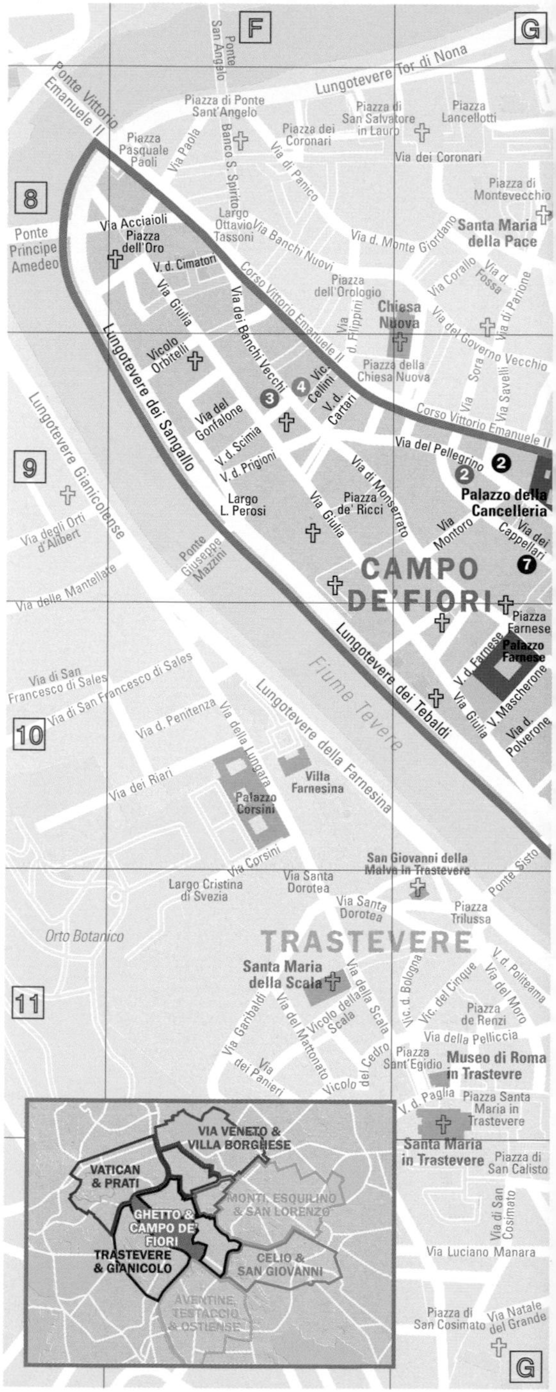

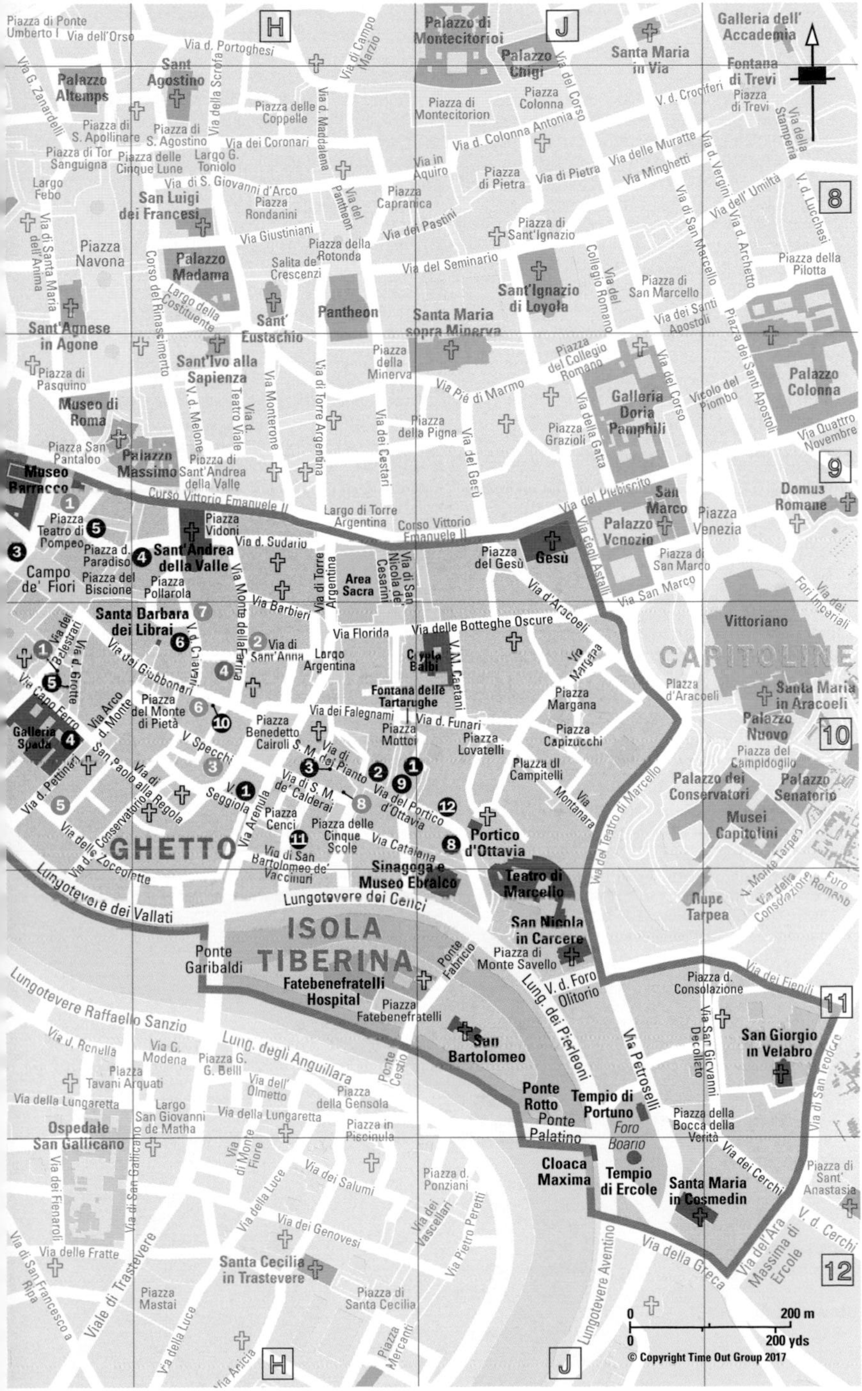
H
J
8
9
10
11
12
Palazzo di Montecitorio
Palazzo Chigi
Santa Maria in Via
Galleria dell' Accademia
Fontana di Trevi
Palazzo Altemps
Sant Agostino
Piazza di Ponte Umberto I
Via dell'Orso
Via d. Portoghesi
Via di Campo Marzio
Via del Corso
Piazza Colonna
Piazza di Montecitorion
Piazza delle Coppelle
Piazza di S. Apollinare
Piazza di S. Agostino
Via dei Coronari
Via d. Colonna Antonia
V. d. Crociferi
Piazza di Trevi
Via della Stamperia
Piazza di Tor Sanguigna
Piazza delle Cinque Lune
Largo G. Toniolo
Via in Aquiro
Piazza di Pietra
Via di Pietra
Via delle Muratte
Via Minghetti
Largo Febo
Via di S. Giovanni d'Arco
Piazza Rondanini
Piazza Capranica
Via del Pantheon
Via dell' Umiltà
V. d. Lucchesi
San Luigi dei Francesi
Via Giustiniani
Via dei Pastini
Piazza di Sant'Ignazio
Via di San Marcello
Via d. Archetto
Piazza Navona
Palazzo Madama
Piazza della Rotonda
Salita de' Crescenzi
Via del Seminario
Piazza della Pilotta
Corso del Rinascimento
Largo della Costituente
Pantheon
Sant'Ignazio di Loyola
Piazza di San Marcello
Via dei Santi Apostoli
Sant'Agnese in Agone
Sant' Eustachio
Santa Maria sopra Minerva
Piazza della Minerva
Piazza del Collegio Romano
Sant'Ivo alla Sapienza
Piazza di Pasquino
Via Pié di Marmo
Vicolo del Piombo
Palazzo Colonna
Museo di Roma
Via Monterone
Via di Torre Argentina
Piazza della Pigna
Galleria Doria Pamphili
Via Quattro Novembre
Piazza San Pantaleo
Palazzo Massimo
Piazza di Sant'Andrea della Valle
Via dei Cestari
Via del Gesù
Piazza Grazioli
Via della Gatta
Museo Barracco
Corso Vittorio Emanuele II
Largo di Torre Argentina
Via del Plebiscito
San Marco
Domus Romane
Piazza Teatro di Pompeo
Piazza Vidoni
Via d. Sudario
Palazzo Venezia
Piazza Venezia
Campo de' Fiori
Piazza d. Paradiso
Sant'Andrea della Valle
Area Sacra
Piazza del Gesù
Gesù
Piazza di San Marco
Piazza del Biscione
Piazza Pollarola
Via degli Astalli
Via San Marco
Via dei Fori Imperiali
Santa Barbara dei Librai
Via Barbieri
Via d'Aracoeli
Vittoriano
Via Florida
Via delle Botteghe Oscure
Via di Sant'Anna
Largo Argentina
Crypta Balbi
V. M. Caetani
CAPITOLINE
Via dei Giubbonari
Via Margana
Fontana delle Tartarughe
Piazza d'Aracoeli
Santa Maria in Aracoeli
Piazza Margana
Via Capo Ferro
Via Arco del Monte
Piazza del Monte di Pietà
Via dei Falegnami
Via d. Funari
Palazzo Nuovo
Galleria Spada
Piazza Benedetto Cairoli
Piazza Mattei
Piazza Capizucchi
V. Specchi
Piazza Lovatelli
Piazza del Campidoglio
Via d. Pettinari
Via di San Paolo alla Regola
Via di S. M. dei Pianto
Piazza di Campitelli
Via Montanara
Palazzo dei Conservatori
Palazzo Senatorio
V. Seggiola
Via di S. M. de' Calderai
Via del Portico d'Ottavia
Via del Teatro di Marcello
Via Arenula
Piazza Cenci
Piazza delle Cinque Scole
Portico d'Ottavia
Musei Capitolini
GHETTO
Via Catalana
Via d. Conservatorio
Via delle Zoccolette
Via di San Bartolomeo de' Vaccinari
Sinagoga e Museo Ebraico
Teatro di Marcello
V. Monte Tarpeo
Via della Consolazione
Foro Romano
Lungotevere dei Vallati
Lungotevere dei Cenci
Rupe Tarpea
ISOLA TIBERINA
San Nicola in Carcere
Ponte Garibaldi
Ponte Fabricio
Piazza di Monte Savello
Fatebenefratelli Hospital
V. d. Foro Olitorio
Piazza d. Consolazione
Via dei Fienili
Lungotevere Raffaello Sanzio
Piazza Fatebenefratelli
Lung. dei Pierleoni
Via Petroselli
Via San Giovanni Decollato
Via d. Renella
Via G. Modena
Piazza G. G. Belli
Lung. degli Anguillara
San Bartolomeo
San Giorgio in Velabro
Piazza Tavani Arquati
Via dell' Olmetto
Ponte Cestio
Piazza della Gensola
Via di San Teodoro
Via della Lungaretta
Largo San Giovanni de Matha
Ponte Rotto
Ponte Palatino
Tempio di Portuno
Foro Boario
Piazza della Bocca della Verità
Ospedale San Gallicano
Piazza in Piscinula
Via dei Cerchi
Via di Monte Fiore
Via dei Salumi
Piazza d. Ponziani
Cloaca Maxima
Tempio di Ercole
Santa Maria in Cosmedin
Piazza di Sant' Anastasia
Via dei Fienaroli
Via di San Gallicano
Via della Luce
Via dei Vascellari
Via Pietro Peretti
Via dei Genovesi
V. d. Cerchi
Via dell'Ara Massima di Ercole
Via delle Fratte
Viale di Trastevere
Santa Cecilia in Trastevere
Via della Greca
Lungotevere Aventino
Via di San Francesco a Ripa
Piazza Mastai
Piazza di Santa Cecilia
Piazza de' Mercanti
Via della Luce
Via Anicia
0
200 m
200 yds
© Copyright Time Out Group 2017

FROM LARGO ARGENTINA TO CAMPO DE' FIORI

In the ancient world, the *Campus martius* (field of war) occupied much of this low-lying area along the River Tiber: here Roman males did physical jerks to stay fighting fit for battle. However, with theatrical entertainment banned in the serious city centre itself, this was also where would have headed to enjoy a bit of low-brow fun.

The **Teatro di Pompeo** – Rome's first permanent theatre, built in the mid first century BC – occupied much of the swathe of land between largo Argentina and campo de' Fiori. The theatres of Marcellus and Balbus also played host to theatrical performances in barbaric times.

Largo Argentina today is a polluted transport hub and rendezvous point for milling teenagers, who rarely give a second thought to the expanse of ancient ruins that fills the hole in the centre of the square. It's officially called largo di Torre Argentina. The name has nothing to do with the Latin American country; it refers to a tower – *torre* – in a nearby street, which was the home of Johannes Burckhardt, the powerful master of ceremonies of the Borgia papacy; Burckhardt's home town was Strasbourg, the diocesan name of which was Argentinensis. The tower which is all that remains of his house is at one corner of the excavations.

Visible when you peer over the railings in largo Argentina are columns, altars and foundations from one round and three rectangular temples dating from the mid third century to the first centuries BC. The surviving frescoes on the taller brickwork are from the 12th-century church of **San Nicola de' Cesarini**, which was built into one of the temples. If you want to take a closer look, you'll have to cosy up to those in charge at the **Rifugio Felino di Torre Argentina** cat sanctuary (www.gattidiroma.net).

To the east of the square, in via delle Botteghe Oscure, is the **Crypta Balbi** (*see p123*), a tribute to Rome's architectural accretions over the ages; in via del Plebiscito is the **Gesù** (*see p124*), mother church of the Jesuit order.

West along corso Vittorio Emanuele II (universally known as corso Vittorio) is the church of **Sant'Andrea della Valle** (*see p126*), topped by Rome's second-tallest dome; the first act of *Tosca* is set here. Further on are the **Museo Barracco** (*see p124*), with its collection of ancient sculpture, and the Vatican-owned Renaissance gem, the **Palazzo della Cancelleria** (*see p125*). To escape the unbreathable air and decibels, take any left off corso Vittorio: in narrow alleys, cramped buildings with chunks of carved ancient stone inserted into their façades are home to countless little shops and cafés whose tables occupy cobbled pavements.

The streets converge on lively **campo de' Fiori**. The *campo* area has for centuries been a fascinating mix of the very smart and the very rough.

The powerful Farnese clan – which spawned Pope Paul III – staked its claim in **piazza Farnese**, a stately square with a pair of fountains made with giant Roman tubs from the Baths of Caracalla. The Renaissance **Palazzo Farnese** (*see p126*) – now the French embassy – sits solidly as the undisputed elder statesman of the square. To the north and west are streets packed with antique stores and eateries. Gold and jewellery shops cluster to the south. **Via dei Giubbonari** (jacket-makers' street) seethes with clothing stores, while the **Galleria Spada** (*see p123*) is in a pretty *palazzo* in parallel via Capo di Ferro.

❤ Time to eat

Snack
Il Forno Campo de' Fiori *p128*

Lunch
Pianostrada Laboratorio di Cucina *p127*

Afternoon beer
Open Baladin *p126*

Blow-out dinner
Il Pagliaccio *p127*,
Il Sanlorenzo *p127*

Wine bar
Il Goccetto *p128*,
Il Vinaietto *p128*

❤ Time to shop

Jewellery
Laboratorio Marco Aurelio *p129*

Kitchenware
Leone Limentani *p133*

Shoes & accessories
Borini *p129*, Marta Ray *p133*

Il Pagliaccio

Sights & museums

Campo de' Fiori

Bus 30Exp, 40Exp, 62, 63, 64, 70, 81, 87, 492, 628, 780, 916, H/tram 8. ***Map** p120 G9.*

Campo de' Fiori has been a hub of Roman life since the 15th century, when the pope moved his chief residence to the Vatican; noble families flocked to this area and built palaces, just across the river from the centre of power. Tradesmen and craftsmen set up shop in via del Pellegrino and via Giulia. And inn-keepers and food purveyors clustered in the *campo.*

Dominating the square is the statue of a brooding, book-clutching Giordano Bruno, the philosopher and mathematician burned at the stake here in 1600 after a run-in with the Inquisition. (Among Rome-dwelling Brits, the dour figure used to be known as 'Gordon Brown'.)

Despite galloping gentrification and a substantial population of foreign students and professionals seeking to soak up *romanitas*, the *campo* has retained some neighbourhood spirit; its friendly, chaotic energy remains magnetic. By day the picturesque but costly food and flower market bustles from about 6am to 2pm (Monday to Saturday), though more tourist tat is sneaking on to the stalls. Restaurant tables ringing the square fill up every lunchtime. Afternoons here are slow and quiet, except for a perpetual group of alternative types with flea-bitten dogs, bongos and an anarchic approach to hairstyling. At sunset the square fills up again, first with sedate wine-quaffers then later on with rowdy Anglo students, making themselves increasingly unpopular with the locals.

❤ Crypta Balbi

Via delle Botteghe Oscure 31 (06 678 0167, archeoroma.beniculturali.it). Bus 30, 40, 46, 62, 63, 64, 70, 87, 190, 492, 780, 810, 916, H/tram 8. ***Open** 9am-7pm Tue-Sun.* ***Admission** €7; €3.50 reductions. Exhibition price varies.* ***Map** p120 J10.*

Part of the Museo Nazionale Romana, the Crypta Balbi displays one of Rome's more interesting recent archaeological finds, and is packed with displays, maps and models that explain (in English) Rome's evolution from its bellicose pre-Imperial era, to early Christian times and on through the dim Middle Ages. The underground ruins themselves – visible occasionally through the day in a tour – show the foundations of the gigantic *crypta*, or theatre lobby, constructed by Cornelius Balbus, a Spaniard much in favour at the court of Augustus. Excavations continue, while upstairs is a display of the minutiae of everyday life in ancient Rome: plates, bowls,

Campo do' Fiori

glasses, amphorae, oil lamps and artisans' tools. The upper levels provide a fantastic view of Roman rooftops.

► *See also p187 The Museo Nazionale Romano collection for more on your combined ticket.*

Galleria Spada

Piazza Capo di Ferro 3 (06 687 4896, www.galleriaspada.beniculturali.it). Bus 23, 63, 280, 780, H/tram 8. ***Open** 8.30am-7.30pm Wed-Mon.* ***Admission** €5; €2.50 reductions. No cards.* ***Map** p120 G10.*

The four rooms containing this collection are charmingly old-fashioned, but little is done to make you forget that most of the contents are second-division 17th-century leftovers. Cardinal Bernardino Spada was an avid art collector. The walls of the four small upstairs *saloni* are crammed and old-style, but notes (in English) in each room help you to make sense of them all. There are some big names here: Domenichino, Guercino and Guido Reni – see his *San Girolamo* and *Slave of Ripa Grande* – plus the father-daughter Gentileschi duo, Orazio and Artemisia. The main attraction, however, is outside the gallery proper: the Borromini perspective, which shows that the manic-depressive architect had a sense,

Gesù

if not of humour, at least of irony. If you're lucky to get there at the right moment (there appears to be no timetable) you'll be taken to a courtyard and misled into believing a 9-metre (30-foot) colonnade is much longer by perspective trickery.

❤ Gesù

Piazza del Gesù (06 697 00232, Loyola's rooms 06 697 001, www.chiesadelgesu.org). Bus 30Exp, 40Exp, 46, 62, 63, 64, 70, 81, 87, 492, 780, 810, 916, H. ***Church*** *7.30am-12.30pm, 4-7.45pm daily.* ***Loyola's rooms*** *4-6pm Mon-Sat; 10am-noon Sun.* ***Admission*** *free.* ***Map*** *p120 J9.*

The Jesuits were the richest Catholic order, founded by Basque soldier Ignatius Loyola in the 1530s. They were also the most energetic, sending teams of fired-up missionaries to the four corners of the (then) known world. This church is the flagship church of the Jesuits, their showcase, and Loyola's final resting place.

The Gesù (built 1568-84) was designed to involve the congregation as closely as possible in the proceedings, with a nave unobstructed by aisles, offering a clear view of the main altar. Giacomo della Porta added a façade that would be repeated *ad nauseam* on Jesuit churches across Italy (and the world) for decades afterwards. A large, bright fresco, *Triumph in the Name of Jesus*, by Il Baciccia (1676-79) – one of Rome's great Baroque masterpieces – decorates the gilded ceiling of the nave, which seems to dissolve on either side as stucco figures (by Antonio Raggi) and other painted images are sucked up into the dazzling light of the heavens. (The figures falling back to earth are presumably Protestants.)

On the left is another spectacular Baroque achievement: the chapel of Sant'Ignazio (1696-1700) by Andrea Pozzo, which is adorned with gold, silver and coloured marble; the statue of St Ignatius entering heaven is now covered the majority of the time with a canvas by Pozzo, but is uncovered at 5.30pm every afternoon in a marvellous piece of baroque theatre (*see right* In the know). Towering above the altar is what was long believed to be the biggest lump of lapis lazuli in the entire world… in fact, the piece is merely covered concrete. Outside the church, at piazza del Gesù 45, you can visit the rooms of St Ignatius, which contain a wonderful painted corridor featuring trompe l'oeil special effects by Pozzo, and mementoes of the saint, including his death mask.

❤ Museo Barracco di Scultura Antica

Corso Vittorio Emanuele 166 (06 687 5657, www.museobarracco.it). Bus 40Exp, 46, 62, 64, 916. ***Open*** *Oct-May 10am-4pm Tue-Sun. June-Sept 1-7pm Tue-Sun.* ***Admission*** *free.* ***Map*** *p120 G9.*

Ignatius Loyola

The story of a Spanish saint

Born in the Spanish Basque Country, Ignatius (Iñigo) Lopez de Loyola (1491-1556) was the aristocratic founder of what was to become arguably the most powerful religious movement of the Catholic Church: the Jesuits. After a dissolute youth and wartime leg injury, the reformed and pious Ignatius experienced a vision at La Storta outside Rome that laid the foundation for the success of his mission: *ego vobis Romae propitius ero* (basically: 'Rome's the place') was God's message. In fact it took Rome a while to see the positive side of Ignatius' teachings, which initially brought him and his band of disciples up against the Inquisition, which had them imprisoned and beaten up.

But the self-flagellatory stance of Ignatius – who preached utter submission, *perinde ac cadaver* ('well-disciplined as a corpse'), to the Church – attracted a large following in Counter-Reformation Catholic Europe, and his Society of Jesus (from whence 'Jesuits') was given the papal seal of approval in 1540. Donations from powerful supporters who followed Loyola's 'Spiritual Exercises' mounted up. His beatification in 1609, and canonisation in 1622, led to an extraordinary flurry of church-building; by then the Jesuits were out in force, pushing to the ends of the world in search of souls to save. The iconography of Bernini's *Four Rivers* fountain (*see p108* Piazza Navona) shows the movement's global reach.

Ignatius' canonisation coincided with the zenith of Roman Baroque architecture: the order's mother-church, the **Gesù** (*see left*), is a jaw-dropping example of theatricality and opulence. **Sant'Ignazio** (*see p114*), the other barn-like Jesuit church, has a trompe l'oeil ceiling that records the ecstasies and agonies of the Spanish saint.

Trompe l'oeil by Andrea Pozzo in Sant'Ignazio *p114*

In the know

Gesù's saintly spectacle

Flashing lights and piped heavenly choirs herald an eye-popping performance of religious theatricality at the Gesù. A bizarre daily *son et lumière* on the life, but mostly the death, of the Jesuits' founder Ignatius Loyola (*see above*) offers 15 minutes' respite from the dizzying frescoes and sheer opulence of the Gesù's fixtures and fittings. Be there at 5.30pm prompt: proceedings start with mechanical precision.

After the recent discovery of the original 9-metre (30-foot) altarpiece painted by Jesuit brother Andrea Pozzo, restoration began on the complex Baroque mechanics once used to raise and lower the giant altarpiece. These were designed as a show to inspire awe and reverence in amazed onlookers. Baroque art is all about trickery, magic, delight and astonishment. Pozzo here (and at nearby Sant'Ignazio) showed himself to be a master.

This small collection of mostly pre-Roman art was amassed during the first half of the 20th century by Giovanni Barracco. The nobleman's artistic interests covered the whole gamut of ancient art, as seen in the collection of Assyrian reliefs, Attic vases, Egyptian sphinxes and Babylonian stone lions, as well as Roman and Etruscan exhibits and Greek sculptures. Don't miss the copy of the *Wounded Bitch* by the fourth-century BC sculptor Lysippus, on the second floor.

Palazzo della Cancelleria

Piazza della Cancelleria. Bus 40Exp, 46, 62, 64, 916. ***Open*** *by appt.* ***Map*** *p120 G9.*

One of Rome's most refined examples of Renaissance architecture, the Palazzo della Cancelleria was built, possibly by Bramante, between 1483 and 1513, for Raffaele Riario. Even though his uncle Pope Sixtus IV made him a cardinal at the tender age of 17, Raffaele did not allow his ecclesiastic duties to cramp his style when collecting art. He is said to have raised a third of the cost of this palace with his winnings from a single night's gambling. He was involved in plotting against the powerful Florentine Medici family; and in retaliation, the palace was confiscated for the Church and is still Vatican property. The *palazzo* incorporates the fourth-century church of San Lorenzo in Damaso and, as archaeologists discovered in the 1940s, sits atop a mithraeum and part of a canal connecting the Baths of Agrippa – located just north of largo Argentina – to the Tiber. These ruins are usually visible with permission (06 6989 3405, economato@apsa.va). From time to time chances arise to enter the *palazzo* for the occasional chamber-music concert or exhibition on religious themes mounted in the magnificently frescoed rooms.

Palazzo Farnese

Piazza Farnese (06 686011, www.ambafrance-it.org). Bus 30Exp, 40Exp, 62, 63, 64, 70, 81, 87, 492, 628, 780, 916, H/tram 8. ***Open*** *(guided tours only) Wed 5pm.* ***Admission*** *€9.* ***Map*** *p120 G10.*

This *palazzo* has housed the French embassy since the 1870s. Considered by many to be the finest Renaissance palace in Rome, the huge building – recently and dramatically restored – was begun for Cardinal Alessandro Farnese (later Pope Paul III) in 1514 by Antonio da Sangallo the Younger. Sangallo died before it was completed, and in 1546 Michelangelo took over. He was responsible for most of the upper storeys, the grand cornice along the roof, and the inner courtyard. Vignola and Giacomo della Porta completed the rear façade, which gives out to a large garden. Tours *must* be pre-booked through www.inventerrome.com at least one week in advance; groups must book three months in advance. Children under ten are not admitted.

Sant'Andrea della Valle

Corso Vittorio 6 (06 686 1339). Bus 30Exp, 40Exp, 46, 62, 63, 64, 70, 81, 87, 492, 628, 810, 916. ***Open*** *7.30am-7.30pm daily.* ***Map*** *p120 H9.*

Many architects got their hands on this church. Originally designed in 1524 by Giacomo della Porta, it was handed over to Carlo Maderno, who stretched the design upward and added the dome, which is the highest in Rome after St Peter's. He left much of the façade design to Carlo Rainaldi, who in turn commissioned artist Giacomo Antonio Fancelli to sculpt two angels to adorn it. When the first one (on the left) was complete, the story goes, it was criticised by Pope Alexander VII. Fancelli quit the job in a huff saying the pope could do the other one himself; it was never done. Giovanni Lanfranco nearly died while painting the dome fresco, allegedly because his rival Domenichino had sabotaged the scaffolding on which he was working. Puccini set the opening act of *Tosca* in the chapel on the left.

Restaurants

Ditirambo €€

Piazza della Cancelleria 74 (06 687 1626, www.ristoranteditirambo.it). Bus 30, 40, 46, 62, 63, 64, 70, 81, 87, 492, 628, 916, H/tram 8. ***Open*** *7.30-11.30pm Mon; 1-3pm, 7.30-11.30pm Tue-Sun. Closed 3wks Aug.* ***Map*** *p120 G9* ❶ Trattoria

This funky trattoria located around the corner from campo de' Fiori serves up good-value food based on mainly organic ingredients. The creative menu changes monthly, offering dishes such as baby octopus and chickpea soup, and veal roulade with a truffle and porcini mushroom sauce. There's a great choice for vegetarians, and fish features heavily on the menu. Service can be slow and occasionally slapdash, but it's friendly enough, and there's usually a good buzz, with a mix of young trendsters and older gourmands.

Emma €€

Via del Monte della Farina 28 (06 6476 0475, www.emmapizzeria.com). ***Open*** *12.30-3pm, 7-11.30pm daily. Bus 30, 40, 46, 62, 63, 64, 70, 81, 87, 492, 628, 916, H/tram 8.* ***Map*** *p120 H10* ❷ Pizzeria

This rather swanky pizzeria opened to great fanfare in 2014 by combining the traditional Roman-style thin-crust pizza with a modern, slightly '80s, black-and-red decor. There is a full menu of pasta and second courses but the pizza is the real winner with a light, airy dough and just the right amount of charring. Toppings range from the conventional margherita to more unconventional creations with international ingredients including French scallops and Spanish chorizo.

❤ Open Baladin €€

Via degli Specchi 6 (06 683 8989, www.openbaladin.com). Bus 30, 40, 46, 62, 63, 64, 70, 81, 87, 271, 492, 628, 780, 916, H/tram 8. ***Open*** *noon-midnight daily. Closed 2wks Aug.* ***Map*** *p120 H10* ❸ International

Dynamic northern Italian brewer Teo Musso is turning more and more of his fellow countryfolk into beer drinkers. Open Baladin, with its 'wall of beer' – about 100 labels served bottled, displayed up one wall of this buzzing venue – and a choice of 40 or more on tap, is his first Roman venture. Bar-snack food, from mounds of chicken wings to gourmet hamburgers, melt-in-the-mouth mozzarella and a signature scrambled egg with bacon helps the brews from many

of Italy's smallest and most interesting producers slip down nicely. This is not a venue for a romantic tryst: most nights, downstairs is utter chaos, upstairs only slightly less so. But if you're seeking beer and bustle, this is your place.

❤ Il Pagliaccio €€€€

Via dei Banchi Vecchi 129 (06 6880 9595, www.ristoranteilpagliaccio.it). Bus 40, 46, 62, 64, 916. ***Open*** *7.30-10.30pm Tue; 12.30-2pm, 7.30-10.30pm Wed-Sat. Closed 1wk Feb, 3wks Aug.* ***Map*** *p120 F9* ❹ *International*

Though prices have climbed – pushed up, perhaps, by a second Michelin star – chef Anthony Genovese still offers a true gourmet experience. The menu successfully incorporates both Mediterranean and oriental influences and his sure touch is evident in innovative combinations such as roasted squid with rhubarb or foie gras served with amberjack. There's also an interesting wine list. Leave plenty of space to try one of the excellent desserts, which are prepared by Alsatian pastry chef-genius Marion Lichtle. Ten-course (€170) and eight-course (€150) taster menus can be arranged.

❤ Pianostrada Laboratorio di Cucina €€

Via delle Zoccolette 22 (06 8957 2296, www.facebook.com/pianostrada). Bus 23, 30, 40, 46, 62, 63, 64, 70, 81, 87, 492, 628, 916, H/tram 8. ***Open*** *1-4pm, 7pm-midnight Tue-Fri, 10am-midnight Sat, Sun. Closed 3wks Aug.* ***Map*** *p120 G10* ❺ *Mediterranean*

The all-female squad of Pianostrada recently left their cramped premises in Trastevere to this new, larger location over the river, complete with a pretty interior garden and large open kitchen. Freshly baked bread and *foccacia* are used to make excellent *panini* (such as the signature burger of salt cod served in a squid-ink bun) and there are creative salads, pastas and *secondi* as well as home-made desserts and cakes.

Roscioli €€€

Via dei Giubbonari 21 (06 687 5287, www.salumeriaroscioli.com). Bus 30, 40, 46, 62, 63, 64, 70, 81, 87, 492, 628, 916, H/tram 8. ***Open*** *12.30-4pm, 7-11.45pm Mon, Sat.* ***Map*** *p120 H10* ❻ *Italian*

Since they began setting up tables in the shop for lunch and dinner this upmarket *salumeria* (delicatessen) has gradually gained fame as one of Rome's top restaurants and nowadays it can be hard to score a table so book well in advance. Service can be brusque but there is no doubting the quality of the cured meats and cheeses which are top-notch (with price tags to match). For something more informal head around the corner to the Roscioli bakery (via dei Chiavari 34) for pizza, or to the Roscioli café and pastry shop up the road (Piazza Benedetto Cairoli 3).

❤ Il Sanlorenzo €€€€

Via dei Chiavari 5 (06 686 5097, www.ilsanlorenzo.it). Bus 30, 40, 46, 62, 63, 64, 70, 81, 87, 492, 628, 916, H/tram 8. ***Open*** *7.30-11.45pm Mon, Sat; 12.45-14.45pm, 7.30-11.45pm Tue-Fri. Closed 1wk Aug.* ***Map*** *p120 H10* ❼ *Seafood*

You'll travel a long way to find fish to rival what is served in this classically elegant restaurant: for both freshness and preparation, Il Sanlorenzo certainly ranks among Rome's finest. From the exquisite raw seafood *antipasto* through the unbeatable spaghetti with sea urchins and the daily catch baked simply in a crust of salt, this is seafood at its very best, brought straight from the island of Ponza, south of Rome. The price tag is high, but it's worth it; and wonderfully graceful service without a hint of smart-dining pomposity makes the whole experience a special one.

Cafés, bars & pubs

L'Angolo Divino

Via dei Balestrari 12 (06 686 4413). Bus 30, 40, 46, 62, 63, 64, 70, 81, 87, 492, 628, 780, 916 H/tram 8. ***Open*** *6pm-1am Mon, Sun; 11am-3pm, 5pm-1am Tue-Sat. Closed 1wk Aug.* ***Map*** *p120 G10* ❶ *Wine bar*

Over 20 red, white and dessert wines are available by the glass (many more by the bottle) at this relaxed wine bar on a quiet street near campo de' Fiori. There's a good range of smoked fish, salami and salads, and a vast selection of cheeses, plus some hot dishes in winter. The furniture is basic and the mood relaxed – stoked by a jazz soundtrack.

Barnum Café

Via del Pellegrino 87 (06 6476 0483, www.barnumcafe.com). Bus 30, 40, 46, 62, 63, 64, 70, 81, 87, 492, 628, 916. ***Open*** *9am-2am Mon-Sat. Closed 10 days Aug.* ***Map*** *p120 G9* ❷ *Café/Bar*

The daytime haunt of freelancers who come for the good coffee, free-wifi and shabby armchairs, Barnum gets lively after sunset when the international *aperitivo* crowd arrive to sample the excellent cocktails. Decent food and snacks are served throughout the day, the prices are reasonable and the service is super-friendly.

Il Goccetto

❤ Il Goccetto

Via dei Banchi Vecchi 14 (06 686 4268, www.facebook.com/Ilgoccetto). Bus 40, 46, 62, 64, 916. ***Open*** *6.30pm-midnight Mon; noon-3pm, 6pm-midnight Tue-Sat. Closed 3wks Aug.* ***Map*** *p120 F9* ❸ *Wine bar*

One of the more serious *centro storico* wine bars, occupying part of a medieval bishop's house, Il Goccetto has original painted ceilings, dark wood-clad walls and a cosy, private-club feel. Wine is the main point here, with a satisfying range by the glass from €4, but if you're peckish, there's a choice of cheeses, salamis and salads too.

❤ Il Vinaietto – Antica Vineria

Via Monte della Farina 37 (06 6880 6989). Bus 30, 40, 46, 62, 63, 64, 70, 81, 87, 492, 571, 628, 780, 916, H/tram 8. ***Open*** *10.30am-3pm, 6.30-10.30pm Mon-Sat. Closed 1wk Aug.* ***Map*** *p120 H10* ❹ *Wine bar*

First and foremost a carry-out bottle shop, this long-running establishment near campo de' Fiori becomes a laid-back bohemian-chic stop of an evening, with standing-only customers spilling out into the picturesque street to sip wine by the glass at very reasonable prices.

Bakeries, pasticcerie & gelaterie

Alberto Pica

Via della Seggiola 12 (06 686 8405). Bus 30, 40, 46, 62, 63, 64, 70, 81, 87, 271, 492, 628, 780, 810, 916, H/tram 8. ***Open*** *Jan-Mar, Oct, Nov 8.30am-2am Mon-Sat. Apr-Sept, Dec 8.30am-2am Mon-Sat; 3pm-midnight Sun. Closed 1wk Aug.* ***No cards. Map*** *p120 H10* ❶ *Café*

Horrendous neon lighting, surly staff… and some seriously good ice-cream: these are the hallmarks of this long-running café close to the justice ministry. The rice specialities stand out: imagine eating frozen, partially cooked rice pudding and you'll get the picture. *Riso alla cannella* (cinnamon rice) is particularly wonderful.

❤ Il Forno Campo de' Fiori

Vicolo del Gallo 14 (06 6880 6662, www.fornocampodefiori.com). Bus 30, 40, 46, 62, 63, 64, 70, 81, 87, 116, 492, 628, 810, 916, H/tram 8. ***Open*** *7.30am-2.30pm, 5-8pm Mon-Sat. Closed Sat pm July & Aug.* ***No cards. Map*** *p120 G9* ❸ *Bakery*

This little bakery does the best takeaway sliced pizza in the campo de' Fiori area by far. The plain *pizza bianca* base, dressed with extra-virgin olive oil, is delicious in itself, but check out the one with *fiori di zucca* (courgette flowers) too. Close by, at campo de' Fiori 22, is the main shop, which turns out a variety of delicious breads, biscuits and cakes.

Pasticceria de Bellis

Piazza del Paradiso 56/57 (www.andreadebellis.it). Bus 30, 40, 46, 62, 63, 64, 70, 81, 87, 492, 628, 780, 916, H/tram 8. ***Open*** *9am-8pm Tue-Sun.* ***Map*** *p120 H9* ❹ *Pasticceria*

Celebrated pastry chef Andrea de Bellis sells his decadent treats from his eponymous bakery close to campo de' Fiori and the choice is as mouthwatering as expected, with flawless works in chocolate and meringue as well as éclairs and fresh fruit tarts, all wrapped up in beautiful packaging.

Zum

Piazza del Teatro di Pompeo 20 (06 6830 7836, www.zumroma.it). Bus 30, 40, 46, 62, 63, 64, 70, 81, 87, 492, 628, 780, 810, 916, H/tram 8. ***Open*** *11am-11pm Mon-Thur, Sun; 11am-1am Fri, Sat. Closed 2wks Aug.* ***Map*** *p120 G9* ❺ *Bakery*

A temple for tiramisu lovers, Zum whips up fresh individual cupfuls of the Italian dessert throughout the day, ranging from the original coffee flavour to more inventive variants. There are also fresh juices, home-made cakes and plenty of gluten- and dairy-free options on offer for a sweet snack to be eaten on the hoof.

Shops & services

Arsenale-Atelier Patrizia Pieroni

Via del Pellegrino 172 (06 6880 2424, www.patriziapieroni.it). Bus 40, 46, 62, 64, 916. ***Open*** *3.30-7.30pm Mon; 10am-7.30pm Tue-Sat. Closed 2wks Aug.* ***Map*** *p120 G9* ❷ *Fashion*

A great place to pick something up to wear back home, Patrizia Pieroni's wonderful designs make for great window displays – not to mention successful party conversation pieces – and have been going down well with the Roman chic luvvy crowd for a fair few years.

❤ Borini

Via dei Pettinari 86 (06 687 5670). Bus 23, 63, 271, 280, 780, H/tram 8. ***Open*** *10.30am-7.30pm Mon-Sat. Closed 2wks Aug.* ***Map*** *p120 G10* ❹ *Shoes*

Franco Borini's shop is busily chaotic, packed with clued-in shoe-lovers. In unusual hues and effortlessly elegant, his durable shoes vary from latest trends to timeless classics. Prices are not low, but for this kind of quality, they're fair.

Farnese Fitness

Vicolo delle Grotte 35 (06 687 6931, www.farnesefitness.com). Bus 40Exp, 46, 62, 64, 916/tram 8. ***Open*** *9am-8pm Mon-Sat; 9am-2pm Sun. Closed Aug.* ***Map*** *p120 G10* ❺ *Gym*

This friendly *centro storico* gym is handily located for a post-sightseeing workout. Classes in the downstairs aerobics studio – a 16th-century cellar – are included in the membership fee which can be purchased at a daily, weekly, monthly or yearly rate.

Ibiz

Via dei Chiavari 39 (06 6830 7297, www.ibizroma.it). Bus 30, 40, 46, 62, 63, 64, 70, 81, 87, 119, 130, 186, 190, 271, 492, 571, 628, 780, 810, 916, C3, H/tram 8. ***Open*** *9.30am-7.30pm Mon-Sat. Closed 2wks Aug.* ***Map*** *p120 H10* ❻ *Bags*

Ibiz bags are made by hand in the on-site workshop: look on as you mull over which of the handbags, briefcases and leather accessories you must have.

❤ Laboratorio Marco Aurelio

Via dei Cappellari 21 (348 276 2842, www.laboratoriomarcoaurelio.it). Bus 30, 40, 46, 62, 63, 64, 70, 81, 87, 492, 628, 780, 810, 916, H/tram 8. ***Open*** *by appt only 4-8pm Tue-Sat. Closed mid Aug-mid Sept.* ***No cards. Map*** *p120 G9* ❼ *Jewellery*

Designer Marco Aurelio creates stunning and often unconventional pieces using hammered and wrought silver, on site. Sizeable stones and intricate patterns vaguely recall the styles of ancient Roman.

Momento

Piazza Benedetto Cairoli 9/via dei Giubbonari (06 6880 8157). Bus 30, 40, 46, 62, 63, 64, 70, 81, 87, 492, 628, 780, 810, 916, H/tram 8. ***Open*** *10am-7.30pm Mon-Fri; 10am-1.30pm, 3.30-7.30pm Sat.* ***Map*** *p120 H10* ❿ *Fashion*

The poshest of princesses and her boho cousin will be equally awed over the collection of clothes and accessories at this treasure trove. Definitely for the fearless and colourful, all pieces from jumpers to evening gowns are flirty, feminine and fun. Also a fabulous spot for knock-'em-dead shoes and handbags in colour combos you've got to see to believe.

GHETTO

Rome's Jews occupy a unique place in the history of the diaspora, having maintained an uninterrupted presence in the city since the second century BC. This makes them Europe's oldest Jewish community; they have enjoyed a surprising degree of security, even at times (such as the years following the Black Death) when waves of anti-Semitism were sweeping the rest of the Continent.

It may seem odd that the city that was the great centre of power for the Catholic Church represented such a safe haven for Jews, but their security came at a price. The popes took on the double role of protectors (curbing popular violence against Jews) and oppressors, bringing Jews under their direct jurisdiction and making sure they paid for the privilege. The first documented tax on Roman Jews, dating back to 1310, set the pattern for the tradition of blackmail that was to characterise the Church's relations with the Jewish community until the 19th century. Payment of this tax exempted Jews from the humiliating *carnevale* games, during which they were liable to be packed into barrels and rolled from the top of Monte Testaccio.

By the 13th century, Rome's Jews had started to cross the river from Trastevere to reach a cramped corner of the *centro storico*, immediately north of the Tiber Island. The Ghetto was walled off from the rest of the city in 1556 after the edict *Cum nimis absurdam*, issued by the anti-Semitic Pope Paul IV, ordered a physical separation between Jewish and Christian parts of the city. Many Jews actually welcomed the protection afforded by the walls and curfews, despite the fact that they were also obliged periodically to attend Mass, to be lectured on their sinfulness.

However, overcrowding, the loss of property rights, and trade restrictions imposed on the community all took their toll, and the Ghetto experienced a long decline from the 16th until the 18th century. When Pius IX became pope in 1848 he opened up the Ghetto gates with a promise of bringing more tolerance and integration. But winds of revolution and secularisation were sweeping across Italy, and he closed them again two years later, issuing a series of race laws that prohibited Jews not only from owning property but from attending secondary school or university, undertaking scientific or artistic careers and receiving treatment in public hospitals. By the time that the Italian Unification took place in 1870, conditions for the more than 5,000 people who lived in the Ghetto had become desperately squalid. The new government ordered that the walls be destroyed.

A series of *leggi raziali* (racial laws) introduced from 1938 by Mussolini's regime made life for Jews increasingly arduous, gradually barring them from marrying Christians, employing Christian servants, becoming civil servants, teaching in universities or being journalists, among other restrictions.

In September 1943 Rome's German occupiers demanded 50 kilograms (110 pounds) of gold from the Jewish community, to be produced in 36 hours. After an appeal – to which both Jews and non-Jews responded – the target was reached, but this time accepting blackmail did not bring security. On 16 October more than 1,000 Jews – mostly women and children – were rounded up and deported in cattle trucks to Auschwitz. A quarter of Rome's Jews died in concentration camps, a proportion that would have been higher had it not been for the help given by wide sections of Roman society, including the Catholic priesthood (though not, many would argue, the Vatican).

Some 15,000 Jews live in Rome now, but few of them choose to reside in the old Ghetto area. They flock there for weekends and holidays, however, and to visit its chief landmark – the imposing **synagogue**, begun in 1874. This incorporates the **Museo Ebraico**, a fascinating museum tracing the history and ritual of Roman Jewish life.

The Great Synagogue and Museo Ebraico

Via Portico d'Ottavia, an anarchic hotchpotch of ancient, medieval and Renaissance architecture leading to the **Portico d'Ottavia** itself (*see p132*), used to mark the boundary of the Ghetto. This street still forms the centre of Rome's Jewish life, even though many of the people you'll see sitting around chatting in the evening or at weekends have travelled into the city from the suburbs. It's also a good place to sample the unique hybrid that is Roman Jewish cuisine. Try *pizza ebraica* (Jewish pizza) at **Il Boccione** (*see p132*) or *torta di ricotta e visciole* – ricotta and damson tart – in a tiny unmarked cornershop, the **Forno del Ghetto** (via Portico d'Ottavia 1).

Sights & museums

Fontana delle Tartarughe

Piazza Mattei. Bus 30, 40, 46, 62, 63, 64, 70, 87, 492, 780, 810, 916, H/tram 8. ***Map*** *p120 H10.*

Four *ephebes* (adolescent boys) cavort around the base of one of Rome's loveliest fountains, gently hoisting tortoises up to the waters above them. Giacomo della Porta and Taddeo Landini built the fountain for the Duke of Mattei at some point in the 1580s. The duke, so the story goes, had lost all his money and hence his fiancée, and wanted to prove to her father that he could still achieve great things. He had the fountain built overnight in the square outside his family *palazzo*; the next morning he triumphantly displayed his accomplishment from a palace window. The wedding was on again, but he had the window walled up, and so it remains. The turtles were probably an afterthought, added by Bernini during a restoration. The ones there today are copies: three of the originals are now in the Capitoline Museums; the fourth was stolen and presumably graces some private fountain.

❤ Museo Ebraico

Lungotevere Cenci (06 6840 0661, www.museoebraico.roma.it). Bus 23, 63, 280, 780/tram 8. ***Open*** *Apr-Sept 10am-6pm Mon-Thur, Sun; 9am-4pm Fri. Oct-Mar 10am-5pm Mon-Thur, Sun; 9am-2pm Fri. Closed Jewish hols.* ***Admission*** *€11; €5 reductions.* ***Map*** *p120 J11.*

Inscriptions and carvings line the entrance passage to this fascinating museum, which holds a collection that details the history of the city's Jewish community. The recently extended and refurbished display is housed beneath the magnificent neo-Assyrian, neo-Greek Great Synagogue that was inaugurated in 1904. As well as luxurious crowns, Torah mantles and silverware, this museum presents vivid reminders of the persecution that was suffered by Rome's Jews at various times throughout the city's history. Copies of the 16th-century papal edicts that banned Jews from a progressively longer list of activities are a disturbing foretaste of the horrors forced on them by the Fascists and Nazis. The Nazi atrocities are in turn represented by stark photographs and heart-rending relics derived from the concentration camps, as well as film footage tracing developments in the post-war period. There are also a number of displays on the ancient Roman synagogue excavated at Ostia in 1964, as well as Jewish items from the city's catacombs. The entrance to the museum includes a guided tour of the two Synagogues housed in the building.

Portico d'Ottavia

Via Portico d'Ottavia. Bus 23, 30Exp, 44, 63, 81, 83, 160, 170, 280, 628, 715, 716, 780, 781, H. ***Open*** *9am-6pm daily.* ***Admission*** *free.* ***Map*** *p120 J10.*

Great ancient columns and a marble frontispiece, held together with rusting iron braces, now form part of the church of Sant'Angelo in Pescheria. They were originally the entrance of a massive colonnaded square (*portico*) containing temples and libraries, built in the first century AD by Emperor Augustus and dedicated to his sister Octavia (this, in turn, had been built over a first-century BC square). The mighty structure was decorated with 34 bronzes by Lysippus depicting bellicose events from the life of Alexander the Great; these are long lost. The isolated columns outside, and the inscription above, date from a later restoration, undertaken by Septimius Severus in AD 213. After lengthy digs and restoration work in the 1990s, a walkway was opened allowing you to stroll through the *forum piscarium* – the ancient fish market, hence the name of the church. The walkway continues through the excavation past a graveyard of broken columns and dumped Corinthian capitals to the **Teatro di Marcello** (*see p135*), passing by three towering columns that were part of the Temple of Apollo, dating from 433 BC.

Restaurants

Sora Margherita €€

Piazza delle Cinque Scole 30 (06 687 4216). Bus 30, 40, 46, 62, 63, 64, 70, 81, 87, 492, 628, 916, H/tram 8. ***Open*** *12.45-2.45pm daily; 7.30-10.30pm Mon, Wed; 8-11.20pm Fri, Sat. Closed 1wk Aug.* ***No cards. Map*** *p120 H10* 8 *Jewish-Roman*

This spit-and-sawdust, hole-in-the-wall trattoria offers one of Rome's great local dining experiences. Tables are crammed into a couple of narrow rooms, and the din generated by 20 simultaneous conversations, with orders shouted over the top, is quite bewildering. Sora Margherita is not for health freaks, and if you're on a diet, forget it; but no one argues with serious Roman Jewish cooking at these prices. The menu of classic pasta and meat dishes includes a great *pasta e fagioli* (pasta and bean stew) and *ossobuco* (veal shank) washed down with rough-and-ready house wine. Dessert consists of home-made *crostate* (jam or ricotta tarts).

Bakeries, pasticcerie & gelaterie

Il Boccione

Via Portico d'Ottavia 1 (06 687 8637). Bus 23, 63, 280, 780, H/tram 8. ***Open*** *7am-2pm, 3.30-7.30pm Mon-Thur; 7am-2pm Fri; 7.30am-5pm Sun. Closed 3wks Aug & Jewish hols.* ***No cards. Map*** *p120 H10* 2 *Bakery*

There is no sign, the decor is plain and the ladies who run it are fierce, but this Jewish bakery in the heart of the Ghetto will usually have a queue of loyal fans snaking out of the door. Come here for the best *torta di ricotta e visciole* (ricotta and wild cherry pie) in town and look out for the scalding hot tray of *pizza ebraica* (Jewish pizza: weighty blocks of spiced dough stuffed with pine nuts, almonds and dried fruit) slapped straight from the oven onto the counter.

Shops & services

Acquamadre

Via di Sant'Ambrogio 17 (06 686 4272, www.acquamadre.it). Bus 23, 30Exp, 40Exp, 46, 64, 70, 81, 87, 280, 492, 628, 780, 810, 916/tram 8. ***Open*** *2-9pm Tue; 11am-9pm Wed-Sun. Closed late July-early Sept.* ***Map*** *p120 H10* 1 *Spa*

What better way to remove the grime of Roman traffic than to sweat it out in this glamorous modern take on the ancient Roman bath house: calm, steamy and offering an array of massages and beauty treatments. On Wednesday and Friday the hammam is women-only.

Beppe e i suoi formaggi

Via Santa Maria del Pianto 9/A (06 6819 2210, www.beppeeisuoiformaggi.it). Bus 23, 40Exp, 46, 62, 64, 916, H/tram 8. ***Open*** *9am-10.30pm Mon-Sat. Closed 1wk Aug.* ***Map*** *p120 H10.* 3 *Delicatessen*

Walking into Beppe Giovale's shop in the Jewish Ghetto is like entering a cheese wonderland. The vast counter displays an overwhelming selection from the familiar parmesan, pecorino and mozzarella, to strong and stinky varieties, many of which hail from Beppe's home region of Piedmont. There is also a small restaurant area which serves cheese tastings and a few seasonal dishes for lunch and dinner.

❤ Leone Limentani

Via Portico d'Ottavia 47 (06 6880 6686). Bus 23, 63, 271, 280, 780, H/tram 8. ***Open*** *10am-7.30pm Mon-Sat. Closed 2wks Aug.* ***Map*** *p120 J10* ❽ *House & home*

A treasure-trove of high-piled crockery and kitchenware is on display here – at bargain-basement prices. Many big-name brands are reduced by up to 20%.

❤ Marta Ray

Via della Reginella 4 (06 6873714, www.martharay.it). Bus 23, 40Exp, 46, 62, 64, 916, H/tram 8. ***Open*** *10am-8pm daily.* ***Map*** *p120 H10* ❾ *Accessories*

Designer Marta Ratajczak's gorgeous leather bags and shoes combine contemporary style with quality materials and craftsmanship. From snazzy ballerina flats to buttery soft satchels and wallets in a spectrum of colours, this stuff is made to last. The practical prices are an added bonus. **Other locations** via dei Coronari 121/122 (piazza Navona); via del Moro 6 (Trastevere).

Il Ponte Contemporanea

Via Beatrice Cenci 9 (06 6880 1351, www.ilpontecontemporanea.com). Bus 23, 40, 46, 62, 64, 870. ***Open*** *Sept-May noon-8pm Tue-Sat; June-July noon-8pm Mon-Fri. Closed Aug.* ***No cards. Map*** *p120 H10* ⓫ *Gallery*

This stylish gallery focuses mostly on photography and installation art. Pierre & Gilles and Tracey Moffat had their first Italian shows here.

Valentina Bonomo Arte Contemporanea

Via Portico d'Ottavia 13 (06 683 2766, www.galleriabonomo.com). Bus 23, 63, 271, 280, 780, H/tram 8. ***Open*** *Oct-May 3-7pm Tue-Sat; June-Sept 3-7pm Mon-Fri. Closed Aug.* ***No cards. Map*** *p120 J10* ⓬ *Gallery*

This space exhibits work by both established international artists and young photographers.

TIBER ISLAND & THE BOCCA DELLA VERITÀ

When the last Etruscan king was driven from Rome, the Romans uprooted the wheat from his fields and threw it in baskets into the river. There the baskets lay, with silt accumulating around them until that silt formed an island. When the Roman god of medicine, Aesculapius, came to Rome on a boat to deal with a plague epidemic in the third century BC, his snake jumped out at that spot, indicating that this was the spot for a sanctuary. That's what the legend says anyway, and from that moment on the island has had a vocation for public health. Today the busy Fatebenefratelli hospital occupies the north end of the island simply called *l'isola tiberina* – the **Tiber Island**. The church of **San Bartolomeo** (*see p134* In the know) – an apostle flayed alive by Armenians – is built over the original sanctuary. Remains of the ancient building can be seen from the wide footpath around the island, down by the muddy, rushing Tiber: a sculpted boat-shaped outcrop of travertine is decorated with a rod and snakes, the symbol of the god of healing. Off the southern tip is the **Ponte Rotto** (Broken Bridge), Rome's oldest, and, on the left, the mouth of the **Cloaca Maxima**, ancient Rome's great sewer.

Across on the east bank of the river stood ancient Rome's cattle market (*forum boarium*) and vegetable market (*forum holitorium*) – a bustling place from the time of the Etruscan kings, chunks of which can be seen beneath the church of **San Nicola in Carcere** (*see p134*). Further south are two delightful Republican-era **temples** and **Santa Maria in Cosmedin** (*see p134*), with its '*bocca della verità*' (mouth of truth). Skirt left around Santa Maria in Cosmedin for the touchingly unadorned Arch of Janus and the church of **San Giorgio in Velabro** (*see p133*).

Sights & museums

Ponte Rotto & Cloaca Maxima

Views from Ponte Palatino, Isola Tiberina & lungotevere Pierleoni. Bus 23, 44, 63, 280, 780, H/tram 8. ***Map*** *p120 J11.*

The Ponte Rotto – literally, 'Broken Bridge' – stands on the site of the Pons aemilius, Rome's first stone bridge, built in 142 BC. It was rebuilt many times – even Michelangelo had a go – before 1598, when great chunks collapsed (yet again) into the river and it was decided to give up trying. To the east of the bridge is a tunnel in the embankment: the gaping mouth of the Cloaca Maxima, the city's great sewer. Built under Rome's Etruscan kings in the sixth century BC to drain the area around the Forum, it was given its final form in the first century BC.

San Giorgio in Velabro

Via del Velabro 19 (06 6979 7536, www.sangiorgioinvelabro.org). Bus 30Exp, 44, 63, 81, 83, 160, 170, 628, 715, 716, 780, 781, H. ***Open*** *10am-12.30pm, 4-6.30pm daily.* ***Map*** *p120 K11.*

The soft light from the windows in the clerestory gives a peaceful aura to this austere

In the know

A temple under a church

You don't need much imagination to picture the ancient temple to Aesculapius (the god of medicine) that lies beneath the church of **San Bartolomeo** (piazza di San Bartolomeo all'Isola, www.sanbartolomeo.org) on the Tiber Island. The precious marble columns in the nave of the church adorned the original temple, which was inaugurated in 293 BC. If you need help to imagine how things were when Otto III built this church in 998, then check out the massive bronze vessel (protected by an iron grille on the right-hand wall of the nave, by the altar) in which the 18-year-old German-born Holy Roman Emperor brought relics of the apostle Bartholomew from Benevento.

little church of the fifth century. A swingeing restoration in 1925 did away with centuries of decoration and restored its original Romanesque simplicity. The 16 columns, pilfered from the Palatine and the Aventine hills, are all different. Pieces of an eighth- or ninth-century choir, including two slender columns, are incorporated into the walls. In the apse is a restored fresco by the school of Pietro Cavallini showing St George with a white horse and the Virgin on one side of the central Christ figure, and St Peter and St Sebastian opposite. The 12th-century altar is a rare example of the Byzantine-inspired 'caged and architraved' ciborium, a canopy on columns. A church was first built here by Greeks and was dedicated to St Sebastian, who was believed to have been martyred in the swampy area hereabouts. It was later re-dedicated to St George of Cappadocia (of dragon-slaying fame); a piece of the skull of the valorous third-century saint is kept under the altar. The portico and bell tower are 12th-century additions. Outside, to the left, is the *arco degli Argentari*, built in AD 204; it was a gate on the road between the main Forum and the *forum boarium* (cattle market), along which money changers (*argenteri*) plied their trade. The church and other monuments were damaged by a Mafia bomb in 1993 but have since been repaired.

San Nicola in Carcere

Via del Teatro di Marcello 46 (06 6830 7198). Bus 30Exp, 44, 63, 81, 83, 160, 170, 628, 715, 716, 780, 781, H. ***Open*** *7am-7pm daily. Closed Aug.* ***Map*** *p120 J11.*

The 12th-century San Nicola was built over three Roman temples: dating from the second and third centuries BC, these were dedicated to two-faced Janus, protector of the gates; to the goddess Juno Sospita, perhaps a protectress of commerce; and to Spes (Hope). If you can find a custodian you can ask to visit the excavations for a small donation. As well as the temples, you descend even deeper to see a slab from the Etruscan *forum holitorium* (vegetable market), a busy commercial exchange near the main river. On the outside of the church, six columns from the Temple of Janus can be seen on the left; the ones on the right are from the Temple of Spes. The church's façade was added by Giacomo della Porta in 1599. The name, in *carcere* (prison), probably comes from a seventh-century jail that stood nearby.

Santa Maria in Cosmedin

Piazza della Bocca della Verità 18 (06 678 7759). Bus 30Exp, 44, 63, 81, 83, 160, 170, 628, 715, 716, 780, 781, H. ***Open*** *9.30am-5.50pm daily.* ***Map*** *p120 J12.*

Despite an over-enthusiastic restoration, this is a lovely jumble of early Christian, medieval and Romanesque church design – with a touch of kitsch. Santa Maria in Cosmedin

Tiber Island

was built in the sixth century and enlarged in the eighth. The beautiful bell tower was a 12th-century addition. Between the 11th and 13th centuries much of the decoration was replaced with cosmati-work, including the spiralling floor, throne, choir and 13th-century *baldacchino*. In the sacristy/souvenir shop is a fragment of an eighth-century mosaic of the Holy Family, brought here from St Peter's. In the crypt are ruins of the Ara maximus, a monument to Hercules over which the church was built. The name Cosmedin comes from the Greek, meaning splendid decoration; this has always been the church of the Greek community, many of whom were expelled from Constantinople in the eighth century: Byzantine rite services are still held here at 10.30am on Sundays.

The church is better known as the *bocca della verità* (the mouth of truth) as, according to legend, anyone who lies while their hand is in the mouth of the mask of the horned man on the portico wall will have that hand bitten off. It was reportedly used by Roman husbands to determine the fidelity of their wives.

In the classic movie *Roman Holiday*, Gregory Peck ad-libs having his hand munched, eliciting a (reportedly) unscripted shriek of alarm from Audrey Hepburn – one of the most delightful moments in cinema. Today there is almost always a long queue of people waiting to follow his example for a euro. The church however requires no queuing and is well worth a visit.

Teatro di Marcello

Via Teatro di Marcello (06 6710 3819). Bus 30Exp, 44, 63, 81, 83, 160, 170, 628, 715, 716, 780, 781, H. ***Open*** *by appt only.* ***Map*** *p120 J11.*

This is one of the strangest sights in Rome: a Renaissance palace grafted on to an ancient, time-worn theatre. Julius Caesar began building a theatre here to rival Pompey's in the *Campus martius*, but it was finished in 11 BC by Augustus, who named it after his favourite nephew. Its 41 arches were topped with marble masks. It seated up to 20,000. Now known as the Palazzo Orsini (little bear – stone symbols of which can be seen on gateposts) after another owner, it is now luxury apartments. The shops that filled the ground-level archways were thrown out in the 1930s, leaving the structure in splendid if rather sad isolation, its travertine blocks looking as though they're suffering from a wasting disease.

Tempii di Ercole & Portuno

Piazza della Bocca della Verità. Bus 30Exp, 44, 63, 81, 83, 160, 170, 628, 715, 716, 780, 781, H. ***Map*** *p120 J12.*

Like the Pantheon, these diminutive Republican-era temples of Hercules and Portunus owe their good state of preservation to their conversion into churches in the Middle Ages.

The round one was built in the first century BC and dedicated to Hercules. Early archaeologists were confused by its shape, which is similar to the Temple of Vesta in the Roman Forum, and dubbed it the Temple of Vesta. Recently restored, it's the oldest marble building still standing in Rome (the marble blocks on the temple's bottom half are what remain of the original). The original upper section, perhaps domed, has been lost, although 19 of its 20 marble columns have survived; the roof is modern.

To its right stands the square temple dedicated to Portunus (god of harbours), as ancient Rome's river port was nearby. (Inexplicably, early archaeologists attributed this one to *Fortuna Virilis* – manly fortune.) The two temples were deconsecrated and designated ancient monuments in the 1920s.

Via Veneto & Villa Borghese

Historically, the area surrounding the city's most central public park, Villa Borghese, was always green: ancient aristocrats built sprawling villas here, and noble families and monastic orders continued the tradition right up until the 1800s. Nowadays, Villa Borghese is all that is left, but it contains splendid sights: a great art repository – the superb Galleria Borghese – along with one of Rome's greatest vistas from the Pincio, over piazza del Popolo to the dome of St Peter's.

South from the park, via Vittorio Veneto (known simply as via Veneto) was the haunt of the glamorous and famous in the *dolce vita* years of the 1950s and '60s. These days, it's home to insurance companies, luxury hotels and visitors wondering where the stars and paparazzi have gone.

❤ Don't miss

1 Galleria Borghese *p142*
A glorious scrapbook of ancient and Baroque art, all in a bucolic setting.

2 The view from the Pincio *p141*
Especially magical at dusk.

3 La Galleria Nazionale *p141*
If the ancient is all a little *too* ancient.

4 Museo Nazionale Etrusco di Villa Giulia *p144*
The world's best Etruscan museum in a villa designed by Michelangelo.

5 Museo Carlo Bilotti *p144*
De Chirico in the park, and it's free.

In the know
Getting around

Via Veneto snakes north from Barberini stop on metro line A up to the Villa Borghese. It takes about ten minutes to walk the length of it, gently uphill. Another way of accessing the park is from the Spagna stop on metro line A. From Spagna, either take the unprepossessing underground walkway and escalator, climb the Spanish Steps, or use the lift just inside the metro station entrance. These lead you to the ridge of the Pincio.

Tempio di Esculapio, Villa Borghese

VIA VENETO & VILLA BORGHESE

Restaurants

1. Marzapane
2. 2 Osteria dell'Arco
3. 3 Pinsere

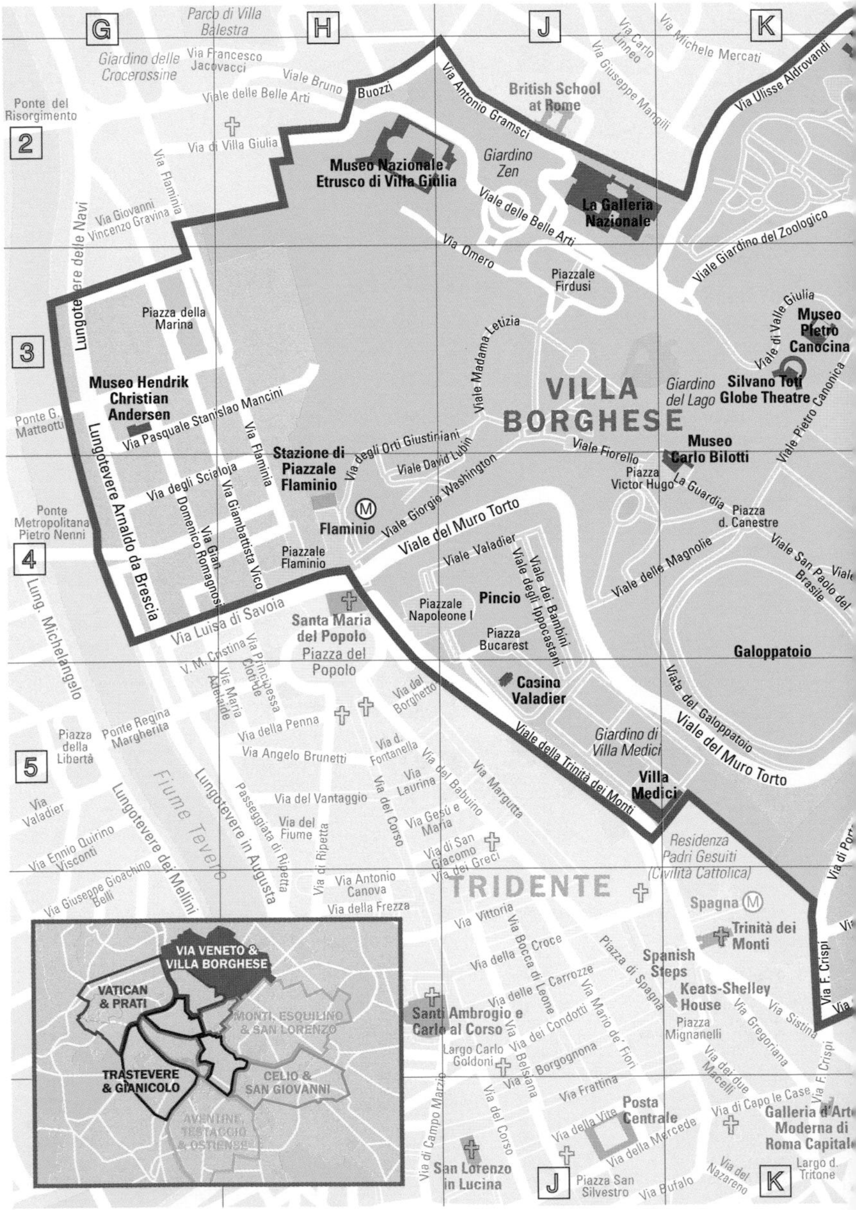

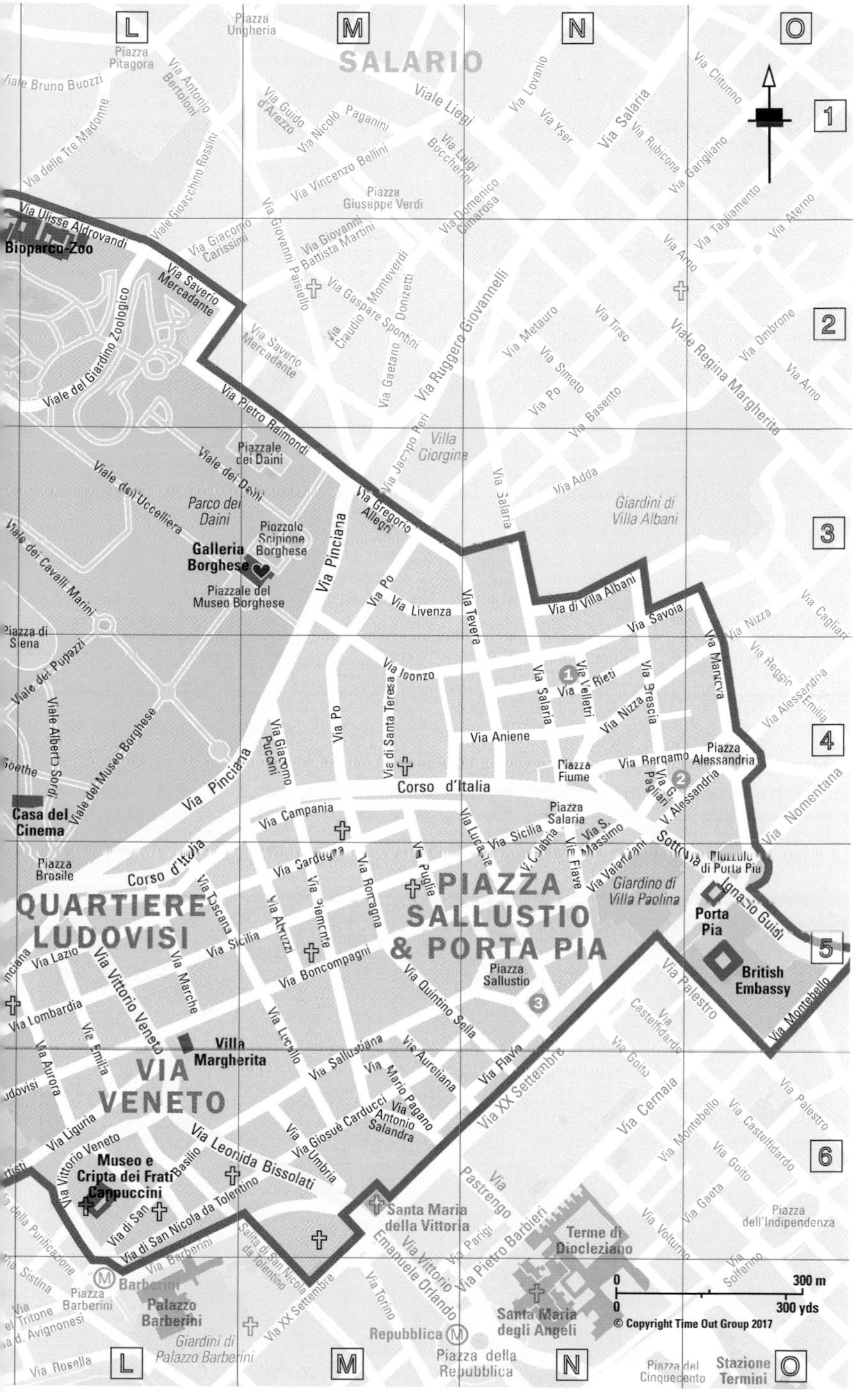
L
M
N
O
1
2
3
4
5
6
SALARIO
QUARTIERE LUDOVISI
VIA VENETO
PIAZZA SALLUSTIO & PORTA PIA
Piazza Ungheria
Piazza Pitagora
Viale Bruno Buozzi
Via Antonio Bertoloni
Via delle Tre Madonne
Viale Gioacchino Rossini
Via Guido d'Arezzo
Via Nicolò Paganini
Viale Liegi
Via Lovanio
Via Yser
Via Salaria
Via Clitunno
Via Rubicone
Via Gangliano
Via Luigi Boccherini
Via Vincenzo Bellini
Piazza Giuseppe Verdi
Via Domenico Cimarosa
Via Tagliamento
Via Aterno
Via Ulisse Aldrovandi
Bioparco-Zoo
Via Giacomo Carissimi
Via Giovanni Paisiello
Via Giovanni Battista Martini
Via Arno
Via Saverio Mercadante
Via Gaspare Spontini
Via Claudio Monteverdi
Donizetti
Via Ruggero Giovannelli
Via Metauro
Via Tirso
Viale Regina Margherita
Via Ombrone
Viale del Giardino Zoologico
Via Gaetano
Via Simeto
Via Po
Via Basento
Via Pietro Raimondi
Via Jacopo Peri
Villa Giorgina
Piazzale dei Daini
Viale dei Daini
Viale dell'Uccelliera
Parco dei Daini
Via Gregorio Allegri
Via Adda
Giardini di Villa Albani
Viale dei Cavalli Marini
Galleria Borghese
Piazzale Scipione Borghese
Piazzale del Museo Borghese
Via Pinciana
Via Livenza
Via Tevere
Via di Villa Albani
Via Savoia
Piazza di Siena
Viale dei Pupazzi
Via Isonzo
Via Salaria
Via Velletri
Via Rieti
Via Brescia
Via Nizza
Via Mantova
Via Cagliari
Via Reggio Emilia
Via Alessandria
Viale Alberto Sordi
Viale del Museo Borghese
Goethe
Via Giacomo Puccini
Via di Santa Teresa
Via Aniene
Piazza Fiume
Via Bergamo
Piazza Alessandria
Via G. Pagliari
V. Alessandria
Via Nomentana
Casa del Cinema
Corso d'Italia
Via Campania
Via Lucania
Via Sicilia
Piazza Salaria
Via Calabria
Via S. Massimo
Via Fiave
Via Valenziani
Sottopassaggio
Piazzale di Porta Pia
Via Ignazio Guidi
Piazza Brasile
Via Sardegna
Via Piemonte
Via Romagna
Via Puglie
Via Toscana
Via Abruzzi
Giardino di Villa Paolina
Porta Pia
British Embassy
Via Lazio
Via Vittorio Veneto
Via Marche
Via Boncompagni
Via Quintino Sella
Piazza Sallustio
Via Palestro
Via Castelfidardo
Via Montebello
Via Lombardia
Via Emilia
Via Aurora
Villa Margherita
Via Lucullo
Via Sallustiana
Via Aureliana
Via Flavia
Via XX Settembre
Via Goito
Via Mario Pagano
Via Antonio Salandra
Via Cernaia
Via Liguria
Via Leonida Bissolati
Via Giosuè Carducci
Via Umbria
Museo e Cripta dei Frati Cappuccini
Via San Basilio
Via Pastrengo
Via Volturno
Via Gaeta
Piazza dell'Indipendenza
Via di San Nicola da Tolentino
Salita di San Nicola da Tolentino
Santa Maria della Vittoria
Via Emanuele Orlando
Via Vittorio
Via Parigi
Via Pietro Barbieri
Terme di Diocleziano
Via Solferino
Via della Purificazione
Via Sistina
Via Barberini
Barberini
Piazza Barberini
Palazzo Barberini
Via del Tritone
Via d. Avignonesi
Via Torino
Santa Maria degli Angeli
Repubblica
0
300 m
300 yds
© Copyright Time Out Group 2017
Giardini di Palazzo Barberini
Piazza della Repubblica
Piazza del Cinquecento
Stazione Termini
Via Rasella

VILLA BORGHESE & THE PINCIO

In the first century BC, Rome's most extensive gardens, the **Horti Sallustiani** (*see p147*), spread over the valley between the Quirinale hill and the Pincio. During the Renaissance, the area was colonised by aristocratic Roman families such as the Borghese and Boncompagni-Ludovisi, who attempted to outdo one another with the lavishness of their vast suburban estates. In fact, up until the building boom in Rome during the late 1800s, only the odd villa or decorative pavilion interrupted the tranquil and leafy parkland that stretched from the Pincio to Porta Pia.

When Rome was made capital of Italy in 1871, this green idyll was seen as prime building land, to be dug up and replaced by street after street of grandiose *palazzi*; of the estates, only the **Villa Borghese** was saved from the property vultures; it is now the city's most central public park.

Shortly after Camillo Borghese became Pope Paul V in 1605, his favourite nephew, 26-year-old Scipione Caffarelli Borghese, was made a cardinal. An obsessive love of the arts led Scipione to embark upon the creation of a pleasure park: the Villa Borghese. What began as a family vineyard was transformed, with the acquisition of surrounding lands, into one of the most extensive gardens in Rome since antiquity. A 'Theatre of the Universe', Scipione's vision was a place where sculpture, painting and music could be enjoyed alongside fossil specimens and technological oddities of the day such as special clocks and lenses. The harmoniously proportioned *Casino nobile* (now the **Galleria Borghese**; *see p142*) was designed to showcase these gems. Begun in 1608, the building was modelled on ancient Roman villas and Renaissance predecessors such as the **Villa Farnesina** (*see p172*).

An impressive aviary (beautifully restored, to the left as you face the Galleria Borghese) acted as a backdrop to the land surrounding the *Casino*, which alternated formal gardens dotted with exotic plants, fountains and statues with wilder stretches of landscape used for hunting. The villa soon became *the* place to be seen in 17th-century Rome, and the magnificent gardens were further embellished until Scipione's death in 1633. The result was a Baroque amusement park, complete with trick fountains that sprayed unwitting passers-by, automata and erotic paintings, menageries of wild beasts, and an al fresco dining room where the cardinal entertained with due magnificence on summer evenings. Successive generations of the Borghese family altered the park according to changing fashions, though Scipione's descendants proved themselves to be less artistically inclined than their keen-eyed predecessor, selling off a good deal of his priceless collection; one of the worst culprits was Prince Camillo, who married Napoleon's notorious sister Pauline in 1807.

When Rome became capital of a unified Italy, the clan looked set to sell off the estate to property speculators. In a rare example of civic far-sightedness, the state stepped in, in 1901, wresting possession of the villa from the family in a bitter court battle and turning it into a public park.

The view from the Pincio at dusk

La Galleria Nazionale

Today, the Borghese family's pleasure grounds are a popular spot for jogging, dog-walking, picnicking and cruising. The entire park has been spruced up in recent years, and a spate of arty projects, such as the opening of the **Museo Carlo Bilotti** (*see p146*), cemented its status as a 'park of the arts', of which its founder would have been proud. A wander around Villa Borghese is a great way to recuperate from an overdose of carbon monoxide. Sporty types will find bicycles and in-line skates for hire, and the park is one big wireless hotspot (see www.romawireless.com). Culture vultures head straight to three of Rome's greatest art repositories: the Galleria Borghese itself, the **Museo Nazionale Etrusco di Villa Giulia** (*see p144*) and **La Galleria Nazionale**. Viale delle Belle Arti and via Omero are crammed with academies and cultural institutes that put on occasional exhibitions and concerts. The **British School at Rome** (www.bsr.ac.uk), in an imposing Lutyens-designed pavilion, hosts contemporary art exhibitions, events and lectures. The park also houses the **Casa del Cinema** (www.casadelcinema.it) and the **Bioparco-Zoo** (www.bioparco.it).

Other sights worth looking out for include the **piazza di Siena**, an elegantly shaped grassy hippodrome that is used for glitzy showjumping events, and, nearby, the pretty **Giardino del Lago**, which has a small lake with rowing boats for hire and faux-ancient temples. There is also a good view of the Muro Torto section of the **Aurelian Wall** from the bridge between the Pincio and Villa Borghese.

Overlooking piazza del Popolo, and now an integral part of the Villa Borghese, is one of the oldest gardens in Rome: the **Pincio**. The Pinci family commissioned the first gardens here in the fourth century. The present layout was designed by Giuseppe Valadier in 1814. The garden is best known for its view of the Vatican at sunset, with the dome of St Peter's silhouetted in gold. The paved area behind the viewpoint is popular with cyclists (bikes can be hired nearby) and skaters.

To the south-east of the Pincio is the **Casina Valadier** (piazza Bucarest, 06 6992 2090, casinavaladier.com), now a pricey restaurant with a to-die-for view. In the manicured green further south sits the **Villa Medici**, since 1804 the French academy in Rome, where many French artists, from Ingres and David to Balthus, found inspiration. The academy hosts occasional art exhibitions (06 67 611, www.villamedici.it) and opens its lovely gardens and some galleries of its art collection in daily guided tours (tours at 11am and 3pm are in English, €12, €6 reductions, booking advisable).

Between Villa Borghese and the river you'll find a striking art nouveau villa housing the **Museo Hendrik Christian Andersen** (*see p144*).

Sights & museums

❤ La Galleria Nazionale

Viale delle Belle Arti 131 (06 3229 8221, www.lagallerianazionale.com). Bus 61, 89, 160, 490, 495/tram 3, 19. ***Open*** *8.30am-7.30pm Tue-Sun.* ***Admission*** *€10; €5 reductions. Exhibition price varies. No cards.* ***Map*** *p138 J2.*

Several of the villas dotted around the park are the remains of a world exposition held here in 1911, and this neo-classical palace

Galleria Borghese

Piazzale del Museo Borghese 5 (06 32 810, www.galleriaborghese.it). Bus 52, 53, 160, 490, 495, 910. ***Open*** *9am-7pm Tue-Sun.* ***Admission*** *€15; €8.50 reductions. Exhibition price varies.* ***Map*** *p138 M3.*

Begun in 1608 by Flaminio Ponzio and continued by Jan van Santen (Italianised to Giovanni Vasanzio) upon his death, the *Casino nobile* was designed to house Cardinal Scipione Borghese's art collection. One of Bernini's greatest patrons, the cardinal had as good an eye for a bargain as for a masterpiece: he picked up many works – including the odd Caravaggio – at knock-down prices after they were rejected by the disappointed or shocked patrons who had commissioned them.

The building's imposing façade was originally adorned with sculptures and ancient reliefs, which, along with many of the gallery's priceless gems, were sold to Napoleon in 1807 and are now conserved in the Louvre. The interior decoration – which was carried out in 1775-90 by Antonio Asprucci and Christopher Unterberger for Marcantonio IV Borghese – was fully restored during the 1990s.

Apollo and Daphne (Bernini, 1625)

A curved double staircase leads to the imposing entrance salon, with fourth-century AD floor mosaics showing gladiators fighting wild animals; the spectacular trompe l'oeil ceiling fresco (Mariano Rossi, 1775-78) shows Romulus received as a god on Olympus by Jupiter and other tales of Roman glory. Also here is the statue of Marcus Curtius throwing himself into a chasm. (According to legend, when a massive crack appeared in the Roman Forum, threatening to swallow up Rome, the only way to stop it was to sacrifice the city's greatest treasure... so in leaped golden-boy Marcus.)

In Room 1 is one of the gallery's highlights: Canova's 1808 waxed marble figure of Pauline, sister of Napoleon and wife of Prince Camillo Borghese, as a topless Venus reclining languidly on a marble and wood sofa, which once contained a mechanism that slowly rotated it. Prince Camillo thought the work so provocative that he forbade even the artist from seeing it after completion. (Asked by a shocked friend how she could bear to pose naked, the irascible Pauline is said to have snapped: 'The studio was heated.')

Rooms 2 to 4 contain some spectacular sculptures by Gian Lorenzo Bernini, made early in his career and already showing flashes of his genius. His *David* (1624) merits observation from different points of view in Room 2; the tense, concentrated face on the biblical hero as he is about to launch his shot is a self-portrait of the artist. Room 3 houses perhaps Bernini's most famous piece: *Apollo and Daphne* (1625), a seminal work of Baroque sculpture. As the nymph flees the amorous sun god, her desperate plea for help is answered by her river-god father; as Apollo reaches her she morphs – fingertips first – into a laurel tree. Ovid's tale was given a moral twist by Maffeo Barberini – later Pope Urban VIII – who composed the Latin inscription on the base: 'When we pursue fleeting pleasures, we reap only bitter fruits.' Bernini's virtuosity is especially evident in the cluster of paper-thin marble leaves separating the god and the girl. In Room 4, Pluto's hand presses fiercely into Proserpine's marble thigh in *The Rape of Proserpine* (1622), as she flexes her toes in tearful struggle.

Room 5 contains important pieces of classical sculpture, many of them Roman copies of Greek originals. Among the most renowned are a Roman copy of a Greek dancing faun and a copy of sleeping Hermaphroditus, who was the offspring of Hermes and Aphrodite, displayed with his/her back to the onlooker so that the breasts and genitals are invisible. Bernini's *Aeneas and Anchises* (1620) dominates Room 6, showing the family fleeing as Troy burns, a theme reflected in the ceiling with Pecheux's painting of the gods deciding the fate of the city. Room 7 is Egyptian-themed: the ceiling paintings by Tommaso Maria Conca (1780) include an allegory of the richness of Egypt, whereas among the classical statues is a second-century Isis that is clad in black marble clothing. The six Caravaggios in Room 8 include the *Boy with a Basket of Fruit* (c1594) and the *Sick Bacchus* (c1593), which is believed to be a self-portrait.

Upstairs, the picture gallery is packed with one masterpiece after another. Look out in particular for: Raphael's *Deposition*, Pinturicchio's *Crucifixion with Saints Jerome and Christopher* and Perugino's *Madonna and Child* (Room 9); Correggio's *Danaë*, commissioned as 16th-century soft porn for Charles V of Spain (as told in Ovid's *Metamorphoses*, Jupiter – disguised as a 'golden shower' – attempted to seduce the reclining, half-naked maiden) and Lucas Cranach's *Venus and Cupid with Honeycomb* (Room 10); a dark, brooding *Pietà* by Raphael's follower Sodoma (Room 12); two self-portraits and two sculpted busts of Cardinal Scipione Borghese by Bernini (Room 14); Jacopo Bassano's *Last Supper* (Room 15); and Rubens' spectacular *Pietà* and *Susanna and the Elders* (Room 18). Titian's *Venus Blindfolding Cupid* and *Sacred and Profane Love*, the work that originally put the gallery on the map, are the centrepieces of Room 20. In 1899, the Rothschilds offered to buy the latter work at a price that exceeded the estimated value of the entire gallery and all its works put together; the offer was turned down. Other highlights of Room 20 include Renaissance paintings by Veronese, Giorgione and Carpaccio, and Antonello da Messina's *Portrait of a Man*.

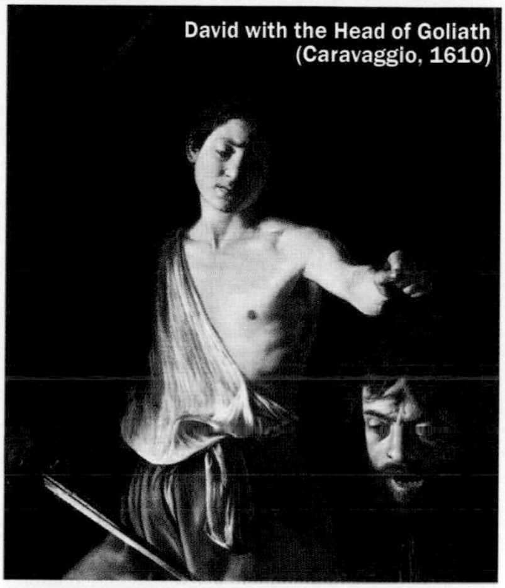
David with the Head of Goliath (Caravaggio, 1610)

► *Booking is obligatory, and if you haven't booked well in advance you may find the gallery fully booked from April to October. You should have no trouble getting in midweek in low season. Visitors are assigned a two-hour slot, entering every two hours from 9am until 5pm. You must leave at the end of your slot.*

Villa Borghese

❤ Don't miss

1 Apollo and Daphne *Room 3*
Bernini's extraordinary and virtuoso Baroque sculpture.

2 David with the Head of Goliath *Room 8*
Caravaggio's bleak last painting of David and Goliath.

3 Deposition of Christ *Room 9*
Raphael's masterpiece, stolen to order by unscrupulous Scipione.

dedicated to 19th- and 20th-century art is one of the most eye-pleasing. (For 21st century *see p224* MAXXI.) A rehang in 2017 broke with the traditional chronological layout.

Major Italian works include the bombast of Canova's *Hercules* (1795), the melancholy of Modigliani, Boldini's society portraits with a twist, the metaphysical masterpieces of De Chirico, and a smattering of Futurism, not to mention Lucio Fontana and Burri.

International stars include *The Three Ages* by Klimt (1905) and *The Gardener* (1889) and *Madame Ginoux* (1890) by Van Gogh. Cézanne, Braque, Rodin and Henry Moore are also represented here.

❤ Museo Carlo Bilotti

Viale Fiorello La Guardia (06 0608, www.museocarlobilotti.it). Bus 61, 89, 160, 490, 491, 495. ***Open*** *Oct-May 10am-4pm Tue-Fri; 10am-7pm Sat, Sun. June-Sept 1-7pm Tue-Fri; 10am-7pm Sat, Sun.* ***Admission*** *free.* ***Map*** *p138 K4.*

This small museum of modern art is housed in a *palazzo* that was bought by Scipione Borghese in 1616 and used as a resting place during hunts. Damaged by French cannon fire in 1849, it was then variously used as a storehouse for oranges, a religious institute and city offices; it opened as a gallery in 2006 to house the superlative collection of billionaire tycoon Carlo Bilotti. The De Chirico paintings and sculptures that form the nucleus of the 22 works in the permanent collection (first floor) perhaps influenced Bilotti to choose Rome as the city in which to display them (De Chirico spent much of his life in Rome, and died here in 1978.) Also on the first floor, an entire room is devoted to the Bilotti family: the highlights are a Larry Rivers portrait of Signor Bilotti posing before a Dubuffet canvas, and a poignant 1981 Warhol portrait of Bilotti's wife and daughter. A wall of photographs capture the family schmoozing with various high-profile figures on the contemporary art scene. The ground floor hosts temporary art exhibitions.

Museo Hendrik Christian Andersen

Via PS Mancini 20 (06 321 9089, www.polomusealelazio.beniculturali.it). Metro Flaminio/bus 89, 490, 495, 628, 926, 19. ***Open*** *9.30am-7pm Tue-Sun.* ***Admission*** *free.* ***Map*** *p138 G3.*

This offshoot of the Galleria Nazionale d'Arte Moderna occupies an art nouveau villa between the river and viale Flaminia. This was the studio-home of Hendrik Christian Andersen, a Norwegian-American whose artistic ambitions were monumental but whose fans were few. Andersen favoured the bombastic homoerotic style of which Mussolini was so fond. His massive bronze and plaster figures stride manfully across the studio; more interesting, perhaps, is his megalomaniacal plan for a 'world city' (1913). Temporary exhibitions in the upper rooms are rather hit-and-miss.

❤ Museo Nazionale Etrusco di Villa Giulia

Piazzale di Villa Giulia 9 (06 322 6571). Bus 52, 926/tram 2, 19. ***Open*** *8.30am-7.30pm Tue-Sun.* ***Admission*** *€8; €4 reductions. No cards.* ***Map*** *p138 H2.*

Founded in 1889 at the splendid Villa Giulia, this collection charts the development of the

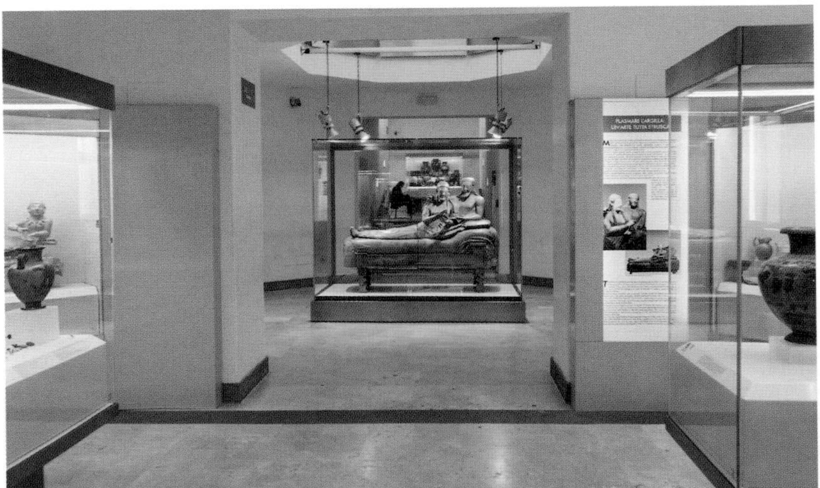

Museo Nazionale Etrusco di Villa Giulia

Capuchins and Cappuccino

The Franciscan coffee connection

In 1520 Franciscan friar Matteo da Bascio decided that his order was no longer sticking faithfully to the penurious lifestyle ordained by its founder St Francis, and broke away to found the Friars Minor. The Franciscans didn't like this criticism, clearly, and hounded the rebels who took refuge with the reclusive Camaldolese monks, adopting their distinctive hood and the habit of never shaving.

When the brown-clad Friars Minor took to the streets again – hirsute, discalced (shoe-less), begging bowls in hand and hoods drawn up over their penitent heads – it was the hoods (*cappucci*) that earned them their popular moniker: *cappuccini* – Capuchins.

Fast-forward 400 years to Milan, where Luigi Bezzera had just come up with a marvellous invention: the espresso machine. The initially simple gadget was honed and whittled throughout the early 20th century, and, by the 1950s, had been transformed: the iconic Gaggia machine was born. This high-pressure boiler was fitted with a little spout to let off steam – handy, *baristi* found, for heating water or whipping milk into a creamy micro-foam-filled addition to the basic coffee: but what to name this concoction?

History does not relate which lateral-thinking wit first compared this brown-coloured beverage with a cap of milky froth to the brown-robed monks with long frothy beards whose main Roman church of Santa Maria della Concezione (*see p146* Museo e Cripta dei Cappuccini) is on worldly, jet-setting via Veneto. But the name stuck. In the space of just a few decades, cappuccino has become not only an Italian icon but an international drink, tainted and corrupted by global chains that insist on taking a perfect recipe – good strong coffee and steamed milk – and adding a lot of unnecessary extras.

In Roman bars, the variations are *cappuccino bollente* (with really really hot milk), *chiaro* (with less coffee and more milk), *scuro* (with less milk) and *al vetro* (in a glass rather than a cup). And it's a breakfast thing: anyone drinking cappuccino after 11am or – heaven help us! – after a meal has 'clueless tourist' written all over them.

sophisticated, mysterious Etruscans. The villa was originally constructed in the mid 16th century as a sumptuous summer residence for Pope Julius III; Michelangelo gave his friend Vignola a hand with the design. The rustic façade leads into an elegantly frescoed loggia. Across the courtyard, stairs go down to the nymphaeum.

In the main body of the museum, a number of rooms are dedicated to objects found at the Etruscan necropolis at Cerveteri; the centrepiece is the almost life size terracotta sarcophagus. Dating from the sixth century BC, it shows a married couple as if they are reclining at a dinner party (or indeed their own funerary banquet). The Etruscan fondness for eating and drinking is apparent from the vast number of bronze cooking utensils, as well as ceramic cups and amphorae (often decorated with scenes from imported Greek myths). The Room of the Seven Hills (a frescoed frieze names them) contains the Castellani collection of extraordinarily delicate jewellery from the eighth century BC right up to the 19th century. Next door is the Room of Venus, with pieces unearthed at the fifth-century BC temples of Pyrgi. The Etruscans went well prepared to their graves, and the majority of the collection comes from excavations of tombs: hundreds of vases, pieces of furniture and models of buildings made to accompany the dead. Detailed notes in English explain the excavation sites and provide information on how gold, bronze and clay were worked in times gone by. The last room before one exits contains one of the museum's absolute masterpieces, the delicate terracotta sixth century BC *Apollo of Veio*. In the gardens there is a reconstruction of an Etruscan temple, and a pleasant café which is sadly only open sporadically.

Museo Pietro Canonica

Viale Pietro Canonica 2 (060608, www.museocanonica.it). Bus 360, 490, 495/tram 3, 19. ***Open*** *Oct-May 10am-4pm Tue-Sun, June-Sept 1-7pm Tue-Sun.* ***Admission*** *free.* ***Map*** *p138 K3.*

In the Villa Borghese, next to the replica of Shakespeare's Globe Theatre (the site of summer productions both Shakespearean and not), is the Museo Pietro Canonica. The faux fortress was once the studio of the late 19th/early 20th century Torinese sculptor, Pietro Canonica. Spookily unaltered since his death in 1959, it contains 19th-century paintings and furniture, Flemish tapestries and the artist's own work, including plaster casts of some of Canonica's grandest and fabulously eclectic projects: Simon Bolivar stares down Faisal I of Iraq, while Edward VII mingles with Attaturk.

VIA VENETO & THE QUARTIERE LUDOVISI

Via Vittorio Veneto (VEH-ne-to) struggles to live up to its *dolce vita* glory days, when Fellini made it Rome's most glamorous hangout. Modern-day Taylors and Burtons, when they're in town, do their hell-raising elsewhere, but this elegant tree-lined slalom curve still manages to rake in the euros, mainly thanks to its vast luxury hotels groaning under the weight of their own chandeliers, and its cripplingly expensive, glass-enclosed pavement cafés, aimed entirely at expense-account travellers and unwitting tourists.

The area either side of via Veneto is known as the **Quartiere Ludovisi**, after the 17th-century Villa Ludovisi, the palace and gardens of which stood here until the 1870s. Following the unification of Italy, the Ludovisi family, like other aristocratic landowners of the day, sold off their property to building speculators; what had once been a slope of verdant tranquillity was swiftly gobbled up by pompous Piedmontese *palazzi* (nearby Villa Borghese only narrowly escaped the same fate).

Prince Boncompagni-Ludovisi put the proceeds of the sale of his glorious estate towards building a huge palace on part of his former grounds. Crippled by running costs and the capital gains bill on the sale of his land, he was forced to sell his new abode to Margherita, widow of King Umberto I, who was to give her name to the classic pizza as well as to this monument to the prince's lack of financial acumen. Halfway along via Veneto, at number 121, **Villa Margherita** is now part of the massively barricaded US embassy.

As the new *palazzi* sprang up, the area began to acquire the reputation for luxury that it retained throughout the mid 20th century. Its fame in the 1950s was due mostly to the enormous American presence at Cinecittà (*see p250*). Fellini's 1960 film *La Dolce Vita*, starring Marcello Mastroianni, consecrated the scene and coined the term 'paparazzo', the surname of a character in the film modelled on legendary photographer Tazio Secchiaroli who made his name snapping away in this glam neighbourhood.

The lower reaches of via Veneto are home to the eerie **Museo e Cripta dei Cappuccini** and to the **Fontana delle Api** (Bee Fountain) by Bernini.

Pope-spotting

Keep your eyes peeled for these papal emblems

Noble, pope-producing families liked to make their presence felt by stamping their family crests on monuments around the city.

• Eagles and dragons, emblems of the Borghese family (Paul V, 1605-21), are the silent sentinels of **Villa Borghese**.

• The dragon of the Boncompagni family (Gregory XIII, 1572-85) can be spied on the façade of **Palazzo Margherita**, now the US embassy. The family later sold the building to Italy's royal Savoia family, whose crest can also be seen on the building's exterior, along with that of the US armouries.

• The bees of Bernini's patron Maffeo Barberini (Urban VIII, 1623-44) decorate the sculptor's **Fontana delle Api** at the lower end of via Veneto. The original inscription read that the pope built it 'in the XXII year of his papacy', though it was in fact completed two months before the date inscribed. A stone-cutter was hastily dispatched to remove an 'I', an action which was judged a curse on the pope... who duly popped his clogs eight days before reaching his 22nd year.

• Michelangelo placed the emblem of the Medici family (Pius IV, 1599-1565) – balls on a shield – on the façade of the **Porta Pia**. The emblem is variously thought to represent pawnbrokers' coins, a dented (but unyielding) shield or, most likely considering the family's origins as apothecaries, medicinal pills.

Detail from Fontana delle Api

Sights & museums

Museo e Cripta dei Cappuccini

Via Veneto 27 (06 4201 4995, www.cappucciniviaveneto.it). Metro Barberini, bus 52, 53, 61, 63, 80, 83, 1160. ***Open*** *Church 7am-noon, 3pm-7pm daily. Museum & crypt 9am-7pm daily.* ***Admission*** *Church free. Museum & crypt €8.50; €5 reductions.* ***Map*** *p138 L6.*

The spooky Capuchin crypt that unsuspecting tourists once happened across has become a well-packaged tourist attraction – sad, but inevitable. Fortunately, the monks have done the transformation with some taste. Visitors are channelled through a series of rooms full of artefacts (a knotted whip for self-flagellation, anyone?) and minor artworks celebrating the order, its saints and missions. Here, too, is the early 17th century painting of *St Francis in Meditation*, which the monks are still, bravely, defending as a work by Caravaggio, though this is almost certainly wishful thinking. The real draw comes at the end, in the crypt, which holds Rome's most macabre sight: the skeletons of thousands of monks, meticulously dismantled and arranged in swirls, sunbursts and curlicues through four subterranean chapels. Delicate ribs hang from the ceiling in the form of chandeliers, and inverted pelvic bones make the shape of hourglasses – a reminder (as a notice states) that 'you will be what we now are'.

The Baroque church upstairs – officially the church of Santa Maria dell'Immacolata Concezione, but known to all as *i Cappuccini* (the Capuchins) after the long-bearded, brown-clad Franciscan sub-order to which it belongs – has a *St Michael* (1635) by Guido Reni (first chapel on the right), a major hit with English Grand Tourists, and a fine *St Paul's Sight Being Restored* (1631) by Pietro da Cortona (first chapel on the left). *See also p145* Capuchins and Cappuccino.

PIAZZA SALLUSTIO & PORTA PIA

East of Villa Borghese, you'll find street after street of imposing, late 19th-century *palazzi* that cover what was once ancient Rome's greatest garden: the **Horti Sallustiani**. The garden was built on land that passed from Julius Caesar to the historian and politician Gaius Crispus Sallustius around 40 BC. Ruins are still visible in the hexagonal **piazza Sallustio**, but it's not what it once was and you will need a good imagination to get an idea of the lost grandeur by peering at the masonry in the hole in the middle of the piazza.

A couple of streets north-east is **Porta Pia**, its city-facing façade designed by Michelangelo for the Medici Pope Pius IV in 1561. It was by this monumental entrance gate that a hole was blown on 20 September 1871, allowing unification troops to march along what is now via XX Settembre and evict the pope from his last stronghold in the Quirinal palace. Next to the gate is the **British Embassy** (via XX Settembre 80). Completed in 1971, the travertine-clad structure designed by architect Sir Basil Spence replaced a 19th-century villa demolished after a bomb explosion in 1946. It has a Henry Moore sculpture in its decorative pool, which can be viewed from the street.

Restaurants

Marzapane €€€

Via Velletri 39 (06 6478 1692, www.marzapaneroma.com). Bus 38, 63, 92, 360, 490, 495. ***Open*** *8-11pm Tue, Wed, Sat; 1-3pm Thur, Fri, Sun. Closed 3wks Aug.* ***Map*** *p138 N4* ① *International*

Young Spanish chef Alba Esteve Ruiz cut her teeth at the famed *El Celler de Can Roca* (twice voted the world's best restaurant) before opening this swish, bistro-style location. The food is doubtlessly aiming for Michelin-star recognition with a modern, creative take on Italian and Mediterranean classics. While the various tasting menus on offer are great value for this level of dining, the opposite must be said for the wine list where prices are a little over-hiked.

Osteria dell'Arco €€

Via G Pagliari 11 (06 854 8438, www.osteriadellarco.net).Bus 38, 60, 62, 80, 90, 490, 495. ***Open*** *1-3pm, 8-11pm Mon-Fri; 8-11pm Sat. Closed lunchtime in Aug.* ***Map*** *p138 N4* ② *Osteria*

The lively neighbourhood just outside Porta Pia is on the up and up, with a sprinkling of new places to eat. One of the best is this wine-oriented *osteria*, all brick vaulted ceiling and bottle-lined walls, which offers creative *trattoria* cooking at competitive prices. A frequently changing menu might have ravioli with broccoli and anchovies, while desserts are mostly play-safe standards such as *crema catalana*. Vegetarians will find a better-than-average selection here, and the worthwhile wine list includes several by-the-glass options.

Pinsere €

Via Flavia 98 (06 4202 0924, www.pinsaromana.info/pinsere-roma). Bus 38, 60, 62, 90, 492, 910. ***Open*** *9am-8pm Mon-Fri. Closed 2wks Aug.* ***Map*** *p138 N5* ③ *Pizzeria*

Named after *la pinsa*, an ancient Roman forerunner of pizza, Pinsere sells its oval flatbreads individually with generous, great-quality toppings which range from the classic margherita to more unique seasonal creations such as prosciutto with fresh figs. It's a tiny place with a handful of seats but with prices hovering around the €4-€5 mark for a whole *pinsa* it's a great value and satisfying lunch spot.

Vatican & Prati

It goes without saying that no visit to Rome is complete without a trip to the Vatican City – the world's smallest state – home to St Peter's and the Vatican Museums. The area where the Vatican now stands was once a marsh, stretching from the Gianicolo to modern-day Monte Mario. Today huge crowds of worshippers pack St Peter's square when the pope is in Rome. Its area of half a square kilometre (one fifth of a square mile) also contains one of the world's finest collections of art and antiquities, including the largest array of pagan and non-Christian works.

The bourgeois district of Prati (meaning meadows, which these were until the 19th century) offers a pleasing antidote to all that history and culture with its excellent shopping and bustling streets.

❤ Don't miss

1 Cappella Sistina, Musei Vaticani *p154*
The private chapel of the popes, and the place of papal elections still today.

2 Stanze di Raffaello, Musei Vaticani *p156*
Painted by Raphael for Pope Julius II and his successor Leo X, these gloriously frescoed rooms were once the popes' private apartments.

3 Michelangelo's *Pietà*, in St Peter's *p159*
The first major piece of Michelangelo's career, completed when he was 24.

4 A glimpse of the pope *p158*
On a Wednesday morning or on a Sunday at noon if the Pope is in town, you too can be blessed by him (along with a few other people).

In the know
Getting around

The closest metro station to the Vatican is Ottaviano (line A); useful buses include 64, 40 and 23.

Cappella Sistina

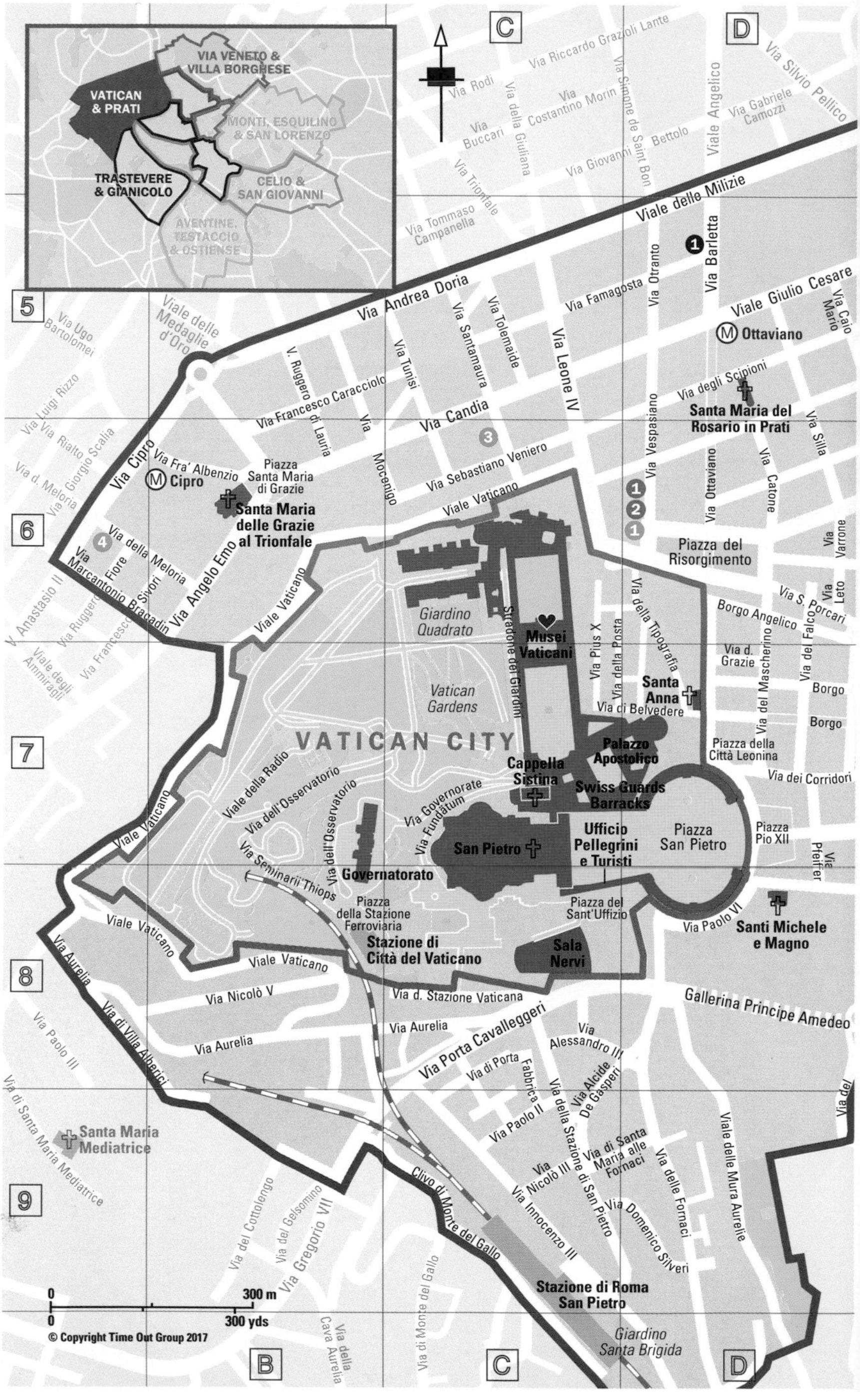
VATICAN & PRATI
VIA VENETO & VILLA BORGHESE
MONTI, ESQUILINO & SAN LORENZO
TRASTEVERE & GIANICOLO
CELIO & SAN GIOVANNI
AVENTINE, TESTACCIO & OSTIENSE
C
D
5
6
7
8
9
B
Viale delle Milizie
Via Andrea Doria
Viale Giulio Cesare
Ottaviano
Via Barletta
Via Otranto
Via Famagosta
Via Leone IV
Via Tolemaide
Via Santamaura
Via Tunisi
Via Candia
Via Sebastiano Veniero
Viale Vaticano
Via Vespasiano
Via degli Scipioni
Santa Maria del Rosario in Prati
Via Ottaviano
Via Catone
Via Silla
Via Cipro
Cipro
Via Fra' Albenzio
Piazza Santa Maria di Grazie
Santa Maria delle Grazie al Trionfale
Via della Meloria
Via Angelo Emo
Via Francesco Caracciolo
V. Ruggero di Lauria
Via Mocenigo
Viale delle Medaglie d'Oro
Via Trionfale
Via Tommaso Campanella
Via Rodi
Via Buccari
Via della Giuliana
Via Costantino Morin
Via Riccardo Grazioli Lante
Via Simone de Saint Bon
Via Giovanni Bettolo
Viale Angelico
Via Gabriele Camozzi
Via Silvio Pellico
Via Caio Mario
Piazza del Risorgimento
Giardino Quadrato
Stradone dei Giardini
Musei Vaticani
Via Pius X
Via della Posta
Via della Tipografia
Santa Anna
Via di Belvedere
Vatican Gardens
VATICAN CITY
Palazzo Apostolico
Cappella Sistina
Swiss Guards Barracks
Ufficio Pellegrini e Turisti
Piazza San Pietro
San Pietro
Governatorato
Via Governorate
Via Fundatum
Viale della Radio
Via dell'Osservatorio
Via Seminarii Thiops
Piazza della Stazione Ferroviaria
Stazione di Città del Vaticano
Piazza del Sant'Uffizio
Sala Nervi
Via Paolo VI
Santi Michele e Magno
Piazza Pio XII
Via Pfeiffer
Via dei Corridori
Piazza della Città Leonina
Borgo Angelico
Via d. Grazie
Via del Mascherino
Via del Falco
Borgo
Via S. Porcari
Via Leto
Via Varrone
Viale Vaticano
Via Aurelia
Via Nicolò V
Via d. Stazione Vaticana
Gallerina Principe Amedeo
Via Porta Cavalleggeri
Via Alessandro III
Via di Porta Fabbrica
Via Paolo II
Via Alcide De Gasperi
Via della Stazione di San Pietro
Via di Santa Maria alle Fornaci
Via Nicolò III
Via Innocenzo III
Via delle Fornaci
Via Domenico Silveri
Viale delle Mura Aurelie
Via di Villa Alberici
Via Paolo III
Via di Santa Maria Mediatrice
Santa Maria Mediatrice
Clivo di Monte del Gallo
Via del Cottolengo
Via del Gelsomino
Via Gregorio VII
Via di Monte del Gallo
Via della Cava Aurelia
Stazione di Roma San Pietro
Giardino Santa Brigida
Via Ugo Bartolomei
Via Luigi Rizzo
Via Rialto
Via Giorgio Scalia
Via d. Meloria
Via Marcantonio Bragadin
Via Fiore
Via Sivori
Via Ruggero
Via Francesco
V. Anastasio II
Viale degli Ammiragli
0
300 m
300 yds

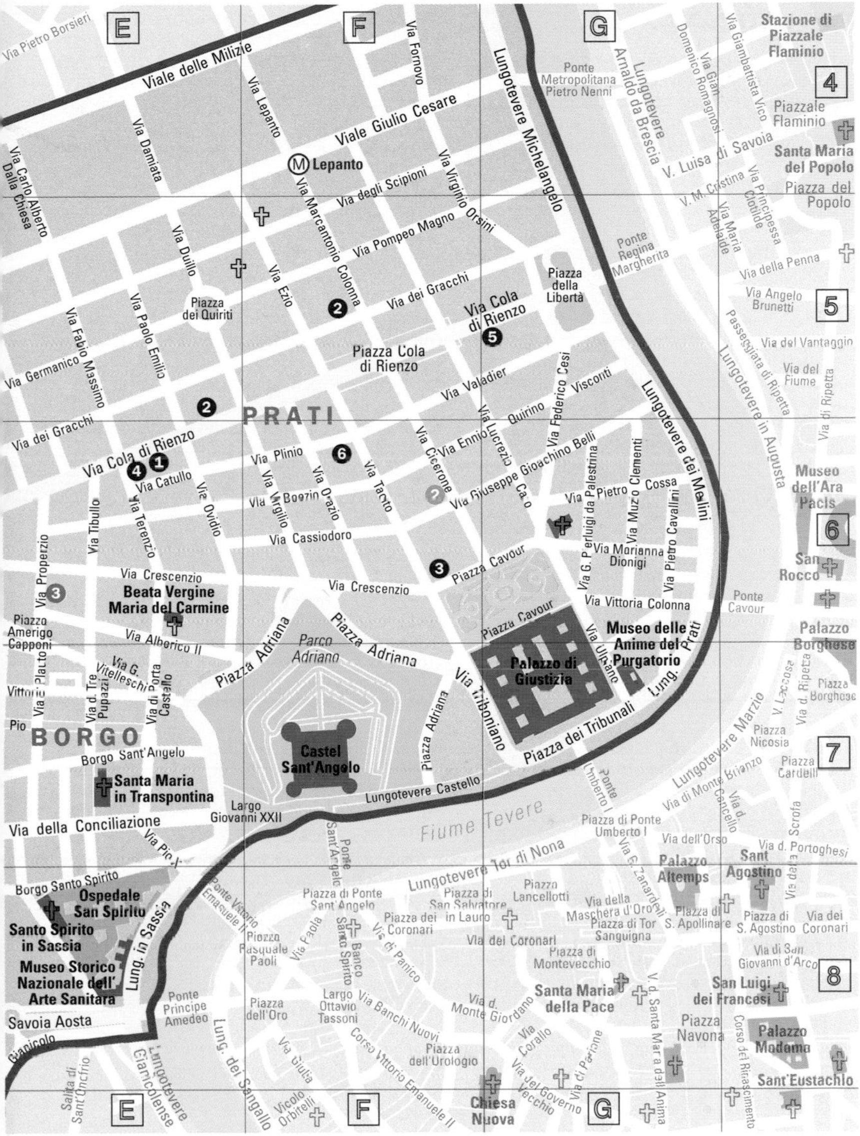

VATICAN & PRATI

Restaurants

1. 200 Gradi
2. L'Arcangelo
3. Osteria delle Commari
4. Pizzarium

Cafés, bars & pubs

1. Be.Re
2. Pergamino Caffè
3. Il Sorpasso

Bakeries, pasticcerie & gelaterie

1. Dolce Maniera
2. Gelateria dei Gracchi

Shops & services

1. Castroni
2. Coin Excelsior
3. Costantini
4. Franchi
5. Iron G
6. El Spa

THE VATICAN

Once the *Ager* or *Campus vaticanus* was marshland lying between the Monti Vaticani and the Tiber, across the river from the city centre and known mainly for its poor-quality wine. Then, in the first century AD, mad, bad Emperor Caligula decided it would be a good spot for a circus and a practice-ground for the most glamorous of sports, chariot-racing.

Nero completed Caligula's circus in AD 54 and built a bridge, the Pons Neronianus, to connect it with the centre. In the summer of AD 64, a fire destroyed half of the city. When people starting muttering that Nero was the arsonist, he in turn blamed the Christians – and the persecution of this pesky new cult began in earnest. Nero's circus was the main venue for Christian-baiting: legend says they were covered in tar and burned alive here. Top apostle Peter is traditionally believed to have been crucified in the circus then buried close by on the spot where, 250 years later, in AD 326, Constantine built the first church of St Peter.

Not all of the following 264 popes resided here – they began in the Lateran (*see p206* San Giovanni in Laterano), in fact, before history drove them to many other places, including Viterbo (*see p234*), Anagni (south of Rome) and Avignon, France – but throughout the Christian era, pilgrims have continued to flock to the tomb of the founder of the Roman Church.

All around, the **Borgo** area grew up to service the burgeoning Dark Age tourist industry. Pope Leo IV (847-55) enclosed the Borgo with the 12-metre-high (40-foot) Leonine Wall, following a series of Saracen and Lombard raids. Pope Nicholas III (1277-80) extended the walls and provided a papal escape route, linking the Vatican to the impregnable **Castel Sant'Angelo** (*see p161*) by way of a long *passetto* (covered walkway). He never used his getaway, but Clement VII did, in 1527, during fierce fighting with the troops of Emperor Charles V. The nine-month siege and Sack of Rome (*see p284* Sack of Rome) was a watershed: things in the papal stronghold were never the same again. Almost the whole papal army was slaughtered, the city was burned and looted, and the Sistine Chapel was used as stables by the Protestant mercenaries – their graffiti in the Papal Suite (*see p156* Stanze di Raffaello) is still visible. After Paul III got Michelangelo in to build bigger, better walls, the popes withdrew across town to the old Lateran palace, and then to the grand new **Quirinale palace** (*see p82*), where they stayed until the troubles of 1870 forced them back across the Tiber once more.

In 1870, when the troops of newly united Italy breached Rome's walls at Porta Pia, centuries of rule by the occupant of the throne of St Peter were put to an end. Over the years, foreign despots had been either seen off or paid off but in 1870 it all went wrong: the pope lost control of a vast part of central Italy and was ignominiously forced back into the Vatican palace behind the hefty walls. Between 1870 and 1929 the pope pronounced the Italian state to be sacrilegious and national elections to be illegal. Something had to be done, and on 11 February 1929 Pius XII and Mussolini signed the Lateran Pacts, a treaty designed to sort out the status of the Vatican once and for all. The terms of the reconciliation treaty (*La Conciliazione*) awarded the Church a huge cash payment, tax-free status and a constitutional role that led to an important continuing moral influence over future legislation on social issues such as education and divorce. To commemorate the historic agreement, Mussolini decided to demolish a particularly picturesque part of the medieval Borgo, replacing it with a short but 'modern' approach road to St Peter's: **via della Conciliazione**.

The **Vatican City** occupies an area of less than half a square kilometre, making it the smallest state in the world. Despite having fewer than 800 residents, it has its own diplomatic service, postal service, army (the Swiss Guard), heliport, railway station, supermarket, and radio and TV stations. It has observer status at the UN, and issues its own stamps and currency (Vatican euros have a tiny circulation; the Holy See keeps a few collectors happy with occasional issues of coins that increase exponentially in value).

❤ Time well spent

The Vatican walls surround splendid formal gardens, which can be glimpsed from some windows in the Vatican Museums or visited on guided tours (a two-hour walking tour costs €32, €24 reductions; the price includes admission to the Vatican Museums), which must be booked at least one week in advance either at the Vatican tourist office (*see p153*) or through www.biglietteriamusei.vatican.va.

Vatican gardens

Vatican Essentials

It pays to be prepared

Dress code

The Vatican enforces its dress code strictly, both in St Peter's and in the Vatican Museums. Anyone wearing shorts or a short skirt, or with bare shoulders or midriff, will be turned away.

Must-haves

- **Sensible shoes**: these are absolutely essential if you are to attempt the ascent of the dome, as the 320 marble stairs after you emerge from the lift are worn and slippery.
- **Water**: in the Vatican Museums, only the Galleria degli Arazzi and the Sistine Chapel are air-conditioned and people have been known to keel over in the summer months. There are vending machines selling water at the museum entrance (by the lavatories and by the lifts), and there is a drinking fountain to fill up a bottle for free on the large terrace at the top of the entrance escalator.
- **Binoculars**: a good idea for looking at the details of frescoes in the Sistine Chapel, as well as for appreciating the view if you're planning an ascent of the dome.

Remember

- Entrances to St Peter's basilica and to the Vatican Museums are in separate places and involve two lengthy queues, as well as a ten-minute hike around the outside of the Vatican walls to get from one to the other. You can significantly cut your waiting time at the museums by pre-booking a date and time for your visit online (mv.vatican.va; there's a €4-per-ticket surcharge) up to 60 days in advance.
- To minimise the often long security queue to enter St Peter's arrive before 8.30am, or after 5.30pm. Before you join the queue, make sure you're not going to be turned away once you get there because you're unsuitably dressed (no shorts above the knee, very short skirts, or bare midriffs or shoulders) and bear in mind that the doors close at the advertised times, no matter how many people are waiting outside.

Tourist information

The Vatican's tourist information office (06 6988 1662, open 8.30am-6.30pm Mon-Sat), situated on the left of St Peter's square as you face the basilica, dispenses information, organises guided tours, has a bureau de change, offers postal and philatelic services, and sells souvenirs and publications. The number of the Vatican switchboard is 06 6982; the general Vatican website, with information on papal activities, church business and museums and so on is vatican.va; www.vaticanstate.va has information about the Holy See in general.

Piazza San Pietro

Musei Vaticani

Viale del Vaticano (06 6988 3860, mv.vatican.va). Metro Ottaviano or Cipro-Musei Vaticani/bus 23, 32, 34, 49, 81, 492, 913, 990/tram 19. ***Open*** *9am-6pm Mon-Sat; 9am-2pm last Sun of mth. Also open May-Sept 7pm-11pm Fri, pre-booking essential. Closed Catholic hols.* ***Admission*** *€16; €8 reductions. Free last Sun of mth.* ***Map*** *p150 C7.*

One of the world's largest museums is a sometimes overwhelming maze incorporating areas, like the incomparable Sistine Chapel, which were here long before you could buy a ticket. The museum began as a collection of ancient sculpture begun by Pope Julius II in his private summer palace in 1503, and it's been added to ever since. The immense collection represents the accumulated fancies and obsessions of a long line of strong, often contradictory personalities. As well as the celebrated work of Michelangelo and Raphael, the collections include Etruscan grave goods, cut outs by Matisse, a piece of the moon donated by Nixon, and a 120m-long (390ft) gallery painted with the most accurate maps in the world from the late 16th century.

The following are selected highlights.

Appartamento Borgia
This six-room suite, known as the Borgia Rooms, was adapted for the Borgia Pope Alexander VI (1492-1503) and decorated by Pinturicchio with a series of frescoes on biblical and classical themes.

Biblioteca Vaticana
Founded by Pope Nicholas V in 1450, this is one of the world's most extraordinary libraries, with 100,000 medieval manuscripts and books, and over a million other volumes. It is open to doctoral students and specialists on application to the Admissions office (06 6987 9403, www.vaticanlibrary.va).

Cappella Sistina (Sistine Chapel)
The world's most famous frescoes cover the ceiling and one immense wall of the Sistine Chapel, built for Sixtus IV in 1473-84. For centuries it has been used for papal elections. In the 1980s and '90s, the 930sq m (10,000sq ft) of *Creation* – on the ceiling – and the *Last Judgement* – on the wall behind the altar – were subjected to the most controversial restoration job of all time. The result is very blue.

In 1508 Michelangelo was commissioned to paint a simple decoration on the ceiling of the Sistine Chapel. Julius II may have been egged on to employ a sculptor with no experience in fresco by his architect Bramante, who was jealous of the pope's admiration for Michelangelo and desperately wanted to see him fail. Michelangelo responded by offering to do far more than mere decoration, and embarked upon his massive venture alone. He spent the next four and a half years standing (only Charlton Heston lay down)

Biblioteca Vaticana

on 18m-high (60ft) scaffolding with paint and plaster dripping into his eyes. Despite a fairly handsome payment (in four years he earned as much as a regular artist could expect to earn in 15), he complained to his brother in 1511, 'I could well say that I go naked and barefoot.'

The ceiling work was completed in 1512, just seven months before the death of Julius, and is exemplary of the confident pursuit of beauty of the High Renaissance. Beginning at the *Last Judgement* end, scenes depict the *Separation of Light from Darkness*, the *Creation of Sun, Moon and Planets*, the *Separation of Land and Sea* and the *Creation of Fishes and Birds*; the *Creation of Adam*, the *Creation of Eve*, the *Temptation and Expulsion from Paradise*; the *Sacrifice of Noah* (which should have appeared after the *Flood*, but for lack of space), the *Flood* and the *Drunkenness of Noah*. Michelangelo painted these scenes in reverse order, beginning with Noah's drunkenness. They are framed by monumental figures of Old Testament prophets and classical sibyls foretelling the birth of Christ.

Ceiling of the Cappella Sistina (Michelangelo, 1508-1512)

Twenty-three years later, aged 60, Michelangelo was dragged back by Paul III in 1535. Between the completion of the ceiling and the beginning of the wall, Rome had suffered. From 1517, the Protestant Reformation threatened the power of the popes, and the sack of the city in 1527 was seen by Michelangelo as the wrath of God descending on the corrupt city. The *Last Judgement* dramatically reflects this gloomy and pessimistic atmosphere. Hidden among the larger-than-life figures that stare, leer and cry out from their brilliant ultramarine background, Michelangelo painted his own frowning, miserable face on the wrinkled human skin held by St Bartholomew, below and to the right of the powerful figure of Christ the Judge.

Before Michelangelo set foot in the chapel, the stars of the 1480s had created the paintings along the walls. On the left-hand wall (as you look at the *Last Judgement*) are: the *Journey of Moses* by Perugino; *Events from the Life of Moses* by Botticelli; *Crossing the Red Sea* and *Moses Receives the Tablets of the Law* by Cosimo Rosselli; the *Testament of Moses* by Luca Signorelli; and the *Dispute over Moses' Body* by Matteo da Lecce. On the right-hand wall are the *Baptism of Christ* by Perugino; the *Temptations of Christ* by Botticelli; the *Calling of the Apostles* by Ghirlandaio; *Handing over the Keys* by Perugino; the *Sermon on the Mount* and the *Last Supper* by Cosimo Rosselli; and the *Resurrection* by Hendrik van den Broeck. The portraits are by the same masters.

Galleria Chiaramonte
Founded by Pius VII in the early 19th century and laid out by the sculptor Canova, this is an eclectic collection of Roman statues, reliefs and busts. Don't miss the replica of a Greek statue by Polyeuctos of stuttering orator Demosthenes or the copy of a *Resting Satyr* by the Greek sculptor Praxiteles.

Gallerie dei Candelabri & degli Arazzi
The long gallery studded with candelabra contains Roman marble statues, while the next gallery is home to ten huge tapestries (*arazzi*), woven by Flemish master Pieter van Aelst.

Galleria delle Carte Geografiche
Pope Gregory XIII (who was responsible for the introduction of the Gregorian calendar) had a craze for astronomy, and built this

❤ Musei Vaticani *continued*

120m-long (394ft) gallery, with its Tower of the Winds observation point. Ignazio Danti of Perugia drew the maps, which were then frescoed (1580-83), and show each Italian region, city and island with extraordinary precision.

Museo Egiziano
Founded by Gregory XVI in 1839, in rooms that are partly decorated in Egyptian style, this is a representative selection of ancient Egyptian art from 3000 BC to 600 BC. It includes statues of a baboon god, painted mummy cases and a marble statue of Antinous, Emperor Hadrian's lover, who drowned in Egypt and was declared divine by the emperor. There are a couple of mummies too.

Museo Etrusco
Founded in 1837 by Gregory XVI, this collection contains Greek and Roman art as well as Etruscan masterpieces, including the contents of the Regolini-Galassi Tomb (c650 BC), the Greek-inspired fourth-century BC *Mars*, and the fifth-century BC *Young Man and Small Slave*. This section is usually only open in the mornings.

Museo Pio-Clementino
In the late 18th century Pope Clement XIV and his successor Pius VI began the world's largest collection of classical statues; it now fills 16 rooms. Don't miss the first-century BC *Belvedere Torso* by Apollonius of Athens; the *Apollo Sauroctonos*, a Roman copy of the bronze *Lizard Killer* by Praxiteles; and, in the octagonal Belvedere Courtyard, the exquisite *Belvedere Apollo* and *Laocoön*, the latter being throttled by the sea serpents Athena had sent as punishment for warning the Trojans to beware of the wooden horse.

Pinacoteca
Founded by Pius VI in the late 18th century, the Pinacoteca (picture gallery) includes many of the pictures that the Vatican hierarchy managed to recover from Napoleon after their forced sojourn in France in the early 19th century. The collection ranges from early paintings of the Byzantine School and Italian primitives to 18th-century Dutch and French old masters, and includes Giotto's *Stefaneschi Triptych*; a *Pietà* by Lucas Cranach the Elder; several delicate *Madonnas* by Fra Filippo Lippi, Fra Angelico, Raphael and Titian; Raphael's very last work, the *Transfiguration*; Caravaggio's *Entombment*; and a chiaroscuro *St Jerome* by Leonardo da Vinci. The Pinacoteca usually closes at 3.30pm.

Stanze di Raffaello & Cappella di Niccolò V
The Raphael Rooms were part of Nicholas V's palace, and were originally decorated by Piero della Francesca. Julius II then let Perugino and other Renaissance masters

Museo Egiziano

loose on them. He later discovered Raphael, and gave the 26-year-old carte blanche to redesign four rooms of the Papal Suite. The order of the visit changes from time to time; if possible, try to see the rooms in the order in which they were painted. The Study (Stanza della Segnatura) was the first one Raphael tackled (1508-11), and features philosophical and spiritual themes – the triumph of Truth, Good and Beauty. Best known is the star-packed *School of Athens* fresco, with contemporary artists as classical figures: Plato is Leonardo; glum Heraclitus with the big knees on the steps at the front is Michelangelo; Euclid is Bramante (note the letters RUSM, Raphael's signature, on his gold collar); and Raphael himself is on the far right-hand side just behind a man in white, believed to be his pupil Sodoma. Raphael next turned his hand to the Room of Heliodorus (Stanza di Eliodoro) (1512-14), frescoed with *The Expulsion of Heliodorus*. The portrayal of God saving the temple in Jerusalem from the thieving Heliodorus was intended to highlight the divine protection that was enjoyed by Julius himself (the pope's portrait is shown twice: both as the priest of the temple in the centre wearing blue and gold, and as the red-capped figure carried on a bier on the left).

The Dining Room (Stanza dell'Incendio, 1514-17), painted after Julius's death, is dedicated to his successor, Leo X (the most obese of the popes, he died from gout aged 38), and shows other Pope Leos with the face of Leo X. The room is named after a fire in the Borgo, which Leo IV apparently stopped with the sign of the cross. (Note that the first church of St Peter's is in the background.)

The Reception Room (Sala di Constantino, 1517-24) was completed by Giulio Romano after Raphael's death in 1520, but was originally based on Raphael's sketches of the Church's triumph over paganism, and tells the legend of Constantine's miraculous conversion.

The long Loggia di Raffaello (only open by special appointment) has a beautiful view over Rome. Started by Bramante in 1513, and finished by Raphael and his assistants, it features 52 small paintings on biblical themes, and leads into the Sala dei Chiaroscuri (Gregory XIII obliterated Raphael's frescoes here, but the magnificent ceiling remains). The adjacent Cappella di Niccolò V (Chapel of Nicholas V, only open by special appointment) has outstanding frescoes of scenes from the lives of saints Lawrence and Stephen by Fra Angelico (1448-50).

Visiting information

Note that pre-booking through the Vatican website is always advised and reduces what can be a lengthy wait to get into the museums. You can book for the date and time of your choice, for up to ten people at a time. Bookings can be made up to 60 days in advance. There is a €4 surcharge for each ticket booked. Midweek is always less busy than Saturdays and Mondays. In high summer the Friday evening opening is a good option to minimise crowds.

It's a brisk ten-minute walk around the Vatican walls from St Peter's to the Vatican Museums. If you're planning to purchase tickets on the day, note that the ticket office shuts two hours before closing time.

One-way routes cater for anything from a dash to the Sistine Chapel to a five-hour plod around the lot. There are also a number of itineraries for wheelchair users, with facilities en route. Wheelchairs can be borrowed at the museum: book them by phone or email (1196921703, accoglienza.musei@scv.va), though booking is not essential and they can almost always be picked up on spec.

Stanze di Raffaello

Papal audiences

The pope plays an active role in Rome's religious life. When he is in town, crowds gather in St Peter's square at noon on Sunday to hear him address pilgrims from the window of his study in the Apostolic Palace. This is by far the easiest way to spot the pope during your visit, and the scale of the piazza means that even if you arrive a few minutes before noon you'll find a spot with a view of the distant pope in his window. On Wednesday mornings he holds a general audience in St Peter's square, if the weather is fine; if the weather isn't good, it's in the modern Sala Nervi audience hall.

Outside, you can join the back of the crowd and watch the goings-on on a big screen. If you want to be close up to the pope, or attend an audience in the **Sala Nervi**, apply well in advance to the Prefettura della Casa Pontificia for tickets (06 6988 3114, open 9am-1.30pm Mon-Sat), which are free and can be picked up the afternoon before the audience. Entry to the Sala Nervi is through the gate, just to the left of the basilica. Even with a ticket you will need to arrive well in advance to secure a decent spot. The audience lasts about an hour and a half.

For a private audience, your local bishop will have to make a written request for you. This may take up to a year to be granted.

San Pietro

Sights & museums

❤ San Pietro

Piazza San Pietro (06 6988 1662). Metro Ottaviano/bus 23, 34, 40Exp, 62, 64, 280. ***No cards. Map*** *p150 C7.*
Basilica ***Open*** *Apr-Sept 7am-7pm daily. Oct-Mar 7am-6.30pm daily.* ***Admission*** *free.*
Dome ***Open*** *Apr-Sept 8am-6pm daily. Oct-Mar 8am-5pm daily.* ***Admission*** *€6 (€8 with lift). Note: there are 320 steps to climb after the lift has taken you to the first level.*
Grottoes ***Open*** *Apr-Sept 8am-6pm daily. Oct-Mar 8am-5pm daily.* ***Admission*** *free.*
Necropolis *Apply at the Ufficio degli Scavi (06 6988 5318, scavi@fsp.va).* ***Open*** *Guided tours 9am-5pm Mon-Sat.* ***Admission*** *€13. Note: English-language tours must be booked at least 25 days in advance. Under-12s are not admitted; 12- to 15-year-olds must be accompanied by an adult.*
Treasury museum ***Open*** *Apr-Sept 9am-6.15pm daily. Oct-Mar 9am-5.15pm daily.* ***Admission*** *€7.*

After 120 years as a building site, the current St Peter's was consecrated on 18 November 1626 by Urban VIII – exactly 1,300 years after the consecration of the first basilica on the site.

The earlier building was a five-aisled classical basilica, fronted by a large courtyard and four porticoes. Enlarged and enriched, it became the finest church in Christendom. By the mid 15th century, however, its south wall was collapsing. Pope Nicholas V had 2,500 wagonloads of masonry from the Colosseum carted across the Tiber, just for running repairs. No one wanted to take responsibility for demolishing Christianity's most sacred church. It took the arrogance of Pope Julius II and his pet architect Donato Bramante to get things moving. In 1506 some 2,500 workers tore down the 1,000-year-old basilica, and Julius laid the foundation stone for its replacement.

Following Bramante's death in 1514, Raphael took over the work and scrapped his predecessor's design for a basilica with a Greek-cross plan, opting for an elongated Latin cross. In 1547 Michelangelo took command and reverted to a Greek cross. He died in 1564, aged 87, but not before coming up with a plan for a massive dome and supporting drum. This was completed in 1590, the largest brick dome ever constructed, and still the tallest point of any building in Rome. In 1607 Carlo Maderno won the consent of Pope Paul V to demolish the remaining fragments of the old basilica and put up a new façade, crowned by enormous statues of Christ and the apostles.

Dome of San Pietro

After Maderno's death Bernini took over and, despite nearly destroying both the façade and his reputation by erecting towers on either end (one of which fell down), he became the hero of the hour with his sumptuous *baldacchino* and elliptical piazza. This latter was built between 1656 and 1667, its colonnaded arms reaching out towards the Catholic world in a symbolic embrace. The oval measures 340m by 240m (1,115ft by 787ft), and is punctuated by the central Egyptian obelisk (erected by a workforce of 800 in 1586) and two symmetrical fountains by Maderno and Bernini. The 284-column, 88-pillar colonnade is topped by 140 statues of saints.

In the portico (1612), opposite the main portal, is a mosaic by Giotto (c1298) from the original basilica. Five doors lead into the basilica: the central ones come from the earlier church, while the others are all 20th-century. The last door on the right is opened only in Holy Years by the pope himself (and, as seen from the inside, is firmly cemented shut).

Inside, the basilica's size is emphasised on the marble floor, where a boastful series of brass lines measure the lengths of other churches around the world that haven't made the grade (second longest is St Paul's, London). But it is Bernini's vast *baldacchino* (1633), hovering over the high altar, that is the real focal point. Cast from bronze purloined from the Pantheon by Bernini's patron, Pope Urban VIII, of the Barberini family, it prompted local wits to quip *'quod non fecerunt barbari, fecerunt Barberini'* ('what the barbarians didn't do, the Barberini did'). An extraordinary piece of Baroque design, it takes its form from a Mesopotamian tradition in which woven silken cloth was draped over a framework to mark a sacred spot. In Bernini's hands it became a hundred feet of gilded bronze. The canopy stands over the high altar officially reserved for the pope; below, two flights of stairs lead beneath the altar to the *confessio*, where a niche contains a ninth-century mosaic of Christ, the only thing from old St Peter's that stayed in the same place when the new church was built. Far below lies the site of what is believed to be St Peter's tomb, discovered in 1951.

Pilgrims head straight for the last pilaster on the right before the main altar, to kiss the big toe of Arnolfo da Cambio's brass statue of St Peter (c1296), worn down by centuries of pious lips, or to say a prayer before the crystal casket containing the mummified remains of much-loved Pope John XXIII, who was beatified in 2002. Tourists, on the other hand, make a beeline for the first chapel on the right, where Michelangelo's first major work, the *Pietà* (1499), is found. He signed his name on the thin sash across the Virgin's chest in response to cynics who claimed that he was too young at 24 to have produced the piece himself. The statue's position behind bullet-proof glass means the signature is only visible with strong binoculars or on postcards. Proceeding around the basilica in an anti-clockwise direction, notice Carlo Fontana's highly flattering monument to the unprepossessing Queen Christina of Sweden, a convert to Catholicism in 1655, to the left of the *Pietà* chapel. The third chapel has a tabernacle and two angels by Bernini, plus St Peter's only remaining painting: a *Trinity* by Pietro da Cortona (the others have been replaced by mosaic copies). In the first chapel beyond the right transept is a tear-jerker of a neo-classical tomb (1792), the last resting place of Pope Clement XIII, by Antonio Canova.

Bernini's Throne of St Peter (1665), flanked by papal tombs, stands at the far end of the nave beyond the high altar, under a stained-glass window. Encased within Bernini's creation is a wood and ivory chair, probably dating from the ninth century but for many years believed to have belonged to Peter himself. To the right of the throne is Bernini's 1644 monument to his patron Urban VIII, who commissioned the bronze portrait (between statues of *Charity* and *Justice*) before his death. On the pillars supporting the main dome are much-venerated relics, including a chip off the True Cross above the statue of St Helena bearing the cross she is said to have brought back from the Holy Land.

Pietà (Michelangelo, 1499)

In the left aisle, beyond the pilaster with St Veronica holding the cloth with which she wiped Christ's face, Bernini's tomb for Pope Alexander VII (another of his patrons) shows the pope seated above a doorway shrouded with a cloth of reddish marble, from beneath which struggles a skeleton clutching an hourglass: a grim reminder of the fleeting nature of life.

Near the portico-end of the left aisle is a group of monuments to the Old Pretender James Edward Stuart (the 18th-century claimant to the throne of England and Scotland, here called King James III), his wife Maria Clementina Sobieski and their sons Charles Edward (Bonnie Prince Charlie) and Henry Benedict. They are buried in the grottoes below.

Beneath the basilica are the **Vatican Grottoes** – Renaissance crypts containing papal tombs. The **Necropolis**, where St Peter is said to be buried, lies under the grottoes. You must pre-book guided tours to the Necropolis, although if you're in Rome without a reservation it's always worth asking at the Ufficio degli Scavi (beyond the Swiss Guard post on the left of St Peter's as you face the basilica) for any spaces.

The small **treasury museum** off the left nave of the basilica contains some stunning liturgical relics. The **dome**, reached via hundreds of stairs (there's a cramped lift as far as the basilica roof), offers fabulous views of the Vatican gardens.

► *For restaurants and cafés surrounding the Vatican, see p161.*

BORGO & PRATI

In the 1930s Mussolini's broad avenue, **via della Conciliazione**, was bulldozed through much of the medieval Borgo. A few of the streets remain, however, and salt-of-the-earth Romans mingle here with off-duty Swiss Guards and immaculately robed priests from the Vatican *Curia* (administration). Before his elevation, Josef Ratzinger lived above souvenir tat in a gloomy Fascist-era building just outside Bernini's colonnade and near the raised, covered *passetto*, the 13th-century escape route to **Castel Sant'Angelo**. In medieval Rome's Anglo-Saxon enclave, to the south of via della Conciliazione, you'll find the **Museo Storico Nazionale dell'Arte Sanitaria**.

After Rome became capital of the unified Italian state in 1871, the meadows (*prati*) around the Renaissance ramparts north of the Borgo were suddenly required for housing for the staff of the new ministries and parliament across the Tiber. The largest of the *piazze* by the Vatican walls was provocatively named after the Risorgimento, the movement that had destroyed the papacy's hold over the whole of central Italy. Broad avenues were laid out and named after anti-papal figures such as 14th-century 'freedom fighter' Cola di Rienzo, and decidedly pre-Christian (ie pagan) leaders such as Octavian and Julius Caesar.

Still a solidly bourgeois district, Prati's main drag, **via Cola di Rienzo**, provides ample opportunities for retail therapy – a good antidote to a surfeit of culture. Endless imposing military barracks line **viale delle Milizie**; quiet, tree-lined streets lead towards the river; and the massive **Palazzo di Giustizia** (known as *il palazzaccio*, 'the big ugly building') is between piazza Cavour and the Tiber. On the riverbank is one of Catholic Rome's truly weird experiences: the **Museo delle Anime del Purgatorio** (*see below*).

Sights & museums

Castel Sant'Angelo

Lungotevere Castello 50 (06 6819 111, castelsantangelo.beniculturali.it). Bus 23, 34, 40Exp, 87, 280, 926, 990. ***Open*** *9am-7.30pm daily.* ***Admission*** *€10; €5.5 reductions. Exhibition price varies.* ***Map*** *p150 F7.*

Begun by Emperor Hadrian in AD 135 as his own mausoleum, Castel Sant'Angelo has variously been a fortress, prison and papal residence. Puccini had Tosca hurl herself to her death from the upper terraces, from which there are excellent views. There is much to see: lavish Renaissance salons, decorated with spectacular frescoes and trompe l'oeil; the glorious chapel in the Cortile d'Onore, designed by Michelangelo; and, halfway up an easily missed staircase, Clement VII's tiny personal bathroom, painted by Giulio Romano. In the summer the *passetto* – linking the castle to the Vatican – is occasionally open (to the halfway point) and worth a visit.

Museo delle Anime del Purgatorio

Lungotevere Prati 12 (06 6880 6517). Bus 30Exp, 70, 81, 87, 130, 186, 280, 492, 913, 926. ***Open*** *Sept-July 7.30-11.30am, 3.30-6.30pm daily. Aug 8-11.30am, 5-7.30pm daily.* ***Map*** *p150 G7.*

This macabre collection, attached to the neo-Gothic church of Sacro Cuore di Gesù in Prati, contains hand- and fingerprints left on the prayer books and clothes of the living by dead loved ones, to request Masses to release their souls from purgatory. Begun just over a century ago, the collection includes a handprint supposedly left by Sister Clara Scholers on the habit of a fellow-nun in

Castel Sant'Angelo

Westphalia in 1696, and scorched bank notes left by a dead soul outside a church where he wanted a Mass said.

Museo Storico dell'Arte Sanitaria

Lungotevere in Sassia 3 (06 689 3051). Bus 23, 40Exp, 62, 280. ***Open*** *Mon, Wed, Fri 10am-noon. Pre-booking required.* ***Admission*** *€7.* ***Map*** *p150 E8.*

This hostel and church was established around 726 by King Ine of Wessex to cater for weary and sick pilgrims who descended from the north. Known as the *burgus saxonum* or *in Sassia*, this district became the nucleus of the world's first purpose-built hospital. The name *in Sassia* persists although British funds for the hostel were cut off with the Norman invasion of England in 1066, after which it passed into papal hands and thence to the Templar knight Guy de Montpellier, who founded the Order of the Holy Spirit (Santo Spirito). A few rooms of the modern hospital of Santo Spirito house a gruesome collection of medical artefacts, dating from ancient times to the 19th century. The two massive 15th-century frescoed wards, the gloriously elegant fruit of a rebuilding programme in Renaissance times, were only recently emptied of their beds to provide space for itinerant exhibitions. If they are open, any opportunity to visit them should be seized. The admission price includes a guided tour.

Restaurants

200 Gradi €

Piazza del Risorgimento 3, Prati (06 3975 4239, www.duecentogradi.it). Metro Ottaviano/bus 23, 32, 49, 81, 492, 590, 990/ tram 19. ***Open*** *11am-3am daily.* ***Map*** *p150 D6* ① *Sandwich shop*

Walk right by the Vatican tourist traps and head to this little sandwich shop for very decent *panini* at very honest prices. With over

60 types of (generously sized) sandwiches to choose from there are also plenty of vegetarian and vegan options. Everything is made to order from the immense counter of fillings so the staff are also happy to make up your own creation. Space is tight so grab your order to take away and sit in the adjacent piazza del Risorgimento.

L'Arcangelo €€€

Via GG Belli 59/61, Prati (06 321 0992, www.larcangelo.com). Bus 30, 34, 70, 81, 87, 280, 913, 926, 990. ***Open*** *1-2.30pm, 8-10.30pm Mon-Fri; 8-11pm Sat. Closed Aug.* ***Map*** *p150 F6* ❷ *Italian/Creative*

L'Arcangelo is a restaurant that divides: for every diner who exits feeling disappointed, you'll find another who rates it among Rome's best gourmet restaurants. Wood panelling, tobacco-coloured walls and a soft jazz soundtrack set the mood. On the plate, you will find a selection of chef Arcangelo Dandini's creative dishes such as squid with peaches or roasted *baccalà* (salt cod) with vanilla: combinations which are, on the whole, successful and always unique, often riffing on Roman culinary traditions. Service is generally cordial but can turn vague when things get busy. Prices are on the high side. The wine list includes some real discoveries from small Italian producers.

Osteria delle Commari €€

Via Santamaura 23, Prati (06 3972 9557, www.osteriadellecommari.it). Metro Ottaviano/bus 23, 70, 492, 913, 990. ***Open*** *noon-11.30pm daily.* ***Map*** *p150 C6* ❸ *Trattoria*

Good, honest food in a convenient location makes Osteria delle Commari a cut above the, mostly, rip-off restaurants nearby. There are some great fried *antipasti* while Roman staples such as carbonara and *saltimbocca* (veal with prosciutto and sage) are cooked with care. Prices are the norm for the area. The wine list has some local gems from Lazio and plenty of by-the-glass options. Open non-stop from noon until late it is a handy address if you find yourself hungry outside of the usual Roman dining hours.

Pizzarium €

Via della Meloria 43, Prati (06 3974 5416, bonci.it/portfolio/pizzarium). Metro Cipro-Musei Vaticani/bus 31, 33, 247, 492. ***Open*** *11am-10pm daily.* ***Map*** *p150 A6* ❹ *Pizzeria*

Rome's revolutionary pizza maker Gabriele Bonci started his astronomic rise to stardom at this unassuming pizza shop and it has consistently remained top of the list of Rome's best *pizza al taglio*. The focus on the perfect dough and only the best, seasonal ingredients along with a creative eye for toppings have deservedly seen the Bonci brand expand across the city. Despite a recent renovation to double the size of the shop, the place is usually heaving so join the throng and eat on the pavement outside. The location near the entrance to the Vatican Museums is ideal for a post-Sistine Chapel carb fix.

Cafés, bars & pubs

Be.Re

Piazza del Risorgimento 7/A, Prati (06 9442 1854, www.facebook.com/BeRe-541249312736140). Metro Ottaviano/bus 23, 32, 49, 81, 492, 590, 990/tram 19. ***Open*** *noon-2am daily.* ***Map*** *p150 D6* ❶ *Pub*

A newcomer on the Prati pub scene, Be.Re brings the craft beer trend to the Vatican area with this modern drinking den which was opened under the expert guidance of beer guru Manuele Colonna (of Trastevere's lauded craft beer pub Ma Che Siete Venuti a Fà). The immense bar serves over 20 different beers and ales on tap, hailing from both Italy and the rest of the world. To accompany your brew there is also the, now ubiquitous, *Trapizzino*, a pizza dough pocket stuffed with Roman stews.

Pergamino Caffè

Piazza del Risorgimento 7, Prati (06 8953 3745, www.facebook.com/PergaminoCaffe). Metro Ottaviano/bus 23, 32, 49, 81, 492, 590, 990/tram 19. ***Open*** *8am-8pm daily.* ***Map*** *p150 D6* ❷ *Coffee shop*

The folk at Pergamino take their coffee very seriously and indeed, they serve little else. As Rome's first 'third wave' coffee shop top-quality selected beans are ground to order and preparations range from traditional espressos to nitro, aeropress and syphon variations: the very friendly (and very well-versed) staff are more than happy to explain and advise if necessary. The laid-back vibe is the antidote to the usual, rushed, swig-it-at-the-counter, Italian coffee experience.

Il Sorpasso

Via Properzio 31, Borgo (06 8902 4554, sorpasso.info). Bus 23, 32, 49, 81, 492, 590, 990/tram 19. ***Open*** *7.30am-1am Mon-Fri, 9am-1am Sat. Closed 3wks Aug.* ***Map*** *p150 E6* ❸ *Café/Bar*

Far enough from the Vatican to escape the crowds (and rub shoulders with some locals), Il Sorpasso is still within an easy stroll of St Peter's. The shabby chic interior of this café-bar creates a cool, relaxed ambience for dining or drinking at any time. Food options range from sandwiches and snacks, including hand-cut prosciutto and cheeseboards, to a full menu at lunch and dinner, while the bar churns out some very passable cocktails. Around 6pm the place gets jammed with young professionals from the nearby offices who swing by for *aperitivo* at the outside tables.

Bakeries, pasticcerie & gelaterie

Dolce Maniera

Via Barletta 27, Prati (06 3751 7518, www.dolcemaniera.it). Metro Ottaviano/bus 23, 32, 70, 81, 492, 590, 990/tram 19. ***Open*** *24hrs daily.* ***Map*** *p150 D5* ❶ *Bakery*

Most young Romans are aware of this 24-hour basement bakery as a popular haunt for night owls picking up warm *cornetti* (croissants) on the way home from the clubs in the early hours. As well as freshly baked bread and pastries, there are also fried snacks, sandwiches and *pizza al taglio*, all at excellent prices. The entrance can be easy to miss but just follow your nose as the enticing smell wafts down the street.

Gelateria dei Gracchi

Via dei Gracchi 272, Prati (06 321 6668, www.gelateriadeigracchi.it). Metro Lepanto/bus 30, 70, 81, 87, 280, 492, 913. ***Open*** *11am-12.30am daily.* ***No cards. Map*** *p150 F5* ❷ *Gelateria*

Wander off the main shopping thoroughfare of via Cola di Rienzo for some of the best gelato in the area. Gracchi combines traditional ethics and know-how with excellent ingredients. The strictly artisanal flavours range from evergreen classics (the pistachio is superb) and fresh, seasonal fruits to more interesting blends such as almond with orange and pear with caramel.

Shops & services

Castroni

Via Cola di Rienzo 196, Prati (06 687 4383, www.castronicoladirienzoshop.it). Metro Ottaviano/bus 23, 32, 49, 81, 492, 982/tram 19. ***Open*** *8am-8pm daily. Closed Sun mid June-mid Sept.* ***Map*** *p150 E6* ❶ *Food & drink*

In business for over 85 years, this wonderful shop roasts its own espresso beans and has lots of Italian regional specialities and imported foodstuffs: it's the place for expats hankering after anything from Chinese noodles to HP Sauce. Online shopping available.

Coin Excelsior

Via Cola di Rienzo 173, Prati (06 3600 4298, www.coinexcelsior.com). Metro Lepanto/bus 30, 70, 81, 87, 280, 492, 913. ***Open*** *10am-10pm daily.* ***Map*** *p150 E5* ❷ *Department store*

The high-class 'excelsior' version of Italian chain Coin, this department store with its gilt escalators and pristine displays looks right at home in the prosperous Prati district. Here you will find top international brands in clothing, shoes, toiletries and homewares and, handily, there is also a small supermarket on the lower level.

Costantini

Piazza Cavour 16, Prati (06 321 3210, enotecacostantinipiero.it). Bus 23, 30, 34, 81, 87, 280, 492, 913, 926, 990. ***Open*** *Shop 4.30-8pm Mon; 9am-1pm, 4.30-8pm Tue-Sat. Wine bar 11am-3pm, 6.30pm-midnight Mon-Fri; 6.30pm-midnight Sat. Closed Aug.* ***Map*** *p150 F6* ❸ *Food & drink*

This cavernous cellar has a seriously comprehensive collection of wines and a huge range of both Italian and international spirits and liqueurs, as well as some gourmet extras such as chocolate, olive oil and pasta. You can order online and have wines sent to your home.

Franchi

Via Cola di Rienzo 200, Prati (06 687 4651, www.franchi.it). Metro Ottaviano/bus 23, 32, 49, 81, 271, 492, 982/tram 19. ***Open*** *8am-9pm daily.* ***Map*** *p150 E6* ❹ *Food & drink*

A dream of a deli, for just about anything you could ever want to eat – cheeses from everywhere, cured meats, and ready-to-eat meat and seafood dishes are freshly prepared.

Iron G

Via Cola di Rienzo 50, Prati (06 321 6798, irongsuperstore.blogspot.it). Bus 30, 70, 81, 130, 186, 224, 280, 590, 913, 926. ***Open*** *10.30am-8pm Mon-Sat; 11am-1.30pm, 2.30-8pm Sun. Closed 1wk Aug.* ***Map*** *p150 G5* ❺ *Fashion*

This warehousey boutique with trashy chandeliers supplies clubwear to the fashion victims of this well-heeled neighbourhood. The hippest labels mix with ethnic and local hand-made accessories.

El Spa

Via Plinio 15, Prati (06 6819 2869, www.elspa.it). Bus 30Exp, 34, 49, 70, 81, 130, 280, 492, 926, 990. ***Open*** *10am-9pm Mon-Thur; 10am-10pm Fri-Sun; noon-9pm Sun.* ***Map*** *p150 F6* ❻ *Spa*

Decorated in warm, Middle Eastern style, this spa specialises in holistic treatments. Try the *mandi lulur*, an ancient Indonesian treatment that leaves you with blissfully silky-soft skin.

Trastevere & Gianicolo

Trastevere is a great treat if you've spent your time diligently observing ancient ruins and admiring statuary on the other, serious side of the river. Although the district's once-boisterous, communal street life and artisan feel has at least partly given way to tourist-oriented wine bars and eateries, Trastevere still feels very Roman.

Across the Tiber (*trans tiberim*), your main tasks include rambling through narrow, cobbled streets and selecting a bar for *aperitivi* and people-watching.

Up above Trastevere, the Gianicolo is central Rome's highest hill and a park with spectacular views over the *centro storico* runs most of its length, making it a great place to get your bearings or take a breather.

❤ Don't miss

1 Orto Botanico *p170*
An oasis nestling behind Palazzo Corsini.

2 Santa Cecilia in Trastevere *p177*
Medieval mosaics and a gloriously tranquil courtyard.

3 Santa Maria in Trastevere *p169*
A grand basilica built upon the legendary site of a miraculous fountain of oil.

4 Festa de' Noantri *p246*
In late July, *Trasteverini* celebrate the 'Festival of We Others': music, food stalls and general carousing.

In the know
Getting around

Trastevere is on the west side of the River Tiber (a short stroll across the pedestrian Ponte Sisto from the campo de' Fiori area), and south of the Vatican. Either work up an appetite climbing the Gianicolo, or take a bus (no.44, 75) up the hill and walk down.

TRASTEVERE & GIANICOLO

Restaurants

1 Alle Fratte di Trastevere
2 Antico Arco
3 Casa Mia
4 Da Enzo al 29
5 Dar Poeta
6 La Gensola
7 Glass Hostaria
8 Le Mani in Pasta
9 I Supplì

Cafés, bars & pubs

1 Bar Gianicolo
2 Bar San Calisto
3 Baylon Café
4 Cioccolata e Vino
5 Enoteca Ferrara
6 Freni e Frizioni

Bakeries, pasticcerie & gelaterie

1 Biscottificio Innocenti
2 Fior di Luna
3 Sora Mirella
4 Valzani

Shops & services

1 L'Albero e la Mano
2 Almost Corner Bookshop
2 Antica Caciara
4 Centro Estetico Malò
5 Elvis Lives
6 Innocenzi
7 Mercato San Cosimato
8 Open Door Bookshop
9 Porta Portese
10 Romastore Profumi
11 Studio Stefania Miscetti
12 Les Vignerons

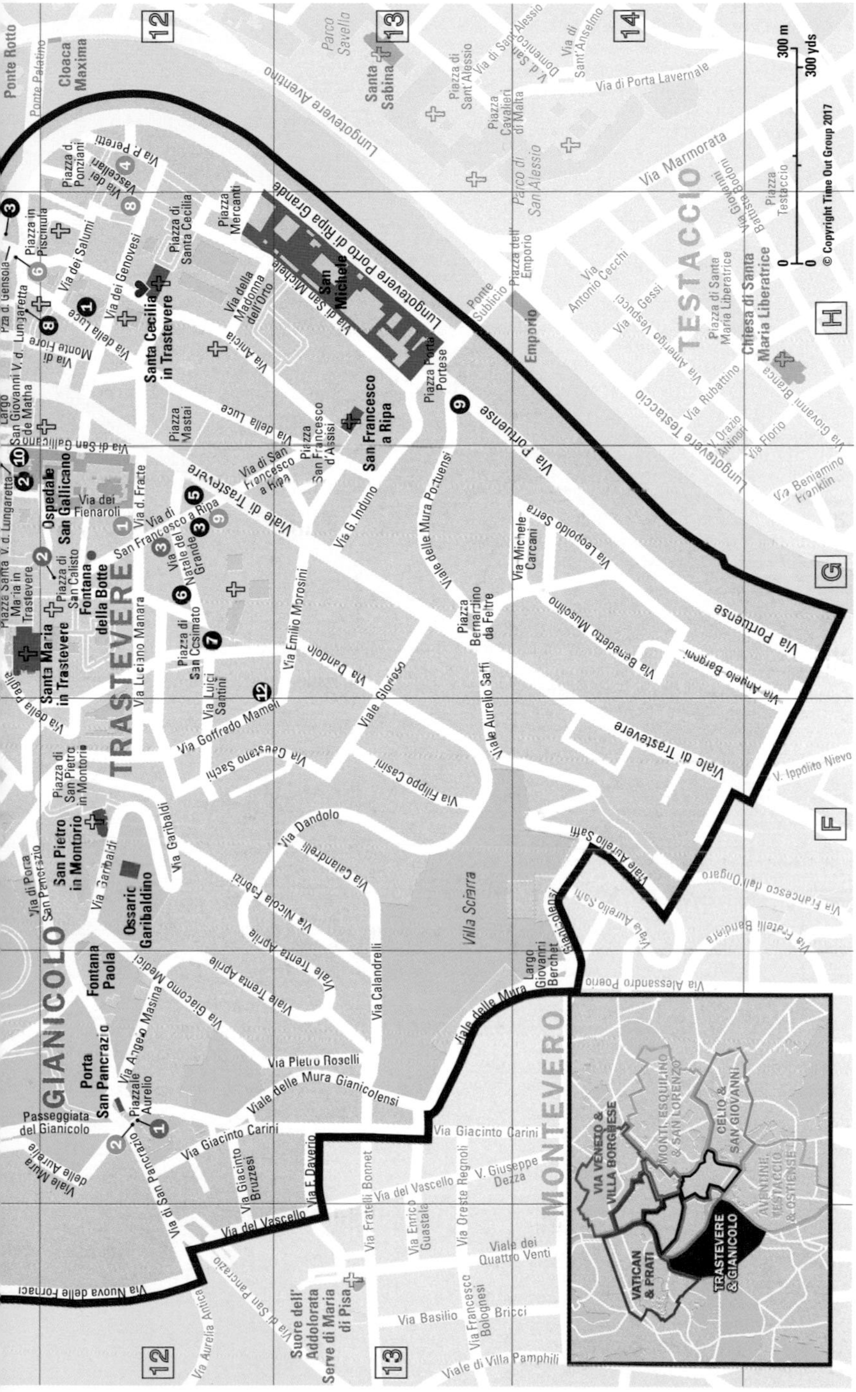

TRASTEVERE
GIANICOLO
MONTEVERO
TESTACCIO
Santa Maria in Trastevere
Santa Cecilia in Trastevere
San Francesco a Ripa
San Michele
Ospedale San Gallicano
Fontana della Botte
San Pietro in Montorio
Ossario Garibaldino
Fontana Paola
Porta San Pancrazio
Passeggiata del Gianicolo
Piazzale Aurelio
Villa Sciarra
Santa Sabina
Parco Savello
Parco di Sant'Alessio
Cloaca Maxima
Ponte Rotto
Ponte Palatino
Ponte Sublicio
Emporio
Chiesa di Santa Maria Liberatrice
Suore dell' Addolorata Serve di Maria di Pisa
Lungotevere Aventino
Lungotevere Portuense
Lungotevere Porto di Ripa Grande
Lungotevere Testaccio
Viale di Trastevere
Via Portuense
Via Marmorata
Via Garibaldi
Via Luciano Manara
Via Goffredo Mameli
Via Dandolo
Viale Glorioso
Via Emilio Morosini
Viale Aurelio Saffi
Via Pietro Roselli
Viale delle Mura Gianicolensi
Via Giacinto Carini
Via di San Pancrazio
Via del Vascello
Via Nuova delle Fornaci
Viale delle Mura Aurelie
Via Aurelia Antica
Viale di Villa Pamphili
Via Basilio Bricci
Via Calandrelli
Via Nicola Fabrizi
Viale Trenta Aprile
Via Giacomo Medici
Via Angelo Masina
Via della Luce
Via dei Genovesi
Via della Lungaretta
Via dei Salumi
Via Anicia
Via di San Michele
Piazza Mastai
Piazza di Santa Cecilia
Piazza dei Mercanti
Piazza di San Cosimato
Piazza Bernardino da Feltre
Piazza di Porta Portese
Piazza di San Francesco d'Assisi
Piazza di Santa Maria in Trastevere
Piazza di San Calisto
Piazza di San Pietro in Montorio
Piazza dell' Emporio
Piazza Testaccio
Piazza di Santa Maria Liberatrice
Piazza di Sant'Alessio
Piazza Cavalieri di Malta
Via di Porta Lavernale
Via Ippolito Nievo
Via Francesco dall'Ongaro
Via Fratelli Bandiera
Via Alessandro Poerio
Largo Giovanni Berchet
VIA VENETO & VILLA BORGHESE
MONTI, ESQUILINO & SAN LORENZO
CELIO & SAN GIOVANNI
VATICAN & PRATI
TRASTEVERE & GIANICOLO
AVENTINE, TESTACCIO & OSTIENSE
300 m
300 yds
© Copyright Time Out Group 2017

AROUND TRASTEVERE

Trastevere (pronounced Tras-TEV-ver-ray) lives up to your oh-so *pittoresco* Roman fantasy – at least partially. Its transformation has been somewhat inevitable: for centuries the area has attracted artists and writers, brawlers and hookers, drawn by its lively, langorous quality.

Notoriously proud of their identity, *Trasteverini* claim descent from indigenous Etruscans as well as slave stock. Through the Imperial period, much of the *trans tiberim* area was agricultural with farms, vineyards, country villas and gardens laid out for the pleasure of the Caesars. Later, Syrian and Jewish trading communities set up here before moving in the Middle Ages to the Ghetto. Trastevere was a working-class district in papal Rome and remained so until well after the unification in 1870. Today, *Trasteverini* boast they are the only true Romans, and celebrate their exclusive heritage in a two-week-long street festival each July called the *Festa de' Noantri* ('we others', *see p246*).

Hugging the river from **Ponte Sublicio** in the south almost to the Vatican in the north, the district has at least three distinct personalities.

The streets and *piazzette* to the east of thundering **viale Trastevere**, with their vines and creepers, are the quiet part of the neighbourhood – contemplative, rather than party-going.

A different demographic gathers to the west of viale Trastevere: by day, action centres on the food market in **piazza di San Cosimato**; come late afternoon, a buzz begins around **piazza Santa Maria in Trastevere**, growing in intensity as the evening progresses. Night brings an international crowd to the scores of cafés, pubs and restaurants. By the wee hours, the result can be charmingly picturesque – or can degenerate unpleasantly into a rowdy frat party, especially around **piazza Trilussa**.

Moving towards the Vatican, **via della Lungara** is flanked by stately villas once owned by some of papal Rome's most illustrious families.

WEST OF VIALE TRASTEVERE

Ponte Sisto, an elegant footbridge that was constructed by Pope Sixtus IV, links Trastevere to Rome 'proper'. Alternatively, you can cross the heavily trafficked **Ponte Garibaldi** and take via della Lungaretta to the heart of Trastevere and **Santa Maria in Trastevere** (*see right*).

South of piazza Santa Maria in Trastevere, the market square of **piazza San Cosimato** attracts children, elderly residents and football-playing youngsters day and night. To the north, on the other hand, **piazza Sant'Egidio** is the site of the unassuming **Museo di Roma in Trastevere** and home to

In the know
A fountain for each neighbourhood

Water splashes merrily from wine cask to barrel in the charming **Fontana delle Botte** on via della Cisterna. It may look venerable but it's a 20th-century tribute to the wine-loving spirit of the locals. In 1927, Rome authorities got architect Pietro Lombardi to design a series of fountains to define various neighbourhoods: these also include the Fontana delle Anfore (amphorae) in Testaccio and the Fontana dei Libri (books) near Palazzo Madama (*see p109*), as well as many others.

❤ Time to eat & drink

Breakfast
Baylon Café *p173*

Lunch
Da Enzo al 29 *p176*

Snack
I Supplì *p173*

Gelato
Fior di Luna *p175*

Blow-out dinner
Antico Arco *p179*, Glass Hostaria *p172*

❤ Time to shop

Bookshop
Almost Corner Bookshop *p175*, Open Door Bookshop *p178*

Perfume
Romastore Profumi *p176*

Retro gadgets
Elvis Lives *p175*

Wine shop
Les Vignerons *p176*

Christina Bowerman, Glass Hostaria

lively open-air stalls where trinkets of varying quality from faraway places are peddled.

Further north still, the backstreets nestled against the Gianicolo (Janiculum hill, *see p178*) allow you a glimpse of the less-commercial side of Trastevere. Smoggy via della Lungara leads to the lovely **Orto Botanico** (botanical gardens; *see p170*), the **Villa Farnesina** (*see p172*), with its frescoes by Raphael, and **Palazzo Corsini** (*see p169*), which houses part of the national art collection.

Sights & museums

Museo di Roma in Trastevere

Piazza Sant'Egidio 1B (060608, www.museodiromaintrastevere.it). Bus 23, 44, 75, 280, 780/tram 3, 8. ***Open*** *10am-8pm Tue-Sun.* ***Admission*** *€8.50, €6.50 reductions. Exhibition price varies.* ***Map*** *p166 G11.*

This modest museum makes a pleasant visit, especially with children in tow. A small collection of watercolours by Ettore Roesler Franz illustrates scenes of everyday 19th-century Roman life; a series of rooms with waxwork tableaux shows humble folks drinking in the *osteria*, dancing the *saltarello* or playing the *zampogne* (bagpipes). There are also occasional photographic exhibitions.

Palazzo Corsini – Galleria Nazionale d'Arte Antica

Via della Lungara 10 (06 6880 2323, www.barberinicorsini.org). Bus 23, 280. ***Open*** *8.30am-7pm Wed-Mon.* ***Admission*** *€10 (incl Palazzo Barberini, valid 10 days); €5 reductions. No cards.* ***Map*** *p166 F10.*

In the 1933 film *Queen Christina*, Greta Garbo played the former owner of this palace as a graceful tussler with existential angst; in real life, the stout 17th-century Swedish monarch smoked a pipe, wore trousers and entertained female – and a fair number of (ordained) male – lovers. 'Queen without a realm, Christian without a faith, and woman without shame' ran one of the contemporary epithets on Christina. But, in addition to being brilliantly scandalous, Christina was also one of the most cultured and influential women of her age. The century's highest-profile convert to Catholicism, she abdicated her throne and established her glittering court here in 1662, filling what was then Palazzo Riario with her fabled library and an ever-expanding collection of fabulous old masters. She threw the best parties in Rome and commissioned many of Scarlatti and Corelli's hit tunes before dying here in 1689.

Today the palace – later redesigned by Ferdinand Fuga for the Corsini family – houses part of the national art collection. The galleries have beautiful frescoes and trompe l'oeil effects, and contain paintings of the Madonna by Van Dyck, Filippo Lippi and Orazio Gentileschi, two *St Sebastians* (one by Rubens and one by Annibale Carracci) and a pair of *Annunciations* by Guercino. Among the works by Caravaggio is an unadorned *Narcissus*. There's also a triptych by Fra Angelico and a melancholy *Salome* by Guido Reni.

❤ Santa Maria in Trastevere

Piazza Santa Maria in Trastevere (06 581 4802, www.santamariaintrastevere.org). Bus 23, 44, 75, 280, 780/tram 3, 8. ***Open*** *Sept-July 7.30am-9pm daily. Aug 8am-1pm, 3-9pm daily.* ***Map*** *p166 G11.*

This stunning church, with its welcoming portico and façade with shimmering 13th-century mosaics, overlooks the traffic-free piazza of the same name. Santa Maria is the heart and soul of Trastevere. According to legend, a well of oil sprang miraculously from the ground where the church now stands the moment Christ was born, and flowed to the Tiber all day. A small street leading out of the piazza, via della Fonte dell'Olio, commemorates this.

The façade we see today was designed by Carlo Fontana in 1692, but the mosaics pre-date it by four centuries: they show Mary breastfeeding Christ on a solid gold background.

The present 12th-century Romanesque church, built for Pope Innocent II, replaced a basilica from the late third or early fourth century (though legend has it that it was founded by Pope Callistus I, who died in 222) – one of the city's oldest and the first dedicated to the Virgin. That in turn probably topped the site of a *titulus* – a place of worship in the house of an early Christian. The apse is made magnificent by a 12th-century mosaic of Jesus and the Virgin Mary; the figure on the far left is Pope Innocent. Further down, between the windows, are mosaics of the Virgin from the 13th century, attributed to Pietro Cavallini, whose relaxed, realistic figures represent the re-emergence of a Roman style after long years of the hegemony of stiff Byzantine models. The *Madonna and Child* with rainbow overhead is also by Cavallini. Through the wooden door on the left, just before entering the transept, there are two tiny, exquisite fragments of first-century AD mosaics, and in the Altemps chapel to the left of the high altar is a very rare seventh-century painting on wood of the Virgin, known as the *Madonna of Clemency*. Still on the left side is the 17th-century Avila chapel with its elaborate cupola by Antonio Gherardi. The wood-carved ceiling and centrepiece painting of the *Assumption* is by Domenichino. Throughout the nave, fine

Top 20

❤ Orto Botanico

Largo Cristina di Svezia 24 (06 4991 7107, www.ortobotanicoitalia.it). Bus 23, 280. ***Open*** *Apr-Oct 9am-6.30pm Mon-Sat. Nov-Mar 9am-5.30pm Mon-Sat. Closed public hols.* ***Admission*** *€8; €4 reductions. No cards.* ***Map*** *p166 E11.*

Providing nearly 30 acres (121,000sq m) of greenery hiding in central Rome (plus 21,500sq ft – 2,000sq m – of greenhouses), the city's Botanical Gardens were established in 1833 when the Italian state acquired the gardens of the Villa Corsini. However, this verdant area at the foot of the Gianicolo has had a much longer botanical past. It was first planted in the 13th century, by order of Pope Nicholas III, when it was devoted to simples (medicinal plants) and citrus groves. Its fortunes rose and fell under successive popes, but thanks to the aqueduct of Trajan, restored in the early 17th century, it would become one of the leading botanical gardens in Europe under Pope Alexander VII. Today the Orto Botanico is run by the University of Rome's Environmental Biology department as a living museum, and offers a delicious haven from the rigours of a hot, dusty day, with its Baroque stairs flanked by cascading waterfalls, formal tableaux around fountains and statues, its bamboo grove, and varieties of exotic plants and flowers. Check out the cactus garden, the orchids and the touching and smelling collection for the vision-impaired. You may find it to be one of Rome's most under-appreciated gems.

marble mosaic style graces the floor, but the original 12th-century work was almost totally replaced in the late 18th century.

Villa Farnesina

Via della Lungara 230 (06 6802 7268, www.villafarnesina.it). Bus 23, 280. ***Open*** *9am-2pm Mon-Sat; 9am-5pm 2nd Sun of mth.* ***Admission*** *€6; €3 reductions.* ***Map*** *p166 F10.*

Villa Farnesina was built between 1508 and 1511 to a design by Baldassare Peruzzi as a pleasure palace and holiday home for the fabulously rich papal banker Agostino Chigi. Treasurer to Pope Julius II, Chigi was one of Raphael's principal patrons. In its day the villa was stuffed to the rafters with great works of art, although many were later sold to pay off debts. Chigi was known for his extravagant parties, where guests had the run of the palace and the magnificent gardens. Just to make sure his guests knew that money was no object, he would have his servants toss the silver and gold plates on which they dined into the Tiber – into underwater nets, to be fished out later and used again. The powerful Farnese family bought the villa and renamed it in 1577 after the Chigis went bankrupt.

The stunning frescoes are homages to the pagan and classical world; the works on the ground-floor Loggia of Psyche were designed by Raphael but executed by his friends and followers, including Giulio Romano; according to local lore, the master himself was too busy dallying with his mistress, *la fornarina* (baker's girl), to apply any more paint than was strictly necessary. The *Grace* with her back turned, to the right of the door, is attributed to him, though. Around the corner in the Loggia of Galatea, Raphael took brush in hand to create the victorious goddess in her seashell chariot. Upstairs, the Salone delle Prospettive was decorated by Peruzzi with views of 16th-century Rome. Next to it is Agostino Chigi's bedroom, with a fresco of the *Marriage of Alexander the Great and Roxanne* (1517) by a contemporary of Raphael, known by the nickname Il Sodoma. Like most of his paintings, this is a rather sordid number showing the couple being undressed by vicious cherubs.

Restaurants

Alle Fratte di Trastevere €€

Via delle Fratte di Trastevere 49-50 (06 583 5775, www.allefratteditrastevere.com). Bus 23, 280, 780, H/tram 8. ***Open*** *noon-11.30pm Mon, Tue,Thur-Sat; noon-3.30pm, 6-11.30pm Sun. Closed Aug.* ***Map*** *p166 G12* ❶ *Trattoria*

This cheerful eaterie with its eye firmly on the tourist trade does honest Roman trattoria fare with Neapolitan influences. The service is friendly, attentive and bilingual. First courses, such as *gnocchi alla trasteverina* (gnocchi with tomato and basil), are served up in generous portions. *Secondi* include oven-roasted sea bream, veal escalopes in marsala and a good grilled beef fillet. Desserts are home-made; the postprandial *digestive* flow freely. In summer there are a few outdoor tables. If you're missing your bagels, call ahead and the trattoria's bakery operation will bake you up a batch.

Casa Mia €€

Via della Renella 88-90 (06 8697 4870, www.casamiaintrastevere.com). Bus 23, 280, 780, H/tram 8. ***Open*** *noon-11pm daily.* ***Map*** *p166 G11* ❸ *Trattoria*

A friendly, relaxed trattoria off the main drag, Casa Mia offers solid Roman cuisine and seasonal blackboard specials. On Thursdays there are usually home-made gnocchi while on Fridays the focus is on fish. There is a decently priced wine list to match. Unlike most places the restaurant stays open between lunch and dinner for a quick afternoon drink or snack. Snag a table in the delightful courtyard to dine *al fresco* or sit at the front to peer through the large window to see the chefs at work.

Dar Poeta €€

Vicolo del Bologna 45 (06 588 0516, www.darpoeta.com). Bus 23, 280, 780, H/tram 8. ***Open*** *noon-midnight daily.* ***Map*** *p166 F11* ❺ *Pizzeria*

Dar Poeta does a quality pizza, based on an innovative slow-rise dough which places it somewhere between the Roman crispy-thin style and the Neopolitan thick-crust version. Creative assemblages include the house pizza (with courgettes, sausage and spicy pepper). The varied *bruschette* are first-rate, and healthy salads offer a break from all those carbs. Leave room for dessert, as the sweet calzone stuffed with Nutella and ricotta is the ultimate in indulgence. You can eat until late and the waiters are genuinely friendly, but do be prepared to queue, since Dar Poeta doesn't take bookings.

❤ Glass Hostaria €€€€

Vicolo del Cinque 58 (06 5833 5903, www.glass-hostaria.it). Bus 23, 280, 780, H/tram 8. ***Open*** *8pm-midnight Tue-Sun. Closed 1wk Jan/Feb & 2wks July/Aug.* ***Map*** *p166 G11* ❼ *Italian/Fusion*

Despite the place being ultra-modern and vigorously kicking against the traditional Trastevere dining scene, Glass offers surprisingly warm service, an interesting wine list and a menu that is, yes, experimental and fusion-tinged but rather less pretentious than you might expect. Chef Cristina Bowerman's Michelin star has pushed prices up somewhat in the past couple of years. The menu changes frequently: expect novelties along the lines of chestnut tagliatelle with pumpkin, sausage and sage, or sumac-scented lamb with quinoa, beluga lentils and nuts. There are three tasting menus including one for vegetarians.

❤ I Supplì €

Via di San Francesco a Ripa 137 (06 589 7110, www.lacasadelsuppli.it). Bus 23, 280, 780, H/tram 8. ***Open*** *10am-9.30pm Mon-Sat. Closed 3wks Aug.* ***No cards. Map*** *p166 G12* ❾ *Streetfood*

A hole-in-the-wall institution, you can spot the entrance to I Supplì from the crowd of people hovering outside devouring the famed *supplì* (a deep-fried ball of rice and ragù stuffed with mozzarella). Aside from the excellent *fritti* (fried snacks) there is also some very good pizza-by-the-slice and a daily-rotating selection of pasta and rice dishes which are scooped into aluminium containers and sold by portion.

Cafés, bars & pubs

Bar San Calisto

Piazza San Calisto (06 583 5869). Bus 23, 280, 780, H/tram 8. ***Open*** *7.30am-2am Mon-Sat.* ***No cards. Map*** *p166 G12* ❷ *Coffee shop/Bar*

Green tourists get their coffee or beer on Piazza Santa Maria in Trastevere; locals who know better go to this bar. The place's harsh lighting would make Sophia Loren look wan, and the dingy space – inside and out – is no picture postcard. But it's cheap and as such it has always been the haunt of arty and fringe types (plus many questionable characters after sundown). The bohemian crowd will be here downing beers or an *affogato* (ice-cream swamped with liqueur), or savouring some of the best hot chocolate in Rome: deliciously thick with fresh whipped cream.

❤ Baylon Café

Via di San Francesco a Ripa 151-153 (06 581 4275, www.facebook.com/bayloncaferoma). Bus 23, 280, 780, H/tram 8. ***Open*** *7am-2am daily.* ***Map*** *p166 G12* ❸ *Café/Bar*

Good for all day drinking and dining, Baylon has a casual, shabby vibe and a few rickety outside tables on the bustling street. A vast international menu is served throughout the day and the free wifi is a bonus, but it is the well-priced *aperitivo* deal that drawls in the crowds between 6pm and 9pm. Try the cocktails which are well-made with some creative additions to the classics.

Cioccolata e Vino

Vicolo del Cinque 11 (06 5830 1868). Bus 23, 280, 780, H/tram 8. ***Open*** *6.30pm-2am Mon-Fri; 2pm-2am Sat, Sun.* ***No cards. Map*** *p166 G11* ❹ *Café/Shop/Bar*

Half-shop, half-bar, this tiny emporium is a joy to visit at almost any hour: for hot chocolate, a delicious espresso with chocolate in the bottom of your cup, a chocolate tasting or a glass of wine from a small but interesting selection. Late at night the pub-crawlers stop here to grab one of the renowned chocolate shots: liqueurs and cocktails served in a tiny chocolate cup.

Enoteca Ferrara

Piazza Trilussa 41 (06 5833 3920, www.enotecaferrara.it). Bus 23, 280, 780, H/tram 8. ***Open*** *6pm-midnight daily.* ***Map*** *p166 G11* ❺ *Wine bar*

Ignore the rather expensive restaurant in this Trastevere stalwart and stick with the wine bar by the entrance, with its good choice of wines by the glass and an encyclopaedic bottle menu – with big markups. You can pick at the range of snacks on the counter for €7-€10.

Freni e Frizioni

Via del Politeama 4-6 (06 4549 7499, www.freniefrizioni.com). Bus 23, 280, 780, H/tram 8. ***Open*** *6.30pm-2am daily.* ***Map*** *p166 G11* ❻ *Bar*

With its unlikely ex-garage surroundings – the name means 'brakes and clutches' – this

Glass Hostaria

Bernini's Babes

All hail the master of racy religious art

One hand clutches her breast, her body writhes and her face looks heavenwards in rapturous agony. Is she in the throes of death or in the midst of an erotic encounter with the Holy Spirit?

Beata Ludovica Albertoni (1671), who graces the church of **San Francesco a Ripa** (*see p176*), is just one of many sexually and spiritually charged marble women scattered around Rome by Baroque genius Gian Lorenzo Bernini. An equal in celestial swooning, *L'estasi di Santa Teresa*, draws crowds to the church of **Santa Maria della Vittoria** (*see p191*).

Lusty Bernini – father of 11 – was a highly religious individual for whom the distinction between the sensual and the sublime was blurred. Sculptor, architect and darling of a string of popes, Bernini (1598-1680) attended Mass every morning, took communion twice a week, and on the way home from work stopped by regularly at the church of the **Gesù** (*see p124*) where he reportedly underwent the rigorous Spiritual Exercises of the Jesuits.

Evidently, though, that didn't preclude a first-hand understanding of female joys and fears. Just look at the terror on the face of Proserpine as Pluto grabs her fleshy thigh in *The Rape of Proserpine* (1621-22); the woeful desperation of Daphne as she turns into a laurel tree to escape Apollo's embrace in *Apollo and Daphne* (1622-25); or the come-hither look of the laid-back *Truth Unveiled by Time* (1646-52), all of which can be admired in the **Galleria Borghese** (*see p142*).

Bernini designed – though his workshop may have carved – the *Four Virtues* group in **Sant'Isidoro** (via degli Artisti 41, 06 488 5359, by appt only), in which *Charity* offers her ample naked bosom with an encouraging smile – an outright solicitation that Bernini's patrons in 1662 didn't seem to find out of place in a church. (It was too much for 19th-century sensibilities, though: the bronze tunics that were added to cover her and one of her buxom sisters were not removed until 2002).

Energetic and disciplined, an indefatigable worker who was at home with popes and princes, Bernini lost his head just once, for Costanza Bonarelli, the wife of a fellow artist. So steamy was the affair that Urban VIII had to step in to put out the fire. Bernini subsequently married, had his numerous brood and lived happily until the age of 82. But not before completing, for himself, an exquisite bust of his beloved Costanza (1635, in the Bargello museum in Florence), with an intelligent face and loose blouse.

Beata Ludovica Albertoni (Bernini, 1671)

is one of Rome's hippest early evening spots, frequented by arty types and a creative, studenty crowd. A grand vegetarian buffet is laid out from 7pm to 10pm: baskets of *focaccia*, ceramic bowls of couscous and pasta, guacamole and raw vegetables. Help yourself while you sip a cocktail (€8), a beer (€6), or a glass of well-priced wine (around €5) in the crowded interior or the equally crowded square overlooking the *lungotevere* riverside road outside.

Bakeries, pasticcerie & gelaterie

❤ Fior di Luna

Via della Lungaretta 96 (06 6456 1314, www.fiordiluna.com). Bus 23, 280, 630, 780, H/tram 8. ***Open*** *11.30am-12.30am daily.* ***Map*** *p166 G11* ❷ *Gelateria*

Gelato connoisseurs will find little to criticise at this popular location in the heart of Trastevere. Small-batch production and attention to quality are the bywords here and the choices rotate according to season and availability of fresh produce. The fresh fruit sorbets are heavenly (look out for the fig in July). For something unique try the flavours made with donkey milk.

Valzani

Via del Moro 37B (06 580 3792, www.valzani.it). Bus 23, 30, 44, 83, 115, 125, 130, 170, 716, 280, 781, H/tram 8. ***Open*** *2-8pm Mon, Tue; 10am-8pm Wed-Sun. Closed Aug.* ***Map*** *p166 G11* ❹ *Bakery*

A Trastevere institution and rightly so. Come here for *sachertorte* (Viennese chocolate cakes) and spicy, nutty *pangiallo* ('yellow bread'), which are the specialities. But they are just the tip of an iceberg of chocolatey delights, including the must-try chocolate with chilli.

Shops & services

L'Albero e la Mano

Via della Pelliccia 3 (06 581 2871, www.lalberoelamano.it). Bus 23, 280, 630, 780, H/tram 8. ***Open*** *timetable varies. Closed Aug Sat, Sun.* ***Rates*** *€12-€15/class. No cards.* ***Map*** *p166 G11* ❶ *Yoga*

This incense-scented studio offers Ashtanga and Hatha yoga, as well as in t'ai chi chuan, belly-dancing and Shiatsu, Ayurvedic and Thai massage.

❤ Almost Corner Bookshop

Via del Moro 45 (06 583 6942). Bus 23, 30, 44, 83, 170, 716, 280, 781, H/tram 3, 8. ***Open*** *10am-8pm Mon-Sat; 11am-1.30pm, 3.30-8pm Sun.* ***Map*** *p166 G11* ❷ *Books*

Not an inch of space is wasted in this English-language bookshop: a good selection of fiction, as well as history, art, archaeology and more is displayed on every surface. Check the noticeboard if you're seeking work, lodgings or Italian lessons.

Antica Caciara

Via di San Francesco a Ripa 140 A/B (06 581 2815, www.anticacaciara.it). Bus 23, 280, 630, 780, H/tram 8. ***Open*** *7am-8pm Mon-Sat. Closed Aug.* ***Map*** *p166 G12* ❸ *Delicatessen*

Follow your nose to this cured meat and cheese institution which has been in business since 1900. Look out for the bunches of salami and slabs of *guanciale* (cured pork jowl) hanging in the doorway and be sure to purchase the best *pecorino romano* (sheep's cheese) in town, which is always served with a smile from the affable owner Roberto Polica.

Centro Estetico Malò

Piazza Tavani Arquati 120 (06 589 8950, www.centroesteticomalo.com). Bus 23, 115, 280, 780, H/tram 8. ***Open*** *10am-8pm Tue-Sat.* ***Map*** *p166 H11* ❹ *Health & beauty*

This friendly Trastevere beautician offers great deals on waxing, manicures and pedicures. It also features a whole range of face and body treatments for relaxation and glowing skin.

❤ Elvis Lives

Via di San Francesco a Ripa 27 (06 4550 9542, www.elvislives.it). Bus 23, 280, 630, 780, H/tram 8. ***Open*** *10am-2pm, 3.30-8pm Mon-Sat. Closed 3wks Aug.* ***Map*** *p166 G12* ❺ *Accessories/Tech*

Run by two graphic designers this small shop sells all your hipster needs from slogan t-shirts, watches and sunglasses to cutting-edge Polaroid cameras and retro record players. **Other locations** via dei Volsci 48 (San Lorenzo).

Innocenzi

Via Natale del Grande 31 (06 581 2725). Bus 23, 44, 83, 115, 170, 716, 280, 781, H/tram 8. ***Open*** *8am-1.30pm, 4.30-8pm Mon-Wed, Fri, Sat; 8am-1.30pm Thur. Closed 2wks Aug.* ***No cards.*** ***Map*** *p166 G12* ❻ *Food & drink*

Pulses spill from great sacks stacked around this treasure trove of foodie specialities that come from all over the world.

Mercato San Cosimato

Piazza San Cosimato. Bus 23, 75, 83, 280, 716, 781/tram 3, 8. ***Open*** *6.30am-2.30pm Mon-Sat.* ***No cards.*** ***Map*** *p166 G12* ❼ *Market*

Trastevere's lively morning market offers a glimpse into the daily life of the local *Trasteverini* as they peruse the mountains of fresh produce while catching up on the neighbourhood gossip. There are also a few fixed stalls at the back selling meat, fish and cheeses.

❤ Romastore Profumi

Via della Lungaretta 63 (06 581 8789, www.romastoreprofumi.com). Bus 23, 115, 280, 780, H/tram 8. ***Open*** *10am-8pm daily.* ***Map*** *p166 G11* ⑩ *Health & beauty*

Passers-by are always drawn in by the artistic window displays of this elegant perfume shop. A blissful sanctuary of lotions and potions, they stock an array of gorgeous scents: old-school Floris, Creed and Penhaligon's rub shoulders with modern classics such as home-grown Acqua di Parma and Lorenzo Villoresi. Staff can be very abrupt.

Studio Stefania Miscetti

Via delle Mantellate 14 (06 6880 5880, www.studiostefaniamiscetti.com). Bus 23, 280. ***Open*** *4-8pm Tue-Sat; or by appt. Closed July-Sept.* ***No cards.*** ***Map*** *p166 E9* ⑪ *Gallery*

One of the more established of Trastevere's commercial art galleries, Miscetti holds unusual shows of sculpture and installations.

❤ Les Vignerons

Via Mameli 61/62 (06 6477 1439, www.lesvignerons.it). Bus 23, 280, 630, 780, H/tram 8. ***Open*** *4-9pm Mon; 11am-9pm Tue-Thur; 11am-9.30pm Fri, Sat. Closed 2wks Aug.* ***Map*** *p166 G12* ⑫ *Wine shop*

Friendly wine shop with a focus on natural and biodynamic wines from small producers in Italy and beyond. The staff here are more than happy to discuss and recommend bottles from the extensive selection. There is also a good choice of craft beers.

EAST OF VIALE TRASTEVERE

In this achingly charming part of Trastevere, you won't have to battle crowds or hawkers as you wander between pretty *piazze* and washing-festooned streets. Nowhere near as showy as some of Rome's districts, it's easy, here, to imagine Roman life as it was two or three centuries ago. The area is dominated by the basilica of **Santa Cecilia** with its underground treasures and Cavallini frescoes, but look out for unexpected gems, too, which can be found at the church of **San Francesco a Ripa**.

This was a busy commercial area from the 15th century through to unification in the late 19th century, due to its proximity to the busy **Ripa Grande** port. The port is commemorated in a statue on the riverside façade of the huge structure of San Michele, a former hospice, orphanage and reform school, now housing offices of the cultural heritage ministry.

Sights & museums

San Francesco a Ripa

Piazza San Francesco d'Assisi 88 (06 581 9020). Bus 23, 44, 75, 115, 280, 780, H/tram 3, 8. ***Open*** *7am-1pm, 3-7pm daily.* ***Map*** *p166 H13.*

Rebuilt in the 1680s, this church took the place of a 13th-century one that held now-lost frescoes by Pietro Cavallini chronicling the life of St Francis of Assisi. The saint stayed in the adjoining convent when he visited Rome in 1229: if you ask the sacristan, he may show you the cell where St Francis lived and the rock on which he placed his head to sleep. An orange tree in the garden was supposedly planted by the saint. The metaphysical artist Giorgio de Chirico is buried here behind a gate off the first chapel on the left; ask the sacrestan if you can have a look. *See p174* Bernini's Babes.

Restaurants

❤ Da Enzo al 29 €€

Via dei Vascellari 29 (06 581 2260, www.daenzoal29.com). Bus 23, 280, 780, H/tram 8. ***Open*** *12.30-2.30pm, 7.30-11pm Mon-Sat. Closed 3wks Aug.* ***Map*** *p166 J12* ④ *Trattoria*

Don't expect a long, leisurely experience at this diminutive family-run trattoria. Space is limited, the noise level is high and the service is fast and furious but for typical *cucina romana* it is a reliable and atmospheric option. Prices are a little above the average but the quality of ingredients is assured and there is a nice selection of lesser-known Lazio wines. Bookings are taken, but only for the early evening seating so to catch one of the outside tables get there for an early lunch or be prepared to join a very long queue.

La Gensola €€€

Piazza della Gensola 15 (06 5833 2758, www.osterialagensola.it). Bus 23, 280, 780, H/tram 8. ***Open*** *12.30-3pm, 7.30-11pm daily.* ***Map*** *p166 H11* ⑥ *Seafood*

The fish served in this buzzy little place hidden in an off-the-track piazza in the quiet side of Trastevere is fresh and well prepared, and comes with a reasonable price tag – not always easy to find in Rome. Family-run and traditional in style, with tables packed closely and a high decibel level most meal times, La Gensola blends Roman cuisine with Sicilian

❤ Santa Cecilia in Trastevere

Piazza Santa Cecilia 22 (06 589 9289). Bus 23, 44, 75, 115, 280, 780, H/tram 3, 8. ***Church*** *9.30am-12.30pm, 4-6pm Mon-Sat; 11.30am-12.30pm, 4-6pm Sun.* ***Cavallini frescoes*** *10am-12.30pm Mon-Sat; 11.30am-12.30pm Sun.* ***Archaeological site*** *9.30am-12.30pm, 4-6pm daily.* ***Admission*** *Frescoes €2.50. Archaeological site €2.50. No cards.* ***Map*** *p166 H12.*

The current 16th-century church of this magnificent religious complex was built above a fifth-century basilica, which in turn incorporated a *titulus*, or house where early Christians met. In this case, gruesome legend relates, that house belonged to Roman patrician Valerio, who lived at the time of Emperor Marcus Aurelius. So impressed was Valerio by his wife Cecilia's vow of chastity that he too converted to Christianity. Valerio was murdered for his pains, and Cecilia was arrested while she tried to bury him. Doing away with the saintly Cecilia proved a difficult job for the Romans. After a failed attempt to suffocate her in the house's hot baths they tried to behead her. But only three strokes of the axe were permitted by law, and after the third failed to do the job, as she was slowly dying she sang, securing her place as the patron saint of music. When her tomb was reopened in 1599, her body was uncorrupted. Sculptor Stefano Maderno portrays her with her head turned away in an exquisite marble rendering beneath the altar. Her sarcophagus is in the crypt.

The excavations below the church provide extensive evidence of early Roman and palaeo-Christian buildings; here, too, is the pretty decorated crypt where Cecilia's body lies.

On the first floor, on the other hand, is a choir from where nuns from the adjoining convent could look down over the interior of the basilica from behind a grill. On one wall is what remains of what was possibly Rome's greatest 13th-century fresco – a *Last Judgement* by little-known genius Pietro Cavallini. With its rainbow-winged angels of all ranks and desperate sinners writhing hellwards, the once-monumental fresco shows Cavallini breaking away from the Byzantine style and giving new light and humanity to the figures.

touches, and if the presentation is *osteria*-style, the quality of what's on the plate is a notch higher.

Le Mani in Pasta €€

Via dei Genovesi 37 (06 581 6017, www.lemaniinpasta.net). Bus 23, 280, 780, H/tram 8. ***Open*** *12.30-2.30pm, 7.30-11pm Tue-Sun. Closed 2wks Aug & 1wk Dec.* ***Map*** *p166 H12* ❽ *Trattoria*

This little trattoria offers decent, creative home cooking in large portions, friendly informal service and great value for money. A meal might begin with some nicely chargrilled vegetables and a sauté of clams and mussels, followed by giant mounds of spaghetti with *seppioline* (baby cuttlefish) and *carciofi* (artichokes). The *secondi*, if you get that far, include a good fillet steak with green peppercorns. The ground-floor room has a ringside view of the kitchen action. Unusually for Rome, there's a *salafumatori* (smoking area), though it's in the basement. Be sure to book ahead.

Bakeries, pasticcerie & gelaterie

Biscottificio Innocenti

Via della Luce 21 (06 580 3926, www.facebook.com/BiscottificioInnocenti). Bus 23, 44, 83, 170, 716, 280, 781, H/tram 8. ***Open*** *10am-8pm Mon-Sat; 9.30am-2pm Sun. Closed mid July-Aug.* ***No cards. Map*** *p166 H12* ❶ *Bakery*

This backstreet biscuit shop can be easy to miss due to a lack of signage and a very unassuming entrance but inside is an Aladdin's cave of sweet baked goods, including many unique recipes which have evolved through the years since the place opened in 1929. Centre-stage is a fabulous 52-foot oven which, along with owner Stefania Innocenti's infectious smile, is the secret to the shop's ongoing success.

Sora Mirella

Lungotevere degli Anguillara, corner of Ponte Cestio. Bus 23, 280, 780, H/tram 8. ***Open*** *10am-3am daily. Closed Oct-Feb.* ***No cards. Map*** *p166 H11* ❸ *Gelateria*

Mirella styles herself as *la regina della grattachecca* (the Queen of Water Ices), and there appears to be no reason to disagree. The place gives you an opportunity to sit on the Tiber embankment wall as you tuck into the *speciale superfrutta* – fresh melon, kiwi fruit and strawberry (or whatever fruit happens to be in season) with syrups served in a specially designed glass.

Shops & services

❤ Open Door Bookshop

Via della Lungaretta 23 (06 589 6478, www.books-in-italy.com). Bus 23, 44, 83, 115, 170, 716, 280, 781, H/tram 3, 8. ***Open*** *Sept-June 10.30am-8pm Mon-Sat; July 4-8.30pm Mon, Sat; 11.30am-8.30pm Tue-Fri. Closed Aug.* ***Map*** *p166 H11* ❽ *Books*

Second-hand and antiquarian English books have been sold from this cramped, welcoming little space on the 'other', quieter side of Trastevere since 1976.

Porta Portese

Via Portuense, southwards from Porta Portese. Bus 23, 44, 83, 115, 170, 716, 280, 781, H/tram 3, 8/train to Trastevere. ***Open*** *5am-2pm Sun.* ***Map*** *p166 H13* ❾ *Market*

Rome's biggest and most famous flea market grew out of the city's thriving black market after the end of World War II. A lingering air of illegality still persists here, so watch out for pickpockets. Dealers peddle all manner of items: bootleg CDs, furniture, clothes, fake designer gear and car stereos of dubious origin.

GIANICOLO

This luxuriously verdant hilltop neighbourhood is one of Rome's most beautiful. A couple of winding roads lead up from Trastevere past decidedly patrician villas, many of which are now embassies and cultural institutions. Up **via Garibaldi** is Bramante's lovely **Tempietto**, in the courtyard of the church of **San Pietro in Montorio** (which is part of a complex that also includes the Spanish cultural centre). It contrasts oddly with the squat Fascist-era monument across the road: the **Ossario Garibaldino** (open 9am-1pm Tue-Sun). Inscribed with the words *Roma o morte* (Rome or death) – the rallying cry of Unification hero Giuseppe Garibaldi – the monument contains the remains of Risorgimento heroes, including Goffredo Mameli, composer of Italy's stirring national anthem.

A grand belvedere at the **Fontana Paola** is one of the best places to gaze down over the Eternal City.

At the top of the hill, the imposing bronze statue of **Giuseppe Garibaldi** on his dashing steed is a reminder of his role in the creation of Italy as a nation – in 1849 this breathtaking lookout spot was the scene of one of the fiercest battles in the struggle for Italian unity (**the Risorgimento**; *see p287*). Freedom fighter Garibaldi and his makeshift army of red-shirted *garibaldini* – a hotch-potch of former papal troops and starry-eyed young enthusiasts – tried valiantly (but ultimately failed) to defend the short-lived Roman Republic against French troops sent to restore papal rule. From beneath this balcony a cannon fires one shot each day at noon. To the north, Garibaldi's South American wife Anita sits astride her own bronze horse, baby in one hand and pistol in the other. The busts that line the road depict Risorgimento martyrs. A lighthouse donated by Italian emigrants to Argentina flashes its light from this promontory.

Sights & museums

Fontana Paola

Via Garibaldi. Bus 44, 75, 115. ***Map*** *p166 F12.*

This grandiose fountain, which sends lavishly splashy cascades into an equally grand-looking pool, is fed by water that has travelled 35km (22 miles) through a Trajan-era aqueduct from Lake Bracciano, to the north of Rome. Pope Paul V had Flamino Ponzio and Giovanni Fontana design the fountain for him in 1621, in a bid to outdo his predecessor Sixtus V, who had harnessed a third-century AD aqueduct to supply his Fontana dell'Acqua Felice (*see p190*) 20 years earlier.

Tempietto di Bramante & San Pietro in Montorio

Piazza San Pietro in Montorio 2 (06 581 3940, Tempietto 06 581 2806). Bus 44, 75, 115. ***Tempietto*** *10am-6pm Tue-Sun.* ***Church*** *8am-noon, 3-4pm daily.* ***Map*** *p166 F12.*

Located on one of the various spots where St Peter is believed to have been crucified (St Peter's is another), San Pietro in Montorio conceals one of Rome's greatest architectural jewels in its courtyard: the Tempietto, designed by Donato Bramante in 1508 for Cardinal Giuliano della Rovere, who was to become Pope Julius II (and who also got him working on St Peter's basilica). The small circular structure, with its Doric columns, has classical symmetry that was subsequently imitated by many architects. Bernini got his hands on it in 1628, adding the staircase that leads down to the crypt. The church next door, founded in the late ninth century and rebuilt in the late 15th century, contains a chapel by Bernini (second on the left) and one by Vasari (fifth on the right). Paintings include Sebastiano del Piombo's *Flagellation* (c1516). The name Montorio, or golden hill, refers to the way the sun hit sand on the Gianicolo, turning it gold.

Restaurants

❤ Antico Arco €€€€

Piazzale Aurelio 7 (06 581 5274, www.anticoarco.it). Bus 44, 75, 115, 710, 870, 871. ***Open*** *noon-midnight daily.* ***Map*** *p166 E12* ❷ *Italian*

The minimalist yet warm interior of Patrizia Mattei's Gianicolo restaurant provides the perfect backdrop for sampling the carefully creative menu which changes according to the season. Although prices have risen somewhat in recent years, Antico Arco remains steadfast in its popularity and reputation. The seven-course *degustazione* menu (€78) is good value and the wine list offers up some sensibly priced gems. Until 6pm there is also a fixed finger food menu of miniature versions of the main dishes. Book well in advance.

Cafés, bars & pubs

Bar Gianicolo

Piazzale Aurelio 5 (06 580 6275). Bus 115, 870. ***Open*** *6am-1am Tue-Sat; 6am-9pm Sun. Closed 2wks Aug.* ***No cards. Map*** *p166 E12* ❶ *Café*

If you've slogged up here to visit Villa Pamphilj (*see p229*) or the site of Garibaldi's doomed battle with the French on the Gianicolo, rest your weary bones on the wooden benches of this tiny bar with an intimate, chatty feel. Carrots and apples are juiced on the spot and there's a good range of interesting sandwiches and light meals.

The view from the Gianicolo

Monti, Esquilino & San Lorenzo

The Esquilino hill, around Termini railway station (if you've come to Rome on a budget deal there's a good chance you'll find yourself staying in a hotel around here), was once where the rich and powerful had their gardens and villas. Today – despite municipal attempts to bring about a 'renaissance' – there's no escaping the fact that Esquilino's *palazzi* are grimy and its after-dark denizens can be on the dodgy side. There are, however, gems here – you just have to know where to look. The spur of the Esquiline closest to the Colosseum is the Colle Oppio with its grubby park amid the ruins of Trajan's Baths.

More picturesque and a whole lot buzzier, Monti has chaotic streets full of ethnic shops and eateries, lively bars and plenty of after-hours activity to keep night owls satisfied.

Meanwhile, students and artists keep neighbouring San Lorenzo lively.

❤ Don't miss

1 Nuovo Mercato Esquilino *p193*
Italian and exotic produce jostle cheek-by-jowl in this lively market.

2 Santa Maria Maggiore *p191*
With a foundation dating to the fourth century, like Rome Santa Maria Maggiore most certainly wasn't built in a day.

3 Trimani *p194*
Rome's oldest and best wine shop.

4 Palazzo Massimo alle Terme *p190*
Extraordinary frescoes from the dining hall of Augustus' wife Livia are a highlight of this fabulous collection.

In the know
Getting around

For Esquilino, *see p316* Transport to Termini, which lists all transport options going to or passing by the station. For Monti, metro Cavour (line B) is the closest station, or it's just a short walk from the Forum area. Colle Oppio is best served by the metro stop Colosseo (line B). A little further afield, San Lorenzo is served by tram 3 which wends its (often picturesque) way from Trastevere to Villa Borghese.

Nero's head on the entrance to the Domus Aurea

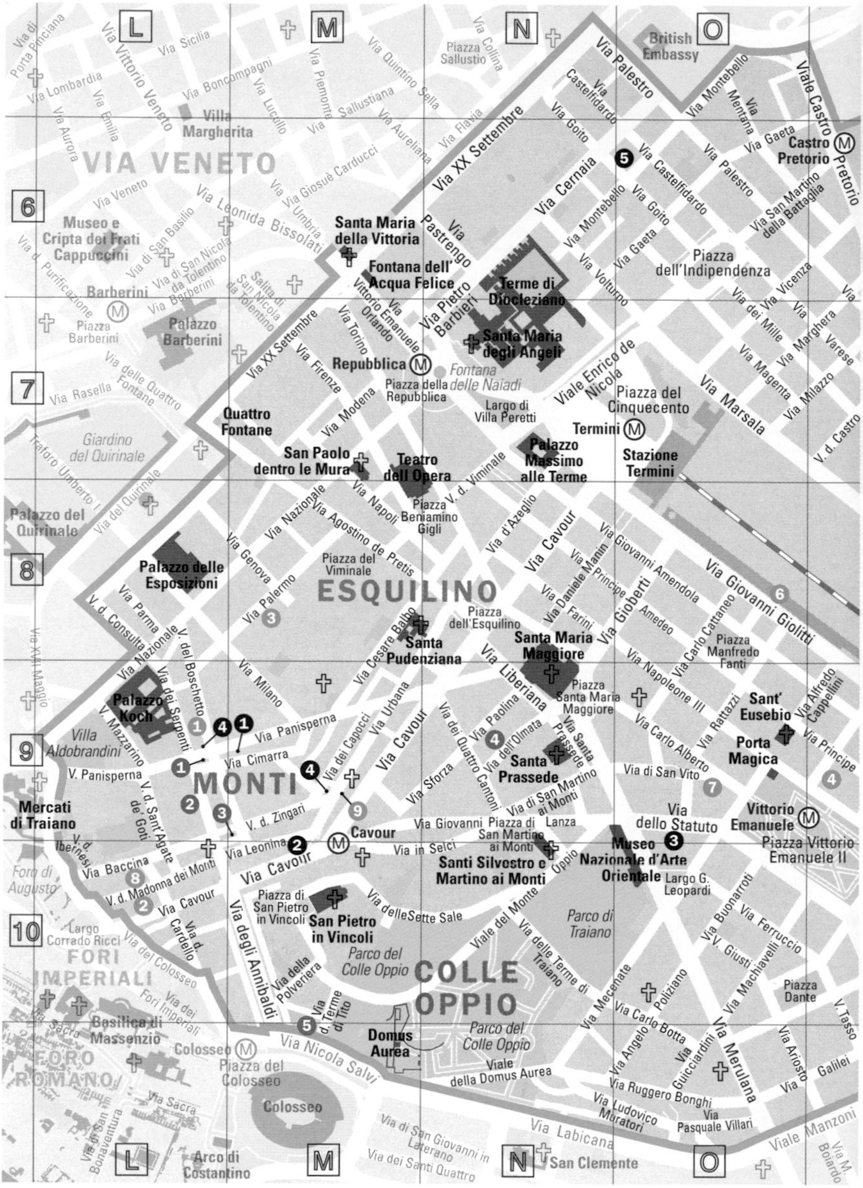

MONTI, ESQUILINO & SAN LORENZO

Restaurants

1. L'Asino d'Oro
2. Cavour 313
3. Doozo
4. JantaFast Food
5. Marcello
6. Mercato Centrale
7. Trattoria Monti
8. Taverna dei Fori Imperiali
9. Zia Rosetta

Cafés, bars & pubs

1. Ai Tre Scalini
2. Al Vino Al Vino
3. La Bottega del Caffè
4. Fiddler's Elbow
5. Oppio Caffè

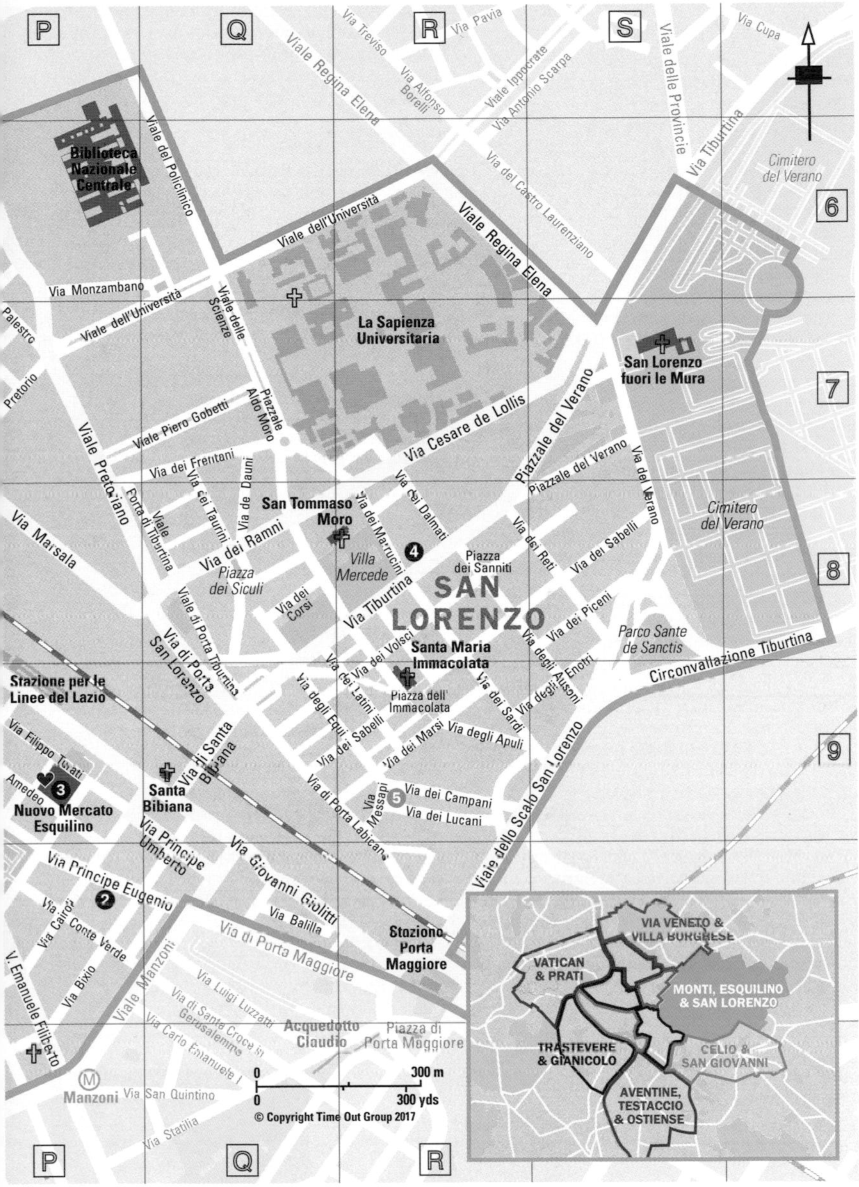

Bakeries, pasticcerie & gelaterie

1. Fatamorgana
2. Il Palazzo del Freddo di Giovanni Fassi
3. Regoli
4. Said

Shops & services

1. Abito – Le Gallinelle
2. Mercato Monti
3. Nuovo Mercato Esquilino
4. Tina Sondergaard
5. Trimani

MONTI

The marshy ground between the Quirinal, Viminal and Esquiline hills was home to the steamy, overcrowded Suburra, which was described by Roman writers fond of excursions into the *demi-monde*. Propertius spent time here waiting for his mistress Cynthia to climb out of a first-floor window, down a rope and into his arms. Juvenal, who lived in the heart of this hottest, noisiest and most chaotic quarter of the city, reported in his *Satires* that the most common cause of death here was insomnia.

The area of Monti that was the Suburra – the enclave stretching east from the Forum between *vie* Nazionale and Cavour – is just as noisy, cosmopolitan and full of life today as it was then. Streets are cleaner, and property prices higher, but the narrow, chaotic streets full of funky clothes shops, wild bars and ethnic restaurants pulsate with the same kind of activity.

The post-unification developers who did their worst to the Esquiline (*see p189*) also left their mark on parts of Monti: **via Nazionale** has roaring traffic, drab carbon-copy high-street fashion emporia and rip-off tourist restaurants; **via Cavour** is singularly bland. The laboratory on undulating via Panisperna where Enrico Fermi and Ettore Majorana first split the atom in 1934 and the lumpen Bank of Italy HQ in Palazzo Koch on via Nazionale are oppressive; the bombastic, windowless **Palazzo delle Esposizioni** (*see p184*), also on via Nazionale, is redeemed only by some good exhibitions.

There's relief, however, in the streets surrounding **Santa Maria Maggiore** (*see p191*), where two stunning early churches dedicated to two sister saints, **Santa Prassede** and **Santa Pudenziana** (for both, *see p185*), glow with extraordinary mosaics.

For a verdant break and splendid views, head for the **Villa Aldobrandini** gardens high up above the south-western end of via Nazionale (access from nearby via Mazzarino). Built in the 16th century, the garden's formal lawns and gravel paths are juxtaposed by homeless people sleeping on benches (and the traffic noise below).

Sights & museums

Palazzo delle Esposizioni

Via Nazionale 194 (06 3996 7500, www.palazzoesposizioni.it). Bus 40Exp, 60, 64, 70, 71, 170, H. ***Open*** *10am-8pm Tue-Thur, Sun; 10am-10.30pm Fri, Sat.* ***Admission*** *€8-€12.* ***Map*** *p182 L8.*

This imposing 19th-century purpose-built exhibition space continues to produce excellent shows on a host of historical, artistic and contemporary-icon themes. Often more than one exhibit is running simultaneously around the 10,000sq m (108,000sq ft) space. If you're under 30, it's free from 2pm to 7pm on the first Wednesday of the month. You don't need a ticket to access the basement bookshop and café – this latter a great place to grab a light lunch.

Santa Prassede

Via Santa Prassede 9A (06 488 2456). Bus 16, 70, 71, 75, 84, 360, 590, 649, 714. ***Open*** *7.30am-noon, 4-6.30pm Mon-Sat; 8am-noon, 4-7pm Sun.* ***Map*** *p182 N9.*

This church was built in the ninth century on the spot where St Praxedes is said to have harboured Christians. The saint, the story says, sponged up the blood of 23 martyrs who were discovered and killed before her, throwing the sponge into a well; its location is now marked by a porphyry disc on the floor of the nave. This tale is depicted in the 1735 altarpiece by Domenico Muratori. The church is a scale copy of the old St Peter's, a ninth-century attempt to recreate an early Christian basilica, although uneven brickwork shows that the Romans had lost the knack.

Pope Paschal I was looking for artists to decorate the chapel of San Zeno as a mausoleum dedicated to his mother,

❤ Time to eat & drink

Morning coffee
La Bottega del Caffè *p186*

Gelato
Fatamorgana *p186*

Wine Bar
Ai Tre Scalini *p186*, Al Vino Al Vino *p186*

Dinner
Taverna dei Fori Imperiali *p185*, Trattoria Monti *p194*

❤ Time to shop

Food market
Nuovo Mercato Esquilino *p193*

Retro accessories
Mercato Monti *p187*

Vintage fashion
Abito – Le Gallinelle *p187*

Wine
Trimani *p194*

Fatamorgana

St Theodora. With the Roman Empire long dead, the pick of mosaic artists was thriving across in Byzantium, where the traditionally Roman art of mosaic took on a flashier and more colourful style, with coloured glass tesserae often backed with gold or silver. Undoubtedly the finest expression of Byzantine art in Rome, the chapel is topped with a vault showing a fearsome Christ supported by four angels, while around the walls are various saints, including St Theodora herself with the blue square halo that tells us she was still alive when she posed for her mausoleum mosaic. On the right the Anastasis shows Christ reaching into hell to rescue Adam, Eve and assorted Old Testament characters. In a room to the right of the chapel of St Zeno is a portion of column said to be part of the very one that Jesus was tied to for the flagellation.

In the apse, Christ riding on a cloud is being introduced to the martyr St Praxedes by St Paul on the right, while St Peter is doing the honours on the left for her sister St Pudenziana. Pope Paschal is there too, holding a model of the church.

Santa Pudenziana

*Via Urbana 160 (06 481 4622). Metro Cavour/ bus 16, 70, 71, 75. **Open** 8.30am-noon, 3-6pm daily. **Map** p182 M8.*

Tradition says St Pudenziana was the sister of St Praxedes; their father Pudens was a senator who harboured St Peter in a house on the spot where this church now stands. A purpose-built church was constructed in the fourth century, restored in the eighth and 11th centuries and brutally remodelled in the 16th century. Still very active, the church is now used by Rome's Filipino community (Pudenziana is the patron of the Philippines). Among the glowing sacred hearts, the undoubted star is the apse mosaic.

Dating from the early fifth century (although damaged in the 16th century) this is a marvellous example of the continuity between pagan and Christian art. Christ is enthroned in majesty and the apostles on either side are depicted as wealthy Roman citizens in a Roman cityscape (albeit with the symbols of the Evangelists flying over their heads). Santa Pudenziana herself is very naturalistically depicted on the right wearing a gold cloak.

Restaurants

L'Asino d'Oro €€

*Via del Boschetto 73 (06 4891 3832, www.facebook.com/asinodoro). Bus 40, 60, 64, 70, 71, 117, 170, H. **Open** 12.30-3pm, 7.30-11pm Tue-Sat. Closed 2wks Aug. **Map** p182 L9* ❶
Trattoria

Chef Luca Sforza moved his restaurant 'The Golden Donkey' from the Umbrian town of Orvieto to Rome back in 2011 and continues to pull in the crowds, making it difficult to get a table. The short, Tusco-Umbrian-inspired menu changes regularly, based on what is freshest and best at any given time. There is often a touch of sweet and sour in his creations: wild boar in chocolate sauce, cod with raisins and chestnuts, or goose with stewed apple are frequently featured. The €16 fixed lunch menu is arguably one of Rome's best gourmet offers, but even during the evening the price/quality ratio of both the food and wine is exceptional.

Cavour 313 €€

*Via Cavour 313 (06 678 5496, www.cavour313.it). Metro Cavour/bus 75, 117. **Open** 12.30-2.45pm, 7.30pm-midnight Mon-Sat. Closed 3wks Aug. **Map** p182 L10* ❷
Enoteca

A friendly atmosphere, a serious cellar and good wine bar food explain the enduring popularity of this wood-panelled, bottle-lined place near the Forum. Prices are reasonable, and there's a selection of hot and cold snacks; in winter, soups are a strong point. With over 500 bottles on the wine list, choosing is the only problem.

❤ Taverna dei Fori Imperiali €€€

*Via della Madonna dei Monti 9 (06 679 8643, www.latavernadeiforiimperiali.com). Metro Cavour/bus 75, 117. **Open** 12.30-3pm, 7.30-10.30pm Wed-Mon. Closed 2wks Aug, 1wk Sept. **Map** p182 L10* ❽ *Trattoria*

This cosy, family-run restaurant hidden behind the Imperial Forum has gained a legion of loyal fans thanks to the warm, friendly atmosphere and focus on quality cuisine. The family's menu always features several seasonal specials and a few creative combinations alongside more standard Roman fare. The attention to detail and popularity have pushed the prices a little above the average trattoria but the ambience, location and food make it worth the extra splurge.

Zia Rosetta €

*Via Urbana 54 (06 3105 2516, www.ziarosetta.com). Metro Cavour/bus 75, 117. **Open** 11am-4pm Mon-Thur, 11am-10pm Fri-Sun. Closed Aug. **Map** p182 M9* ❾
Sandwich shop

Specialising in Roman *rosette* (typical bread rolls in the shape of a rose) stuffed with a selection of fillings, Zia Rosetta has put a very Monti-esque, hipster spin on one of the city's traditional products. Using fresh seasonal ingredients means there are always new combinations on the menu, and there are even dessert versions filled with strawberry tiramisù or sweet ricotta with cherry. Good, fresh salads and fruit smoothies are also on offer. The tiny shop has just a few stools so grab your food to eat in nearby piazza della Madonna dei Monti.

Cafés, bars & pubs

❤ Ai Tre Scalini

Via Panisperna 251 (06 4890 7495, www.facebook.com/aitrescalini). Bus 40, 60, 64, 70, 117, 170, H. ***Open*** *12.30pm-1am daily. Closed 1wk Aug.* ***Map*** *p182 L9* ❶ *Wine bar*

This atmospheric, rustic wine bar is the *aperitivo* destination of choice for Monti arty, creative types. It is always packed on summer evenings when crowds spill out onto pretty, vine-covered Via Panisperna and it is a struggle to get through the door, let alone the bar. Earlier in the day it is an altogether calmer affair with friendly staff, excellent wines (many also served by the glass) and an all-day menu of food chalked up on the blackboard.

❤ Al Vino Al Vino

Via dei Serpenti 19 (06 485 803). Bus 40, 60, 64, 70, 117, 170, H. ***Open*** *10.30am-2.30pm, 6pm-1am daily. Closed 2wks Aug.* ***Map*** *p182 L9* ❷ *Bar*

This hostelry on lively via dei Serpenti has a range of over 500 wines, with more than 25 available by the glass. But its speciality is *distillati*: dozens of fine grappas, whiskies and other strong spirits. The food is so-so but light snacks are fine for soaking up the alcohol. Shame the staff can be less than charming.

❤ La Bottega del Caffè

Piazza Madonna dei Monti 5 (06 474 1578). Metro Cavour/bus 53, 75, 80, 85, 87, 117. ***Open*** *8am-2am daily.* ***Map*** *p182 L9* ❸ *Café*

With tables outside on the pretty square (patio heaters keep them warm through winter) this café draws locals – and weary sightseers from the nearby Roman and Imperial Fora – for breakfast, lunch and *aperitivi*. Friendly staff serve morning coffee or afternoon tea with tiny *cornetti* or biscuits. There's generally a cooked option alongside the usual range of sandwiches and filled rolls at lunch.

Bakeries, pasticcerie & gelaterie

❤ Fatamorgana

Piazza degli Zingari 5 (06 4890 6955, www.gelateriafatamorgana.it). Metro Cavour/bus 40, 60, 64, 70, 75, 117, 170, H. ***Open*** *1pm-midnight daily.* ***Map*** *p182 M9* ❶ *Gelateria*

Organic, no additives, gluten-free and superb: the wonderful product whipped up by Maria Agnese Spagnuolo for her Fatamorgana mini-chain (and previously only available in the 'burbs) can now be found in several new easily accessible *centro storico* locations, including this one in the hip Monti district's pretty piazza degli Zingari. There are all the classic flavours (with twists), plus specialities such as black cherries and beer, pears and gorgonzola, and baklava. **Other locations** via Roma Libera 11, Trastevere; via Laurina 10, Tridente ; piazza degli Zingari 5, Monti; via Aosta 3, San Giovanni; via Leone IV 50, Prati; via dei Chiavari 37, Campo de' Fiori.

Abito – Le Gallinelle

Shops & services

❤ Abito – Le Gallinelle

Via Panisperna 61 (06 488 1017, www.facebook.com/ABITO61). Metro Cavour/bus 40, 60, 64, 70, 71, 117, 170. ***Open*** *11am-8pm Mon-Sat. Oct-Jan also open noon-8pm Sun. Closed 2wks Aug.* ***Map*** *p182 M9* ❶ *Fashion*

Wilma Silvestri founded Le Gallinelle in 1989 and sells gorgeous, reworked vintage and ethnic garments along with new contemporary designs which she creates in her workroom at the back of the shop. Items can be tailored or made-to-measure on demand. For those who shun the outlandish, there are classic linen suits for men and women.

❤ Mercato Monti

Via Leonina 46 (www.mercatomonti.com). Metro Cavour/bus 40, 64, 70, 75, 117. ***Open*** *Sept-June 10am-8pm Sat, Sun.* ***Map*** *p182 M10* ❷ *Market*

Mercato Monti perfectly reflects the arty, hipster vibe of the Monti district. Almost every weekend young creatives set up shop at the back of the Hotel Palatino to sell their wares which include innovative jewellery and accessories, vintage-inspired clothing and unique crafts and homewares. Check the website for dates.

Tina Sondergaard

Via del Boschetto 1D (06 8365 5761, www.tinasondergaard.com). Bus 40, 60, 64, 70, 117, 170. ***Open*** *10.30am-7.30pm Mon-Sat. Closed 2wks Aug.* ***Map*** *p182 L9* ❹ *Fashion*

This Danish designer and her team whip up delightfully stylish one-off 1960s-inspired women's clothes on the premises in this compact pared-back space on trendy via del Boschetto. Fabrics are eye-catching and Tina will do on-the-spot alterations to make sure that your purchases fit perfectly. Space is tight here, so last season's leftovers are sold off at extremely interesting prices.

COLLE OPPIO

The serene, green **Parco del Colle Oppio** was the site of Nero's **Domus Aurea** (Golden House), an all-too-vivid reminder of the hated emperor that was torn down, filled in and replaced with bath complexes, first by Titus (on the south-west side of today's park) and later by Trajan (on the northern side). On **via Terme di Traiano** is a structure – closed to the public – called the *Sette sale* (seven rooms), which was in fact a nine-chamber water tank estimated to have held eight million litres of water. Nowadays the lower reaches of the Colle Oppio park, towards via Labicana, are peopled by swarms of Roman mums and their toddlers during the day. A string of unpleasant incidents involving far-right local youths, homeless immigrants and a sprinkling of the city's foolhardy cruisers has resulted in the park being locked after darkness falls.

On the western slope of the park, **San Pietro in Vincoli** (*see p188*) contains important relics and a mighty Michelangelo. Further north, on the border with Monti, the church of **Santi Silvestro e Martino ai Monti** (*see p189*) stands above a Roman house. Nearby, on via Merulana, the **Museo Nazionale d'Arte Orientale** (*see p188*) provides an exotic break from ancient Rome.

Sights & museums

Domus Aurea

Via della Domus Aurea (06 3996 7700, www.coopculture.it). Metro Colosseo/bus 53, 75, 80, 85, 87, 117, 810/tram 3. ***Open*** *Sat, Sun 8.45am-6pm by appt only.* ***Map*** *p182 M11.*

► *At present, access is only possible by following guided tours pre-booked online. Visits may be suspended or cancelled in the winter months or in case of bad weather.*

In the summer of AD 64 fire devastated a large part of central Rome. (Some blame Nero for setting the blaze intentionally but fire was a real risk and a common occurrence.) The ashes of patrician palaces mingled with those of slums. Afterwards, anything in the area east of the Forum left unsinged was knocked down to make way for a home fit for the sun-god that Nero liked to imagine he was.

Work began on the emperor's Domus Aurea (Golden House) immediately after the fire had died down. A three-storey structure, its main façade faced south and was entirely clad in gold; inside, every inch not faced with mother-of-pearl or inlaid with gems was frescoed by Nero's pet aesthete Fabullus. Fountains squirted perfumes, and baths could be filled with sea or mineral water. In one room, Suetonius claimed, an immense ceiling painted with the sun, stars and signs

In the know

The Museo Nazionale Romano combined ticket

Visit any of the venues in the Museo Nazionale Romano collection and you'll buy a combined ticket (€7; €3.50 reductions), which includes entry to the Palazzo Massimo alle Terme (*p190*), Palazzo Altemps (*p108*), Crypta Balbi (*p123*) and Terme di Diocleziano (*p192*). The ticket is valid for three days.

of the zodiac revolved constantly, keeping time with the heavens. Lakes were dug, forests planted and a 35-metre-high (116-foot) gilded bronze statue of Nero erected.

After Nero's death in AD 68, a *damnatio memoriae* was issued and work was begun to eradicate every vestige of the hated tyrant. Vespasian drained the lake to build his amphitheatre (the tight-fisted emperor kept Nero's colossus, simply putting a new head on it, and so the stadium became known as the Colosseum), and Trajan used the brickwork as a foundation for his baths. So thorough was the cover-up job that for decades after the house's frescoes were rediscovered in 1480, no one realised it was the Domus Aurea that they had stumbled across. The frescoed 'grottoes' became an obligatory stopover for Renaissance artists, inspiring – among other things – Raphael's weird and wonderful frescoes in the Vatican (and also giving us the word 'grotesque'). The artists' signatures can still be seen scratched into the ancient stucco.

Museo Nazionale d'Arte Orientale

Via Merulana 248 (06 4697 4832 www. museorientale.beniculturali.it). Bus 16, 714, 717, C3/tram 3. ***Open*** *8am-7pm Tues-Sun.* ***Admission*** *€6; €3 reductions. No cards.* ***Map*** *p182 O10.*

If you've had enough of ancient and papal Rome, try this impressive collection of Oriental art, in a dusty *palazzo* near Santa Maria Maggiore. It's arranged geographically and roughly chronologically. First are ancient artefacts from the Near East – pottery, gold, votive offerings – some from the third millennium BC. Then come 11th- to 18th-century painted fans from Tibet, sacred sculptures, and some Chinese pottery from the 15th century. Perhaps most unusual are artefacts from the Swat culture, from Italian-funded excavations in Pakistan.

San Pietro in Vincoli

Piazza di San Pietro in Vincoli 4A (06 9784 4950). Metro Cavour/bus 16, 75, 117. ***Open*** *8am-12.30pm, 3-6pm daily.* ***Map*** *p182 M10.*

First mentioned in 431, the church was rebuilt in 439 by Sixtus III with backing from Emperor Valentian III's wife Eudoxia, and dedicated to Saints Peter and Paul. In 442 Eudoxia gave Pope Leo I the chains that had held Peter in prison in Jerusalem; he put them together with the chains that had bound the saint at the Carcere Mamertino (*see p67*), whereupon they miraculously fused. It was only in the 11th century, however, that Gregory VII changed the dedication to St Peter *ad vinculum* – in chains. The church

Domus Aurea *p187*

was repaired in the 15th century, and then modified and restored in the 19th.

The chains are in a reliquary beneath the high altar and are the objective of the pilgrims who flock to the church. Secular tourists head for the funerary monument of Pope Julius II with Michelangelo's imposing *Moses* (c1513) as its central figure. Julius had wanted an enormous sepulchre with 40 life-size statues in a vast free-standing architectural framework. The proposed scale of the tomb was one of the reasons for the rebuilding of St Peter's, but it quickly became clear that neither the tomb nor the basilica would be finished before the sickly pope expired. So Julius shifted Michelangelo to work on another pet project: redecorating the ceiling in the Sistine Chapel. After the completion of the ceiling Michelangelo went back to work on the tomb, but seven months later syphilis got the better of Julius and the tomb was put on a back-burner. This considerably abbreviated version was cobbled together by Michelangelo's pupils. The magnificent *Moses* (horned, from an archaic mistranslation of an Old Testament phrase really meaning 'with light emanating from his head') dominates the composition. The master's hand can be seen in the statues of Leah and Rachel to either side of the patriarch. After a recent restoration, experts came to the conclusion that he may have carved the pope's head too, although he clearly had nothing to do with the rest of poor Julius, which is by Maso del Bosco. When completed, the monument was placed here where Julius had been titular cardinal. His body ended up in an unmarked grave across the river in the Vatican.

Santi Silvestro e Martino ai Monti

Viale del Monte Oppio 28 (06 4784 7048). Metro Cavour or Vittorio/bus 16, 714, 717. ***Open*** *8.30am-noon, 4-7pm daily.* ***Map*** *p182 N10.*

The first church on this site was founded by St Sylvester in the fourth century. It was in that earlier church in 325 that the findings of the Council of Nicea (which established God the Father and Christ as one and the same) were presented to Constantine: the event is commemorated in the fresco on the left as you enter. The church was rebuilt in the ninth century and remodelled in c1650. On the far left and right of the left-hand aisle, two frescoes show respectively San Giovanni in Laterano (*see p206*) as it was before Borromini's changes and the interior of the original St Peter's (*see p158*). On the wall of the right-hand aisle, the mid 17th-century frescoes by pioneering landscape artist Gaspard Dughet caught the eye of many a Roman aristocrat, sparking the fashion for landscaped rooms in grand residences such as *palazzi* Colonna (*see p80*) and Doria Pamphilj (*see p115*). Beneath the ninth-century church is a third-century *titulus* (Roman house used as a place of worship); if the sacristan is about, ask him to unlock the gate for you (donation welcome). It's a spooky place, littered with bits of sculpture, decaying mosaics and frescoes. But it doesn't have the usual jungle of newer foundations sunk through Roman brickwork, so it's not difficult to picture this as an ancient dwelling and/or place of worship.

Cafés, bars & pubs

Oppio Caffè

Via delle Terme di Tito 72 (06 474 5262, www.oppiocaffe.it). Metro Colosseo/bus 53, 75, 80, 85, 87, 117/tram 3. ***Open*** *7am-2am daily.* ***Map*** *p182 M11* ❺ *Café*

This vintage-chic venture is worth frequenting mainly for its view over the Colosseum. Food and drinks are served throughout the day but from 5.30pm to 10pm the hip crowd descend for the €12 drink plus all-you-can-eat *aperitivo* buffet. You may have to put up with slow, grumpy service, and you may not feel the standard of the food matches the price tag but the spectacular Colosseum panorama makes up for a lot.

ESQUILINO

If you've come to Rome on a budget package or picked up a last-minute deal, chances are you'll end up in a hotel on the Esquilino, around Termini railway station. Despite assurances from local authorities that the area is on the up, the Esquilino's grimy *palazzi* and after-dark characters may not be what you expected of the Eternal City. But the Esquilino's charms and attractions are many.

The ancient ruins and Renaissance villas that dotted the area were swept away, and a whole new city-within-a-city built in the grid mode favoured by the Torinese planners who followed Italy's new royal family from the north after Italian Unification in the 1870s. Piazza Vittorio Emanuele II – the city's biggest square and always known simply as **piazza Vittorio** – was the new capital's showcase residential area. From optimistic beginnings the once-proud *palazzi* saw a steady decline into characterless slumhood. In the 1980s the first arrivals of a multi-ethnic community settled in the area, injecting life and colour, but no prosperity, into the run-down streets around the square. The noisy, smelly and characterful market that once occupied the pavements around the garden at the centre of the square now occupies more salubrious covered quarters in a former army barracks in via Lamarmora. The piazza's shady central gardens have been valiantly brought back into play. In the gardens, have a go at breaking the still-encoded recipe for changing base metal into gold on the **Porta Magica** in the northern corner; this curious door, with hermetic inscriptions dating from 1688, is all that remains of the **Villa Palombara**, an estate that once occupied this site.

North-west of the piazza, **Santa Maria Maggiore** (*see p191*) is one of the four patriarchal basilicas, and has splendid mosaics.

Due north of piazza Vittorio is **Termini railway station**. The railway reached Termini (the name comes from the nearby Terme di Diocleziano, and has nothing to do with its being a terminus) in the 1860s. The first station (1864-71) was demolished to make way for what is one of Italy's most remarkable modern buildings, a triumph of undulating horizontal geometry. Architect Angiolo Mazzoni designed the lateral wings, complete with tubular towers of metaphysical grace straight out of a De Chirico painting; building began in 1937 as a key part of feverish preparations for the Fascist Universal Expo planned for 1942 (World War II stymied the Expo). In 1947 a judging commission hedged its bets by selecting two projects in a competition for the design for a new main station building. Despite the compromise, the result is staggering. The great reinforced concrete 'wave' was completed in time for the 1950 Holy Year. In the late '90s the station – and **piazza del Cinquecento** with its bus terminus – underwent a major facelift but the whole area remains less than charming. Pass through piazza del Cinquecento as dusk approaches and you'll see swirling clouds of starlings driven to insanity by the constant light and diesel fumes.

Proximity to the railway terminus made the surrounding area particularly interesting to developers. Architect Gaetano Koch designed a ministerial and administrative district, focusing on the semicircular arcaded **piazza della Repubblica** (1888), once the *exedra* (anteroom) of the massive **Terme di Diocleziano** bath complex (*see p192*) and still frequently referred to as piazza Esedra by locals.

This heavily trafficked roundabout is the traditional starting point for many major demonstrations. The **Fontana delle Naiadi** at its centre was due for unveiling in 1901, but the nudity of the art nouveau sea-nymphs (naiad, a female water spirit) cavorting seductively with sea monsters so shocked the authorities that it was boarded up again for years. Locals, fed up with the eyesore, eventually tore the planks down – a rather undignified inauguration.

The extraordinary Museo Nazionale Romano collection of ancient artefacts, which used to be confined to the Terme di Diocleziano, has spilled over into the **Palazzo Massimo alle Terme** (*see p190*) on the south-east fringe of the square.

To the north-west is the church of **Santa Maria della Vittoria** (*see p191*), containing one of Bernini's most extraordinary sculptures, and the **Fontana dell'Acqua Felice.** Designed by Domenico Fontana in the form of a triumphal arch, this fountain was completed in 1589. It was one of many urban improvements that were commissioned in Rome by Sixtus V, and provided this district with clean water from an ancient aqueduct. The statue of Moses in the central niche of the fountain, by Leonardo Sormani, has been condemned as an atrocity against taste ever since it was unveiled in 1586.

To the south-west of piazza della Repubblica, via Nazionale descends to the old centre, passing the American church of **San Paolo dentro le Mura** (via Napoli 58, 06 488 3339, www.stpaulsrome.it, open 9am-4.30pm Mon-Fri), with its Arts and Crafts movement mosaics, along the way. If you've had your fill of the picturesque and need a shot of the Kafkaesque, take a look at such monolithic examples of Italian public architecture as the Interior Ministry in piazza del Viminale or the **Teatro dell'Opera** (*see p271*) along via Firenze.

Sights & museums

❤ Palazzo Massimo alle Terme

Largo di Villa Peretti 1 (06 480 201, www.archeoroma.beniculturali.it). See p316 Transport to Termini. ***Open*** *9am-7.30pm Tue-Sun.* ***Admission*** *€7; €3.50 reductions. Free 1st Sun of mth.* ***Map*** *p182 N7.*

Part of the Museo Nazionale Romano collection, Palazzo Massimo has a basement display of coins from Roman times to the euro. On the ground and first floors are busts of emperors, their families and lesser mortals, in chronological order (allowing you to track changing fashions in Roman hairstyles). The ground floor covers the period up to the end of the Julio-Claudian line. In Room 5 is a magnificent statue of Augustus as *pontifex maximus*. Room 7 houses the undoubted stars of the ground floor, two bronzes found on the Quirinale showing a Hellenistic hero in the triumphant pose of Hercules and an exhausted boxer.

The first floor begins with the age of Emperor Vespasian (AD 69-79); portrait busts in Room 1 show the gritty no-nonsense soldier. Room 5 has decorations from Imperial villas – statues of Apollo and of a young girl holding a tray of religious objects are both from Nero's coastal villa at Anzio, and a gracefully crouching Aphrodite taking her bath is from Hadrian's Villa (*see p235*) at Tivoli. Room 6 has two discus throwers, second-century marble copies of a Greek bronze original from the fifth century BC. In Room 7 is a peacefully sleeping hermaphrodite, another second-century AD copy of a Greek original.

The real highlight of the Palazzo Massimo, though, lies on the second floor, where rare wall paintings from assorted villas have been reassembled. The spectacular fresco from the *triclinium* (dining room) of the villa of Livia shows a fruit-filled garden bustling with animal life and displays a use of perspective that was rarely seen again until the Renaissance. Another, from the *triclinium* of the Roman Villa Farnesina (in Room 3), has delicate white sketches on a black background, surmounted by scenes of courts handing down sentences that have baffled experts for centuries. Also in Room 3 is a lively naval battle, from a frescoed corridor in the same villa. The three *cubicoli* (bedrooms) in Room 5 all have decorative stuccoed ceilings.

Santa Maria degli Angeli

Piazza della Repubblica (06 488 0812 www. santamariadegliangeliroma.it). See p316 Transport to Termini. ***Open*** *7.30am-6.30pm Mon-Sat, 7am-7.30pm Sun.* ***Map*** *p182 N7.*

Another reminder of the vast scale of the Baths of Diocletian, the church of Santa Maria degli Angeli was slotted into the main hall of the complex by none less than Michelangelo, though his designs were modified on various occasions, including eighteenth century modifications at the hands of Vanvitelli. It is also famous for Clement XI's magnificent 45-metre-long (148-foot) bronze meridian (1702), which runs across the marble floor, marking the zodiac signs of the constellations and, importantly, the exact point of the spring equinox, from which the date of Easter (first Sunday after the first full moon following the spring equinox) was calculated. Until 1870, all clocks in Rome took their cue from this sophisticated time-piece.

Santa Maria della Vittoria

Via XX Settembre 17 (06 4274 0571, www. chiesasantamariavittoriaroma.it). Metro Repubblica/bus 16, 60Exp, 61, 62, 85, 492, 590, 910. ***Open*** *8.30am-noon, 3.30-6pm daily.* ***Map*** *p182 M6.*

This modest-looking Baroque church, its interior cosily candlelit and adorned with marble and gilt, holds one of Bernini's most famous works. The *Ecstasy of St Teresa*, in the Cornaro chapel (the fourth on the left), shows the Spanish mystic floating on a cloud in a supposedly spiritual trance after a teasing, androgynous angel has pierced her with a burning arrow; the result is more than a little ambiguous. (Writing of the angel incident in her *Life*, Teresa recalled: 'so intense was the pain I uttered several moans; so great was the sweetness caused by the pain that I never wanted to lose it.') When the chapel is seen as a whole, with the heavens painted in the dome, the light filters through a hidden window reflecting gilded rays and bathing Teresa in a heavenly glow. She is surrounded by members of the Cornaro family.

❤ Santa Maria Maggiore

Piazza Santa Maria Maggiore (06 6988 6800, www.vatican.va). Bus 16, 70, 71, 75, 105, 360, 590, 649, 714, 717/tram 5, 14. ***Church*** *7am-7pm daily. Museum 8.30am-6.30pm daily.* ***Loggia*** *(booking essential, groups only) 8.30am-6.30pm daily.* ***Admission*** *Church free. Museum €3. Loggia €5. No cards.* ***Map*** *p182 N9.*

Behind this blowsy Baroque façade is one of the most striking basilica-form churches in Rome. Local tradition says a church was built on this spot in c366; documents place it almost 100 years later. The fifth-century church was first extended in the 13th century, then again prior to the 1750 Holy Year, when Ferdinando Fuga redid the interior and attached the façade that we see today. Inside, a flat-roofed nave shoots between two aisles to a triumphal arch and apse. Above the columns of the nave, heavily restored fifth-century mosaics show scenes from the Old Testament. There are also 13th-century mosaics in the apse by Jacopo Torriti, which show Mary, dressed as a Byzantine empress, being crowned Queen of Heaven by Christ.

The Virgin theme continues in fifth-century mosaics on the triumphal arch. The ceiling in the main nave is said to have been made from the first shipment of gold extracted from the Americas by Ferdinand and Isabella of Spain, and was presented to the church by the Borgia Pope Alexander VI. The Borgias' heraldic device of a bull is very much in evidence. In the 16th and 17th centuries two incredibly flamboyant chapels were added. The first was the Cappella Sistina (last chapel on the right of the nave), designed by Domenico Fontana for Sixtus V (1585-90), and decorated with multicoloured marble, gilt and precious stones. Directly opposite is the Cappella Paolina, an even gaudier Greek-cross chapel, designed in 1611 by Flaminio Ponzio for Paul V to house an icon of the Madonna (dating from the ninth, or possibly the 12th, century) on its altar. To the right of the main altar a plaque marks the burial place of Rome's great Baroque genius, Gian Lorenzo Bernini. In the loggia, high up on the front of the church (book tours in advance; notes are provided in English), are glorious 13th-century mosaics that decorated the façade of the old basilica, showing the legend of the foundation of the church. The lower row shows Mary appearing to Giovanni the Patrician, who, with Pope Liberius, then sketches the plan for the basilica. The legend goes that the Virgin told Giovanni to build a church on the spot where snow would fall the next morning. The snow fell on 5 August 352, a miracle that is commemorated on that day every year, when thousands of flower petals are released from the roof of the church in the Festa della Madonna delle Neve (*see p246*). The Cappella Paolina also contains a relief (1612) by Stefano Maderno showing Liberius tracing the plan of the basilica in the snow.

Terme di Diocleziano

Via Enrico de Nicola 79 (06 3996 7700, archeoroma.beniculturali.it). See p316 Transport to Termini. ***Open*** *9am-7.45pm Tue-Sun.* ***Admission*** *€7; €3.50 reductions. Free 1st Sun of mth.* ***Map*** *p182 N6.*

Part of the Museo Nazionale Romano, Diocletian's baths were built in AD 298-306, and were the largest bath complex ever built in the Roman Empire able to accommodate an estimated 3,000 people at a time. For an idea of the immense size of the structure, tour the remaining fragments: the tepidarium and part of the central hall are in Santa Maria degli Angeli (*see p191*); a circular hall can be seen in San Bernardo alle Terme (piazza San Bernardo); and the Aula Ottagona (octagonal hall) – which used to house Rome's planetarium and now is occasionally used for exhibitions – is in via Romita.

A convent complex was built around the largest surviving chunk of the baths by Michelangelo in the 1560s: it now contains inscriptions and other items from the Museo Nazionale Romano ancient artefacts collection, including some of the hut-shaped funerary urns found in Lazio, which give an idea of what eighth-century BC houses looked like. *See p187* The Museo Nazionale Romano combined ticket.

Restaurants

Doozo €€€

Via Palermo 51 (06 481 5655, www.doozo.it). Metro Repubblica/bus 40, 60, 64, 70, 71, 117, 170, H. ***Open*** *12.30-3pm, 7.30-10.30pm Tue-Sat; 7.30-10.30pm Sun. Closed 1wk Aug.* ***Map*** *p182 M8* ❸ *Japanese*

Defining itself as an 'art books and sushi' gallery, this Japanese restaurant (the name means 'welcome') is an oasis of quality in an area dominated by tourist-oriented eateries. The interior is airy and cultured (tables spill over into the bookshop and gallery, where art and photography exhibitions are held), but we especially like the small Zen garden out at the back, with its magnolia tree. A Japanese chef produces genuine dishes, rather than watered-down Italo-Nipponic, with good sushi, sashimi, tempura and *karaage* chicken served in wooden bento boxes. Doozo is also open in the afternoon for tea.

JantaFast Food €

Via Mamiani 11 (06 446 0792). Metro Vittorio/bus 70, 71, 360, 105, 150, 649/tram 5, 14. ***Open*** *11am-4pm, 5.30-10pm daily.* ***No cards.*** ***Map*** *p182 P9* ❹ *Indian/Fast food*

A little piece of India transplanted to Rome's multi-ethnic zone, just off piazza Vittorio,

Santa Maria Maggiore

❤ Nuovo Mercato Esquilino

Via Lamarmora. Metro Vittorio/bus 70, 71, 105, 150, 360, 590, 649/tram 5, 14. ***Open*** *5am-3pm Mon-Sat.* ***Map*** *p184 P9* ❸ *Market*

Tucked between the jumble of ancient and industrial archeology (railway lines, tram lines, aqueduct, part of a grand Roman dining pavilion) by Termini and the faded *fin de siècle* grandeur of piazza Vittorio Emanuele is the lively and chaotic Esquiline market. The area has long been a multicultural hub, and that is reflected in the market's rich arrays of produce both wildly exotic and as Roman as they come. African and Asian stalls stock fruits, vegetables and spices which are hard to come by in other parts of the city while alongside them more traditional greengrocers, fishmongers and butchers noisily vie to attract customers. It all starts winding up by lunchtime so get there early, and then pop over to nearby Mercato Centrale (*see below*) for a snack. In a separate building there are exotic fabrics, and rather less interesting selections of clothes and household goods.

Janta serves some of the most authentic Indian food in the city. You can take away or eat in; what you'll find on your plastic plates is every bit as good as what you'll find at the capital's more upmarket Indian restaurants – and here it comes accompanied by gloriously kitsch Indian music videos.

Mercato Centrale €

Termini Station, Via Giolitti (www.mercatocentrale.it). See p316 Transport to Termini. ***Open*** *8am-midnight daily.* ***Map*** *p182 O8* ❻ *Fast food*

More food court than market, the Roman answer to Florence's celebrated Mercato Centrale opened to great fanfare in late 2016. Located at the rear of Termini train station, it injected a much-needed culinary boost in an area previously not famed for its dining establishments. The lower level of the market is divided into sections selling dishes and foodstuffs by some of Italy's top producers including pizza, steak, fish and vegetable dishes, salads and pastries as well as craft beers and wines. On the upper level of the huge hall is a considerably fancier (and much pricier) restaurant run by Michelin-starred chef Oliver Glowig.

❤ Trattoria Monti €€

Via di San Vito 13A (06 446 6573). Metro Vittorio/bus 16, 70, 71, 75, 105, 360, 590, 649, 714, 717/tram 5, 14. ***Open*** *12.45-2.45pm, 7.45-11pm Tue-Sat; 12.45-2.45pm Sun. Closed 1wk Aug, Dec.* ***Map*** *p182 O9* ❼ *Trattoria*

This upmarket trattoria is more difficult to get into than many top restaurants – so book well in advance. The reasons for its popularity are simple: friendly service and ambience, excellent food and a huge wine list with reasonable markups. The cuisine, like the family that runs the place, is from the region of Le Marche – so meat, fish and game all feature on the menu. Vegetarians are well served by a range of *tortini* (pastry-less pies); pasta-hounds can enjoy such treats as *tagliolini* with anchovies, pine nuts and pecorino cheese.

Cafés, bars & pubs

Fiddler's Elbow

Via dell'Olmata 43 (06 487 2110, www.thefiddlerselbow.com). Metro Cavour/bus 16, 70, 71, 75, 360, 590, 649, 714, 717. ***Open*** *4pm-1.30am daily.* ***Map*** *p182 N9* ❹ *Pub*

One of the oldest, best-known pubs in Rome, the Fiddler's Elbow has a basic wooden-benched interior that hasn't changed for years. Though Italy's smoking ban means it's no longer a fume-filled dive, it still succeeds in giving the impression of being one. Check the website for live music dates.

Bakeries, pasticcerie & gelaterie

Il Palazzo del Freddo di Giovanni Fassi

Via Principe Eugenio 65/67 (06 446 4740, www.palazzodelfreddo.it). Metro Vittorio/bus 70, 71, 105/tram 5, 14. ***Open*** *noon-midnight daily.* ***Map*** *p182 P10* ❷ *Gelateria*

With its breathtakingly kitsch interior and splendid ices, Fassi is a Roman institution. Established in 1880, its walls are adorned with Edwardian adverts and Fascist-era posters, which extol the virtues of the shop's wares. Service is often irascible, and the crowds can be daunting, but the ices are very good, in an old-school way: best of all are *riso* – the English translation, 'rice pudding', hardly does it justice – and the Palazzo's own invention, *la caterinetta*, a mysterious concoction of whipped honey and vanilla.

Regoli

Via dello Statuto 60 (06 487 2812, www.pasticceriaregoli.com). Metro Vittorio/bus 70, 71, 105, 714/tram 5, 14. ***Open*** *6.30am-8pm Wed-Mon. Closed Aug.* ***No cards. Map*** *p182 O9* ❸ *Pasticceria*

With a history spanning over a century the Regoli family know their cakes, and Romans will happily cross town to their little *pasticceria* near piazza Vittorio Emanuele to taste the delectable selection. The *maritozzi con panna* (sweet brioche buns filled with freshly whipped cream) are widely considered to be the best in Rome and certainly merit a special trip.

Shops & services

❤ Trimani

Via Goito 20 (06 446 9661). Metro Termini/bus 38, 85, 92, 140, 217, 360. ***Open*** *9am-8.30pm Mon-Sat. Closed 1wk Aug.* ***Map*** *p182 O6* ❺ *Food & drink*

In the family since 1821, Trimani is Rome's oldest and best wine shop with a spectacular choice of labels from all over Italy which can be shipped anywhere in the world. Around the corner at Via Cernaia 37/b the same family recently opened a wine bar to serve wines by the glass as well as lunch and dinner.

SAN LORENZO

Colourful and hopping, the San Lorenzo neighbourhood still retains some of its original threadbare working-class character. Its proximity to Rome's La Sapienza university keeps it youthful and lively. A constant influx of students and artists mingles with a (diminishing) local population proud of its unswerving anti-Fascist and partisan history.

Constructed in the 1890s as a ramshackle ghetto for the poor, San Lorenzo became a hotbed of anarchist and left-wing activity. Hemmed in by urban infrastructure, such as the freight train depot and the sprawling cemetery of Il Verano, *sanlorenzini* were isolated in poverty from the rest of the city. Maria Montessori, who opened her first school here in 1907, said, 'When I first came to this quarter where respectable people only come when they're dead, I had the impression that some huge disaster had struck.'

Unbowed by their circumstances, the locals were ready with rocks and bricks to hurl from buildings when Fascists first came calling some years later. Alas, their anti-Fascism didn't help them in World War II: on 19 July 1943, Allied planes launched a strike on the Nazi-occupied train station – in the process knocking out several buildings, including the lovely (now restored) **San Lorenzo fuori le Mura**, and killing 3,000 civilians. The scars show, as do other vestiges of the district's history. But besides the many emporia selling tombstones, coffins and memorial lanterns, there's a happy mix of artisans, second-hand clothing shops, clubs and restaurants, plus purveyors of food and hardware to show that real people still live here. It's also home to Rome's only converted-loft artists' community.

To the north-east, some 120,000 students study at **La Sapienza university**, a sprawling complex of Fascist-era buildings by the likes of Marcello Piacentini and Arnaldo Foschini.

Sights & museums

San Lorenzo fuori le Mura

*Piazzale del Verano 3 (06 491 511). Bus 71, 88, 163, 492/tram 3, 19. **Open** Apr-Sept 7.30am-noon, 4-8pm daily. Oct-Mar 7.30am-12.30pm, 3.30-7pm daily. **Map** p182 S7.*

This spacious church, with its unusual chancel and ethereal light, gives an atmosphere of calm, a feature of the Romanesque tradition to which it belongs. Like most Roman places of worship, the building has been formed from a patchwork of 'improvements' over the centuries. St Laurence, whose remains lie in a crypt beneath the church, was martyred in the mid third century; convert-Emperor Constantine had a basilica built over his tomb during the fourth century. Several popes were subsequently laid to rest in the same underground catacombs.

In the late sixth century, Pope Pelagius II rebuilt the basilica; from this incarnation comes the broad chancel with its Corinthian columns, marble ciborium and stylised Byzantine mosaic of Pelagius and St Laurence, with Christ seated on an orb. The nave is a 13th-century addition by Pope Honorius, even though much is a faithful restoration undertaken after it was demolished by American bombs in 1943. In the portico are 13th-century frescoes depicting the life of the saint. A lovely courtyard encloses gardens and a piece of the errant bomb that wreaked havoc on the church. A ramp on the right leads behind the chancel, to the crypt of Blessed Pope Pius IX, the last pope to rule over the Vatican States; his reportedly uncorrupted body lies with a creepy silver mask over his face.

San Lorenzo fuori le Mura

Restaurants

Marcello €€

*Via dei Campani 12 (06 446 3311, www.osteriadamarcello.com). Bus 71, 140, 492, C2, C3/tram 3, 19. **Open** June-Sept 7.30-11.30pm Mon-Sat. Closed Fri. **No cards. Map** p182 R9* ❺ *Tratttoria*

From outside, this San Lorenzo eaterie looks like one of those spit-and-sawdust places that Romans refer to as *un buco* – a hole-in-the-wall. Inside, hordes of students from the nearby university occupy the old wooden tables. Alongside Roman offal specialities such as tripe and *pajata* (calf intestines) feature lighter, seasonal dishes such as *straccetti ai carciofi* (strips of veal with artichokes). Besides reliable traditional recipes (*spaghetti alla carbonara, all'amatriciana* or *alla gricia*), you can try home-made *ravioloni* filled with fresh cheese, ricotta and walnuts. There's a surprisingly extensive wine list, strong on big reds.

► *San Lorenzo has several great live music venues worth checking out. See p258 Live music venues.*

Bakeries, pasticcerie & gelaterie

Said

*Via Tiburtina 135 (06 446 9204, www.said.it). Bus 71, 492/tram 3, 19. **Open** noon-midnight Mon-Sat. Closed Aug. **Map** p182 R8* ❹ *Chocolatier*

This chocolate factory – in operation since 1923 – is enveloped in the glorious scent of its exquisite core product. But scattered among the antique chocolate-making equipment are tables and chairs at which to enjoy a warming hot chocolate in winter, a coffee any time, an *aperitivo* with buffet snacks (in which chocolate pops up in odd places) or – if you wish – a meal at the (rather overpriced and nothing to write home about) restaurant. We recommend you stick to the simpler pleasures.

Celio & San Giovanni

There are few finer places than San Giovanni and Celio to get a feel for the clash between powerful pagan Rome and early Christianity. After Emperor Constantine legalised Christianity in the fourth century, he donated land on which the basilica of San Giovanni in Laterano (originally dedicated to the Saviour) was built. This was ground-breaking in that it brought the new religion out into the open, but was fence-sitting in the sense that, at the time, this neighbourhood was as far as you could get from the city's centre of power. Today, the basilica continues to attract religious visitors, while the Celio retains the bucolic character that made it the area of choice for wealthy Romans.

❤ Don't miss

1 San Giovanni in Laterano *p206*
Cathedral of Rome, and off the beaten tourist trail (though a favourite for pilgrims).

2 Villa Celimontana *p203*
A stone's throw from the Colosseum, but a million miles from the crowds lies this tranquil, timeless, ever so slightly unkempt park.

3 San Clemente *p200*
Three layers of history in one church, a real-life time machine.

4 Li Rioni *p204*
A loud, raucous Roman dining experience.

In the know

Getting around

Close to the Colosseum, the Celio is a great place to escape the crowds into a real neighbourhood – the most convenient metro stop is Colosseo (line B). At the far end of via San Giovanni in Laterano (or more easily accessed by the San Giovanni stop on metro line A) is the Cathedral of Rome, and to the east of it, the area of San Giovanni.

Mosaic in Santa Maria in Domnica *p202*

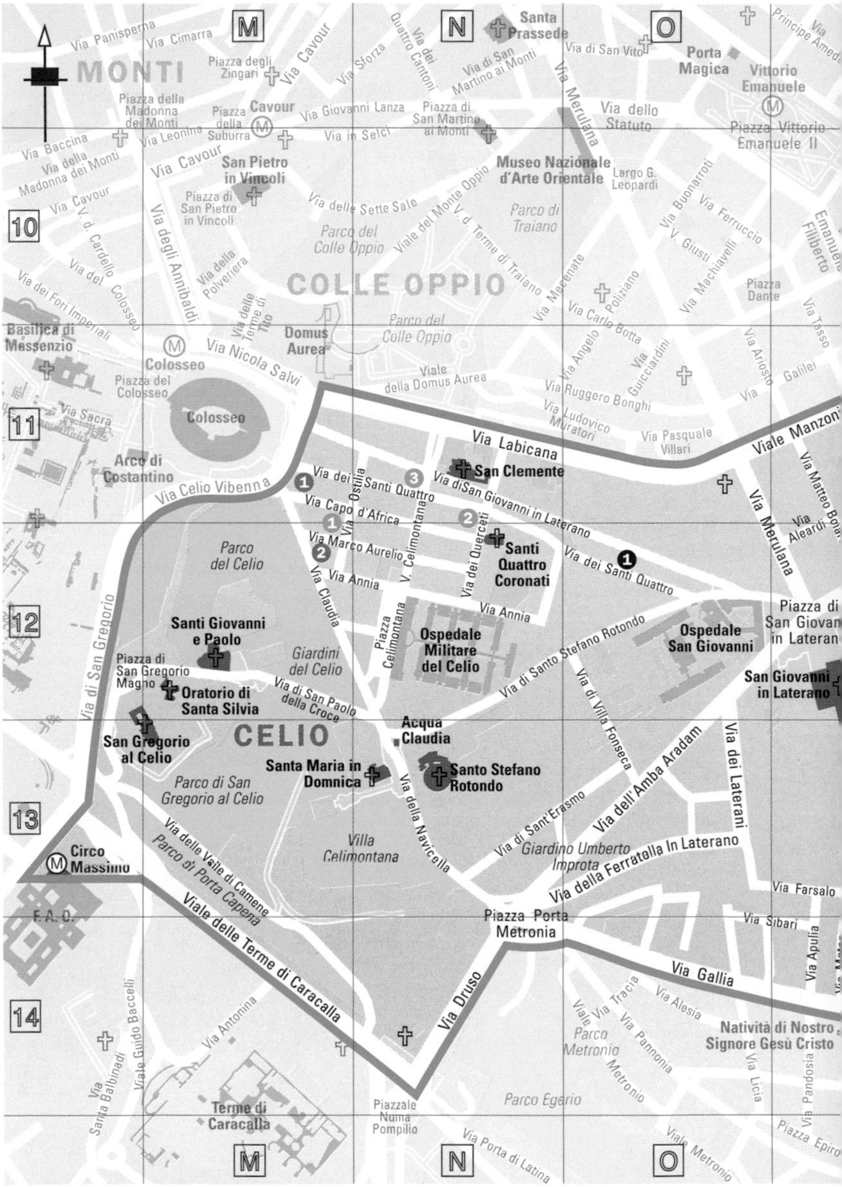

CELIO & SAN GIOVANNI

Restaurants

1. Il Bocconcino
2. Li Rioni
3. Luzzi

Cafés, bars & pubs

1. Café Café
2. Caffè Propaganda

Shops & services

1. Soul Food
2. Mercato via Sannio

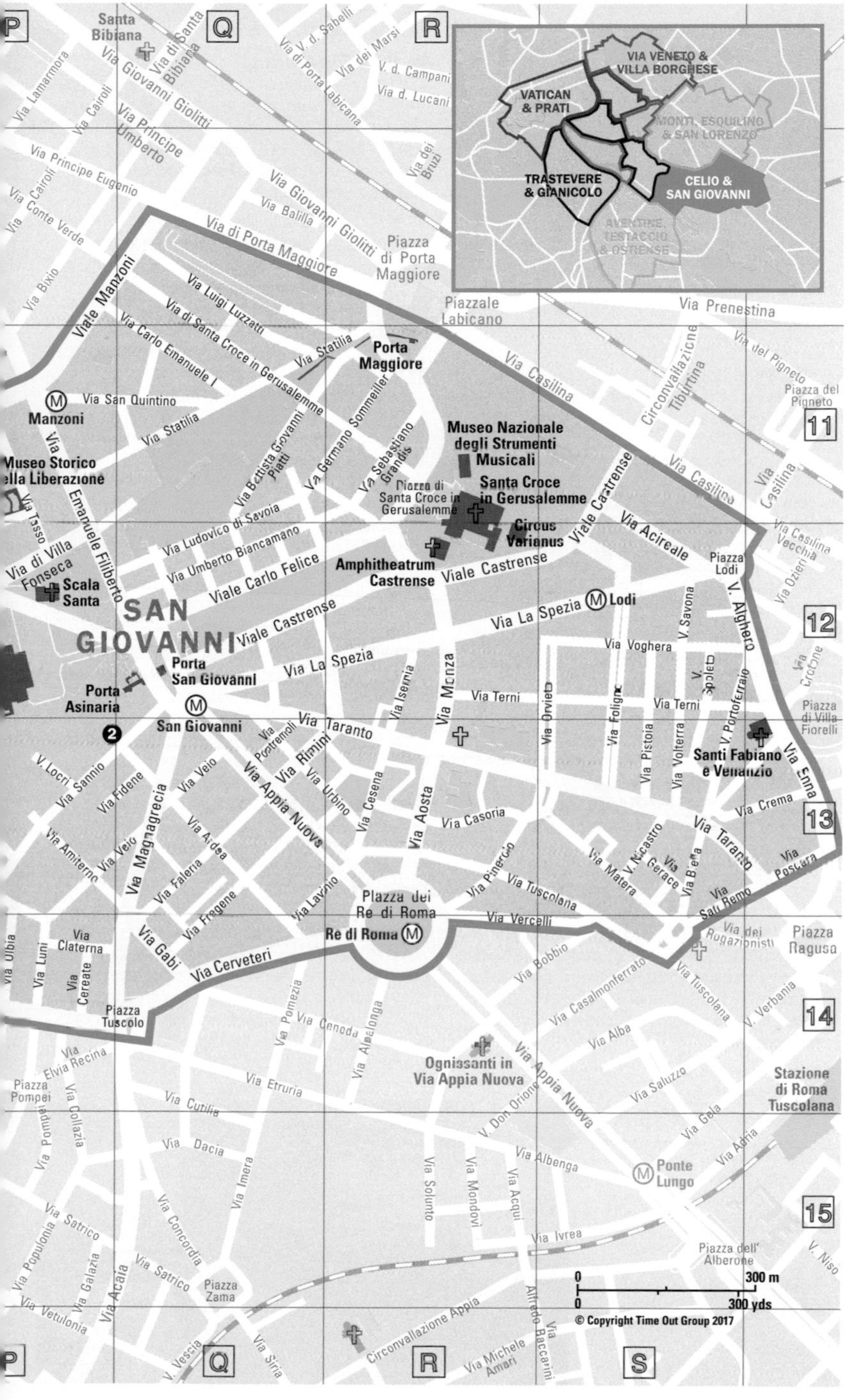

CELIO & SAN GIOVANNI

CELIO

Once home to Roman senators, nobility and wealthy entrepreneurs, the Caelian hill (one of the famous seven) was – like the rest of Rome – overrun in AD 410 by Alaric the Goth. Its patrician villas and shops remained largely deserted for centuries afterwards, crumbling back to nature. Today, the hill itself retains a bucolic character; much of it is occupied by monasteries and convents, churches and nursery schools.

The greater Celio neighbourhood stretches roughly from the via delle Terme di Caracalla to the south, to the Palatine to the west, the Colosseum to the north and **San Giovanni in Laterano** (*see p206*) to the east. An arduous but rewarding (and crowd-free) walking tour of the area could begin at the church of **San Gregorio al Celio** , pass under the medieval arcade to the church of **Santi Giovanni e Paolo** (*see p202*), with its fabulous Roman house underneath, and on to the lovely, leafy **Villa Celimontana** (*see p203*) park – a good place to rest your feet.

The high-walled road along the park's northern edge leads to a chunk of the **Acqua Claudia** aqueduct. At the top of the supporting arch is a blue and red Greek cross, the symbol of the Trinitarian order whose 12th-century mission was to raise money to pay the ransom of crusaders captured by the infidels.

Past that arch, and right into **via della Navicella**, two churches face off across the street. On the west, **Santa Maria in Domnica** (*see p202*) has pretty ninth-century mosaics and a delicate sculpture of a little Roman boat (*navicella*) in front of it. Across the road, assorted martyrdoms are depicted in the odd and gruesome frescoes in **Santo Stefano Rotondo** (*see p203*). North of here, the monolithic **Santi Quattro Coronati** (*see p203*) complex comes into view, with its charming cloister and secret chapel. Nearby is the multi-layered **San Clemente**.

Sights & museums

❤ San Clemente

Via San Giovanni in Laterano (06 774 0021, www.basilicasanclemente.com). Metro Colosseo/bus 53, 75, 80, 85, 87, 117, 810/ tram 3. ***Open*** *9am-12.30pm, 3-6pm Mon-Sat; noon-6pm Sun.* ***Admission*** *Church free. Excavations €10; €5 reductions.* ***Map*** *p198 N11.*

A favourite with kids for its dungeon-like underground level, this 12th-century basilica is a three-dimensional Roman timeline, a church above a church above an even older Imperial building – a full 18 metres (60 feet) of Roman life separate the earliest structure from the one we see today.

In 1857 the Irish Dominicans – who have run the church since the 17th century – began digs that unearthed the church's fourth-century predecessor, and, beneath, an early Christian *titulus* (meeting place). The fourth-century structure was razed in the Norman sack of 1084, but the *schola cantorum* (choir), with its exquisite carving and mosaic decorations, survived and was moved upstairs to the new church, where it still stands.

Also in the upper church is the 12th-century mosaic in the apse, still in Byzantine style but with a theological complexity unusual for its period. Against a gold backdrop, cobalt blues, deep reds and multi-hued greens make up the crucified Christ. From the drops of Christ's blood springs the vine representing the Church, which swirls around peasants at their daily tasks, Doctors of the Church spreading the divine word and a host of animals. Above the cross, the hand of God links heaven and earth, while below, sheep represent Christ and the 12 apostles. The Latin inscription above the sheep says 'I am the vine, you are the branches'. Towards the back of the church, in the chapel of St Catherine of Alexandria, a series of frescoes by Masolino (c1430), possibly with help from Masaccio, depict the life of the saint – she is shown calmly praying as her torturers prepare

❤ Time to eat & drink

Morning coffee
Café Café *p205*

Lunch
Luzzi *p205*

Dinner
Li Rioni *p204*

Cocktails
Caffè Propaganda *p205*

Café Café

the wheel to which she was strapped and stretched to death (and for which the firework was later named) – as well as Christ on the cross in between the two thieves.

From the sacristy, steps lead down to the fourth-century basilica, the space broken up by walls supporting the structure above. Fading frescoes show scenes from the life of St Clement, the fourth pope, exiled to the Crimea by Emperor Trajan. Even in exile, he didn't give up proselytising and so was hurled into the Black Sea, tied to an anchor. A year later, the sea receded, revealing a tomb containing Clement's body. After that, the sea would recede once a year and another miracle would occur.

Near the far end of the underground basilica is a modern shrine to St Cyril; the inventor of Cyrillic script was a great figure of the Orthodox churches and credited with bringing Clement's body to Rome.

A stairway leads down to an ancient Roman alley. On one side are the remains of a second-century Roman insula, or apartment building, containing a site where the Persian god Mithras was worshipped (*see p204* Blood and Sperm: the Cult of Mithras). There are three rooms devoted to the cult. In the sanctuary, a fresco depicts the god killing a bull. On the other side of the lane are the ground-floor rooms of a Roman house used by early Christians as a *titulus*. At one of the turns in this warren of antiquity, you can hear water rushing through an ancient sewer on its way down to the Tiber.

San Gregorio al Celio

Piazza di San Gregorio Magno 1 (06 700 8227). Bus 75, 80, 81, 673/tram 3. ***Open*** *9am-noon, 4-7pm daily.* ***Map*** *p198 M13.*

This impressive Baroque church with a grandiose staircase, finished by Giovanni Battista Soria in 1633, stands on the site of the home of one of the most remarkable popes, Gregory I (the Great; 590-604). Gregory was steered by his affluent family towards a career in public administration, but instead he embraced the monastic life and converted his house into a monastery. He became Pope Pelagius II's right-hand man and was tapped for the papacy when Pelagius died. Popular lore says he fled Rome when he heard the news; dragged back, he spent his 14-year pontificate vigorously reorganising the Church.

Inside the church, in a chapel on the right, is a marble chair dating from the first century BC, said to have been used by Gregory as his papal throne. Also here is the tomb of diplomat Sir Edward Carne, who visited Rome several times to persuade the pope to annul the marriage of Henry VIII and Catherine of Aragon, so that the king would be able to marry Anne Boleyn.

Outside, across a pine-scented garden, stand three chapels, or *oratori*. The chapels of Santa Barbara and Sant'Andrea are medieval structures, heavily restored in the early 17th century and popularly believed to have been part of the house of Gregory the Great and his mother St Sylvia; Sant'Andrea has frescoes by Guido Reni and

Sack of Rome 1084

Normans on the rampage

Decades before William led his Normans across the Channel to conquer England, another freebooting Norman, Robert de Hauteville – aka Robert Guiscard – was rampaging through Italy. With his brother Roger, he took control of all southern Italy and became a major power broker. In 1084 Pope Gregory VII called for the Normans' help when the Holy Roman Emperor Henry IV laid siege to Rome. But though the Normans successfully beat back Imperial troops, the Romans weren't happy having the swaggering northerners about, and showed it. So the Normans went on the rampage, looting, pillaging and setting fire to large swathes of the city. When Robert and his men scaled the city walls and broke into *caput mundi*, the Palatine (*see p67*) still bristled with ancient Roman palaces – a little down-at-heel perhaps, but standing, and with their original roofs more or less intact. To vent their anger fully, Roman legend has it, the ransackers painted the *palazzi* with pitch, to ensure that, once set alight, they would burn for days. The rich ecclesiastical properties on the Caelian hill were another key target for Norman pillage. **Santi Quattro Coronati** (*p203*), **San Clemente** (*p200*) and **Santi Giovanni e Paolo** (*p202*) all suffered devastating attacks, and the terrified residents of the Celio high-tailed it down towards the river, to huddle around **Castel Sant'Angelo** (*p161*) and the poorer, more densely populated area near the river. Centuries would pass before the Celio shook off its ghost-town feel.

For further rape and pillage, *see p284*.

Domenichino. The chapel of Santa Silvia itself dates from the 17th century. Behind the chapels are remains of shops that once lined this ancient road, the Clivus Scauri.

Santa Maria in Domnica

Via della Navicella 10 (06 7720 2685). Bus 81, 117, 673. ***Open*** *9am-noon, 3.30-6pm daily.* ***Map*** *p198 N13.*

Santa Maria in Domnica is known to the locals as the *navicella* (little ship), after the Roman statue that stands outside (which was the inspiration for the 16th-century *barcaccia* fountain at the Spanish Steps). A church was built here in the seventh century, over the barracks of a corps of Roman *vigiles* (firefighters). It was reconstructed in the ninth century by Pope Paschal I, who commissioned the apse mosaic – one of the most charming in Rome. The pope is portrayed sitting at the feet of the Virgin and Child with a square halo that indicates he was living when the mosaic was made. What sets this lovely design in gold and rich blues, reds and aquamarines apart is that Mary and Jesus don't show the melancholy prescience of what was to befall them as did most such depictions until then: the cherry-red daubs of blush on their cheeks give them a healthy and cheerful glow. They are surrounded by a host of angels; above, the apostles appear to be skipping through a meadow. The interior of the church is austere and peaceful, with 18 ancient marble columns supporting the graceful arches of the nave. The carved wood ceiling and porticoed façade are the result of a 16th-century restoration.

Santi Giovanni e Paolo

Piazza Santi Giovanni e Paolo 13 (church 06 700 5745, excavations 06 7045 4544, www.case romane.it). Bus 75, 80, 81, 673/tram 3. ***Church*** *8.30am-noon, 3.30-6pm daily.* ***Excavations*** *10am-1pm, 3-6pm Mon, Thur-Sun.* ***Admission*** *Church free. Excavations €8; €6 reductions. No cards.* ***Map*** *p198 M12.*

In the fourth century, a church was built over the house (and probably the bones) of John and Paul, two officers at the Imperial court who were martyred in 362. The original church was hacked away, first by Goths and later by Normans (*see above* Sack of Rome), but traces of it can still be seen in the 12th-century façade on lovely piazza Santi Giovanni e Paolo, which is overlooked by a 12th-century bell tower attached to the nearby convent. Two time-worn lions flank the entrance; one seems to be gnawing on a helpless babe.

An 18th-century restoration left the church with its present lugubrious ambience inside. The elaborate chandeliers were donated by Cardinal Spellman in the 1950s, a hand-me-down from the Waldorf Astoria in New York. Outside the church, head around the corner, beneath the medieval buttresses of Clivus Scauri to locate the door leading to the labyrinthine excavations of the martyrs' house. Digs in the 19th century and others in the final years of the 20th led to the discovery of more than 20 rooms on several levels. From four different buildings, and dating from the first century AD, these rooms include some evidently used for secret Christian worship. Among these are spaces bought in the fourth century by wealthy senator Pammachius, who, after embracing Christianity, donated generously to the poor and made his home into a church. Three other Christian martyrs are said to be buried there; a well-preserved fresco from the late fourth century in the *confessio* honours them. In the nymphaeum, putti in brightly coloured boats flank a naked female divinity, perhaps Proserpine. There are several other frescoes preserved in good condition throughout the site. This is an especially rewarding and little-visited place to time-travel through Roman history.

The sacristan may let you in through the gates at the foot of the bell tower: from there you'll get a glimpse of the massive foundations of the Temple of Claudius.

Santi Quattro Coronati

Via dei Querceti (06 7047 5427, www.monacheagostinianesantiquattrocoronati.it). Bus 53, 85, 117/tram 3. ***Church*** *6.30am-12.45pm, 3-7.45pm daily.* ***Cloister*** *10-11.45am, 4-5.45pm Mon-Sat.* ***Oratory*** *8.30-11.45am, 4-5.45pm daily.* ***Map*** *p198 N12.*

The secret places in the basilica of the Four Crowned Saints make it a good candidate for dragging listless kids to. The church dates from the fourth century and was probably named after four Roman soldiers who refused to pray before the statue of Esculapius, the Roman god of healing. Another version has it dedicated to early stonemasons who refused to sculpt the aforementioned deity, making the church especially dear to present-day masons. Like San Clemente and Santi Giovanni e Paolo, it was burned down by rampaging Normans in 1084 (*see left* Sack of Rome). It was rebuilt as a fortified monastery, with the church itself reduced to half its original dimensions; the outsize apse, visible as you look uphill along via dei Santi Quattro, remains from the original church. The early basilica form is still discernible, and the columns that once ran along the aisles are embedded in the walls of the innermost courtyard. The church has a fine cosmatesque floor and an upper-level *matronium*, to which women were relegated during religious functions. There is also one of Rome's most beautiful cloisters, dating from about 1220, with lovely, slender columns supporting delicate arches and a double-cupped fountain amid its flowerbeds. The musty chapel of Santa Barbara conceals a pair of frescoes: a 12th-century *Madonna and Child* and a ninth-century unidentified saint. Just ring the bell at the door on the left side of the nave and a kind-hearted nun will probably let you have a peek.

In the oratory outside the church (ring the bell and ask for the key) is a fresco cycle depicting the *Donation of Constantine* – a false story put forward for centuries by the papacy as justification for its authority. According to the legend, an early pope, Sylvester, cured Emperor Constantine of leprosy, after which the august personage was so grateful that he granted the Bishops of Rome spiritual and worldly authority over the whole of the Western Empire (Constantine, from his capital at Constantinople, lorded it over the Eastern Empire). The frescoes, a first-class example of political propaganda, were painted in the 13th century. They show a pox-ridden Constantine being healed by Sylvester, crowning him with a tiara and giving him a cap to symbolise the pope's spiritual and – more importantly – earthly power. In one scene, Constantine's mother, Helen, indicates Christ's cross on the hill of Golgotha. Visitors are asked to be as silent as possible: the monastery is home to an enclosed order of Augustine nuns.

Santo Stefano Rotondo

Via di Santo Stefano Rotondo 7 (06 4211 9132, www.santo-stefano-rotondo.it). Bus 81, 117, 673. ***Open*** *Apr-Sept 10am-1pm, 3.30-6.30pm daily. Oct-Mar 10am-1pm, 2.30-5.30pm daily.* ***Map*** *p198 N13.*

Perhaps inspired by the Church of the Holy Sepulchre in Jerusalem, this unusual round church dates from the fifth century; in its measurements, some say, lies the secret of the Holy Number of God. It rests on parts of a patrician Roman villa and a mithraeum, one of many in this area of Rome. In its original form, the church must have been exceptionally beautiful, with its Byzantine-inspired simplicity – three concentric naves separated by rings of antique columns set within a Greek cross – and play of natural light. This effect was disturbed when arches were built to shore it up in the 12th century, and the portico was added. The outer ring was walled in 1450, and the atmosphere changed definitively with a 16th-century attempt at mind control: 34 horrifically graphic frescoes of martyrs being boiled, stretched and slashed were added to the interior walls for the edification of the faithful. Visit when the sun is streaming in from the upper windows and you'll catch something of the original contemplative aura.

❤ Villa Celimontana

Via della Navicella/via San Paolo della Croce. Bus 75, 80, 81, 117, 673/tram 3. ***Open*** *dawn-dusk daily.* ***Map*** *p198 N13.*

This is a pretty, leafy walled garden, with a rather pokey playground; which does not stop swarms of local kids from climbing, running and holding birthday picnics here. The pleasant lawns are dotted with pieces of marble from the collection of the Mattei

Blood and Sperm

The cult of Mithras

Mithras was an ancient Persian god, mentioned in cuneiform texts from as far back as the 15th century BC. A sun deity, god of contracts and loyalty, Mithras was ordered by Apollo to sacrifice a bull which he apparently did quite unwillingly – his face is always averted from the animal in portrayals of the act. The bull became the moon, Mithras' cape became the starry sky, the bull's blood was transformed into grapes and corn and its semen was the seed from which everything else sprung. But awoken by the celestial light of the sacrifice, evil appeared in the shape of a scorpion and a snake, and so began the eternal struggle between good and evil. Or so says the myth.

As gentler turn-the-other-cheek Christianity, with its promise of a happier afterlife, spread across the Roman world, so did this messier men-only cult: the former slowly among women and slaves, the latter rampantly among the military. Battle-weary troops were encouraged by emperors and generals to aspire to the loyalty demanded by this deity. There were initiation rites, quite a bit of chastisement, enthusiastic animal sacrifices and a ladder of seven cult ranks to climb. Meetings were held in long narrow caverns, with members facing off from long benches along the side. Mithraeums can be seen beneath the churches of **San Clemente** (*see p200*) and **Santo Stefano Rotondo** (*see p203*), as well as in the ancient port of **Ostia Antica** (*see p232*).

The cult of Mithras was still going strong in the early fourth century, but Christianity was slowly gaining the upper hand. Unfortunately for the grisly Persian god, it was a burning cross rather than a blazing bull that led the Emperor Constantine to victory in 312 (*see p281*). The emperor threw his weight behind Jesus. By the time it was banned in 395, Mithraism was the religion of a handful of reactionary pagan cranks.

Mithraeum, Ostia Antica

family, which owned the property from 1553 until 1928, when it became a public park. The graceful family villa, now housing the Italian Geographic Society, was built in the 16th century. Forlorn and forgotten at the southern end is one of Rome's Egyptian obelisks. During the summer, the villa becomes the gorgeous venue for evening jazz concerts (*see p261* Summer Nights).

Restaurants

Il Bocconcino €€

Via Ostilia 23 (06 7707 9175, www.ilbocconcino.com). Bus 53, 75, 80, 81, 85, 87, 117, 673/tram 3. ***Open*** *12.30-3.30pm, 7-11pm Mon, Tue, Thur-Sun. Closed 3wks Aug.* ***Map*** *p198 M11* ❶ Tratttoria

With its red-check tablecloths and brick vaulted ceilings, this trattoria within a slingshot's range of the Colosseum feels like the definition of tradition. The welcome is friendly, the menu mixes Roman classics such as *tonnarelli cacio e pepe* or *abbacchio brodettato* (braised lamb) with a sprinkling of more adventurous, Slow-Food-style dishes (the former are a safer bet). On Tuesdays and Fridays, fish dominates the menu. The wine list is limited but honestly priced. The desserts are worth leaving space for.

❤ Li Rioni €€

Via dei Santi Quattro 24 (06 7045 0605, lirioni.it) Metro Colosseo/bus 53, 75, 80, 81, 85, 87, 117, 673/tram 3. ***Open*** *7pm-midnight Wed-Mon. Closed 2wks Aug.* ***Map*** *p198 N11* ❷ Pizzeria

A hit with locals and tourists alike, Li Rioni churns out wafer-thin *pizza romana* from its wood-fired oven at an impressive rate, and at more than reasonable prices given its location just a short stroll from the Colosseum. The (slightly kitsch) interior is decked out like a Roman street with shuttered windows and terracotta hues and in summer extra tables are set up outside on the pavement. Expect it to be packed, and very noisy; exactly as a Roman pizzeria should be.

❤ Luzzi €€

Via Celimontana 1 (06 709 6332, www. trattorialuzzi.it). Metro Colosseo/bus 53, 75, 80, 81, 85, 87, 117, 673/tram 3. ***Open*** *noon-midnight Mon, Tue, Thur-Sun. Closed 2wks Aug.* ***Map*** *p198 N11* ❸ *Trattoria*

When it's busy (and it almost always is), this heaving neighbourhood trattoria is the loudest and most crowded 40sq m in the whole of Rome. It isn't the place for a romantic tête-à-tête, nor for gourmet dining, but it is cheap, lively and handy for the Colosseum. And the menu's range of Roman staples and pizzas is competently done, though expect the service to be a little erratic. The outdoor tables operate all year round.

Cafés, bars & pubs

❤ Café Café

Via dei Santi Quattro 44 (06 700 8743, www. cafecafebistrot.it). Metro Colosseo/bus 53, 75, 80, 81, 85, 87, 117, 673/tram 3. ***Open*** *9.30am-4.30pm daily. Closed 1wk Aug.* ***Map*** *p198 M11* ❶ *Café*

This attractive place offers smoothies, teas, wines, salads and sandwiches for travellers weary after a romp around the Colosseum. There's a brunch buffet from 11.30am to 4pm on Sundays.

❤ Caffè Propaganda

Via Claudia 15 (06 9453 4255, www.caffe propaganda.it). Metro Colosseo/bus 53, 75, 80, 81, 85, 87, 117, 186, 271, 571, 673, 810/tram 3. ***Open*** *noon-2am daily.* ***Map*** *p198 M12* ❷ *Café*

With its leather banquettes, monochrome décor and French artwork, Caffè Propaganda looks more Paris bistro than Roman drinking hole. Its diverse clientele consists of well-heeled Romans mixed with tourists who stumble in after a trek around the Colosseum down the road. Lunch and dinner are served but prices are high and the service can be patchy making it best to drop by for afternoon tea or coffee (accompanied by one of the exquisite pastries).

Shops & services

Soul Food

Via San Giovanni in Laterano 192/194 (06 7045 2025, www.haterecords.com). Metro Colosseo/bus 53, 85, 75, 80, 87, 117, 673/ tram 3. ***Open*** *10.30am-1.30pm, 3.30-8pm Tue-Sat. Closed 3wks Aug.* ***Map*** *p198 O12* ❶ *Music*

A cool vintage record shop, stocking indie, punk, beat, exotica, lounge, rockabilly and more. Heaven.

SAN GIOVANNI

Seat of the Bishop of Rome (ie the Pope in his local role), and the first and foremost of the four great Roman basilicas, **San Giovanni in Laterano** (*see p206*) is high on any pilgrim's must-do list. However, many non-religious visitors are liable to write it (and the area that surrounds it) off as too far from the *centro storico*, a state of affairs not helped by the fact that first-class sights are thin on the ground here. This is a pity because a stop at this grandiose – if rather impersonal – cathedral and nearby monuments provides a good picture of Christianity as a fledgling state religion.

San Giovanni stands on the spot donated in the third century by Emperor Constantine for the construction of the first Christian basilica: he wasn't keen to rock the boat too much – note its location inside the city walls but in a then-quiet corner far away from the centre of political power. For centuries it was to be the papal seat and residence, its importance underscored by the presence of many holy souvenirs carted here from the Holy Land by Constantine's mother Helena, an early convert to the new faith. The 28 steps of the **Scala Santa**, for example, across the road to the north of the basilica, were said to be the very ones that Christ climbed to hear Pontius Pilate's non-verdict that essentially condemned him to death. At the top is the **Sancta Sanctorum**, containing super-sacred relics. A few blocks north of here is the **Museo Storico della Liberazione**, a grim testament to the notorious prison where Nazi SS officers tortured and killed suspected partisans.

On the west side of San Giovanni are the Lateran palace, now used for the administration of the Church in Italy, the Pontifical University and the octagonal baptistry. Stranded in the middle of thundering traffic in the unappealing piazza is another of Rome's Egyptian obelisks (*see p85* Obelisks). South-east of the church are the sunken ruins of **Porta Asinaria**, an ancient gate belonging to the third-century Aurelian Wall. The **Porta San Giovanni** is the starting point of the modern via Appia Nuova, a retail-intensive main drag that leads south out of town to the Alban Hills.

A park has been created beneath the impressive stretch of Aurelian Wall running from San Giovanni east towards **Santa Croce in Gerusalemme**, a basilica that bristles with relics brought back by the redoubtable St Helena after her pilgrimage to the Holy Land at the age of 80: pieces of the cross, a nail and thorns from Christ's crown among them.

Dotted around is a panoply of minor Roman ruins: through the opening in the Aurelian Wall to the right of the church is the **Amphitheatrum Castrense**, and part of the **Circus Varianus**, both dating from the reign of Elagabalus; the Baths of Helena, of which only the cistern is visible; and the monumental travertine archway built by Emperor Claudius in the first century AD to mark the triumphal entrance of the aqueducts into the city (it was later incorporated into the Aurelian Wall).

To the east of Santa Croce is the delightful **Museo Nazionale degli Strumenti Musicali** (Museum of Musical Instruments, piazza Santa Croce in Gerusalemme 9a, www.museostrumentimusicali.it) which contains an astonishing variety of drums, lutes, flutes and spinets.

The oven-shaped **Tomb of Eurysaces** (an ancient Roman baker) stands just outside the well-preserved third-century **Porta Maggiore**.

Sights & museums

Museo Storico della Liberazione

Via Tasso 154 (06 700 3866, www. museoliberazione.it). Metro San Giovanni/ bus 16, 85, 87, 186, 218, 650, 665, 714/tram 3. ***Open*** *9.30am-12.30pm, 3.30-7.30pm Tue-Fri; 9.30am-12.30pm Sat, Sun. Closed Aug.* ***Admission*** *free.* ***Map*** *p198 P11.*

A stone's throw from the Holy Staircase, this small museum occupies the house where the Gestapo interrogated suspected Resistance fighters during the wartime occupation. From the messages carved into cell walls to the rows of photos of victims, it is a haunting place.

❤ San Giovanni in Laterano

Piazza San Giovanni in Laterano 4 (06 6988 6409, www.vatican.va). Metro San Giovanni/ bus 16, 81, 85, 87, 117, 218, 650, 714/tram 3. ***Church*** *7am-6.30pm daily.* ***Baptistry*** *7.30am-12.30 pm, 4-6.30pm daily.* ***Cloister*** *9am-6pm daily. Museum 10am-5.30pm daily.* ***Admission*** *Church free. Cloister €3. Museum €4. No cards.* ***Map*** *p198 P12.*

The Catholic faithful earn indulgences for visits to this major basilica. Along with the Lateran palace, it was the site of the original papal headquarters until the move across the river to St Peter's and the Vatican during the 14th century. Constantine's second wife, Fausta, gave the plot of land to Pope Melchiades to build the papal residence and church in 313. There are few traces of the original basilica, which was destroyed by fire, earthquake and barbarians. It has been heavily restored and reconstructed: the end result is a vast, impersonal, over-decorated hangar.

The façade, with its 15 huge statues of Christ, the two Johns (Baptist and Evangelist) and 12 Doctors of the Church, is part of the 1735 rebuilding by Alessandro Galilei. The interior bears the stamp of Borromini, who transformed it in 1646. A few treasures from earlier times survive: a much restored 13th-century mosaic in the apse, a fragment of a fresco attributed to Giotto (hidden behind the first column on the right) showing Pope Boniface VIII announcing the first Holy Year in 1300, and the Gothic *baldacchino* over the main altar.

Off the left aisle is the 13th-century cloister, with delicate twisted columns and fine cosmatesque work by the Vassalletto family. A small museum off the cloister contains papal vestments and some original manuscripts of music by Palestrina.

The north façade was designed in 1586 by Domenico Fontana, who also placed Rome's tallest Egyptian obelisk outside. This was part of Pope Sixtus V's 16th-century urban renewal scheme. Also on this side is the octagonal baptistry that Constantine had built. The four chapels surrounding the font have mosaics from the fifth and seventh centuries, and bronze doors said to come from the Baths of Caracalla.

Santa Croce in Gerusalemme

Piazza Santa Croce in Gerusalemme 12 (06 7061 3053, www.santacroceroma.it). Bus 81, 649/tram 3. ***Open*** *7am-12.45pm, 3.30-7.30pm daily.* ***Map*** *p198 R11.*

Founded in 320 by St Helena, mother of Emperor Constantine (who legalised Christianity in 313), this church began as a hall in her home, the Palatium Sessorium, a palace that originally belonged to the Emperor Septimius Severus (193-211). The church was rebuilt and extended in the 12th century, and again in 1743-44. Helena had her church constructed to house relics brought back from the Holy Land by the redoubtable lady herself. The emperor's *mamma* came back with an enviable shopping-bagful: three chunks of Christ's cross, a nail, two thorns from his crown and the finger of St Thomas – allegedly the very one that the doubting saint stuck into Christ's wound. All these are displayed in a chapel at the end of a Fascist-era hall at the left side of the nave. Apart from the wood, those venerable objects are rather hard to identify, inside their gold reliquaries. In the mosaic-ceilinged lower chapel (under the altar) is Helena's stash of soil from

Jerusalem. Helena's Holy Land souvenir collecting sparked a relic-craze exploited to the full for centuries by the wily merchants of the Holy Land; when Jesus-related bits were in short supply, scraps of saints and martyrs were fair game too.

The basilica's gorgeous vegetable garden, restored and lovingly tended by monks of the adjoining monastery, is unfortunately closed to the public.

► *The grave of St Helena can be seen in the Aracoeli (see p63)... though the pretty little church of Sant'Elena in Venice also claims to have the great lady's body.*

Scala Santa & Sancta Sanctorum

Piazza di San Giovanni in Laterano 14 (06 772 6641, www.scala-santa.com). Metro San Giovanni/bus 16, 85, 87, 218, 650, 665, 714/ tram 3. ***Scala Santa*** *Apr-Sept 6.15am-1pm, 3-6.30pm Mon-Sat; 7am-12.30pm Sun. Oct-Mar 6.15am-1pm, 3-6pm Mon-Sat; 7am-12.30pm Sun.* ***Sancta Sanctorum*** *(booking obligatory) 9.30am-12.30pm, 3-5.10 pm Mon-Sat.* ***Admission*** *Scala Santa free. Sancta Sanctorum €3.50. No cards.* ***Map*** *p198 P12.*

According to tradition, these steps (now covered with wooden planks) are the very ones Jesus climbed in the house of Pontius Pilate only to see the Roman governor wash his hands of the self-styled messiah. Emperor Constantine's mother St Helena brought these back in the fourth century. A crawl up the Scala Santa (on your knees) has been a fixture on every serious pilgrim's list ever since. In 1510 Martin Luther gave it a go, but halfway up he decided that relics were a theological irrelevance and walked back down again. Don't climb them unless you know 28 different prayers (one for each step); walking up is not allowed. Prepare for a queue on Good Friday.

At the top of the Holy Stairs (but also accessible by non-holy stairs to the left) is the Sancta Sanctorum ('Holy of Holies'), the *privatissima* chapel of the popes and one of the only monuments around here that escaped Sixtus V's revamping. Some of the best early Christian relics were kept in the crypt under the altar at one time – including the heads of saints Peter, Paul and young Agnes. Most of them have been distributed to other churches around the city, but displayed in a glass case on the left wall is a fragment of the table on which the Last Supper was supposedly served. The real treasures here, however, are the 13th-century frescoes in the lunettes and on the ceiling, attributed to Cimabue. Once, no one but the *pontifex maximus* himself was allowed to set foot in the Sancta Sanctorum.

Shops & services

Mercato via Sannio

Via Sannio. Metro San Giovanni/bus 16, 53, 81, 85, 87, 218, 360, 650. ***Open*** *8.30am-1.30pm Mon-Fri; 8.30am-6pm Sat.* ***Map*** *p198 P13* ❷ *Market*

Via Sannio market is made up of long corridors of stalls piled high with new, low-priced clothes, and a large second-hand section behind. Those prepared to sort through the slagheap of cut-price day- and eveningwear, bags and shoes, will be rewarded with rare gems.

San Giovanni in Laterano

Aventine, Testaccio & Ostiense

The leafy, upmarket Aventine hill couldn't be more different from the busy, workaday districts of Testaccio and Ostiense that lie at its southern feet, yet there's a grudging respect between them that runs both ways. Without the proximity of Testaccio's bars and markets, and Ostiense's burgeoning cultural and nightlife scene, the Aventine would be nothing but a lifeless enclave of privilege; whereas inhabitants of the hectic lower areas are grateful for a respite from the bustle and din that surrounds them with a wander up to the peaceful hill that overlooks them. Quiet attractions abound here, from the Terme di Caracalla (Baths of Caracalla) to the Cimitero Acattolico.

❤ Don't miss

1 Centrale Montemartini *p213*
Ancient sculptures meet early 20th-century power station.

2 Cimitero Acattolico *p216*
Pay your respects to Keats and Shelley, in gloriously verdant surroundings nestling at the foot of the Aurelian Wall.

3 Terme di Caracalla *p214 & p269*
Visit the Baths on summer evenings to take in an opera surrounded by antiquity, or just marvel at the vast scale in silence.

4 Da Remo *p217*
For the best *pizza romana* in town pay a visit to this Testaccio institution.

In the know
Getting around

South of the centre of town, the Aventine is eminently walkable from the Colosseum area. Alternatively metro stop Circo Massimo on line B is the closest. For Testaccio and Ostiense, Piramide is the most convenient stop.

Centrale Montemartini

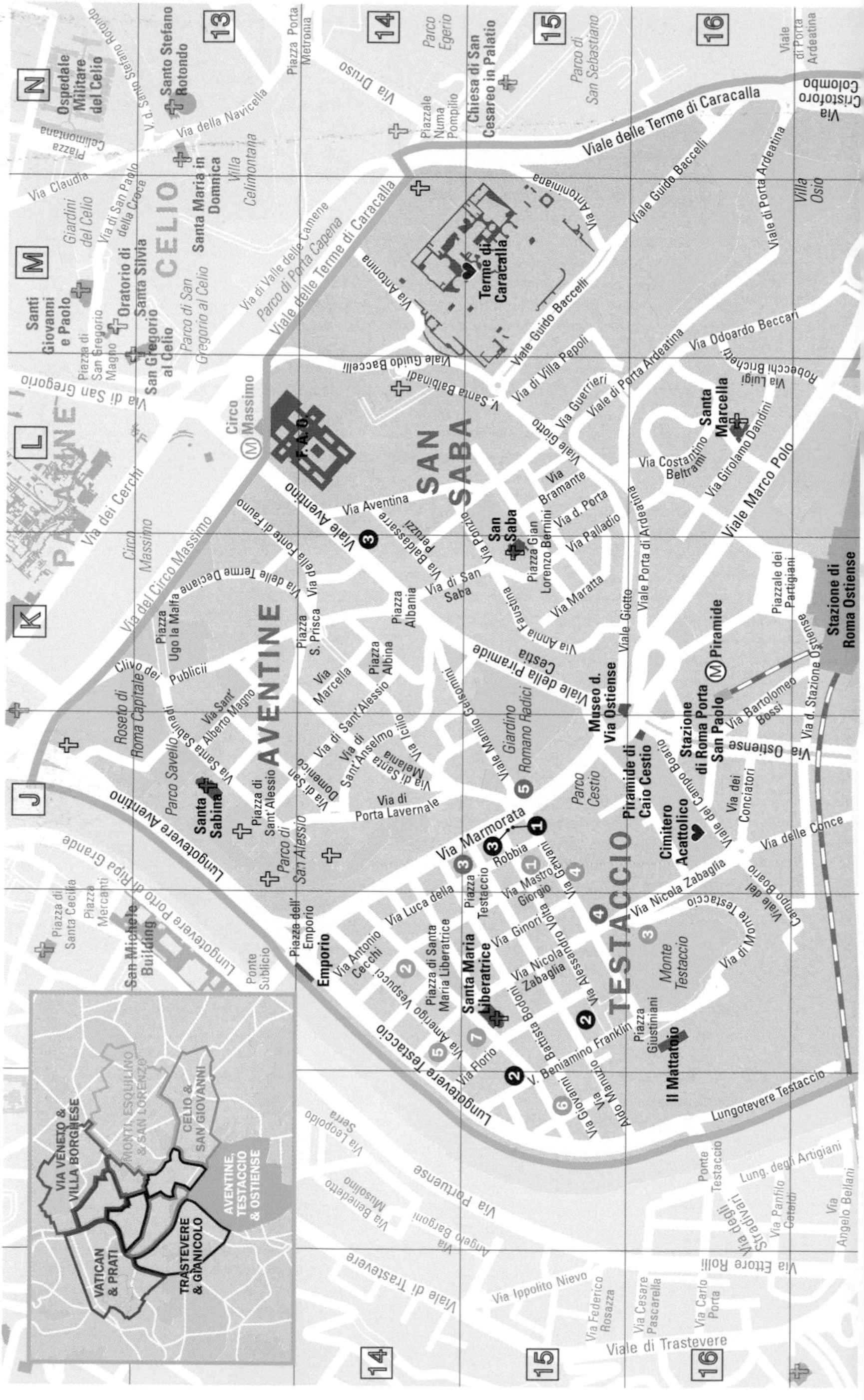
AVENTINE
TESTACCIO
SAN SABA
CELIO
PALATINE
Terme di Caracalla
F.A.O.
Circo Massimo
Santa Sabina
San Saba
Santa Maria Liberatrice
Museo d. Via Ostiense
Piramide di Caio Cestio
Cimitero Acattolico
Stazione di Roma Porta San Paolo
Piramide
Stazione di Roma Ostiense
Il Mattatoio
Monte Testaccio
Emporio
San Michele Building
Santa Marcella
Santi Giovanni e Paolo
Oratorio di Santa Silvia
San Gregorio al Celio
Santa Maria in Domnica
Santo Stefano Rotondo
Ospedale Militare del Celio
Chiesa di San Cesareo in Palatio
Roseto di Roma Capitale
Parco Savello
Giardino Romano Radici
Parco Cestio
Villa Celimontana
Parco di San Gregorio al Celio
Parco di Porta Capena
Parco Egerio
Parco di San Sebastiano
Villa Osio
Lungotevere Aventino
Lungotevere Testaccio
Viale Aventino
Via Marmorata
Viale della Piramide Cestia
Viale Marco Polo
Viale delle Terme di Caracalla
Viale Guido Baccelli
Via Ostiense
Via Cristoforo Colombo
Viale di Trastevere
Via Portuense
Via del Circo Massimo
Via dei Cerchi
Via di San Gregorio
Via Nicola Zabaglia
Via Galvani
Via Luca della Robbia
Via Aventina
Via Antoniniana
Via Druso
Via della Navicella
Via Claudia
VIA VENETO & VILLA BORGHESE
MONTI, ESQUILINO & SAN LORENZO
CELIO & SAN GIOVANNI
VATICAN & PRATI
TRASTEVERE & GIANICOLO
AVENTINE, TESTACCIO & OSTIENSE
J
K
L
M
N
13
14
15
16

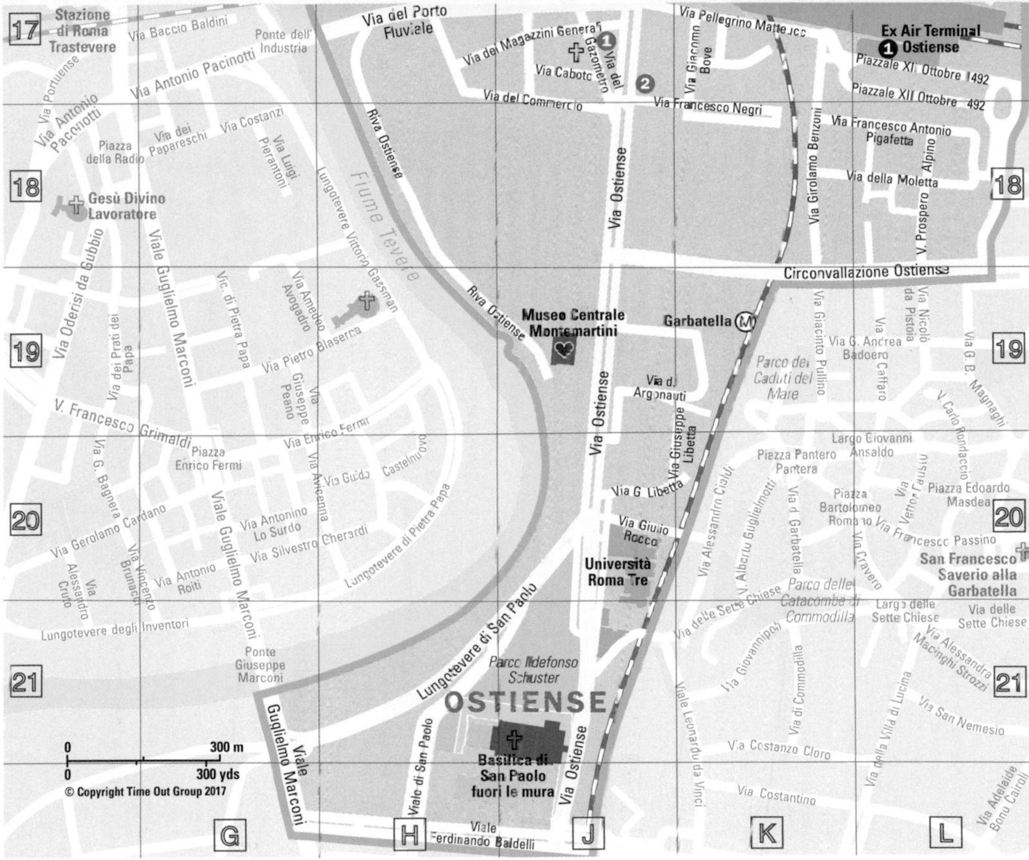

AVENTINE, TESTACCIO & OSTIENSE

Restaurants

1. Da Felice
2. Da Remo
3. Flavio al Velavevodetto
4. Masto
5. Piccolo Alpino
6. La Torricella
7. Trapizzino

Cafés, bars & pubs

1. Andreotti
2. Caffè Letterario
3. L'Oasi della Birra
4. Il Seme e la Foglia
5. Tram Depot

Bakeries, pasticcerie & gelaterie

1. Barberini
2. Chiosco Testaccio
3. Il Gelato di Claudio Torcè

Shops & services

1. Eataly
2. Mercato Testaccio
3. Volpetti

AVENTINE

First settled by King Ancius Marcius in the seventh century BC, the Aventine was later colonised by sailors, merchants and other undesirables who crept inexorably up the hill from the rough-and-tumble port below.

In 456 BC the whole of the Aventine hill was earmarked for plebeians to construct homes. And there the plebs remained, organising their guilds and building their temples. As they became more successful, so their villas became gentrified. By the time the Republic gave way to the Empire in 27 BC, this had become an exclusive neighbourhood. By the fifth century AD there were two bath complexes here and many luxurious *palazzi*.

What the Aventine is best for nowadays is a walk: the **Parco Savello**, still surrounded by the crenellated walls of a 12th-century fortress of the Savello family, has dozens of orange trees and a spectacular view. Contemplate the beauty of the basilica of **Santa Sabina** or peek through the keyhole of the **priory of the Knights of Malta** at nearby **piazza Cavalieri di Malta** to enjoy the surprise designed by Gian Battista Piranesi: a telescopic view of St Peter's dome.

Across thundering viale Aventino is the *piccolo Aventino*, aka the **San Saba** district – a leafy neighbourhood with a morning market in its main square, piazza Bernini, not far from the eighth-century church of San Saba. Beyond the white cuboids of the UN's Food and Agriculture Organisation – once Mussolini's Colonies Ministry – stand the towering remains of the **Terme di Caracalla** (**Baths of Caracalla**, *see p214*).

Sights & museums

Santa Sabina

Piazza Pietro d'Illiria 1 (06 5794 0600). Bus 81, 160, 175, 628, 715. **Open** *7am-6.30pm daily.* **Map** *p210 J13.*

Try to visit Santa Sabina on a sunny day, when the light shines softly into this magnificent, solemn basilica. It was built in the fifth century over an early Christian titulus believed to have belonged to a martyred Roman matron named Sabina; the only trace of this ancient place of worship is a bit of mosaic floor visible through a grate at the entrance. The church was subjected to a merciless restoration in the 1930s: nevertheless, what you see today is arguably the closest thing – give or take a 16th-century fresco or two – in Rome to an unadulterated ancient basilica. The late fifth-century cypress-wood doors are carved with biblical scenes, including one of the earliest renderings of the Crucifixion; ten of the original 28 panels have been lost. The high nave's elegant Corinthian columns support an arcade decorated with ninth-century marble inlay work; the *schola cantorum* (choir) dates from the same period. Selenite has been placed in the high, stone-grated arched windows, as it would have been in the ninth century. Above the entrance, the fifth-century mosaic recalls that the priest Peter of Illyria built the church while Celestine was pope; two figures on either side of the inscription represent the church members converted from paganism and Judaism. Later additions in the church include Taddeo Zuccari's 16th-century fresco in the apse.

A tiny window in the entrance porch looks on to the place where St Dominic is said to have planted an orange tree that had been brought from Spain in 1220. The adjoining monastery contains a cell where the saint stayed. A peaceful 13th-century cloister is reached along a sloping corridor near the main door. Excavations here in the 19th century unearthed parts of the fourth-century BC Servian Wall, a house from the second century BC, a third-century AD bath complex and a third-century BC temple (which can be seen by appointment only).

❤ Time to eat & drink

Morning coffee
Barberini *p218*

Snack
Trapizzino *p217*

Aperitivo
Masto *p217*, Tram Depot *p218*

Dinner
Da Remo *p217*, Flavio al Velavevodetto *p217*

Flavio al Velavevodetto

❤ Centrale Montemartini

Via Ostiense 106 (06 574 8030, 06 0608, www.centralemontemartini.org). Metro Garbatella/bus 23, 769. ***Open*** *9am-7pm Tue-Sun.* ***Admission*** *€7.50, €5.50 reductions.* ***Map*** *p210 J19.*

Once a state of the art power station, the early 20th-century Centrale Montemartini was chosen in the late 1990s to house part of the collection of the Capitoline Museums during work on the atrium (which was being built to house Marcus Aurelius). The temporary exhibition 'Machines and Gods' was such a success that it became permanent. Ancient statuary is set off beautifully by the industrial setting; fauns and Minervas, bacchic revellers and Apollos are all oddly at home against the imposing machinery of the decommissioned generating station. Highlights include incredibly detailed mosaics depicting marine themes, a spectacular early fourth century mosaic depicting a hunting scene, pediment decorations which once adorned the Temple of Apollo Sosianus next to the Theatre of Marcellus (*see p135*), and the giant head and foot of a goddess found at Largo Argentina. Occasional musical events, including jazz concerts among the statues, are not to be missed.

You can buy a combined ticket for €12.50, which also gives you entry to the Capitoline Museums (€16 when a temporary exhibition is on).

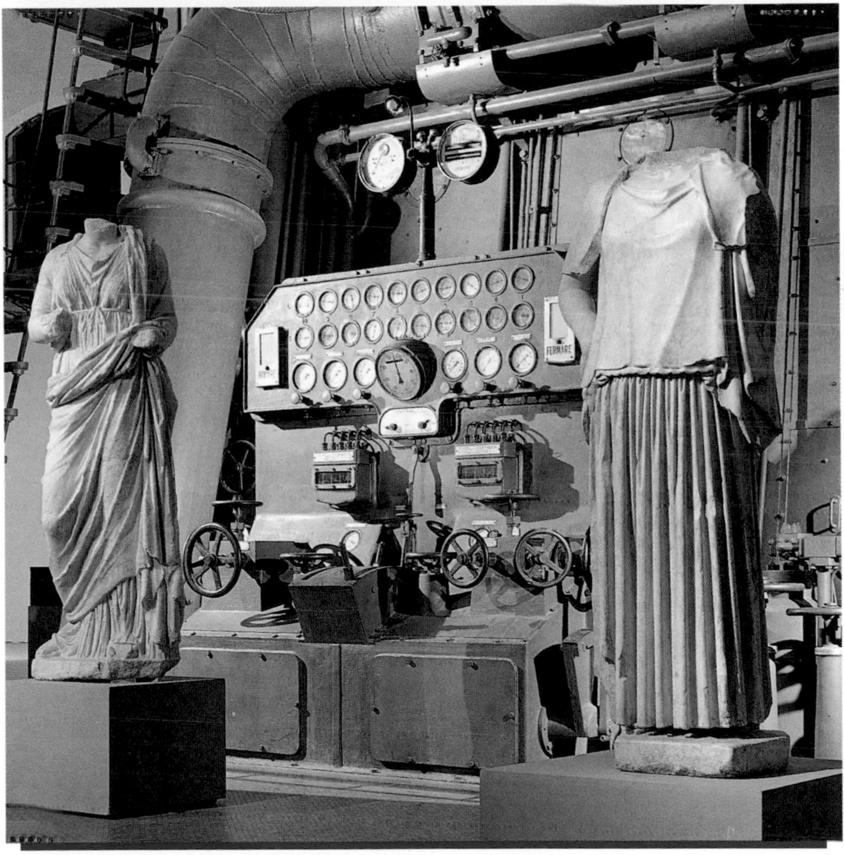

Terme di Caracalla

❤ Terme di Caracalla

Viale delle Terme di Caracalla 52 (06 3996 7700, www.coopculture.it). Bus 118, 160, 628. **Open** *9am-2pm Mon; 9am-sunset Tue-Sun.* **Admission** *€6; €3 reductions. No cards.* **Map** *p210 M15.*

The high-vaulted ruins of the Baths of Caracalla, surrounded by trees and grass, are pleasantly peaceful today, but were anything but tranquil in their heyday, when up to 1,600 Romans could sweat it out in the baths and gyms. You can get some idea of the original splendour of the baths – built between AD 213 and 216 – from the fragments of mosaic and statuary littering the grounds, although the more impressive finds are in the Vatican Museums (*see p154*) and the Museo Archeologico in Naples.

The two cavernous rooms down the sides were the *gymnasia*, where Romans engaged in strenuous sports like toss-the-beanbag. There was also a large open-air *natatio* (pool) for lap-swimming. After exercising, they cleansed themselves in saunas and a series of baths of varying temperatures. The baths were usually open from noon until sunset and were social centres where people came to relax after work. The complex also contained a library, a garden, shops and stalls. Underneath it all were 9.5km (six miles) of tunnels, where slaves scurried about, treading the giant wheels that pumped clean water up to bathers and tending to huge braziers that heated the chambers from below the tiles and through pipes in the walls. Caracalla's baths were in use for more than 300 years: the fun dried up in 537 when the Visigoths sacked Rome and severed the city's aqueducts.

Discovered in 1912 but never opened to the public, Rome's largest mithraeum (*see p204* Blood and Sperm: the Cult of Mithras) is situated in the tunnels beneath the baths; it is currently open for evening guided tours. See www.coopculture.it or www.060608.it for information.

► *If visiting in summer, try to catch an opera at the Caracalla – even if you're not an opera lover, the setting will convince you (see p269).*

Bakeries, pasticcerie & gelaterie

Il Gelato di Claudio Torcè

Viale Aventino 59 (06 574 6876, www.ilgelatodiclaudiotorce.com). Bus 75, 673, 715/ tram 3. **Open** *Oct-Apr 11am-9.30pm daily. May-Sept 11am-11.30pm daily. Closed Jan & 1wk Aug.* **Map** *p210 K14* ❸ *Gelateria*

If weird and wonderful gelato is your thing then master gelato maker Claudio Torcè is your man. The all-natural, strictly artisanal gelato comes in a dizzying array of flavours from familiar chocolates, fruits and creams to altogether more unusual, savoury creations to challenge your taste buds, including habanero chilli, celery, brie with berries and even mortadella sausage with pistachio. **Other locations** piazza del Risorgimento 51 (Prati).

TESTACCIO & OSTIENSE

Tucked below the quiet heights of the Aventine is bustling **Testaccio**, where long-time residents are stridently – even brusquely – Roman (though a more recent influx tends to be urban and professional). The produce market (**Mercato Testaccio**; *see p219*), in a purpose-built structure between *vie* Volta and Galvani, is one of Rome's best.

Today's Testaccio is strictly residential-commercial. Historically, though, Testaccio was a place of industry and trade. This was the site of ancient Rome's great inner-city port. With the decline of Rome as a trading power, so Testaccio became a tranquil place of vegetable gardens and vineyards belonging to the great religious orders up on the Aventine, only to be built over after Italian Unification in the 1870s: dwellings went up for the underclass who manned the municipal slaughterhouse – **il Mattatoio** – and the other noisy industries shifted here from the *centro storico*. Testaccio has no wondrous monuments, just sites that tell of its industrious past, such as the ancient port – **Emporio** – and a rubbish tip of carefully stacked pieces of an estimated 50 million amphorae – **Monte Testaccio**. Wander the grubbily bucolic **via di Monte Testaccio**, deserted during the day when the night spots are firmly shut up, and keep an eye out for hens roaming the greenery which sprouts from between the carefully stacked potsherds.

Other noteworthy stops include the charming **Museo della via Ostiense**; the **Cimitero Acattolico** (non-Catholic cemetery; *see p216*), with its illustrious company of defunct foreign artists and writers; and the totally out-of-place **Piramide di Caio Cestio**, the mausoleum of a Roman with an inflated ego.

Testaccio also boasts the city's best nightlife, with clubs, eateries and bars dug into the base of **Monte Testaccio**: you can see the broken clay pieces piled up in some of the establishments on via Galvani. If you have a strong stomach, try a typical *testaccino* meal in the vicinity of the old slaughterhouse: bits that no one else wanted go into specialities such as *rigatoni alla pajata*, *trippa alla romana* and *coratella ai carciofi* (*see p43* Decoding the Menu).

Due south from Testaccio, **via Ostiense** slices through the once-run-down area of the same name, now destined for greater things. To the east of this ancient road is a concentration of nightspots, especially around **via Libetta**, the shiny, bustling new campus of the Università Roma Tre and the former wholesale fruit and veg market, slowly being transformed into an arts and entertainment hub designed by Dutch architect Rem Koolhaas.

Also off the via Ostiense, the classical statuary displayed against gleaming power station machinery in the **Centrale Montemartini** (*see p213*) is a wonderful combination and well worth the trek.

Sights & museums

Il Mattatoio

Piazza Giustiniani/via di Monte Testaccio, Testaccio. Bus 83, 170, 673, 719, 781. ***Map** p210 H16.*

The bizarre statue of a winged hero slaughtering an ox atop the Mattatoio (slaughterhouse) leaves little doubt about its mission. Hailed as Europe's most advanced abattoir when it opened in 1891, the 24-acre complex extending from the Tiber to Monte Testaccio and the Aurelian Walls coped with an eightfold increase in the city's population, was the source of meat for the whole of central Italy and provided Testaccio's residents with work until 1975. For decades, bickering between politicians, architects and planners left the structure in picturesque abandon: now, the whole area – including the *campo boario* (cattleyards) – is gradually being reclaimed and transformed into a university architecture department, an art school, a fair-trade and organic food store, and spaces for multimedia projects and exhibitions (*see p222* MACRO.

Museo della via Ostiense

Via Raffaele Persichetti 3, Testaccio (06 574 3193, archeoroma.beniculturali.it). Metro Piramide/bus 23, 30Exp, 75, 83, 118, 271, 280, 716, 769/tram 3. ***Open** Sept-July 9am-1.30pm Tue-Sun; Aug 9am-1.30pm Tue-Sat.* ***Admission** free.* ***Map** p210 K15.*

This humble but oddly charming museum contains artefacts and prints pertaining to via Ostiense and Ostia Antica, the ancient port to which this consular road led.

Restaurants

Da Felice €€€

Via Mastro Giorgio 29, Testaccio (06 574 6800, www.feliceatestaccio.com). Bus 23, 30, 75, 83, 170, 280,673, 716, 719, 781/tram 3. ***Open** 12.30-2.45pm, 8-11pm daily. Closed 1wk Aug.* ***Map** p210 J15* ❶ *Trattoria*

This trattoria in the heart of trendy Testaccio was once rather basic, but it has had a makeover that turned it into a stylishly *moderne* neo-osteria. The quality of the cooking has not changed, although there are

Top 20

❤ Cimitero Acattolico

Via Caio Cestio 6, Testaccio (06 574 1900, www.cemeteryrome.it). Metro Piramide/bus 23, 30Exp, 75, 83, 118, 280, 716, 769/tram 3. ***Open*** *9am-5pm Mon-Sat; 9am-1pm Sun. Closed 10 days Aug.* ***Admission*** *€3 donation requested.* ***Map*** *p210 J16.*

This heavenly oasis of calm in the midst of a ruckus of traffic has been Rome's final resting place for non-Catholic foreigners since 1784. Verdant and atmospheric, it's popular with modern-day travellers keen to recapture the atmosphere of the Grand Tour. Unofficially known as the Protestant Cemetery, this charmingly old-world corner of the city also hosts Buddhists, Russian Orthodox Christians and atheists: a sign points to the grave of Antonio Gramsci, founder of the Italian Communist Party. In the older sector, close to the first century Pyramid of Caius Cestius, is the grave of John Keats, who coughed his last at the age of 25, after only four months in Rome; in fine Romantic fashion his anonymous epitaph concludes: 'Here lies one whose name was writ on water.' This was all the poet wanted; his executors added the rest. Next to him lies the friend who ministered to him on his death bed, Joseph Severn (who died six decades later). The larger, newer section is much more crowded, and slopes up to the crenellations of the Aurelian Wall. At the top, slightly to the left of the tower, is the tomb of Shelley, who died a year after Keats in a stormy shipwreck in the Bay of la Spezia, having unfortunately ignored a shipbuilder's advice in favour of his personal modifications to his boat. Just in front of his tombstone is the small monument to Belinda Lee, a Devon-born film star who lived in Rome but was killed in a car accident in California in 1961, aged 25.

now a few lighter and more creative dishes alongside the Roman classics – *tonnarelli cacio e pepe* (pasta with pecorino and black pepper), *abbacchio al forno con patate* (roast lamb with potatoes) – which first made the name of this Testaccio institution. The desserts are excellent – especially the tiramisù – and the wine list has improved since the days when it was cloudy Castelli Romani or nothing.

❤ Da Remo €€

Piazza Santa Maria Liberatrice 44, Testaccio (06 574 6270). Bus 23, 75, 95, 170, 280, 716, 781/tram 3. ***Open*** *7pm-1am Mon-Sat. Closed 3wks Aug.* ***Map*** *p210 H14* 2 *Pizzeria*

The best place in town for authentic *pizza romana*, Remo is a Testaccio institution, with a prime location on the district's main piazza. You can sit at wonky tables balanced on the pavement, or in the cavernous interior, overseen by Lazio players in various team photos. The *bruschette al pomodoro* are the finest in Rome. A park with swings right across the road makes this a great place to eat with kids. You can try booking but they probably won't accept: get here early if you don't want to queue.

❤ Flavio al Velavevodetto €€

Via Monte Testaccio 97, Testaccio (06 574 4194, www.flavioalvelavevodetto.it). Bus 23, 30Exp, 75, 95, 170, 280, 716, 781/tram 3. ***Open*** *12.30-3pm, 7.45-10.45pm daily.* ***Map*** *p210 H16* 3 *Trattoria*

With its rear walls made of the piled-up amphora sherds that constitute the strange urban feature called Monte Testaccio, Flavio al Velavevodetto (the name means 'I told you so') has all the hallmarks of a genuine Testaccio osteria. The traditional fare is hearty and *onesto* – not hugely refined but filling and generally good – the service is friendly in a hurried Roman way, and the atmosphere is buzzy, noisy and young (with a strong contingent from the nearby music school as well as clubbers starting their night out). There are some outside tables for warm-weather dining.

❤ Masto €€

Via Galvani 39/41, Testaccio (06 9521 5816, www.facebook.com/MASTO-1734866006762281). Bus 23, 30, 75, 83, 170, 280, 673, 716, 719, 781/tram 3. ***Open*** *9am-midnight Mon-Sat, noon-11pm Sun. Closed 1wk Aug.* ***Map*** *p210 J15* 4 *Delicatessen/Wine bar*

During the morning Masto operates as a delicatessen with the locals wandering in to stock up on the excellent prosciutto, salami and cheese. At mealtimes it transforms into an informal dining spot serving light meals, salads and their signature *taglieri*: huge wooden chopping boards loaded with cured meats and cheeses. Towering shelves display a decent selection of wines and the exuberant owners Rita and Emiliano keep clients entertained with their lively antics.

Piccolo Alpino €€

Via Orazio Antinori 5, Testaccio (06 574 1386). Bus 23, 75, 95, 170, 280, 716, 781/tram 3. ***Open*** *12.30-2.30pm, 6-11pm Wed-Sun. Closed 2wks Aug.* **No cards.** ***Map*** *p210 H14* 5 *Pizzeria*

This no-frills trattoria-pizzeria in a Testaccio sidestreet is as far as you can get from the tourist herd. There's a telly (with live football on Sunday evenings), beer on tap and rough wine in the fridge; but the pizzas are good, and the pasta, too, as long as you stick to the house specialities: *spaghetti con le vongole* or *penne all'arrabbiata*; for restaurant fare, expect to pay a little more. In summer, tables invade the road and it all feels like a scene from Fellini's *Roma*.

La Torricella €€

Via Evangelista Torricelli 2/12, Testaccio (06 574 6311, www.la-torricella.com). Bus 83, 170, 781. ***Open*** *12.30-3pm, 7.30-11.30pm.* ***Map*** *p210 G15* 6 *Seafood/Trattoria*

In the slaughterhouse district of Rome it may seem odd to opt for fish but the daily seafood menu at La Torricella makes a welcome change from the heavier, offal-based fare usually on offer in Testaccio. The waiters are a little gruff and the decor rather old-fashioned but that just adds to the charm. Aside from the fresh catch there are also plenty of non-fish options and the home-made desserts are worth the extra calories.

❤ Trapizzino €

Via G Branca 88, Testaccio (06 4341 9624, www.trapizzino.it). Bus 23, 30, 75, 83, 170, 280, 673, 716, 719, 781/tram 3. ***Open*** *Sept-July noon-1am Tue-Sun; Aug 6pm-1am Tue-Sun. Closed 1wk Aug.* ***Map*** *p210 H15* 7 *Streetfood*

Pizza maker Stefano Callegari took Rome by storm in 2009 when he invented the *trapizzino* from his tiny pizza joint in Testaccio. Almost a decade and a major refit later, the expanded shop now focuses almost solely on these triangular pockets of pizza dough stuffed with classic recipes ranging from oxtail stew to cuttlefish and peas, and several more offshoots of the Trapizzino brand have popped up throughout the city. Also on offer are a range of *supplì* (deep-fried rice balls) and a selection of Italian craft beers.

Cafés, bars & pubs

Andreotti

Via Ostiense 54/56, Ostiense (06 575 0773, www.andreottiroma.com). Bus 23, 769. ***Open*** *7am-9.30pm daily. Closed 1wk Aug.* ***Map*** *p210 J17* ❶ *Café/Bar*

The Andreotti family claims to serve up to 700 cups of its excellent coffee every day – and that was before a refit that doubled the space, lengthened the counter and gave this bustling neighbourhood bar a cool retro atmosphere. All of which provided more space for sampling excellent breakfast *cornetti*, cakes, light lunchtime snacks and evening *aperitivi* with delicious nibbles.

Caffè Letterario

Via Ostiense 95, Ostiense (06 5730 2842, www.caffeletterarioroma.it). Bus 23, 769. ***Open*** *10am-2am Tue-Sun. Closed Aug.* ***Map*** *p210 J17* ❷ *Coffee shop*

In an area swarming with students from the Terza Università campus, Caffè Letterario is a style temple showcasing not only the latest books but also the contemporary arts in general. Enjoy your morning coffee, light lunch or *aperitivo* perusing new titles, exhibitions and design-related happenings of many and various descriptions.

L'Oasi della Birra

Piazza Testaccio 41, Testaccio (06 574 6122). Bus 23, 30, 75, 83, 170, 280, 716, 781/tram 3. ***Open*** *4.30pm-12.30am Mon-Sat, 6pm-12.30am Sun. Closed 1wk Aug.* ***Map*** *p210 J15* ❸ *Bar*

In the basement of an *enoteca* on Testaccio's market square, this 'Oasis of Beer' has more than 500 brews on offer – or so it claims – though in fact when you put your order in, you may find that the one(s) you want are temporarily unavailable... In fact, the wine collection upstairs (where an off-licence is open all day) is more impressive and can be enjoyed by the glass. From 7pm to 9pm every night, customers can pile up a plate from the very generous *aperitivo* buffet to accompany their glass of wine. An à la carte menu includes snacks, cheese and cured meat platters, as well as dishes with a Teutonic slant. The outdoor tables operate year-round, weather permitting.

Il Seme e la Foglia

Via Galvani 18, Testaccio (06 574 3008). Bus 23, 30, 75, 83, 170, 280, 673, 716, 719, 781/tram 3. ***Open*** *8am-2am Mon-Sat; 11am-2am Sun. Closed Sun in July & 3wks Aug.* ***No cards. Map*** *p210 H15* ❹ *Bar*

Right-on and alternative, this lively daytime snack bar and evening pre-club stop is always packed with students and teachers from the Scuola Popolare di Musica across the road. At lunchtime there's generally a pasta dish, plus large salads (€6-€8) and creative filled rolls.

❤ Tram Depot

Via Marmorata 13, Testaccio (06 575 4406, www.facebook.com/tramdepotroma). Bus 23, 30, 75, 83, 170, 280, 716, 781/tram 3. ***Open*** *mid Mar-Oct 8am-2am daily.* ***Map*** *p210 J15* ❺ *Café/Bar*

With drinks and *panini* served from a disused tram carriage on the corner of via Marmorata to be consumed at the outside tables (accompanied by a frantic soundtrack of traffic and sirens), Tram Depot is certainly a quaint place to take a break. The most evocative time to visit is after sunset when young folk stop by for pre-dinner cocktails, the trees are bedecked with fairy lights and the atmosphere is one of friendly conviviality.

Bakeries, pasticcerie & gelaterie

❤ Barberini

Via Marmorata 41 (06 5725 0431, www.pasticceriabarberini.it). Bus 23, 30Exp, 75, 95, 170, 280, 716, 781/tram 3. ***Open*** *6am-9pm daily. Closed pm in Aug.* ***Map*** *p210 J15* ❶ *Café/Pasticceria*

The *testaccini* have been flocking to Barberini for their morning coffee and pastries for almost a century, and continue to do so despite a recent refit which saw the rather charming old bar replaced with a sparkling modern counter and the previous dusty decor transformed into a slick, pastel interior. The mouth watering array of cakes are all made onsite and include fresh fruit tarts, decadent cream-filled creations and a feather-light mini tiramisù served in a tiny chocolate cup.

Chiosco Testaccio

Via Giovanni Branca, corner of via Beniamino Franklin, Testaccio. Bus 83, 170, 781/tram 3. ***Open*** *noon-1.30am daily. Closed mid Sept-Apr.* ***No cards. Map*** *p210 G15* ❷ *Gelateria*

Still going strong after more than 80 years in this working-class neighbourhood, the Chiosco Testaccio has the unusual selling point of being painted in a different colour each year. You have to push past the lounging local youth to order a hand-grated ice, but the unusual flavours are worth the jostling. The selection is as varied as the outside paint job is colourful; tamarind and *limoncocco* (lemon-coconut) are among the specialities that you will find at this unique place.

Shops & services

Eataly

Air Terminal Ostiense, piazzale XII Ottobre 1492, Ostiense (06 9027 9201, www.roma.eataly.it). Metro Piramide (follow signs to Ostiense, then air terminal) or Garbatella/bus 670, 673, 715, 716. ***Open*** *10am-midnight daily.* ***Map*** *p210 L17* ❶ *Food & drink/House & home*

The three sprawling floors of this temple to Italian cuisine is a food lover's paradise. On offer are kitchenware and cookbooks to dedicated sections of produce, meat, fish, cheese, wine and much more. Dotted throughout are a myriad of specialist eateries serving food throughout the day as well as a wine bar and craft beer pub. Food festivals, cooking classes and tastings are held frequently so check the website for the programme of events.

Mercato Testaccio

Between via Galvani and via A Volta, Testaccio (www.mercatoditestaccio.it). Bus 23, 30, 75, 83, 170, 280, 716, 781/tram 3. ***Open*** *7am-3.30pm Mon-Sat.* ***Map*** *p210 H15* ❷ *Market*

In 2012 Testaccio's slightly dilapidated market moved into squeaky-clean new premises. Almost all the old vendors made the move and the eccentric selection of stalls selling shoes, clothes, household goods and fresh produce are all still in business. However an influx of new gastronomic stalls have created a delightful juxtaposition of old and new as well as breathing a new lease of life into the market. Michelin-starred chef Cristina Bowerman's modern delicatessen Romeo (box 30/44), delicious Roman sandwiches at Mordi e Vai (box 15) and gourmet snacks and streetfood at FoodBox (box 66), along with many more, have all contributed to raising the modern profile of both the market and the Testaccio neighbourhood.

Volpetti

Via Marmorata 47, Testaccio (06 574 2352, www.volpetti.com). Bus 23, 30, 75, 83, 280, 716, 781/tram 3. ***Open*** *8am-2pm, 5-8.15pm Mon-Wed, 8am-8.15pm Thur-Sat.* ***Map*** *p210 J15* ❸ *Food & drink*

In business since 1973, Volpetti is still considered to be one of the finest gourmet food shops in Rome, although the departure of the congenial Volpetti brothers and the arrival of new ownership has shifted the focus from friendly family-run deli to an altogether more aloof affair. However, the shop is still stuffed to the rafters with the very best Italy has to offer from exquisite prosciutto and salamis, a tremendous selection of cheeses, fine olive oils, balsamic vinegars, wine and truffles. The prices will make your eyes water but the quality is undisputed. The shiny new Volpetti brand has also extended around the corner on via Alessandro Volta 8 where Taverna Volpetti serves sit-down meals created to show off the shop's stock.

Mercato Testaccio

Suburbs

In 1871, when Rome became the capital of united Italy, its 212,000 residents rattled around inside the Aurelian Wall, where vast swathes were still given over to vegetable gardens. By 1901 the population had almost doubled to 422,000; by 1971 it was well over two million. These new *romani* were only too happy, in the interests of having a roof over their heads, to endorse the destruction of the countryside that was swiftly gobbled up, at first by pompous turn-of-the-century *palazzi* and, later, by unauthorised – and often unplumbed – apartment buildings.

Today the result mostly looks grim, with a few notable exceptions. There are Liberty (art nouveau) *palazzi* along *vie* Salaria and Nomentana, for example, and some memorable Fascist urban planning in EUR. Elsewhere, even some of the most architecturally uninspired districts hide surprises worth travelling for.

❤ Don't miss

1 A match at the Stadio Olimpico *p223*
Flares and chanting, when in Rome... go to a football match.

2 Auditorium-Parco della Musica *p273*
Geographically, it's far flung, but it's at the heart of Rome's cultural life.

3 Museo delle Mura *p227*
Wander the ramparts of Rome's ancient walls, and it's free.

4 MAXXI *p224*
Zaha Hadid's 21st-century gallery, for when the ancient is too much.

5 La Pergola *p224*
Rome's only three-star Michelin restaurant atop the Monte Mario.

In the know
Getting around

Where possible, take the metro out to the suburbs; otherwise trams provide the swiftest route beyond the walls.

MORE
THAN
MEETS
THE
EYE

NORTH

► *For Flaminio and the Foro Italico, take tram 2 up the via Flaminia from piazzale Flaminio (metro line A), and then walk across the Ponte della Musica to the Stadio Olimpico and Foro Italico. For Quartiere Coppedè, take tram 3 along viale Regina Margherita to piazza Buenos Aires. For transport to other sites, see individual listings.*

For centuries the route along which most travellers entered the Eternal City, the dead-straight via Flaminia nowadays passes through affluent residential *Roma nord*, or **Flaminio**, as it shoots north from piazza del Popolo to a hopping new hub of art and culture at the hyperactive **Auditorium-Parco della Musica** (*see p273*) and the Zaha Hadid-designed **MAXXI** art gallery (*see p224*).

Via Flaminia crosses the Tiber at the ancient **Ponte Milvio**; now open to pedestrians only, the second-century BC bridge offers a good view of the neighbouring **Ponte Flaminio** designed by Armando Brasini, a glorious example of Fascist rhetorical architecture. Across the river are the **Foro Italico** sports complex and **Stadio Olimpico**. The impressive new **Ponte della Musica** footbridge, designed by the UK's Buro Happold, crosses the Tiber from piazza Gentile da Fabriano to the sports complex.

Via Salaria – the salt road – existed before Rome, when ancient tribes brought vital salt supplies from saltpans on the east coast. Today the road begins at piazza Fiume. The real treasures of the area **Salario** are the delightful art nouveau **Quartiere Coppedè** – centred on piazza Mincio – and the leafy shade of the **Villa Ada** public gardens and the **Catacombe di Priscilla** (via Salaria 430, www.catacombepriscilla.com). In via della Moschea, between vie Salaria and Flaminia, lies Paolo Portoghesi's **mosque** (*see p327*).

To the north-east, Via Nomentana leads out of Rome, flanked on either side by another middle-class area, **Nomentano**, with some charming art nouveau buildings. Its green lung is the **Villa Torlonia**; its art prevalent in the **MACRO** gallery and perhaps the earliest Christian mosaics in **Santa Costanza**, part of the atmospheric complex which includes **Sant'Agnese fuori le Mura** (*see p224*). The area around via Tiburtina is more low-rent.

Sights & museums

Foro Italico

Piazza de Bosis/via del Foro Italico, Flaminio. Bus 32, 48, 53, 69, 200, 201, 220, 280, 910/ tram 2.

A marble obelisk, 36m (120ft) high, with the words 'Mussolini Dux' carved on it, greets visitors to the Foro Italico, a sports complex (which includes the Stadio Olimpico) conceived in the late 1920s by architect Enrico Del Debbio. The avenue leading west of the obelisk is paved with black-and-white mosaics of Fascists flying warplanes and saluting *il Duce*. It's a wonderfully camp sight today, and well preserved considering the feet that trample the tiles on their way to the Stadio Olimpico beyond. Surrounding the Stadio dei Marmi track to the north – also by Del Debbio – are 60 marble statues of naked athletes, each with some kind of sports apparatus.

MACRO

Via Nizza 138, Nomentano (06 6710 70400, www.museomacro.org). Bus 38, 60Exp, 62, 80Exp, 82, 84, 89, 90Exp. ***Open*** *10.30am-7.30pm Tue-Sun.* ***Admission*** *€10; €8 reductions. Exhibition price varies.*

In a stunningly converted brewery, the Museo d'Arte Contemporaneo di Roma covers 10,000sq m (107,500sq ft). MACRO brings big international names to Rome, and gives space to young and local artists.

ella Musica

❤ A match at the Stadio Olimpico

Viale dello Stadio Olimpico, Flaminio (06 323 7333). Bus 32, 48, 53, 168, 186, 224, 271, 280, 690, 910, 911, C2, C3/tram 2. ***Tickets*** *€11-€115. No cards,* ***Map*** *p8.*

Rome has two first-class football clubs – AS Roma (www.asromacalcio.it) and SS Lazio (www.sslazio.it) – which share the Stadio Olimpico. Set in the Fascist-era Foro Italico (*see p222*), it was originally built for the 1960 Olympic Games before being rebuilt for the 1990 World Cup, and it's definitely showing its age.

When Roma and Lazio play each other tension is thick across the city. derbies are an excuse for *romanisti* and *laziali* to attempt to out-do each other with the wittiest banners, the rudest chants and the most impressive displays of team-colour pyrotechnics. Lazio was founded in 1900, the younger Roma in 1927. Both teams are a solid presence in Serie A. Whilst only the most intrepid visitor may want to attend a Roma-Lazio game, a trip to the stadium is an interesting addition to a trip to Rome for football fanatics: a spectacle of flares and chanting and a touch of atmospheric drama a million miles away from the elegant *bella figura* of the *centro storico*. For some of the atmosphere without the possibility of too much hooliganism, skip the derbies and choose another meet.

As part of measures to curb stadium violence, tickets can no longer be purchased directly from the Stadio Olimpico box office. Get them online from www.listicket.it, or from registered ticket sellers through the team websites; other sites are not always reliable. Tickets are personal and non-transferable. You can buy tickets for a limited number of other people but you will need a photo-ID document (some outlets will accept photocopies) for each ticket-holder. Each must then present photo ID (corresponding, obviously, with the name on the ticket) at the turnstiles when they get to the stadium. Important matches sell out quickly. All seats have a decent view but bear in mind the cheap seats in the Curva are favoured by the 'Ultras' and can be extremely rowdy.

It's not possible to visit the stadium outside games, but a stroll around the arena is still a worthwhile trip.

Roma far

❤ MAXXI

Via Guido Reni 10, Flaminio (06 321 0181/06 3996 7350, www.maxxi.art). Bus 53, 233, 280, 910/tram 2. ***Open*** *11am-7pm Tue-Fri, Sun; 11am-10pm Sat.* ***Admission*** *€11; €8 reductions; free under-14s.*

Designed by Anglo-Iraqi architect Zaha Hadid and inaugurated in 2009, the Museum of the Arts of the 21st Century displays a permanent collection of works by mainly – but not exclusively – Italian contemporary artists and stages a changing programme of shows on artistic and architectural topics. It's the dramatic building itself, however, that holds centre stage here.

Sant'Agnese fuori le Mura & Mausoleo di Santa Costanza

Via Nomentana 349, Nomentano (06 8620 5456, www.santagnese.org). Bus 60Exp, 82, 90Exp, 140, 233. ***Church*** *7.30am-noon, 4-7.30pm daily.* ***Catacombs*** *(guided tours) &* ***Santa Costanza*** *9am-noon, 4-6pm Mon-Sat; 4-6pm Sun. Closed Nov.* ***Admission*** *Church & Santa Costanza free. Catacombs €8; €5 reductions. No cards.*

The circular fourth-century mausoleum of Santa Costanza, 2km (1.25 miles) along via Nomentana, was built for Constantine's daughters, Constance and Helen. The sarcophagus here, containing the remains of Constance, is a plaster cast of the porphyry original, now in the **Vatican Museums** (*see p154*). The barrel-vaulted ambulatory, whose arcades rest on exquisite 'pillows' of marble, is decorated with perhaps the world's earliest surviving Christian mosaics. In the adjoining church of Sant'Agnese, dating from the seventh century, is an original apse mosaic showing a diminutive figure of St Agnes standing on the flames of her martyrdom, flanked by two popes. St Agnes was almost certainly buried in the catacombs below this church, though her skull was later moved to the church of **Sant'Agnese in Agone** (*see p110*).

Villa Torlonia

Via Nomentana 70, Nomentano (06 0608, www.museivillatorlonia.it). Bus 60Exp, 62, 82, 90Exp. ***Open*** *9am-7pm Tue-Sun.* ***Admission*** *€9.50; €7.50 reductions. Exhibition price varies.*

The Villa Torlonia, with its verdant palm-filled park, was the elegant home of the aristocratic Torlonia family from 1797, glorified as Mussolini's suburban HQ in the 1930s and trashed by Anglo-American forces when they made it their high command base (1944-47). When Rome city council bought it in 1978, it was in a disastrous state; but this is now a truly worthwhile hike. The main house – the pretty *Casino nobile* – was revamped in 1832 by architect Giovan Battista Caretti. Mussolini's bunker beneath the house can be visited by appointment. The *Casina delle civette*, a wacky Swiss chalet-folly, was endowed with all kinds of stupendous stained glass and boiseries in 1916-20; the art nouveau fittings have been beautifully restored. The Limonaia – where lemon trees were kept through the winter – is now a pleasant café-restaurant.

Restaurants

❤ La Pergola €€€€

Via Cadlolo 101, Monte Mario (06 3509 2154, www.romecavalieri.com). Bus 907, 913, 991, 999. ***Open*** *7.30-11.30pm Tue-Sat. Closed 4wks Jan & 3wks Aug. International*

Heinz Beck is, without a doubt, the most talented chef in Rome, with three – merited

– Michelin stars. His technical dexterity and unerring instinct for taste and texture combinations never fail to impress. The setting, on the top floor of the Cavalieri hotel with its panoramic view over the city, is simply breathtaking. But what emerges from Beck's kitchen – every dish dictated by seasonal availability – is equally so: amberjack tartare with tomato mousse and olives, potato gnocchi with caviar and chives or sea bass with olive oil-marinated vegetables are infinitely more sophisticated than they sound. The remarkable cellars are said to hold 53,000 bottles; markups on wine are very steep. But around €350 for two with a good bottle still compares favourably with restaurants at the top of the gourmet ladder in other capitals. There are seven- (€210) and ten-course (€245) tasting menus.

Il Tiepolo €€

Via GB Tiepolo 3/5, Flaminio (06 322 7449, www.iltiepolo.com). Bus 910, C3, M/tram 2. ***Open*** *12.30pm-1am daily. Closed 1wk Aug.*
International

If you're catching a concert at the **Auditorium-Parco della Musica** (*see p273*) or an exhibition at **MAXXI** (*see p224*), this brightly coloured bistro with retro touches is a fun place to grab an *aperitivo* or a bite before or after the performance. Non-meat-eaters and vegans are unusually well catered for here.

Shops & services

Borghetto Flaminio

Piazza della Marina 32, Flaminio (www.creativitalia.com). Metro Flaminio/bus 61, 89, 120, 150, 160, 490, 495, 628, 926/tram 2, 19. ***Open*** *Sept-mid July 10am-7pm Sun.*
Market

An upmarket garage sale in a former bus depot, with stalls selling bric-a-brac, costume jewellery and vintage designer clothes. Much loved by the well-heeled denizens of this prosperous part of town.

Lazio Style 1900

Via G Calderini 66C, Flaminio (06 3254 1745, www.sslazio.it). Bus 48, 53, 280, 910, 911/tram 2. ***Open*** *4-8pm Mon; 10am-1.30pm, 2.30-8pm Tue-Sat; 5hrs prior to home matches Sun.*
Sport

The official store of SS Lazio football team sells shirts, scarves and a huge selection of merchandise stamped with the eagle emblem of the *biancocelesti*. Tickets for matches can also be purchased.

La Pergola

EAST

► *To reach Pigneto, take bus 81 or 105, or tram 5, 14 or 19 from Termini.*

Bordered by via Prenestina to the north and via Casilina to the south, the eastern **Pigneto** district sprang up in haphazard fashion between the 1890s and 1930s as railwaymen and artisans used micro-credits from workers' co-operatives to build dwellings amid the warehouses and railway sheds.

The district (along with nearby **San Lorenzo**; *see p194*) suffered heavy wartime bombing and when development came it was piecemeal and barely regulated. The anarchic, bohemian feel of the place attracted artsy types including director Pier Paolo Pasolini, who shot much of his acclaimed film *Accatone* (1960) in the area. Rossellini's *Roma città aperta* (1945) and Visconti's *Bellissima* (1951) were also largely shot here.

Formerly renowned as the home of sketchy late-night drinking dens and drug dealers, Pigneto has dusted itself down in the last few years, emerging as one of Rome's trendiest areas – with property prices going through the roof and a host of restaurants and bars springing up to make the trek out here worthwhile. It retains much of its unique appeal, thanks in large part to the fruit and vegetable market (Monday to Saturday) and a sprinkling of grocers and artisan shops along pedestrianised **via del Pigneto**, which gives way to bars and restaurants in the evening.

Restaurants

Pigneto 41 €€

Via del Pigneto 41, Pigneto (06 7039 9483, www.pignetoquarantuno.it). Bus 81, 105, 150, 412/tram 5, 14, 19. ***Open*** *6pm-midnight Tue-Sat, noon-midnight Sun. Closed May-Sept Sun.* *Trattoria*

Situated on the lively pedestrianised hub of the Pigneto nightlife, Pigneto 41 is the perfect place to sit outside and people watch. The classic Roman dishes here are good, but even better are the daily specials scribbled on the blackboard which incorporate seasonal ingredients, often with a creative twist (think pasta with pancetta and fig, or duck breast with peach chutney).

Cafés, bars & pubs

Bar Necci dal 1924

Via Fanfulla da Lodi 68, Pigneto (06 9760 1552, www.necci1924.com). Bus 81, 105, 150, 412/tram 5, 14, 19. ***Open*** *12.30-3pm, 7.30-11pm daily.* *Café/Bar*

This former old-blokes' bar is now a shabby-chic café/bar, usually frequented by Pigneto creative types. The interior has a great 1960s-style decor but the laid-back, leafy terrace is the real draw; ideal for a long lazy breakfast or early evening aperitif. A full lunch and dinner menu is also served, although quality and service can be a little inconsistent.

SOUTH

San Paolo

► *To get to San Paolo, take the metro line B to San Paolo or buses 23, 128, 769 or C6.*

Heading south along the via Ostiense from Piramide metro, **San Paolo** is a district of mainly uninspiring 1950s-70s high-rises, but is home to one of Rome's major basilicas, **San Paolo fuori le Mura**.

Via Appia Antica

To the south of the city, to the east of **Ostiense** (*see p215*), lies the beginning of the **Appian Way**. Appius Claudius Caecus, censor of 312 BC, had the inspired idea of building a road (taking advantage of a lava stream from a volcanic eruption 270,000 years earlier in the Alban Hills to the south) to move troops and goods easily between towns. In ancient times, the Appian Way was a prime spot for the real estate of the afterlife; the remains of the dead – whether cremated or buried – had to be kept outside the *pomerium* (a sacred city boundary), and well-to-do Roman families set up family mausoleums alongside this major road into the city. It was once lined with tombs, vaults, sarcophagi and every kind of magnificent decoration imaginable.

Christians, too, began burying their dead here, initially in common necropoli. Later, as land became too expensive, they laid them to rest underground, creating the estimated 300-kilometre (200-mile) network of underground cemeteries known as the **catacombs**. Jews also used the catacomb method for their burials; a Jewish catacomb can still be visited at **Vigna Rondanini** (via Appia Antica 119).

From the Middle Ages, via Appia Antica suffered at the hands of marauding Goths and Normans; successive popes did as much damage as barbarians had, filching any good pieces of statuary or marble that remained. Miraculously, there are mausoleums that maintain more or less their original shape.

Although it once started at the south-eastern end of the Circo Massimo, the beginning of the Appia Antica is now considered to be at the **Porta San Sebastiano**, the best-preserved of the gates that were built by Aurelian when he walled the city in AD 270. Inside the gate is the little **Museo delle Mura**, which allows access to a section of the wall. On the right, ten minutes' walk beyond the gate, is the **Parco Appia Antica Punto Informativo** (via Appia Antica 58/60, 06 513 5316, www.parcoappiaantica.it, open 9am-sunset daily).

Sights worth visiting include the tiny, austere church of **Domine Quo Vadis** (open 8am-6pm daily) and several notable catacombs. Nearby is the **Fosse Ardeatine** (via Ardeatina 174), a moving memorial to the 355 Italians shot by the occupying Nazis in 1944 in retaliation for a Resistance ambush.

The further south you go, the more the Appian Way returns to almost as it was. The original volcanic paving stones that lie exposed beneath a canopy of pines and cypresses are those trod by the Roman infantry. On either side of the road are remains of funerary ornaments, and you'll find the vast **Circo di Massenzio** (*see p228*), one of the best-preserved Roman circuses.

► *Follow the Appia Antica south, past a stretch of traffic-clogged highway (as it joins via Appia Nuova), and you'll find charming countryside to explore. See p236 Via Appia.*

❤ Museo delle Mura

Via di Porta San Sebastiano 18 (06 0608, www.museodellemuraroma.it). Bus 118, 218. ***Open*** *9am-2pm Tue-Sun.* ***Admission*** *free.* ***Map*** *p8.*

Rome's ancient walls run an 18-km (12-mile) circuit around the city. Built by Aurelian in the third century, a desperate sign of the city's imminent decline, they were subsequently reinforced and modified. They remained the fortifications defending the papal city until they were breached at Porta Pia in 1870 (*see p147*), 16 centuries after their construction. This small and free museum is housed in the ancient Porta San Sebastiano. There is a small collection of artefacts associated with Roman walls and roads, including a couple of nice models. But the main attraction is undoubtedly the fine view from the ramparts of the gate, looking out across the verdant Parco dell'Appia Antica towards the Alban Hills in the distance. There is also a walkway that leads along a section of the wall, complete with arrow slits to peer out at advancing invaders.

EUR

► *The quickest way from the city centre to EUR is by metro (line B; get off at EUR Magliana), b411ut approaching the district from the surface, along via Cristoforo Colombo (bus 30Exp, 130, 170, 714, 791), is the best way to experience the emerging-from-greenery feel of EUR, which was a significant part of the original architects' design411411.*

Italian Fascism managed to be simultaneously monstrous and absurd, but its delusions of grandeur helped to produce some of the most interesting European architecture and town planning of the 20th century. In the early 1930s Giuseppe Bottai, governor of Rome and the leading arbiter of Fascist taste, had the idea of expanding landbound Rome along via Ostiense towards the sea. Imperial Rome had its monuments; papal Rome had its churches. Fascist Rome (*la terza Roma*), Bottai thought, should have its architectural spaces as well. He combined this with the notion of a universal exhibition, pencilled in for 1942, and intended to combine cultural exhibition spaces with a monument to the regime.

Architect Marcello Piacentini was charged with co-ordinating the ambitious project but few of the original designs were ever built. The planning committee became so embroiled in argument that little had been achieved by the outbreak of World War II. After the war, work resumed with a different spirit. With its bombastic modernism, the EUR (Esposizione Universale Romana) lets you know you're not in Kansas anymore.

On either side of axial via Cristoforo Colombo, Fascist-inspired buildings such as Guerrini's **Palazzo della Civiltà del Lavoro**, popularly known as *il colosseo quadrato* (the square Colosseum), and Arnaldo Foschini's church of **Santi Pietro e Paolo** (piazzale Santi Pietro e Paolo) can be seen alongside post-war *palazzi* like Adalberto Libera's **Palazzo dei Congressi** (piazza JF Kennedy). A slew of museums allow a glimpse inside these striking monuments to Fascist grandeur. A futuristic new congress centre designed by Massimiliano Fuksas and opened in 2016, known as *La Nuvola* (the cloud), stands glistening and proud at the southern end of the avenue.

The 1960 Olympics offered another stimulus for filling out the area. The masterpiece is Nervi and Piacentini's flying-saucer-like **Palazzo dello Sport** (piazza dello Sport), hovering over EUR's artificial lake and now often used for big rock concerts and political conventions. The area contains other attractions, such as the **LunEur Park** funfair (www.luneurpark.it) and the **Piscina delle Rose** swimming pool (www.piscinadellerose.it).

For relief from EUR's relentless modernity, head for the leafy charm of the **Abbazia delle Tre Fontane**.

Sights & museums

Abbazia delle Tre Fontane

Via Acque Salvie 1 (06 540 1655). Bus 671, 716. ***Santi Vincenzo e Anastasio*** *6.30am-1pm, 3-7.30pm daily.* ***San Paolo*** *8am-12.30pm, 3-6pm daily.* ***Shop*** *(06 540 2309) 9am-2pm, 3.30-7.30pm daily.*

To the east of the Tre Fontane sports facilities lies a haven of ancient, eucalyptus-scented green, with three churches commemorating the points where St Paul's head supposedly bounced after it was severed from his body in AD 67. (Being a Roman citizen, Paul was eligible for the relatively quick and painless head-chop, as opposed to the long, drawn-out crucifixion.) These are the grounds of the Trappist monastery of Tre Fontane, where water has gurgled and birds have sung since the fifth century. The church of San Paolo delle Tre Fontane is said to be built on the spot where the apostle was executed; apart from a column to which Paul is supposed to have been tied, all traces of the fifth-century church were done away with in 1599 by architect Giacomo della Porta, who was also responsible for the two other churches.

In the know
Getting around

The first section of the via Appia Antica is pavementless and best avoided on foot. Take bus 660 from Colli Albani metro station (line A) to the junction of via Appia Antica and via Cecilia Metella and either walk or hire bikes at **Appia Antica Caffé** (via Appia Antica 175, appiaanticacaffe.it) or from **Parco Appia Antica Punto Informativo** (see p226).

Other buses that service the area include no.118 (from Piramide metro) and no.218 (from piazza San Giovanni).

Catacombe di San Callisto

Via Appia Antica 110 & 126 (06 513 0151, www.catacombe.roma.it). ***Open*** *9am-noon, 2-5pm Mon, Tue, Thur-Sun. Closed late Jan-late Feb.* ***Admission*** *€8; €5 reductions.*

Buried in the 29km (18 miles) of tunnels were nine popes (venerated in a chapel known as *il piccolo Vaticano*), dozens of martyrs and thousands of Christians. Named after third-century Pope Callixtus, the area became the first official cemetery of the Church of Rome.

Circo & Villa di Massenzio, & Mausoleo di Romolo

Via Appia Antica 153 (06 0608, www.villadimassenzio.it). ***Open*** *10am-4pm Tue-Sun.* ***Admission*** *free.*

This large area of lovely green countryside contains one of the best-preserved Roman circuses. It was built by Emperor Maxentius for his private use, before his defeat and death at the hands of co-ruler Constantine in AD 312. Remains of the Imperial villa are perched above the track, at its northern end. Also at the north end is the mausoleum Maxentius built for his beloved son Romulus.

Museo dell'Alto Medioevo

Viale Lincoln 3 (06 5422 8199, archeoroma.beniculturali.it). Metro EUR Fermi/bus 30Exp, 170, 714, 791. ***Open*** *9am-7pm Tue-Sun. Closed Aug Sun, Mon.* ***Admission*** *€4; €2 reductions.*

Tomb of San Sebastiano (Giuseppe Giorgetti, 1672)

Focusing on the decorative arts between the fall of the Roman Empire and the late Middle Ages, this museum has intricate gold- and silver-decorated swords and buckles. The absolute highlight of the collection is a spectacular reconstructed room decorated in *opus sectile* (stone inlay) from a very Late Imperial building at Ostia Antica, well worth the journey all by itself.

► *There is a cumulative ticket for €10 which includes access to the nearby Museo Preistorico ed Etnografico Pigorini and the Museo delle Arti e Tradizioni Popolari below.*

Museo delle Arti e Tradizioni Popolari

Piazza G Marconi 8 (06 592 6148). Metro EUR Fermi/bus 30Exp, 170, 714, 791. ***Open*** *9am-8pm Tue-Sun.* ***Admission*** *€4; €2 reductions.*

This enormous collection is dedicated to Italian folk art and rural tradition. Exhibits include elaborately decorated carts and horse tackle, as well as a bizarre collection of votive offerings left to local saints. Malevolent-looking puppets fill one room; another has *carnevale* artefacts.

Museo Preistorico ed Etnografico L Pigorini

Piazza G Marconi 14 (06 5495 2269, www.pigorini.beniculturali.it). Metro EUR Fermi/bus 30Exp, 170, 714, 791. ***Open*** *9am-6pm Mon-Sat; 9am-1.30pm Sun. Closed July, Aug Sun.* ***Admission*** *€6; €3 reductions.*

This museum displays prehistoric Italian artefacts together with material from a range of world cultures, including the anthropological collection of 17th-century Jesuit polymath Athanasius Kircher. The lobby contains a genuine Neanderthal skull.

San Paolo fuori le Mura

Piazzale San Paolo 1 (06 541 0341, www.basilicasanpaolo.org). See arrow text above. ***Basilica*** *7am-6.30pm daily.* ***Cloister*** *9am-6pm daily.* ***Admission*** *Church free. Cloister €4. No cards.*

Constantine founded San Paolo to commemorate the martyrdom of St Paul at nearby Tre Fontane in EUR (*see p228*). The church is a mix of different styles, having been destroyed, rebuilt and restored several times; most of the present basilica – the largest in Rome after St Peter's – is only 150 years old. The greatest damage to the building occurred in a fire in 1823, but restorers also contributed to the destruction of the older church. Features that have survived include 11th-century doors decorated with biblical scenes; a strange 12th-century Easter candlestick featuring human-, lion- and goat-headed beasts spewing the vine of life from their mouths; and the elegant 13th-century ciborium above the altar, by Arnolfo di Cambio. In the *confessio* beneath the altar is the tomb of St Paul, topped by a stone slab pierced with two holes through which devotees stuff bits of cloth to imbue them with the apostle's holiness.

The cloister is a good example of Cosmatesque work, its twisted columns inlaid with mosaic and supporting an arcade of sculpted reliefs. In the sacristy are the remnants of a series of papal portraits that once lined the nave. The modern church has carried on this tradition, replacing the originals with mosaic portraits of all the popes from Peter to the present incumbent. There are only eight spaces left; once they are filled, the world, apparently, will end.

San Sebastiano & Catacombe di San Sebastiano

Via Appia Antica 136 (06 788 7035/06 785 0350, www.catacombe.org). ***Church*** *8am-1pm, 2-5.30pm daily.* ***Catacombs*** *10am-5pm Mon-Sat. Closed mid Nov-mid Dec.* ***Admission*** *Church free, Catacombs €8; €5 reductions.*

The name 'catacomb' originated in this spot, where a complex of underground burial sites situated near a tufa quarry was described as being *kata kymbas* – 'near the quarry'. The guided tour will take you into the crypt of St Sebastian, the martyr always depicted nastily pierced by a hail of arrows, who was buried here. Visitors usually ignore the fourth-century basilica built over the catacombs; pilgrims taking a tour of Rome's great basilicas understand its importance: the remains of apostles Peter and Paul were hidden in the underlying catacombs in the third century, during the persecutions by Emperor Valerian.

WEST

► *To get to Monteverde Vecchio, take buses 44, 75, 115, 710 or 870.*

To the west of the city, climbing the steep hill behind **Trastevere** and the **Gianicolo** (*see pp164-179*) is **Monteverde Vecchio**, a leafy, well-heeled suburb that is home to the vast, green, tree-filled expanse of the **Villa Doria Pamphilj** park (*fold-out map E14*). Here, children will enjoy feeding the turtles – if you can find the pond – and riding the ponies (if they're not at their other haunt, the Gianicolo). Nearby, to the south-east, is the smaller but equally lovely **Villa Sciarra** garden, with its rose arbours, children's play area and miniature big dipper.

Day Trips

Heading into the Lazio countryside, chances are you'll be travelling along a route that has been trodden for millennia. The *consolari* (the consular roads) of the Romans were well paved and well maintained. Today the *consolari* are still key traffic corridors; but along them you'll find Roman (and earlier) remains, grand *palazzi*, quaint villages, lovely countryside and some perfectly acceptable beaches.

❤ Don't miss

1 Ostia Antica *p232*
Wander the streets of Rome's ancient port.

2 Villa Adriana *p235*
The extraordinary complex built by Hadrian as his country retreat.

3 Villa d'Este *p236*
Marvel at the fountains at the Renaissance gardens of Cardinal d'Este, an extravagant exercise in conspicuous consumption.

4 Castelgandolfo *p236*
Explore the gardens of the summer retreat of the popes, on the breezy banks of Lake Albano.

In the know
Getting around

The network of local railways, the **Ferrovie Regionali** and **Ferrovie Urbane** (06 7205 7205/ 800 431 784 free of charge, www.atac.roma.it), is handy for destinations outside Rome. For more on mainline services, *see p316*.

The Lazio transport authority **COTRAL** (06 7205 7205/800 174 471 free of charge, www. cotralspa.it) covers the region efficiently. Buses leave from several city termini (see 'Getting there' in each area).

For **car hire**, *see p320*.

Via Appia Antica *p236*

❤ Ostia Antica

Scavi di Ostia Antica, viale dei Romagnoli 717 (www.ostiaantica.beniculturali.it). Train to Ostia Antica (see right In the know). ***Open*** *varies, see website. Closed Mon.* ***Admission*** *€8; €4 reductions.*

Forget attempting the punishing trip to Pompeii during your Rome stay ,and do a comfortable day-trip to the ancient port of **Ostia Antica** instead – just as good a site for getting a feel for everyday life in a working Roman town.

Legend says that Ostia was founded by Ancus Martius, the fourth king of Rome, in the second half of the seventh century BC, although the oldest remains date 'only' from c330 BC. Ostia was Rome's main port for over 600 years, until its decline in the fourth century AD. Abandoned after sackings by barbarians in the fifth century, the town was gradually buried by river mud.

Admission gives you access to the remains below, and the Museum; ideally, visit on a sunny weekday. (Admission is also free the first Sunday of every month.) Purchasing a site plan at the ticket office (€4) is a good idea.

The *decumanus maximus* (high street) runs from the entrance at the **Porta Romana** (Roman Gate) for almost a kilometre (half a mile), past the theatre and forum (*see below*), before forking left to what used to be the seashore (now three kilometres/two miles away at modern-day Ostia). The right fork, **via della Foce**, leads to the Tiber. On either side of these main arteries is a network of intersecting lanes, where the best discoveries can be made.

Undoubtedly one of the grandest structures at Ostia is the **theatre** which once housed around 5000 spectators. Behind the theatre is the **piazza of the Corporations.** Here the various trade guilds had their offices, and mosaics on the floor of small shops that ring the open square refer to the products each guild dealt in – shipowners had ships on the floor; ivory dealers had elephants. Further along on the right is the **old mill**, where both the grindstones and the circular furrows ploughed by the blindfolded donkeys that turned them are still visible. In the tangle of streets between the *decumanus* and the museum, don't miss the **thermopolium** – an ancient Roman bar, complete with marble counter,

Theatrical mask at the Roman theatre

Roman Theatre

a fresco advertising the house fare and a garden with a fountain.

The **Forum** is dominated by the imposing brick skeleton of the Capitolium, once clad in marble and the seat of the veneration of Rome's three major deities: Jupiter, Juno and Minerva. Located off the forum to the south-east are the **Forum baths** – the terracotta heating pipes are still visible. Nearby is the **forica**, or ancient public latrine. In mostly residential districts off via della Foce, the **House of Cupid and Psyche** is an elegant fourth-century construction; the **House of the Dioscuri** has beautiful mosaics; the **Insula of the Charioteers** still has many of its frescoes. The wealthy lived in the garden apartments at the western end of the site, set back from the busy streets; recently restored, these can be visited on tours on Sunday morning at 10.30am by booking on 06 5635 2830.

The **Museo della Via Ostiense** (open 9.30am-1hr before sunset Tue-Sun) has a model of Ostia Antica in its heyday, and a good collection of artefacts from the site, including bas-reliefs of scenes of ordinary life; there's a café and bookshop next door.

In the know
Ostia Antica essentials

From Rome, take the local train from Porta San Paolo (the suburban part of Piramide metro station, line B) to Ostia Antica (30mins). (Bear in mind the small café outside the station is the last chance for refreshments until the café at the excavations which is quite a long way into the site.) Cross the footbridge over the road and follow the road, cross the pedestrian crossing, pass the restaurant on your right and the site entrance is ahead and on your left.

Piazza of the Corporations

Gladiator fresco

VIA AURELIA

From Rome's western suburbs, the via Aurelia travels due west, curving north to follow the coast. Despite the occasional unfortunate outbreak of modern eyesores – including the entire town of **Ladispoli** – the Aurelia today remains a pretty drive through rolling hills and by the sea, with the occasional Roman tomb or medieval watchtower along the way. Unless you're looking for a beach, ignore signposts to the seaside towns of **Maccarese**, **Fregene** and Ladispoli, and head straight for the town of **Cerveteri** with one of the most important sites in Etruscan Lazio.

With three ports, **Cerveteri** was one of the great Mediterranean trading centres from the seventh to fifth centuries BC. Most interesting is the **Necropoli di Banditaccia** (via della Necropoli, www.etruriameridionale.beniculturali.it). This town of the dead – with streets, *piazze* and tidy little houses – is one of the most touching archaeological sites in Italy. There's plenty of ancient atmosphere here, with a wilderness of vines, cypresses and oaks growing on and around tufa-cut tumuli (mound-shaped tombs).

Northwards, past the family resort of **Santa Marinella** and the port of Civitavecchia, **Tarquinia** lies three kilometres (two miles) inland from the Aurelia, bristling with medieval defensive towers. Once a major Etruscan stronghold, the **Necropoli dei Monterozzi** (via Ripagretta) contains some 100 tombs, hidden beneath a grassy hill about two kilometres (1.25 miles) out of town. Housed in the impressive, 15th-century Palazzo Vitelleschi, the **Museo Archeologico Nazionale di Tarquinia** (Palazzo Vitelleschi, piazza Cavour, www.archeologialazio.beniculturali.it) has one of the best Etruscan collections outside Rome.

VIA CASSIA

Leading north-west out of Rome, via Cassia winds through Lazio's lakeland – gentle hilly countryside dotted with picturesque towns. It also passes by a number of glorious gardens.

From the GRA ring road, the modern via Cassia Veientana parallels it to the east. Between the old and new roads (but best reached from the former), the **Parco Regionale di Veio** – just before the medieval village of Isola Farnese – surrounds **Veio**, an Etruscan city founded in the eighth century BC. The site contains rare examples of Etruscan houses and temples, plus a striking sixth-century BC sanctuary of Apollo.

In the crater of an extinct volcano, pretty **Lago di Bracciano** – about 40 kilometres (24 miles) north of Rome – is Rome's emergency water supply, so it's kept reasonably clean; the best swimming spots are just north of Bracciano town on the western shore, and on the eastern side near Trevignano. Boats run around the lake from Bracciano in summer (see www.consorziolagodibracciano.it). A handful of pretty villages overlook this body of water.

Just to the south-east is tranquil **Lago di Martignano**, with a beach where you can hire sailing boats, pedalos and canoes. You'll need your own transport to reach it. Further north on the Cassia is the town of **Sutri**, which sits on a tufa rock outcrop above its ancient amphitheatre. The amphitheatre is located in the pretty **Parco Urbano dell'Antica Città di Sutri**.

Just past Sutri, a winding local road heads north off the Cassia towards medieval **Ronciglione** and on to **Lago di Vico**; most of the area is a natural park.

North lies **Viterbo**, an important Etruscan town and an insignificant Roman one. Today, Viterbo's *centro storico* is a jumble of narrow streets concealing a mix of rather grand *palazzi*, medieval laundries and ancient porticoes. The medieval quarter lies

In the know
Via Aurelia essentials

For **Tarquinia**, take the train from Termini, Ostiense or Trastevere (journey time 1hr15mins).

For **Cerveteri**, take the train to Marina di Cerveteri station (approx 30mins from Termini, Ostiense or Trastevere) where a local bus will connect you.

COTRAL runs bus services along the Aurelia from Cornelia station.

In the know
Via Cassia essentials

By car, follow the Cassia (SS2). For **Lago di Bracciano**, exit at La Storta and take via Claudia-Braccianense (SS493).

Trains to this region originate mostly from Ostiense, Trastevere, or Valle Aurelia (with the exception of trains to **Viterbo**, which leave from Flaminio).

at the city's southern edge, flanked by piazza della Morte. Across the bridge is the elegant 12th-century cathedral of **San Lorenzo**, and next door is the **Palazzo Papale**, built for the popes in the 13th century. The pretty 12th-century church of **Santa Maria Nuova** has an ancient head of Jupiter on the façade, and a pulpit from which St Thomas Aquinas preached.

VIA TIBURTINA

Via Tiburtina more or less follows the Aniene river, which wends its way east of Rome to join the Tiber north of the city centre.

Just 20 kilometres (12.5 miles) from Rome are two UNESCO World Heritage Sites that are worth a visit – **Villa d'Este**, in via Tiburtina's original, ancient destination of Tibur (modern Tivoli), and **Villa Adriana** (**Hadrian's Villa**), five kilometres (three miles) down the hill, site of the spectacular second-century AD retreat designed and built by Emperor Hadrian.

Tivoli itself was founded by an Italic tribe, and conquered by the Romans in 338 BC. It was littered with temples, and the surrounding territory became a popular location for country villas. The cathedral of **San Lorenzo** (via Duomo) contains a carved 13th-century *Descent from the Cross*. At the town's highest point (piazza delle Nazioni Unite) is **Rocca Pia**, a 15th-century castle built by Pope Pius II. Dominating Tivoli is the **Villa d'Este** (*see p236*), a lavish pleasure palace built over a Benedictine monastery in 1550 for Cardinal Ippolito d'Este, son of Lucrezia Borgia.

Sights & museums

❤ Villa Adriana

Via di Villa Adriana, Villa Adriana (0774 382 733, www.villaadriana.beniculturali.it). ***Open*** *9am-1hr before sunset daily.* ***Admission*** *€8; €4 reductions. Exhibition price varies.*

Strewn across a gentle slope, the Villa Adriana was built from 118 to 134 and has some fascinating architectural spaces and water features. Hadrian was an amateur architect and is believed to have designed many of the unique elements in his villa himself. He drew on inspiration from his travels in Greece and Egypt. In the centuries following the fall of the Empire it became a luxury quarry for treasure-hunters. At least 500 pieces of statuary in collections around the world have been identified as coming from this site, and marble and mosaic finds from the villa now make up a significant portion of the collections of Roman art at the Capitoline and Vatican museums. The restored remains are still impressive, yet the layout of the complex is seemingly haphazard: it's easy to get lost and just as easy to stumble upon charming surprises.

Where the original entrance to the villa lay is uncertain; today the first space you'll encounter from the ticket office is the *pecile* (or *poikile*), a large pool that was once surrounded by a portico with high walls, of which only one remains.

Directly east, the *Teatro marittimo* (Maritime Theatre) is one of the most delightful inventions in the whole villa. A circular brick wall encloses a moat, at the centre of which is an island of columns and brickwork; it was a self-sufficient *domus* (mini-villa) – complete with its own baths, bedrooms and gardens.

Canopus, Villa Adriana

Villa d'Este

South lies a three-storey building known simply as the 'building with a fish pond' (*peschiera*), or the Winter Palace (*Quartiere invernale*). This may have been the emperor's private residence, with a large banquet hall overlooking the plains towards Rome. Continuing south, locate the *Piccole terme* (Small Baths), where intricate ceiling plaster mouldings are amazingly intact, giving an idea of the grandeur of the entire villa's decoration.

In the valley below is the lovely *canopus*. Built to recall the canal that connected Alexandria to the city of Canopus on the Nile delta, this is a long, narrow pool, framed on three sides by columns and statues, including a marble crocodile.

❤ Villa d'Este

Piazza Trento 1, Tivoli (0774 332 920, www.villadestetivoli.info). ***Open*** *Nov-July 8.30am-1hr before sunset Tue-Sun. Aug-Oct also 2pm-1hr before sunset Mon.* ***Admission*** *€8; €4 reductions. Exhibition price varies.*

Mannerist architect Pirro Ligorio made detailed studies of Hadrian's Villa (*see p235*), and he drew on these in his plans for the Villa d'Este and its gardens. The gardens are the main attraction, drawing busloads of day-trippers to admire their ingenious fountains.

Ligorio developed a complex 'hydraulic machine' that channelled water from the Aniene river (still the source today) through a series of canals under the garden. Using know-how borrowed from the Romans, he created a homage to the natural springs on the hillsides of Tivoli in the 51 fountains spread around the terraced gardens. Technological gimmickry was a big feature; the Owl Fountain imitated an owl's song using a hydraulic mechanism. There is a programme of summer evening openings and events at the villa.

In the know
Via Tiburtina essentials

By car, skip the congestion of the first section of via Tiburtina, and take the fast A24 towards **Tivoli**.

COTRAL runs a bus service from Ponte Mammolo to Tivoli (45mins). Get off at the main square (piazza Garibaldi) for **Villa d'Este**. The service also stops at **Villa Adriana** (35mins). Local buses also connect Tivoli town to Villa Adriana (10mins). The site is not very well signposted: ask where to get off.

VIA APPIA

While the start of the **via Appia Antica** – or regina viarum (Queen of Roads) as it was known – offers a plethora of catacombs and churches (*see p226* Via Appia Antica); you'll need to persevere southwards on the SS7 through the smog and traffic fumes of the modern **via Appia Nuova** (SS7) before you are rewarded. Beyond lies the lake-dotted countryside south of Rome, continuing along via dei Laghi (SS217).

Perched on the lip of the **Lago Albano** crater, **Castelgandolfo** is best known as the town where the pontiffs have traditionally spent their summer holidays. (Pope Clement VII began the tradition in the 1500s, though Pope Francis has broken with tradition and stays in Rome). It is now possible to visit the **Palazzo Apostolico** and the splendid **Giardini di Barberini** (Piazza della Libertà, museivaticani.va). On Saturdays there is the option of a full day tour including the Vatican Museums and Gardens and transfer by train to Castelgandolfo from the Vatican City railway station. At the Palazzo's entrance, enjoy enchanting views of the lake from the pretty, cobbled piazza della Libertà. In high summer enjoy the breeze by taking a stroll around the lakeshore, hire a pedalo or take a (brisk) swim.

A few kilometres to the south, **Albano Laziale** was the site of a huge army base built by Septimius Severus for the Second Legion, and its remains can be seen all over the town. The church of **Santa Maria della Rotonda** (which looks a bit like the Pantheon in miniature) was once the nymphaeum of a huge Roman baths complex.

Of all the Castelli Romani villages, **Nemi** is the most picturesque, perched on the edge of a tree-covered crater overlooking a lake.

South-east, the town **Ninfa** was named – local legend says – after a nymph who was so devastated by the loss of her lover that she cried herself a river. Today a stream flows through some of Italy's most beautiful gardens, which ramble around the ruins of a medieval town. In the 1920s, Don Gelasio Caetani decided to plant his vast collection of exotic species here; the result of his botanical dabbling – the **Oasi di Ninfa** (www.fondazionecaetani.org) – is pure magic.

> In the know
> **Via Appia essentials**
>
> To explore by car, take the Appia (SS7) out of Rome. For **Nemi**, exit after Ciampino and take via dei Laghi.
>
> Trains to **Castelgandolfo** run hourly from Termini (journey time 45mins).

VIA PONTINA

Slicing south from the city, via Pontina (SS148) can make no claim to antiquity. It was built in the 1930s to connect Mussolini's capital to the Pontine marshes and 'ideal' Fascist settlements such as Littorio (now Latina, a dingy centre of provincial life) and the smart beach resort of Sabaudia.

Pick the Pontina up just outside EUR (*see p227*) and head through the soulless, high-rise dormitory suburbs. At Aprilia the SS207 forks right to **Anzio**, where the Allies landed in 1944 to launch their victorious march on Rome, and **Nettuno**, with its serried rows of heart-rending white crosses in the British and American military cemeteries.

The first cleanish sea south of Rome is at **Sabaudia**. With its striking 1930s architecture, the town is a favourite with Italy's holidaying intelligentsia. It owes its miles of unspoilt sandy beaches to the fact that it is inside the **Parco Nazionale del Circeo**. Hire bikes or set out on foot for walks and picnics (bring mosquito repellent).

Looming to the south is **Monte Circeo**, where Odysseus was waylaid by the enchantress Circe, who turned his ship's crew into pigs. A hike to the top through cork- and holm-oak forests on the western, seaward side is spectacular. Or drive most of the way up from the landward side to explore the ancient ruins along the ridge. East of the outcrop, a road winds up to **San Felice Circeo**, a pretty little town and a paradise for the permatanned in summer.

The Pontina merges with the Appia (becoming the SS213) at **Terracina**. Modern Terracina is down by the sea, while the medieval town above lies on top of the forum of the Roman port of Anxur. World War II bombing uncovered the ancient remains of a temple to Augustus and made space for the modern town hall and **Museo Civico di Terracina** (piazza Municipio 1). Standing above the town is the first-century BC **Tempio di Giove** (Temple of Jupiter).

Sperlonga is a pretty seaside resort. The whitewashed medieval town on the spur above the two beaches – its narrow lanes lined with potted geraniums, boutiques and restaurants – fills with well-heeled Romans in the summer.

> In the know
> **Via Pontina essentials**
>
> By car, pick up the Pontina (SS148) in EUR. For minor destinations, your own transport is essential.
>
> Take a train to Priverno (journey time 50mins) and change for buses to **Sabaudia** (30mins) and to **Terracina** (20mins).
> Take the train to Fondi (1hr) for buses to **Sperlonga** (20mins).
>
> COTRAL services run from Laurentina in Rome to Terracina (2hrs). For Sperlonga, change in Terracina (20mins).

Nemi

Experience

Opera at Terme de Caracalla *p269*

Events

A rundown of Rome's packed calendar

The Romans, perennial fun-seekers, have never needed much of an excuse for a knees-up; in ancient times a whopping 150 days were set aside every year for R&R. Though modern-day Romans must make do with a paltry ten annual public holidays, the final total is usually quite a bit more: any holiday that falls midweek is invariably taken as an invitation to *fare il ponte* ('do a bridge') – take an extra day or two off between the official holiday and the nearest weekend.

Important religious holidays have different effects on the city (the Assumption on 15 August shuts it down; Easter brings hordes of pilgrims). Districts of Rome hold smaller-scale celebrations of their own patron saints in their own way, from calorific blowouts to extravagant firework displays. Occasional large-scale city-run events make ample use of Rome's endless supply of photogenic venues.

▶ *For a sense of seasonal Rome and advice on when to visit, see p26 When to Visit.*

Festa de' Noantri

Spring

Giornate FAI

Various venues (www.giornatefai.it). ***Date*** *Sat/Sun in Mar/Apr.*

For one weekend each year, the Fondo per l'Ambiente Italiano (FAI) persuades institutional and private owners of historic properties to reveal their spectacular interiors, usually off-limits to the public; see the website for information.

Festa della Donne

Various venues. ***Date*** *8 Mar.*

Rome celebrates International Women's Day by offering women free entry to the state-run museums and attractions. Bright yellow mimosa flowers, the traditional gift, are on sale throughout town.

Festa di Santa Francesca Romana

Basilica di Santa Francesca Romana, Piazza Santa Francesca Romana 4, Capitoline. Metro Colosseo/bus 51, 75, 85, 87, 118/tram 3 ***Date*** *9 Mar.* ***Map*** *p68 L11.*

In 1433 Santa Francesca Romana founded the Oblate di Maria, an order of nuns who never took final vows. She was believed to possess the gift of dislocation (being in different places at once), a quality that so endeared her to Italy's pioneer motorists that they made her their patron saint. Devout Roman drivers get their motors blessed at her church in the Foro Romano (*see p67*) on 9 March.

Palazzo Massimo alle Colonne

Corso Vittorio Emanuele II 141, Piazza Navona. Bus 30, 40, 46, 62, 64, 70, 81, 130, 190, 492, 628, 916. ***Date*** *16 Mar (7am-1pm).* ***Map*** *p104 G8.*

San Filippo Neri performed one of his most famous miracles in the *palazzo* of the Massimo family. Called to give last rites to Paolo Massimo, the saint found the boy already dead; undaunted, he revived Paolo, chatted for a while, then – when the boy was ready to meet his maker – commended him to God. On the anniversary, a procession of family, servants and altar boys escorts the cardinal or archbishop to a private room for a slap-up buffet. Turn up near 11.30am to witness the spectacle in all its Felliniesque glory.

Festa di San Giuseppe

Basilica di San Giuseppe al Trionfale, via Bernadino Telesio 4b, Suburbs: Trionfale. Bus 23, 31, 33, 70, 495. ***Date*** *19 Mar.*

Also known as Father's Day in Italy, the feast of St Joseph is no longer a public holiday but festivities still take place near the basilica di San Giuseppe al Trionfale, north of the Vatican. In the run-up to the feast, the city's *pasticcerie* are piled high with deep-fried, custard-filled, batter-balls called *bignè di San Giuseppe*, a traditional Father's Day gift.

Festa di Primavera – Mostra delle Azalee

Piazza di Spagna (see p88). ***Date*** *late Mar/early Apr.*

Spring arrives early in Rome, bringing masses of blooms. When the azaleas come out, some 3,000 vases of them are arranged on the Spanish Steps.

In the know
Check the details

Details and programmes of many events remain vague until the last minute, and are likely to change from year to year. Check www.turismoroma.it or www.060608.it.

❤ Best Roman festivals

Festa de' Noantri *p246*
A quintessential Roman combo of religious devotion, neighbourhood spirit and raucous merriment.

Natale di Roma *p244*
Rome's birthday blowout, complete with gladiators, parades and pageantry.

Roma Incontra il Mondo *p246 & p259*
A summer series of international and multicultural outdoor events.

Settimana Santa & Pasqua *p244*
The biggest week of the Catholic year.

Stagione Estiva del Teatro dell'Opera *p245*
Dazzling sets, sensational music and a magnificent third-century backdrop.

Natale di Roma

❤ Rome Marathon

Around the city (06 406 5064, www.maratonadiroma.it). ***Date*** *Sun in late Mar/early Apr.*

The annual Maratona della Città di Roma attracts some big-name runners, hordes of amateur pavement-pounders and flocks of locals and visitors just happy to observe the sporting activity along city streets marvellously empty of motor vehicles. A party atmosphere prevails as runners – 16,000 of them in 2017 – set off jubilantly south… then limp back through the *centro storico* to the finishing line. The serious race begins and ends in via dei Fori Imperiali; sign up online (the sooner you register, the lower the fee).

The Stracittadina fun-run, which takes place on the same day, is a five-kilometre (three-mile) jog past some of Rome's most glorious ancient sites: you can wear your skates or bring your dog if you wish. Sign up at the Marathon Village (venue varies – check online) up to a day before the event.

❤ Settimana Santa & Pasqua (Holy Week & Easter)
Vatican (see p152), Colosseo (see p74). ***Date*** *Mar/Apr.*

Tourists and pilgrims flood into the city on the Saturday before Palm Sunday, cramming inside St Peter's square for the open-air Mass. The non-stop services of Holy Week peak in the pope's Stations of the Cross (*Via Crucis*) and Mass at the Colosseum late on the evening of Good Friday. On *Pasquetta* (Easter Monday), tradition coaxes Romans *fuori porta* (outside the city gates) to feast upon lavish picnics of such specialities as *torta pasqualina* (cheesy bread, with salami and hard-boiled eggs) and *fave e pecorino* (broad beans and cheese).

Settimana della Cultura
Various venues (www.beniculturali.it). ***Date*** *1wk in Apr/May.*

For Cultural Heritage Week, state-owned museums and monuments open to the public without charge.

❤ Natale di Roma
Various venues (www.natalidiroma.it). ***Date*** *21 Apr.*

Not all cities celebrate their birthday… but Rome, 'born' in 753 BC, is no ordinary city. The bulk of the festivities take place around the ancient sites with costumed processions, gladiator fighting, historical re-enactments and enormous amounts of fireworks.

Festa della Liberazione
Date *25 Apr.*

This public holiday commemorates the liberation of Italy by Allied forces at the end of World War II.

Primo Maggio
San Giovanni in Laterano (see p206, www.primomaggio.net). ***Date*** *1 May.*

On May Day, trade unions organise a huge, free rock concert, which is traditionally held in front of the basilica of San Giovanni in Laterano. Performers – mainly Italian, with a smattering of international has-beens – belt out crowd-pleasers from mid-afternoon into the small hours.

Campionato Internazionale di Tennis
Foro Italico (see p222, www.internazionalibnlditalia.it). ***Date*** *2wks early May.*

Every May, Rome hosts the Italian Open tennis tournament, one of the most important European clay-court challenges outside the Grand Slam, and a warm-up event for the French Open. Matches take place at the Foro Italico, next-door to the Olympic Stadium, Purchase tickets online at www.ticketone.it.

Concorso Ippico Internazionale di Piazza di Siena
Piazza di Siena, Villa Borghese (see p140, www.piazzadisiena.it). ***Date*** *2nd half of May.*

Natale di Roma

Rome's jetset flock to see this glamorous international show-jumping event in leafy Villa Borghese.

Pentecoste

Pantheon (see p113). ***Date*** *Sun in mid May/early June.*

Exactly 50 days after Easter, the Pentecost mass at the Pantheon spectacularly concludes with tens of thousands of red rose petals scattered through the oculus in the dome upon the heads of attendees.

Art City

Various venues (www.art-city.it). ***Date*** *late May-Sept.*

A circuit of events to promote art, architecture, performing arts and literature in three of the most fascinating and photographed buildings of Rome: Palazzo Venezia (*see p63*), Castel Sant'Angelo (*see p161*), and Vittoriano (*see p64*). Ballet, theatre, jazz and classical music concerts take place in their courtyards or terraces, with breathtaking panoramas. Guided tours allow you to discover the ancient underground layer at Vittoriano or the chemin de ronde and belvedere at Palazzo Venezia.

Summer

Estate Romana

Various venues (www.estateromana.comune.roma.it). ***Date*** *June-Sept.*

During the event-packed Estate Romana (Roman Summer) festival, *piazze*, *palazzi*, parks and courtyards come alive with music from local bands, films are shown on outdoor screens late into the night, and cultural events such as readings and gastronomic events take place in venues around town. Many events are free.

Concerti del Tempietto

Various venues (348 780 4314, www.tempietto.it). ***Date*** *July-Sept.*

The Associazione Il Tempietto organises year-round concerts under the Festival Musicale delle Nazioni banner in various venues, mainly the Sala Baldini (piazza Campitelli 9), in the archaeological site around the Teatro di Marcello (*see p135*) in summer. It's not top quality, musically speaking, but there's a concert almost every evening and the venues are enchanting. You can book online.

Festival delle Letterature

Basilica di Massenzio, Foro Romano (see p67, www.festivaldelleletterature.it). Metro Colosseo/bus 51, 75, 85, 87, 118 or tram 3. ***Date*** *June/July.*

The floodlit basilica of Maxentius in the Roman Forum provides a theatrical backdrop to readings by some of the most important names in contemporary literature; past guests have included Paul Auster, Hanif Kureishi and Zadie Smith.

❤ Stagione Estiva del Teatro dell'Opera

Terme di Caracalla (see p214, www.operaroma.it). ***Date*** *June-Aug.*

The venue for the Opera di Roma's summer season is a breathtaking archaeological site. Set designers usually exploit the backdrop of majestic Roman ruins with few props and dramatic lighting. Back-row seats are very far from the stage – so bring binoculars. Box office at Teatro dell'Opera (*see p271*) or online at www.ticketone.it.

Festa della Repubblica

Via dei Fori Imperiali, Capitoline. ***Date*** *2 June.* ***Map*** *p68 L10.*

The date on which Italy became a republic in 1946 is celebrated with appropriate pomp and circumstance by a military parade along via dei Fori Imperiali and culminates with a patriotic green, white and red fly-by from the national aerobatic team, the *Frecce Tricolori*.

Gay Village

Venue varies (www.gayvillage.it). ***Date*** *early June-early Sept.*

A ten-week open-air bonanza that makes summer the pinkest season of the Roman year: bars, restaurants, live acts, discos, cinema – a great event for boys and girls alike. Venue and contact details change from year to year.

Postepay Rock in Roma

Ippodromo delle Capannelle, via Appia Nuova 1245, Suburbs: Capannelle (www.

In the know
Festive food

Try Rome's feast-day seasonal delicacies: *panettone* – sponge cake with raisins and candied fruit – is ubiquitous around Christmas. The Easter variation is vaguely bird-shaped and called a *colomba* (dove). Around the feast of San Giuseppe (19 March), *pasticcerie* make fried batter-balls filled with custard. During *carnevale* (the run-up to Lent) you'll find compact balls of fried dough called *castagnole* and crispy fried pastry strips dusted with icing sugar called *frappe*.

rockinrome.com). Bus 654 from Cinecittà metro station/664 from Colli Albani metro station/train Fm4 from Termini to Capannelle. ***Date*** *mid June-early Sept.*

If there is a big name from the international rock firmament playing in Rome in summer it is likely to be here. Since its inception in 2008, RinR has hosted Radiohead, the Killers, Snoop Dogg, Placebo, Bruce Springsteen and many others. Transport and traffic can be a nightmare so arrive early.

Just Music Festival

Various venues (www.justmusicfestival.it). ***Date*** *mid June-early Sept.*

Started in 2015, and already a smash due to A-list headliners such as Björk, Massive Attack, Public Enemy, Burt Bacharach, Pet Shop Boys, and Fatboy Slim.

Santi Pietro e Paolo

Basilica di San Pietro (see p158); San Paolo fuori le Mura (see p229). ***Date*** *29 June.*

The two founders of Catholicism are, naturally, also the twin patron saints of Rome, and each of them is honoured in his own basilica on this Roman public holiday. At St Peter's, a solemn mass is the highlight of the festivities; celebrations at San Paolo fuori le Mura focus around an all-night street fair on via Ostiense.

❤ Roma Incontra il Mondo

Villa Ada, Via di Ponte Salrio 28, Suburbs: Parioli (www.villaada.org). Bus 56, 57, 92, 135, 168, 235, 319, 342, 351, 391. ***Date*** *July-Aug.*

The international summer music and theatre festival at picturesque Villa Ada gets bigger and better every year and features artists and performers from all over the globe (*see p259*).

❤ Festa de' Noantri

Trastevere (see p164, www.festadenoantri.it). ***Date*** *2wks mid-end July.*

Though few traces of Trastevere's working-class roots remain today, the area's residents celebrate its humble origins with gusto during the Festa de' Noantri. Festivities kick off with a procession held in honour of the Madonna del Carmine, to whom the whole shebang is theoretically dedicated. Two weeks of arts events and street performances follow, and fireworks round off the closing night.

International Chamber Ensemble

Sant'Ivo alla Sapienza (see p110, 06 6937 8125, icensemble.it). Bus 30, 40, 46, 62, 64, 70, 81, 87, 130, 628, 916. ***Date*** *mid July-mid Aug.*

Chamber and symphonic music, as well as opera, takes place in a splendid example of Renaissance architecture: the courtyard of Sant'Ivo alla Sapienza, the hallowed 15th-century seat of Rome university.

Festa della Madonna della Neve

Santa Maria Maggiore (see p191). ***Date*** *5 Aug.*

There was an unseasonal snowfall on the Esquiline hill on 5 August 352, an event that is still remembered at the basilica of Santa Maria Maggiore. The day is marked with a special Mass, culminating in a blizzard of white rose petals, which flutter down from the roof on to the congregation.

Notte di San Lorenzo

Date *10 Aug.*

On the night of 10 August, Roman eyes turn towards the heavens, hoping to catch a glimpse of one of the night's shooting stars. Some explain the phenomenon as the fall-out of a meteor entering orbit, while the more poetic attribute the falling stars to the tears shed by St Lawrence, martyred in Rome on this day in 258.

Ferragosto

Date *15 Aug.*

Those who haven't scarpered to the coast for the whole of August take a long weekend for the Feast of the Assumption, and most of the city closes down.

Autumn

RomaEuropa Festival

Various venues (06 4555 3050, www.romaeuropa.net). ***Date*** *Sept-Nov.*

Rome's cutting-edge performing arts festival offers music, dance and theatre, with an eclectic mix of international acts and emerging young local talent. You can buy tickets at the venues themselves, by phone or online; book well in advance for big-name acts.

Taste of Rome

Auditorium Parco della Musica (see 273, www.tasteofroma.it). ***Date*** *1 wknd in Sept.*

The city's top chefs unite in the gardens of the Auditorium for this gastronomic festival where visitors can taste a selection of dishes as well as participate in courses and demos by Rome's culinary stars.

Festival Internazionale del Film di Roma

Auditorium Parco della Musica (see p273, www.romacinemafest.it). ***Date*** *10 days Oct-Nov.*

Rome's new-ish film festival is firmly in the serie B of international movie meets, but generous allocations of tickets for the cinema-loving Roman public and all the usual red-carpet glamour ensure plenty of non-professional audience participation and a great atmosphere.

Ognissanti/Giornata dei Defunti

Cimitero del Verano, piazzale del Verano, San Lorenzo. Bus 71, 163, 448, 492, 542, 545/tram 3, 19. ***Date*** *1-2 Nov.* ***Map*** *p182 S8.*

Otherwise known as *Tutti santi*, All Saints' Day (*Ognissanti*) is followed by *La commemorazioni dei defunti* (or *Tutti i morti*), when the pope celebrates Mass at Verano Cemetery in the San Lorenzo district. Romans travel en masse to visit family graves.

Winter

Immacolata Concezione

Piazza di Spagna (see p88). ***Date*** *8 Dec.*

The statue of the Madonna in piazza di Spagna is the focus of the Feast of the Immaculate Conception. With the pope looking on, the fire brigade runs a ladder up Mary's column and one lucky fireman gets to place a wreath over her outstretched arm. At the base of the column, the locals deposit their own elaborate floral tributes.

Natale & Santo Stefano (Christmas & Boxing Day)

Date *25-26 Dec.*

Tickets for the papal midnight Mass at St Peter's can be obtained from the Prefettura (*see p153*); you'll have to put your request in months in advance. Nativity scenes can be found in most churches, but the most impressive are halfway up the Spanish Steps and in piazza San Pietro. The Roman Christmas Day is a gluttonous affair: locals feast upon *fritti* (calorific fried offerings), followed by *panettone* (sponge with dried and candied fruit) and *torrone* (slabs of nutty chocolate or nougat). The pope says a special Mass and gives his '*Urbi et orbis*' blessing at St Peter's.

San Silvestro & Capodanno (New Year's Eve & New Year's Day)

Date *31 Dec-1 Jan.*

Hordes of Romans flock to the city's *piazzas* to see in the new year. There are usually free concerts and a fireworks display; check the city council website (www.comune.roma.it) for a full list of events. Some people add to the fun with home-grown pyrotechnics and flying *spumante* corks, turning the *centro storico* into something resembling a war zone.

Epifania – La Befana (Epiphany)

Date *6 Jan.*

Tradition has it that on the eve of Epiphany Italian children receive a visit from an old witch (*la befana*). The well-behaved wake up to a stocking filled with sweets and chocolate while the naughty will be left lumps of coal (usually a sugary, edible version sold in cake shops).

Festa di Sant'Antonio Abate

Sant'Eusebio, piazza Vittorio Emanuele II 12A, Esquilino. Metro Vittorio Emanuele/bus 50, 105, 150/tram 5, 14. ***Date*** *17 Jan.* ***Map*** *p182 O9.*

Romans commemorate the feast of the protector of animals, Sant'Antonio Abate, in the church of Sant'Eusebio. Anyone who is keen to ensure their pet gets a place in heaven can bring it along to the church for a blessing.

Carnevale

Date *2wks Feb/early Mar.*

The final fling before Lent used to be a much more riotous affair in Rome; in the Middle Ages wild parties were held on Monte Testaccio (*see p215*). Nowadays, for the two weeks leading up to Ash Wednesday, the most fun is had by children who dress up in costume to play in the city's *piazzas*. *Pasticcerie* sell special carnival treats including *castagnole* (fried dough-balls rolled in sugar) and *frappe* (thin strips of pastry doused in icing sugar).

Six Nations Championship

Stadio Olimpico (see p223, www.federugby.it). ***Date*** *Feb-Mar.*

Italy's national rugby team have proudly competed in the Six Nations Championship since 2000 and now even occasionally win a match. Home games are played at the Olympic Stadium. Tickets can be purchased online at www.ticketone.it.

Immacolata Concezione

Film

Basking in past glories, perhaps – but still a great location

Rome's legendary film studio, Cinecittà, opened with Fascist pomp in 1937 on 99 acres of former farmland south-east of the city. After its *dolce vita* heyday, however, the studio would mostly churn out TV variety shows and commercials. Launched over a decade ago, the Rome Film Festival remains in the second division of international movie meets, but the enthusiasm it creates locally is palpable. Romans, like most Italians, are keen filmgoers; and though most still like their movies dubbed, there's a growing roster of original-language offerings.

CINEMA

MAMMA ROMA

Anna Magnani starring in *Mamma Roma*

Cinema then and now

Cinecittà began to make a name for itself after World War II, when US producers discovered how cheap it was to film here and the great era of 'Hollywood-on-the-Tiber' began. The Christians-to-the-lions romp *Quo Vadis?* (1951) opened the floodgates to *gli americani*, much to the delight of the post-war public and nascent paparazzi. *Roman Holiday* (1953) brought Gregory Peck and Audrey Hepburn; *The Barefoot Contessa* (1954) drew Ava Gardner and Humphrey Bogart; and Charles Vidor's *Farewell to Arms* (1957) brought Rock Hudson and Jennifer Jones. Meanwhile, Federico Fellini was consecrating his elaborate visions in Teatro 5, the largest of Cinecittà's studio sheds, sandwiching *La Dolce Vita* (1960) between two US sword-and-sandal blockbusters, *Ben-Hur* (1959) and *Cleopatra* (1963). Spaghetti Westerns and Viscontian epics kept the place riding high through to the mid '60s, but thereafter its decline was rapid.

The 1990s saw something of a revival, with the return of big Hollywood productions, from Sylvester Stallone vehicles *Cliffhanger* and *Daylight* to Anthony Minghella's *The Talented Mr Ripley*. There was even a reprise of the over-budget glory days when Martin Scorsese's *Gangs of New York* roadshow rolled into town with Leonardo DiCaprio and Cameron Diaz. Since then Rome's costume-makers, carpenters, post-production technicians and stuntmen have been kept busy by Mel Gibson's *The Passion*, Wes Anderson's *The Life Aquatic*, all-star crime caper *Ocean's Twelve*, Julia Robert's vehicle *Eat Pray Love* and Woody Allen's *To Rome with Love*. But the biggest productions of recent years have been two HBO TV series: the highbrow ancient-history soap *Rome* – co-produced with the BBC – and *The Young Pope*.

It's not just foreign directors whose cameras are rolling in Rome. Italians are still making around a hundred films a year – though few if any of these are big-budget studio productions. The contemporary Italian director who comes closest to Fellini's knack for making intelligent movies with (relatively) wide audience appeal is Paolo Sorrentino, a Neapolitan-in-Rome whose Oscar-winning *La Grande Bellezza* (*The Great Beauty*, 2013) was a barbed but still passionate love letter to the Eternal City's decadent, complicated charms. More recently, Sorrentino has turned his attention to the Vatican in his HBO series *The Young Pope*, which features Jude Law as a cigarette-puffing American pontiff with an agenda. Other names to watch include Matteo Garrone, director of the bleak but adrenalin-fuelled Neapolitan mafia drama *Gomorra* (2008) and the flawed but original dissection of reality TV culture (*Reality*, 2012). Meanwhile, some directors from an older generation are still going strong, including intense maverick Marco Bellocchio and politicised comedian Nanni Moretti.

In the know
Show times

For a standard 90-minute film, the four daily screenings are usually at 4.30pm, 6.30pm, 8.30pm and 10.30pm.

❤ Best cinemas

Casa del Cinema *p252*
The lastest in arthouse, immersed in the Borghese gardens.

Nuovo Olimpia *p251*
Good original language selection for serious film-lovers.

Nuovo Sacher *p251*
Original language art house films on Monday and Tuesday.

Sala Trevi *p252*
Retrospectives, classics and thought-provoking seasons.

Moviegoing in Rome

Italians are enthusiastic moviegoers. Inner-city miniplexes and vast suburban multiplexes exhibit commercial fare. Arthouse fans are well served by the Circuito Cinema chain (www.circuitocinema.com) which controls several first-run outlets, and by the first-run independent **Nuovo Sacher** owned by cult director Nanni Moretti. Run by the city's historic Centro Sperimentale film school (www.fondazionecsc.it), **Sala**

Nuovo Sacher

Cinecitta Studios

Trevi (*see p252*) is a *centro storico* single-screen space dedicated to retrospectives.

Housed in a former pleasure pavilion in the Villa Borghese gardens, and sponsored by Rome city council, **Casa del Cinema** ('house of cinema', *see p252*) hosts film-related exhibitions, press conferences and presentations. But it also has an eclectic screening programme.

The downside is the dubbing. Films in the original language (*lingua originale* or *versione originale* – VO in newspaper listings) with subtitles are very far from the norm, though the number of screens dedicated to VO has picked up slightly in recent years. The two-screen **Nuovo Olimpia** and the **Fiamma** have regular VO programming. The Nuovo Sacher shows its current attraction in *lingua originale* on Monday and/or Tuesday. Cinemas **Lux** and **Intrastevere** offer frequent VO screenings as do the multi-screen **Multisala Barberini** and **Space Moderno** (*see p252*).

The best source of information for what's on, including summer venues, is the local section of daily newspaper *La Repubblica*, while the paper's website hosts www.trovacinema.it with programme details for first-run cinemas all over Italy. Programmes generally change on Fridays.

First-run cinemas

Fiamma

Via L Bissolati 43, Veneto & Borghese (06 8880 1283, www.circuitocinema.com). Metro Barberini/bus 62, 85, 492. Closed Jul-Aug. ***Map*** *p138 M6.*

Fellini's classic *La Dolce Vita* had its first screening at this historic cinema in 1960; revamped and now part of the Circuito Cinema group, it generally shows an original language film on one of its screens.

Intrastevere

Vicolo Moroni 3, Trastevere (06 588 4230, www.cinemadiroma.it). Bus 23, 125, 280/tram 8. ***Map*** *p166 G11.*

Check the website of this hard-to-locate cinema in Trastevere for their regular roster of films in English.

Lux

Via Massaciuccoli 31, Suburbs: Salario (06 8639 1361, www.cinemadiroma.it). Metro S. Agnese-Annibaliano/bus 63, 80, 83, 310.

It's a bit of a hike from the *centro* to this multi-screen in the northern suburbs but it's worth it to catch the classier type of mainstream films in *lingua originale*.

Multisala Barberini

Piazza Barberini 24/26, Trevi & Quirinale (06 4201 0392, www.facebook.com/Cinema.Barberini). Metro Barberini/bus 62, 63, 80, 85, 492. ***Map*** *p79 L7.*

For splashy blockbusters in their original language look no further than this *centralissimo* cinema which has been operating since 1930.

❤ Nuovo Olimpia

Via in Lucina 16G, Tridente (06 686 1068, www.circuitocinema.com). Bus 62, 63, 80, 83, 85, 117, 160, 492, 628. Closed Jul-Aug. ***Map*** *p89 J7.*

Hidden away just off via del Corso, this two-screener belongs to the arthouse-oriented Circuito Cinema group; both screens usually show films in *lingua originale*.

❤ Nuovo Sacher

Largo Ascianghi 1, Trastevere (06 581 8116, www.sacherfilm.eu). Bus 44, 75, 125, H/tram 3, 8. ***Map*** *p166 H13.*

The Nuovo Sacher is owned and run by veteran director Nanni Moretti, and is a meeting place for local cinematic talent. VO films are usually shown on Mondays or Tuesdays.

Space Moderno

Piazza della Repubblica 43/45, Monti & Esquilino (www.thespacecinema.it). Metro Repubblica/bus 40, 60, 64, 70, 85. ***Map** p182 N7.*

The smell of popcorn overwhelms in this multi-screener which frequently shows mainly big-budget blockbusters in *lingua originale*.

Cinema d'essai and cineclubs

Generally small and cheap, *cinema d'essai* mainly feature classics or contemporary art-house cinema, occasionally in *versione originale*. In these, and even smaller cineclubs, the best of Italy's cinema heritage can be seen. A *tessera* (membership card) is required by many clubs, but these are free or carry a minimal charge.

Azzurro Scipioni

Via degli Scipioni 82, Prati (06 3973 7161, www.silvanoagosti.it). Metro Lepanto/ bus 30, 70, 81, 280, 590, 913, 926. ***Map** p150 D5.*

Azzurro Scipioni is run by director Silvano Agosti. It has two screens showing art-house successes, world cinema classics and themed seasons.

❤ Casa del Cinema

Largo Marcello Mastroianni 1, Veneto & Borghese (060608, www.casadelcinema.it). Bus 61, 89, 120, 150, 160, 490, 495. ***Map** p138 L4.*

In the Villa Borghese park, the Casa is used for film-related presentations and screenings. Many of the films shown during the Casa's festivals and retrospectives are in *lingua originale*. Even if you're not there to see a film, the Cinecaffè inside the Casa del Cinema is a great place for a coffee or lunch.

❤ Sala Trevi

Vicolo del Puttarello 25, Trevi & Quirinale (06 678 1206, www.fondazionecsc.it). Bus 52, 53, 62, 63, 71, 80Exp, 81, 83, 85, 492, 628. ***Map** p79 K8.*

This 100-seater cinema belongs to Italy's national film archive. It shares its basement location with a 400sq m (4,300sq ft) archaeological site based around two ancient Roman *insulae* (apartment blocks), which can be seen through the glass panels at the side of the main screening room.

Festivals and summer programmes

Around the beginning of July, a raft of second-run or arthouse open-air cinema feasts is launched as part of the **Estate Romana** festivities (*see p245*), many of them in breathtaking settings. Scour the local press for details or check www.060608.it.

In addition, several *arene* (open-air screens) – including one behind the **Nuovo Sacher** (*see p251*) – provide a chance to catch that blockbuster you missed or to see that classic.

Two regular mini-festivals – Cannes a Roma and Venezia a Roma – show a selection of original-language films from the Cannes and Venice film festivals a few days after the festivals themselves close (in May and September respectively). The **Festival Internazionale del Film di Roma** (*see p246*) in November is also a great time to catch some new and up-coming releases.

Festival Internazionale del Film di Roma

Essential Roman Films

The city on screen

Roma, Città Aperta
(Roberto Rossellini, 1945)
The horrors and difficulties of war are placed firmly in the context of everyday life in this semi-documentary on the Resistance, shot under difficult circumstances at the end of World War II. Evolving from a documentary about a priest serving with the Resistance, it is considered the foundation stone of neo-realism.

Roman Holiday (William Wyler, 1953)
Endlessly endearing, eternally fresh, the story of not-so-cynical newsman Gregory Peck aiding and abetting bored princess Audrey Hepburn as she goes AWOL to dodge duty and protocol defined Rome for generations. Uniquely for its time, it was filmed on location.

Ben-Hur (William Wilder, 1959)
Though set in the Holy Land, this epic was actually shot mainly in Rome – the most expensive movie ever made at the time. The arena for the famous chariot race took one million dollars and a year to construct. Star Charlton Heston pushes toga-clad sexual ambivalence to its limits.

La Dolce Vita (Federico Fellini, 1960)
Philandering hack Marcello (Marcello Mastroianni) beds starlets and follows sensationalist stories, as a generation misplaces its moral compass in Federico Fellini's unforgettable portrait of life in the high-octane, paparazzo-fuelled Rome of the 1950s and '60s.

Mamma Roma (Pier Paolo Pasolini, 1962)
A stupendous Anna Magnani as the archetypal, almost beatified Roman mamma: a prostitute who strives, and ultimately fails, to keep her son from a bad end in the mean streets of Rome's outskirts. Pasolini's second feature is visually stunning, with scenes echoing works by Caravaggio, among others.

The Talented Mr Ripley
(Anthony Minghella, 1999)
Ripley and Greenleaf move between *piazze* di Spagna and Navona, Tom's pad in the Ghetto, the Capitoline museums and the St Regis Grand hotel in the Roman episode of Minghella's psychological thriller, with Matt Damon and Gwyneth Paltrow.

La Grande Bellezza (Paolo Sorrentino, 2013)
Sorrentino's go-to leading man, Toni Servillo, channels the spirit of Marcello Mastroianni as a jaded cultural journalist in this ravishingly shot and scored cinematic fresco. Scratch the surface and it's an age-old story of Roman decadence; but what a surface.

Audrey Hepburn in *Roman Holiday*

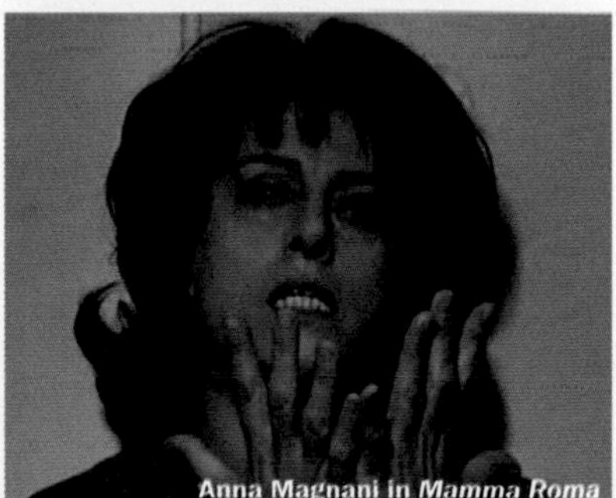
Anna Magnani in *Mamma Roma*

Nightlife

Where to find hot nights and hip DJs

The turn of the millennium saw a growing cultural, artistic and musical vibrancy that began to turn the once sleepy Eternal City into a lively European capital. If things have shown signs of slowing down recently, with the closure of such clubs as Warehouse, Rashomon and Sinister Noise, there's still plenty out there to keep night owls busy. International DJs still pass through Rome's clubs, and some interesting bands can be heard in a host of small clubs and venues. You will, however, need some inside information to avoid the Eurotrash played by the plethora of commercial venues.

Rome gives its best over the long summer, when the breeze makes nights fresh and almost magical. There's always action of one kind or another along the riverbanks, where clubs, shops and restaurants go al fresco for the hotter months.

CLUBBING

By-laws forcing *centro storico* bars to shut at 2am have been lifted, to the great horror of residents and joy of clubbers. But hold your enthusiasm: finicky summer ordinances forbid and fine the sale and consumption of alcohol on the street, starting as early as 10pm in some areas of the city. Application and enforcement is capricious, so be advised and ask around.

Discos and live venues stay open until the small hours. In Rome, evenings tend to start late and end early... the next day. Concerts rarely kick off before 10.30pm and most clubs close after 4am, even on weekdays. When picking a club, bear in mind that many mainstream clubs serve up commercial house or retro 1980s tunes on Fridays and Saturdays.

Established venues like **Goa** (*see p258*) can always be relied upon to offer quality DJ sets. For something alternative, catch one of the itinerant punk/industrial/new wave/metal/EBM parties organised by **Subbacultcha** (see www.facebook.com/SubbacultchaClub for location and skip-the-line entry) and the techno house parties thrown by Rebel Rebel at **Circolo Andrea Doria** (*see p261*). Otherwise, check out what's on at places like **Locanda Atlantide** (*see p262*) or **Ex Dogana** (*see p261*). Watch out for DJ Andrea Esu & Fabrice and guests who spin their electro-house and tech sounds at **L-Ektrica** (Ex Dogana; *see p261*). Vintage enthusiasts will find gold at **Twiggy**, Rome's best 1960s night, with expert DJs Luzy L and Corry X (at **Le Mura**; *see p262*).

Where to go

A growing number of Rome's nightlife venues are in far-flung areas, though there is still quite a lot of action in a few easily accessible areas. Testaccio is one of Rome's liveliest quarters, with nightlife action concentrated around **Monte Testaccio**: you will be spoilt for choice – just walk around until you find the vibe that you're seeking for the evening. The nearby area that lies around **via Libetta**, off via Ostiense in Garbatella, teems with many trendy clubs and is poised to become even more crowded: the city council has been developing the whole district as an arts hub based around the old fruit and vegetable market for the past ten years. Recent projects include plans for more green areas. Even if the future looks uncertain, the area has tons of potential.

Fashionistas head for the *centro storico*: join them in the **triangolo della Pace** to be part of trendy Roman life. **Campo de' Fiori**, once a fashionista meeting spot, has become increasingly chaotic and, as the evening progresses, squalid, with the occasional brawl.

San Lorenzo is less pretentious: drinks are cheaper, and there's always something new going on.

Trastevere has lovely alleys packed with friendly, crowded bars. If you're longing for company but your Italian's weak, this is the place for you: English is the lingua franca. Note, though, that around piazza Trilussa, the scene gets seriously seedy in the small hours.

Getting through the door

Getting into more relaxed, down-to-earth venues is easy enough – just join the chaotic queues at the door and use your elbows. But making it inside fashionable mainstream clubs can be stressful, no matter how elegantly you're dressed. Intimidating bouncers will bar your way, while supposed VIPs are whisked through the door.

In the know
Centri sociali

Until recently, *centri sociali* – disused buildings occupied by dissatisfied youth and transformed into spaces for art, music and politics – were Rome's only spaces hosting avant-garde artists and musicians. With more opportunities elsewhere, their importance has waned, but they still have plenty to offer at bargain prices (admission is usually €5). In recent years, police have raided and shut down a number of them (such as the very central Rialto Sant'Ambrogio), yet many historic ones, like the Forte Prenestino (www.forteprenestino.net), still resist. Check the listings pages of *La Repubblica* for what's on.

In the know
What's on

For details of upcoming events, consult listings in the magazines *Trovaroma* (with the newspaper *Repubblica* on Thursdays) or the websites www.romatoday.it and www.wantedinrome.com.

For an alternative look at Rome's nightlife, check out roma.zero.eu, and 2night.it for gigs. Reggae addicts head to www.reggae.it.

The www.060608.it website has a dauntingly exhaustive what's-on list under 'Events and Shows'.

Clubs and discobars generally charge an entrance fee at weekends but not on weekdays; you often have to pay for a *tessera* (membership card) on top of, or sometimes instead of, the entrance fee. *Tessere* may be valid for a season or for a month, and in some cases they're free. At many clubs it pays to check out the venue's website before going along: some events are cheaper – or indeed only accessible – if you put yourself on the list prior to your arrival. Admission tickets often include a 'free' drink, but you can expect the other drinks you buy to be pricey. Another popular formula is to grant 'free' admission while forcing you to buy a drink (generally expensive). To get out again you have to hand a stamped drink card to the bouncer, so hold on to whatever piece of paper they give you or you'll be forced to pay twice.

Note that many clubs close down for some part of the hotter months, from June to September, though some reappear in summer guise in different, cooler, outdoor or seaside locations. Check the individual venues' website and/or Facebook pages for warm-weather developments.

▶ *Where we have not specified an admission price, entry is free.*

In the know
Ticket agencies

Expect to pay *diritti di prevendita* (booking fees) on tickets bought anywhere except at the venue on the night. Tickets for concerts of all descriptions can be booked online through a number of agencies, the largest of which are **Ticket One** (892 101, www.ticketone.it) and **Viva Ticket** (892 234, www.vivaticket.it).

Nightclubs

Akab

Via di Monte Testaccio 68/69, Testaccio (06 5725 0585, www.facebook.com/akabclubufficiale). Metro Piramide/bus 23, 30Exp, 75, 83, 130, 673, 719, 3N, 9N, 10N, 11N/tram 3. ***Open*** *11pm-3am Tue-Sat.* ***Admission*** *€10-€25 (incl 1 drink).* ***Map*** *p210 H16.*

Formerly a carpenter's workshop, this place is now a busy, long-term fixture of the Testaccio nightlife scene, hosting various well-known international DJs. Depending on the night you choose music may be retro, R&B or house. Akab has two levels: an underground cellar and a street-level room, as well as a garden.

Angelo Mai Altrove

Via delle Terme di Caracalla 55A, Aventine (329 448 1358, www.angelomai.org). Bus 118, 160, 628. ***Open*** *varies.* ***Admission*** *varies. No cards.* ***Map*** *p210 N15.*

This highly active *centro sociale* is one of the few remaining alternative semi-legal arts social, arts and entertainment hubs operating in central Rome nowadays. Check out the website for the programme of live music and dance events, all of which are guaranteed to be very far off the beaten musical track.

❤ Best dance clubs

Goa Club *p258*
Never change a winning horse.

Room 26 *p258*
Smashing sound-system – it's all in the decibels.

Shari Vari Playhouse *p258*
In the heart of the historic centre.

Goa Club

Black Out The Club

Via Anagnina 3, Suburbs: south-east (06 97841880, www.blackoutrockclub.com). Metro Anagnina/bus N1. ***Open*** *11.30pm-4.30am Fri, Sat.* ***Admission*** *€5-€30.*

The Black Out has been Rome's rockers' number one hangout since 1979, first in a dark and gloomy dive near San Giovanni and then on the Casilina. Nowadays in its larger venue close to the Anagnina metro stop, the look is quite different and not as dark and gothic, although the feel is still slightly vintage. Some surprisingly big international names play in this club, and the standard of the DJ sets is generally high.

La Cabala

Via dei Soldati 25c, Pantheon & Navona (06 6830 1192). Bus 30, 70, 81, 87, 492, 628. ***Open*** *Sept-June 11pm-4am Thur-Sat.* ***Admission*** *free (drink purchase required).* ***Map*** *p104 G7.*

Not your standard club. It's hosted in a 15th-century *palazzo*, with Baroque mirrors, ornate chandeliers and leather couches. Stretching across three floors, with a pianobar, a restaurant (Hostaria dell'Orso), and a floor boosting house and commercial music, the doormen can be very picky, and certain nights are invitation only. Elegant attire recommended.

❤ Goa Club

Via Libetta 13, Ostiense (06 9555 8820, www.goaclub.it). Metro Garbatella/bus 23, 271, 769, 770, 2N, 3N, 9N. ***Open*** *Sept-May 11pm-4am Thur-Sat; 5pm-1am Sun.* ***Admission*** *€10-€25.* ***Map*** *p210 K20.*

In trendy Ostiense, this is one of the best of Rome's fashionable clubs. The quality of the Italian and international DJs that it books is generally above the competition. Note that the doormen can be picky.

Planet Roma

Via del Commercio 36, Ostiense (06 574 7826, www.planetroma.com). Metro Piramide/bus 23, 271, 769, 2N, 3N. ***Open*** *10.30pm-4am Fri-Sun; other eves vary.* ***Admission*** *€5-€20.* ***Map*** *p210 H17.*

An eclectic club with a hotch-potch but interesting crowd, Planet (formerly the Alpheus) has four big halls for gigs, music festivals, theatre and cabaret, which are all followed by a disco. The music changes every night and varies depending on the room you're in: rock, chart R&B, Latin, world music, retro and happy trash. Planet also hosts the G I Am gay one-nighter (*see p264*).

❤ Room 26

Piazza Guglielmo Marconi 29, Suburbs: EUR (333 428 9202, www.room26.it). Bus 30Exp, 671, 714, 780, 791, 2N, 21N. ***Open*** *end Sept-beg June 9.30pm-4am Fri-Sun.* ***Admission*** *€10-€20.*

It doesn't get any louder than this. The name derives from the 26 Crown amplifiers that blast the music through the club, from revival night on Friday to house on Saturday. The Fascist-era architecture makes it an unconventional spot. During the summer, it moves across the street, to Piazza John Fitzgerald Kennedy 1, with the open-air dance floor Le Terrazze.

❤ Shari Vari Playhouse

Via De' Nari 14, Pantheon & Navona (06 6880 6936, sharivari.it). Bus 30, 46, 64, 492, 5N, 6N, 8N, H/tram 8. ***Open*** *10pm-4am Tue-Sat, 10pm-2am Sun. Closed Aug.* ***Map*** *p104 H9.*

Its central location – conveniently nestled between campo de' Fiori, the Pantheon, and piazza Navona – has made this restaurant and underground club a very popular destination. It's usually packed during the winter. Getting in is up to the stable of beefy bouncers at the door (best to avoid t-shirts and casual outfits). The music selection in the three dance rooms is very eclectic, from commercial and pop to electro, and from house to hip-hop, to revival.

LIVE MUSIC

To a large extent, the recent rise in the popularity of concert-going in Rome is due to the **Auditorium-Parco della Musica** (*see p273*), a multifunctional complex hosting not only classical music, but also pop, jazz, world music and rock events. Rome's vocation for live music is also being prodded along by a string of smallish live clubs, and by the daring programme of goodies on offer at the cool **Teatro Palladium** (*see p272*). Moreover, city hall continues to fund the exciting **RomaEuropa Festival** (*see p246*) and the occasional free mega-concert. Many of Rome's clubs host local, national and international bands of varying quality. Strangely, a major outdoor venue for musical events is still lacking: really huge acts often play at the **Stadio Olimpico** (*see p223*), the **Ippodromo delle Capannelle** (a racetrack) and, occasionally, at **Circo Massimo** (*see p67*).

❤ Roma Incontra il Mondo

Villa Ada, via di Ponte Salario, Suburbs: north (06 4173 4712/4648, www.villaada.org). Bus 53, 63, 92, 233, 235, 310. ***Date*** *early July-early Aug.* ***Admission*** *€8-€22 per event. No cards.*

Musicians from around the world play on a lakeside stage beneath the venerable trees of the Villa Ada park. Lights reflected in the water and cool breezes make this one of the most atmospheric and relaxing of the summer festivals.

Now in its 24th season, this multicultural series of events is an institution of the Roman summer. Music ranges from reggae to jazz, in a spectacular yet laidback setting. Beyond music, the festival also showcases political debates, art exhibitions, book readings and workshops. A great addition to the 2017 programme is a series of theatrical performances, with an experimental bent. You'll need a ticket for all major events (www.i-ticket.it or onsite, usually from 8pm), but anything taking place at the D'Ada Park space is free. Events are scheduled every day of the week, from the afternoon on, with a dedicated area and programme for kids. What makes the Villa Ada festival stand out is its promotion of world cultures, with a strong political and ethical message permeating each edition. Started as a small production, the outdoor jamboree *kermesse* has become extremely popular, especially among Romans, as it offers the city at large an unparalleled occasion to open up to the rest of the world. Ky-Mani Marley, Femi Kuti, Sun Ra Arkestra, and Wire are some of the names that have recently inflamed the park arena. You'll also find mouthwatering international food, thanks to stellar chefs who prepare delicacies both for aperitif and dinner, and a wide array of street food.

Live music venues

► *See also p273* Auditorium-Parco della Musica *and p272* Teatro Palladium.

Alexanderplatz

Via Ostia 9, Prati (06 8377 5604, www.alexanderplatz.it). Metro Ottaviano/bus 23, 34, 49, 81, 492, 590, 982, 1N, 6N, 11N/tram 19. ***Open*** *8.30pm-1.30am daily.* ***Admission*** *free with monthly (€15) or annual (€45) membership.* ***Map*** *p150 C5.*

The pioneer of jazz in the Eternal City, and *the* jazz club in Rome, is still the Alexanderplatz. This venue offers nightly concerts with famous names from the Italian and foreign jazz scene. Live music starts at 9, 9.30 or 10pm, depending on the gig. Booking is strongly advised. Call ahead or email prenotazioni.alexanderplatz@gmail.com.

Beba do Samba

Via dei Messapi 8, San Lorenzo (339 575 0390, www.bebadosamba.it). Bus 71, 163, 492, 10N, 11N/tram 3, 19. ***Open*** *10pm-2am daily.* ***Admission*** *free with annual membership (€5). No cards.* ***Map*** *p182 R9.*

This popular, buzzing little venue in San Lorenzo attracts a studenty crowd for live music – mostly of an ethnic, world music and jazz variety – almost every night, often followed by a DJ.

Big Mama

Vicolo San Francesco a Ripa 18, Trastevere (06 581 2551, www.bigmama.it). Bus 44, 75, 115, 125, H, 8N, 11N, 19N/tram 3, 8. ***Open*** *Oct-May 9pm-1.30am Tue-Sat.* ***Admission*** *free with membership (€10); extra for big acts.* ***Map*** *p166 G13.*

Rome's blues heart throbs in this pared-back but welcoming venue, which hosts an array of respected Italian and international artists every evening. The blues menu is punctuated with jazz, rock and ethnic music. There are drinks and hot meals to consume while listening to the top-quality music on offer. Book if you want to get a table.

❤ Black Market Art Gallery

Via Panisperna 101, Monti (339 822 7541, www.blackmarketartgallery.it). Metro Cavour/bus 40, 64, 70, 75, 117, 170, H, 8N, 9N, 15N. ***Open*** *6pm-2am daily.* ***Admission*** *free; extra for big acts.* ***Map*** *p182 M9.*

If you're looking for a very intimate concert, this is the place to be. The unplugged live sessions bring to Rome indie-rock and jazz musicians, who play in a tiny space in the back (with roughly 50 seats) fitted with vintage furniture and sofas, for a retro-cool feel. Their website is unreliable, so check their Facebook page for an updated list of events. If you show up impromptu, you might have to stand, but can always grab a cocktail and a bite at the bar. Admission is free, as are most of the concerts. There may be a charge when more popular bands play.

Caruso Café de Oriente

Via di Monte Testaccio 36, Testaccio (06 574 5019, www.carusocafe.com). Metro Piramide/bus 23, 30Exp, 75, 83, 130, 673, 719, 3N, 9N, 10N, 11N/tram 3. ***Open*** *Sept-May 11pm-4am Tue-Sun.* ***Admission*** *€8-€15, free Sun. No cards.* ***Map*** *p210 H16.*

A must for lovers of salsa and the like, this club offers Latin American tunes every night and live acts almost daily. Shimmy your way in between scores of dancing couples to enjoy the warm atmosphere in these three, ethnic-themed, orange-hued rooms – or head up to the roof terrace. It's usually packed (some would say to an annoying degree) and service can be rude. In the summer months from June to August, Caruso moves venue to Fiesta (via delle Tre Fontane 24, Suburbs: EUR, www.fiesta.it).

❤ Casa del Jazz

Viale di Porta Ardeatina 55, San Saba (06 704 731, www.casajazz.it). Bus 160, 715. ***Open*** *10am-midnight on concert eves.* ***Admission*** *€5-€15. No cards.* ***Map*** *p210 M16.*

This city council-owned jazz venue in a plush villa confiscated from a local organised-crime boss and situated behind the Terme di Caracalla (*see p214*) offers a packed programme of high-class Italian and international jazz performers. There's a café and restaurant, too, set in the villa's beautiful grounds.

Charity Café

Via Panisperna 68, Monti (06 4782 5881, www.charitycafe.it). Metro Cavour/bus 40, 64, 70, 75, 117, 170, H, 8N, 9N, 15N. ***Open*** *7pm-2am Tue-Sun.* ***Admission*** *€8-€10 (incl 1 drink).* ***Map*** *p182 M9.*

A tiny laid-back jazz (on Thursday and Friday) and blues venue (on Wednesday

❤ Best live music venues

Black Market Art Gallery *p260*
A couch, a drink, an intimate concert.

Casa del Jazz *p260*
A Roman standard.

Lanificio 159 *p262*
Experimental and trendy.

Roma Incontra il Mondo *p259*
Broaden your boundaries.

In the know
Latin American

Rome has hosted an energetic Latin American community since the 1970s, and Romans swarm to dance courses. *Capoeira* is one of the latest fads, and schools run by resident Brazilians have popped up all over town. As well as clubs, discobars and a few tango cafés, lovers of Latin American tunes head en masse, especially on Thursdays, to **Palacavicchi** (via RB Bandinelli 130, Suburbs: south, 06 7932 1797). **Caruso** (*see above*) offers live bands almost every night.

Summer Nights

Great sounds, glorious settings

Until recently, long summer nights in Rome used to buzz with an embarrassment of top-class cultural riches, often held in such breathtaking locations as Roman ruins, Renaissance villas or ancient amphitheatres. More competition for less funding has created some sorry casualties in the last few years, but despite the constant uncertainties looming over the cultural sector at large in Rome, there are still plenty of events to keep determined revellers busy.

The warm season starts with the free **Labour Day concert**, which is organised by Italy's trade unions on 1 May (*Primo Maggio; see p244*). It's traditionally held in **piazza San Giovanni** in Laterano (*map p198 Q12*) and hosts Italian celebrities, along with a handful of international stars, drawing half a million people from all over Italy.

In mid June, the **Estate Romana** (*see p245*) kicks off. An umbrella for most of Rome's outdoor summer festivals sponsored by city hall, it runs to the end of September. Every year, a couple of major concerts are held in the **Stadio Olimpico** (*see p223*).

Look out for the neighbourhood fairs and religious festivities, like the **Festa de' Noantri** (*see p246*) which takes place in the narrow streets of Trastevere during the summer.

Other summer events to look out for include **Postepay Rock in Roma** (*see p245*), **Just Music Festival** (*see p246*) and **Circolo Andrea Doria** (via del Baiardo, 26) – a sport centre-turned-open-air dance club, right by the Tiber river. **Bouganville Celimontana** also runs a buzzing jazz festival in villa Celimontana (www.bouganvilleroma.it, *map p198 N13*).

Francesco Gabbani, Labour Day concert 2017

and Saturday), with a rustic bar and a small stage. On Sunday enjoy an aperitif with live music from 6.30pm. During the summer, the café moves to a stand by the river (on Lungotevere Sassia).

Ex Dogana

Viale dello Scalo S. Lorenzo 10, San Lorenzo (www.exdogana.com). Bus 71, 163, 492, 10N, 11N/tram 3, 19. ***Open*** *12pm-2am Tue, Wed; 12pm-5am Thur-Sat; 10am-2am Sun.* ***Admission*** *free. Concerts €10-€15.* ***Map*** *p182 R10.*

The post-industrial architecture of this former railway hub constitutes the perfect backdrop to DJ sets and live music concerts, from electronic to indie rock, as well as art shows, movie screenings and cultural events, all served with food and drinks. Happy hour is from 6.30pm every day except Mondays. The L-Ektrica crew (www.l-ektrica.com) also spins discs here for lovers of electronic sounds. Many music events are free; you need a ticket for bigger concerts. It has great potential for the future, if the local residents can bear with the loud decibels.

Gregory's

Via Gregoriana 54, Tridente (06 679 6386, www.gregorysjazz.com). Metro Spagna or Barberini/bus 61, 62, 63, 80, 83, 85, 150, 160,492, 590, 1N, 4N, 5N, 12N, 25N. ***Open*** *7pm-2am daily.* ***Admission*** *€15-€25 (incl 1 drink).* ***Map*** *p89 K6.*

This cosy venue oozes jazz culture from every pore. On the ground floor, sip a glass of whisky from one of Rome's widest selections while admiring old portraits of legendary jazz

Lanificio 159

musicians. In the small upstairs room, you can jazz up your ears to top live acts while sitting comfortably among soft lights and lacquered tables. Concerts start at 10pm but you'll need to be there at least 20 minutes before that. On Fridays and Saturdays there's a double live concert, at 9.30pm and midnight. During the summer Gregory's moves to its location by the river, near Castel Sant'Angelo where sushi is served.

❤ Lanificio 159

Via di Pietralata 159, Suburbs: north-east (06 450 1384, www.lanificio.com). Bus 211. ***Open*** *7pm-4am Thur, Sun; 11pm-4am Fri, Sat. Closed 2wks Aug.*

A former wool factory in Rome's north-eastern suburbs, Lanificio 159 is now a stunning white space with a restaurant and dance school, plus spaces for live music and dancing. There's a lot of boundary pushing experimental music here.

Lettere Caffè

Via San Francesco a Ripa 100/101, Trastevere (340 0044 154 , www.letterecaffe.org). Bus 44, 75, 115, H, 8N, 11N, 19N/tram 3, 8. ***Open*** *5pm-2am daily (concerts begin 10.30pm). Closed Aug-mid Sept.* ***No cards. Map*** *p166 G13.*

As well as a vocation for poetry and literature, the Lettere Caffè has a choice of concerts and DJ sets. From rockabilly to jazz, passing through 1960s beat, the Lettere is both a showcase of new talent and a place to listen to well-known DJs and bands from Rome and beyond. An excellent selection of wines and spirits that won't empty your wallet and yummy own-made cakes complete the picture. There's a €6 vegetarian *aperitivo* buffet from 7pm to 9pm every evening.

Locanda Atlantide

Via dei Lucani 22B, San Lorenzo (06 4470 4540, www.locandatlantide.it). Bus 71, 163, 492, 10N, 11N/ tram 3, 19. ***Open*** *9.30pm-3am Mon, Tue, Thur-Sun.* ***Admission*** *€3-€10. No cards.* ***Map*** *p182 R9.*

This friendly, grungy, unpretentious venue in the buzzing San Lorenzo neighbourhood hosts an array of events, ranging from concerts, gigs and DJ acts to theatrical performances. The venue sometimes opens earlier in the evening for book launches; there are occasional events on Mondays too. It pulls in an alternative crowd and can be relied upon for a good night out.

Le Mura Live Music Club

Via di Porta Labicana 24, San Lorenzo (www.lemuramusicbar.com). Bus 71, 492, 10N, 11N/tram 3. ***Open*** *8.30pm-2am daily.* ***Admission*** *free with annual membership card (€7). No cards.* ***Map*** *p182 Q9.*

Friendly and lively, Le Mura has a policy of encouraging upcoming Italian bands: the quality varies greatly. But this live-music club also fields better-known Italian and international names, as well as offering live-mic nights, jazz, good DJ sets and the occasional '60s event by retro one-night crew Twiggy.

PalaLottomatica

Piazzale dello Sport, Suburbs: EUR (06 540 901, www.palalottomatica.it). Metro EUR Palasport/bus 30Exp, 671, 714, 780, 791, 2N, 21N. ***Open*** *varies.* ***Admission*** *varies.*

The flying-saucer-shaped PalaLottomatica, which was designed by architect and engineer Pierluigi Nervi for the 1960 Rome Olympics, is Rome's leading space for large indoor concerts. Refurbishment has improved the once-appalling acoustics – a little. Tickets are available from the usual outlets for large-scale events (*see p57*).

LGBT ROME

The LGBT scene may lack the excitement of other European capitals and doesn't have its own neighbourhood to speak of, but there are some good bars and clubs, spread across the city.

Italy started recognising same-sex civil unions in 2016, becoming the last major Western country in Europe to do so, overcoming strong opposition from the Catholic Church. Being late to the party may explain why Rome is less LGBT-friendly than other European capitals like Madrid, Berlin or Paris, but things seem to be on the right path, generally speaking.

Don't expect to find one main gay area or gaybourhood: the scene is pretty scattered throughout the city. An historic gathering point is the so-called 'Gay Street' behind the Colosseum, a 300-metre stretch in via di San Giovanni in Laterano, dotted with gay and gay-friendly bars, restaurants and shops. Chief among them is **Coming Out**, Rome's oldest openly gay bar.

Spearheading activities in Rome are the historic **Circolo Mario Mieli di Cultura Omosessuale** (*see p324*) group and the hyperactive **Di'Gay Project** (*see p325*). A diverse gay market continues to cater for distinct clienteles, with restaurants, pubs, clubs and bars attracting punters of all ages. Mixed one-nighters allow men and women to have fun under the same roof – and, for that matter, in the open air. The summer event **Gay Village** (*see p245*) has been all the rage since it launched in the early 2000s. It still soldiers on, but seems to have lost some luster. Critics point to the mixed (and increasingly younger) clientele, high prices, and the dropping quality of the DJ sets. However, with its concerts, various dancefloors and bars, many find it's still worth staying in town for the traditionally becalmed months of July and August.

❤ Best LGBT hangouts

Bunker *p264*
Cruising in a dark maze.

Coming Out *p263*
The rainbow behind the Colosseum.

Muccassassina *p265*
Where LGBT meets TGIF.

The Venus Rising *p265*
The only women-only one-nighter in town.

► *Useful info and Rome listings can be found on azgay.it and gay.it. See also p324 LGBT Resources.*

The most popular and awaited event of the year is the **Gay Pride Parade** (www.romapride.it), usually held on the second weekend of June.

Admission prices to Rome's gay bars and clubs can be confusing. Some places may charge no entrance fee, but will instead oblige you to buy a drink, while others include the first of your drinks in the admission price. Many venues also ask for a membership card: the **Arcigay/Arcilesbica** card costs €15, and the **Anddos** card costs €17 for annual membership (or €10 if you just go to one club). Both cards can be bought at any venue that requires it (you'll need photo ID) and is valid throughout Italy. In most bars you're given a printed slip on which the bar staff tick off what you consume; you pay the total amount on leaving the venue. Where we have not specified an admission price, entry is free.

Gay bars & pubs

❤ Coming Out

Via San Giovanni in Laterano 8, Celio (06 700 9871, www.comingout.it). Metro Colosseo/bus 53, 85, 87, 117, 571, 673, 10N, 11N. ***Open*** *7am-2am daily.* ***Map*** *p198 M11.*

The epicentre of the 'Gay Street' in Rome, this very popular pub offers breakfasts, quick lunches, evening snacks, beers and cocktails to a predominantly youthful crowd of men and women. It's a useful address if you need somewhere to meet before heading off in search of something a bit more adventurous. There's a 6.30-8.30pm happy hour; plus a DJ set from 11pm on Wednesday (and Thursday – but not during the summer, as the place is already quite packed).

Coming Out

Garbo

Vicolo di Santa Margherita 1, Trastevere (06 581 2766, www.garbobar.it). Bus 44, 75, 115, 125, H, 8N, 11N, 19N/tram 3, 8. ***Open*** *10.30pm-4am daily. Closed 2wks Aug.* ***Admission*** *free with membership card (€3).* ***Map*** *p166 G11.*

Right in the heart of touristy Trastevere, this intimate and relaxed bar with exposed-brick walls, dim lights, and a touch of camp offers a good spot for a nightcap, as it closes at 4am. It's a cultural association, so you'll need a card to go in.

Gay clubs

L'Alibi

Via di Monte Testaccio 40-44, Testaccio (06 574 3448, www.lalibi.it). Metro Piramide/ bus 23, 30, 75, 83, 170, 280, 673, 716, 719, 3N, 9N, 10N, 11N/tram 3. ***Open*** *11.30pm-5am Thur-Sun.* ***Admission*** *€10-€20 (incl 1 drink).* ***Map*** *p210 H16.*

The Alibi paved the way for Testaccio's boom as a nightlife quarter with an alternative feel. An increasingly straight-friendly approach, and the fact that it's showing its age rather, has diluted its success with punters. It's still a good place to bop the night away, however, with a well-oiled sound system covering two floors in winter and three in summer, when the roof garden comes into its own. If you can get yourself on to the guest list, admission is cheaper.

❤ Bunker

Via Placido Zurla 68, Suburbs: east (06299929/34 85793760, www. bunkerclubroma.com). Bus 81, 105, N16. ***Open*** *10pm-3am Thur, Sun; 10pm-4am Fri-Sat.* ***Admission*** *free with Acil card.*

The biggest men's disco cruising club in Rome, with glory holes, underground red zone, maze, video screens, dance floor and cocktail bar. On Thursday/Saturday/Sunday underwear/naked night, on Friday free entry and free dress code.

Company

Piazza Manfredo Fanti 40, Esquilino (06 64871292, www.facebook.com/Company. Roma). ***Open*** *10.30pm-3am Sun, Tue-Thur; 10.30pm-5am Fri, Sat.* ***Admission*** *free with Anddos card.* ***Map*** *p182 O8.*

Open in 2014 in the Termini area as a rib of the successful mothership in Milan, this cruising club caters specifically to bears. DJ sets play electro and house on Friday, and 1980s music on Saturday. A darkroom and smoking area complete the scene.

> **In the know**
> **Bear Monday Summer**
>
> Bear Monday Summer takes place at the **Os Club** (via delle Terme di Traiano 4A, www.bearmonday.com), while you'll find the Bears Invasion summer edition (www.bearsinvasion.com) every Saturday at **Qube** (see p265).

Frutta e Verdura

Via di Santa Passera, Suburbs: south (347 879 7063, www.facebook.com/fruttae. verdura.50). Bus 128, 775, 780, 781, 16N. ***Open*** *4.30-10.30am Sun.* ***Admission*** *€15 with Arcigay card (incl 1 drink). No cards.*

This after-hours club has changed its venue several times over the past few years but the faithful continue to turn up. DJs set the rhythm to house, techno, and deep house music on the dance floor, but there are also two dark rooms and private cabins.

Skyline

Via Pontremoli 36, San Giovanni (06 700 9431, www.skylineclub.it). Metro San Giovanni/bus 16, 81, 85, 87, 360, 810, 1N/ tram 3. ***Open*** *10.30pm-3am Mon-Thur, Sun; 10.30pm-4am Fri, Sat.* ***Admission*** *free with Arcigay & Anddos cards (Tue-Fri, Sun), €5 (Mon, Sat; incl 1 drink). No cards.* ***Map*** *p198 Q13.*

The crowd at Skyline ensures there's constant movement between the bar areas, the video parlour and the cruisy maze and dark areas. There are naked parties on Mondays.

One-nighters

Amigdala

Venue varies (www.facebook.com/ amigdalaparty). ***Admission*** *varies.*

LGBT-friendly bimonthly party taking place every second and fourth Saturday of the month at Ex Dogana, and other venues, with a mix of electronic music (house, techno, electro), visual arts and live concerts. Check their Facebook page for updates on which DJ is spinning that night, and where. Admission prices varies. It sometimes depends on when you arrive – before 11.30pm, it could be free; after 1.30am, you may pay €15 a ticket.

G I Am

Planet Roma, via del Commercio 36, Ostiense (340 753 8396, www.facebook. com/GIAMRoma). Metro Piramide/bus 23, 271, 769, 2N, 3N. ***Open*** *11pm-4am Sat.* ***Admission*** *€10. No cards.* ***Map*** *p210 H17.*

This one-nighter, held at the cavernous Planet Roma (formerly the Alpheus) club is a

Sex and the Suburbs

Dark encounters on the outskirts of town

All roads may lead to Rome, but many also lead straight out again to a plethora of cruising clubs that have sprung up on the eastern outskirts of the city. Sex in the suburbs is flourishing – though be warned: there are still some nasty characters out there.

The working-class via Casilina, much loved by Pasolini, was the first to set the trend with **K Men's Club** (Via Amati Amato 6-8, 06 2170 1268, kmenclub.com), the first venue in the capital wholly devoted to the joy of the dark encounter.

Moving to the via Prenestina area, **Il Diavolo Dentro** (Largo Itri 23, 392 8837 397, www.ildiavolodentro.com) is a stark, candlelit basement that opens its doors to weekend thirtysomething hedonists, whose inner devils are tempted at the club's theme nights. Anyone for an orgy or a black mass (hoods free of charge)?

One of Rome's favourite sex clubs, Gate Men's Club, has moved, becoming **Bunker** (*see p264*), with an eclectic programme including an 'extreme naked Thursday', an 'underwear vs naked' evening on Sunday, plus a host of themed evenings.

Some additional words of warning: the harder core and further-flung the club, the greater chance there is for sudden closure – so ring ahead. As well as the 105 bus, the Casilina area is served by the Termini–Pantano tram service. Night buses back to the centre can be irregular so take your chances or ask the doorman to call a taxi.

rather glamorous affair, featuring drag shows and programming a host of good-quality guest and resident DJs. This isn't just one for the boys: there's often a women-only room (La Coco' Room) at the event too, hosted by the Venus Rising crew. During the summer weekends, G I Am is hosted at the Gay Village (*see p245*).

❤ Muccassassina

Qube, via di Portonaccio 212, Suburbs: east (06 541 3985, www.muccassassina.com). Metro Tiburtina/bus 409, 440, 545. ***Open*** *11pm-4am Fri.* ***Admission*** *€15 (incl 1 drink). No cards.*

The Mario Mieli crew (*see p324*) were trailblazers of the gay one-nighter a few years ago – and their Friday-night fest at the Qube still packs them in. Three floors of pop and house create a great atmosphere throughout, which tends to get hot (literally). There are also some one-off events on other evenings: check the website for details.

Lesbian Rome

There are two identifiable factions in *Roma lesbica*: older lesbian groups, which meet at the **Casa Internazionale delle Donne** centre (Via della Lungara 19, www.casainternazionaledelledonne.org), have their roots in 1970s feminism and continue to claim separate identity from men, gay or straight; younger lesbians, on the other hand, tend to favour the less separatist **Arci-Lesbica** association (*see p324*) or join the lads at **Circolo Mario Mieli** (*see p324*) or the **Di'Gay Project** (*see p325*).

Rome has yet to host a permanent lesbian club, but joint ventures like **Gay Village** (*see p245*), **Muccassassina** and other one-nighters get a good turnout from lesbians, and bars like **Coming Out** (*see p263*) are also popular with women. Check noticeboards at gay and women's bookshops or stop by the Casa Internazionale delle Donne. Try www.listalesbica.it, www.arcilesbica.it, and www.arcilesbicaroma.it.

❤ The Venus Rising

See left Alibi club (www.facebook.com/venusrisingroma)

Muccassassina (*see left*) and the Gay Village (*see p245*) attract their fair share of women, but Venus Rising is the only women-only one-nighter in the capital. The crew has been organising the biggest women-only events in Italy since 1989, with DJ sets and dancing all night long. It's changed location several times, from Goa, to Planet, to Alibi.

Muccassassina

Performi
Arts

Some great settings for music and the

Rome is now back on the music-love
century of neglect. This is thanks, m
eclectic programming of the Auditor

Of course, the Auditorium is not
music. Many of the more traditional
have also benefited from the surge o
generated, and many boast high-qua
resident and visiting artists. The nu
are organised throughout the year b
another feather in Rome's cap.

Opera, theatre and dance remain
performing arts scene. Notwithstan
opera programmes tend towards the
can be mediocre. Theatre remains –
exceptions – hidebound. And as for
internationally minded festivals.

THE CULTURAL SCENE

Classical music

The **Accademia Nazionale di Santa Cecilia** (www.santacecilia.it) is Italy's national music academy, with its prestigious *conservatorio*, and choir and orchestra directed by British-born conductor Antonio Pappano. It resides in Rome and plays out its season at the much-admired **Auditorium-Parco della Musica** (*see p273*), a complex of concert and exhibition spaces, designed by internationally acclaimed architect Renzo Piano. Pappano promotes the Accademia's trend of thematic cycles, with a series of mini-festivals dedicated to single composers, artists or themes in bursts throughout the season. Meanwhile, Santa Cecilia also continues to attract some of the world's greatest conductors for its symphonic season, and renowned soloists for its chamber music programme.

Many other institutions of all sizes make their voices heard. The **Accademia Filarmonica Romana** (www.filarmonicaromana.org) – which performs mainly, though not exclusively, at the **Teatro Olimpico** (*see p272*) and **Teatro di Roma – Argentina** (*see p271*) – was founded in 1821 and boasts an illustrious history, with such composers as Rossini, Donizetti, Paganini and Verdi among its founders. It offers a varied programme of chamber music, ancient music, ballet and chamber opera.

In the know
More music

Many churches and basilicas throughout Rome host chamber ensembles, choirs and soloists of differing artistic worth – keep an eye on posters and the daily press for details of events.

❤ Best performing arts venues

Auditorium-Parco della Musica *p273*
This spaceship-like venue never disappoints.

Terme di Caracalla *p269*
The setting says it all.

Oratorio del Gonfalone *p271*
A concert inside a jewel box.

Teatro di Roma – India *p271*
For those undaunted by the experimental.

Teatro Romano di Ostia Antica *p272*
Uncomfortable, but the wow factor makes up for it.

Another major concert provider is the **Istituzione Universitaria dei Concerti** (IUC, www.concertiiuc.it), founded after World War II to inject some life into Rome's university campus. The IUC offers a varied calendar that includes often outstanding – and frequently experimental – international and Italian recitals and chamber music at La Sapienza's main auditorium, the rather stark **Aula Magna** (*see p271*).

The 16th-century **Oratorio del Gonfalone** (*see p271*) hosts a chamber music season. Every concert and recital on the programme, which runs from December to May, seems to have been lovingly chosen to fit the beautiful frescoed surroundings, and to show off the Oratorio's magnificent 18th-century organ. In recent years, it has been giving more concerts and recitals with an ethnic, folk or contemporary flavour.

In 2014, the beloved Orchestra Sinfonica di Roma went out of business. But other acts are making their mark, such as the **Orchestra Internazionale di Roma**, composed of young international talent and catering to a younger crowd. The **Orchestra di Piazza Vittorio** (www.orchestrapiazzavittorio.it) features musicians from ten different countries, with musical styles spanning at least as many genres and cultures.

Rome offers the occasional concert in extraordinary settings. **Roma OperaOmnia** (www.romaoperaomnia.com) organises

Teatro Palladium

❤ Opera at Terme di Caracalla

Terme di Caracalla (see p214, 06 3996 7700, www.ticketone.it). ***Box office*** *at Teatro Costanzi (see p271) or 1hr30mins before show start.* ***Tickets*** *€25-€100.*

Born as a cultural policy experiment in 1937, the Opera di Roma's season at the Baths of Caracalla is now a highlight of the Roman summer, staging world-class performances amid colossal ancient ruins and cool evening breezes. The programme starts in mid to late June and ends in early August, and packs in over 20 opera shows, between opening nights and encore performances. There are also several ballets, and so-called 'extra' events, with a more contemporary spin (recent examples include Neil Young and Bob Dylan). The atmosphere and the dress code are less formal than a traditional theatre setting, which, together with the crowd-pleasing calendar, have helped promote these initiatives among a wider and younger audience.

Gaetano Donizetti's *Lucia di Lammermoor* inaugurated the opera summer season at the Baths of Caracalla on 1 August 1937. The idea was to promote theatre among the public at large with affordable tickets and lesser-known archaeological sites.

The opera most intrinsically associated with the site (and most represented) is Giuseppe Verdi's *Aida*: its triumphal marches, with horses and camels, perfectly fit the monumentality of the stage and its surroundings.

The stage is placed in front of the caldarium, slightly removed from the ruins, which serve as a dramatic backdrop with cinematic lighting. On each side, two

Opera di Roma's season at the Terme di Caracalla is a highlight of the Roman summer, staging world-class performances amid colossal ancient ruins and cool evening breezes

screens project subtitles both in Italian and English, while the orchestra plays live from the pit in front of it.

In case of rain, the show can be delayed or interrupted for up to 100 minutes, before being cancelled. In this case, you can request a ticket refund where you purchased it, within five days. You'll need to show proof of the ticket, by turning it in. However, if the show has run through the first act when it starts raining, you won't be entitled to any refunds.

Performances usually last about three hours, so consider bringing a shawl or a jacket, as it tends to get chilly as the night advances.

Once the opera is over, you can catch a taxi right outside the entrance. The queue tends to be quite long and people don't necessarily respect the order of arrival. The 'Opera Bus' connects the Baths of Caracalla with the Termini train station, with two runs before and after each show.

early music events inside historic sites like the **Museo e Cripta dei Cappuccini** (*see p146*) in Via Veneto and **Palazzo Doria Pamphilj** (*see p115*).

The **Quirinale** palace (*see p82*) also opens its doors to the public, on Sunday mornings, for a cycle of chamber music concerts and recitals in the Cappella Paolina.

Opera

Rome's opera scene is great for fine settings but not always so consistent where quality is concerned. The drab exterior of the Opera di Roma's 19th-century **Teatro Costanzi** (*see p271*) gives way to a beautiful and harmonious interior, with a good-sized stage and perfect acoustics. And in summer the breathtaking majesty of the **Terme di Caracalla** (*see p269*) is a unique backdrop and setting for lyrical productions. But political and financial bungling have always dogged the theatre.

The **Teatro Nazionale** (via del Viminale 51, 06 3570, www.operaroma.it) provides the stage for most of the smaller productions, including chamber opera, contemporary works and ballets. Keep an eye on cast lists to avoid second-rate substitutes after the first night.

Theatre

It isn't easy for an Anglo-Saxon audience to find satisfaction in the Italian theatre scene. The school of drama, with its strong traditions and roots in the *commedia dell'arte*, and the stiff style imposed by its dramatic arts academy, is worlds apart from what you may be used to.

That said, the Roman theatregoing public is becoming ever more sophisticated, its standards raised mainly thanks to some excellent seasonal festivals (in particular the **RomaEuropa** festival; *see p246*) that bring the best national and international fare to the city's excitement-starved stages.

One interesting project is **Casa dei Teatri**. The aim of this centre is to give a multifaceted perspective to drama, integrating performances with training, workshops and research. The complex – which is located inside the Villa Pamphili park (*see p115*) in Monteverde – hosts a library, a space for screenings, conferences, lectures and workshops, and a permanent art collection.

Rome has no lack of performing arts venues: there are some 100 theatres in the city. The Associazione Teatro di Roma, which locally took over the functions of the defunct ETI (the Italian drama board) is responsible for the 18th-century **Teatro di Roma – Argentina**, the modern **Teatro di Roma – India**, and, from 2018, the Silvano Globe Theatre. However, chronic underfunding of theatres has bred turmoil in recent years, from protests, to privatisations, and closures.

Valiant private foundations and organisations offer fare of uneven quality. The **Teatro Vascello** (*see p272*) often hosts international contemporary dance companies and experimental productions; the **Teatro Olimpico** (*see p272*) holds some dance events and concerts as well as musicals; the **Teatro Palladium** (*see p272*) runs an innovative programme; and Rome's own version of Shakespeare's Globe Theatre, the **Silvano Toti Globe Theatre** (*see p272*) in the Villa Borghese, offers its own summer programme of Shakespearean fare and Sunday matinée shows for children.

In the know
Buying tickets

Box offices at some venues have limited hours and many do not accept cards. Pre-booking by phone or online makes life far simpler (though you may incur a booking charge). Some theatre websites have their own built-in booking facilities. In many cases, though, you will be redirected to a ticket agency (*see p57*).

Puppet theatre

Italy's puppet tradition centres on Sicily and Naples, but Rome also offers some good productions. Although Mr Carlo Piantadosi – one of the best-known *burattinai* (puppeteers) – died in 2012, his theatre still operates on the Gianicolo and is identifiable by the sign *Non Tirate Sassi!* (Don't throw stones!). It serves up Pulcinella, just as violent and misogynistic as his English descendant Mr Punch; and don't worry about the language barrier – it's delivered in an accent so thick that most local kids understand it no better than foreigners do: it's the whacks on the head that count, anyway.

Rome's best-known children's theatre, **Teatro Verde** (circonvallazione Gianicolense 10, 06 588 2034, www.teatroverde.it, closed Aug-Sept) offers puppet shows and plays, mostly in Italian. Another popular puppet theatre is the **San Carlino** (www.sancarlino.it), inside the Villa Borghese park (*see p140*).

Dance

Dance has always been the Cinderella of the arts in Italy, notwithstanding a string of influential Italian dancers and choreographers, such as Maria Taglioni and Enrico Cecchetti. An ever-inadequate arts funding package means that many excellent young Italian dancers find fame and fortune abroad, then drop in here occasionally to star as guest artists in Italian corps de ballet. It also means that certain festivals, like the famous Invitation to the Dance, have been forced to shut down.

Dance fans keep an eye on the programme at the **Teatro Olimpico** (*see p272*), which hosts visiting international companies. The **Teatro Greco** (*see p272*), the **Auditorium-Parco della Musica** (*see p273*) and the **Auditorium Conciliazione** (*see p271*) are possible venues for touring Italian and international dance companies.

The **Teatro dell'Opera** and its offspring, the **Teatro Nazionale**, are where the Opera's corps de ballet stretches its limbs. Its seasonal programme invariably includes two or three classics and a handful of contemporary works. The standard leaves much to be desired; in fact, good soloists and sometimes brilliant stars are overshadowed by kitsch productions, mouldy old sets and costumes, and second-rate choreographers. For ticket agencies, *see p57*.

Auditoria & theatres

Auditorium Conciliazione

Via della Conciliazione 4, Borgo (06 6813 4748, www.auditoriumconciliazione.it). Bus 23, 34, 40Exp, 62, 982. ***Box office*** *10am-5pm Mon-Fri and from 2hrs before concerts.* ***Map*** *p150 E7.*

This was Rome's prime serious music venue until the national academy shifted its season to the Auditorium-Parco della Musica. It has since been renovated to reveal a good-sized stage that is suitable for dance. And dance performances – including some star-studded events – make up part of its varied programme, which also includes music.

Aula Magna dell'Università la Sapienza

Piazzale Aldo Moro, Esquilino (06 361 0051, www.concertiiuc.it). Metro Policlinico/bus 71, 88, 310, 492, 649/tram 3, 19. ***Box office*** *from 1hr before concerts.* ***Map*** *p182 Q7.*

With kitsch Fascist decor but reasonable acoustics, this is the main auditorium for the Istituzione Universitaria dei Concerti (*see p268*) season.

Casa dei Teatri

Villino Corsini, Villa Doria Pamphilj, Suburbs: west (06 581 4176, www.comune.roma.it/cultura). Bus 44, 75, 115, 710, 870, 871, 984. ***No cards.***

Elegant 18th-century Villa Corsini inside the Villa Pamphilj park (*see p229*) is a centre for drama and drama-making, with a stage, spaces for workshops and study, and two prestigious libraries, as well as the collection of theatrical documents donated by actor Carmelo Bene. For information on performances, call the Teatro Argot on 06 589 8111 or 06 581 4023.

❤ Oratorio del Gonfalone

Via del Gonfalone 32, Campo (06 687 5952, www.oratoriogonfalone.eu). Bus 23, 40Exp, 46, 62, 64, 116, 190, 280, 870, 916. ***Box office*** *10am-4pm Mon-Fri.* ***No cards. Map*** *p120 F9.*

This beautiful frescoed little auditorium is located in a 16th-century oratory adjacent to the Baroque church of the Gonfalone. It provides a suitable home for one of the city's most precious organs.

Teatro dell'Opera di Roma – Teatro Costanzi

Piazza B Gigli 1, Esquilino (06 4816 0255, www.operaroma.it). Metro Repubblica/bus 40Exp, 60Exp, 64, 70, 71, 170, H. ***Box office*** *9am-5pm Tue-Sat; 9am-1.30pm Sun; until 15mins after performances begin.* ***Map*** *p182 M7.*

The lavish late 19th-century *teatro all'italiana* interior comes as quite a surprise after the grey, angular, Mussolini-era façade. There are towering rows of boxes, and loads of stucco, frescoes and gilding. The acoustics vary: the higher (cheaper) seats are unsatisfactory, so splash out on a box, if you can.

Teatro di Roma – Argentina

Largo Argentina 52, Ghetto & Campo (06 684 0001, www.teatrodiroma.net). Bus 30Exp, 40Exp, 46, 62, 63, 64, 70, 81, 87, 492, 628, 780, 916, H/tram 8. ***Box office*** *10am-2pm, 3-7pm Tue-Sun.* ***Map*** *p120 H9.*

Rome's plush flagship theatre has a wide-ranging programme, including some dance and poetry.

❤ Teatro di Roma – India

Lungotevere Papareschi/via L Pierantoni 6, Suburbs: south (06 6840 00311, www.teatrodiroma.net). Bus 170, 766, 775, 780, 781, C6. ***Box office*** *from 5pm before shows (3pm Sun), or at Teatro di Roma – Argentina (see above).* ***No cards.***

This converted industrial space, with three stages, is used for more experimental offerings.

PERFORMING ARTS

Teatro Greco

Via R Leoncavallo 10, Suburbs: north (06 860 7513, www.teatrogreco.it). Bus 63, 135, 310. ***Box office*** *10am-1pm, 4.30-7pm Mon, Tue, Thur-Sun.*

A well-designed venue that programmes some Italian dance and has a penchant for little-tried writers, both foreign and domestic.

Teatro Olimpico

Piazza Gentile da Fabriano, Suburbs: north (06 326 5991, www.teatroolimpico.it). Bus 53, 280, 910/tram 2, 19. ***Box office*** *10am-7pm daily.*

Great for all types of performances, the Olimpico has good acoustics, even for cheaper seats. Go for the central front and second-row seats in the gallery.

Teatro Palladium

Piazza Bartolomeo Romano 8, Suburbs: south (06 5733 2768, www.teatro-palladium.it). Metro Garbatella/bus 670, 673, 715, 716. ***Box office*** *4-8pm Tue-Sun.* ***No cards.***

This beautiful theatre dates from the 1920s. Now furnished with brightly coloured chairs, it provides a fascinating mix of electronic music, cutting-edge theatre and art performances. It is one of the venues of choice for the exciting and eclectic annual RomaEuropa Festival (*see p246*).

Teatro Vascello

Via G Carini 72, Suburbs: west (06 588 1021, www.teatrovascello.it). Bus 44, 75, 115, 710, 870, 871, 984. ***Box office*** *9am-6pm Mon; 9am-9.30pm Tue-Fri; 4-9.30pm Sat; 2.30-7.30pm Sun.* ***No cards.***

The Teatro Vascello presents decent experimental theatre and dance productions, along with conferences and workshops.

SUMMER IN ROME

Most of Rome's summer festivals take place under the **Estate Romana** umbrella (*see p245*). This event-fest runs from June to September and – despite funding upsets in recent years – still manages to provide an array of entertainment. In 2017 the festival saw a substantial change at organisational level, with fewer events in the centre of the city and more on the outskirts. One casualty was the Anfiteatro della Quercia del Tasso – a standing appointment of the Estate Romana since 1965 – to the great disappointment of Romans.

The **Accademia Nazionale di Santa Cecilia** offers a full summer programme of quality crowd-pleasers, including international orchestras and classical/popular crossovers, in the outside *cavea* of the **Auditorium-Parco della Musica** performing arts complex.

▶ *For the RomaEuropa Festival, see p246.*

Summer venues

Silvano Toti Globe Theatre

Largo Aqua Felix, Villa Borghese (06 0608, www.globetheatreroma.com). Bus 61, 89, 120, 150, 160, 490, 491, 495, C3, M. ***Box office*** *June-Oct 2-7pm Tue-Sun.* ***No cards. Map*** *p138 K3.*

Rome's Elizabethan theatre, a reproduction of London's Globe Theatre, can hold up to 1,250 people, including 420 standing in the stalls. The theatre offers a Shakespearean menu, with a number of incursions into Goldoni and Molière and special performances designed for children.

❤ Teatro Romano di Ostia Antica

Scavi di Ostia Antica, viale dei Romagnoli 117, Ostia Antica (06 0608, www.ostianticateatro.com). Train from Piramide to Ostia Antica. ***Box office*** *from 6pm before shows. Shows Mid June-July 8.*

This superbly preserved Roman theatre fills the summer with prestigious productions of Roman and Greek classics, as well as a range of concerts and ballets. It's an authentic affair, which means the seats are made of stone – so bring a cushion. Some mosquito repellent is a good idea, too. For more on the dramatic remains of ancient Rome's port at Ostia Antica, *see p232.*

Teatro Palladium

❤ Auditorium-Parco della Musica

Via P de Coubertin 15, Flaminio (06 80241281, www.auditorium.com). Bus 53, 217, 223, 910, M/tram 2. ***Box office*** *11am-8pm Mon-Sat; 10am-8pm Sun.* ***Map*** *p8.*

Fifteen years after its much-trumpeted opening, Rome's stunning Auditorium-Parco della Musica continues to take centre stage in the city's cultural life. For anyone who wishes to establish their cultural credentials, it's quite the chic-est place to be seen – once you get there. Romans who can, drive to the leafy residential area north of piazza del Popolo where the lead roofs of the three giant scarab-shaped concert halls rise. Students, tourists and impecunious music-lovers strap-hang on the rattly no.2 tram. But everybody goes because... well, there's something for everybody.

Box office figures, which leap from year to year, show that low ticket prices and eclectic programming are a winning mix. Its programme – which ranges from symphonies to soul, and from jazz to jugglers – has cast its spell over Roman citizens, many of whom have never set foot in a classical-music venue in their lives. All kinds of music – especially jazz – are taken seriously here, as well as poetry and debate, contemporary art, the sciences and cinema.

Most concert halls don't put Nobel laureates and other top number-crunching boffins on the stage for sell-out annual mathematics festivals. They don't

The programme – which ranges from symphonies to soul – has cast its spell over Roman citizens, many of whom have never set foot in a classical-music venue in their lives

gather the world's top philosophers for four days of brainstorming sessions. Or blast Tchaikovsky's 1812 Overture out of extremely well-balanced speakers for the delight of Christmas ice skaters.

But then, the Auditorium is unique. It even has its own Roman villa nestling between starchitect Renzo Piano's trio of cherry-wood halls, besides several museums – two dedicated to archaeological finds and one to musical instruments. The acoustics – and the catering, of course (this is Italy!) – are beyond reproach.

Each day's programme is packed with events. Sunday is family day and the Auditorium's genial director Antonio Pappano (when he's not conducting at Covent Garden) can often be found explaining to rapt youngsters what exactly a bassoon is. On select weekend mornings there's a farmers' market.

Luglio Suona Bene (July Sounds Great) is a series of concerts taking place in the open *cavea* of the auditorium during the summer. Recent artists include legends such as Charles Aznavour, The Pretenders, Philip Glass, Jethro Tull, and The Beach Boys.

The Auditorium draws on its vast treasure trove of historic recordings to stream its own lively radio station, bringing its world-class offerings to an even larger public. If Rome's Auditorium experiment has proved one thing, it's that if you provide a constant diet of excellence you will never be short of an audience.

► *To book a guided tour (€9, €5 reductions, no cards) call 06 8024 1281 for times. Alternatively, wander in (open 10am-6pm on winter weekends, until 8pm during the summer, open from 11am during the week, admission free) and have a look around for yourself.*

Understand

Constantine the Great

History

Myth, might and intrigue

Each year on 21 April, Romans and visitors in their thousands flock to the Campidoglio for extravagant fireworks and illuminations marking the *Natale di Roma* – Rome's birthday. How many other cities boast such a precise foundation date (or as impressive a tale to go with it)? Then again, how many other cities manage to blend myth and history, fact and fiction, past and present quite as seamlessly as Rome? From Julius Caesar to the Treaty of Rome, if you're looking for history, you've come to the right place.

Julius Caesar

The beginning

The city's birth date tale plays out as follows: twins Romulus and Remus were the fruits of a rape by the god of war, Mars, of an Italian princess called Rhea Silvia. Cast adrift as babies and washed into the marshy area below the Palatine hill, the twins were suckled by a she-wolf until found by a shepherd. Romulus became leader of his tribe, quarrelled with and killed his brother, and – on 21 April 753 BC – founded the city of Rome. Then, because his community was short of females, he abducted the women of the neighbouring Sabine tribe, and got to work to raise a nation that would rule the known world.

As for the facts? Ninth-century BC huts have been excavated on the Palatine – proof there was a primitive village there. But the first historically documented king of Rome was not a Roman but an Etruscan (the area north of Rome, consisting of modern day Tuscany, western Umbria and northern Lazio), Tarquinius Priscus, who reigned from 616 BC. And it was probably ingenious Etruscans who drained the marshy area between the seven hills to create the Forum, hub of the city's political, economic and religious life.

The Roman Republic takes over

According to Roman historians, in 509 BC the son of King Tarquinius Superbus raped Lucretia, the wife of Collatinus, a Roman. The next day, before killing herself, she told her husband and his friend Brutus what had happened, and in revenge they led a rebellion against the Tarquins. The Etruscan dynasty was expelled and the Roman Republic founded, with Brutus and Collatinus as its first consuls.

By the end of the second century BC, the Romans were a race of soldiers, engineers, administrators and merchants

This account is doubtless as historically (in)accurate as the city's foundation yarn but, in time, Etruscan influence over the region did wane and authority passed to Rome's magistrates. Chief among these were the two annually elected consuls, who guided a council of elders called the Senate. Only the few ancient families or clans who formed the patrician class could participate in the political life of the Republic. The lower classes, or *plebs* (*see right* Civus Romanus Sum), struggled for a greater say in their own affairs. In 494 BC, the office of Tribune of the Plebeians was created to represent their interests, and by 367 BC a plebeian could hold the office of consul. To keep up standards, rich or successful plebeians were simply designated patricians.

Romans were united by a belief in their right to conquer other tribes. Their superb military organisation and an agile policy of 'divide and rule' allowed them to bring other peoples – including the Etruscans – under Roman control. New cities were established in conquered territories and an extensive infrastructure was created to support the many conquests. The first great consular road, the via Appia (*see p236*), was begun in 312 BC. Shortly afterwards, work started on the Acqua Appia, the first aqueduct to bring fresh water to the city. The port of Ostia (*see*

Romulus and Remus

Civus Romanus Sum

Society's hierarchy explained

Roman society was rigid but bending, enforcing strict social divisions while holding out the possibility of rising through the ranks. Even ex-slaves worked themselves into powerful places.

Roman citizens

Patricii (patricians or aristocrats) A hereditary aristocracy made up of ancient Latin families. Later, anyone elected to the Senate automatically joined this group, and members of other orders could be raised to this class as well.

Equites (knights or equestrians) Originally from families wealthy enough to provide mounted soldiers for Rome's armies, this rank was later open to anyone worth 400,000 sesterces or more. Equites could become bureaucrats, provincial governors or prefects.

Plebeians (the populace) Making up the majority of Roman society, plebeians ranged from peasants to wealthy traders, and were eligible for food hand-outs as well as free seats at official games and entertainments. The *concilium plebes* council could legislate in some areas, and was able to place proposals before the Senate.

Others

Slaves Owners had the power of life and death over their slaves but did pay them a small retainer, which, if they wished, they could use to buy their way out of servitude.

Freedmen Ex-slaves who had bought or earned their way out of servitude could become teachers, bureaucrats and – on occasion – imperial officials.

Young slave serving patricians

p232 Ostia Antica) – founded at the mouth of the Tiber in 380 BC – expanded rapidly. Barges plied the river, bringing corn, wine, oil and building materials into Rome.

Rome's expansion brought the Republic into conflict with two equally powerful peoples: the Carthaginians, who populated North Africa and Spain, and the Greeks, who had colonised southern Italy and Sicily. The latter had been expelled from mainland Italy by 272 BC, but the Punic Wars against the Carthaginians were to last for almost 120 years. In 218 BC Hannibal crossed the Alps, gaining control of much of the Italian peninsula, but was too cautious – and his supply lines were too stretched – to launch an assault on Rome. When Carthage was destroyed in 146 BC, Rome held sway over the whole western Mediterranean.

In the early days of the Republic most Romans, whether rich or poor, had been farmers, tending their own land or raising livestock in the surrounding countryside. Wars like those against Carthage, however, required huge standing armies. At the same time, much of the agricultural land in Italy had been laid waste, either by Hannibal or by the Romans themselves as they attempted to starve the invading Carthaginians into defeat with a scorched-earth policy.

Wealthy Romans bought estates at knock-down prices, while landless peasants flocked to the capital. By the end of the second century BC, the Romans were a race of soldiers, engineers, administrators and merchants, supported by tribute from defeated enemies and the slave labour of prisoners taken in battle. Keeping the mass of the Roman poor content required the exaction of more tribute money from the conquered territories, creating a parasitic relationship in which all classes in Rome lived off conquered peoples.

The political situation in the first century BC became more and more anarchic. Enormous armies were required to fight wars on the distant boundaries of the Republic's empire; soldiers came to owe greater loyalty to their general than to the government back in Rome. The result was a succession of civil wars fought between rival generals.

To hold the Empire together a single central power was needed, and Octavian was that power

Hail Caesar!

Julius Caesar and Pompey, the two greatest generals of the first century BC, tried to bury their differences in a triumvirate with Crassus, but in 49 BC Caesar, then governor of Gaul, defied the Senate by bringing his army into Italy ('crossing the Rubicon', the muddy stream that marked the border). All opposition was swept aside and for the last six years of his life Julius Caesar ruled Rome as a dictator. The Republican spirit was not quite dead, though: in 44 BC he was assassinated.

His death did not lead to the restoration of the Republic: instead, there was a power struggle between Mark Antony and Octavian – the former a Caesar-supporting general, the latter Caesar's nephew – whose initial partnership broke down and escalated into a full-blown civil war. Octavian eventually defeated Mark Antony and Cleopatra at the Battle of Actium in 31 BC. Rome's influence now stretched from Gaul and Spain in the west to Egypt and Asia Minor in the east. To hold it together a single central power was needed, and Octavian was that power. To drive the point home, he took the name of Augustus: 'favoured by the gods'.

To give himself greater authority, Augustus encouraged the cult of his uncle Julius Caesar as a god, building a temple to him in the Forum (the Temple of Divus Julius; *see p71*). The Ara Pacis (*see p101*) was a reminder that it was he who had brought peace to the Roman world. Statues of Augustus sprang up all over the Empire, and he was more than happy to be worshipped as a god himself.

Augustus lived on the Palatine hill in a relatively modest house. Later emperors built extravagant palaces. The last member of Augustus' family to inherit the Empire was the megalomaniac Nero, who built himself the biggest palace Rome had ever seen: the Domus Aurea (Golden House, *see p187*).

When Nero died in AD 68, he had not produced an heir. Suddenly, the Empire was up for grabs. Generals converged from right across the Empire to claim the throne, and the eventual winner was a bluff soldier called Vespasian, the founder of the Flavian dynasty.

Emperor Augustus

The golden age of Pax Romana

Over the next 100 years Rome enjoyed an era of unparalleled stability. The Empire reached its greatest extent during the reign of Trajan (AD 98-117). Thereafter it was a matter of protecting the existing boundaries and avoiding civil war.

Peace throughout the Mediterranean encouraged trade and brought even greater prosperity to Rome, but the power and influence of the capital and its inhabitants declined. Many talented Imperial officials, generals and even emperors were Greeks, north Africans or Spaniards: Trajan and Hadrian were both born in Spain.

To keep an increasingly disparate mass of people content, emperors relied on the policy of *panem et circenses* (bread and circuses). From the first century AD, grain was regularly handed out to the poor, ostensibly to maintain a supply of fit young men for the army, but also to ensure that unrest was kept to a minimum. Such generosity to Rome's poor necessitated further exploitation of the outlying provinces of the Empire.

The other means used to keep more than a million souls loyal to their emperor was the staging of lavish public entertainments. The most famous venue for such spectacles was the Colosseum (*see p74*), built by

To keep an increasingly disparate mass of people content, emperors relied on the policy of 'bread and circuses'

emperors Vespasian and Domitian and completed in AD 80.

In the time of Augustus, Rome was home to about one million people. By the reign of Trajan a century later this had risen to 1,500,000. No other city in the world would even approach this size until the 19th century.

A slow decline

The golden age of Rome ended in 180 with the death of Emperor Marcus Aurelius. Defending the eastern provinces and fortifying the borders along the Danube and the Rhine placed a huge strain on the Imperial purse and legions. Moreover, the exploitative relationship between the Roman state and its distant provinces meant that the latter were unable – or unwilling – to defend themselves.

The threat from barbarian invaders and civil wars became so serious that in the third century Emperor Aurelian (270-75) was obliged to fortify the city of Rome with massive defences. The still-extant Aurelian Wall, which was later reinforced by medieval popes, is a splendid monument to the engineering skills of the ancient Romans. But in its heyday, the city needed no defences: its protection lay in the vastness of the Empire and the security of the *Pax Romana*.

The end of the third century AD was a turning point in the history of Rome. Diocletian (284-305) established new capital cities at Mediolanum (Milan) and Nicomedia (now in Turkey). He divided the Empire into four sectors, sharing power with a second 'Augustus' – Maximian – and two 'Caesars', Constantius and Galerius. The priorities of the over-extended Empire were now to defend the Rhine and Danube borders against invading Germanic tribes and the eastern provinces from the Persians. Rome was, essentially, abandoned.

Christianity and Constantine

The reign of Diocletian is also remembered as one of the periods of most intense persecution of Christians in the Empire. Christian communities had been established in Rome very soon after the death of Jesus. Christianity, though, was just one of many cults that had spread from the Middle East. Its followers were probably fewer than the devotees of Mithraism (*see p204* Blood and Sperm: the Cult of Mithras), a Persian religion open only to men, but Christianity's promise of salvation in the afterlife had great appeal. Within two decades of Diocletian's persecutions, Emperor Constantine (306-37) would first tolerate Christianity and then recognise it as the Empire's official religion.

Life in fourth-century Rome went on much as before; all around, however, the Roman world was falling apart

The early part of Constantine's reign was largely taken up with campaigns against rival emperors, the most powerful being Maxentius, who commanded Italy and north Africa. The decisive battle was fought just to the north of Rome at the Milvian Bridge (Ponte Milvio) in 312. Before the battle a flaming cross is said to have appeared in the sky, bearing the words *in hoc signo vinces* (by this sign shall you conquer). As the legend goes, Constantine's cavalry then swept Maxentius' superior forces into the Tiber. The Senate built the triumphal Arch of Constantine (*see p66*) to celebrate the victory. The following year, in the Edict of Milan, Constantine decreed that Christianity be tolerated throughout the Empire. Later in his reign, when he had gained control of the Eastern Empire and started to build his new capital city at Byzantium/Constantinople (now Istanbul), it became the state religion.

Christianity's effect on Roman life was at first limited, the new faith simply co-existing with other religions. Constantine's reign saw the building of three great basilicas, all on the outskirts of the city. St Peter's and St Paul's Without the Walls (San Paolo fuori le Mura; *see p229*) were built over existing shrines, whereas Constantine donated land to build a basilica – San Giovanni in Laterano (*see p206*) – beside the Aurelian Wall. To give Rome credibility as a centre of its new religion, fragments of the 'True' cross were brought from the Holy Land by Constantine's mother, St Helena.

Meanwhile, life in fourth-century Rome went on much as before. The departure of part of the Imperial court to Constantinople was a heavy blow, but the old pagan holidays were still observed, games staged and bread doled out to the poor.

All around, however, the Roman world was falling apart. Constantine learned nothing from the conflicts created by Diocletian's division of power: on his death he left the Empire to be split between his three sons. From this point on, the Western Empire and the Byzantine Empire were

Visigoths sack Rome in 410

two separate entities, united for the last time under Theodosius in the late fourth century. Byzantium would stand for another 1,000 years, while Rome's glories were soon destroyed by waves of invaders.

The fall of the Western Empire

The first great shock came in 410, when Alaric's Visigoths marched into Italy and sacked Rome. Even more significant was the conquest of north Africa by the Vandals in 435, which cut Rome off from its main grain supply. In 455 the Vandals sacked Rome, removing everything they could carry. After this the Western Empire survived in name only. The great aqueducts supplying water to Rome ceased to function. Emperors in Rome became nothing more than puppets of the assorted Germanic invaders. The last emperor, Romulus, was given the nickname Augustulus, since he was such a feeble shadow of the Empire's founder. In 476 he was deposed by the German chieftain Odoacer, who styled himself King of Italy. Odoacer was in turn deposed by Theodoric the Ostrogoth, who invaded Italy with the support of Byzantium and established an urbane court in Ravenna, which was to provide stable government for the next 30 years.

In the sixth century much of Italy was reconquered by the Eastern Empire. Then, in around 567, yet another Germanic tribe swept in. The Lombards overran much of the centre of the peninsula, but when they threatened to besiege Rome they met their match in Pope Gregory the Great (590-604), who bought them off. Gregory was a tireless organiser, overseeing the running of the Church's estates around Europe, encouraging the establishment of new monasteries and sending missionaries as far afield as pagan Britain.

He also did a great deal to build up the prestige of the papacy. Rome had been merely one of the centres of the early Church, the others – Byzantium, Jerusalem, Antioch and Alexandria – all being in the East. Disputes were sometimes referred to the Bishop of Rome, but many Christians did not accord him overall primacy. The collapse of secular government in the West meant that the papacy emerged almost by default as the sole centre of authority, with the pope a political leader as well as head of the Roman Church.

A shadow of itself

The Dark Ages must have been a particularly galling period for the inhabitants of Rome, living as they did among the magnificent ruins of a golden age that had vanished. The population had no fresh water, and disease was rife. Formerly built-up areas reverted to grazing land, or were planted with vegetables by religious orders. Fear of attack meant that the countryside around the city was practically deserted. Having reached well over a million at its zenith, Rome's population by the sixth century could be counted in hundreds. The city's ancient ruins became little more than convenient quarries: marble was burned to make cement, most of which was used to repair fortifications.

For several centuries the city still owed nominal allegiance to the emperor in Byzantium and his representative in Italy, the exarch, whose court was at Ravenna. However, the exarch's troops were normally too busy defending their own cities in north-east Italy to be of much help. Rome had a military commander – a *dux* – and a *comune* (city council). But the papacy also had its courts and administration. In the end, the power of the Church prevailed; this would lead to a permanent rift with Byzantium and the Eastern Orthodox churches.

When the Lombards seized Ravenna in 751 and threatened to do the same to Rome, Pope Stephen II enlisted Pepin, King of the Franks, as defender of the Church. The papacy's alliance with the Franks grew with the victories of Pepin's son, Charlemagne, over the Lombards and was sealed on Christmas Day 800, when the pope caught Charlemagne unawares in St Peter's and crowned him Holy Roman Emperor.

Holy Roman politics

Now Rome had the protection of an emperor (with a power base comfortably far away in Aachen) anointed by the pope, who in return was rewarded with the gift of large areas of land in central Italy. As things turned out, this arrangement caused nothing but trouble for the next 500 years, as popes, emperors and other monarchs vied to determine whose power was greatest. Roman nobles took sides in the disputes, taking advantage to promote members of their own families to the papacy, frequently reducing the city to a state of anarchy.

Papal independence was reasserted in the second half of the 11th century by Pope Gregory VII (1073-85), who also established many of the distinctive institutions of the Church. It was Gregory who first made celibacy obligatory for priests; he set up the College of Cardinals, giving it sole authority to elect all future popes. He also insisted that no bishop or abbot could be invested by a lay ruler, which led to a cataclysmic struggle for power with the Holy Roman Emperor Henry IV.

When Henry marched on Rome in 1084, bringing with him a new papal candidate, Gregory demanded help from Robert Guiscard, leader of the Normans who had a strong power base in southern Italy. By the time Robert arrived, Rome had already capitulated to Henry's army; in protest, the Normans indulged in a three-day orgy of looting, then torched what was still standing. From the Palatine to San Giovanni in Laterano, little remained but smoking ruins. Gregory slunk out of his hiding place in Castel Sant'Angelo and left Rome a broken man; he died the following year. *See also p202* Sack of Rome.

Despite conflict between rival factions, the 12th and 13th centuries were times of great architectural innovation. The creative spirit of the Middle Ages is preserved in beautiful cloisters such as those of San Giovanni and in Romanesque churches with graceful brick bell towers and floors of finely wrought mosaic.

Rome's prestige suffered a severe blow in 1309, when the French overruled the College of Cardinals and imposed their own papal candidate, who promptly decamped to Avignon. A pope returned to Rome in 1378, but the situation became farcical, with three pontiffs laying claim to St Peter's throne. Stability was restored only in 1417, when

Pope Gregory VII

Sack of Rome 1527

Bloodshed and devastation as the imperial army descends

On 5 May 1527 an ill-disciplined force gathered beneath Rome's walls. Some 14,000 were Germans with Martin Luther's fulminations against the papacy ringing in their ears; 6,000 were Spanish troops; the rest were a rabble of Italian deserters and free-booters. All of them were angry. It was months since their nominal commander-in-chief the Holy Roman Emperor Charles V (aka Charles I of Spain) had paid them. And all of them knew that Rome was bursting with treasure.

In many ways, Pope Clement VII had brought this situation on himself: he had spurned tradition and turned his back on the Holy Roman Emperor, allying himself with France, England and Venice. Not that Charles was giving much thought to the pope: with Ottomans battering his eastern borders, he had left this particular force very much up to its own devices. When the attack on Rome's walls was launched on 6 May, the imperial army's nominal leader the Duke of Bourbon was killed, leaving his men to wreak havoc unchecked.

What the attackers found as they piled over the walls must have seemed an El Dorado of stupendous villas and sumptuously appointed churches. As Clement high-tailed it to his fortress at Castel Sant'Angelo (*see p161*) the soldiers ran amok. Women were dragged into churches to be raped by Lutherans dressed in priests' robes; children were hurled from high windows; priests suffered unspeakable tortures; the corpses piled up on the streets.

Clement was forced to capitulate on 6 June, and was fined 400,000 ducats. But it was months before any semblance of order returned to the devastated city.

In a 1526 census, Rome had 55,000 residents. By the end of 1527, there were no more than 10,000. Many had fled, but as many as 20,000 died – both in the sack and in the plague that swept through the city towards the end of the year.

Not content with this bloodshed, Romans looked for a scapegoat for their misfortunes. They found it in the Jews, who were accused of saving their own skins and profiteering by buying up looted goods from the attackers. In fact, the Jewish community was responsible for salvaging Roman treasures that would otherwise have been lost.

The Sack of Rome put an abrupt end to the Renaissance popes' dream of making Rome a formidable political power

Oddo Colonna was elected as Pope Martin V (1417-31) at the Council of Constance. He returned to Rome in 1420 to find the city and the surrounding Papal States in a ruinous condition.

With the reign of Martin, some semblance of dignity was restored to the papacy. City councillors were nominees of the pope, who made the Vatican his principal residence: it offered greater security than their traditional seat in the Lateran Palace. Successive popes took advantage of this new sense of authority; Rome became an international city once more.

The renewed prestige of the papacy enabled it to draw funds from all over Europe in the form of tithes and taxes. The papacy also developed the money-spinning idea of the Holy Year, which had been instituted in 1300. Such measures financed the lavish artistic patronage of Renaissance Rome.

Renaissance is born

Nicholas V (1447-55) is remembered as the pope who brought the Renaissance to Rome. A lover of philosophy, science and the arts, he founded the Vatican Library and had many ancient Greek texts translated. He also made plans to rebuild St Peter's, the structure of which was perilously unstable. The Venetian Pope Paul II (1464-71) built the city's first great Renaissance *palazzo*, the massive Palazzo Venezia (*see p63*), and his successor Sixtus IV (1471-84) invited leading artists from Tuscany and Umbria to fresco the walls of his new Sistine Chapel (*see p154*) in the Vatican.

Since the papacy had become such a fat prize, the great families of Italy redoubled their efforts to secure it. The French and Spanish kings usually had their own candidates too. Political clout, rather than spirituality, was the prime concern of Renaissance popes. Sixtus IV and his successors Innocent VIII (1484-92) and Alexander VI (the infamous Rodrigo Borgia; 1492-1503) devoted far more of their energies to politics and war than to spiritual matters.

The epitome of the worldly Renaissance pope, Julius II (1503-13) made a strong papal state a reality. He began the collection of classical sculpture that formed the nucleus of today's Vatican Museums (*see p154*) and invited the greatest architects, sculptors and painters of the day to come to Rome, including Bramante, Michelangelo and Raphael.

Julius' successors accomplished far less than he did. Some were simply bon viveurs, like Giovanni de' Medici, who, on being made Pope Leo X in 1513, said to his brother, 'God has given us the papacy. Let us enjoy

The papacy was such a fat prize that political clout, rather than Christian spirituality, was the prime concern of Renaissance popes

it.' Enjoy it he did. A great patron of the arts, Leo's other passions were hunting, music, theatre and throwing spectacular dinner parties. He plunged the papacy into debt, spending enormous sums on French hounds, Icelandic falcons and banquets of nightingale pies and dishes involving peacocks' tongues.

Protestants and Imperialism

Later popes had to face two great threats to the status quo of Catholic Europe: the protests of Martin Luther, and the growing rivalry between Francis I of France and Spanish King/Holy Roman Emperor Charles V.

The year 1523 saw the death of Pope Adrian VI, a Flemish protégé of Charles V. He was succeeded by Clement VII (1523-34), formerly Giulio de' Medici, who rather unwisely backed France against the all-powerful emperor. Charles took the Duchy of Milan in 1525 and threatened to annex all Italy in retaliation for the pope's disloyalty. In 1527 an ill-disciplined Imperial army, many of whom were Germans with Lutheran condemnations of Rome ringing in their ears, sacked Rome (*see opposite*). Chiefly interested in gold and ready money, the looters also destroyed churches and houses, burned or stole countless relics and works of art, looted tombs, and killed indiscriminately. The dead rotted in the streets for months.

Pope Clement held out for seven months in Castel Sant'Angelo, but eventually slunk away in disguise. He returned the following year, crowning Charles as Holy Roman Emperor in Bologna shortly afterwards. In return, Charles grudgingly confirmed Clement VII's sovereignty over the Papal States.

The 1527 Sack of Rome put an abrupt end to the Renaissance popes' dream of making Rome a formidable political power. The primary concerns now had to be the rebuilding of the city and pushing forward the Counter-Reformation, the Catholic Church's response to Protestantism. *See also left* Sack of Rome 1527.

Reshaping Rome

Bulldozing the buildings of the past

When Rome became the capital of united Italy in 1870, its new masters – the Savoy royal house with its court of northern bureaucrats – set out to mould the ancient city to their image of a major metropolis. The results, many felt, were disastrous.

'Twelve years of rule by the Savoias have done more for the destruction of Rome, with its beauty and interest, than all the invasions of the Goths and Vandals,' wrote Augustus Hare in his *Walks in Rome* (1883), the guide book for the discerning late 19th-century traveller. 'The whole aspect of the city is changed, and the picturesqueness of the old days must now be sought in such obscure corners as have escaped the hand of the spoiler.'

Rome in 1870 was a magnificent jumble of the medieval, the Renaissance and the Baroque, interspersed with the nature-engulfed ruins of the ancient world. To architects used to the Gallic-style order of Turin, this was anarchy at its worst, and certainly not fit for their showpiece capital. Moreover, the hordes of northern pen-pushers who flooded in to man the new country's ponderous bureaucracy had to be provided with offices and accommodation. The consequences, Hare believed, were devastating.

'Precious street memorials of medieval history have been swept away; ancient convents have been levelled with the ground or turned into barracks; the glorious cloisters of Michelangelo have been walled up; the pagan ruins have been denuded of all that gave them picturesqueness or beauty.'

The highest-profile blow was the demolition of a whole medieval quarter on the slopes of the Capitoline hill to make way for the Vittoriano (*see p64*), the massively disproportionate monument in piazza Venezia to Italy's famously diminutive first king, Vittorio Emanuele II.

Many stones that were left unturned by the Savoys were later heaved well out of the way by Mussolini, whose obsession with the glories of the Empire led him not to preserve its remains but to stamp his mark upon them with a characteristically heavy hand. The great sweep of via dei Fori Imperiali was knocked through a forest of *fora* to link – geographically and symbolically –*il Duce*'s HQ at Palazzo Venezia with the Colosseum.

Via dei Fori Imperiali

Counter-Reformation

The first great Counter-Reformation pope was Alessandro Farnese, Paul III (1534-49). He summoned the Council of Trent to redefine Catholicism and encouraged new religious groups such as the Jesuits – founded by the Spaniard Ignatius of Loyola and approved in 1540 – over older, discredited orders. From their mother church in Rome, Il Gesù (*see p124*), the Jesuits led the fight against heresy.

Pope Paul IV (1555-59), the next major reformer, was a firm believer in the Inquisition. He expelled Jews from the Papal States, except for those in Rome itself, where they were confined to the Ghetto in 1556.

By the end of the 16th century the authority of the papacy was on the wane, and the treasury was increasingly dependent on loans. But in the following century popes continued to spend money wildly, commissioning architects such as Bernini and Borromini to design the churches, *palazzi* and fountains that would transform the face of the Eternal City forever. The economy of the Papal States became chronically depressed.

Poor locals and rich tourists

If two centuries of papal opulence had turned monumental Rome into a spectacular sight, squalor and poverty were still the norm for most of its people: the streets of Trastevere and the Suburra – ancient Rome's great slum – in what is now the Monti district were filthy and dangerous. The city was, however, a more peaceful place to live. The rich no longer shut themselves up in fortress-like *palazzi*, but built delightful villas in landscaped parks, such as Villa Borghese (*see p142*). A Europe-wide resurgence of interest in the classical past was under way, and shortly the city would discover the joys – and earning power – of tourism.

By the 18th century a visit to Rome as part of a 'Grand Tour' (*see p90* Grand Tourists) was near obligatory for any European gentleman, and Romans responded eagerly to the influx. The city produced little great art or architecture at this time. The two great Roman sights that date from this period, the Spanish Steps and the Fontana di Trevi, are a late flowering of Roman Baroque. The few big building projects undertaken were for the benefit of tourists, notably Giuseppe Valadier's splendid park on the Pincio (*see p141*) and the neo-classical facelift he gave to piazza del Popolo (*see p97*).

Although on the surface Rome was a cultured city, it remained a place where many customs reeked of medieval superstition. Executions were mostly staged in piazza del Popolo, and they were often timed to coincide with *carnevale*, a period of frantic merrymaking before Lent. For a few days, via del Corso was one long, masked ball. Here bands played and people would shower one another with confetti, flour, water and more dangerous missiles.

Indeed, Rome was a city of spectacle for much of the year. In summer, piazza Navona was flooded by blocking the outlets of the fountains, and the nobility sploshed around in their carriages. The only time the city fell quiet was in late summer, when everyone who could left for their villas in the Alban hills to escape the stifling heat and the threat of malaria.

Occupation, then unification

In 1798 everything changed. French troops under Napoleon occupied the city and Rome became a republic once more. Pope Pius VI (1775-99), a feeble old man, was exiled from the city and died in France. Like most attempts to restore the Roman Republic, this one was short-lived. The next pope, Pius VII (1800-23), elected in Venice, signed a concordat with Napoleon in 1801, which allowed the pontiff to return to Rome. The papacy was expelled for a second time when French troops returned in 1808. Napoleon promised the city a modernising, reforming administration, but Romans were not keen to be conscripted into his armies. When the pope finally reclaimed Rome after the fall of Napoleon in 1814, its noble families and many of the people welcomed his return.

The Papal States were returned to Pius VII. But the brief taste of liberty under the French had helped to inspire a movement for unification, modernisation and independence from the domination of foreign rulers.

The *Risorgimento* was a movement for the unification of the country, but in itself it was very diverse. Its supporters ranged from liberals who believed in unification for economic reasons, to conservatives who looked to the papacy itself to unify Italy. Initially, the most prominent players were the idealistic republicans of the *Giovine Italia* (Young Italy) movement, headed by

The brief taste of liberty had helped to inspire a movement for unification, modernisation and independence

Vittorio Emmanuele II

Giuseppe Mazzini. They were flanked by more extreme groups and secret societies, such as the Carbonari.

Two reactionary popes, Leo XII (1823-29) and Gregory XVI (1831-46), used a network of police spies and censorship to put down any opposition. Most of the unrest in the Papal States, though, was in the north; in Rome, life went on much as before. Travellers continued to visit; Shelley and Dickens expressed horror at the repressive regime.

The election of a new pope in 1846 aroused great optimism. Pius IX came to the throne with a liberal reputation and immediately announced an amnesty for over 400 political prisoners. But the spate of revolutions throughout Europe in 1848 radically altered his attitude. In November that year his chief minister was assassinated and Pius fled. In his absence, a popular assembly declared Rome a republic. Seizing the chance to make his dream reality, Mazzini rushed to the city, where he was chosen as one of a triumvirate of rulers. Meanwhile, another idealist arrived in Rome to defend the Republic, at the head of 500 armed followers. He was Giuseppe Garibaldi, a former sailor who had gained military experience fighting in wars of liberation in South America.

Ironically, it was Republican France, with Napoleon I's nephew Louis Napoleon as president, that decided it was duty-bound to restore papal rule to Rome. Louis Napoleon did so in order to stop Austrian power spreading further within Italy. A French force marched on Rome, but was repelled by the ragtag army of *garibaldini* (followers of Garibaldi). The French attacked again in greater numbers, mounting their assault from the gardens of Villa Pamphili. For the whole of June 1849 the defenders fought valiantly from their positions on the Gianicolo, but the end of the Republic was by now inevitable.

For the next 20 years, while the rest of Italy was being united under King Vittorio Emanuele II of Savoy, a garrison of French troops protected Pope Pius from invasion. Garibaldi protested vainly to the politicians of the new state – it was, he said, a question of *Roma o morte* ('Rome or death') – but the Kingdom of Italy, established in 1860, was not prepared to take on Napoleon III's France.

Meanwhile, the former liberal Pius IX was becoming more and more reactionary. In 1869 he convened the first Vatican Council in order to set down the Catholic Church's response to the upheavals of the industrial age. It did so with intransigence, making the doctrine of papal infallibility an official dogma of the Church for the first time.

A capital once more

Though still under papal rule, Rome had been chosen as the capital of the newly unified kingdom. In 1870, with the defeat of Napoleon III in the Franco-Prussian War, the French withdrew from Rome and unification troops occupied the city.

There followed the most rapid period of change Rome had experienced since the fall of the Empire. The new capital needed government buildings and housing for the civil servants who worked in them. Church properties were confiscated and for a time government officials worked in converted monasteries and convents. Two aristocratic *palazzi* were adapted to house the Italian parliament: Palazzo di Montecitorio (*see p96*) became the Lower House, and Palazzo Madama (*see p109*) the Senate.

The city's great building boom lasted for over 30 years. New avenues appeared: via Nazionale and via Cavour linked the old city with the new Stazione Termini, and corso Vittorio Emanuele was driven through the historic centre. The new ministries were often massive piles quite out of keeping with their surroundings; still more extravagant was the monstrous Vittoriano (*see p64*), the marble monument to Vittorio Emanuele erected in piazza Venezia. (*See also p286* Reshaping Rome.)

Fascism and the post-war era

Though Rome was little affected by World War I, social unrest broke out following the war, with the fear of Socialism encouraging the rise of Fascism. Benito Mussolini was a radical journalist who, having become alienated from the far left, shifted to the extreme right. He turned to ancient Rome to find an emblem to embody his idea of a totalitarian state: *fasces*, bundles of rods tied round an axe, were carried by the Roman *lictors* (marshals) as they walked in front of the city's consuls. In 1922 Mussolini sent his Blackshirt squads on their 'March on Rome', demanding – and winning – full power in government. Mussolini made the 'march' by train.

Mussolini's ambition was to transform the country into a dynamic, aggressive society. His ideas for changing the face of Rome were far-fetched. He planned to rebuild the city in gleaming marble, with fora, obelisks and heroic statues proclaiming *Il Duce* ('the Leader') as a modern Augustus at the head of a new Roman Empire. The most prominent surviving monuments to his megalomania are the suburb of EUR (*see p227*) and the Foro Italico sports complex (*see p222*).

When put to the test in World War II, Fascist Italy rapidly foundered. Mussolini was ousted from power in 1943 and Romans switched their allegiance. During the period of German occupation that followed, Italian partisans showed themselves capable of acts of great courage. Rome was declared an 'open city' meaning that the Germans agreed not to defend it, pitching their defence south of the city. While other Italian cities and towns were pounded by bombs, Rome suffered only one serious bombing raid during the whole war.

Mussolini's ambition was to transform the country into a dynamic, aggressive society

After the war Italy voted to become a republic and Rome quickly adapted to the new political structures. *Partitocrazia* – government by a group of political parties sharing power and dividing up lucrative government jobs and contracts between them – suited the Roman approach to life.

Meanwhile Italy was staking its claim as a leading player in a new united Europe. The Treaty of Rome – the founding document of the European Economic Community – was signed in the Campidoglio (Capitoline, *see p60*) on 25 March 1957.

The political unrest that hit Italy in the 1970s and '80s – a spate of right-wing bomb attacks, and kidnappings of key figures by the far-left Red Brigades – affected Rome less than it did Milan or Turin. Romans simply swam with the political tide: they voted in their first Communist mayor in 1976.

The city benefited greatly from Italy's post war economic boom, spreading out along its major arterial roads. The problem for the post-war city authorities has been how to preserve the old city yet encourage development. Rome's main industry remains itself, whether capital of Italy or historical relic, and the city continues to thrive, trading – as it has done for the millennium and a half since the Empire fell – on its unforgettable past.

Benito Mussolini during the march on Rome 1922

Architecture

Classical ruins, futuristic design, and everything in between

---

There has never been a time in Rome when architecture wasn't about making a statement – and the statement has always been, first and foremost, political. From the ancient *fora* with their marbled temples and towering statues, to the overwhelming churches of the Baroque and the gleaming white EUR district – a Fascist ideal city – the goal was always to awe. More recently, city councils of all political hues have summoned international archistars to show their clout. The long slump in new architecture between the late 1980s and 2000 came to an impressive end at the start of the new millennium. But recent political uncertainty in the city has significantly slowed this trend. Can Rome keep adding to its already-significant architectural heritage?

Palazzo della Civiltè Italiana

The ancient city

The classical ruins we see today are, to an extent, misleading. What's missing (besides roofs and walls) is colour: there was nothing minimalist about ancient Rome. Statues were multi-hued: buildings and temples were a riot of variegated marbles; bas-reliefs were painted in garish shades. What they still give is an idea of size: major buildings were designed to express the might of Rome. Perhaps for this reason, it was a while before the Romans developed much in the way of architectural style.

The Romans had the Etruscans to thank for insights into hydraulics and town planning. The Greek system of orders was followed for important façades. The main Greek orders – with columns of different proportions based on their width – were Doric (plain and sturdy), Ionic (more slender and ornate) and Corinthian (the most delicate and ornate of all). The **Colosseum** (*see p74*) is a good example of how they were used: hefty Doric at the bottom to support the construction; lighter, more elegant Ionic in the middle; and the decorative Corinthian top layer. It wasn't only columns that were copied from Greece: whole genres of building were based on Greek models: temples were colonnaded and either rectangular or circular; theatres were derived from their Greek counterparts.

Eventually, however, the Romans came up with some ideas of their own: elliptical arenas – known as amphitheatres – designed for blood sports; rectangular meeting houses flanked by columns, known as basilicas; and efficient plumbing and heating systems, complete with hot running water. Perhaps most importantly, the Romans took the arch to unprecedented heights of perfection, giving the world its first large-scale, free-standing masonry.

Villa Adriana

The most common stone found around Rome was soft, volcanic tufa. This was not an ideal building material, and as early as the third century BC a form of concrete was developed, made of *pozzolana* (volcanic ash), lime and tufa rubble. Without concrete, constructing the **Pantheon** (*see p113*) would have been impossible: the huge hemispherical dome was the largest cast-concrete construction made before the 20th century. Other feats of cast-concrete engineering include the **Terme di Diocleziano** (*see p192*) and **Terme di Caracalla** (*see p214*). But concrete was not aesthetically pleasing, so buildings were faced with veneers of coloured marble or travertine. Brick, another fundamental Roman building material, was used to face buildings, to lend internal support to concrete walls and as a material in its own right. The most impressive example is the **Mercati di Traiano** (*see p73*).

Early Christian Rome

Stylistically speaking, the transition from pagan to paleo-Christian was a smooth one, though this isn't always immediately apparent. The earliest Christian meeting places – known as *tituli* – were in very ordinary private houses. The first churches happily adopted the basilica form. Churches founded in the fourth and fifth centuries such as **San Giovanni in Laterano** (*see p206*), **Santi Quattro Coronati** (*see p203*) and **Santa Maria in Trastevere** (*see p169*) are the most tangible connection we have with the interiors of ancient civic Rome. Most are rectangular, with a flat roof and a colonnade separating a tall nave from lower aisles. Natural light enters the nave through high windows. Behind the altar, opposite the entrance, is an apse topped by a conch (domed roof). Perhaps the best example of all is **Santa Sabina** (*see p212*), which was shorn of later additions in a no-holds-barred restoration in the 1930s.

You can trace the fortunes of the Catholic Church in Rome's architecture. When it was poor, as in the fifth century, buildings were plain and functional; when it was rich, in the eighth and 12th centuries, churches were adorned with brilliant mosaics. The

The Romans took the arch to unprecedented heights of perfection

Santa Sabina

most magnificent to have survived are in **Santa Maria Maggiore** (*see p191*), **Santa Prassede** (*see p184*) and **Santa Maria in Trastevere** (*see p169*). Many churches were decorated with Cosmati-work: choirs, candlesticks and floors inlaid with dazzling patterns in chips of coloured marble and glass. Very occasionally, circular churches were built: **Santa Costanza** (*see p224*) – with its swirling mosaics, which owe much to pagan symbolism – was probably built in the fourth century as a mausoleum for the daughters of Emperor Constantine; its contemporary, **Santo Stefano Rotondo** (*see p203*), may have been inspired by the church of the Holy Sepulchre in Jerusalem.

During the Middle Ages, Rome's influential families were engaged in an almost constant battle for power – something reflected in the city's architecture. Anyone who could, opted for a fortress-home with lookout towers like **Torre delle Milizie**, behind Trajan's market (*see p66*).

The quarrels between the families were to have long-lasting effects: with daggers constantly drawn, they failed to impose a Roman candidate on the throne of St Peter's. France stepped in, had Clement V elected, and helped him to shift the papacy to Avignon in 1309, where it remained until 1378. The international funds that had shored up the spendthrift papacy were diverted to the French city and Rome was left bankrupt. The Gothic period passed the city by (the one exception being the church of **Santa Maria sopra Minerva**, *see p114*). The earlier years of the Renaissance, too, were lost on the shadow of its former self that Rome had become.

Renaissance

In the late 14th century a revolution in art, architecture and thought was under way in Tuscany. In crumbling, medieval Rome it was not until the following century that the Renaissance began to gather momentum (the sole exception being the group of artists around genius Pietro Cavallini). In 1445 the Florentine architect Antonio Filarete created one of Rome's first significant Renaissance works: the magnificent central bronze doors of **St Peter's** (*see p158*).

It was Pope Nicholas V (1447-55) who realised that if Rome was to take on fully its role as the focus of Christianity, she had to look the part. As a first step, Nicholas commissioned extensive restoration work on the fourth-century basilica of St Peter, which was in imminent danger of collapse. Meanwhile, those with lucrative church connections built fabulous palaces: papal banker Agostino Chigi commissioned a lavish villa in 1508 (it's now the **Villa Farnesina**, *see p172*) and in 1515 work started on **Palazzo Farnese** (*see p126*) for Cardinal Alessandro Farnese.

Pope Pius II (1458-64), a cultured Tuscan, banned the quarrying of ancient buildings for construction materials for the new. Sixtus IV (1471-84) had roads paved and widened, churches such as **Santa Maria della Pace** (*see p107*) and **Santa Maria del Popolo** (*see p98*) rebuilt, and the **Sistine Chapel** (*see p154*) built and decorated by the best artists of the day.

Rome's Renaissance reached its peak with Julius II (1503-13), who made Donato Bramante (1444-1514) his chief architect. Bramante came to Rome from Milan in 1499, and in 1502 built the **Tempietto** (*see p179*). With its domed cylinder surrounded by a Tuscan Doric colonnade, the Tempietto came closer than any other building to the spirit of antiquity. Julius also commissioned Michelangelo (1475-1564) to sculpt his tomb and fresco the ceiling of the Sistine Chapel. Raphael (1483-1520) was called in to decorate the *stanze* (private apartments) in the Vatican palace.

Not satisfied with the restoration of St Peter's initiated by his predecessors, the supremely self-assured Julius decided to scrap the basilica that for twelve centuries had been one of the holiest sites in Christendom and start again. The job was given to Bramante, and in 1506 the foundation stone was laid. Work began on Bramante's Greek-cross design, but was halted after his death in 1514. In 1547 Michelangelo took over, increasing the scale tremendously. During the papacy of Sixtus V (1585-90) – an obsessive planner responsible for the layout of much of modern Rome – Giacomo della Porta (1533-1602) erected the dome to a design by Michelangelo. The second half of the 16th century in Rome was dominated by the austere reforms of the Council of Trent (1545-63), designed to counter the ideas of the Reformation, and by the establishment of heavy-handed new religious orders such as the Jesuits. With the dictates of the Counter-Reformation in mind, Paul V (1605-21) finally scuppered the original Greek-cross design for St Peter's and instead commissioned Carlo Maderno (1556-1629) to lengthen the nave to create a Latin cross.

Central bronze doors, St Peter's

The earliest churches of the period, such as the **Chiesa Nuova** (*see p106*), were plain and provided with long naves suitable for processions. **Il Gesù** (*see p124*) was ideal for the purposes of the Jesuits, as no architectural obstacles came between the preacher and his flock.

As the Counter-Reformation gathered pace, great cycles of decoration teaching the mysteries of the faith or inspiring the onlooker to identify with the sufferings of martyrs (as in the bloodthirsty frescoes of Santo Stefano Rotondo) began to appear.

Baroque

This austerity gave way to an exuberant, theatrical Baroque. It is to a great extent the endlessly inventive confections of this period that make Rome what it is today. Architects such as Giacomo della Porta and Domenico Fontana (1543-1607) set the scene for the real shapers of the Baroque: Gian Lorenzo Bernini, Francesco Borromini and Pietro da Cortona.

Bernini (1598-1680) virtually made the Roman Baroque his own, with his imaginative use of marble, bronze and stucco. He was jealously guarded by his Barberini family patrons, carrying out much of the decoration of the interior of St Peter's for the Barberini Pope Urban VIII.

Bernini said that quarrelsome, neurotic Borromini (1559-1667) 'had been sent to

For centuries Borromini was vilified; today he is recognised as one of the great masters of the period

Discover Borromini

A walking tour to illuminate the dark horse of the Baroque

Budget €120
Getting around Walking

If architect and sculptor Gian Lorenzo Bernini was the bright star of the Roman baroque, Francesco Borromini (1599-1667) was its troubled, brooding dark horse. There's no truth in the popular legend that the veiled Nile figure in Bernini's Four Rivers fountain in piazza Navona is recoiling in horror from Borromini's church of Sant'Agnese in Agone across the square (the statue predates the church), but rivalry between the two certainly kept Borromini firmly in the shadows for centuries. Now he's recognized as a true genius.

Sant'Andrea delle Fratte

Morning

A good starting point for getting to know Borromini is the exquisite **San Carlo alle Quattro Fontane** (*see p84*), a tiny church occupying the same surface area as one of the columns supporting the dome of St Peter's. A short walk downhill from here, **Palazzo Barberini** (*see p83*) is considered a Bernini masterpiece but in fact Borromini gave the building its fine proportions and glorious oval staircase when working with the first architect on the project, his uncle Carlo Maderno.

From Palazzo Barberini walk down to the homonymous piazza and up via Sistina. If you're peckish, side-track slightly to via della Panetteria for a fantastic ice-cream at **Il Gelato di San Crispino** (*see p81*).

On via Sistina, turn into the second street on the left, then right into via Capo le Case where one of Rome's least known architectural gems comes into view: **Sant'Andrea delle Fratte** with its belltower and dome. The contrast between the dome's convex and concave walls – a characteristic Borromini feature – is striking. Around the corner in via di Propaganda is another Borromini masterpiece: the chapel of the **Palazzo di Propaganda Fide.** To build this chapel Borromini ordered – probably with some satisfaction – the demolition of an existing one, erected only a few years earlier by Bernini. The chapel's façade dominates the building's elevation on the narrow street with great theatrical effect.

Palazzo Barberini

Afternoon

You'll need to do some winding through the narrow streets of the *centro storico* – perhaps stopping for a spot of lunch at **Ginger** (*see p99*) or **Armando al Pantheon** (*see p114*) – to reach the next stop on your Borromini tour: **Sant'Ivo alla Sapienza** (*see p110*). This small but grand church – built as the chapel of Rome University – stands at the end of a beautiful porticoed courtyard. From Sant'Ivo it's a short walk to the church of **Sant'Agnese in Agone** (*see p110*) in piazza Navona.

Borromini's **Oratorio dei Filippini** stands next to the **Chiesa Nuova** (*see p106*), its slightly concave façade embracing a large square off corso Vittorio Emanuele. To get here, take via dei Banchi Vecchi and walk as far as the piazza dell'Orologio (Clock Square), so-called because of the tower that dominates it. The tower marks the rear of the *oratorio* complex and is one of Borromini's most successful brick structures.

On the river Tiber beyond corso Vittorio Emanuele, the church of **San Giovanni dei Fiorentini** contains a plaque commemorating the architect, but it's unlikely that his remains are inside what some call his tomb. Stormy and tormented to the end, Borromini took his own life in the summer of 1667.

destroy architecture', and for centuries Borromini was vilified; today he is recognised as one of the great masters of the period, perhaps the greatest in the inventive use of ground plan and spatial effects (*see p295* Borromini). The most startling examples of his work are **San Carlo alle Quattro Fontane** (*see p84*) and **Sant'Ivo alla Sapienza** (*see p110*).

Like Bernini, Pietro da Cortona (1597-1669) created some of his greatest works for the Barberini popes. At Santa Maria della Pace he combined opposing convex forms that, curving sharply at the ends, are nearly flat in the middle. The result is overwhelmingly theatrical.

Throughout the Baroque period the patronage of papal families and religious orders sustained an explosion of architectural and artistic fervour. Several popes commissioned the decoration of St Peter's (Urban VIII, 1623-44); the colonnade in front of it (Alexander VII, 1655-67) and the layout of **piazza Navona** (*see p109*). Their cardinal nephews inspired lesser building schemes: the redecoration or restoration of existing churches, and private villas, gardens and palaces. The Jesuit church of

Obelisk dedicated to Guglielmo Marconi

Il Gesù, though begun in the 1560s, was completed decades later with a façade by Giacomo della Porta.

Neo-classicism and unification

During the 18th century the Baroque gained a rococo gloss, as demonstrated by Nicola Salvi's **Fontana di Trevi** (*see p78*) and Francesco de Sanctis' **Spanish Steps** (*see p92*). Giovanni Battista Piranesi imposed his neo-classical theories on the city in the later part of the 18th century, creating a striking tableau in **piazza dei Cavalieri di Malta** (*see p25*).

The French occupation of the city (1809-14) brought a flurry of Gallic town planning. Some plans – such as Giuseppe Valadier's magnificent reorganisation of **piazza del Popolo** (*see p97*) and the **Pincio** (*see p141*) – were carried out under French rule. Others were adopted after 1815 by the restored papacy.

In 1870 the city became capital of a united Italy, ruled by the Savoy dynasty, which sought to impose order on the chaotic cityscape, providing it with a road system and structures to accommodate the burgeoning bureaucracy... even if this meant razing entire medieval and Renaissance quarters in the process. **Piazza Vittorio** (*see p189*), Palazzo delle Esposizioni and the jingoistic **Vittoriano** monument (*see p64*) in piazza Venezia are fine examples of the period. Occasional relief from the pomposity comes in the shape of lovely Liberty (art nouveau) outcrops, such as the **Casina della civette** (*see p224* Villa Torlonia), the palazzo housing **Museo Hendrik Christian Andersen** (*see p144*), and the whole, extraordinary **Coppedè** district (*see p222*) around piazza Mincio in the northern suburbs.

20th-century and contemporary

During the Fascist period (1922-43) the expansion of Rome was given a push by several large-scale projects. One of the most impressive was Luigi Moretti's **Foro Italico** (*see p222*), a sports complex with two stadiums and an army of towering statues of naked athletes. To celebrate the 20th anniversary of the Fascist revolution, construction began on a whole new district, initially called E42 but later renamed Esposizione universale romana (**EUR** for short; *see p227*). It is one of the most striking examples of town planning anywhere in Europe.

With construction under way at EUR, Mussolini turned his attention to the *centro storico*: here, according to his Grand Plan, chunks of the medieval and Renaissance

A growing population with money to spend was to have dire effects on the capital's outskirts

urban fabric would be destroyed, making room for a network of boulevards to improve sight lines between major monuments. Thankfully, the outbreak of war stopped *il Duce* wreaking too much havoc. He did, however, manage to bludgeon the via dei Fori Imperiali through the ruins of ancient fora from the Colosseum to piazza Venezia.

During his rule, however, some of Rome's most interesting modern buildings were built, with a philosophy that was dubbed *razionalismo*, a blend of European functionalism with the elegance of Mediterranean/classical tradition. In the state-sponsored building spree of the 1920s and '30s, architects working in this style contributed some gems: post office buildings in via Marmorata by Adalberto Libera and in piazza Bologna by Mario Ridolfi, and Moretti's Casa della Gioventù in largo Ascianghi (all 1933-35) are masterpieces of the modern movement. By the 1930s, the *razionalisti* realised that they were propaganda pawns. Their last great works of the period were in the Città universitaria campus. Libera stayed on to design the Palazzo dei Congressi in EUR.

After the war, with Italians from all over the country drifting to the capital, a number of successful public-housing projects were developed. Economic prosperity in the 1950s allowed unfinished projects to be completed: **Termini railway station** was given a magnificent wave-like canopy, and building resumed in EUR. The prosperity fuelled many elegant modernist projects, including the sports venues built by Pier Luigi Nervi for the 1960 Olympics.

A growing population with money to spend was to have dire effects on the capital's outskirts, where property speculators had a zoning-free field day. From the 1960s to the '80s, high-rise blocks galloped across previously unspoilt countryside. Though the *centro storico* was spared atrocities, there was a distinct lack of anything new: work on the first major post-war building project within the Aurelian Walls (the **Ara Pacis** museum, *see p101*), only began in 2000.

The slump in new architecture came to an end as the new millennium dawned, with talented and original architects at work. Rome's **mosque**, one of the largest in Europe, was completed in 1995 to a design by postmodernist Paolo Portoghesi. In 2002 Renzo Piano's **Auditorium-Parco della Musica** (*see p273*) opened and has been a resounding success. Richard Meier's slick container for the Ara Pacis was inaugurated in 2006 to much trumpeting and a lot of criticism.

In the **Mattatoio** (*see p215*), the former slaughterhouse in Testaccio, the old holding pens and fridge units have been transformed into a MACRO exhibition space, a branch of the Academy of Fine Arts and an organic outlet.

The year 2010 saw the inauguration of Odile Decq's new building for **MACRO** (*see p222*) and Zaha Hadid's Stirling prize-winning **MAXXI** (*see p224*). Massimiliano Fuksas' 'Cloud' – the new **Centro Congressi Italia** in EUR – was inaugurated with much fanfare in 2016, though has been slow to swing into action. A plan to build a new stadium for the AS Roma football team has been dogged by political in-fighting.

▶ *For a glossary of architectural terms, see p331.*

MAXXI

Art

An aesthetic education

From the Renaissance through to the 19th century, an artist's education was not complete without a journey to Rome. The whole city was seen as an overflowing 'studio' with classical ruins and copious, ancient statues.

Few travellers today have such lofty artistic goals, but looking closely at the art of Rome still offers a stirring aesthetic experience – and a great education. Art in Rome embraces both quality and stunning chronological range. That the city displays art covering nearly 3,000 years is staggering; that almost all of it was produced right here even more so.

With so many artistic treasures to take in, visitors can find Rome overwhelming. Take it slowly, stick with aspects you particularly love, and enjoy Rome's unique continuum of past and present in your own chosen way.

Belvedere Torso in Vatican Museums

Art of the ancients

Although the art of Rome has furthered the needs of the Catholic Church for nearly two millennia, the single strongest influence has always been the weighty legacy of the ancient world. Ancient Rome harvested or created much of the best art of antiquity. Those who sacked or occupied the city – from Alaric in 410 to Napoleon in 1808 – pillaged much of this patrimony, but the fraction that survives continues to amaze.

Egyptian obelisks transported across the Mediterranean still mark key squares in Rome (*see p85* Obelisks) and, despite a lack of Greek originals, the miracle of Greek art can be studied and appreciated in scores of important Roman copies. These marbles – often copies of bronzes that have long since been destroyed – display the Greek flair for endowing the body with beauty, purpose and a sense of movement. The classical ideal, combining striking naturalism with idealised body types, offered a standard of beauty that was hard to ignore.

The classical ideal, combining striking naturalism with idealised body types, offered a standard of beauty that was hard to ignore

Although the most famous Greek sculpture in Rome is the *Ludovisi Throne* – in the Ludovisi family collection housed in Palazzo Altemps – many works are transitional in nature, between Greek and Roman. An outstanding example in this category is the hulking *Belvedere Torso* – a superhuman physique from about 50 BC that inspired Michelangelo – now housed in the Vatican Museums (*see p154*).

The Etruscans, the pre-Roman peoples who dominated central Italy from the sixth to the third century BC, produced an exuberant, violent and sensuous art. Villa Giulia (*see p144*) offers an extraordinary selection, including life-size terracotta sculptures from Veio and a tender terracotta sarcophagus of a married couple. Equally important is the Etruscan bronze work known as the *Lupa Capitolina* (the 'Capitoline She-Wolf'), which is in the Musei Capitolini (*see p60*).

Come the Romans

From the third century BC the Romans literally built upon this Greek and Etruscan legacy with an unprecedented construction boom. New structural techniques – notably the arch and poured-concrete technology – gave birth to daring and spacious buildings. The Romans were also responsible for monumental forms that blur the boundary between architecture and art, such as the triumphal arch ornamented with reliefs (those of Septimus Severus and Titus in the Forum, *see p67*; and Constantine's, *see p66*) and the independent column ornamented with a spiral band (Colonna di Traiano, *see p72*; Colonna di Marco Aurelio, *see p96*). A further Roman innovation on a smaller scale was the portrait bust, which recorded facial features of the great and the average with arresting honesty.

Much of the best classical art is now concentrated in a few major museums. The Palazzo Altemps (*see p108*), which contains the statue of the Gaul's Suicide, is an ideal first stop. The Palazzo Massimo alle Terme (*see p242*) houses important works of Roman painting and sculpture. The large collections of the Musei Capitolini feature the Dying Gaul and beautiful centaurs from Hadrian's Villa (*see p235*). Today the sheer size of the classical collection of the Vatican Museums (*see p154*) can be demoralising, and the galleries may seem a distraction in one's march towards the Sistine Chapel, but two centuries ago the Vatican's Pio Clementino sculpture gallery was undoubtedly the most famous museum in the world. Even today one sculpture there gives modern tourists the same frisson that countless other classical works imparted to 18th-century visitors: this is *Laocoön and His Sons* (AD c27-68), a Hellenistic sculpture showing a powerful man and his sons struggling for their lives against serpents. It remains perhaps the most dynamic statue in the whole history of art.

Holy inspiration

Christian art flourished in Rome after AD 313, when Emperor Constantine's Edict of Milan legitimised the new religion. Rome was transformed from a city of temples to one of churches. Little of the devotional apparatus of the newly recognised religion survives, but stunning mosaics decorate a number of venerable churches: including Santa Costanza (fourth century; *see p224*), Santa Maria Maggiore (fifth century; *see p191*), Santi Cosma e Damiano (sixth century; *see p73*), and Santa Prassede (ninth century; *see p184*). Two of the most atmospheric early churches are the austere, lovely Santa

Laocoön and His Sons in the Vatican Museums

Sabina (*see p212*), and San Clemente (*see p200*), with its 12th-century mosaics.

Later medieval art can be enjoyed in Santa Cecilia in Trastevere (*see p177*), which contains a ciborium (1283) by Arnolfo di Cambio (best known as the architect of the Duomo in Florence) and a pioneering fresco of the *Last Judgement* (1293) by **Pietro Cavallini** above the nun's choir. The little-known Cavallini – who perhaps deserves to rank with Giotto as an early initiator of the Renaissance – also impresses with his narrative mosaics (1291) in nearby Santa Maria in Trastevere (*see p169*).

From 1309 to 1377 the papacy was based in Avignon; Rome withered, and only a fraction of the population remained. Thus the Gothic is largely absent in the Eternal City. The lack of late-medieval art, however, is compensated for by the wealth of Renaissance, and particularly High Renaissance, art of the 15th and 16th centuries.

Laocoön and His Sons remains perhaps the most dynamic statue in the whole history of art

Renaissance begins in Rome

The definitive return of the papacy in 1420 permitted the Renaissance and its doctrine of humanism to take root and eventually flourish in the primary seat of classical glory.

Humanism was preoccupied with reviving the language and art of the ancient Greeks and Romans, and reconciling this pagan heritage with Christianity. Renaissance ideas began to leave their mark on the city with architecture based on ancient examples, and sculpture and painting that assimilated the grace and naturalism of the best classical statues. In 1455, on his deathbed, Pope Nicholas V informed his successors that 'noble edifices combining taste and beauty with imposing proportions would immensely conduce to the exaltation of the chair of St Peter'.

Nicholas' extant contribution to Vatican beautification – the little chapel of Nicholas V, frescoed by **Fra Angelico** and **Benozzo Gozzoli** (1447-79) – may be modest in the light of his ambitions, but it remains an extraordinary jewel of the early Renaissance. Later popes undertook grander campaigns: Sixtus IV (1471-84) engaged the greatest painters of the day – **Perugino**, **Botticelli**, **Ghirlandaio** and **Cosimo Rosselli** – to fresco the walls of his Sistine Chapel in 1481-82. And think what you may of the morals of the Borgia pope, Alexander VI, his taste in art was exquisite, as seen in the frescoes (1493-95) by **Pinturicchio** that perpetuate Perugino's sweet style throughout the many rooms of the Borgia Apartments (*see p154*).

Frescoes in Santa Maria sopra Minerva (Filippino Lippi, 1489)

Outside the Vatican the grace of 15th-century Florentine art can also be seen in the joyful and energetic frescoes (1489-93) of **Filippino Lippi** in the Caraffa chapel in the church of Santa Maria sopra Minerva (*see p114*).

If Michelangelo was unsurpassed in depicting the human body in complex poses, the Stanze show Raphael's superiority in arranging compositions

High Renaissance

In the 16th century art and architecture took a monumental turn. In painting, the human figure grew in relation to the pictorial field: the busy backgrounds of 15th-century art were eliminated. Sculptors took their cue from ancient statues, making the human body newly heroic. Florentine **Michelangelo** (1475-1564) first worked in Rome from 1496 to 1501 for clerics and businessmen. He carved his first *Pietà* (1499, now in St Peter's) for a French cardinal. Michelangelo positioned the dead Christ gracefully in his mother's lap, creating an eternal meditation on death.

Under Julius II (1503-13) papal patronage called ever greater artists to work on ever larger projects at the Vatican, shifting the centre of the Renaissance from Florence to Rome. Julius summoned Michelangelo back from Florence to begin work on a monumental tomb, a work destined for the choir of the old St Peter's and crammed with larger-than-life statues. The headstrong Julius soon changed his mind, insisting that the young sculptor paint the ceiling of the Sistine Chapel instead. Complaining bitterly that he was 'no painter', Michelangelo rapidly frescoed the ceiling (1508-11), retelling the first nine chapters of Genesis with a grandeur and solidity previously associated with sculpture.

Although a later campaign to fresco the chapel's altar wall produced the awe-inspiring *Last Judgement* (1534-41), the tomb for Julius limped to an unsatisfactory conclusion in the early 1540s in San Pietro in Vincoli (*see p158*), using the powerful *Moses* (c1515) as its centrepiece.

Julius initiated his most ambitious plan of all when he called upon **Donato Bramante**

Sacred Art

Ten of the best churches with jaw-dropping pieces

Santa Maria del Popolo *p98*
This 15th-century church has works by Pinturicchio (below right), Raphael and some massive Caravaggios.

Chiesa Nuova *p106*
Exuberant scenes by Pietro da Cortona dominate this 16th-century church, but there are some unexpected works by Flemish artist Peter Paul Rubens too.

Sant'Agostino *p110*
Caravaggio's startlingly beautiful *Madonna of the Pilgrims* (1604; below left) scandalised viewers with its realism.

San Luigi dei Francesi *p111*
Rome's French church has lovely frescoes of St Cecilia by Domenichino, and dramatic scenes from the life of St Matthew by Caravaggio.

Santa Maria sopra Minerva *p114*
Filippino Lippi's frescoes in the Carafa chapel are simply charming.

San Pietro *p158*
The hub of the Catholic Church contains surprisingly little original art (much of what you see is mosaic copy) but Michelangelo's *Pietà* (1499) is superb.

Santa Cecilia in Trastevere *p177*
Only part of the *Last Judgement* fresco by proto-renaissance dark horse Pietro Cavallini remains, but what there is, is spectacular.

Santa Prassede *p184*
This ninth-century church – a scale model of the first St Peter's – glimmers with splendid Byzantine mosaics.

Santa Maria della Vittoria *p191*
Bernini's dramatic *Ecstasy of St Theresa* statue (1652) is an ambivalent work, with the saint swooning in a fit of (spiritual?) passion.

Santi Quattro Coronati *p203*
A marvellous 13th-century fresco spins the spurious *Donation of Constantine* legend.

(1444-1514) to design a new basilica of St Peter's. The stateliness of Bramante's style inspired painters as well as other architects. The most influential of the former was **Raphael** (1483-1520).

Julius would not occupy the apartments of his dissolute Borgia predecessor; he insisted on a new suite of rooms – the so-called Stanze di Raffaello (*see p154*). These were decorated by Raphael starting in 1508. The presence of Michelangelo working next door on the Sistine ceiling was a spur to the young painter: the elegant *School of Athens* (1510-11) exemplifies the notion of the High Renaissance, with its re-creation of the philosophers of ancient Greece against a backdrop of imaginary architecture borrowed from Bramante.

If Michelangelo was unsurpassed in depicting the human body in complex poses, the *Stanze* show Raphael's superiority in arranging compositions. The latter's astonishingly swift development can be appreciated in a single room of the Vatican Pinacoteca. There, three masterful altarpieces – *The Coronation of the Virgin* (1505), *The Madonna of Foligno* (c1511) and *The Transfiguration* (c1518-20) – chart the amazing shift from a sweetness reminiscent of Perugino to a brooding, dramatic late style. In the same room, you can also take note of the lavish tapestries, designed by Raphael for the lower walls of the Sistine Chapel.

The Transfiguration (Raphael, 1518-20)

The Sack of Rome in 1527 halted the artistic boom of the High Renaissance, as frightened artists sought employment elsewhere. The spread of the Protestant Reformation prompted a more hardened, pessimistic spirit that gave preference to mannerist art, a style of exaggerated proportions and contorted poses that developed out of the mature work of Raphael and Michelangelo. Frescoes (c1545) by Raphael's assistant **Perino del Vaga** (1501-47) in the Castel Sant'Angelo (*see p161*) depict both hyper-elegant humans and statues, playing with the viewer's sense of what is real.

Going for Baroque

By the second half of the 16th century, the mannerist style had lost its energy. Baroque rescue came through the works of **Annibale Carracci** (1560-1609) of Bologna and the shocking naturalism of Michelangelo Merisi, better known as **Caravaggio** (1571-1610; *see p302*). Carracci, who sought a buoyant version of High Renaissance harmony, is best experienced at the Galleria Doria Pamphilj (*see p115*) which has a lovely *Flight into Egypt* (c1604). Carracci's contemporary, Caravaggio, left paintings throughout the city during his stormy career. These works, with their extreme *chiaroscuro*, can be seen in the churches of Sant'Agostino (*see p110*) and Santa Maria del Popolo (*see p98*). His masterpiece may be the *Calling of St Matthew* (c1599-1602) in the church of San Luigi dei Francesi (*see p111*).

The Galleria Borghese (*see p142*) houses a fine nucleus of Caravaggio paintings, from the coy secular works of his early years to the brooding religious canvases of his maturity, notably the powerful *David with the Head of Goliath* (c1609), in which the severed head is Caravaggio's self-portrait. The cruelty often depicted in Caravaggio's paintings mirrored his violent life, and altercations with police and patrons marked his Roman years. After losing a tennis match and killing his opponent, Caravaggio fled south. His bold style persisted for a generation, though, as witnessed in the Vatican Pinacoteca's extraordinary room of Baroque altarpieces by **Domenichino**, **Guido Reni** and **Nicolas Poussin**. Equally weighty Baroque altarpieces can be seen in the Pinacoteca of the Musei Capitolini (*see p60*), with **Guercino**'s *Burial of St Petronilla* (c1623) winning the prize.

The most faithful followers of Caravaggio's style were **Orazio Gentileschi** (1563-1639) and his daughter **Artemisia** (1593-1652). Artemisia had to endure male prejudice to pursue her career, and both artists left Rome, resurfacing together in London in the late 1630s to work for Charles I. Canvases by father and daughter can be seen in the Galleria Spada (*see p123*).

The consummate artist of the Roman Baroque, however, was primarily a sculptor: **Gian Lorenzo Bernini** (1598-1680). The confident energy inherent in Baroque art is revealed in Bernini's greatest religious sculpture: *The Ecstasy of St Theresa* (1647-52) in Santa Maria della Vittoria (*see p191*) brilliantly captures a split second of sensual rapture. The theatricality of such works as *Apollo and Daphne* (1622-25) in the Galleria Borghese (*see p142*) pushed back the boundaries of sculpture, capturing whole narratives in a frozen instant, and describing textures more vividly than any previous carver.

Similarly, the Galleria Doria Pamphilj (*see p115*) evokes the epoch with outstanding pictures in a magnificent setting. One small room forces a comparison of two portraits of the Pamphilj Pope Innocent X (1644-55): a bust by Bernini and a canvas by the Spaniard Diego Velázquez (the pope found the painting 'too truthful'). Both museums are awash with aristocratic atmosphere.

Art moves on

Subsequent generations insisted further upon the artistic unity of architecture, sculpture and painting pioneered by Bernini. Illusionistic ceiling decoration became more and more elaborate. Ceiling paintings – like those in the Palazzo Barberini and the church of Il Gesù (*see p124*) – depicted heavenly visions: assemblages of flying figures bathed in celestial light. Perhaps the most inventive practitioner of ceiling painting was **Andrea Pozzo** (1642-1709), a Jesuit painter, architect and stage designer. In Sant'Ignazio di Loyola (*see p114*), Pozzo painted both a fresco of the *Glory of St Ignatius Loyola* (c1685) on the vault of the nave and a false dome on canvas. The latter fools the viewer only from the ideal viewing point, which is marked by a disc on the floor. The Baroque style and the interest in illusionism limped on well into the 18th century.

The final great artistic movement born in Rome was neo-classicism, a nostalgic celebration of ancient Greek art, expressed in stark white statues and reliefs. **Antonio Canova** (1757-1822) created enormous, muscular statues like *Hercules and Lichas* (1796), which can be seen in the Galleria Nazionale d'Arte Moderna (*see p141*), dignified tombs in St Peter's, and plaster wall panels now on show at the Villa Torlonia (*see p224*).

Later movements of the 19th and 20th centuries can be seen at the Galleria Nazionale d'Arte Moderna (*see p141*) and the Galleria d'Arte Moderna Roma Capitale (*see p91*). For contemporary art, the MAXXI (*see p224*) and MACRO (*see p222*) galleries show that – at least as far as exhibiting goes – the city isn't entirely trapped in its past.

The Apotheosis of St Ignatius (Andrea Pozzo, 1685)

Plan

Accommodation

Once a city of polar-opposite accommodation options – exorbitantly expensive luxury hotels on the one hand, cheap *pensioni* of dubious cleanliness on the other – Rome now has the range of hotels you might expect in one of the most-visited destinations on the planet. But they are, on the whole, considerably more expensive than in other tourist hubs. For a dirt-cheap hotel bed these days – and even that concept is relative – you may have to accept a less salubrious part of town, or even an out-of-the-way convent. On the positive side, though, the general standard of accommodation has improved in recent years. At the top of the market, chic boutique offerings are creating fierce competition to the large, often soulless, luxury chains, while older-style mid-range hotels and *pensioni* have been forced to upgrade to keep pace. Small, stylish B&Bs are ever more numerous, and some great deals are to be found in this sector.

Hotel Eden

Where to stay

The area around Termini station in the **Esquilino** district has a slew of five-star hotels, but the vast majority in the area are cheap *pensioni* swarming with budget backpackers. It's not Rome's most picturesque corner, and almost certainly not what you dreamed of for your Roman holiday. Unless you snag the smart budget offerings at little gems such as **Casa Romana** (*see p314*) or the **Beehive** (*see p314*) it's well worth considering looking further afield, even if it costs you a bit more.

For atmosphere and convenience, go for a room in the historic centre, around **piazza Navona**, the **Pantheon** or **campo de' Fiori**. A shower between sightseeing and dinner and a

In the know
Price categories

We have included a selection of the best hotels in the city in four pricing categories. Categories are based on a standard double room per night including taxes and breakfast (not including seasonal offers or discounts).

Luxury	€400+
Expensive	€250-€400
Moderate	€100-€250
Budget	up to €100

wander (rather than the bus) back to the hotel afterwards can make all the difference.

Moving distinctly up the price range, Rome's top-end hotels have traditionally clustered around **via Veneto** – though bear in mind that it's not as lively as it was in its much-hyped *dolce vita* heyday, and there's a strong whiff of expense account in the air. The **Tridente** area near the Spanish Steps, hub of designer shopping, is full of elegant hotels at the upper end of the price scale.

If you're looking for some peace, the **Celio**, just beyond the Colosseum, offers a break from the frantic activity of the city centre while residential **Prati** offers some great deals just a short walk from the Vatican. The trendy neighbourhoods of **Monti** and **Trastevere** are becoming ever-more popular bases, thanks to their picturesque streets and abundance of bars and restaurants.

For atmosphere and convenience, go for a room in the historic centre – a shower between sightseeing and dinner can make all the difference

Booking a room

Always reserve a room well in advance, especially at peak times, which now means most of the year, with lulls during winter (January to March), and in the dog days of August. If you're coming at the same time as a major Christian holiday (Christmas or Easter) it's wise to book weeks, or even months, ahead and expect to pay full whack.

Many of Rome's hotels now model their pricing policy on low-cost airlines: the same room in an empty hotel may cost you less than half what it does in heavily booked high season. It is worth shopping around and contacting the hotels directly for deals.

Keats-Shelley Memorial House

Stars and standards

Italian hotels are classified on a star system, from one to five. The more stars, the more facilities a hotel will have, but bear in mind that a higher rating is no guarantee of friendliness, cleanliness or even decent service. B&Bs, on the other hand, can sometimes prove to be very

Luxury

Eden

Via Ludovisi 49, Villa Borghese (06 478121, www.dorchester collection.com). Bus 52, 53, 61, 63, 80, 83, 150, 160. ***Map*** *p138 K6.*

Originally opened in 1889, a recent 18-month restoration project has upped the Eden's opulence level to a new high. Glitzy gold and marble abound alongside the original art nouveau features and the result is one of Rome's most sumptuous hotels. The 98 rooms and suites are adorned with bespoke furniture, rich fabrics and Murano glass light fittings in a refined palette of warm neutrals. The brand new spa offers state-of-the-art treatments while the top-floor restaurant affords spectacular views across the Roman rooftops.

Hassler

Piazza Trinità dei Monti 6, Tridente (06 699 340, www. hotelhasslerroma.com). Metro Spagna/bus 117. ***Map*** *p89 K6.*

Looking down from the top of the Spanish Steps, the Hassler remains the *grande dame* of Rome's deluxe hotels – ageing a little, but still charming. With acres of polished marble and abundant chandeliers, the relentless luxury may make your head spin, but the attentiveness of the staff distinguishes this place from the impersonal service often found at Rome's top hotels. A stay in one of the 92 rooms includes top-notch amenities (including a spa, Michelin-starred restaurant and several bars) as well as spectacular views over the Roman rooftops.

JK Place Roma

Via Monte d'Oro 30, Tridente (06 982 634, www.jkroma.com). Metro Spagna/bus 70, 81, 117, 492, 628, 913. ***Map*** *p89 H7.*

Art-deco-inspired JK Place opened in 2013 following its sister branches in Florence and Capri. The elegant, townhouse feel, complete with original fireplaces, wooden bookshelves and leather-bound chairs, is far more intimate than many of the sprawling luxury hotels usually found in Rome, and the 23 rooms and seven suites all offer wireless internet and bucketfuls of opulent charm. The lack of outside space is compensated for by the excellent location just a short walk from the Spanish Steps.

Portrait Suites

Via Bocca di Leone 23, Tridente (06 6938 0742, www. lungarnocollection.com/portrait-roma). Metro Spagna/bus 117, 628, 913. ***Map*** *p89 J6.*

Portrait Suites is one of the luxury boutique hotels owned by fashion designer Salvatore Ferragamo. Black and white photos and memorabilia from the designer's archives decorate the hallways, yet the rooms themselves carry little clue of the hotel's fashion pedigree (though eagle-eyed fans might spot the designer's *gancino* emblem on the curtains). A black-and-slate colour scheme is offset with touches of pink and lime, and the 14 studios and suites all have spacious marble bathrooms, as well as walk-in wardrobes and even a glamorous kitchenette. Breakfast is served in the rooms or outside on the spectacular terrace.

Rome Cavalieri

Via Alberto Cadlolo 101, Suburbs: Monte Mario (06 35091, romecavalieri.com). Bus 913.

Although situated a little way out of the action, the Cavalieri's majestic position on top of the leafy Monte Mario hill north of the Vatican is worth the extra travel time (there is a free shuttle bus for guests), especially if you like to spend time away from the bustle of central Rome. However, with almost 400 rooms and suites, this is more about palatial extravagance than intimate escape. Amenities are what you would expect from a hotel of this grandeur: three swimming pools, a full spa and fitness centre and Rome's only three Michelin-star restaurant, La Pergola (*see p224*) to name but a few.

Villa Spalletti Trivelli

Via Piacenza 4, Quirinale (06 4890 7934, www.villaspalletti.it). Bus 40, 60, 64, 70, 71, 117, 170, H. ***Map*** *p79 L8.*

The aristocratic Spalletti Trivelli clan has turned its family home – with views across a little park to the *manica lunga* of the Quirinale palace – into a sumptuously elegant 12-room hotel with such high-class extras as an historic library with a preservation order, a formal garden where breakfast or *aperitivi* can be served, and a marvellous spa in the basement. Some of the large rooms can be linked together to form immense suites. Service is charmingly discreet; and there's a chef on hand to whip up special meals on request. Across the garden, two large and similarly elegant suites offer all the same services plus self-catering facilities and gorgeous private terraces.

Expensive

Crossing Condotti

Via Mario de' Fiori 28, Tridente (06 6992 0633, www. crossingcondotti.com). Metro Spagna/bus 117. ***Map*** *p89 J6.*

A short stroll from Prada, Bulgari and other fashion heavyweights, Crossing Condotti is remarkably central. The owner's gorgeous antiques are set against a cool contemporary background, and attentive staff are unfailingly helpful. It is more Roman hideaway than fully fledged hotel, though; there are just eight rooms and public spaces are limited to a handy kitchenette with coffee-making facilities and a fridge stocked with (free) soft drinks.

Donna Camilla Savelli

Via Garibaldi 27, Trastevere (06 588 861, hoteldonnacamilla savelli.com). Bus 115, H/tram 8. ***Map*** *p166 F11.*

This former convent, designed by Borromini, has been transformed into an upmarket hotel by an Italian chain – though there's still a slight air of nunnery around the echoing corridors. The position – in a quiet corner beneath the Gianicolo hill but a short stroll from Trastevere's lively alleyways – is great, there's a pretty garden, and the view from the roof terrace is quite spectacular. A few of the 78 rooms are very pokey so specify your needs when booking.

Grand Hotel Via Veneto
*Via Veneto 155, via Veneto (06 487 881, www.ghvv.it). Bus 52, 53, 61, 63, 80, 83, 150, 160. **Map** p138 L5.*
Award-winning Grand Hotel Via Veneto is just as flashy as you'd expect, with an art deco theme worked to the hilt in the striking public spaces, and given a slightly more contemporary modernist bent in the 116 bedrooms and suites, even the smallest of which are spacious by Rome standards. The huge bathrooms are done out in Carrara marble and the walls are dotted with the hotel's own art collection. The street-level bar-restaurant Time buzzes at cocktail hour with great *aperitivi* and there is also a 500sq m wellness centre with hammam.

Hotel Art
*Via Margutta 56, Tridente (06 328 711, www.hotelart.it). Metro Spagna/bus 117. **Map** p89 J5.*
On a street famed for its arty, crafty studios, the Hotel Art sticks to its theme throughout. The lobby area – with white pods serving as check-in and concierge desks – sets the modern tone; only the ceiling retains a touch of the classic (the building was once a chapel). Hallways are in acidic shades of orange, yellow, green and blue, while the rooms themselves are decorated in a serene palette of neutrals, with parquet floors and chunky wood furniture. Free Wi-Fi (and a wireless keyboard) can be found in each of the 46 rooms.

Inn at the Roman Forum
*Via degli Ibernesi 30, Monti (06 6919 0970, www.theinnattheromanforum.com). Metro Cavour/bus 51, 75, 85, 87, 117. **Map** p182 L10.*
The location of this boutique hotel, close to the Forum but on a picturesque street that is comfortably off the tourist trail, gives the place an exclusive feel. The 12 rooms are a suave combination of rich fabrics and antiques; the spacious deluxe double rooms – some of which have fireplaces – have canopied beds and marble bathrooms. Breakfast is served on the roof terrace or in a cosy room with open fire in the winter. An ancient *cryptiporticus* has been excavated on the ground floor.

Sole al Pantheon
*Piazza della Rotonda 63, Pantheon (06 678 0441, www.hotelsolealpantheon.com). Bus 30, 40, 46, 62, 64, 70, 81, 87, 130, 190, 492, 628, 916. **Map** p104 H8.*
Dating back to the 15th century, this – management will tell you – is the oldest hotel in Europe. The 32 rooms have been painstakingly restored and are fresh and uncluttered, with tiled floors and frescoes. All bathrooms have whirlpool baths. Ask for one of the rooms at the front for superb views over the Pantheon; otherwise console yourself by seeking out the glorious roof terrace, where breakfast is served in the warmer months.

Moderate

Abruzzi
*Piazza della Rotonda 69, Pantheon (06 9784 1351, www.hotelabruzzi.it). Bus 30, 40, 46, 62, 64, 70, 81, 87, 130, 190, 492, 628, 916. **Map** p104 H8.*
The splendid location is really this hotel's selling point. Most of its 26 rooms have breathtaking views of the Pantheon (specify that you want a view when you book), and all are outfitted in bright white decor with splashes of vivid colour. Guests are provided with a complimentary smartphone with unlimited local and international calls. Breakfast is taken nearby, in a café in piazza della Rotonda.

Capo d'Africa
*Via Capo d'Africa 54, Celio (06 772 801, www.hotelcapodafrica.com). Metro Colosseo/bus 51, 75, 81, 85, 87, 117, 118, 673/tram 3. **Map** p198 N12.*
Artfully arranged bamboo? Tick. Pastel armchairs? Tick. The Capo d'Africa is perfect for the design-conscious, and the hotel's location, on a quiet street near the Colosseum, is another thing in its favour. The 65 rooms are spacious and comfortable, and the rooftop breakfast room and terrace has knock-out views of the Colosseum and the fourth-century basilica dei Santi Quattro Coronati.

Daphne Trevi
*Via degli Avignonesi 20, Fontana di Trevi (06 8953 8471, www.daphne-rome.com). Metro Barberini/bus 52, 53, 62, 63, 80, 83, 85, 160, 492. **Map** p79 L7.*
Owned by dynamic Italo-American couple Elyssa and Alessandro, Daphne Trevi sets the standard for inexpensive but stylish accommodation in Rome. The hotel is decorated in modern, earthy tones throughout, and the seven tastefully furnished bedrooms have high ceilings, terracotta or parquet floors and decent-sized bathrooms. Guests are lent a smartphone for the duration of their stay and staff are endlessly helpful. Adjoining rooms can be arranged to create a significant range of family and group accommodation.

Hotel Santa Maria
*Vicolo del Piede 2, Trastevere (06 589 4626, www.hotelsantamariatrastevere.it). Bus 23, 280, H/tram 8. **Map** p166 G11.*
Just off piazza Santa Maria in Trastevere, the Santa Maria stands on the site of a 16th-century convent. Each of the 19 bedrooms has a tiled floor, colourful decor and a spacious bathroom, and they all open on to a charming, sunny central courtyard planted with orange trees. Complimentary bicycles are available for guests to use for exploring Trastevere's winding alleys.

Teatro Pace
Via del Teatro Pace 33, piazza Navona (06 687 9075, www.

hotelteatropace.com). Bus 30, 40, 46, 62, 64, 70, 81, 87, 130, 492, 628, 916. ***Map*** *p104 G8.*
This 16th-century former cardinal's residence lies down a cobbled alley near piazza Navona. An impressive Baroque stone spiral staircase winds up four floors (no lift). The 23 rooms are spacious and elegantly decorated with wood floors, heavy drapes and marble bathrooms. The original, wood-beamed ceilings are intact in all rooms, but higher on the top two floors. Breakfast is served in the rooms.

Torre Colonna

Via delle Tre Cannelle 18, Capitoline (06 8360 0192, www.torrecolonna.it). Bus 40, 60, 64, 70, 117, 170, H. ***Map*** *p68 K9.*
Quirky little Torre Colonna is just what the name implies: a medieval tower. Five stylish, comfortable bedrooms, with painted wood-beamed ceilings and jaunty artwork, are stacked one on top of the other and crowned with a leafy roof terrace complete with hot tub and a dramatic view across a huge swathe of the *centro storico*. Miraculously, they've also managed to squeeze a lift into this difficult space. The Forum and Palatine are short strolls away. Owner Sarah Hawker and her English-speaking staff are fabulously informative and helpful.

Budget

Arco del Lauro

Via dell'Arco de' Tolomei 27, Trastevere (06 9784 0350, www.arcodellauro.it). Bus 23, 125, 280, 780, H/tram 8. ***Map*** *p166 H12.*
On a picturesque Trastevere backstreet, Arco del Lauro has four rooms, all with private bathrooms, decorated in modern, fresh neutrals. Budget accommodation is hard to find in chi-chi Trastevere, so the Arco del Lauro, with its airy and spotlessly clean rooms and free Wi-Fi, is all the more of a find. Breakfast is taken in a bar in a nearby *piazza*.

Beehive

Via Marghera 8, Esquilino (06 4470 4553, www.the-beehive.com). Metro Termini/bus 40, 64, 75, 492, 910, H. ***Map*** *p182 O7.*
American owners Steve and Linda Brenner mix design-icon furnishings with reasonable rates and basic amenities, to create a 'youth hostel meets boutique hotel' vibe with both dormitory beds and private rooms scattered throughout the main building and in equally stylish nearby structures. All have internet access, air-conditioning or ceiling fans and use of the communal areas including the sunny garden with comfy patio. Breakfast (at an extra cost) is served in their own organic restaurant.

Casa Romana

Via dei Mille 41a, Esquilino (329 228 0626, www.myromeapartment.com). Metro Termini/bus 40, 64, 75, 492, 910, H. ***Map*** *p182 P7.*
Simply stylish, this three-room B&B hideaway not far from Termini station offers excellent facilities for this price bracket and each room has internet and air-conditioning. The welcome is friendly, the breakfast is excellent and owner Fulvia's many years of experience in the travel sector make her expert advice consistently spot-on.

The Beehive

Colors

Via Boezio 31, Prati (06 687 4030, www.colorshotel.com). Metro Ottaviano/bus 23, 34, 40, 49, 492, 982, 990. ***Map*** *p150 E6.*
A short walk from St Peter's and the Vatican Museums, Colors offers bright, clean dormitory and hotel accommodation that's well above the average quality for this price bracket. The first two floors, decorated in zingy colours, have self-catering kitchen facilities, with cornflakes and coffee provided for guests to make their own breakfast. More neutral tones have been used in the superior rooms on the third floor (all with private bathroom, flat-screen TV, air-conditioning and breakfast). There's a sunny terrace, and members of staff are multilingual and very friendly.

La Finestra sul Colosseo

Via Labicana 72, Monti & Esquilino (389 126 4301, www.lafinestrasulcolosseo.com). Metro Colosseo or Manzoni/bus 51, 85, 87, 117/tram 3. ***Map*** *p182 O11.*
The very white, very stylish accommodation in this five-room B&B is surprisingly spacious for Rome, and the well-equipped, mosaic-tiled bathrooms are similarly large. On a busy artery leading up to the Colosseum, the B&B lives up to its name: two of the rooms do have windows overlooking the ancient arena. All rooms have internet, air-conditioning and striking arched brick ceilings and the price includes breakfast at a nearby café.

Pensione Panda

Via della Croce 35, Tridente (06 678 0179, www.hotelpanda.it). Metro Spagna/bus 117, 301, 628, 913. ***Map*** *p89 J6.*
Panda's excellent location, just west of the Spanish Steps, is its main selling point. Rooms are very basic but clean; ask for one of the more recently renovated rooms, which have terracotta floors and high, wood-beamed ceilings. There's no lift and you'll have to go elsewhere for your morning cappuccino, but bargains in this area are hard to come by and Panda's 28 rooms are usually booked solid in high season.

Getting Around

ARRIVING & LEAVING

By air

Rome has two major airports: Fiumicino, about 30km (18 miles) west of the city, handles scheduled flights; Ciampino, 15km (9 miles) south-east of the city, is for low-cost airlines and for charter flights.

Aeroporto Leonardo Da Vinci, Fiumicino *Via dell'Aeroporto di Fiumicino 320 (06 65 951, information 06 65 951, www.adr.it). **Open** 24hrs daily.*
There's an express rail service between Fiumicino airport and Termini railway station (run by **Trenitalia**, *see p316*). It takes 31mins and runs every 30mins from 6.23am until 10.35pm daily (5.35am-10.35pm back to Fiumicino). Tickets in either direction cost €14. Note that at the Termini end, the airport train departs from platform 23 or 24, a good 10-min walk from the main concourse; tickets bought at the departure platforms cost €15. For security reasons, you must have a ticket to access the platform area.

The regular service from Fiumicino takes 25-40mins, and stops at Trastevere, Ostiense, Tuscolana and Tiburtina stations. Trains leave about every 20mins (less often on Sun) between 5.57am and 11.27pm (5.05am-10.33pm back to Fiumicino). Tickets cost €11.

You can buy tickets for both these services with cash or card from automatic machines in the airport lobby and rail stations, and the airport *tabacchi*. Some carriages have wheelchair access (*see p322*). You must stamp your ticket in the machines on the platform before boarding.

SIT (06 591 6826, www.sitbusshuttle.it) runs frequent buses from Fiumicino to Termini railway station (in front of the Hotel Royal Santina on via Marsala, Termini exit near platform 1, 8.30am-12.30am) and vice versa (5am-8.30pm). Tickets cost €6 each way.

Terravision (www.terravision.eu; journey time 55mins) covers the same route, and leaves from via Giolitti (*map p182 O8*, Termini exit near platform 24); tickets booked online cost €4 one way; bought on the bus, they cost €6.

A **COTRAL** (www.cotralspa.it) night bus service runs between Fiumicino (Terminal C) and Termini and Tiburtina railway stations in Rome. Tickets cost €5 from newsstands or €7 on the bus. Buses leave Tiburtina at 12.30am, 1.15am, 2.30am and 3.45am, stopping at Termini railway station 10mins later. Departures from Fiumicino are at 1.15am, 2.15am, 3.30am and 5am. Neither Termini nor Tiburtina are attractive places at night, so it's advisable to get a taxi from there to your final destination.

Aeroporto GB Pastine, Ciampino *Via Appia Nuova 1650 (06 65 951, www.adr.it). **Open** 24hrs daily.*
The most hassle-free way to get into town from Ciampino is to take the **Terravision** coach service (www.terravision.eu) to Termini station (journey time 45mins). Buses leave from outside the arrivals hall after each arrival. Buses from Termini to Ciampino leave from via Giolitti (*see above*). This is a dedicated service for the low-cost airlines, so you will need to show your ticket or boarding pass. Bus tickets (€4 online, €6 at the airport) can be booked online, or bought (cash only) in the arrivals hall at Ciampino or at the Terravision office in the Termini forecourt (next to Benetton) or on the bus.

SIT Bus Shuttle (www.sitbusshuttle.it) also does the Termini (via Marsala, *map p182 O7*) to Ciampino route (€4 one way). Tickets can be purchased on the bus or online.

Alternatively, **Schiaffini** buses (800 700 805, www.romeairportbus.com) runs a service between the airport and Termini (€4.90 one way). Buy tickets on board the bus, which leaves from in front of the arrivals hall; at Termini, it departs from via Giolitti. The same bus goes to Ciampino station from where frequent trains depart for Termini; this costs €1.20.

COTRAL (www.cotralspa.it) buses run regularly between the airport and Anagnina metro station (€1.20 one way), between the airport and Termini station (€3.90 one way) and between the airport and Ciampino town's railway station (€1.20 one way). The onward trains from Ciampino station to Termini cost €1.30.

After the last bus has departed, getting into the city is well-nigh impossible, as taxis don't bother to pass by the airport. If you are arriving late, phone ahead and organise a taxi before your arrival (*see p319*).

Major airlines

Alitalia *89 2010, www.alitalia.it.*
British Airways *reservations 02 6963 3602, www.ba.com.*
Easyjet *199 201 841, www.easyjet.com.*
Ryanair *899 552 589, www.ryanair.com.*

By bus

The long-distance bus station in Rome is **Autostazione Tibus**, an easy walking distance from Stazione Tiburtina, in largo Guido Mazzoni. Most services terminate outside these (metro) stations: Saxa Rubra (routes north); Cornelia, Ponte Mammolo and Tiburtina (north and east); Anagnina and Laurentina (routes south). For more details, *see p318*.

By train

Mainline trains are operated by **Ferrovie dello Stato (FS)/Trenitalia** (892 021, www.trenitalia.it). Most long-distance trains arrive at Termini, the hub of Rome's transport network (and its pickpockets, so beware). Night trains arrive at Tiburtina or Ostiense, both some way from the *centro storico*. If you arrive after midnight, take a taxi.

Some daytime trains bypass Termini, while others stop at more than one station in Rome.

Stazione Ostiense *Piazzale dei Partigiani, Testaccio. Metro Piramide/bus 30Exp, 80Exp, 83, 175, 280, 719, 9N. **Map** p210 K17.*

Stazione Piazzale Flaminio (Roma Nord) *Piazzale Flaminio, Veneto & Borghese. Metro Flaminio/bus 61, 89, 120, 150, 160, 490, 491, 495, C31N, 25N/tram 2. **Map** p138 H4.*

Stazione Termini *Piazza dei Cinquecento, Esquilino. See above Transport to Termini. **Map** p182 O7.*

Stazione Tiburtina *Circonvallazione Nomentana, Suburbs: south. Metro Tiburtina/bus 71, 111, 120, 135, 163, 168, 211, 309, 409, 443, 448, 490, 491, 492, 495, 649, C3, 2N, 17N, 23N.*

Stazione Trastevere *Piazzale Biondo. Bus 170, 228, 719, 766, 773, 774, 780, 781, 786, 871, H, C3, 8N, 14N, 16N/tram 3, 8.*

> **In the know**
> **Transport to Termini**
>
> For convenience, we have indicated 'Transport to Termini' in the listings in this guide, as all of the following services pass by (or terminate at) Termini rail station.
>
> **Metro Termini**; Repubblica is also within easy walking distance.
>
> **Buses** 16, 38, 40Exp, 64, 70, 71, 75, 82, 85, 90Exp, 92, 105, 150, 170, 175, 217, 310, 360, 590, 649, 714, 910, C2, C3, H, M.
>
> **Night buses** 2N, 5N, 7N, 8N, 9N, 13N, 15N.
>
> **Trams** 5, 14.

Trains & tickets

For bookings and information on Italian rail services, see **Trenitalia** (892 021, 199 166 177 from mobiles, 24hrs daily, www.trenitalia.it). Tickets can be bought at stations (over the counter or from machines; both accept cards), from travel agents with an FS sign, or online; many trips booked online are ticketless (*see right*). Under-12s pay half fare; under-4s travel free. For wheelchair access, *see p322*.

Train timetables can be purchased at *edicole* (newsstands) but are best checked online. Slower trains (*espressi*, *regionali* and *regionali veloci*) are cheap; faster services – InterCity (IC), EuroCity (EC), Eurostar Italia (ES) and the new super-fast Alta Velocità (AV) – are closer to European norms. Advance seat reservation is automatic on most faster services; check and obtain reservations at peak times to avoid standing in packed corridors. If your plans change, partial refunds are given (phone Trenitalia).

Queues at Termini ticket desks can be lengthy; speed things up by using one of the many automatic ticket machines (all accept cards). You'll often find an unofficial 'helper' by the machines, keen to show you how it's done for a euro or so; if they seem threatening, report them to the station police.

Trenitalia's Ticketless service allows you to book tickets with a card online (www.trenitalia.it) or by phone up to 10mins before the train's departure time. Either way, you'll be provided with a carriage and seat number, and a booking code. The service is available on all AV, ES and some IC trains. Seat reservation is obligatory for all passengers using this service.

Note: with paper tickets, you *must* stamp your ticket and supplements in the yellow machines at the head of the platform, before boarding. You risk being fined if you don't.

PUBLIC TRANSPORT

Rome's transport is operated by **Atac** (06 57 003, www.atac.roma.it). The bus, tram, metro and urban train services of the city centre and inner suburbs are relatively easy to use and as efficient as the traffic-choked streets allow. Pickpocketing is a problem on buses and metros, particularly major tourist routes, notably the 64 and 40 Express between Termini and the Vatican.

Children travel free on Rome's city transport until their tenth birthday; older children pay the full price for single-journey and one- or three-day bus passes.

Information

Atac's website has a handy route-planner for bus and metro travel, and detailed downloadable transport maps.

For real-time information on bus movements as you wait at a stop, go to muovi.roma.it and key in the stop ID number (a five-digit code at the bottom left corner of the information panel); alternatively key in the bus number for which you need information.

Tickets

The same tickets are valid on all city bus, tram and metro lines, whether operated by Trambus, MetRo or regional transport authority COTRAL (*see p230*), but not on airport services (*see p315*). Tickets must be bought before boarding, and are available from

Rome Metro

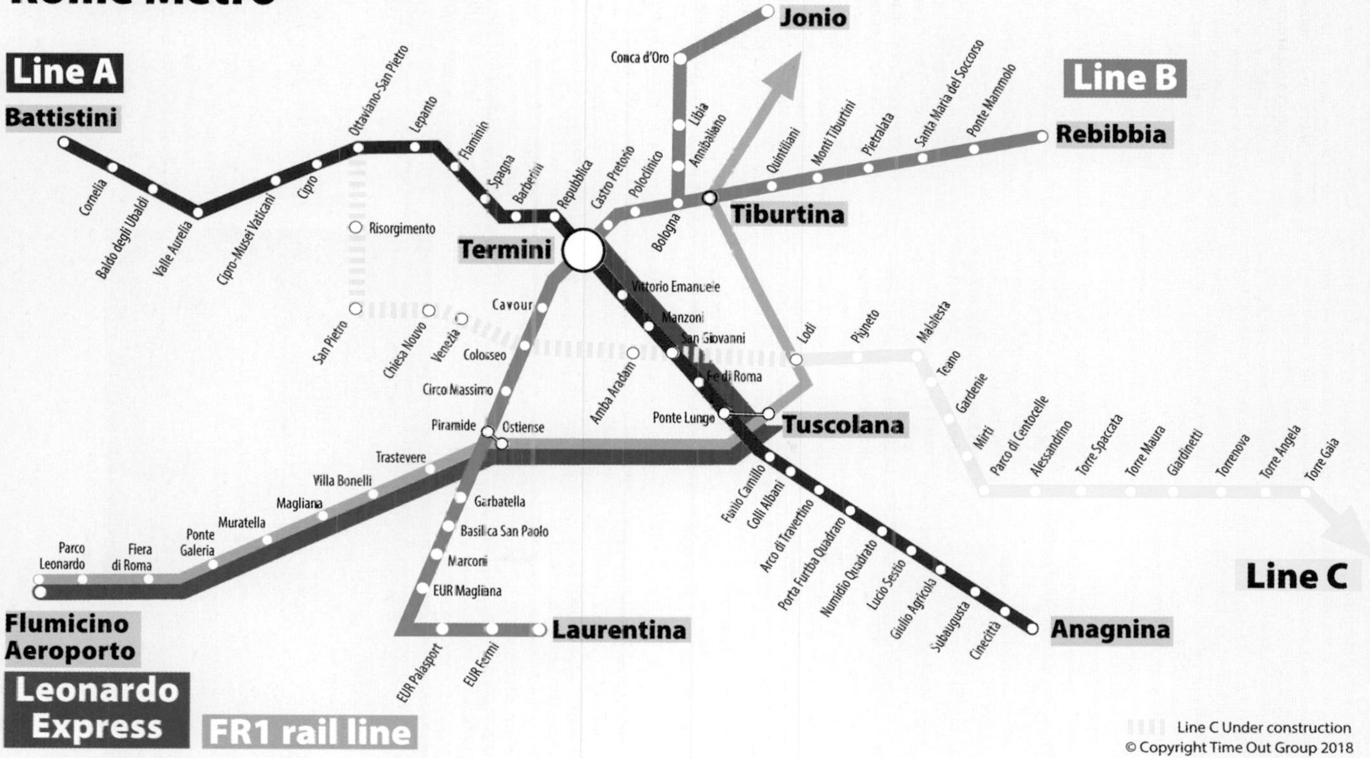
Line A
Battistini
Cornelia
Baldo degli Ubaldi
Valle Aurelia
Cipro-Musei Vaticani
Cipro
Ottaviano-San Pietro
Lepanto
Flaminio
Spagna
Barberini
Repubblica
Termini
Vittorio Emanuele
Manzoni
San Giovanni
Re di Roma
Ponte Lungo
Furio Camillo
Colli Albani
Arco di Travertino
Porta Furba Quadraro
Numidio Quadrato
Lucio Sestio
Giulio Agricola
Subaugusta
Cinecittà
Anagnina
Line B
Rebibbia
Ponte Mammolo
Santa Maria del Soccorso
Pietralata
Monti Tiburtini
Quintiliani
Tiburtina
Bologna
Policlinico
Castro Pretorio
Cavour
Colosseo
Circo Massimo
Piramide
Ostiense
Garbatella
Basilica San Paolo
Marconi
EUR Magliana
EUR Palasport
EUR Fermi
Laurentina
Jonio
Conca d'Oro
Libia
Annibaliano
Line C
Risorgimento
San Pietro
Chiesa Nuovo
Venezia
Amba Aradam
Lodi
Pigneto
Malatesta
Teano
Gardenie
Mirti
Parco di Centocelle
Alessandrino
Torre Spaccata
Torre Maura
Giardinetti
Torrenova
Torre Angela
Torre Gaia
Tuscolana
Trastevere
Villa Bonelli
Magliana
Muratella
Ponte Galeria
Fiera di Roma
Parco Leonardo
Flumicino Aeroporto
Leonardo Express
FR1 rail line
Line C Under construction
© Copyright Time Out Group 2018

Atac ticket machines, information centres and all *tabacchi* (*see p328*). Newer buses have ticket dispensers on board, requiring exact change.

BIT (*biglietto integrato a tempo*): valid for 100mins, during which you can take an unlimited number of city buses, plus a metro trip; €1.50.

ROMA 24H: valid for one day, until midnight, and covers the urban network; €7

ROMA 72H: 3-day pass, covering all bus and metro routes, and local mainline trains (second class) to Ostia; €18. (Before purchasing, consider whether the 3 day Roma Pass might not be better value; *see p57*.)

BIRG (*biglietto integrato regionale giornaliero*): valid for 1 day on rail journeys in the Lazio region. Depending on the zones covered, it costs €2.50-€10.50, and is valid on metro, buses and local mainline trains (second class), but not Fiumicino airport lines.

CIS (*carta integrata settimanale*): valid for 7 days; it covers all bus routes and the metro system, including the lines to Ostia; €24.

Abbonamento mensile: valid for unlimited travel on the entire metropolitan transport system during the calendar month in which the ticket was bought; €35.

Note: when you get on, you *must* stamp tickets in the machines on board.

Under-10s travel free; older kids have to pay the adult fare, as must pensioners. Discounts for students, the disabled and pensioners are only available for residents. Fare-dodging is common, but if caught without a validated ticket, you'll be fined €51 on the spot, or €101 if you pay later at a post office.

Buses

Buses are by far the best way to get around the city for tourists. Bus routes are added or suspended and numbers change with some regularity: regularly updated bus maps can be bought at news kiosks. The Atac website (*see above*) has a journey planner and maps to download.

Regular bus services run 5.30am-midnight daily, every 10-45mins, depending on the route. The doors for boarding (usually front and rear) and alighting (usually centre) are clearly marked. A sign at each bus stop displays the lines and routes they take.

Note that the 'Express' buses make few stops along their route: check before boarding so you don't get whisked past your destination.

A small fleet of electric minibuses also serves the centre, navigating *centro storico* alleys too narrow to accommodate regular buses. Only bus 117 operates from piazza del Popolo to piazza San Giovanni. The main stops are piazza di Spagna, via Nazionale, via Cavour and Colosseo.

Mosaics at Spagna Metro Station

Metro

Rome has three metro lines. Line A runs from south-east to north-west; Line B runs from EUR to the north-eastern suburbs; the interchange is beneath Termini mainline station. Line C runs from the eastern suburbs as far as Lodi, but will eventually link with Line A at San Giovanni and with Line B at Colosseo. *See map p317*.

Trams

Tram routes mainly serve suburban areas. An express tram service – no.8 – links largo Argentina to Trastevere and the western suburbs. The first stop is now in via delle Botteghe Oscure, on the corner with piazza Venezia.

Suburban transport

Atac's suburban railway lines are integrated with local lines of the Trenitalia (the state railway). Regular bus, tram and metro tickets are valid on trains as far as the stations in red on the *metro e ferrovie metropolitane* map. COTRAL coaches cover more distant destinations.

Tour buses

The red **City Sightseeing Roma** (www.roma.city-sightseeing.it) buses can be seen throughout the city (9.30am-7.40pm daily), taking in the major basilicas and pilgrim sites. Options include 24, 48 or 72hr tickets. A 24hr stop-and-go ticket is €28 (reductions €14, free under-5s). Wheelchairs welcome.

The **Roma Cristiana** service (06 698 961 www.operaromanapellegrinaggi.org/it/roma-cristiana/open-bus) departs from Termini and St Peter's regularly through the day (9.30am-6.30pm daily). Tickets can be bought on board, at Termini, San Giovanni in Laterano or at piazza Pia near St Peter's. A 24hr stop-and-go ticket costs €20 (under-10s free).

TAXIS

Licensed taxis are painted white and have a meter. Touts are rife at Termini and other major tourist magnets; ignore them if you don't want to risk an extortionate fare.

Fares & surcharges

When you pick up a taxi at a rank or hail one in the street, the meter should read zero. As you set off, it will indicate the minimum fare – currently €3 (€4.50 on Sun and public holidays; €6.50 10pm-7am).

Each kilometre (half mile) after that is €1.10. The first piece of luggage put in the boot is free, then it's €1 per piece. Tariffs outside the GRA, Rome's major ring road, are much higher. There's a 10% discount for trips to hospitals, and for women travelling alone 10pm-6am.

Fixed airport tariffs from anywhere inside the Aurelian walls (ie most of the *centro storico*) are €48 to/from Fiumicino; €30 to/from Ciampino. This is for up to four people and includes luggage: don't let taxi drivers tell you otherwise.

Most of Rome's taxi drivers are honest; if you do suspect you're being fleeced, take down the driver's name and number from the metal plaque inside the car's rear door. The more ostentatiously you do this, the more likely you are to find the fare returning to its proper level. Report complaints to the drivers' co-operative (phone number on the outside of each car) or, in serious cases, the police (*see p326*).

Taxi ranks

Ranks are indicated by a blue sign with 'Taxi' written on it in white. In the centre, there are ranks at largo Argentina, the Pantheon, piazza Venezia, piazza San Silvestro, piazza Sonnino (Trastevere), piazza di Spagna and Termini station.

Phone cabs

When you phone for a taxi, you'll be given the taxi code-name (always a location followed by a number) and a time, as in *'Bahama 69, in tre minuti'* ('Bahamas 69, in three minutes'). There's a set call fee of €3.50 from 6am until 10pm Mon-Sat; €4.50 Sun and holidays; €6.50 from 10pm until 6am after which radio taxis start the meter from the moment your phone call is answered. There's a city-run single phone cabs service: 06 0609. Or else try one of the companies below.

Cooperativa Autoradio Taxi Roma 06 3570, www.3570.it.

Cooperativa Samarcanda 06 5551, www.samarcanda.it.

Società la Capitale Radio Taxi 06 49 94.

Citysightseeing Roma at piazza Venezia

DRIVING

Think twice before bringing a vehicle to Rome. Most of the *centro* is off-limits to all but permit holders, and on-street parking (if you can find a space) in most areas costs €1-€1.20 per hour, depending on the area.

Then there are Roman drivers: if you don't have nerves of steel and lightning-quick reactions, then the Eternal City is not somewhere you should be driving.

Short-term visitors should have no trouble driving with their home licence, but if it is in a less common language an international licence can be useful. All EU citizens are obliged to get an Italian licence after being resident for one year.

- You are required by law to wear a seat belt at all times, in both front and back, and have a reflective jacket and warning triangle in the car.
- Outside urban areas, you must drive with headlights on at all times.
- You must keep your driving licence, vehicle registration and personal ID on you at all times.
- Do not leave anything of value in your car. Take all luggage into your hotel when you park.
- Flashing your lights in Italy means that you will not slow down (contrary to British practice).
- Traffic lights flashing amber mean stop and give way to the right.
- Beware death-defying mopeds and pedestrians. Pedestrians assume they have the right of way in the older, quieter streets without clearly designated pavements.

Restricted areas – ZTL

Large sections of the city centre (marked ZTL – *Zona a Traffico Limitato*) are closed to non-resident traffic during business hours, and sometimes in the evening. Police and video cameras guard these areas; any vehicle without the required pass will be fined €84 if it enters at restricted times.

If your accommodation is in a restricted area, make arrangements with your hotel before arrival.

Petrol

Petrol stations sell unleaded petrol (*senza piombo* or *verde*) and diesel (*gasolio*). Liquid propane gas is *GPL*. Most stations offer full service on weekdays; pump attendants don't expect tips. At night and on Sun many stations open self-service pumps that accept €5, €10, €20 and €50 notes, in good condition; some also accept cards. Unofficial 'assistants' may offer to do the job for you for a small tip (€1).

Breakdown services

Before taking a car to Italy it's advisable to join a national motoring organisation, like the AA or RAC in Britain or the AAA in the US. They have reciprocal arrangements with the Automobile Club d'Italia (ACI), offering breakdown assistance and giving general information. Even if you're not a member, it's still best to call the ACI if you have any kind of breakdown.

If you require major repairs, pay a bit more to use the manufacturer's official dealer: the reliability of any garage depends on having built up a good client-mechanic relationship. Dealers are listed in the phone book under *auto*, along with specialist repairs such as *gommista* (tyres), *marmitte* (exhausts) and *carrozzerie* (bodywork). The *English Yellow Pages* has a list of garages at which English is spoken.

Automobile Club d'Italia (ACI) *803 116 (free of charge), www.aci.it.*
The ACI has English-speaking staff and provides services for all foreign drivers. Members of associated organisations get basic repairs for free, and other services at lower rates; non-members will be charged, but prices are reasonable.

Parking

A system in which residents park for free and visitors pay is in place in many areas of the city. It's efficiently policed, so watch out for the tell-tale blue lines. Buy parking tickets (€1-€1.20/hr) at pay-and-display ticket dispensers or *tabacchi*. In some areas parking is free after a certain time (usually 8pm or 11pm) or on Sun – check instructions on the machine.

Your vehicle may be clamped if it's improperly or illegally parked: you will have to pay a fine, plus a charge to have the clamp removed. If your car's in a dangerous position or blocking trams and buses, it will be towed (call the municipal police on 06 67 691 and quote your number plate to find out which car pound it's in).

In zones with no blue lines, anything resembling a parking place is up for grabs, but with some exceptions: watch out for signs saying *Passo carrabile* ('access at all times') or *Sosta vietata* ('no parking'), and disabled parking spaces (yellow stripes on the road). The sign *Zona rimozione* ('tow-away area') means no parking, and is valid for the length of the street or until the sign is repeated with a red line through it. If a street or square has no cars parked in it, assume it's a strictly enforced no-parking zone. In some areas, self-appointed *parcheggiatori* will 'look after' your car for a small fee; it may be illegal and an absurd imposition, but it's probably worth paying up to preserve your tyres.

Cars are fairly safe in most central areas, but you may prefer the hefty rates for underground car parks to keep your vehicle off the street.

Villa Borghese *Viale del Galoppatoio 33, Veneto & Borghese (06 322 5934, www.sabait.it). Metro Spagna/bus 61, 89, 116, 120, 150, 160, 490, 491, 495, C3, M.* ***Open*** *24hrs daily.* ***Rates*** *Cars €2.20/hr, max 24hr rate of €18* ***Map*** *p138 K5.*
Vehicle entrances are on via del Muro Torto (both sides of the road). The car park is linked to the Spagna metro station, with 24hr pedestrian access to piazza di Spagna.

Car hire

To hire a car you must be over 21 – in some cases 23 – and have held a licence for at least a year. You will be required to leave a credit card number or substantial cash deposit. It's advisable to take out collision damage waiver (CDW) and personal accident insurance (PAI) on top of basic third-party cover. Companies not offering CDW are best avoided.

Avis *199 100 133, 06 4521 08391, www.avisautonoleggio.it.*
Europcar *199 307 030, 06 488 2854, www.europcar.it.*
Maggiore *06 2245 6060, 199 151 120, www.maggiore.it.*

CYCLES, SCOOTERS & MOPEDS FOR HIRE

To hire a scooter or moped (*motorino*) you need a driving licence, photo ID, credit card and/or a cash deposit. Helmets are required on all motorbikes, scooters or mopeds (the police are very strict about this). For hiring bicycles, you can usually leave ID rather than pay a deposit.

Rome's bus company, Atac, runs a city-wide cycle hire scheme called Atac-Bikesharing. It is so badly run, and so few bikes remain, that it's hardly worth signing up.

Bici & Baci *Via del Viminale 5, Monti (06 482 8443, www.bicibaci.com). Metro Repubblica/bus 40Exp, 60Exp, 64, 70, 170, H.* ***Open*** *8am-7pm daily.* ***Rates*** *(per day) €11 bicycles; €28-€35 mopeds (50cc); €45-€72 scooters (125cc).* ***Map*** *p182 N8.*
This friendly outlet also offers hourly and weekly rates. Another branch is in vicolo del Bottino 8, piazza di Spagna. Metro Spagna. Open 8am-7pm daily.
TopBike Rental *via Labicana 49, Celio (06 488 2893, www.topbikerental.com). Metro Colosseo or bus 87.* ***Rates*** *(per day) €19-€45 bicycles. Bike tours in Rome and outskirts.* ***Map*** *p198 N11.*
Scooters for Rent *Via della Purificazione 84, Tridente (06 488 5485, www.rentscooter.it). Metro Barberini/bus 52, 53, 62, 63, 80Exp, 83, 85, 116, 160, 175, 492, 590.* ***Open*** *9am-7pm daily.* ***Rates*** *(per day) €12 bicycles; €40 mopeds (50cc); €50-€70cooters (125cc).* ***Map*** *p89 L6.*

Resources A-Z

Travel Advice

For up-to-date information on travel to a specific country – including the latest on safety and security, health issues, local laws and customs – contact your home country government's department of foreign affairs. Most have websites with useful advice for would-be travellers.

Australia
www.smartraveller.gov.au

Canada
www.voyage.gc.ca

New Zealand
www.safetravel.govt.nz

Republic of Ireland
www.foreignaffairs.gov.ie

UK
www.fco.gov.uk/travel

USA
www.state.gov/travel

ACCIDENT & EMERGENCY

Emergency numbers

Ambulance *Ambulanza 118.*
Fire service *Vigili del fuoco 115.*
Police *Carabinieri (English-speaking helpline) 112; Polizia di Stato 113.*

A&E departments

If you need urgent medical care, go to the *pronto soccorso* (casualty department). All the hospitals listed here offer 24hr casualty services. If your child needs emergency treatment, head straight for the excellent Ospedale Pediatrico Bambino Gesù.

Ospedale Fatebenefratelli *Isola Tiberina, Ghetto (06 68 371, www.fatebenefratelli-isolatiberina.it). Bus 23, 63, 280, 780, H/tram 8. **Map** p120 I11.*
Ospedale Pediatrico Bambino Gesù *Piazza Sant'Onofrio 4, Gianicolo (06 68 591, www.ospedalebambinogesu.it). Bus 115, 870. **Map** p166 G12.*
Ospedale San Camillo-Forlanini *Via Portuense 332, Suburbs: west (06 55 551, 06 58 701, www.scamilloforlanini.rm.it). Bus 228, 710, 719, 773, 774, 786, 791, H/tram 8.*
Ospedale San Giovanni *Via Amba Aradam 8, San Giovanni (06 77 051, www.hsangiovanni.roma.it). Metro San Giovanni/bus 81, 85, 117, 650, 673, 714, 717. **Map** p198 O12.*
Policlinico Umberto I *Viale Policlinico 155, Suburbs: north (06 49 971, www.policlinicoumberto1.it). Metro Policlinico/bus 61, 88, 310, 495, 649/tram 3, 19.*

ADDRESSES

Rome addresses follow the standard Italian format with the street name coming before the number on the first line, and the postcode preceding the name of the town or city on the second; the two-letter code in brackets after the city name indicates the province.

AGE RESTRICTIONS

Cigarettes and alcohol cannot be sold to under-18s. Over-14s can ride a moped or scooter of 50cc, but 14-18s are required to pass a practical test and obtain a pre-licence first (*see p319* Driving). The age of heterosexual and homosexual consent is 14.

CLIMATE

Spring and autumn are the best times to see Rome; the weather's pleasantly balmy and the city is bathed in a glorious yellow light. To visitors arriving from chillier climes, the weather in May, June, Sept and Oct may seem like a fairly convincing approximation of summertime, but the actual Roman summer is a different matter altogether: searing, 40°C heat and energy-sapping humidity mark July and Aug, when the city empties as Romans scurry for the hills and sea.

Between Nov and Feb the weather in Rome is very unpredictable: you might strike it lucky with a run of crisp, bright, sunny days, maybe punctuated by the odd icy blast of wind buffetting in from northern Europe... or you may arrive in the midst of a torrential downpour that shows no sign of letting up, putting a dampener on your sightseeing plans. But there is some compensation: you'll find there's a relative scarcity of other tourists. *See also p26* When to Visit.

CONSUMER

Rome city council's general helpline (060606) is the best place to go in the first instance for advice. In serious cases, ring the Carabinieri police on 112, where you should find English-speaking switchboard staff. The city council's **Ufficio Tutela del Consumatore** (Consumer Protection Office, via dei Cerchi 6, 06 6710 4282, open 9am-1pm, 2-4.30pm Tue, Wed; 9am-1pm Thur) advises on shoppers' rights.

CUSTOMS

People travelling between EU countries are not required to declare goods imported into or exported from Italy if they are for personal use. For those arriving from non-EU countries, these limits apply:

- 200 cigarettes/100 cigarillos/50 cigars/250g of tobacco.
- 1l of spirits (over 22% alcohol) or 2l of wine.

Pharmacies

Farmacie (identified by a green cross) give informal medical advice, as well as making up prescriptions. Most also sell homeopathic and veterinary medicines, and all will check your height/weight/blood pressure on request. Make sure you know the generic as well as the brand name of your regular medicines: they may be sold under a different name here. The best-stocked pharmacy in the city is in the Vatican (*see below*): it has a whole range of medicines not found elsewhere in Italy.

Normal pharmacy opening hours are 8.30am-1pm, 4-8pm Mon-Sat. Outside these hours, a duty rota system operates. A list displayed by the door of any pharmacy (and in local papers) indicates the nearest ones open at any time. A surcharge applies when only the special duty counter is open.

Farmacia della Stazione *Piazza dei Cinquecento 50, Esquilino (06 488 0019). See p316 Transport to Termini.* ***Open*** *8am-11.20pm daily.* ***Map*** *p182 O7.*
Farmacia del Vaticano *Porta Sant'Anna entrance, Vatican (06 6988 3422). Metro Ottaviano/bus 23, 32, 34, 40Exp, 49, 62, 64, 81, 271, 490, 492, 590, 982, 990/tram 19.* ***Open*** *8.30am-1pm Mon-Sat.* ***Map*** *p150 D7.*
Piram *Via Nazionale 228, Esquilino (06 488 4437). Metro Repubblica/bus 40Exp, 60Exp, 64, 70, 170, H, N7, N8, N9, N15, N18.* ***Open*** *24hrs daily.* ***Map*** *p182 M8.*

Water

Rome's water is safe to drink. Some areas of the *centro storico* still get water through ancient aqueducts that draw from the springs in the countryside. Take advantage of the drinking fountains located on street corners and in *piazze* all over the city: unless they say *non potabile*, they all have excellent quality drinking water.

ID

You are required by law to carry photo ID with you at all times. You must produce it if stopped by traffic police (along with your driving licence, which you must carry when you're in charge of a motor vehicle) and when you check into a hotel. Smaller hotels may try to hold on to your passport/ID card for the length of your stay; you are within your rights to ask for it back.

INSURANCE

EU citizens are entitled to reciprocal medical care in Italy provided they leave their own country with an **EHIC** (European Health Insurance Card), which has replaced the old E111 form. In the UK, you can apply for an EHIC online (www.ehic.org.uk) or by post using forms available at any post office. If you use it for anything but emergencies (which are treated free anyway in casualty departments; *see p321*), you'll need to deal with the intricacies of the Italian state health system. For short-term visits, it is advisable to take out private travel/health insurance. Non-EU citizens should take out private medical insurance before setting off.

Visitors should also take out adequate insurance against loss or theft. If you hire a car, motorcycle or moped, make sure you pay the extra for full insurance cover and, for a car, sign the collision damage waiver (CDW).

LANGUAGE

Romans always appreciate attempts at spoken Italian, no matter how incompetent. In hotels and all but the most spit-and-sawdust restaurants, there's likely to be someone with basic English. *See also p332* Vocabulary.

LEFT LUGGAGE

The left-luggage office by platform 24 in Termini station (06 474 5421) is open 6am-11pm daily. A suitcase costs €6/hr (for up to 5hrs); €1/hr from the 6th to the 12th hour; thereafter, 50¢/hr.

At Fiumicino airport, left luggage in Terminal 3 is open 6.30am-11.30pm daily. Each item costs €6 for up to 24hrs. Hotels will generally look after your luggage during the day, even after you've checked out.

LEGAL HELP

Legal advice should first be sought at your embassy or consulate (*see p323*).

LGBT

There are over 70 gay activist organisations in Italy. Foremost among these are the organisations belonging to the Bologna-based Arcigay network. For up-to-the-minute information on LGBT events, plus gay-friendly listings of all kinds, check out www.friendlyroma.it; it's (kind of) in English too. Another good source for events listings is www.gayvillage.it.

Organisations & resources

Arcigay Roma *Via Zabaglia 14, Testaccio (06 6450 1102, free helpline 800 713 713, www.arcigay roma.it/www.gaycenter.it). Metro Piramide/bus 23, 30, 75, 83, 170, 280, 673, 716, 719, 3N, 9N, 10N, 11N/tram 3.* ***Map*** *p210 H15.*
The local group gets together on Wed 7-9pm for those over 27; on Fri 6-8pm for those under 27.
Arci-Lesbica Roma *Via Zabaglia 14, Testaccio (06 6450 1102, free helpline 800 713 713, www.arcilesbica.it/roma). Metro Piramide/bus 23, 30, 75, 83, 170, 280, 673, 716, 719/tram 3.* ***Map*** *p210 H15.*
Arci-Lesbica organises once-monthly women-only meetings (third Tue of mth 9-11pm). Phone or see the website for other events.
Circolo Mario Mieli di Cultura Omosessuale *Via Efeso 2A, Suburbs: south (06 541 3985, 800 110 611 free of charge, www.mariomieli.org). Metro San Paolo/bus 23, 761.* ***Open*** *10.30am-6.30pm Mon-Fri.*
Named after the pioneer author and thinker Mario Mieli, this is the most important gay, lesbian and transgender group in Rome.

It provides a base for debates and events, and offers counselling and care facilities. Its Muccassassina one-nighter (*see p265*) is highly popular, and it also organises Pride events (www.romapride.it) during the summer.

Di'Gay Project *Via Costantino 82, Suburbs: south (06 513 4741, www.digayproject.org). Metro San Paolo/bus 670, 715, 766, 769.* ***Open*** *10am-6pm Mon-Fri.*
Hosts the summer Gay Village (*see p245*) as well as a series of other worthy events. There's a welcome group, a film club, a youth group and a theatre workshop.

La Foresteria Orsa Maggiore *Via San Francesco di Sales 1A, Trastevere (06 689 3753, www.orsamaggiorehostel.com). Bus 23, 280.* ***Map*** *p166 F10.*
The women-only Orsa Maggiore (Great Bear) hostel provides 13 brightly decorated rooms priced at €26-€42.50 per person per night.

Publications

Edicole (newsstands) are often good for gay books and videos; the *edicole* in piazze dei Cinquecento (*map p182 O7*) and Colonna (*map p79 K9*) are treasure troves of porn: discreet amounts are displayed by day, but piles of it come out at night.

The online magazine www.prideonline.it is a great resource for news and key events in the gay calendar.

LIBRARIES

Rome's libraries are dogged by red tape, restricted hours and patchy organisation. All libraries listed are open to the public; other specialist libraries can be found under *Biblioteche* in the phone book. Always take some ID along; in some cases, a letter from your college stating the purpose of your research will be required.

Archivio Centrale dello Stato (State Archives) *Piazzale Archivi 27, Suburbs: EUR (06 545 481, www.archiviocentraledellostato.beniculturali.it). Metro EUR Fermi/bus 703, 707, 765, 767.* ***Open*** *9am-6.45pm Mon-Fri; 9am-1pm Sat.*
The original documents, historical correspondence and many other items at this efficiently run archive have to be consulted in situ (but most can be photocopied). Material must be requested by 12.20pm.

Biblioteca dell'Università Gregoriana *Piazza della Pilotta 4, Trevi & Quirinale (06 6701 5131, www.unigre.it/newbiblio). Bus 40Exp, 53, 60Exp, 62, 63, 64, 70, 81, 83, 85, 160, 170, 175, 204, 492, 628, 630, 850, H.* ***Open*** *8.30am-6.30pm Mon-Fri; 8.30am-12.30pm Sat. Closed mid July-Aug.* ***Map*** *p79 K8.*
Books here are not allowed off the premises.

Biblioteca Nazionale *Viale Castro Pretorio 105, Esquilino (06 49 891, www.bncrm.beniculturali.it). Metro Castro Pretorio/bus 310, 492, 649, C2.* ***Open*** *Sept-June 8.30am-7pm Mon-Fri; 8.30am-1.30pm Sat. Mid July-Aug 8.30am-1.30pm Mon-Sat. Closed 2wks Aug.*
The national library holds a large proportion of all that's in print in Italy, plus books in other languages.

Biblioteca Vaticana *Via di Porta Angelica, Vatican (06 6987 9411, www.vatlib.it). Metro Ottaviano/bus 23, 32, 49, 62, 81, 492, 982, 990/tram 19.* ***Open*** *(postgrads only) 8.45am-5.15pm Mon-Fri.* ***Map*** *p150 D7.*
To obtain an entrance card, students need a letter on headed paper, signed by a professor, stating their research purpose. Go between 8.45am and noon to get a membership card. The library is frequently closed: check the website.

British School at Rome Library *Via Gramsci 61, Veneto & Borghese (06 3264 9380, www.bsr.ac.uk). Bus 52/tram 3, 19.* ***Open*** *9am-6.45pm Mon-Fri. Closed mid July-Aug.* ***Map*** *p138 J2.*
The library has 60,000 English and Italian books on all aspects of Rome, especially art history, archaeology and topography. Annual membership costs €30, monthly €10; you must present a photo, a valid document and a letter of introduction from a museum or university. No lending facilities.

LOST PROPERTY

Anything lost on Metro lines A and B, on FS trains or at Termini station may turn up at this council-run lost property office.

Ufficio oggetti smarriti *Circonvallazione Ostiense 191, Suburbs: south (06 6769 3214). Metro Garbatella/bus 670, 673, 716, 715.* ***Open*** *8.30am-1pm Mon, Wed, Fri; 8.30am-5pm Thur.*

MEDIA

National print & online dailies

Corriere della Sera *www.corriere.it.*
To the centre of centre-left, this serious but often dull Milan-based paper is good for foreign news.

La Repubblica *www.repubblica.it.*
Rome-based, centre-ish, left-ish, and providing a good selection of supplementary inserts.

Il Sole-24 Ore *www.ilsole24ore.it.*
This business, finance and economics daily has a great arts supplement on Sun.

La Stampa *www.lastampa.it.*
Part of the massive empire of Turin's Agnelli family; it offers good (albeit pro-Agnelli) business reporting.

Local print & online dailies

La Repubblica and *Corriere della Sera* (*see above*) have large daily Rome sections.

Il Messaggero *www.ilmessaggero.it.*
The Roman daily *per eccellenza*. Particularly useful classified ads – with many flat rents – on Sat.

L'Osservatore Romano *www.vatican.va.*
The Vatican's official newspaper reflects conservative orthodoxies issuing from the top. Weekly English edition on Wed.

Magazines

Panorama and *L'Espresso* each provide a generally high-standard round-up of the week's news, while *Magazine* and *Venerdì* – the colour supplements of *Corriere della Sera* (Thur) and *La Repubblica* (Fri) respectively – have nice photos but are textually rather weak; *La Repubblica*'s rather glossy Sat supplement D is the best of the lot. For tabloid-style scandal, try the weird mix of sex, glamour and religion in *Gente* and *Oggi*, or even the compulsively awful *Eva 3000* and *Cronaca Vera*. Far more highbrow, *Internazionale* (www.internazionale.it) provides a readable digest of articles gleaned from the world's press over the previous week. *Diario della Settimana* (www.diario.it) offers informed investigative journalism. But the biggest-seller is *Famiglia Cristiana* – readily available from newsstands and in most churches – which alternates between Vatican line-toeing and Vatican-baiting, based on the current state of relations between the Holy See and the idiosyncratic Paoline monks who produce it.

Listings & small ads

American Magazine
www.theamericanmag.com.
A monthly online English-language magazine that covers cultural and political life in Italy, and runs useful classified ads.

Italian Insider
www.italianinsider.it.
In print and online, this daily provides Italian political and economic coverage, as well as general features, aimed at English-speakers doing business in Italy.

Porta Portese
www.porta-portese.it.
Essential reading for flat-hunters in Rome (whether you're planning to rent or to buy). Published Tue and Fri, it also has sections on household goods and cars. Place ads free on 06 70 199.

Roma C'è
Comprehensive listings for theatre, music, dance, film and nightlife every Wed, with a small English-language section as well.

Trovaroma
Comes free with *La Repubblica* every Thurs; its English-language section covers the week's concerts, exhibitions and tours.

Wanted in Rome
www.wantedinrome.com.
Essential information and upmarket housing ads for English-speaking expats; out fortnightly.

Radio

These state-owned stations (RAI, www.rai.it) play a programme of classical and light music, interspersed with chat shows and regular, excellent news bulletins:

RAI 1 *89.7FM, 1332AM*
RAI 2 *91.7FM, 846AM*
RAI 3 *93.7FM, 1107AM*

For UK and US chart hits, mixed with home-grown offerings, try:

Radio Capital *95.8FM, www.capital.it.*
Radio Centro Suono *101.3FM, www.radiocentrosuono.it.*
Radio Città Futura *97.7FM, www.radiocittafutura.it.*
Italy's most PC 24hr station.
Radio Kiss Kiss Network *97.2FM, www.kisskiss.it.*
Radio 105 *96.1FM, www.105.net.*
Vatican Radio *105FM, 585MW, www.vaticanradio.org.*
World events, as seen by the Catholic Church, and broadcast in English.
Virgin Radio *98.7FM, www.virginradio.it.*

Television

Italy has six major networks (three are owned by the state broadcaster RAI, three by Silvio Berlusconi's Mediaset group), and two channels that operate across most of the country: La7 and MTV. Local stations provide hours of tacky programming, from tarot-reading to zero-budget soaps.

TV in Rome and the Lazio region is now digital.

MONEY

The Italian currency is the euro, with banknotes of €5, €10, €20, €100, €200 and €500, and coins worth €1 and €2, plus 1¢, 2¢, 5¢, 10¢, 20¢ and 50¢ (*centesimi*). Money from any Eurozone country is valid tender. Vatican euros are a highly collectable rarity.

Banking hours

Opening hours vary, but most banks operate 8.30am-1.30pm, 2.45-4.30pm Mon-Fri. Some central branches now also open until 6pm Thur and 8.30am-12.30pm Sat. All banks close on public holidays, and work reduced hours the day before a holiday (many close by 11am).

Banks & ATMs

Most banks have 24hr cash-point (*Bancomat*) machines. The vast majority accept cards with the Maestro, Cirrus and Plus logos, and will dispense up to a daily limit of €250.

Bureaux de change

Banks usually offer better exchange rates than private bureaux de change (*cambio*). Take a passport or other photo ID. Commission rates vary (from nothing to €5 per transaction). Beware 'no commission' signs: the rate is likely to be terrible.

Many city-centre bank branches have automatic cash-exchange machines, which will accept most currencies (notes in good condition only).

Credit & debit cards

Nearly all hotels of two stars and above now accept at least some of the major credit cards; all but the cheapest local eateries will take them too.

Should you lose a credit or debit card, phone one of the 24hr emergency numbers below.

American Express *06 7290 0347.*
Diner's Club *800 393 939.*
MasterCard *800 870 866.*
Visa *800 819 014.*

OPENING HOURS

For information on shop opening hours, *see p49*.

POLICE

The principal Polizia di Stato station, the **Questura Centrale**, is at via San Vitale 15 (06 46 861, www.poliziadistato.it, *map p182 M8*). Others, and the Carabinieri's Commissariati, are listed in the phone book under Polizia and *Carabinieri*. Incidents can be reported to either. For emergency numbers, *see p321*.

POSTAL SERVICES

For postal information, call 803 160 (8am-8pm Mon-Sat; Italian only) or visit www.poste.it.

The once-notorious Italian postal service is now generally efficient. If you still have any doubts, the Vatican Post Office (*see p153*) is run in association with the Swiss postal service.

Most postboxes are red and have two slots, *per la città* (for Rome) and *tutte le altre destinazioni* (everywhere else).

On the whole, mail arrives swiftly – up to 48hrs delivery in Italy, three days for EU countries and 5-9 days for other countries (in zones 2 and 3). A letter of 20g or less to Italy costs 60¢; to other countries in the EU costs 75¢; to zone 2 costs 1.60¢; to zone 3 costs €2.

Registered mail (ask for *raccomandata*) starts at €4.80 for a letter of 20g or less.

Parcels can be sent from any post office. It is advisable to send any package worth more than €50 insured.

There are local post offices (*ufficio postale*) in each district; opening hours can vary, but they are generally 8.30am-6pm Mon-Fri (Aug 8.30am-2pm), 8.30am-12.35pm Sat and any day preceding a public holiday. They close 2hrs earlier than normal on the last day of each month. Main post offices in the centre have longer opening hours.

Several postal services are available online; visit www.poste.it to avoid the queues.

Posta Centrale *Piazza San Silvestro 19, Tridente (06 6973 7205, information 803 160). Bus 52, 53, 62, 63, 71, 80Exp, 83, 85, 117, 160, 492, 590.* ***Open*** *8.20am-7pm Mon-Fri, 8am-12.35pm Sat.* ***Map*** *p89 J7.*
The hub of Rome's postal system has been treated to a facelift: shiny new internet terminals, numerous counters, an information desk... and vastly reduced queues.

PUBLIC HOLIDAYS

On public holidays (*giorni festivi*) virtually all shops, banks and businesses close, although (with the exception of May Day, 15 Aug and Christmas Day) bars and restaurants tend to stay open. There's only limited public transport on 1 May and Christmas afternoon.

New Year's Day *(Capodanno) 1 Jan*
Epiphany *(La Befana) 6 Jan*
Easter Monday *(Pasquetta)*
Liberation Day *(Liberazione) 25 Apr*
May Day *(Primo Maggio) 1 May*
Patron Saints' Day *(Santi Pietro e Paolo) 29 June*
Feast of the Assumption *(Ferragosto) 15 Aug*
All Saints *(Tutti i santi) 1 Nov*
Immaculate Conception *(Festa dell'Immacolata) 8 Dec*
Christmas Day *(Natale) 25 Dec*
Boxing Day *(Santo Stefano) 26 Dec*

RELIGION

For information about papal audiences, *see p158*.

There are over 400 Catholic churches in Rome, but few hold Mass in English. The main English-speaking Catholic church is **San Silvestro** (piazza San Silvestro 17A, 06 697 7121, *map p89 J7*); **San Patrizio** (via Boncompagni 31, 06 4290 3787, www.stpatricksrome.com, *map p138 M5*) is the principal Irish church; the American Catholic church is **Santa Susanna** (via XX Settembre 15, 06 4201 4554, www.santasusanna.org, *map p138 M6*).

Anglican *All Saints, via del Babuino 153, Tridente (06 3600 1881, www.allsaintsrome.org). Metro Spagna/bus 117. Services morning prayer 8.30am Wed, Fri; 8am, 10.30am Sun; 6pm 4th Sun of mth.* ***Map*** *p89 J5.*
All Saints hosts a programme of cultural events, including regular concerts and activities for children.
Episcopal *St Paul's Within the Walls, via Napoli 58, Esquilino (06 488 3339, www.stpaulsrome.it). Metro Repubblica/bus 40Exp, 60Exp, 64, 70, 71, 170, H. Services 9am, 10.30am, 1pm (in Spanish) Sun.* ***Map*** *p182 M7.*
Jewish *Comunità Israelitica Ebraica di Roma, lungotevere Cenci, Ghetto (06 6840 0661, www.romaebraica.it). Bus 23, 63, 280, 780, H.* ***Map*** *p120 J11.*
There are daily services, but times vary. Guided tours of the synagogue are offered from the Museo Ebraico (*see p131*).
Methodist *Ponte Sant'Angelo Church, via del Banco di Santo Spirito, Pantheon & Navona (06 686 8314). Bus 40Exp, 46, 62, 64, 98, 280, 870, 881, 916. Services 10.30am Sun.* ***Map*** *p104 F8.*
Muslim *Moschea di Roma, viale della Moschea, Suburbs: north (06 808 2167, www.moscheadiroma.it). Train to Campi Sportivi/bus 230.*
Paolo Portoghesi's masterpiece is always open to Muslims for prayer. Non-Muslims can visit 9-11.30am Wed, Sat; €2, €1 reductions.
Presbyterian *St Andrew's, via XX Settembre 7, Trevi & Quirinale (06 482 7627, www.presbyterianchurchrome.org). Bus 16, 60Exp, 61, 62, 75, 85, 492, 590, 910. Services 11am Sun.* ***Map*** *p79 M7.*

SAFETY & SECURITY

Thefts should be reported immediately at the nearest police station. Report the loss of credit cards immediately to your credit card company (*see p326*), and of passports to your consulate/embassy (*see p323*).

Muggings are fairly rare in Rome, but pickpocketing is rife in the main tourist areas. Below are a few basic precautions:

- Don't carry wallets in back pockets, particularly on buses. If you have a bag or camera with a long strap, wear it across the chest.
- Keep bags closed, with your hand on them. If you stop at a pavement café or restaurant, don't leave bags or coats where you cannot see them.
- When walking down a street, hold cameras and bags on the side of you towards the wall – you're less likely to become the prey of a motorcycle thief.
- Avoid groups of ragged children brandishing pieces of cardboard, or walk by quickly keeping hold of your valuables. The cardboard is to distract you while accomplices pick your pockets or bags.

If you are the victim of crime, call the police (*see p326*) or go to the nearest police station and say you want to report a *furto* (theft). A *denuncia* (written statement) of the incident will be made. It's unlikely your things will be found, but you will need the *denuncia* for insurance claims.

SMOKING

Smoking is prohibited in all public places in Italy except for those that provide a distinct, ventilated smokers' room. Occasionally you'll find a restaurant or club which has a dedicated smoking room, specifically marked as such, but these are becoming less and less common. Smoking in hotels is almost universally banned.

Tabacchi

Tabacchi or *tabaccherie* (identifiable by signs with a white 'T' on black or blue) are the only places you can legally buy tobacco products. They also generally sell stamps, telephone cards, tickets for public transport, lottery tickets and the stationery required for dealing with Italian bureaucracy. Most *tabacchi* keep shop hours, but some are attached to bars and so stay open into the night.

STUDY

The state universities – **La Sapienza** (www.uniroma1.it), **Tor Vergata** (www.uniroma2.it) and **Roma Tre** (www.uniroma3.it) – plus the private LUISS (www.luiss.it) offer exchanges with other European universities. All EU citizens have the same right as Italians to study in Rome's universities, paying the same fees. Get your certificates translated and validated by the Italian consulate in your own country before lodging your application at the *ufficio stranieri* (foreigners' department) of the university of your choice.

Several US universities have campuses in Rome, which students attend on exchange programmes. Private Catholic universities run some of Italy's most highly respected medical faculties.

Italiaidea *Corso Vittorio Emanuele II 184, campo de' Fiori (06 6994 1314, www.italiaidea.com). **Map** p120 G9.*
Minutes from campo de' Fiori, Italiaidea runs intensive, full-immersion and evening courses, as well as special courses in art history and business Italian. They also run social events and can help accommodate you. An intensive one-week group class costs €170.

Scuola Leonardo Da Vinci *Piazza dell'Orologio 7, Pantheon & piazza Navona (06 6889 2513, www.scuolaleonardo.com). **Map** p104 F8.*
Located near piazza Navona, this language school offers individual or group classes, as well as extra, educational 'free time' activities in history of art, fashion and food. An intensive one-week group class costs €210.

Torre di Babele *Via Cosenza 7, Nomentano (06 4425 2578, www.torredibabele.com).*
This friendly, buzzy school near Villa Torlonia offers intensive Italian language courses, plus a host of 'cultural' courses – from cooking to handbag design. They'll also find you accommodation. An intensive one-week group class costs €210.

TELEPHONES

Dialling & codes

There are three main types of phone number in Rome:

- Landlines have the area code 06, which must be used whether calling from within or outside the city. Numbers generally have 8 digits. If you can't get through, it may be an old number; check the directory or ring enquiries (*see below*). When phoning Rome from abroad, keep the initial 0.
- Numbers beginning 800 are free. Numbers beginning 840 and 848 are charged at low set rates, no matter where you're calling from or how long the call lasts. These numbers can be called from within Italy only; some of them function only within a single phone district.
- Mobile numbers begin with a 3.

Mobile phones

GSM phones can be used on both 900 and 1800 bands; British, Australian and New Zealand mobiles work fine, but US mobiles are on a different frequency that doesn't work (unless it's a tri-band phone). The main mobile phone networks in Italy are **Tim** (www.tim.it), **Vodafone** (www.vodafone.it), **Tre** (www.tre.it) and **Wind** (www.wind.it). All have numerous branches located throughout the city.

Public phones

Rome has no shortage of public phone boxes and many bars have payphones, most of which are readily available as locals are addicted to mobiles. Most only accept phone cards (*schede telefoniche*); a few also accept major credit cards. Phone cards cost €5, €15 and €30 and are available from *tabacchi* (*see p48* Life's Essentials), some news-stands and some bars.

TIME

Italy is one hour ahead of London, six hours ahead of New York, eight hours behind Sydney and 12 hours behind Wellington. In all EU countries clocks are moved forward one hour in early spring and back again in late autumn.

TIPPING

Foreigners are generally expected to tip more than Italians, but the 10%+ that is customary in many countries is considered generous even for the richest-looking tourist in most eateries, where anything between €1 and €5 is normal; some smarter places, however, now include a 10-15% service charge. For drinks, follow the example of many locals, who leave a 10¢ or 20¢ coin on the counter when ordering at a bar. Taxi drivers will be happy if you round the fare up to the nearest whole euro.

TOILETS

If you need a toilet, the easiest thing to do is to go to a bar (it won't necessarily be clean or provide toilet paper). There are modern lavatories at or near most major tourist sites, some with attendants to whom you must pay a nominal fee. Fast-food restaurants and department stores may also meet the need. For wheelchair-accessible toilets, *see p322*.

TOURIST INFORMATION

For tours, *see p57* Tour buses.

Rome's city council operates a number of well-stocked green-painted tourist information kiosks (PIT) that are open 9.30am-7/7.30pm daily.

For Rome tourist information on your mobile appliance, see mobile.turismoroma.it. The excellent, exhaustive www.060608.it website is the city council's one-stop shop for information on museums, galleries, events, hotels and much more besides.

The website of the city council-affiliated APT (Azienda per il Turismo di Roma), www.romaturismo.com, contains plenty of useful information.

PITs *(Punti Informativi Turistici) are located in the following places:*
Piazza Pia, Vatican & Prati. Bus 23, 34, 40Exp, 62, 280, 982. ***Map*** *p150 E7.*
Piazza delle Cinque Lune, Pantheon & Navona. Bus 30Exp, 70, 81, 87, 186, 492, 628. ***Map*** *p104 G8.*
Piazza del Tempio della Pace, Capitoline & Palatine. Bus 53, 75, 80Exp, 85, 87, 117, 186, 810. ***Map*** *p68 L10.*
Via Nazionale, Trevi & Quirinale. Bus 40Exp, 60Exp, 64, 70, 71, 117, 170, H. ***Map*** *p182 L8.*
Piazza Sonnino, Trastevere. Bus 23, 280, 780, H/tram 8. ***Map*** *p166 H12.*
Via Minghetti, Tridente. Bus 53, 62, 63, 80Exp, 81, 83, 85, 117, 160, 175, 204, 492, 628, C3. ***Map*** *p79 J8.*
Termini station, platform 24, Esquilino. See p316 Transport to Termini. ***Map*** *p182 O7.*
Fiumicino airport, Terminal 3, see p315.
Ciampino airport, Arrival Hall, see p315.

Ufficio Pellegrini e Turisti *Piazza San Pietro, Vatican (06 6988 2350, www.vaticanstate.va). Metro Ottaviano/bus 23, 32, 34, 40 Exp, 49, 62, 64, 81, 490, 492, 590, 982, 990/tram 19.* ***Open*** *8.30am-6.30pm Mon-Sat.* ***Map*** *p150 D7.*
The Vatican's tourist office.

VISAS & IMMIGRATION

EU nationals and citizens of the US, Canada, Australia and New Zealand do not need visas for stays of up to three months. For EU citizens a passport or national ID card valid for travel abroad is sufficient; non-EU citizens must have full passports. In theory, all visitors must declare their presence to the local police (*see p326*) within eight days of arrival. If you're staying in a hotel, this will be done for you.

WOMEN

Rome is generally a safe city for women. Stick to central areas and if you do find yourself being hassled, take comfort in the fact that Italian men are generally all mouth and no trousers. Common sense is usually enough to keep potential harassers at bay: if you're not interested, ignore them and they'll probably go away.

You may feel harassed around major tourist magnets, such as piazza Navona, piazza di Spagna and the Trevi Fountain. Stick to the areas around campo de' Fiori, Testaccio or Trastevere for a quieter night. The Termini station area gets seriously seedy after the sun has gone down.

WORKING & LIVING IN ROME

Foreign nationals residing in Italy are obliged to pick up a series of forms and permits. The basic set is described below. EU citizens should have no difficulty getting their documentation once they are in Italy (see www.portaleimmigrazione.it, or contact the free number 800 309 309), but non-EU citizens are advised to enquire at an Italian consulate before travelling. There are agencies that specialise in obtaining documents for you if you can't face the procedures yourself – but at a price (see *Pratiche e certificati – agenzie* in the phone book).

Carta d'identità (identity card) You will need three passport photographs, the original and one photocopy of your *permesso di soggiorno* (*see below*), your passport and a form that will be given to you at your *circoscrizione* – the local branch of the central records office, which eventually issues the ID card. You will also need to be officially resident in Rome (*see p330*). Consult the phone book (*Comune di Roma: Circoscrizioni*) for your area's office.

Codice fiscale (tax code) A *codice fiscale* is essential for opening a bank account or setting up utilities contracts. Take your passport and *permesso di soggiorno* (*see below*) to your local tax office (*ufficio delle entrate*). Fill in a form and return a few days later to pick up the card. It can be posted on request.

Permesso/carta di soggiorno (permit to stay) You need a *permesso di soggiorno* if you're staying in Italy for over three months; you should, in theory, apply for one within eight days of arrival in Italy. Requirements vary depending on whether or not you are an EU citizen. You'll need four passport photographs, your passport (and a photocopy), proof that you have some means of support (eg a bank statement) and reason to be in Italy (preferably a letter from an employer or certificate of registration at a school or university), and a stamp (*marca da bollo*) costing €14.62, available at *tabacchi*.

Both EU and non-EU citizens can now, in theory, apply for their *permesso/carta di soggiorno* at main post offices. For information, call 06 4686 3098.

The *carta* (card) *di soggiorno* is similar to the *permesso* but allows you to stay in Italy indefinitely – though it has to be renewed every five years. EU citizens who have been resident in Italy for at least five years and who also have a renewable *permesso di soggiorno* can request a *carta*.

Permesso di lavoro (work permit) Most EU citizens do not require a work permit; only those from new member states, as well as non-EU citizens, are legally obliged to have one, though many don't. Employers are required to put in a request to the *Direzione Provinciale del Lavoro* (www.lavoro.gov.it) before taking such employees on. Once authorisation has been granted, a passport and *permesso di soggiorno* (plus photocopies) are needed for a *permesso di lavoro*, obtained from the *Direzione's* office at via dei Vestini 13 (06 4487 1642, open 9am-noon Mon, Wed, Fri; 9am-noon, 2.45-4.30pm Tue, Thur). The whole business is fiendishly complicated, and you may feel that it's worth leaving it in the hands of an agency (*see above*) or a lawyer.

Residenza (residency) This is your registered address in Italy. It's required to buy a car, get customs clearance on goods brought here from abroad and for many other transactions. You'll need your *permesso di soggiorno* (it must be valid for at least another year), your passport and a residency request form (downloadable from www.comune.roma.it). Take everything to your local *circoscrizione* (*see p329*).

Work

Casual employment can be hard to find, so try to sort out work in advance. English-language schools and translation agencies are mobbed with applicants, so qualifications and experience count. The classified ads paper *Porta Portese* (*see p326*) has lots of job ads; try also *Wanted in Rome* (*see p326*). You can also place ads in any of the media above. For serious jobs, check newspapers *Il Messaggero* and *La Repubblica*.

Glossary

Amphitheatre oval open-air theatre in ancient Rome
Apse large recess at the high-altar end of a church
Atrium courtyard
Baldacchino canopy supported by columns
Baroque artistic period in the 17th–18th centuries, in which the decorative element became increasingly florid, culminating in the rococo
Basilica ancient Roman rectangular public building; rectangular Christian church
Campanile bell tower
Caryatid supporting pillar carved in the shape of a woman
Cavea step-like seating area found in an amphitheatre or theatre
Chiaroscuro from Italian *chiaro* (light) and *scuro* (dark), juxtaposition of light and shade to bring out relief and volume
Ciborio dome-shaped canopy on columns over high altar
Clivus ancient name for a street on the side of a hill
Cloister exterior courtyard surrounded on all sides by a covered walkway
Column upright architectural element that can be round, square or rectangular; usually structural, but sometimes merely decorative, and usually free-standing; conforms to one of the classical orders
Confessio crypt under raised altar
Cosmati, cosmatesque mosaic technique using coloured marble chips, usually to decorate floors and church fittings
Cryptoporticus underground corridor
Cubicolum bedroom
Decumanus main road, usually running east–west
Domus Romane city house
Entablature section above a column or row of columns that includes the frieze and cornice
Ex-voto an offering given to fulfil a vow; often a small model in silver of the limb, organ or loved one cured as a result of prayer
Fresco painting technique in which pigment is applied to wet plaster
Giallo antico yellowish marble
Gothic architectural and artistic style of the late Middle Ages (from the 12th century), of soaring, pointed arches
Greek cross (of a church) in the shape of a cross with arms of equal length
Grisaille painting in shades of grey to mimic sculpture
Insula an ancient multi-storey city apartment block
Intarsio form of mosaic made from pieces of wood of different colours; also known as intaglio
Largo square
Latin cross (of a church) in the shape of a cross with one arm longer than the others
Loggia gallery open on one side
Lunette semicircular area, usually above a door or window
Maiolica fine earthenware with coloured decoration on an opaque white glaze
Mannerism High Renaissance style of the late 16th century; characterised in painting by elongated, contorted human figures
Matronium gallery (usually screened) where women sat in early Christian and Byzantine basilicas
Mithraeum temple, usually underground, to the deity Mithras
Narthex enclosed porch in front of a church
Nave main body of a church; the longest section of a Latin-cross church
Necropolis literally, 'city of the dead'; graveyard
Nymphaeum grotto with pool and fountain dedicated to the Nymphs (female water deities)
Ogival (used of arches, windows and so on) curving in to a point at the top
Orders rules governing the proportions and decoration of columns, the most common being the very simple Doric, the curlicue Ionic, and the Corinthian, which is decorated with stylised acanthus leaves
Palazzo large and/or important building (not necessarily a palace)
Pendentives four concave triangular sections on top of piers supporting a dome
Peristyle temple or court surrounded by columns
Piazza square
Pilaster a rectangular column designed to project slightly from a wall
Pillar upright architectural element, always free-standing, but not conforming to classical orders
Rococo highly decorative style of the 18th century
Romanesque architectural style of the early Middle Ages (c500-1200), drawing on Roman and Byzantine influences
Rosso antico red-coloured marble brought from Matapan, Greece, by the Romans
Sarcophagus a coffin made of stone or marble
Spandrel the near-triangular space between the top of two adjoining arches and the ceiling resting above them
Tepidarium warm (as opposed to hot), steam-filled room in a Roman baths complex
Theatre in ancient times, a semicircular open-air theatre
Titulus an early Christian meeting place
Transept as per the **Latin-cross** shape of a church but with shorter arms
Travertine cream-coloured calcareous limestone
Triclinium dining room
Triumphal arch arch in front of an apse, usually over the high altar; monumental victory arch
Trompe l'oeil decorative painting effect that makes a flat surface appear three-dimensional

Vocabulary

There are two forms of address in the second person singular: *lei* (formal, used with strangers and older people) and *tu* (informal). In practice, the personal pronoun is usually omitted.

Pronunciation

a *as in* **a***sk*
e *like a in* **a***ge or e in s***e***ll*
i *like ea in* **ea***st*
o *as in h***o***tel or h***o***t*
u *as in b***oo***t.*
Romans have a lot of trouble with their consonants. **C** often comes out nearer **g**; **n**, if in close proximity to an **r**, disappears. Remember: **c** and **g** both go soft in front of **e** and **i** (becoming like the initial sounds of **ch**eck and **g**iraffe respectively). An **h** after **c** or **g** makes it hard – *chiuso* (closed) is pronounced 'kiuso'.
c *before* **a**, **o** *and* **u**: *as in* **c***at*
g *before* **a**, **o** *and* **u**: *as in* **g***et*
gl *like mi***lli***on*
gn *like ca***ny***on*
qu *as in* **qu***ick*
r *always rolled*
s *has two sounds, as in* **s***oap or ro***s***e*
sc *like* **sh***ame*
sch *like* **sc***out*
z *can be* **ts** *or* **dz**.

Useful phrases

Basics

hello/goodbye (informal) *ciao/salve*
good morning *buon giorno*
good evening *buona sera*
good night *buona notte*
please *per favore/per piacere*
thank you *grazie*
you're welcome *prego*
excuse me/sorry *mi scusi (formal)/scusa (informal)*
I'm sorry, but... *mi dispiace...*
I don't speak Italian (very well) *non parlo (molto bene) l'italiano*
do you speak English? *parla inglese?*
can I use/where's the toilet? *posso usare/dov'è il bagno/la toilette?*
open *aperto*
closed *chiuso*
entrance *entrata*
exit *uscita*

Female self-defence

no thank you, I can find my own way *no grazie, non ho bisogna di una guida*
can you leave me alone? *mi vuole lasciare in pace?*

Directions

(turn) left *(giri a) sinistra*
(it's on the) right *(è a/sulla) destra*
straight *on sempre diritto*
where is...? *dov'è...?*
could you show me the way to...? *mi potrebbe indicare la strada per...?*
is it near/far? *è vicino/lontano?*

Transport

car *macchina*
bus *autobus/auto*
coach *pullman*
taxi *tassì/taxi*
train *treno*
tram *tram*
plane *aereo*
bus stop *fermata (d'autobus)*
station *stazione*
platform *binario*
ticket/s *biglietto/biglietti*
one way *solo andata*
return *andata e ritorno*
(I'd like) a ticket for... *(vorrei) un biglietto per...*
where can I buy tickets? *dove si comprono i biglietti?*
are you getting off at the next stop? (ie get out of my way if you're not) *che, scende alla prossima?*
I'm sorry, I didn't know I had to stamp it *mi dispiace, non sapevo che lo dovevo timbrare*

Communications

phone *telefono*
stamp *francobollo*
how much is a stamp for England/Australia/the US? *quanto viene un franco-bollo per l'Inghilterra/l'Australia/gli Stati Uniti?*
can I make a phone call? *posso telefonare?*
letter *lettera*
postcard *cartolina*

Shopping

I'd like to try the blue sandals/black shoes/ brown boots *vorrei provare i sandali blu/le scarpe nere/gli stivali marroni*
do you have it/them in other colours? *ce l'ha in altri colori?*
I take (shoe) size... *porto il numero...*
I take (dress) size... *porto la taglia...*
it's too loose/too tight/just right *mi sta largo/stretto/bene*
can you give me a little more/less? *mi dia un po' di più/meno?*
100 grams of... *un etto di...*
300 grams of... *tre etti di...*
one kilo of... *un kilo/chilo di...*
five kilos of... *cinque chili di...*
a litre/two litres of... *un litro/ due litri di*

Eating, drinking & accommodation

I'd like to book a table for four at eight *vorrei prenotare una tavola per quattro alle otto*
that was poor/good/delicious *era mediocre/buono/ottimo*
the bill *il conto*
is service included? *è incluso il servizio?*
I think there's a mistake in this bill *credo che il conto sia sbagliato*
a reservation *una prenotazione*
I'd like to book a single/twin/double room *vorrei prenotare una camera singola/doppia/ matrimoniale*
I'd prefer a room with a bath/shower/ window over the courtyard *preferirei una camera con vasca da bagno doccia/finestra sul cortile*
can you bring me breakfast in bed? *mi può portare la colazione al letto?*

Days, nights & times

Monday *lunedì*
Tuesday *martedì*
Wednesday *mercoledì*
Thursday *giovedì*
Friday *venerdì*
Saturday *sabatò*
Sunday *domenica*
yesterday *ieri*
today *oggi*
tomorrow *domani*
morning *mattina*
afternoon *pomeriggio*
evening *sera*
night *notte*
weekend *fine settimana/weekend*
could you tell me the time? *mi sa (formal)/ sai (informal) dire l'ora?*
it's... o'clock *sono le (number)*
it's half past... *sono le (number) e mezza*
when does it (re)open? *a che ora (ri)apre?*
does it close for lunch? *chiude per pranzo?*

Numbers & money

0 *zero*; **1** *uno*; **2** *due*; **3** *tre*; **4** *quattro*; **5** *cinque*; **6** *sei*; **7** *sette*; **8** *otto*; **9** *nove*; **10** *dieci*; **11** *undici*; **12** *dodici*; **13** *tredici*; **14** *quattordici*; **15** *quindici*; **16** *sedici*; **17** *diciassette*; **18** *diciotto*; **19** *diciannove*; **20** *venti*; **30** *trenta*; **40** *quaranta*; **50** *cinquanta*; **60** *sessanta*; **70** *settanta*; **80** *ottanta*; **90** *novanta*; **100** *cento*; **200** *duecento*; **1,000** *mille*; **2,000** *duemila*
how much is it/does it cost? *quanto costa/ quant'è/quanto viene?*
do you take credit cards? *si accettano le carte di credito?*
can I pay in pounds/dollars? *posso pagare in sterline/dollari?*

Further Reference

BOOKS

Classics

Catullus *The Poems* Sometimes malicious, sometimes pornographic.

Juvenal *Satires* Contemporary view of ancient Rome's seedy underbelly.

Ovid *The Erotic Poems* Handbook for cynical lovers that got Ovid banished from Rome.

Suetonius *The Twelve Caesars* Salacious biographies of rulers from Julius Caesar to Domitian.

Virgil *The Aeneid* Rome's foundation myth is a great yarn.

Fiction & literature

Lyndsey Davis *The Falco series* Ancient detective romps.

Michael Dibdin *Vendetta* A thriller set in contemporary Rome.

George Eliot *Middlemarch* Dorothea's big honeymoon let-down takes place in 19th-century Rome.

Nathaniel Hawthorn *The Marble Faun* A quaint, moralising novel about two female artists in Rome.

Henry James *The Portrait of a Lady* It's also worth trying *Daisy Miller* and a couple of essays in *Italian Hours*.

Elsa Morante *History* Compelling evocation of life for the very poor in wartime Rome.

Shakespeare *Julius Caesar, Antony and Cleopatra, Titus Andronicus, Coriolanus.*

Non-fiction

Mary Beard *SPQR* This sprawling history of Rome from Republic to Empire is hugely readable.

Donald Dudley *Roman Society* Culture, politics and economics from the ninth century BC to the fourth century AD.

Paul Ginsborg *Italy and its Discontents* A fine introduction to the ups and downs of life in post-war Italy.

Michael Grant *History of Rome* Highly readable and full of facts.

Christopher Hibbert *Biography of a City* Engaging account of the history of Rome.

Tobias Jones *The Dark Heart of Italy* An exploration of some of the country's recent and contemporary secrets.

John Kelly *The Oxford Dictionary of Popes* Life stories of the pontiffs.

Georgina Masson *Queen Christina* Biography of the Catholic Church's illustrious Protestant convert, giving some great insights into 17th-century Rome.

Alexander Stille *The Sack of Rome, Excellent Cadavers* Studies of Italy under Berlusconi, and of the Mafia.

Rudolf Wittkower *Art and Architecture in Italy 1600-1750* All about the Baroque..

WEBSITES

060608.it Exhaustive information on museums, archaeological sites and events.

www.archeoroma.beniculturali.it A handy source of information about Rome's city-administrated archeological sites.

www.atac.roma.it Transport in and around the city, with downloadable maps and a useful journey planner.

www.coopculture.it Information and bookings for museums and exhibitions.

www.romaturismo.com Theatres, exhibitions and things to do with children.

APPS

CNT Rome *Condé Nast Traveller*'s guide has extensive practical and sights listings, plus audio tours.

Eat Rome Food writer Elizabeth Minchilli's guide to the restaurants, wine bars and gelaterie of Rome.

I Nasoni di Roma This free app locates drinking fountains.

Rome Bus A free app that allows you to plan routes in real time.

Rome for Foodies Food historian and blogger Katie Parla shares 150 of her favourite Rome eateries.

FILMS

Italian

► *See also p253* Essential Roman Films.

Accattone *(Pier Paolo Pasolini, 1961)* No-hoper Franco Citti careers from bad to worse to ignominious early death in Testaccio in this devastating portrait of the lives of the lowest of Rome's low.

Bellissima *(Luchino Visconti, 1951)* Screen-struck mamma Anna Magnani pushes her plain, ungifted daughter through the agony of the film-studio casting circuit.

Caro Diario *(Dear Diary, Nanni Moretti, 1994)* As much a wry love letter to Moretti's home town as a diary.

Fellini's Roma *(Federico Fellini, 1972)* A patchwork of cameos with visual gems that only the master of cinema could pull off.

La Grande Bellezza *(The Great Beauty, Paolo Sorrentino, 2013)* This Oscar winner explores the seamy underbelly of aristos and social climbers in a decadent, emotionally sterile Rome.

International

The Agony and the Ecstasy *(Carol Reed, 1965)* Charlton Heston daubs the Sistine ceiling as pope Rex Harrison looks on.

Gladiator *(Ridley Scott, 2000)* Russell Crowe's general Maximus flexes his muscles in the Colosseum, watched by Emperor Commodus.

Quo Vadis? *(Mervyn Le Roy, 1951)* Blood, sand and love in the lions' den; a huge (and hugely long) epic.

The Roman Spring of Mrs Stone *(Jose Quintero, 1961)* Fading, widowed Vivien Leigh tries to spice up her Roman holiday with an affair with gigolo Warren Beatty.

Spartacus *(Stanley Kubrick, 1960)* Kirk Douglas does his best to get the slaves revolting.

The Talented Mr Ripley *(Anthony Minghella, 1999)* Jude and Matt play out part of their tortuous relationship in Rome.

Three Coins in the Fountain *(Jean Negulesco, 1954)* Rome looks like a luscious postcard in this 1950s film

Index

INDEX

Picture credits

Inside front cover zebra0209/Shutterstock.com; Pages 2 (top); © Alberto Novelli/Gallerie Nazionali di Arte Antica di Roma - Palazzo Barberini; 2 (bottom), 96 InnaFelker/Shutterstock.com; 3 Anton Chalakov/Shutterstock.com; 5, 95 JJFarq/Shutterstock.com; 7 LuisPinaPhotography/Shutterstock.com; 11 (bottom), 37, 307 Catarina Belova/Shutterstock.com; 11 (top) Christian Mueller/Shutterstock.com; 12 (bottom) Marco Iacobucci EPP/Shutterstock.com; 12 (top) Ivana D' Orlanda/Shutterstock.com; 13 (bottom) DimaSid/Shutterstock.com; 13 (top), 18 (bottom), 83, 142, 214 Luxerendering/Shutterstock.com; 14 (top), 224 Nattakit Jeerapatmaitree/Shutterstock.com; 14 (bottom), 227 Museo delle Mura; 15 (top), 26 (bottom), 259 Lorenzo Vecchio/Roma Incontro il Mondo; 15 (bottom) tkunited/Shutterstock.com; 16 (top) francesco de marco/Shutterstock.com; 16 (bottom) JLOrtin/Shutterstock.com; 16 (middle), 240, 269 Yasuko Kageyama-Teatro dell'Opera di Roma; 17 (top) Gal Csilla/Shutterstock.com; 17 (bottom), 232 (right) ValerioMei/Shutterstock.com; 18 (top), 84, 111, 115, 125, 157, 197 photogolfer/Shutterstock.com; 20 Alessandra Santorelli / Time Out; 21 (bottom), 85 Valery Rokhin/Shutterstock.com; 21 (top) Marco Rubino/Shutterstock.com; 22 (bottom) Sergei Afanasev/Shutterstock.com; 22 (top) Zabotnova Inna/Shutterstock.com; 23 (bottom) Vladimir Melikiants/Shutterstock.com; 23 (top) red-feniks/Shutterstock.com; 24 (bottom) alessandro pinto/Shutterstock.com; 24 (top) travelview/Shutterstock.com; 25 (top), 188, 204, 232 (left) marcovarro/Shutterstock.com; 25 (bottom), 255, 263, 265, 267, 268, 272, 313, 314 Gianluca Moggi/Time Out; 26 (top), 27 (top), 243 Polifoto/Shutterstock.com; 27 (bottom) irisphoto1/Shutterstock.com; 29, 165, 235 Diego Fiore/Shutterstock.com; 30 MikeDotta/Shutterstock.com; 31 Westermak/Shutterstock.com; 32 (bottom) Ana del Castillo/Shutterstock.com; 32 (top), 207 Artography/Shutterstock.com; 33 (top) Marzia Giacobbe/Shutterstock.com; 33 (bottom) Vladimir Mucibabic/Shutterstock.com; 34 (top) Matteo Gabrieli/Shutterstock.com; 34 (bottom) alexandre zveiger/Shutterstock.com; 35 Lasse Ansaharju/Shutterstock.com; 38 Da Enzo al 29; 39 Antico Arco; 40, 128 Il Goccetto; 41, 184 Fatamorgana Gelato; 42 Trapizzino; 45 Heracles Kritikos/Shutterstock.com; 46 Roman Babakin/Shutterstock.com; 47, 48, 219 Mercato di Testaccio; 49 rihards/Shutterstock.com; 51 SAPhotog/Shutterstock.com; 53 Stuart Crump/age fotostock/SuperStock.com; 54 PitK/Shutterstock.com; 55 Lucky Team Studio/Shutterstock.com; 56 (top) DeAgostini/SuperStock.com; 56 (middle) Flavia al Velavevodetto; 56 (bottom) Viacheslav Lopatin/Shutterstock.com; 59 iofoto/Shutterstock.com; 61 Photos are property of the Administration of the Metropolitian City of Rome Capital; 62 Mark Schwabacher/Shutterstock.com; 64, 247 muratart/Shutterstock.com; 66 Henning Marquardt/Shutterstock.com; 72 anyalvanova/Shutterstock.com; 74 Leonid Andronov/Shutterstock.com; 77 Jon Chica/Shutterstock.com; 78 (top) lucarista/Shutterstock.com; 78 (bottom), 297 (top), 303 (right) Zvonimir Atletic/Shutterstock.com; 80 Galleria Colonna, Roma; 87 Vladislav Gajic/Shutterstock.com; 88, 231, 297 (bottom) Gimas/Shutterstock.com; 90 Keats Shelley House Quadro Biblioteca; 91, 309 jm/Landmark Trust; 92 gdvcom/Shutterstock.com; 94 Rocco Forte Hotels/Hotel de Russie; 97 wjarek/Shutterstock.com; 98 Phant/Shutterstock.com; 100 Denis Aminev/Shutterstock.com; 103 red-feniks/Shutterstock.com; 109 Roman Belogorodov/Shutterstock.com; 113 Shevchenko Andrey/Shutterstock.com; 117 Le Tartarughe, 119 Bill Perry/Shutterstock.com; 122 AROMI www.aromicreativi.com.; 123 Belt944/Shutterstock.com; 124 Alexander Mazurkevich/Shutterstock.com; 127 Open Baladin; 130 Helissa Grundemann/Shutterstock.com; 131 Museo Ebraico di Roma; 134, 280 futureGalore/Shutterstock.com; 137 Kiev.Victor/Shutterstock.com; 140 gnoparus/Shutterstock.com; 141 Courtesy Galleria Nazionale d'Arte Moderna e Contemporanea; 143 (bottom) pisaphotography/Shutterstock.com; 143 (top) SuperStock.com; 144 vvoe/Shutterstock.com; 146 Jule_Berlin/Shutterstock.com; 151 Juanma Aparicio/age fotostock/SuperStock.com; 152 Anna Malinowska/Shutterstock.com; 153 natalia_maroz/Shutterstock.com; 154 Francesco Dazzi/Shutterstock.com; 155 Andrisk/Shutterstock.com; 156 Viktor Gladkov/Shutterstock.com; 158 Mateusz_Szymanski/Shutterstock.com; 159 salajean/Shutterstock.com; 160 starryvoyage/Shutterstock.com; 161 Nattee Chalermtiragool/Shutterstock.com; 168 Aromi Creativi; 170 Flavio Tarquini; 173 Mjrka Boensch Bees/Aromi Creativi; 174 Bjanka Kadic/age fotostock/SuperStock.com; 177, 303 (left), 306 Renata Sedmakova/Shutterstock.com; 179 trabantos/Shutterstock.com; 181 Antony McAulay/Shutterstock.com; 186 Le Gallinelle; 192 manjik/Shutterstock.com; 193 (bottom left) Baloncici/Shutterstock.com, 193 (top), 193 (bottom right) ChiccoDodiFC/Shutterstock.com; 195 Tupungato/Shutterstock.com; 200 Davide Dragonetti; 201 Vlad G/Shutterstock.com; 209 Foto Zeno; 212 Flavio al Velavevodetto; 213 Sovrintendenza Capitolina ai Beni Culturali; 216 Anthony Shaw Photography/Shutterstock.com; 221 Tita.ti/Shutterstock.com; 222 Albert Noib/Shutterstock.com; 223 bestino/Shutterstock.com; 227 Courtesy of Rome Cavalieri; 228 Zoran Karapancev/Shutterstock.com; 233 (top) Marco Mariani/Shutterstock.com; 233 (bottom) Millionstock/Shutterstock.com; 236 Claudiovidri/Shutterstock.com; 237, 292 Stefano_Valeri/Shutterstock.com; 241 Gari Wyn Williams/age fotostock/Superstock.com; 242 cherry-hai/Shutterstock.com; 244 GTS Productions/Shutterstock.com; 249 neftali/Shutterstock.com; 250 Nuovo Sacher; 251 nito/Shutterstock.com; 252 Fondazione Cinema per Roma; 253 (top), 253 (bottom) Wikicommons, 153 (middle) fototeca gilardi/Marka/SuperStock.com; 257 ©Fabio Germinario; 261 (top) Gloria Imbrogno/Shutterstock.com; 261 (bottom) Cineberg/Shutterstock.com; 262 LORENZO_M; 273 Vladimir Volodin/Shutterstock.com; 275 CervelliInFuga/Shutterstock.com; 277 Sergiy Zavgorodny/Shutterstock.com; 278 abxyz/Shutterstock.com; 279 Album/Prisma/SuperStock.com; 282 World History Archive/SuperStock.com; 283 Universal images Group/SuperStock.com; 284 Emilia Ereza/age fotostock/SuperStock.com; 286 lornet/Shutterstock.com; 288 Iberfoto/SuperStock.com; 289 World History Archive/SuperStock.com; 291 pio3/Shutterstock.com; 293 Circumnavigation/Shutterstock.com; 295 Alexander Mazurkevich/Shutterstock.com; 296 Marcello Scopelliti/Shutterstock.com; 298 laura zamboni/Shutterstock.com; 299 SimoneN/Shutterstock.com; 301 gabriele gelsi/Shuttestock.com; 302 Stockafisso/Shutterstock.com; 304 Aleks49/Shutterstock.com; 308 Niall Clutton; 310 feat est; 318 JopsStock/Shutterstock.com; 319 Lucian Milasan/Shutterstock.com.

Credits

Crimson credits
Authors Fulvia Angelini, Agnes Crawford, Luisa Grigoletto, Anne Hanley, Kate Zagorski
Editor Beth Bishop
Proofreader Liz Hammond
Layouts Patrick Dawson, Emilie Crabb, Mihaela Botezatu
Cartography Gail Armstrong, John Scott, Simonetta Giori

Series Editor Sophie Blacksell Jones
Production Manager Kate Michell
Design Mytton Williams

Chairman David Lester
Managing Director Andy Riddle

Advertising Media Sales House
Marketing Lyndsey Mayhew
Sales Joel James

Acknowledgements
The authors and editor would like to thank contributors to previous editions of *Time Out Rome*, whose work formed the basis of this guide.

Photography credits
Front cover Hao Liang/Getty Images
Back cover left Mariia Golovianko/Shutterstock.com; centre wjarek/Shutterstock.com; right Diego Fiore/Shutterstock.com
Fold-out map (from top) S-F/Shutterstock.com; Henning Marquardt/Shutterstock.com; Gal Csilla/Shutterstock.com; bellena/Shutterstock.com; Elijah Lovkoff/Shutterstock.com; Dave Carroll/Shutterstock.com.
Interior Photography credits, *see p343.*

Publishing information
Time Out Rome City Guide 11th edition

February 2018

ISBN 978 1 780592 55 8
CIP DATA: A catalogue record for this book is available from the British Library

Published by Crimson Publishing 21d Charles Street, Bath, BA1 1HX (01225 584 950, www.crimsonpublishing.co.uk) on behalf of Time Out England.

Distributed by Grantham Book Services
Distributed in the US and Canada by Publishers Group West (1-510-809-3700)

Printed by Replika Press, India.